I RODE WITH FORREST!

~~ THE LOCHLAINN SEABROOK COLLECTION ~~

AMERICAN CIVIL WAR
Abraham Lincoln Was a Liberal, Jefferson Davis Was a Conservative: The Missing Key to Understanding the American Civil War
Confederacy 101: Amazing Facts You Never Knew About America's Oldest Political Tradition
Confederate Blood and Treasure: An Interview With Lochlainn Seabrook
Everything You Were Taught About African-Americans and the Civil War is Wrong, Ask a Southerner!
Everything You Were Taught About the Civil War is Wrong, Ask a Southerner!
Give This Book to a Yankee! A Southern Guide to the Civil War For Northerners
Lincoln's War: The Real Cause, the Real Winner, the Real Loser
The Great Yankee Coverup: What the North Doesn't Want You to Know About Lincoln's War!
The Ultimate Civil War Quiz Book: How Much Do You Really Know About America's Most Misunderstood Conflict?
Women in Gray: A Tribute to the Ladies Who Supported the Southern Confederacy

CONFEDERATE MONUMENTS
Confederate Monuments: Why Every American Should Honor Confederate Soldiers and Their Memorials

CONFEDERATE FLAG
Confederate Flag Facts: What Every American Should Know About Dixie's Southern Cross

SECESSION
All We Ask Is To Be Let Alone: The Southern Secession Fact Book

SLAVERY
Everything You Were Taught About American Slavery is Wrong, Ask a Southerner!
Slavery 101: Amazing Facts You Never Knew About America's "Peculiar Institution"

CHILDREN
Honest Jeff and Dishonest Abe: A Southern Children's Guide to the Civil War
Saddle, Sword, and Gun: A Biography of Nathan Bedford Forrest For Teens

NATHAN BEDFORD FORREST
A Rebel Born: A Defense of Nathan Bedford Forrest - Confederate General, American Legend (winner of the 2011 Jefferson Davis Historical Gold Medal)
A Rebel Born: The Screenplay (film about N. B. Forrest)
Forrest! 99 Reasons to Love Nathan Bedford Forrest
Give 'Em Hell Boys! The Complete Military Correspondence of Nathan Bedford Forrest
I Rode With Forrest! Confederate Soldiers Who Served With the World's Greatest Cavalry Leader
Nathan Bedford Forrest and African-Americans: Yankee Myth, Confederate Fact
Nathan Bedford Forrest and the Battle of Fort Pillow: Yankee Myth, Confederate Fact
Nathan Bedford Forrest and the Ku Klux Klan: Yankee Myth, Confederate Fact
Nathan Bedford Forrest: Southern Hero, American Patriot - Honoring a Confederate Icon and the Old South
Saddle, Sword, and Gun: A Biography of Nathan Bedford Forrest For Teens
The God of War: Nathan Bedford Forrest As He Was Seen By His Contemporaries
The Quotable Nathan Bedford Forrest: Selections From the Writings and Speeches of the Confederacy's Most Brilliant Cavalryman

QUOTABLE SERIES
The Alexander H. Stephens Reader: Excerpts From the Works of a Confederate Founding Father
The Quotable Alexander H. Stephens: Selections From the Writings and Speeches of the Confederacy's First Vice President
The Quotable Jefferson Davis: Selections From the Writings and Speeches of the Confederacy's First President
The Quotable Nathan Bedford Forrest: Selections From the Writings and Speeches of the Confederacy's Most Brilliant Cavalryman
The Quotable Robert E. Lee: Selections From the Writings and Speeches of the South's Most Beloved Civil War General
The Quotable Stonewall Jackson: Selections From the Writings and Speeches of the South's Most Famous General
The Unquotable Abraham Lincoln: The President's Quotes They Don't Want You To Know!

CONSTITUTIONAL HISTORY
The Articles of Confederation Explained: A Clause-by-Clause Study of America's First Constitution
The Constitution of the Confederate States of America Explained: A Clause-by-Clause Study of the South's Magna Carta

VICTORIAN CONFEDERATE LITERATURE
Rise Up and Call Them Blessed: Victorian Tributes to the Confederate Soldier, 1861-1901
The God of War: Nathan Bedford Forrest As He Was Seen By His Contemporaries
The Old Rebel: Robert E. Lee As He Was Seen By His Contemporaries
Victorian Confederate Poetry: The Southern Cause in Verse, 1861-1901

ABRAHAM LINCOLN
Abraham Lincoln: The Southern View - Demythologizing America's Sixteenth President
Lincolnology: The Real Abraham Lincoln Revealed in His Own Words - A Study of Lincoln's Suppressed, Misinterpreted, and Forgotten Writings and Speeches
The Great Impersonator! 99 Reasons to Dislike Abraham Lincoln
The Unholy Crusade: Lincoln's Legacy of Destruction in the American South
The Unquotable Abraham Lincoln: The President's Quotes They Don't Want You To Know!

CIVIL WAR BATTLES
Encyclopedia of the Battle of Franklin - A Comprehensive Guide to the Conflict that Changed the Civil War
Nathan Bedford Forrest and the Battle of Fort Pillow: Yankee Myth, Confederate Fact
The Battle of Spring Hill: Recollections of Confederate and Union Soldiers

PARANORMAL
Carnton Plantation Ghost Stories: True Tales of the Unexplained from Tennessee's Most Haunted Civil War House!
UFOs and Aliens: The Complete Guidebook

FAMILY HISTORIES
The Blakeneys: An Etymological, Ethnological, and Genealogical Study - Uncovering the Mysterious Origins of the Blakeney Family and Name
The Caudills: An Etymological, Ethnological, and Genealogical Study - Exploring the Name and National Origins of a European-American Family
The McGavocks of Carnton Plantation: A Southern History - Celebrating One of Dixie's Most Noble Confederate Families and Their Tennessee Home

MIND, BODY, SPIRIT
Autobiography of a Non-Yogi: A Scientist's Journey From Hinduism to Christianity (Dr. Amitava Dasgupta, with Lochlainn Seabrook)
Britannia Rules: Goddess-Worship in Ancient Anglo-Celtic Society - An Academic Look at the United Kingdom's Matricentric Spiritual Past
Christ Is All and In All: Rediscovering Your Divine Nature and the Kingdom Within
Christmas Before Christianity: How the Birthday of the "Sun" Became the Birthday of the "Son"
Jesus and the Gospel of Q: Christ's Pre-Christian Teachings As Recorded in the New Testament
Jesus and the Law of Attraction: The Bible-Based Guide to Creating Perfect Health, Wealth, and Happiness Following Christ's Simple Formula
Seabrook's Bible Dictionary of Traditional and Mystical Christian Doctrines
The Bible and the Law of Attraction: 99 Teachings of Jesus, the Apostles, and the Prophets
The Book of Kelle: An Introduction to Goddess-Worship and the Great Celtic Mother-Goddess Kelle, Original Blessed Lady of Ireland
The Goddess Dictionary of Words and Phrases: Introducing a New Core Vocabulary for the Women's Spirituality Movement
The Way of Holiness: The Story of Religion and Myth From the Cave Bear Cult to Christianity

WOMEN
Aphrodite's Trade: The Hidden History of Prostitution Unveiled
Princess Diana: Modern Day Moon-Goddess - A Psychoanalytical and Mythological Look at Diana Spencer's Life, Marriage, and Death (with Dr. Jane Goldberg)
Women in Gray: A Tribute to the Ladies Who Supported the Southern Confederacy

Five-Star Books & Gifts From the Heart of the American South

I RODE WITH FORREST!

CONFEDERATE SOLDIERS WHO SERVED WITH THE WORLD'S GREATEST CAVALRY LEADER

COLLECTED, EDITED, & ARRANGED, WITH AN INTRODUCTION, BY "THE VOICE OF THE TRADITIONAL SOUTH," COLONEL

LOCHLAINN SEABROOK

JEFFERSON DAVIS HISTORICAL GOLD MEDAL WINNER

Diligently Researched and Generously Illustrated for the Elucidation of the Reader

2018

Sea Raven Press, Nashville, Tennessee, USA

I RODE WITH FORREST!

Published by
Sea Raven Press, Cassidy Ravensdale, President
PO Box 1484, Spring Hill, Tennessee 37174-1484 USA
SeaRavenPress.com • searavenpress@gmail.com

Copyright © 2018 Lochlainn Seabrook
in accordance with U.S. and international copyright laws and regulations, as stated and protected under the Berne Union for the Protection of Literary and Artistic Property (Berne Convention), and the Universal Copyright Convention (the UCC). All rights reserved under the Pan-American and International Copyright Conventions.

1st SRP paperback edition, 1st printing, September 2018 • ISBN: 978-1-943737-71-0
1st SRP hardcover edition, 1st printing, September 2018 • ISBN: 978-1-943737-72-7

ISBN: 978-1-943737-71-0 (paperback)
Library of Congress Control Number: 2018955134

This work is the copyrighted intellectual property of Lochlainn Seabrook and has been registered with the Copyright Office at the Library of Congress in Washington, D.C., USA. No part of this work (including text, covers, drawings, photos, illustrations, maps, images, diagrams, etc.), in whole or in part, may be used, reproduced, stored in a retrieval system, or transmitted, in any form or by any means now known or hereafter invented, without written permission from the publisher. The sale, duplication, hire, lending, copying, digitalization, or reproduction of this material, in any manner or form whatsoever, is also prohibited, and is a violation of federal, civil, and digital copyright law, which provides severe civil and criminal penalties for any violations.

I Rode With Forrest! Confederate Soldiers Who Served With the World's Greatest Cavalry Leader, by Lochlainn Seabrook. Includes an index, endnotes, and bibliographical references.

Front and back cover design and art, book design, layout, and interior art by Lochlainn Seabrook. All images, graphic design, graphic art, and illustrations copyright © Lochlainn Seabrook. All images selected, placed, manipulated, and/or created by Lochlainn Seabrook. Cover images and design copyright © Lochlainn Seabrook.

All persons who approve of the authority and principles of Colonel Lochlainn Seabrook's literary work, and realize its benefits as a means of reeducating the world about the South and the Confederacy, are hereby requested to avidly recommend his books to others and to vigorously cooperate in extending their reach, scope, and influence around the globe.

The views on the American "Civil War" documented in this book are those of the publisher.

PRINTED & MANUFACTURED IN OCCUPIED TENNESSEE, FORMER CONFEDERATE STATES OF AMERICA

DEDICATION

To the soldiers who rode with the mighty Forrest, among whom were a number of my relatives. Freedom-lovers everywhere will forever honor you in prose, verse, song, and stone. May this little book aid in the preservation of your names; fearless patriots who defended the Founding Fathers' "Confederate Republic," the original Constitution, and the Conservative principles that serve as their foundation.

EPIGRAPH

Hero in the old town of Gainesville, Alabama, Forrest, the grand warrior, whose very name evoked love and admiration from his followers, fear and consternation to his foes, fought the hardest battle he ever fought, when he sheathed his sword and laid down his arms he had so valiantly used in the defense of his country. He and his dauntless men who had not quailed before the cannon's blast, who without a murmur endured cold, hunger, and hardships, were now to face defeat, for General Canby, of the U.S. army, came to offer them terms of surrender and issue their paroles. These men, some of them mere boys, were as grand in defeat as they were in war. They accepted their paroles in good faith, returned to their desolated homes to face life with a noble courage, fostered and strengthened by four years of service to their country, and took up the task of restoring a ruined country.

Many of these men who rode with Forrest have achieved success in life; many have served their country in the legislative halls and in the senate chamber; some have attained to highest ranks in medicine, law, and literature, and all became good citizens of the United States.

Many years have passed since that day Forrest and his men were paroled at Gainesville. Time has marked more than half a century, many have crossed over the river to rest under the trees of Paradise, but many of Forrest's men are yet to be seen at every Confederate reunion and love to talk over the days of the sixties. To see these veterans at the reunion in Richmond, with the snow of many winters on their heads, but the glow of health in their faces, rejuvenated by war memories and renewed friendship, with agile and graceful step dance the old Virginia Reel, you would not have thought them old and feeble, worn with life's burdens, but men who had fought the good fight with age resting on them like a benediction.[1]

Confederate Veteran
1923

CONTENTS

Notes to the Reader - 11
Military Biography of, and List of Staff Officers Under, Forrest - 17
Introduction, by Lochlainn Seabrook - 19

A - 23
B - 35
C - 65
D - 89
E - 111
F - 117
G - 127
H - 143
I - 171
J - 175
K - 191
L - 201

M - 217
N - 257
O - 265
P - 269
Q - 285
R - 287
S - 303
T - 333
V - 345
W - 349
Y - 375
Z - 379

Appendix A: Forrest's Escort - 383
Appendix B: Annual Reunion of Forrest's Escort - 384
Appendix C: Confederate Generals of Tennessee - 385
Appendix D: A Remarkable Group of Men - 386
Appendix E: Where Forrest Surrendered - 387
Appendix F: General Forrest's Grandson Vs. Public School - 388
Appendix G: Company G, Forrest's Cavalry - 389
Appendix H: At the Birthplace of General Forrest - 390
Notes - 391
Bibliography - 405
Index - 411
Meet the Author - 417

"General Forrest made infantrymen of cavalrymen and cavalrymen of infantrymen with results equally brilliant."

A Confederate veteran, 1900

Nathan Bedford Forrest has been characterized

- By Robert E. Lee as "the most remarkable genius produced in the Confederate army, and a man that I never saw."

- By Theodore Roosevelt as "the most remarkable man produced in either the Union or Confederate armies."

- By George Creel as "the Gray Ghost of the South, whose terrible harassing embarrassed the Union forces beyond their expectations."

- By one of Europe's greatest military strategists as "the greatest cavalry leader of all times."

These characterizations of Nathan Bedford Forrest could be multiplied without limit.[2]

ART & GRAPHIC DESIGN COPYRIGHT © LOCHLAINN SEABROOK

NOTES TO THE READER

"NOTHING IN THE PAST IS DEAD TO THE MAN WHO WOULD
LEARN HOW THE PRESENT CAME TO BE WHAT IT IS."

WILLIAM STUBBS, VICTORIAN ENGLISH HISTORIAN

THE TWO MAIN POLITICAL PARTIES IN 1860
☛ In any study of America's antebellum, bellum, and postbellum periods, it is vitally important to understand that in 1860 the two major political parties—the Democrats and the newly formed Republicans—were the opposite of what they are today. In other words, the Democrats of the mid 19th Century were Conservatives, akin to the Republican Party of today, while the Republicans of the mid 19th Century were Liberals, akin to the Democratic Party of today.[3]

Thus the Confederacy's Democratic president, Jefferson Davis, was a Conservative (with libertarian leanings); the Union's Republican president, Abraham Lincoln, was a Liberal (with socialistic leanings).[4]

This is why, in the mid 1800s, the conservative wing of the Democratic Party was known as "the States' Rights Party."[5]

Hence, the Democrats of the Civil War period referred to themselves as "conservatives," "confederates," "anti-centralists," or "constitutionalists" (the latter because they favored strict adherence to the original Constitution—which tacitly guaranteed states' rights—as created by the Founding Fathers), while the Republicans called themselves "liberals," "nationalists," "centralists," or "consolidationists" (the latter three because they wanted to nationalize the central government and consolidate political power in Washington, D.C.).[6]

The author's cousin, Confederate Vice President and Democrat Alexander H. Stephens: a Southern Conservative.

Since this idea is new to most of my readers, let us further demystify it by viewing it from the perspective of the American Revolutionary War. If Davis and his conservative Southern constituents (the Democrats of 1861) had been alive in 1775, they would have sided with George Washington and the American colonists, who sought to secede from the tyrannical government of Great Britain; if Lincoln and his Liberal Northern constituents (the Republicans of 1861) had been alive at that time, they would have sided with King George III and the English monarchy, who sought to maintain the American colonies as possessions of the British Empire. It is due to this very comparison that Southerners often refer to their secession as the Second Declaration of Independence and the "Civil War" as the Second American Revolutionary War.

Without a basic understanding of these facts, the American "Civil War" will forever remain incomprehensible. For a full discussion of this topic see my book, *Abraham Lincoln Was a Liberal, Jefferson Davis Was a Conservative: The Missing Key to Understanding the American Civil War.*

THE TERM "CIVIL WAR"

☞ As I heartily dislike the phrase "Civil War," its use throughout this book (as well as in my other works) is worthy of explanation.

Our entire modern literary system refers to the conflict of 1861 using the Northern term the "Civil War," whether we in the South like it or not. Of course, this is purposeful, for America's book industry, which determines everything from how books are categorized and designed to how they are marketed and sold, is almost solely controlled by Liberals, socialists, globalists, collectivists, and communists, individuals who will do anything to prevent the truth about Lincoln's War from coming out. An important aspect of this wholesale revisionism of American history is the use of the phrase "Civil War," which Yankee Liberals thrust into the public forum even as big

The American "Civil War" was not a true civil war as Webster defines it: "A conflict between opposing groups of citizens of the *same* country." It was a fight between two individual countries; or to be more specific, two separate and constitutionally formed confederacies: the U.S.A. and the C.S.A.

government Left-winger Lincoln was diabolically tricking the Conservative South into firing the first shot at the Battle of Fort Sumter in April 1861.

The progressives' blatant American "Civil War" coverup continues to this day, one of the more overt results which pertains to how books are coded, indexed, and identified.[7] Thus, as all book searches by readers, libraries, and retail outlets are now performed online, and as all bookstores categorize works from or about this period under the heading "Civil War," honest book publishers and authors who deal with this particular topic have little choice but to use this deceptive term. If I were to refuse to use it, as some of my Southern colleagues have suggested, few people would ever find or read my books.

Confederate General Nathan Bedford Forrest, just one of many Southern officials who referred to the conflict of 1861 as the "Civil War."

Add to this the fact that scarcely any non-Southerners have ever heard of the names we in the South use for the conflict, such as the "War for Southern Independence"—or my personal preference, "Lincoln's War." It only makes sense then to use the term "Civil War" in most commercial situations, distasteful though it is.

We should also bear in mind that while today educated persons, particularly educated Southerners, all share an abhorrence for the phrase "Civil War," it was not always so. Confederates who lived through and even fought in the conflict regularly used the term throughout the 1860s, and even long after. Among them were Confederate generals such as Nathan Bedford Forrest, Richard Taylor, and Joseph E. Johnston, not to mention the Confederacy's vice president, Alexander H. Stephens.

In 1895 Confederate General James Longstreet wrote about his military experiences in a work subtitled, *Memoirs of the Civil War in America*, while in 1903 Confederate General John Brown Gordon entitled his autobiography, *Reminiscences of the Civil War*. Even the Confederacy's highest leader, President Jefferson Davis, used the term "Civil War,"[8] and in one case at least, as late as 1881—the year he wrote his brilliant exposition, *The Rise and Fall of the Confederate Government*.[9] Authors writing for *Confederate Veteran* magazine sometimes used the phrase well into the early 1900s,[10] and in 1898, at the Eighth Annual Meeting and Reunion of the United Confederate Veterans (the forerunner of today's Sons of Confederate Veterans), the following resolution was proposed: that from then on the Great War of 1861 was to be designated "the Civil War Between the States."[11]

A WORD ON EARLY AMERICAN MATERIAL

☞ In order to preserve the authentic historicity of the antebellum, bellum, and postbellum periods, for the most part I have retained the original spellings, formatting, and punctuation of the early Americans I quote. These include such items as British-English spellings, long-running paragraphs, obsolete words, and various literary devices peculiar to the time. However, I have corrected misspelled names to prevent confusion, and also *where possible*, inaccurate dates and locations (the inevitable result of old faulty memories). Bracketed words within quotes are my additions and clarifications, while italicized words within quotes are (where indicated) my emphasis.

PRESENTISM

☞ As a historian I view *presentism* (judging the past according to present day mores and customs) as the enemy of authentic history. And this is precisely why the Left employs it in its ongoing war against traditional American, conservative, and Christian values. By looking at history through the lens of modern day beliefs—and,

Judging our ancestors by our own standards is unfair, unjust, misleading, and unethical.

just as heinous, fabricating obviously fake history based on emotion, opinion, and political ideology—they are able to distort, revise, and reshape the past into a false narrative that fits their ideological agenda: the liberalization *and* Northernization of America, the enlargement and further centralization of the national government, and total control of American political, economic, and social power, the same agenda that Lincoln championed.[12]

This book rejects presentism and replaces it with what I call *historicalism*: judging our ancestors based on the values of their own time. To get the most from this work the reader is invited to reject presentism as well. In this way—along with casting aside preconceived notions and the bogus "history" churned out by our left-wing education system—the truth in this work will be most readily ascertained and absorbed; truth that has been rigorously researched and forensically uncovered by myself using the scientific method. As Confederate Colonel Bennett H. Young noted in 1901:

> History is valuable only as it is true. Opinions concerning acts are not history; acts themselves alone are historic.[13]

LEARN MORE
☞ Lincoln's War on the American people and the Constitution can never be fully understood without a thorough knowledge of the South's perspective. As this book is only meant to be a brief introductory guide to these topics, one cannot hope to learn the complete story here. For those who are interested in additional material from Dixie's viewpoint, please see my comprehensive histories listed on pages 2 and 3.

Keep Your Body, Mind, & Spirit Vibrating at Their Highest Level

YOU CAN DO SO BY READING THE BOOKS OF

SEA RAVEN PRESS

There is nothing that will so perfectly keep your body, mind, and spirit in a healthy condition as to think wisely and positively. Hence you should not only read this book, but also the other books that we offer. They will quicken your physical, mental, and spiritual vibrations, enabling you to maintain a position in society as a healthy erudite person.

KEEP YOURSELF WELL-INFORMED!

The well-informed person is always at the head of the procession, while the ignorant, the lazy, and the unthoughtful hang onto the rear. If you are a Spiritual man or woman, do yourself a great favor: read Sea Raven Press books and stay well posted on the Truth. It is almost criminal for one to remain in ignorance while the opportunity to gain knowledge is open to all at a nominal price.

We invite you to visit our Webstore for a wide selection of wholesome, family-friendly, well-researched, educational books for all ages. You will be glad you did!

Five-Star Books & Gifts From the Heart of the American South

SeaRavenPress.com

A Brief Military Biography of
GEN. NATHAN BEDFORD FORREST

Gen. Nathan Bedford Forrest.—May, 1861, captain of a company of cavalry; 1861-62, Colonel Forrest's Regiment of Cavalry; July 21, 1862, appointed brigadier general; December 4, 1863, appointed major general; February 28, 1865, appointed lieutenant general. Commands: August 1, 1862, commanded brigade composed of 4th, 8th, and 9th Tennessee Regiments of Cavalry, 4th Alabama Regiment of Cavalry, and Freeman's Battery of Artillery. In December, 1863, assigned to the command of all the cavalry in West Tennessee and North Mississippi, consisting of the brigades of J. R. Chalmers, Ben McCullough, Tyree H. Bell, J. M. Jeffries, R. V. Richardson, and H. B. Lyon, the whole organized into two divisions, commanded by J. R. Chalmers and Abe Buford; in February, 1865, commanded the divisions of J. R. Chalmers, W. H. Jackson, Abe Buford, and Ben McCullough, together with the militia of Mississippi and East Louisiana.[14]

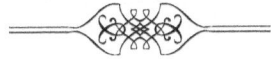

OFFICERS UNDER FORREST
A List of Forrest's Regular Staff Officers

Major John P. Strange: assistant adjutant-general
Major Charles W. Anderson: aide-de-camp and assistant inspectorgeneral
Major Gilbert Vincent Rambaut: chief commissary
Major George Dashiell: chief paymaster
Major Charles S. Severson: chief quartermaster
Major A. Warren: quartermaster
Major Richard M. Mason: quartermaster
Captain Matthew C. Galloway: aide-de-camp2166
Captain William Montgomery "Willie" Forrest (the General's only son): aide-de-camp
Dr. James B. Cowan: chief surgeon
Captain John G. Mann: chief engineer
Captain Charles S. Hill: chief of ordnance
Lieutenant Samuel Donelson: aide-de-camp[15]

Loyalty to the truth of Confederate history.

U.D.C. MOTTO, 1921

INTRODUCTION

Why should you care about Confederate Gen. Nathan Bedford Forrest, and more particularly about the men who served with and under him? America's War for the Constitution, purposefully misnamed the "Civil War" by 19th-Century Liberals, ended more than 150 years ago.

Forrest and his men are important today, and will always be important, because they were the premier 19th-Century personifications of *conservatism*, a political philosophy at whose heart lies that most sacred of all the Founding Fathers' principles: *constitutionalism*. As such, it is vital that Forrest's men never be forgotten, and that their valorous service in the Confederate army be recognized, honored, and perpetuated. For the "Southern Cause" was itself conservatism, an idea that was forged in the soul of Conservative Dixie even before the formation of our country in 1776. And it is in the modern Christian South where conservatism continues to serve as the foundation of traditional American society.

Who were these amazing patriots, the men who rode with Forrest? Contrary to the Liberals' fabricated anti-South propaganda, Ol' Bedford, a political Conservative, was one of the most socially tolerant Victorians in America—which is why his soldiers were without question the most diverse group any army has ever seen. Racially, for example, they ranged from white to black to red; nationally they ranged from American-born to foreign-born; sectionally they ranged from easygoing Southrons to uptight Yankees; politically they ranged from dyed-in-the-wool Conservatives (then Democrats) to zealous Liberals (then Republicans)—though, it should be pointed out, nearly all from the latter group quickly converted to conservatism when their states seceded and Lincoln's troops invaded. Educationally, Forrest's men ranged from those with no formal schooling to those with multiple college degrees; economically they came from all walks of life, from the poorest backwaters to the wealthiest neighborhoods; from farm boys to corporate tycoons. It was indeed a diverse group of very special individuals!

Nonetheless, they all shared two things in common: a passionate reverence for (as well as a strict interpretation of) the U.S. Constitution, and an unshakable faith in their leader, one, as the reader will see, that verged on pagan-like idolatry.

While wishing to fairly represent the men of Forrest's "Critter Company," my encyclopedia is not meant to contain a complete list of the soldiers who served under or with the General. Indeed, since at one time or another 50,000 men (many unnamed) came under his command—including some 100 organizations, such as regiments, battalions, and batteries[16]—a book of this type would be impossible to compile. Thus, instead, I have concentrated on those men whose biographies and obituaries were most widely chronicled by earlier writers. Despite this limitation, I have attempted to include as many individuals as possible, from the obscure and unsung to the universally lionized, in order to give an accurate idea of Forrest's soldiers—as well as the immortal Confederate chieftain who led them.

With the Left's ongoing campaign to further humiliate Dixie and both erase and rewrite Southern history, it will be obvious to even the casual reader why a book of this kind is necessary. However, if more clarification on this matter is required, I end my Introduction with the pen of Dr. John Ware of Rome, Georgia, whose poignant article "Taps" was published in 1930. In his essay Dr. Ware is speaking of *all* Confederate soldiers and not specifically of those who rode with Forrest. However, his words convey special meaning for American patriots, and in particular for individuals such as myself, a Southern historian whose ancestors fought and died for the Confederate Cause, *the conservative constitutional principles of the Founding Fathers*—the most noteworthy who were Southerners:

> Sixty-five years ago a ragged, shoeless, starved handful of men, the pitiful remnant of a once mighty host, laid down their arms and dispersed to their homes. Worn down by years of valiant struggle against a foe whose resources in men and materials were inexhaustible, to the very end they held their heads high, as befitted men who had fought the good fight, who had never questioned the fact that their cause was just; who had nothing to regret but that they had not been finally successful. They had followed leaders worthy of any man's devotion and reverence; they had continued to wage what they knew was a losing fight as long as those leaders had not told them it was time to stop, and when the word came that that time had come, they laid down their arms before a worthy and appreciative enemy, and went back to ruined homes and desolation and a lifetime of grim labor to keep the soul and body together. Such men need no praise; no historian to record their deeds. They have written their names in the heavens and in the hearts of all men who honor valor both in time of war and of peace.
>
> . . . We have always known that the survivors of the armies of the Confederacy would some day lay down their earthly arms and go on to join Lee and Johnson and Johnston and Jackson and Forrest, but somehow it did not seem that we had to face it at any definite time. And now it has come. Quietly and unobtrusively a half dozen tired old men, bowed under the weight of more than fourscore years, have folded for the last time their beloved banner and have placed it for honored keeping in the hands of others. It is now only a memory, and, with the passing of the years, it will become fainter and fainter memory. The last protagonists of a heroic epic have passed away. An era has written *Finis* and has closed its books. They will never be opened again save by historians, who will honor the actors for their roles, for they played them well in war and peace, and merit honor.
>
> . . . We, their descendants, live in happier times materially. We consider as commonplace necessities of life what were to them unattainable luxuries; we have in our power to do things that they could never have dreamed of doing. But we shall be fortunate indeed, if we, in passing, leave as rich a heritage and as honored a name as they, humble citizens though many of them were. Shall not we, then, we of a later generation, pause a moment to do honor to the passing of a flag and to those who fought worthily under its folds? For in so doing, we honor ourselves.
>
> Dear gray ghosts of the Confederacy, clear-eyed and head erect, marching steadily down the misty corridors of the past, we wave to you a reverent salute. Hail and farewell![17]

LOCHLAINN SEABROOK
Nashville, Tennessee, USA
September 2018
In Nobis Regnat Christus

ENTRIES

"To be of Forrest's command was to laugh at danger and defy privations."

A Confederate veteran, 1916

HERE LIES A STRAINGER BRAVE

Here lies a strainger braive,
Who died while fighting the Southern Confederacy to save.
Piece to his dust.
Braive Suthern frind,
From iland 10,
You reached a Glory us end.
We plase these flowers above the strainger's hed,
In honor of the shiverlus ded.
Sweet spirit, rest in Heven,
Ther'l be no Yankis there.[18]

INSCRIPTION ON THE HEADSTONE OF AN UNRECONSTRUCTED CONFEDERATE VETERAN IN THE METHODIST CEMETERY, ST. LOUIS, MISSOURI.

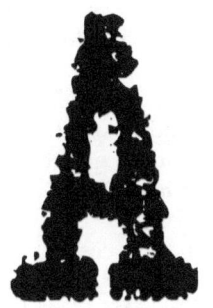

ABERNATHY, THOMAS E.: Thomas E. Abernathy, who died in Navasota, Tex., on the 4th of November, 1920, was born on the 24th of February, 1847, in Pulaski, Giles County, Tenn. He was married to Miss Nannie E. Ivey in September, 1867.

Comrade Abernathy volunteered his services for the Confederacy on the 5th of February, 1864, and was enrolled as a private in Company F, 14th Tennessee Cavalry, serving under General Forrest until the surrender. He participated in the many skirmishes and battles while under Forrest and surrendered at Gainesville, Ala., on the 27th of April, 1865, receiving his parole from General Canby. He made a good soldier.

After his marriage he moved to Texas and located in Navasota, where he lived for more than forty years. He was a member of the Hannibal Boon Camp, U.C.V., of Navasota, and attended the last Reunion at Atlanta. Many friends mourn his death. His many good qualities as a friend, neighbor, and citizen will keep his memory green.

Comrade Abernathy joined the Methodist Church when a young man and was a steward for a number of years.[19]

William Wirt Adams.

ADAMS, WILLIAM WIRT: William W. Adams was born on March 22, 1819, at Frankfort, Ky., later becoming a banker and planter in Mississippi. Confederate President Jefferson Davis offered him the job of postmaster-general, which he turned down, preferring to "work" on the battlefield fighting the Northern invaders. After raising a cavalry regiment (the 1st Mississippi), Adams was promoted to brigadier general in 1863, and in 1864 his brigade was attached to Forrest's corps (paroled at Gainesville, Ala., May 12, 1865). After the War he removed to Jackson, Miss., where he was killed on May 1, 1888, during a quarrel with a local newspaper editor.[20]

ADEN, JAMES S.: After a long illness, Judge James S. Aden died at his home, in Paris, Tenn., in his seventy-ninth year. He was born in that city on February 13, 1842, and had practically spent all his life in Henry County, where he was widely known and beloved. He had been honored by the people of his county by election to office, having served as county court clerk and also as county judge; but most of his life had been spent on his farm, near Paris.

He was a gallant soldier of the Confederacy, serving under Forrest as a member of Company G, 7th Tennessee Cavalry. At one time he was with Stark's company and again with his uncle, Capt. F. F. Aden. He was captured and paroled at Paducah, Ky.

In early life he became a Christian and so remained through his long and useful life. As a minister of the gospel he brought salvation to many. It was the work he loved, and he used his gift to the glory of God, toiling with his hands for the support of his family. He was the father of twelve children and is survived by seven sons and a daughter, also the faithful, beloved wife.

He was laid to rest in Maplewood Cemetery, attended by his Confederate comrades and many friends and relatives. In his passing his community and State have lost a noble citizen.[21]

ALCORN, MILTON STEWART: When the war broke out, Milton S. Alcorn, a youth of not quite eighteen years, was at school in Lexington, Va., under the immediate instruction of the afterwards famous Stonewall Jackson. Volunteering in Virginia with other cadets of the military institute, his father, James Lusk Alcorn (afterwards Governor of Mississippi and United States Senator), had him transferred at the request of Bedford Forrest, and the youthful Milton was made Sergeant in Capt. Forrest's company, and gave to them their first lessons in the manual of arms.

The education of Milton had been largely military. He had spent two years at Frankfort. Ky., where his military taste had been cultivated, and when transferred to Lexington, Va., he found a school no less adapted to his chivalrous nature, so when brought to Forrest's company at Memphis, he, naturally polite, with the breeding of a Southern gentleman, won the admiration of Forrest and his men as well. With Forrest's command he remained until December, 1861, when he was elected and commissioned a captain in the First Regiment of Mississippi Infantry under Col. J. M. Simonton, which regiment was then stationed at Hopkinsville, Ky. The young captain lost no time in joining the company that had honored him so unexpectedly. These boys had never seen him, but had heard well of him. He found the company composed of a propertyless class, and he used his father's purse to equip them, and soon the drill made his Ittawamba boys the crack company of that brave regiment.

In the battle at Fort Donelson this regiment won the admiration of the army, and no man did more to achieve the result than did Milton S. Alcorn. He was then the youngest captain in the Confederate service. Before the surrender was consummated he escaped with as many of his men as would follow him out of the fortifications and safely into Nashville. The gallant Captain was soon again before the enemy in the battle of Corinth. When the Fort Donelson prisoners were released, in the fall of 1862, their rendezvous on their return was at Vicksburg, where the troops were reorganized for the war. Capt. Alcorn was reelected to the command of his old company, which was selected as the color company of the regiment. Now began the thunderstorms of war.

The Federal army had now been disciplined to the work of regular troops; by the hundred thousand they came, with banners flying and bayonets fixed, as if sent to break the proud heart of a master race. Whether in the bivouac or on the march or in the charge of battle, Capt. Alcorn was at the front, not once complaining, nor did he ever falter in that terrific campaign from Baker's Creek or Champion Hill to the surrender at Port Hudson. Of his old company, numbering over a hundred men, more than sixty had been killed or wounded, and the company never had a fight in his absence. In prison at Johnson's Island, his strength succumbed to the rations of a Federal contractor, and the cold climate with scanty fare brought on disease from which he never recovered. Notwithstanding this, after being exchanged he returned to the army, and with his decimated command was soon at Chattanooga, thence with Joseph E. Johnston on his retreat to Atlanta, thence under Hood over the hills of Georgia to Nashville, then again under Johnston. In the meantime he had been promoted to the rank of Major, and in every fight that he was engaged he moved in the front ranks of the deadly assault. At the close of the war he surrendered his sword in Georgia and returned home a broken fragment of a cruel war.[22]

ALDRICH, ED: This valiant old soldier came to an untimely death on March 21 [1907?] while walking on the railroad near Gulfport, Miss. Captain Aldrich enlisted in the 2nd Missouri Cavalry (Col. Robert McCulloch) early in the war, remaining with that regiment, in Forrest's Cavalry, until 1863, when he was transferred to the staff of Gen. Frank Armstrong, with whom he served with distinction the remainder of the war. After the war closed, Captain Aldrich settled near Byhalia, Miss., from whence he removed to Gulfport, Miss., about one year ago. He was nearing his eightieth year, and, being very deaf, was an easy prey to a passenger train. His remains were interred at the Soldiers' Home, Beauvoir, Miss.[23]

ALEXANDER, J. P.: J. P. Alexander, who died at Coronado, Cal., October, 1902, enlisted in the Confederate service as a private in the Third Texas Cavalry June 10, 1861, and served until the end of the war. Upon the reorganization of his company he was elected lieutenant. The Third Regiment soon thereafter, being assigned to Ross's Brigade, became a portion of Gen. Forrest's command, at which period Lieut. Alexander was promoted to the rank of major and appointed inspector general of the command. He was reared in the famous blue grass region of Kentucky, graduated with honor at the Danville University, and at the time of his death was sixty years of age. Upon the termination of the war he became extensively engaged in cotton-planting in Carroll Parish, La., subsequently also in Chico County, Ark., in which latter place he resided at the time of his death. He was thoroughly honorable in his dealings, genial in his associations, ever making stanch [meaning staunch] friends. His wife died some twenty years prior to his death, and he left no immediate family, his nearest relatives being a sister residing in Texas and three nieces residents of Louisiana and Mississippi. He generously remembered Camp J. H. Morgan in the distribution of his property.[24]

ALEXANDER, SAMUEL J.: Maj. S. J. Alexander, whose death occurred at his home, in Macon, Tenn., March 19, 1912, was born in Henderson County, Tenn., in 1833, a descendant of a Charlotte (N.C.) family who signed the famous Mecklenburg Declaration of Independence. He entered Forrest's Cavalry as a private and rose to the rank of major.

Major Alexander was educated in the old Masonic College at Macon. He was self-made, having amassed a splendid estate. He was very active and contributed much to the improving of his community. He was an ardent and devoted member of the Church and true in every relation of life. He leaves the rich legacy of an honorable and well-spent life.

Of four brothers who served faithfully in the Confederate army, he was the last to pass away. An adopted niece lives in Macon, Ga., and he had expected to attend the Reunion there, for he loved to mingle with the survivors of those days of sacrifice, suffering, and achievement.

In a personal letter John H. Hineman, of Morrell, Ark., who sent the foregoing, writes: "Major Alexander was a first cousin to my mother. Of all the group of my kinsmen who went out at the call of the grand old Volunteer State, only one survives, John Smith, of Oakland. My mother's brother was killed in the battle of Belmont, Mo., another of the group was killed at Franklin, a third was desperately wounded at Shiloh and again at Chickamauga, and a fourth was seriously shot at Murfreesboro. Major Alexander passed through the war without receiving a wound."[25]

ALLEN, J. G.: J. G. Allen died in Plain Dealing, La., in September, 1906, in his seventy-second year. He joined the Confederate army at Monroe, La., in April, 1861, as private in Company B, 1st Louisiana Squadron of Cavalry, went direct to Corinth, Miss., and was promoted to second sergeant just after a battle at Denmark, Tenn. He served in Forrest's Cavalry until the later part of 1864, when he was transferred to west of the Mississippi River, was promoted to first lieutenant in Company D, of the 1st Louisiana Cavalry, and surrendered at Shreveport May 25, 1865. His life, both military and civil, was characterized by religious fidelity.[26]

ALLEN, SAMUEL: Sam Allen was born February 28, 1838, in Williamson County, Tenn., and lived there until his death, November 22, 1911. He served in the 11th Tennessee Cavalry, C.S.A., under Forrest. A few weeks before his death he moved to Franklin. The Confederate flag was placed in his casket.[27]

ALLEN, WADE: Among the many gallant and brave soldiers of the Confederate States' Armies, perhaps few were more conspicuous for gallantry and devotion to the Southern cause than Lieutenant Wade Allen, who was one of the first to respond to the call for volunteers. Early in the spring of 1861, Mr. Allen enlisted in Company L, 30th Tennessee Infantry Regiment, and served in that gallant command until its reorganization after the battle of Shiloh (April, 1862), when he was transferred to Capt. Pete Williams' Company (I), 15th Tennessee Brigade, Forrest's Cavalry.

Lieutenant Allen participated in nearly all of the great battles fought by Forrest and his brave followers, and was many times complimented for gallantry displayed in battle. He was made Lieutenant of Company I immediately after joining the Regiment, which was then at Tupelo, Miss., in which capacity he ever served with distinction. When Gen. Forrest raided the city of Memphis, Aug. 21, 1864, Lieutenant Allen was at the head of the charging column which came so near making a "prisoner" of the Federal General Washburne. It was Lieutenant Allen who captured Gen. W.'s fine horse soon after he escaped to Fort Pickering in south Memphis. Lieutenant Allen rode this fine horse to the end.

Wade Allen is now a prominent citizen of Collierville, Tenn., where he is engaged in mercantile and agricultural pursuits, but he has been a resident of Shelby County nearly all his life—57 years.[28]

ALLEY, RICHARD B.: Though Mr. Alley had been failing in health for a year, his decline was more rapid than his friends had anticipated, the end coming quietly after an illness of ten days.

As a Confederate soldier Mr. Alley was distinguished for bravery. The Montgomery (Va.) *Messenger* quotes the following incident . . .: "In December, 1864, General Forrest engaged the Federals near Murfreesboro, when the onslaught of the enemy was so fierce that the Confederate lines began to waver. General Forrest, seeing the danger, seized the colors wherever he could reach them, and carrying them himself tried with them to check the retreat of his men. Riding up to the 54th Virginia Regiment, he said to the color bearer, Richard Alley, 'Hand me your flag.' Though barefooted, thinly clad, and shivering in the December wind, Alley, scarcely more than a lad, holding tightly his flag, replied: 'General Forrest, I can take care of my flag; just show me where to put it.' Pointing to some hills crowned with Federal batteries, the General said: 'Put it there.' The flag was planted where ordered, and, reenforced by the regiments, the hill was taken. General Forrest never forgot the color bearer of the 54th Virginia Regiment as 'that little fellow that totes his own flag.'"

Comrade Alley had been a resident of Montgomery County for over thirty years. During a part of this period he taught school at different places, but in recent years had lived on his farm near Rogers, Va. He is survived by his wife and nine children. A member of the Presbyterian Church for many years, he died in faith of the redeeming grace of Jesus Christ.

The funeral was conducted at Union Valley Church by Rev. E. E. Lane, pastor of the Presbyterian Church at Christianburg, Va., and was largely attended. The burial service at the grave was conducted by the Masonic order.[29]

Robert Allen Allison.

ALLISON, ROBERT ALLEN: At his home, at Winona, Miss., on January 9 [1908], passed to his reward Maj. Robert Allen Allison, aged seventy-one years, one month, and twelve days. Major Allison had had a severe spell of pneumonia during the fall of 1907, from which he had never fully recovered. On the day the summer of the grim reaper reached him he had expressed himself as feeling even better than usual and had spent some time in his office. After gently protesting to the anxious ministrations of his always devoted wife that he was "all right," he seated himself in a reclining chair, and almost immediately and without a struggle quietly passed away. It was truly a fitting end to his long, gentle, and unobtrusive life, evidencing even in his last hours the same earnest devotion to duty, the same courteous regard for those about him, the same gentle self-effacement and brave self-control that had characterized his whole life.

Robert Allen Allison, the second son of Andrew and Rebecca Allison, was born at the home of his maternal grandfather, Robert Allen (who was a distinguished officer of the War of 1812), in Carthage, Tenn., on November 28, 1836. He graduated at Cumberland University, in Lebanon, in the class of 1857, and soon thereafter became associated with his father and elder brother in the wholesale trade of Nashville. In early boyhood he became a member of the Presbyterian Church, and even at that early age manifested that piety of heart and purity of mind that distinguished him throughout his entire life. His faith was ever that of a child trusting a good and tender father, and his service to his Church was faithful as member, deacon, and elder.

In February, 1861, he married Miss Belle Kelso, of Lincoln County, Tenn., a beautiful and noted belle, and entered upon that loving and tender companionship for which his loving heart and exquisitely refined nature so eminently fitted him and which was ended only with his death in her arms after almost a half century of ideal love and devotion.

In the very morning of his wedded life, with a brilliant and successful business career just opening before him, with the tender kiss of his firstborn upon his lips, he heard the call of his country to her sons, and, turning aside from all thought of personal pleasure, sternly set his face to duty, sprang to her defense, and enlisted in the Provisional Army of Tennessee in the early spring of 1861. When the State seceded and the State troops were transferred to the army of the Confederacy, he was made adjutant on the staff of that distinguished preacher-soldier, Col. Wyley M. Reid, in whose Church he had long been a devoted member, and remained with him until his chief fell, in the forefront at Shiloh.

Upon the reorganization of the army after Shiloh he went to Lincoln County, saw his girl wife with her baby, and assisted in the organization and equipment of a company for the mounted artillery service, and marched them one hundred and ten strong, on their own horses and furnished with their own uniforms, side arms, camp furniture, and rations, to Lavergne, where they were sworn into the service and offered themselves to that "Wizard of the Saddle," Gen. N. B. Forrest. But, alas for the poverty of the cause upon the altar of which they had offered themselves! there were no guns for them, and the only thing to be done was for officers and privates alike to take service in the ranks and, as the grim chieftain expressed it, "wait until they could capture, a [Yankee] battery." This they manfully did, and thus became a part of that glorious troop . . .[30]

ALLISON, THOMAS F. P.: Was born April 28, 1832, in Williamson County, Tenn. His education was received at the academies at Triune and Franklin; Western Reserve College, Hudson, Ohio; Jackson College, Columbia, Tenn., and the Lebanon Law School. He obtained a license, but never practiced. He farmed in Williamson County for some years, sold out and engaged in cotton planting in Tunica County, Miss. When the war broke out he returned to Middle Tennessee and enlisted as private in the Fourth Tennessee Cavalry (Starnes' Regiment). When Company "F" was formed, he was elected Second Lieutenant, and was later appointed on the staff of Colonel Starnes, where he remained until the Colonel died in 1863. He was then ordered to report to General Forrest for duty on his staff, remaining with him until the formation of Gen. Tyree H. Bell's brigade. He served on General Bell's staff—in Forrest's Cavalry—until the surrender. He was with Forrest in all his campaigns, battles and raids, and was paroled at Gainesville, Ala., April 11, 1865.

Thomas F. P. Allison.

After the close of the war he resumed farming in Williamson County, and in 1871 was elected to the Legislature, and to the State Senate from Williamson and Maury Counties in 1873.

Major Allison was appointed Commissioner of Agriculture by Governor Turney in 1893, and reappointed in 1895; which position he still holds [1896].[31]

Charles W. Anderson.

ANDERSON, CHARLES W.: Maj. Chas. W. Anderson was, perhaps, more constantly by the side of Forrest than any of his Staff Officers being his Private Secretary—in camp, on the march, and in battle. He resides still [in 1896] on his farm that he left as Railroad Superintendent before going into the war.[32]

ANDERSON, DEWITT: Capt. DeWitt Anderson died at his home near Marianna, Ark., August 21 [1902?]. Capt. Anderson was a representative scion of one of the oldest and most distinguished families of Tennessee, where he was reared to manhood. He enlisted at the age of seventeen as a soldier in the Confederate army in the company of his brother, Capt. Monroe Anderson, Seventh Tennessee Infantry Regiment, and was in active service in Virginia until he was discharged, having succumbed to a severe attack of rheumatism, which unfitted him for service.

Returning home and having recruited his health, he enlisted in a company commanded by Capt. Paul Anderson, in the memorable Fourth Tennessee Cavalry Regiment, which was brigaded with the Third Arkansas, Eleventh Texas, and Terry's Texas Rangers at various times under Gens. Tom Harrison, John A. Wharton, Paul Anderson, Joseph Wheeler, and Bedford Forrest. No soldier ever did more severe service or participated in more active fighting than did Capt. DeWitt Anderson. He was an ideal soldier, ever ready for duty, brave and resolute. Six months before the close of the war he was taken prisoner and confined at Johnson's Island.

As a citizen and civilian he was strong in his convictions, resolute of purpose, with a magnetic force and energy of intellect that made his influence felt in the community in which he lived. His care and attention were absorbed in the management of the affairs of his plantation on Langville River, in Arkansas. Courteous and cordial of manner, generous and hospitable, in conversation earnest, forceful, and fluent, his recital of events attracted the undivided attention of his hearers. His companionship was ever sought for, and he drew around him a coterie of the best citizenship of the country.

His eventful life closed at the age of fifty-nine, and in accord with his expressed desire his remains were interred beside his brothers, Col. Paul and Capt. Monroe Anderson, at Helena, Ark. Capt. Anderson was the youngest of seven brothers, all of whom wore the gray. Two sisters survive him—Mrs. Andrew McGregor, of Lebanon, Tenn., and Mrs. Sam S. Ashe, of Houston, Tex.[33]

ARMSTRONG, FRANK CRAWFORD: May 16, 1861, appointed second lieutenant of cavalry, but declined the commission; March 6, 1862, appointed assistant adjutant general to Gen. Ben McCulloch; May 14, 1862, elected colonel 3rd Louisiana Infantry; January 30, 1863, appointed brigadier general. Commands: In 1863 commanded brigade in Forrest's Division, Van Dorn's Cavalry, consisting of Tennessee, Kentucky, and Arkansas troops; commanded a division consisting of G. G. Dibrell's and Thomas Harrison's brigades under Gen. James Longstreet, in East Tennessee; afterwards commanded a brigade in J. R. Chalmers's division, under Gen. Richard Taylor.[34]

ARNOLD, JAMES: Comrade James Arnold departed this life at his home, in Wartrace, Tenn., July 29, 1915, and was laid to rest in Hollywood Cemetery beside his dearly loved wife and two noble sons, who had preceded him to the spirit land.

James Arnold was born near Shelbyville, Tenn., October 25, 1843. When he was eleven years old his parents moved to Belton, Tex., where they both died. Soon afterwards the War between the States came on, and James Arnold, though not eighteen years of age, enlisted in the 6th Texas Cavalry, Ross's Texas Brigade, which was subsequently a part of Forrest's Cavalry. Comrade Arnold made a splendid record as a soldier, taking part in many of the engagements of his command, and was noted for his activity and bravery. In recognition of his valued services he was attached to Forrest's staff. He was captured near the close of the war and placed in prison at Camp Chase, but was shortly taken to Point Lookout, where he remained until the war was over. He then returned to Tennessee and made his home in Shelbyville.

In 1870 he was married to Miss Nannie Francis, of Winchester, and to them were born two sons and two daughters, of whom the daughters survive him. He is also

James Arnold.

survived by his brother, J. O. Arnold, with whom he was associated in the merchandise business for over thirty years.

Having accumulated quite a large fortune, Comrade Arnold retired from business several years ago. He was a member of the Baptist Church and served faithfully as deacon, Sunday school superintendent, and clerk. He was a relative by marriage of the late editor and founder of the *Confederate Veteran* [Sumner A. Cunningham], and they were close personal friends.[35]

ARNOLD, JAMES M.: James M. Arnold entered the military service of the Confederate States as a private in the Columbus Riflemen, of Columbus, Miss., on May 1, 1861, which company afterward became Company K, Fourteenth Mississippi Infantry, commanded by Col. W. E. Baldwin. He was with his company in the battle of Fort Donelson, and there became a prisoner and was sent to Camp Douglas. He was exchanged with his regiment in 1862, which reorganized at Raymond, Miss., where he was made sergeant. He served with this company in the skirmishes and small fights in North Mississippi and in the defense of Jackson.

In January, 1864, the Sixth Mississippi Cavalry was organized, with Col. Isham Harrison commanding, at which time Arnold was elected second lieutenant of Company I; C. A. Johnson was captain. The regiment was attached to Mabry's Brigade, which was in service under Gen. Forrest during the skirmishes in and around Vicksburg, and was at the taking of the transports and gunboats on the Tennessee River, near Johnsonville. This campaign having disabled the horses of Mabry's Brigade, it was for a while left in garrison at Corinth, Miss. Later the brigade was in the lead of the charge at the battle of Harrisburg, Miss., one of the bloodiest of the war, where cavalry alone were engaged. The brigade was dismounted and marched in line of battle to within fifty steps of the Federal line, entrenched, where Mabry's horse was shot down and Col. Isham Harrison and Lieut.-Col. Nelms, of Arnold's Regiment, were killed, his captain slightly wounded, and over one-half of the privates were killed or wounded. The regiment was afterward united with two others, forming Stark's Mississippi Brigade, in Chalmers' Division, and was engaged in skirmishes with Gen. Wilson's command en route to Selma, Ala. The other brigade of Chalmers' Division (Armstrong's) met Wilson's command in the last battle of the war.

James M. Arnold surrendered with his command under Forrest at Livingston, Ala. He was never sick nor absent during the four years of the war, except while sitting as a member of the Mississippi Legislature. Being a member of that body, he was exempt from military service, but remained with his command all the while, except during the sessions of the Legislature. After the war he returned to Columbus, Miss., where he commenced the practise of law, and continued to practise until 1877, when he was appointed circuit judge of the district by Gov. Stone. He held that position for a number of years, and then was appointed one of the justices of the Supreme Court of Mississippi, and was afterward made chief justice of that court, from which position he resigned, when he returned to the practise of law at Birmingham, Ala.[36]

ASHCRAFT, JOHN W.: John W. Ashcraft, Commander of Bill Dawson Camp, United Confederate Veterans, at Dyersburg, Tenn., and one of Dyer County's most highly esteemed citizens, died on June 20, 1932, at his home in Newbern, Tenn., at the age of eighty-five years. He was born in Decatur County, April 5, 1847; moved to Dyer County in 1890, where he lived until his death.

John W. Ashcraft volunteered and went to war at fifteen years of age. He served three years, staying till the close of the war. He was with General Forrest, Company I, 1st Tennessee Cavalry. He was captured and spent one year at Rock Island prison. Again captured, he was for several months at Camp Chase, Ohio. Near the close of the war, he was exchanged and at the close was somewhere in North Carolina. On account of the bushwhackers in East Tennessee, he walked to his home in Middle Tennessee by way of South Carolina, Georgia, Alabama, and Mississippi.

Comrade Ashcraft . . . attended every Confederate reunion except two. He failed to attend these on the account of sickness. But just as the veterans were gathering and answering the Roll Call at the Richmond Reunion, he answered the Roll Call in Heaven.

He was a man of noble purposes, ever loyal to all that was good and true. He was also a loyal and faithful member of the Methodist Church.

In his Confederate uniform, which he loved and which represented the beloved cause for which he fought, he was laid to rest in Fair View Cemetery at Newbern. Surviving are his wife, two sons and three daughters.[37]

ASHWORTH, CARLTON: Carlton Ashworth, of Wills Point, Tex., [served in] Forrest's command. . . . He belonged to Company I, 1st Confederate Cavalry, under command of Colonel Cox, Captain Bettis, and First Lieutenant Estes. He joined the army at sixteen years of age, was in the battle of Franklin, and later captured.[38]

ATKISSON, G. J.: Capt. G. J. Atkisson, a brave and true Southern soldier, died March 17, 1915, at the age of eighty-three years, and he was laid to rest by his comrades, friends, and associates at Memphis, Tex. Captain Atkisson was commander of his company, in the 9th Tennessee Regiment, a good part of the time under General Forrest. Men who knew him report that he was a good and faithful officer, always ready to do his duty. At the close of the war he went to Texas, and for a number of years he had been an honored citizen of Memphis, where he organized the U.C.V. Camp, which was named in his honor. He is survived by two sons and three daughters—D. D. and G. B. Atkisson, Mrs. J. A. Whaley, Mrs. T. A. Hart, and Miss Biffie Atkisson.[39]

G. J. Atkisson.

BABB, D. W.: On the 14th of December, 1929, Comrade D. W. Babb answered to the last roll call. He was born on October 12, 1841, hence was eighty-eight years old. On December 17, 1867, he was most happily married to Miss Mattie Atkins, a devout Christian woman, always in hearty sympathy and helpfulness in his beloved work. He was converted early in life, and joined the Methodist Episcopal Church, South. In 1872, he was called to preach, joined the North Mississippi Conference, served various charges most acceptably for fifty-two years, and was superannuated at his own request in 1924, at the age of eighty-three years.

Comrade Babb joined the Confederate army in July, 1863, and was assigned to Company B, 6th Mississippi Cavalry and served till the close of the war under the leadership of General Forrest. In the early part of 1864, he was elected captain of his company, and a braver officer never drew sword.

Captain Babb was a man of fine mind and a most remarkable memory. He sleeps beside his wife in the old family burying ground, a few miles from Corinth, Miss. So a great and good man has "passed over the river," a great man because he was a wonderfully good man. Scores who knew him best greatly mourn his departure.[40]

BALCH, L. C.: L. C. Balch, born in Panola County, Miss., is the son of R. C. Balch, Captain of Cavalry under Forrest, and grandson of John Bloomer Balch, who was a private in the Confederate service. He is a great-grandson of Amos Balch, a soldier from North Carolina in the Revolutionary army. Comrade Balch enlisted as a private in the "Sardis Blues" May 8, 1861, which was company E of the Twelfth Mississippi Regiment, thus making three generations serving the Confederacy at one time. He was severely wounded at the battle of Seven Pines, which confined him to his bed for two months. From this wound he is now a cripple. He himself cut the Minie ball out with his pocket knife in December, 1865, and soon thereafter went to work. Although a

L. C. Balch.

constant sufferer from this still unhealed wound, he has never felt that he would exchange places with the man who refused to fight for his country.

Comrade Balch married Miss E. F. Walker in Copiah County, Miss., July 3, 1867, commenced the practice of law in 1871, and moved to Little Rock in 1881. He is a member of Omer R. Weaver Camp, U.C.V., of this city, and of the Sons of the American Revolution. He was a member at large of the Domestic Control Committee of Mississippi, and took part in the campaigns in that State from 1875 to 1880; was a member of the Lower House of the General Assembly of Arkansas in 1887, and was the originator of the railroad commission bill in that State.[41]

BANKHEAD, L. J.: L. J. Bankhead, long-time resident of Paris, Tex., died at his home there at the age of eighty-six, following a long period of ill health. Funeral services were from the First Christian Church, and burial at Evergreen Cemetery. He is survived by his wife, formerly Miss Susan Alcinda Miller, three sons, and a daughter. He also leaves a sister.

Comrade Bankhead was born December 8, 1845, at Holly Springs, Miss. In 1862, he joined the Confederate army, serving with Rucker's Brigade, 18th Mississippi Militia, later joining Captain Mitchell's Independents. After a year's service with the latter, he was transferred to General Forrest's command, Russell's Brigade, and took part in many of the major engagements of that command.

Going to Texas, he was married in August, 1874, and ten years later he moved to Paris, making his home there continuously from that time. He took active part in civic and other community affairs and served several years on the school board and as a member of the city council. He was engaged in farming and other business enterprises for many years, until impaired health interfered with his activities.

As a member of the Confederate Veterans' Camp, he was prominent in its work and attended all gatherings of that body.[42]

BARGER, W. GLEASON: W. G. Barger died at his home, near Martin, Tenn., in July, 1906, aged sixty-six years. He served throughout the war in Company H, 7th Tennessee Cavalry, under General Forrest, which is proof of his service as an active soldier. He was married in 1873 to Miss S. E. Carlin, daughter of Elder John H. D. Carlin, A.B., D.D., one of the most noted scholars and ablest divines of the Baptist denomination in West Tennessee. Ten children blessed this happy union. Comrade Barger, by industry and economy, became one of the wealthy men of Weakley County, and had many friends.[43]

BARLOW, JOSEPH CANTRILL: Capt. J. C. Barlow, a beloved citizen of Phillips County, Ark., died at the home of his daughter, Mrs. A. P. Coolidge, in Helena, on September 17, 1920.

Joseph Cantrill Barlow was born in Scott County, Ky., on January 3, 1836. He went to Helena from Georgetown, Ky., in 1859 and made that his home until the beginning of the War between the States. In February, 1861, he participated in the movement which resulted in the capture of the arsenal at Little Rock from the United States troops. In April, 1861, he enlisted as a private in Gen. Patrick Cleburne's command and served with that distinguished Confederate officer until the State troops were reorganized and transferred to the service of the Confederate States of America. He then joined the 2nd Arkansas Battery, having selected the artillery as his arm of the service, and served under Maj. F. A. Shoupe until that officer was transferred to the Army of Tennessee. The battery was a part of Gen. N. B. Forrest's command. Captain Barlow served with General Forrest until within a few months of surrender. He was sent to Mobile and was there during the siege of that city. After the fall of Mobile he went to Meridian, Miss., where he was paroled on May 13, 1865, as a member of Gen. Dick Taylor's command. Captain Barlow was thought to be the last of the commissioned officers serving under General Forrest.

After the war Captain Barlow went to Memphis, Tenn., and later returned to Helena. During the days of Reconstruction Captain Barlow organized a section of artillery and patrolled Phillips County, every township furnishing a company of cavalry, serving under Col. Paul Anderson. The result of this movement was to take official affairs of the county out of the hands of the carpetbaggers [meaning, in general, Yankee Liberals].

Captain Barlow served several terms as mayor of Helena, and throughout his life after the war he was identified with the business interests and welfare of Phillips County. No citizen of Helena was more highly respected and none more popular personally. He is survived by one daughter and one son, J. C. Barlow, Jr., of Trenton, and seven grandchildren.[44]

BARNETT, JOHN W.: John W. Barnett, of V. Y. Cook Camp No. 1474, United Confederate Veterans, Newark, Ark., died at the residence of his daughter at that place September 10, 1921, aged seventy-four years. He entered the Confederate Army in December, 1862, a private in Company E, 7th Tennessee Cavalry, Forrest's Corps, with which he served until the end in May, 1865. He was wounded at Tupelo, Miss., July 15, 1864. He was faithful as a soldier and as a citizen and died as he had lived, in affectionate allegiance to the will of his Maker.[45]

BARRON, S. B.: On February 2, 1912, one of the oldest and most respected citizens of Rusk, Tex., answered the last roll call. He was born in Gurley, Ala., November 9, 1834. His father, Samuel B. Barron, was a native of South Carolina, a soldier of the War of 1812, and a captain under Andrew Jackson.

His parents died early, thus leaving him to work his way through the world as best he could. Having studied law, he came to Texas in 1859 and located at Rusk, where he continuously resided until the time of his death, excepting the time he was a soldier in the Confederate army.

When the call to arms was made, in 1861, he volunteered with the first company that left the county for the front, Company C, 3rd Texas Cavalry, participating in the battles of Oak Hill, Elkhorn, Corinth, Farmington, Iuka, Hatchie Bridge, Oakland, Holly Springs, and he was wounded at Davis's Mill. He was promoted for courage and gallantry to the rank of second lieutenant, and later fought at Jackson, Miss., Liverpool, and Yazoo City. He was in the Georgia Campaign of 1864 from start to finish. He was captured at Lovejoy Station, but made his escape by playing dead.

He was with General Hood's army in Tennessee in 1864-65, and under General Forrest in the battles near Pulaski, Tenn., and Sugar Creek, said to have been the last battle of the war in that department. He was detailed by Gen. S. L. Ross to be judge advocate of the permanent brigade court-martial, and served as such with credit. The regiment to which Captain Barron belonged was one among the best that was mustered into the Confederate service—a regiment dubbed "Old Ironsides" and given a post of honor and of danger in every advance and retreat by the army which it served, and he endured all the dangers to which his command was exposed.

S. B. Barron.

When the war ended Captain Barron returned to his home, in Rusk, Tex., and again resumed the practice of law. He held many positions of trust and honor, having been county clerk, county judge, and justice of the peace. He was a man in whom people had great confidence, a member of the Presbyterian Church, the Masonic order, and Knights of Honor. He spent several years during the latter part of his life in writing a book, *The Lone Star Defenders*, which relates in a plain, unvarnished way the dangers, trials, and hardships through which the Confederate soldier passed while on the march, in camp, or on the battle field.

On September 5, 1865, Captain Barron was married to Miss Eugenia Wiggins, daughter of Col. James M. Wiggins, who died in 1882. The only surviving child of that union is Dr. W. P. Barron, of Carmona, Tex. In 1884 he was married to Mrs. Olympia Miller (née Scott), who died in 1893, leaving a daughter, Miss Anna, now of Ladonia, Tex. His third marriage was to Mrs. Agatha Leftwich (née Scott), formerly of Huntsville, Ala. He was greatly esteemed by his comrades.[46]

BASKERVILLE, GEORGE BOOTH: Rev. George Booth Baskerville, the son of Dr. John Tabb and Margaret Malone Baskerville, was born near Somerville, Tenn., March 29, 1847, where he lived until his death, July 31, 1928.

As a boy, he had the best educational advantages in his time and section. Imbued with the high and noble traditions of the South, and knowing that her cause was just, he joined Company E, 12th Tennessee Cavalry, on October 11, 1862, when only fifteen years old. He served with this command until the spring of 1865, when the 12th Tennessee was consolidated with Forrest's Old Regiment. He surrendered with General Forrest at Gainesville, Ala., May 11, 1865, after following that peerless leader through all his campaigns.

Returning home at the close of hostilities, he entered college, and, in 1868, joined the Methodist Church under the ministration of his distinguished father, Rev. John Tabb Baskerville, and was soon himself an ordained minister. For sixty years, Dr. George Baskerville was a foremost leader of Methodist divines in Tennessee; for twelve years, he was presiding elder, and for four years, pastor of the Second Methodist Church in Memphis.

Failing health caused him to retire from active duties as a minister, nevertheless he continued to preach throughout his section of Tennessee until his death.

On November 29, 1869, he married Sallie Lewis Read, of Brownsville, who died in 1921. Five children survive them, three sons and two daughters. Dr. Baskerville was buried in the cemetery at Stanton, Tenn.

A gallant, fearless soldier in youth, defending his native Southland throughout the four years of incessant warfare; a militant disciple of Christ, carrying the gospel all his life by his words and his personal character to unnumbered multitudes; a devoted husband and father in his own home, finding a hearty welcome everywhere and in every other home, the life of this beloved comrade was long in the land which the Lord, his God, gave him; his individual record was part of the history of the Confederacy and of the Methodist Church; his memory is cherished by the thousands in the different Christian flocks he served and saved as a minister; and his own soul will enjoy eternally the peace and happiness of the blessed and the faithful.[47]

BAZZELL, ROBERT I.: Comrade Robert I. Bazzell died at his home in Clinton, Ky., Saturday, June 7, 1902. He had been in feeble health for a long time, and had constant and loving attention from children and friends. The end came very peacefully, as he died in the triumphs of a living faith. He was a faithful member of the Methodist Church, a Mason of long standing, and a Confederate veteran who did well his part.

Comrade Bazzell was born in Maury County, Tenn., April 22, 1843, and came to Kentucky in his boyhood. He enlisted in the Seventh Kentucky Infantry, C.S.A., at the beginning of the war. He was with his regiment at Shiloh, Vicksburg, and on other hard fought fields. Later he was transferred to the Twelfth Kentucky Cavalry, and served under Gen. Forrest until the sad, sad end.

Returning to Kentucky after the surrender, he served his people in many positions of trust, among others that of sheriff of Hickman County for four years, trustee of the jury fund, etc. He was a member of our Camp (the Col. Ed Crossland, 1228), and served one year as its Commander. Bob has "passed over the river," leaving another vacant place in "the thin gray line." It is well with him. May our God bless and save all "our boys" left behind![48]

BELL, ISAAC THOMAS: Isaac T. Bell was born at Gallatin, Tenn., July 17, 1841, the son of Gen. Tyree H. Bell, brigadier general under Forrest in the war. Enlisting first as a member of Company H, 7th Tennessee Cavalry, Col. I. T. Bell was transferred to Company A, 12th Tennessee Infantry, Col. T. H. Bell commanding, in 1862; and after the battle of Chickamauga he was promoted to aid-de-camp and assigned to Gen. Tyree Bell's brigade, Forrest's Cavalry, in 1863, and so served to the end of the war. He was twice wounded—in the arm at Tishomingo, and in the side at Bryce's Crossroads.

Isaac Thomas Bell.

After the war Comrade Bell served eight years as County Court Clerk of Henderson County, Tenn., and located later at McKenzie. He was married at Lexington, Tenn., in 1868 to Miss Seraphine Elizabeth Smith, who survives him with the four children born in Tennessee—three sons and a daughter. In the latter part of 1883 he removed his family to California and located at Sanger. A son was born there, who died as an infant. In 1886 he removed to Visalia and there served as clerk in the land office under his father. In later years he was interested in the real estate business and also handled land office cases. At Visalia he organized the Gen. Joseph E. Johnston Camp, U.C.V., and also served as the Adjutant of the Pacific Division, U.C.V. He was for years prominent as an Odd Fellow, having joined the organization in 1866, and throughout his life was actively interested. He was Grand Senior Warden of the State and would have become Grand Patriarch of the order in a little more than a year. He was also a prominent Forester from 1899 and served many years as its Financial Secretary.

As a citizen of Visalia none stood higher than Captain Bell. He was an honest, sincere, big-hearted man and Christian, and was universally loved and respected. All California Daughters [U.D.C.] remember the beautiful welcome to Visalia that was given by Captain Bell as Commander of Joe Johnston Camp when the annual convention of the California Division was held there during the time that his daughter, Mrs. Samuel Cary Dunlap, was President of the Division.

Captain Bell was one of the first subscribers to the *Confederate Veteran* in California, and throughout the years of its existence his interest had not waned.

His death occurred on June 3, 1914, and in his going there is the loss of one of the most prominent and best-beloved of the Confederate veterans.[49]

BELL, TYREE, H.: Tyree H. Bell was born September 6, 1815, and was reared in Sumner County, Tenn. In 1858 he moved with his family to Dyer County, same State. At the beginning of the war he raised the first company of volunteers that went from Newbern, in his adopted county, and was elected captain. At Jackson, Tenn., they were organized into the Twelfth Tennessee Infantry, and Capt. Bell was elected its lieutenant. Robert Milton Russell, of Trenton, Tenn., was chosen colonel.

This regiment fought at Belmont, the first battle in the West at least, and Lieut. Col. Bell was in command of the regiment (Col. Russell being in command of the brigade). Two horses were shot from under Col. Bell in this battle. In the battle of Shiloh he commanded the regiment (as Col. Russell was still in command of the brigade). In this battle, in which his regiment was constantly engaged, he lost three horses, all shot from under him while he escaped unhurt, except that the first horse (that was shot from under him) fell on one of his legs, which lamed him for a short time; but he was soon remounted, and continued through the battle.

Tyree H. Bell.

In the reorganization of the army at Corinth, Miss., the Twelfth and Forty-Seventh Tennessee Regiments, the latter number becoming obsolete, were consolidated and Bell was elected colonel. He led his command in that famous raid into Kentucky under Kirby Smith, and was in all of the engagements. His regiment fought a brigade at LaVergne, Tenn., and it was also in the great battle of Murfreesboro under his leadership. In the LaVergne fight he completely routed the enemy, capturing many prisoners. After this he was sent as a recruiting officer into West Tennessee, where he raised a brigade of cavalry. With it he reported to Gen. N. B. Forrest in the fall of 1864, and was soon commissioned as brigadier general. From that time he "was with Forrest on every raid and in every battle that was fought during the remainder of the war." Although in many battles, he only received one severe wound. That was in the breast and face, at Pulaski, Tenn., from the explosion of a bombshell. That disabled him for only a few days, when he resumed command again. With that exception he was on duty throughout the entire war, surrendering at Gainesville, Ala., with his brigade, May 14, 1865. In 1875 Col. Bell moved to Fresno County, Cal., with his family, where he now resides, hale and hearty in his eighty-fourth year.[50]

[After Gen. Bell's death on August 30, 1902, Gen. George Moorman wrote:] "A famous general in the Confederate army and one of Tennessee's most distinguished sons, his name will always be linked with the history of each as one of 'Forrest's men,' and his fame will go sounding down the ages entwined with laurels won by his dauntless courage and bright deeds."[51]

BEMISS, JAMES HAMILTON: James H. Bemiss, a veteran of the Confederacy, died in Birmingham, Ala., on December 30, 1919, from injuries received in an auto accident shortly before. He was born near Bloomfield, Nelson County, Ky., on June 5, 1842, the eldest son of William H. and Mary Bedford Bemiss. Early in 1861 he enlisted in the Confederate army, going out from Bloomfield with Capt. William Davis McKay's company. This company was sent to Memphis, Tenn., and temporarily attached to the 40th Tennessee Regiment, serving with that command until the fall of Memphis. They were captured at Island No. 10 and after six months in prison at Camp Douglas, Ill., were exchanged, and the company was placed with the 8th Kentucky Infantry, Colonel Lyon.

Comrade Bemiss was elected lieutenant of the company at its organization, and shortly after it was placed with the 8th Kentucky he was made adjutant. His brigade (Lyon's) was mounted late in the summer of 1863 and placed with the intrepid Forrest. Young Bemiss did a good deal of staff duty in the latter part of the war, as his colonel, Shacklett, often commanded the brigade. He was badly wounded at Selma, Ala., Forrest's last great fight. As he was carrying an order to a certain part of the line late in the evening the whole line gave way before the overwhelming force of the enemy. It became a complete rout, and in getting out of this he was passing through the outskirts of the town when he was confronted by a Federal trooper and ordered to surrender. Concluding that he had an equal chance to win, he decided to fight it out; so with his pistol against the Federal's carbine matters soon came to a close, both falling from their horses. After dark both were taken into a house near by, the Federal soldier dying in a few minutes, and the war closed before Lieutenant Bemiss recovered from his wounds.

James Hamilton Bemiss.

After the war he went to Rodney, Miss., and there passed through the days of Reconstruction, helping to redeem the State from carpetbag and negro rule [Note: Yankee Liberals had purposefully placed illiterate racist blacks in powerful political positions in order to disrupt Southern society].[52]

He married there, but, his wife dying in a few years, he removed to Bardstown, Ky., and became connected with a dry goods firm. In 1887 he married again and located in Birmingham, Ala., where he engaged in banking and other lines of business.

Since his younger days Comrade Bemiss had been a member of the Presbyterian Church. He was a true Christian and noble patriot. He was laid to rest with honors by Camp Hardee, U.C.V., of Birmingham, of which he was a member. His wife, two sons (one adopted), and a grandson survive him.

Thus has passed a noble character, a Christian gentleman, a brave Confederate soldier.[53]

BENNETT, W. H.: On April 25, 1903, at Lebanon, Tenn., the place of his birth and life work, Dr. W. H. Bennett, a true soldier and gentleman, went to join the ranks of the faithful who have passed away. When a youth he was a member of Hatton's Seventh Tennessee Regiment, and served in Virginia until the spring of '62, when ill health caused his discharge. In the summer of that year he became, with many of his neighbor boys, a member of the Cedar Snags, commanded by Capt. (afterwards Col.) Paul Anderson.

W. H. Bennett.

This company did escort and courier service first for Gen. Forrest, then for Gen. Wharton, until his transfer to the Trans-Mississippi Department, and he was then chosen by Gen. Hood to do like service for him on the celebrated campaign from Dalton to Jonesboro, Ga., and the subsequent advance into Tennessee.

This service required intelligence and courage of no small degree, and so faithfully was it performed that Capt. Anderson was promoted and gained celebrity throughout the cavalry branch of the service; and his successor, Capt. J. H. Britton, also became widely and favorably known.

The company was then attached to Smith's Fourth Tennessee Cavalry Regiment, and Dr. Bennett served faithfully therein until the end by Gen. Joseph E. Johnston's surrender.

On returning to his home in the spring of '65 he began the great battle of life with the same fortitude previously shown. He chose dentistry for his profession, and graduated from the Baltimore Dental College, and for more than a third of a century practiced skillfully and faithfully, gaining a competence and maintaining the respect of all who knew him. He was a soldier of the cross also, and brought to that service the same faithfulness exhibited elsewhere.

Dr. Bennett was twice married. He leaves his widow and two sons the heritage of a successful, honest, Christian life. On Monday, April 6, his birthday, his former pastor paid him merited tribute to a large concourse of sympathizing friends and a goodly company of old comrades.[54]

BERRY, T. F.: At the age of eighty-five years Dr. T. F. Berry, a veteran of seven wars, including the War between the States, died in Oklahoma City, Okla., on December 24, 1917. He was a native of Kentucky, but had lived in Oklahoma for about eight years, the last two in Oklahoma City. He was prominently connected with the Oklahoma Division, U.C.V., and had been surgeon of the Oklahoma City Brigade during the past year.

While serving with Gen. John H. Morgan's famous command Dr. Berry was captured by the Union forces and confined at Rock Island, Ill. However, during the last year of the war he escaped and made his way back South, where he joined Forrest. Following the surrender at Appomattox, Dr. Berry, with hundreds of other Confederate soldiers, refused to surrender, but went to Mexico. He then went to South America and served in various armies, and he served with the American forces during the Boxer War in China. His book entitled *My Four Years with Morgan* has been widely circulated in Oklahoma and the South. Two children survive him, a son and daughter, the former thought to be serving with Pershing's forces in France.[55]

BETHELL, WILLIAM DECATUR: Capt. William Decatur Bethell was born on February 2, 1840, at Saint Mary's Parish, La., being the son of an extensive sugar planter, who was subsequently engaged in business in Memphis, Tenn.

In 1860 Captain Bethell married the third daughter of Jerome B. Pillow, Cynthia Saunders Pillow, of Maury County, Tenn. At the breaking out of the war, in the spring of 1861, he went to Louisiana and raised a company which his father equipped and which became a part of the 22nd Tennessee Regiment, Captain Bethell being made drillmaster of the regiment. He was in the battles of Belmont and Shiloh, and also Murfreesboro. He was wounded at Shiloh. He afterwards served under General Forrest, and subsequently was appointed and served as a member of General Pillow's staff until the end of the war.

William Decatur Bethell.

The writer of this sketch knew him for many years most intimately, and gladly attests his many noble attributes of heart. He was a man of the people, and never turned his back on friend or foe. Some of his most intimate associates were among the poor men of Memphis. He loved the South, and was true to the instincts of his birth, faithful to the teachings of his father, and constant in his love for the State.

Captain Bethell was a man of fine business capacity. Shortly after the war he engaged in sugar-planting in his native State, thence moved to Maury County, Tenn., where he remained until the death of his father. Then his business interests called him to Memphis, where he became connected with the State National Bank as President, proving himself a man of exceptional capacity, energy, and enterprise. He took a prominent part in many departments of business, banking, insurance, manufacturing, railroads, real estate, etc. He was successful in whatever he undertook, his last public service being in the interest of the "Taxing District," of which he was elected president in 1890. Later, resigning on account of ill health, he moved to Denver, Colo., where he lived until his death, in August, 1906. Three children survive him. His eldest daughter is Mrs. John M. Foster, of Denver, Colo.; his other daughter is Mrs. John P. Edrington, of Memphis, Tenn.; and his son, W. D. Bethell, resides at Redlands, Cal.[56]

Bell G. Bidwell.

BIDWELL, BELL G.: The name of Maj. Bell G. Bidwell brings to memory one of the noblest, bravest, and most lovable of the many true men who graced the Confederate army, and he certainly merits distinguished mention in the veteran's roll of honor.

Bell G. Bidwell was a native of Robertson County, Tenn., born February 19, 1837, and there he grew to young manhood. Developing a brilliant intellect, he soon acquired a fine education, graduating at the Nashville Medical University. Medicine not being the profession he desired to follow, he at once entered the Law School at Lebanon, Tenn., from which he graduated in 1860 with distinguished honor.

Finding himself thus early in life the possessor of diplomas in two of the professions, medicine and law, he at once impressed his personality upon the community in which he lived, and early after the war came to the front as the most brilliant orator in the State, a strong rival in debate with John F. House, long a distinguished member of Congress.

With the fall of Fort Sumter, in 1861, Bidwell was among the first to call for volunteers and to leave Robertson County as captain in command of men, who were of the noblest and truest soldiers that ever marched to battle; and every man was devoted to the captain from the beginning, to the end of the struggle. Other companies were soon formed, and the 30th Tennessee Regiment was formed of nine hundred and seventy-five men from Robertson and Sumner Counties, in which Captain Bidwell's company was assigned to first rank (Company A). He was then the youngest officer in the command. John W. Head, of Gallatin, was Colonel; R. H. Murphy, Lieutenant Colonel; J. J. Turner, Major. The regiment went into camp at Red Springs for drill, and in November was ordered to Fort Henry, and later to Fort Donelson, which battle began on February 13, 1862. The 1st Tennessee Brigade was formed, composed of the 30th, 49th, and 50th Tennessee Regiments, and McCoot's company of cavalry under Forrest.

Sometime previous General Tilghman had asked for a company from the 30th Tennessee for heavy artillery service, and at Captain Bidwell's request his company was chosen. The companies of Captains Beaumont and Bidwell were assigned to take charge of the water batteries, with Captain Dixon, of the Engineer Corps, as chief of artillery. Captain Beaumont being absent on furlough, Captain Bidwell was placed in command of the batteries. The large Federal fleet had steamed up to within three hundred yards of the little fort. The battle was terrific, with all the odds in favor of the Federal fleet; so this was a test which demonstrated Captain Bidwell's extraordinary military capacity. His coolness, courage, and great skill in handling the situation secured the admiration of that fine officer, General Forrest, and received his highest commendation in report of that battle.

    . . . [After the War] Major Bidwell returned to his home broken in health, suffering from malaria, and for almost a year was a confirmed invalid. He opened a law office at Springfield, Tenn., but was later drawn to Paducah, Ky., where he again opened an office, and soon secured a lucrative practice. He always won the confidence and esteem of the people. Major Bidwell was married in 1871 to Miss Eleanor Patrick Flournoy, and a son and daughter came to bless their home. He served two terms in the Kentucky Legislature, 1873-76, where he made a record for himself and became a leader in the House. That he served with distinction was evidenced by a statement in the *Courier-Journal* that "if we had a man of his talent in Louisville we would push a man out of place to push him on."

    Friends urged Major Bidwell to run for Congress; but circumstances decided him to remove to Texas, which he did in the fall of 1879, locating in Weatherford, where he soon established a lucrative law practice and made friends. He was shortly afterwards employed by the Texas and Pacific Railway, and held a prominent position in the law department of the road for twenty years. As a corporation lawyer, he became eminent. The company manifested many evidences of esteem and friendship for him; while the confidence, friendship, and regard of the managers for him was unbounded. In his home town of Weatherford no man was held in higher esteem or loved and trusted more. After several years of illness, his old enemy, rheumatism, having once more attacked him, he quietly passed away on the 30th of June, 1904, leaving a memory that will live green and bloom in the hearts of his friends during life.[57]

BIGGS, GEORGE TALLY: George Tally Biggs was born June 17, 1830, and died on June 17, 1918, at his home, in Lauderdale County, Miss. He had made this county his home since early manhood. He was a farmer by choice, a law-abiding citizen, a true friend, and a Christian gentleman. As a Confederate soldier he served in Company H, 2nd Mississippi Regiment, Armstrong's Brigade, Forrest's command. He was true to every trust and never ashamed of the laurels he won as such.[58]

BIRDSONG, THOMAS LOGAN: Thomas L. Birdsong was born in Giles County, Tenn., January 23, 1845; and died at his home, near Pulaski, on February 17, 1911. In his early life the family removed to Alabama, where he lived until the breaking out of the war. At the age of sixteen years he enlisted in the 4th Alabama Regiment, and bravely followed the lead of Forrest until paroled and honorably discharged as a soldier of the Confederacy. No less honorable and true has he been as a private citizen since he laid down his arms.

    His loyalty to the [Conservative] principles for which he fought and the leader whom he followed never faltered; and though a sufferer for many years past, his pleasure has been to receive his old comrades and meet them in reunion. His attractive disposition drew people to him, and his home was long known as the "Home for the Weary," be they rich or poor, and the good that he has done in his unpretentious life cannot be estimated. A devoted wife, three sons, and a host of friends mourn for him who now sleeps "the sleep that knows no waking" until the resurrection morn.[59]

BISHOP, DAVID: David Bishop, aged eighty-five years, died February 11, 1922, at his home in Lacy, Tenn. He was also born, reared, and spent his life in the same district. His hospitality was unbounded, and his home was seldom without guests. He was a man of the highest sense of honor, thoughtful and considerate of others. As a brave Southern soldier, he followed wherever the gallant Forrest led. In 1856 he was married to Miss Louisa Grantham, and to them were born eleven children, his wife and eight children surviving him. He was a member of the Baptist Church for thirty-five years.[60]

BITTICK, JOHN HOLLAND: John Holland Bittick, son of Green and Sallie Brownlow Bittick, was born November 16, 1839, at the family home near Pulaski, in Giles County, Tenn.; and at Rives, Tenn., on June 17, 1924, he was promoted to the heavenly home, in his eighty-sixth year.

In his early boyhood the family removed to Gibson County, near Kenton, where he grew to manhood. At the age of nineteen years, he professed religion and united with the Cumberland Presbyterian Church and remained a faithful Christian throughout his long and useful life.

When he was but fourteen, his lovely Christian mother slipped away to heaven, leaving him and a younger sister to care for a large family of younger brothers and sisters, a task which they performed faithfully and well.

In April, 1861, he was among the first volunteers for service in defense of our Southland, joining Company H, of the 9th Tennessee Infantry. He was severely wounded at the battle of Shiloh, which incapacitated him for further infantry service, and he joined Forrest's Cavalry, was elected lieutenant at Corinth, Miss., and followed that dauntless leader throughout all the hard-fought campaigns of his matchless career.

On returning home he married Miss Harriett Alice Latimer, daughter of Andrew Jackson and Harriett Underwood Latimer, with whom he traveled life's rugged pathway more than fifty-nine years. Together they reared six children, three sons and three daughters.

When help was needed in reconstruction days to hold our Southland for its rightful possessors, he joined the [Conservative pro-Constitution organization known as the] "Invisible Empire" [the Ku Klux Klan] and followed his old beloved leader until the task was done.[61] He was a member of Warren McDonald Camp, U.C.V., and no time was more joyful to him than that with his old comrades.

He became a Mason in early manhood and was raised to the Royal Arch degree more than thirty years ago. After funeral services at the old Beech Church, the Masons took charge and tenderly laid his body away beneath a mound of beautiful flowers.[62]

Robert J. Black.

BLACK, ROBERT J.: Maj. Robert J. Black, A.D.C. on staff of Gen. A. J. Vaughan, commanding Tennessee Division, U.C.V., was born in Fayette County, Tenn., in 1841. Prior to our great war his family removed to Haywood County, near Stanton. Young Robert promptly joined Hill's Cavalry, from Tipton County, which became Company B, of Logwood's Battalion, afterwards merged into the Second Tennessee Regiment. He was soon made orderly sergeant, and then elected lieutenant of the company, and so continued to the end. His regiment served under Gens. W. H. Jackson, James R. Chalmers, Earl Van Dorn, Edmund W. Rucker, A. W. Campbell, and Lieut. Gen. N. Bedford Forrest, in numerous scouts, skirmishes, and battles, Lieut. Black always being on hand for active service. His company served as escort for Gen. G. B. Loring while the division was about Canton, Jackson, Yazoo City, Miss. Later Lieut. Black was detailed to act as commissary on Gen. E. W. Rucker's staff. Comrade Black notes that the most complete victory he ever witnessed was at the battle of Tishomingo Creek, when Gen. Forrest, with about twenty-eight hundred men, cleaned up about eighty-five hundred well-equipped Federal troops, capturing their entire wagon train and army stores, together with all their artillery. It is said a majority of the command were killed, wounded, or captured.

Lieut. Black was cut by a sailor at Lockridge's Mill, shot through the left leg in a cavalry charge near Hernando, Miss., and shot through the left arm at Union City while preparing for its capture. He had two horses shot under him at Oxford and at Tishomingo Creek, Miss. His son, Joe Stonewall Black, is now with the Second Tennessee Infantry. Maj. Black is a member of the Confederate Historical Association of Memphis. Its camp number is 28, U.C.V. He was predecessor as Adjutant General and Chief of Staff with Gen. A. J. Vaughan to Col. Hickman.[63]

BLACK, WILLIAM FERROL: Comrade William Ferrol Black was born near Waverly, Tenn., on June 6, 1846. His parents, William and Jane Teas Black, moved to the Solomon Mill neighborhood, Fayette County, in 1851, and from there to Bellemont and finally to Stanton, Haywood County, in 1860. In June, 1862, he joined Company B, 7th Tennessee Cavalry, then encamped near Holly Springs. J. P. Russell was captain; H. P. Sale, first lieutenant; and his brother, R. J. Black, second lieutenant. This regiment became a part of Gen. N. B. Forrest's command when he was transferred to the command of West Tennessee, North Mississippi, and Alabama.

Comrade Black served under General Forrest the rest of the war, being in all of his raids, skirmishes, and battles, and was paroled at Gainesville, Ala., with General Forrest on May 11, 1865. He was married by Rev. A. R. Wilson on April 17, 1872, to Miss Sallie I. Coppedge, of Dancyville, Tenn. Their children were: Henrietta, W. F., and R. E. Black. He died in Memphis on January 14, 1920.

As a man he was quiet, modest, amiable, and just; as a soldier, without fear or reproach; as a husband and father, faithful and devoted; as a friend, true and steadfast. His memory is cherished by all and most by those who knew him best.

A beautiful set of resolutions were adopted by the Confederate Historical Association, Camp 28, which were ordered spread upon the minutes and a copy sent to his family.[64]

William Ferrol Black.

BLACKBURN, JAMES K. POLK: James K. Polk Blackburn was born in Tennessee, but at the age of nineteen he went to Texas with his father's family and was teaching school in Lavaca County, Tex., when the war came on in the sixties. He was enrolled with Terry's Texas Rangers, which command, with a unanimity never surpassed, enlisted "for the war." Young Blackburn fought bravely in the battles of Shiloh, Perryville, Murfreesboro, Chickamauga, and was with General Forrest in numerous raids. He was given a saber by General Morgan for valuable service rendered during a scout at Murfreesboro under hazardous circumstances. At the battle of Farmington he was wounded and his horse killed. This was his last battle, for he was a prisoner on parole during the rest of the war. The chaplain of his regiment, in writing of the battle of Farmington, said: "And the noble Blackburn fell at the head of the column, leading a charge upon the enemy." After his wounds healed, he visited Brick Church, Tenn., where he met the daughter of Robert H. Laird, a wealthy planter, and a few years later they were married. He was a model husband and a good father to the seven sons and two daughters born to this union.

Captain Blackburn took a leading part in building up his country after the war. He represented Giles County, Tenn., with honor in both houses of the State legislature. He was a brave soldier for his beloved South, but it was as a Christian soldier that his character shines brightest. His place at church was never vacant except when hindered providentially, and he taught a Sunday school class for over thirty years in the Christian Church at Lynnville. He was a good neighbor, ever ready to help in time of need, and his passing leaves a vacancy in his community that cannot be filled. On July 6, 1923, he fell asleep peacefully at the ripe age of eighty-six years, and his comrades in arms laid him to rest in Lynwood Cemetery to await the resurrection of the just.[65]

BLANTON, J. C.: Rev. J. C. Blanton died at his home, in Nettleton, Miss., October 8, 1908, aged seventy years. He was licensed to preach just before the beginning of the Civil War, and after hostilities began he entered the cavalry service in the Confederate army, enlisting as a private in Forrest's Regiment.

He rose by gallant conduct to a captaincy, and was recommended for promotion to major just before the surrender. The colonel of Forrest's old cavalry regiment, widely known as Rev. D. C. Kelley, of Tennessee, wrote this of him: "For the sake of a duty which I owe to truth and comradeship, it is a great pleasure to write this tribute to the soldierly excellence of J. C. Blanton, who as a member of Company C, Forrest's old cavalry regiment, I saw rise from the position of private to that of captain of the company. He had been recommended to the position of major by the commanding general before the surrender at Gainesville, Ala. Stonewall Jackson never rode with more seeming coolness into the thickest of the battle than did Blanton. We knew always when the tug of war became hardest and an officer reliable for desperate enterprise was in demand that Blanton was the man to plan and execute the most difficult feat. In camp his men were devoted to him. As an officer he bore his duties not after the ideas of a military martinet, not so much a strict disciplinarian in camp, but as a friend. His men trusted his judgment and unhesitatingly obeyed his orders when battle was hottest."

Soon after the close of the war Dr. Blanton resumed his ministerial work, and was ordained in 1867. His active ministerial life covered a period of forty-two years, twenty-two of which were spent in Alabama, two in Texas, and sixteen years in Mississippi. In all this he endured hardships as a good soldier of Jesus Christ, preaching among the destitute and visiting the afflicted, sacrificing much for the good of others. He was deeply grateful for kindnesses shown to him, and his last public appearance was in a thanksgiving service in which he had been kindly remembered by his friends. He was pastor of the Cumberland Presbyterian Church at Nettleton for some years, and was Chaplain of the U.C.V. Camp there from its organization. He fought a good fight and kept the faith.[66]

BOGGS, DAVID C.: David C. Boggs was born March 15, 1834, and died January 10, 1922, at the Confederate Home of Missouri, of which institution he had been an inmate for a number of years, having long been deprived of his sight. He was a true and tried soldier of the South, having served through the entire four years of bloody war. He was a member of the 2nd Missouri Corps under General Forrest; was in the battles of Elk Horn, Iuka, Corinth, Harrisburg, Fort Pillow, and many others. May his long sleep be the slumber of a faithful soldier is the wish of his old comrades.[67]

BOGY, JOSEPH VITOL: Joseph Vitol Bogy was born in Pine Bluff, Ark., October 29, 1841, and died in Bridgeport, Tex., July 29, 1914. He is survived by his wife, three sons, and a daughter. Comrade Bogy enlisted in Pine Bluff with Captain McNally's battery in 1861 and surrendered at Gainesville, Ala., in April, 1865, under General Forrest, in the 2nd Missouri Battery, commanded by Captain King. He was captured at Vicksburg, Miss., was paroled, and went into camp at Demopolis, Ala., until exchanged. While there he met the young lady, Miss Ruth Smith, who became his wife in November, 1865; and their home was at Pine Bluff until 1874, when they went to Hillsboro, Tex., and then to Willow Point, where he engaged in farming and stock-raising, as well as merchandising. He was also postmaster there for nine years, when his health failed, and he removed to Bridgeport to be with his sons. After going through the war with only two slight wounds, he had the misfortune of injuring his knee with a drawing knife, which crippled him for life.

The ancestors of Joseph Bogy were French, who came from Gascony long before the Revolution and settled in Canada, where they prospered until the British took possession of that country. They were of those four thousand unfortunate families whose sad wanderings are immortalized in Longfellow's *Evangeline*. His mother died when he was two years old, and his education was limited to country schools and one term in college, when he answered the call to fight for the South. He was a member of the Methodist Episcopal Church, South, and lived a consistent Christian life.[68]

BOLING, M. L.: M. L. Boling died at his home, in Sherman, Tex., on April 3, 1921, at the age of seventy-three years. He is survived by his wife and one son, of that city, also a sister of Tuscon, Ariz. Comrade Boling was born on April 10, 1847, in Marshall County, Miss. He enlisted in April, 1864, at Holly Springs, Miss., in Company C, 18th Mississippi Cavalry, Chalmers's Brigade, Forrest's Division, Wheeler's Corps. His company was escort for General Chalmers. He participated in the Harrisburg or Tupelo fight, also in the battles of Johnsonville, Franklin, and Nashville, and many other smaller engagements, the last being at Selma, Ala., and surrendered at Gainesville, Ala. He went to Texas in 1876 and settled in Grayson County, where he had since lived.[69]

BOMAR, WILLIAM S.: William S. Bomar, pioneer citizen of Henry County, Tenn., and member of Fitzgerald-Kendall Camp, U.C.V., of Paris, Tenn., died at the home of his daughter, Mrs. Isom Comer, in the Manleyville community, on November 5 [1929?], after a short illness. He was in his eighty-fifth year.

Born in Henry County, in 1845, of one of the most prominent families in that section, he became a leading citizen of his county and community, and was a lifelong member of the Baptist Church. At the outbreak of the war in 1861, he enlisted and served throughout the conflict as a member of a company under Captain Pettyjohn, Forrest's Cavalry.

After the war, Comrade Bomar was married to Miss Dora Iron, and three sons and two daughters of that marriage survive him. His second wife was Miss Mary Doty, who also survives with their daughter. A large number of grandchildren and great-grandchildren are also left, and there are many friends to mourn the passing of one who had won their respect and love by his upright Christian character.[70]

BONE, H. P.: On September 2, 1911, at his home, near Maysville, Ala., occurred the death of Dr. H. P. Bone in the seventy-fourth year of his age. He was a native of Kentucky, having been born at Elkton in 1838, but grew to manhood and spent his life in Madison County, Ala., where he became a most substantial citizen. He was graduated from Cumberland University in 1857, later taking a degree from the Baltimore College of Dental Surgery.

Upon the outbreak of the War between the States he joined a cavalry company that was organized at New Market, Ala., with Dr. D. C. Kelley for captain. This company was known as "Kelley's Troopers," and became a part of Forrest's original command, serving through the operations around Fort Donelson.

After taking part in the great battle of Shiloh, Dr. Bone was on sick furlough for a time. When sufficiently recovered he was appointed steward in the hospital at Tullahoma, Tenn., Cleburne's Division, under General Bragg. He served in this capacity all through Bragg's Chickamauga campaign.

Field hospitals were abandoned after the battle of Chickamauga, and Dr. Bone was then attached to the staff of D. A. Linthicum, chief surgeon of Cleburne's Division. He was placed in charge of all medical and hospital supplies for the army, and remained at this post throughout Johnston's memorable campaign in Georgia, and also under Hood when he superseded Johnston.

After the disaster of Hood at Franklin and the consequent disorganization, many of his men rallied to the command of General Johnston in North Carolina, Dr. Bone among the number; and when Johnston surrendered, he was paroled and returned to his home in North Alabama, where he devoted the remainder of his life to the peaceful pursuits of agriculture.[71]

BONNER, N. S.: N. S. Bonner, of Roby, Tex., one of the few Confederate veterans in that section of Texas, died at his home on March 5, 1927, in his eighty-second year. He was born in Warren County, Tenn., October 2, 1845.

Though too young to enlist at the beginning of the War between the States, N. S. Bonner served in the Confederate army throughout the war, the last two years being regularly enlisted in the cavalry under Gen. N. B. Forrest. He was the last survivor of his company, and it is thought that his passing completes the roll call for his regiment. He was considered the most expert marksman and one of the most able horsemen in his company; he was twice wounded.

In 1868, Comrade Bonner removed his family to Texas and settled in Falls County. In 1897, he removed to Fisher and engaged in farming in the western part of the county. He served Fisher County as surveyor for eight years and his duties in this regard caused him to remove his family to Roby in 1905, where he lived until death. He was elected to the office of county treasurer of Fisher County for four consecutive terms; and again was elected in 1924, when he was seventy-nine years of age. He was very active, both in mind and body up to within a few days of his death.

Comrade Bonner was married three times, and is survived by his wife, two sons, and two daughters, one son being by his first marriage. There are also eighteen grandchildren and seven great-grandchildren.

Comrade Bonner was a member of the Church of Christ, having obeyed the gospel before he entered the army, and he had always taken an active part in Church work. He was a Mason for almost half a century, and was also an Odd Fellow.[72]

BOONE, HUGH L. W.: Hugh L. W. Boone died March 5, 1899, at his home near Booneville, Lincoln County, Tenn. Entering the Confederate service as a private in the Eighth Tennessee Regiment at its organization, he served with that regiment until Forrest's escort was raised. He was transferred to this company, and served with it until the surrender at Gainesville, Ala., May 12, 1865. Hugh was one of the bravest of Forrest's Cavalry, discharging every duty with a cheerfulness that showed his heart was in his work, he was known in the company as "Uncle John," and was a favorite with his comrades. He was a member of the Shackelford Fulton Bivouac, Fayetteville, Tenn., and a brother of Captain [Nathan S.] Boone.[73]

BOONE, NATHAN S.: Capt. Nathan S. Boone's parents were among the pioneer settlers of Lincoln County [Tenn.], and he was a descendant of the famous Daniel Boone. When sixteen years old he responded to his country's call for volunteers, and enlisted for the Mexican war, in which he served to the end. Returning home, he remained until the war between the States.

In 1862, "Nath" Boone, as he was familiarly called, volunteered as a private in Forrest's escort, but at the organization of the company was chosen first lieutenant. After Capt. Montgomery Little was killed he was made captain, and commanded the company for a long while. He was wounded at Somerville, Tenn., and also at Plantersville, Ala. During the memorable saber charge upon Gen. Forrest and his escort by Wilson's Cavalry, Capt. Boone was the only wounded man in his company, he having been cut on the head with a saber while trying to capture the flag from the color bearer. The killed on the Federal side numbered fifty-four. His courage knew no bounds, his heart no fear. He was a brave, chivalrous man and soldier; yet he was gentle, social, and kind-hearted as a woman. During the three or four days in which Gen. Forrest fought Wilson's Cavalry, Capt. Boone with less than one hundred men killed more Federal soldiers than the entire Spanish army killed during the recent war, and that without the loss of a man. He surrendered with Gen. Forrest at Gainesville, Ala., May 12, 1865. [Capt. Boone passed away at his home in Booneville, Tenn., November 21, 1898].[74]

BOOTON, DANIEL F.: Maj. Daniel F. Booton was born in Madison County, Va., September, 1834. He removed to Georgia in 1857, and resided for several years in Floyd County. Early in 1861 he made up a cavalry company from Floyd Springs and Calhoun, and as Captain of the company was assigned to duty in the Third Georgia Regiment of Cavalry. He did active and valiant service in the Army of the West, and was for time on the staff of Gen. N. B. Forrest, following his forces in the hard-fought battles of Murfreesboro and Chickamauga. For gallantry in action at the latter battle he was promoted to the

Daniel F. Booton.

rank of Major. He followed Bragg's army in the memorable campaign in Kentucky, participated in the battle of Perryville and other engagements, and shared in the hardships and dangers of the retreat from that State. About the close of 1863 he was captured near McMinnville, Tenn., and for eighteen months was held as prisoner of war at Camp Chase and Fort Delaware. Soon after the war he settled in Marshallville, Ga., where he resided till his death, in July, 1900. Maj. Booton was gallant soldier, and nobly illustrated Georgia on many hard-fought battlefields. In civil life he was a courteous, generous, and affable gentleman.[75]

BOTTOM, THOMAS A.: Died, at his home, Victoria, Marshall County, Miss., on Thursday, August 23, 1900, Capt. Thomas A. Bottom, aged fifty-eight years.

Capt. Bottom was a Missourian by birth, and when very young entered the Confederate army as a private soldier in the Second Missouri Cavalry (Col. Robert McCulloch's Regiment), in which he served during the war.

By conspicuous gallantry he was early promoted to the captaincy of his company; was severely wounded at the storming of Fort Pillow, and participated in most of the engagements fought under Gen. Forrest's command.

At the close of the war Capt. Bottom married Miss Mary Hardy, near Byhalia, Miss., and became a citizen of that community, later removing to Victoria, where he resided for a number of years.

By his energy, industry, and fine business judgment he soon acquired more than he deemed needful for his own purposes, and his generosity and liberality were freely exercised by continuous contributions to the wants of the unfortunate in his immediate vicinity. The son of a Methodist minister, he was always faithful to his early religious training, and whether in camp or on the march was studious in the performance of his religious obligations.

Within recent years much of his time was actively spent in the interest of his Church, the "Holiness Methodist," of which he was a faithful and zealous member. Some ten years ago he donated to his Church the Victoria Camp Ground, and chiefly out of his own means erected the tabernacle thereupon, which will doubtless be maintained a lasting monument to his memory, as it forms the center of interest for annual open-air worship for those of his immediate faith from all sections of the country.

As a soldier, citizen, or friend Capt. Bottom had few equals for constancy and fidelity. He was truly a man of peace, and his entire life was spent in doing good. It has been some four weeks since he followed the remains of his aged mother to the grave. Of his family there survives him only his widow, Mrs. Mary A. Bottom, who has been his constant coworker in the service of God and of his fellow-man.[76]

BOWLES, JOHN JAMES: John James Bowles, born in Henry County, Tenn., January 15, 1841, died at the home of his son near Elkhorn on April 21 [1928], survived by his wife, three sons, and two daughters. He was a gallant Confederate soldier, serving under Forrest and taking part in many notable engagements of that famous command. When the war closed, he returned to his native county, married, and reared a splendid family; he was a successful farmer and good citizen.[77]

BOYD, J. C.: J. C. Boyd, for many years Adjutant of Camp James McIntosh, U.C.V., of Lonoke, Ark., died in Little Rock on June 28, 1913. He was born in South Carolina February 8, 1839; but in 1851 the family removed to Tennessee, where our comrade was reared, married, and enlisted in the Confederate army, serving throughout the war in Forrest's command as private and orderly sergeant. He was in the battles of Harrisburg, Yazoo City, and several others, and was wounded twice. After the war he removed to Arkansas and settled in what is now Lonoke County, living in and near the towns of Cabot and Lonoke. He practiced law and served as justice of the peace and as school director for more than twenty years. He was a prominent Mason and Church member. A short time before his death he removed to Little Rock.

J. C. Boyd.

Comrade Boyd was married three times—to Miss Minerva Jane Foster in 1858, to Miss Elizabeth J. Scott, and to Mrs. Emma V. Alexander, who survives him with four of fourteen children, ten of whom blessed the first two unions. He was laid to rest in his Confederate uniform, according to his request, by his comrades and brothers of the U.C.V. and A.F. and A.M.[78]

BRADWELL, THOMAS MARION: Thomas Marion Bradwell was a Confederate soldier from March 17, 1861, to May 6, 1865. He was the oldest son of Dr. Daniel Bradwell and Jane Gordon Bradwell, born February 5, 1835, and was eighty-five years old at the time of his death, May 4, 1920.

Before the War between the States there was a military company at Bainbridge, Ga., called the "Bainbridge Independents," made up of young men of the most prominent families of the town and county. They were handsomely uniformed, well armed and drilled. When the State seceded, they offered their services to Governor Brown and were organized as a part of the 1st Georgia Regiment. This command was sent to Pensacola, Fla., and thence to the mountains of West Virginia, where they suffered untold hardships from hunger and cold. Thomas Bradwell was of this command and was among those Confederates who were surrounded and captured at Cheat Mountain; but his company and regiment made their escape after marching many days without food in the mountains until they got back into the Southern lines. They were afterwards with Stonewall Jackson in his winter campaign in West Virginia, when he marched to Romney. The suffering of the men on this occasion from cold was almost beyond human endurance. Many of the men died from exposure. Jackson was ordered to withdraw from that advanced position, very much against his judgment, to the vicinity of Winchester.

The 1st Georgia had gone into the service of the Confederacy for twelve months, and their time expired before the conscript act was passed. The regiment was mustered out at Lynchburg, Va., and the men returned to their homes to join other commands. Tom Bradwell joined Captain Dunlap's company of the 2nd Georgia Cavalry, Col. C. C. Crews. With this command he served first under Forrest, part of the time in the artillery. His regiment was then put under Wheeler, with whom he served until the surrender in North Carolina. He was in many battles and skirmishes, but was never wounded, although he had seven horses killed under him.

In 1873 Thomas Bradwell moved to Texas, where he married Miss Bird, and from this union there were three daughters and a son, all surviving. In 1891, to educate his children, he went to Kerrville, where he lived respected by all his acquaintances for his learning and kindly disposition and also for the service he had rendered to his country.

There was but one Confederate veteran to march at the head of the procession that laid his body to rest. Adieu, my brother.[79]

BRAGG, HENRY TALBOT: Henry Talbot Bragg, who died Match 15, 1909, at his home, near Eads Station, in Shelby County, Tenn., was born in Florence, Ala., in August, 1839. His father, Henry A. Bragg, and his mother, Frances Armstead Bragg, were Virginians, the former a native of Norfolk and the latter born in Loudoun County. They moved in the early thirties to North Alabama, where Henry T. Bragg was born. He went with his parents in 1848 to Memphis, where he was educated in the private schools of that city.

When Henry Bragg had just attained his majority, the great Civil War broke out with intense fury. The young man was strongly attracted, being chivalrous in his nature, though quiet in his habits, but bold to the point of rashness, and quickly determined to take up arms in behalf of his country.

At that time a cavalry company, the first organized in the Southwest, was being recruited by Capt. Thomas H. Logwood and named the Memphis Light Dragoons. While it was the first company offered by Memphis to the service of the South, it was not mustered in regularly until the 16th of May, 1861, with several other commands. His company became A of the 7th Tennessee Cavalry. It was perhaps the most splendidly equipped and mounted company which entered first the State and then the Confederate service. Young Bragg himself was an ideal trouper. Tall, splendidly formed, with massive shoulders and the erectness of an Indian, he added more than a unit to the splendid aggregate of the company. And his subsequent career proved him to be a perfect type of the Confederate cavalry soldier which made Forrest famous and enabled him to accomplish such grand results.

His career was that of the Confederate private. Under the lead of W. H. (Red) Jackson, Van Dorn, and Forrest his company was in the forefront of battle throughout the war. Beginning with the initial engagement at Belmont, Mo. in November, 1861, young Bragg took part with his company in thirty-seven heavy engagements and battles, and was more than two hundred times under fire, in one campaign alone with Forrest being engaged thirty-three times in forty days.

In all these emergencies he was the same cool, brave, determined young soldier, never faltering when danger called and never lagging when the word was "Forward." After the war he was married to Miss Sallie S. Star, became a farmer, and accumulated a handsome estate.[80]

BREATHITT, JOHN B.: John B. Breathitt, who was buried in Tucson, Ariz., on April 1, one day before he attained his seventy-ninth year, was born in Kentucky, but his father's family settled in Arrow Rock, Mo., in 1852. He left school early in 1861 and enlisted in the Confederate army under Gen. Sterling Price, serving in the battle of Elk Horn, March 7 and 8, 1862, also in the battles of Iuka and Corinth. The 2nd Missouri Cavalry, in which he enlisted, was transferred to the command of that matchless cavalry soldier, Gen. N. B. Forrest, and was in numerous battles with that general, surrendering under him.

John Breathitt was a grandson of ex-Governor Breathitt, of Kentucky. He was prosecuting attorney of Saline County, Mo., and was for four years railroad commissioner of Missouri. We were schoolmates when the war began. Eight of us left school and enlisted early in the Confederate army, and I hope to meet the only survivor, except myself, at our reunion at New Orleans. Genial and beloved schoolmate and comrade, farewell.[81]

BRIAN, JAMES PRUETT: James Pruett Brian, son of James Henry and Caroline Gertrude Brian, was born in Hopkinsville, Ky., September 3, 1840. When the War between the States came on he was among the first to enlist on the side of the South, and he entered the service as a member of Company A, 3rd Kentucky Regiment, and served throughout the entire war. In the organization of Forrest's Cavalry Corps he became a member of that immortal command and remained with it until its banner, emblem of a hundred glorious victories, was furled forever. He attained to the rank of first lieutenant. To say that Lieutenant Brian was a Kentuckian is to say that he was a hero. Forrest never suffered any uneasiness when he knew that he was supported by a Kentucky regiment.

After the war was over, Lieutenant Brian took up the duties of civil life with as much heroism as he had entered the war, and he made a commendable success. He married a splendid woman, Miss Hermina Bush, who, with four children, survives him.

Young Brian belonged to a Southern family not one of whom ever showed the white feather or proved traitor to the cause. His noble brother, Western

Brian, who preceded him to the heavenly home, was also a Confederate veteran of the most royal type. The wife and daughter of the latter now live in Kansas City and are active and zealous members of the U.D.C. there.

Comrade James Brian was a worthy and exemplary member of the Church of the Disciples. He sleeps in honor at Palmer, Ky.[82]

BRIGGS, JOSEPH B.: Gen. J. B. Briggs is a native of Franklin, Tenn., and was born November 20, 1842. Early in the war he joined Col. J. W. Starnes's Fourth Tennessee Cavalry, Forrest's Brigade. He was soon appointed quartermaster-sergeant and then quartermaster of the regiment, later on of the brigade. Gen. Briggs was with Forrest at the siege of Knoxville, Tenn., and with Gen. Dibrell at the surrender at Washington, Ga., May 12, 1865, where he paid off the brigade with the last gold and silver in the Confederate treasury, paying each man $26.25—officer and private the same.

Joseph B. Briggs.

Since the war he has been a banker at Russellville, Ky., where he now resides. Several years ago he organized the J. W. Caldwell Camp No. 139, U.C.V. at Russellville, Ky., and is yet its Commander. Several years ago he was appointed General commanding the first Kentucky Brigade, U.C.V. At the Richmond reunion he was elected the Kentucky trustee of the Confederate Memorial Association (or Battle Abbey), and at the Lookout Mountain meeting was appointed one of the five of the Executive Committee. He holds all of these offices at present. He is an enthusiastic U.C.V.[83]

BROWN, JOSEPH TALIAFERRO: Joseph Taliaferro Brown died at St. Luke's Hospital, St. Louis, Mo., of heart disease on October 16, 1908.

When the Civil War commenced Joseph T. Brown was a boy of twelve residing at his home, in Mississippi, and naturally his sympathies were with the South. He remained at home for two years; but when fourteen years of age he shouldered a gun and took his place in line to assist in repelling the famous Grierson Cavalry raid in May, 1863. On that occasion he was really captured by some Federal soldiers; but his youth and the plausible excuse he made about being out squirrel hunting saved him not only from being taken into custody but the gun as well. When but fifteen years of age he participated in the battle of Coleman's Lane with the command of Gen. Wirt Adams against four regiments of United States colored troops and a regular battery, for which action he was highly mentioned in the dispatches of Lieut. Col. Calvit Roberts, under whose immediate command he served. In February, 1865, he was regularly enlisted and mustered into the Confederate army in the 4th Mississippi Cavalry, under command of Gen. N. B. Forrest, in which command he served until the declaration of peace.

In 1886 he settled on Tongue River, in Custer County, Mont., where he was engaged in the cattle business until mustered into the United States Volunteer Cavalry May 19, 1898. He served with his troop at Chickamauga Park, Ga., until he was mustered out September 8, 1898. After leaving the volunteer service, Captain Brown returned to Montana, where he represented Custer County in the State Legislature, and was at the time of his death one of the presidential electors from that State.[84]

BROWN, JOSHUA: Joshua Brown, a native of Tennessee and resident of Nashville, whose death occurred suddenly in Florida in February, 1924, was the son of Joshua and Evalina Bailey Brown, born at Clarksville on December 25, 1843. His paternal ancestors came from the north of Ireland, settling in Maryland and Pennsylvania, and they were represented in the Revolutionary War. Later the family removed to Kentucky, at the present site of Louisville, afterwards going to Bardstown, where Joshua Brown's father was born in 1800. He located in Clarksville in 1825, and as farmer and merchant remained there for sixty years.

Joshua Brown was a student at the Southwestern University at Clarksville when Fort Donelson fell, and Clarksville was the first place afterwards captured by General Grant. The next fall young Brown joined the 2nd Kentucky Cavalry, under Colonel Woodward. At the battle of Stone's River he was captured and taken to Nashville, being confined in the old penitentiary with some two thousand other Confederate prisoners. He escaped by climbing the wall, got a pass out of the city, and joined Forrest's command at Columbia. Some weeks later he was put on detached service and ordered to report to the chief of the secret service in the Army of Tennessee, and after the battle of Chickamauga he was ordered into Tennessee for scout duty under Captain Coleman, also known as Dr. Shaw, chief of the secret service inside the Federal lines at Pulaski; and in that service young Brown was associated with Sam Davis, Tennessee's boy hero and martyr. He was captured at the same time as Davis, but no papers were found on him, and he was in jail at Pulaski when Sam Davis was executed. He was sent to prison in Nashville, then to Louisville, to Chicago, and then to Rock Island. Later on, when being transferred to Elmira, N.Y. he escaped by jumping from the train, made his way to Canada, and remained there until July, 1865. Returning to Tennessee, he was in business in Nashville for some years, going to New York in 1870 and entering business there. He returned to Nashville in 1911, and that city had since been his home. One brother only of the large family survives him.

The following comes from an old friend, W. J. Bohon, of Kentucky: "The sudden summons of my old friend, comrade, and one-time fellow prisoner in Rock Island, Joshua Brown, who was very dear to me, speaks in no uncertain terms that they are 'gathering home one by one,' and that soon the last leaf of the roses will have fallen and only their memory remain. I loved him as a brother, and shall cherish his memory as something sacred. His record as a soldier speaks for itself. He was one of the scouts captured with Sam Davis, and one of the last to grasp his hand as he started to make that heroic sacrifice which stamped him as the hero of the War between the States."[85]

BROWN, R. U.: R. U. Brown, of Lytle, Tex. . . . belonged to Company E, 7th Regiment, Tennessee Cavalry, under Forrest.[86]

BROWN, TULLY: Tully Brown is the son of Gov. Neil S. Brown. He joined the Confederate army in the spring or early summer of 1861. He left the school desk to do so, being in his seventeenth year. He became a member of the battery of Capt. Monsarratt, and remained in that company until the fall of 1862, when he was promoted to a first lieutenancy of artillery, was assigned to duty on the staff of Gen. John C. Brown, and remained with him until the spring of 1863, when he obtained an order to report to Bedford Forrest, with whom he remained until the end of the war, as a lieutenant of artillery in the battery commanded by Capt. John W. Morton.

Tully Brown.

Soon after the war ended he adopted the profession of his father, and with the opportunity thus offered for the exercise of his rare and exceptional ability as an advocate and debater, he very soon won high rank as a lawyer. He was appointed, and served four years, as District Attorney-General of the Federal Court for the Middle District of Tennessee under the administration of President [Grover] Cleveland.[87]

William Hugh Brown.

BROWN, WILLIAM HUGH: W. H. Brown was born in 1843 in Maury County, Tenn., in the ancestral home where his grandfather, Col. Hugh Brown, settled in 1762. Colonel Brown was a leader in the organization of Jackson College, where his grandson and great-nephews, John C. and Neil S. Brown, and many other distinguished citizens were educated.

William H. Brown entered the Confederate army at sixteen in Capt. Henry Pointer's company, 3rd Tennessee Infantry. After the fall of Fort Donelson he did staff duty in Forrest's Cavalry, and was paroled at Gainesville, Ala., in 1865.

Returning home, he became a prosperous

farmer. He was actively interested in churches and schools, like his distinguished ancestor, giving assistance liberally. For many years he taught a Bible class in the Presbyterian Church, which he joined at the age of fourteen years. He is survived by his wife and two worthy children.[88]

BRUCE, JAMES B. F.: James B. F. Bruce was born in Laurens District, S.C., February 25, 1825; and died near Hattiesburg, Miss., August 25, 1910. He was buried at Decatur, Miss. In 1848 he was married to Miss Emily Brown. He served in Company H of the 1st Regiment, commanded by General Forrest.[89]

BUCHANAN, CHARLES M.: Charles M. Buchanan died at his home in Fayetteville, Tenn., on December 19, 1922, at the age of eighty-three years. He enlisted in the Confederate army at the beginning of the War between the States as a member of the 8th Tennessee Infantry, and served with it until wounded. After that he was transferred to Forrest's Cavalry, where he served with distinction and courage as one of Forrest's scouts until the surrender at Gainesville, Ala., in May, 1865. He was one of Forrest's most trusted and efficient scouts, spending much time within the enemy's lines.

Soon after the war, Comrade Buchanan was made deputy sheriff of Lincoln County, and later was chief of police in Fayetteville, and still later was deputy United States Marshall, all of which positions he filled with courage and satisfaction. He was a member of the Methodist Episcopal Church, South, and was treasurer of the Shackelton-Fulton Bivouac and the 8th Tennessee Consolidated Association U.C.V.—honest, faithful, and true. His wife, a son, and grandchildren survive him.[90]

BUCHANAN, WILLIAM FLETCHER: After a year of failing health William Fletcher Buchanan died at Shelbyville, Tenn., at the age of seventy years. He was one of the most prominent and widely known farmers of Bedford County, owning a fine farm near Pleasant Grove. In years past the home was noted for its hospitality. He was twice married, his first wife being Miss Kercheval, of Lewisburg. To them were born thirteen children, nine of whom survive him. He is also survived by his second wife. His father was a prominent merchant of Shelbyville before and after the war.

As a mere youth Fletcher Buchanan served in the Confederate army as a member of Forrest's escort. . . . He was a man of pleasant address, genial and affable to all with whom he came in contact, a generous neighbor, and a kind and obliging friend. Of his immediate family, a brother, Robert Buchanan, of Franklin, and Mrs. J. H. Woods, of Shelbyville, are left.

Prior to the union of the Presbyterian and Cumberland Presbyterian Churches he was a faithful and leading member of the latter Church.[91]

BUFORD, ABRAHAM: The late General Abe Buford was born in Woodford County, Ky., January 20, 1820. He was a graduate of West Point in class of 1841, and was appointed second lieutenant of dragoons in May, 1842. He served in the Mexican war, and for distinguished bravery at Buena Vista he was brevetted a captain. In 1854 he retired from the service.

In the summer of 1862 he offered his services to the Confederate Government, and was commissioned a brigadier general of cavalry and served in the Army of Tennessee. In 1864 he organized a brigade, consisting of the Third, Seventh, and Eighth Kentucky Regiments of mounted infantry, and was assigned to the division of Forrest. He was badly wounded on Hood's retreat from Nashville in 1864, and surrendered at Gainesville, Ala., in May, 1865. Gen. Buford died in Danville, Ind., June 9, 1894.[92]

Abraham Buford.

BURKE, MICHAEL: M. Burke was born October 11, 1827, in County Limerick, Ireland, and emigrated to this country when quite young. He enlisted in the Confederate army early in 1861 as a member of Company G, 8th Kentucky Infantry. He was captured at Fort Donelson, exchanged at Vicksburg, returned to duty with his command, and was in many hard-fought battles afterwards. He was badly wounded at Jackson, Miss., and was in the hospital three months. The regiment having been reorganized, he was next in Company A. In 1864 the regiment was mounted and sent to General Forrest, and was with him until the surrender.

Comrade Burke returned to Kentucky, and in 1869 was married to Miss Hannah Warner, from which union were born six daughters and three sons, who, with their mother, survive him. He was an honorable Christian gentleman. He died at his home, on Red River, near Adams, Tenn., September 11, 1911, aged eighty-three years and eleven months.[93]

BUSBY, JOHN S.: John S. Busby [fought with] Forrest's Cavalry, and [was] a courier for General Forrest . . . serving with the 17th Louisiana Infantry as band leader . . .[94]

BUSH, WILLIAM GEORGE: .Maj. William G. Bush, for many years one of the leading brick manufacturers and contractors of the South, a Confederate veteran, and a lifelong resident of Davidson County, Tenn., died in Nashville in October, 1911, in his eighty-third year.

Major Bush came to Nashville as a penniless boy and served as an apprentice to a brick layer. When the war began, he joined the Confederate forces, and served throughout the struggle under General Forrest. He ever took an active interest in Confederate matters and was an esteemed member of Frank Cheatham Bivouac at Nashville, and ever lent liberal aid in any undertaking by the members. He was affectionately called "Major" by his employees and friends. As a soldier he had a distinguished career, and as a citizen and businessman he will long be remembered for his sterling integrity.

Immediately after the war he went into business for himself as a brick manufacturer and contractor. He was eminently successful in his business, and at the time of his retirement, some fifteen years ago, the firm of W. G. Bush & Co. was known throughout the South. His son-in-law, T. L. Herbert, at whose home he died, succeeded him in the business.

Of his family, only a daughter, Mrs. T. L. Herbert, survives, his only son having died some years ago.[95]

CALLAWAY, WILLIAM ANDERSON: Many hearts were saddened by the death of William A. Callaway at his home in Atlanta, Ga., on September 26 [1931], after some months of failing health. He had passed into his eighty-sixth year vigorous of mind and body, actively engaged in business almost to the last. After funeral services conducted by the pastor of the Ponce de Leon Baptist Church in Atlanta, his body was taken to Lagrange, his old home, and interred in the family plot of the cemetery there.

William Anderson Callaway was born August 10, 1845, youngest child of the large family of the Rev. W. A. and Martha Pope Callaway, whose ancestry went back to the grandmother of George Washington, who was Ann Pope. When war came on in 1861, he was too young to enlist, but at the age of sixteen, he ran away and joined a company known as the "Judge Bull Invincibles".... In 1863, he was regularly enrolled as a member of Young's Battery of Light Artillery, of Columbus, Ga., and gave devoted and valiant service to the end, taking part in the battles of Chickamauga, Murfreesboro, Vicksburg, and under General Forrest in the engagements at Franklin and Nashville, Tenn., his battery being a part of the rearguard for the Confederate retreat from Tennessee.

... Returning home at the close of war, he found his father on his deathbed and the family dependent upon him. He met the situation squarely and made good, and, in the fall of 1865, took unto himself a wife, sixteen-year-old Mary Elizabeth Patillo, of Atlanta. Of this union there were four children. Since his wife's death in 1921, he had married twice, the last wife, who was Mrs. Bessie Harris Callaway, surviving him, with a son and daughter of the first marriage, also four grandchildren and two great-grandchildren. Comrade Callaway had been successful in his business and built up a fine estate.

Coming of a long line of distinguished Baptists, his church affiliations were with that denomination from early youth, and he had a prominent part in its work both in Lagrange and Atlanta.[96]

CAMPBELL, ALEXANDER WILLIAM: Born June 4, 1828, at Nashville, Tenn. In 1861 elected colonel 33rd Tennessee Infantry; 1862-63, colonel and inspector general on the staff of Gen. Leonidas Polk; March 15, 1864, appointed brigadier general. Commands: Commanded a brigade in W. H. Jackson's division, Forrest's Cavalry.[97] After the War he ran unsuccessfully as a Democratic [then a Conservative] candidate for governor of Tennessee. He died June 13, 1893, and is buried at Jackson, Tenn.[98]

CAMPBELL, THOMAS: Sixty odd years ago Dr. John D. Smith, the founder of Henderson, Tenn., took his crop of cotton to Memphis on a Hatchie River boat. One of the deck hands was a red-headed Irishman, a cheerful, tireless worker, already approaching middle age. Dr. Smith was so impressed with this man's capability that he engaged him to return with him and help on his farm. Tommy Campbell, or "Uncle Tommy," as he was soon called, became a member of the Smith family and one of its strongest adherents.

Thomas Campbell.

In 1861 Tommy Campbell enlisted with the 2nd Tennessee Infantry, Col. J. Knox Walker, and later the 5th Confederate Regiment. In 1862 he was discharged at Tupelo, Miss., as over age. A year later he joined Captain May's company, Bell's Brigade, Forrest's Cavalry. In 1864 he was wounded in a fight at Athens, Ala. The wound was on top of his head and "Uncle Tommy" was gratified that he was so low, for if otherwise the bullet would have struck him in the head.

After the war he returned to Tennessee, and that State had no better nor more zealous citizen than the little red-headed Irishman who seems to have found the fountain of youth.

In early September of this year Judge G. W. Smith, of Fresno, Cal., who was the youngest son of Dr. John Smith, came back to Henderson to visit the scenes of his boyhood, and "Uncle Tommy Campbell" came from his home in Pinson to see him, hale and hearty, little the worse for the summers and winters of one hundred and two years. The old gentleman and the silver-haired judge, whom he regards as a boy, spent happy days together in recalling incidents of the Judge's youth. This old man was reported in [good] health late in September [1909].[99]

CAMPBELL, WILLIAM A.: On October 27, 1909, in Columbus, Miss., after a long period of declining health, William A. Campbell answered the last roll call and joined the ranks of those faithful soldiers who have won the crown.

Comrade Campbell was a true soldier of the Confederacy and also of the

William A. Campbell.

cross of the Lord Jesus Christ, and his life was devoted to the defense and upholding of truth and right. He was born in Franklin County, Tenn., near Winchester, in 1836. He was a descendant of the noble clan Campbell of which the Dukes of Argyle are the hereditary head and which has stood in Scotland for the crown and covenant of Jesus Christ and against the encroachments of kings and priests. His immediate ancestors were Lairds of Dennaboden House in the North of Ireland, so that he came legitimately by his fighting blood.

His father was Arthur Campbell and his mother Virginia Young, a typical Southern lady.

His family moved to Memphis when William was a child, and after his father's death moved to Columbus, Miss., in 1851. There he was in business until 1861. When the call to arms in defense of the South was made, he responded with enthusiasm. He enlisted in Captain Fort's company of Muldrow's Regiment of Cavalry. He was made orderly sergeant of the company, and under Generals Forrest and Wheeler he served to the end, never missing a roll call of his company.

After the war he went into business in Columbus; but in 1871 he removed to Memphis, where he engaged in business until 1879. He was there during the terrible epidemic of yellow fever in 1878, and as a member of the Howard Association he rendered service as valiant as any when a soldier in battle.

In 1879 he returned to Columbus and engaged in business until his failing health forced his retirement. In 1891 he was married to his cousin, Miss Alicia Campbell, of Nashville. She was a true-hearted sympathizer with him in all his aims and ideals. Her death in October, 1908, was an affliction which hastened his own death.

For many years he was a ruling elder and clerk of session of the Presbyterian Church in Columbus. It could be truly said that his highest aim in life was to make his Church a true exponent of the gospel and a blessing to the entire community. He was a consistent Christian.

His devotion to the Confederacy never wavered, and he strove to keep fresh in the hearts of the Southern people those great principles [conservatism and constitutionalism] for which he fought and of those heroic souls who gave their lives for the cause.[100]

CARMICHAEL, GEORGE WASHINGTON: In sorrow over the loss of another good comrade, Troop A, Forrest's Cavalry, of Nashville, Tenn., passed resolutions in tribute to George W. Carmichael, a charter member of the Troop, from which the following is taken:

"George Washington Carmichael, one of the charter members of Troop A, Forrest's Cavalry, was born near Nolensville, in Williamson County, Tenn., on the 8th of September, 1843. He joined Capt. (afterwards Col.) J. W. Starnes's company of cavalry in October, 1861, when stationed at Sacramento, Ky., and was one of the forty members of the company who took part with Forrest's command in the battle near Sacramento, Ky. Soon after the battle of Chickamauga young Carmichael was sent with others across the Tennessee River near Loudon on a scout, during which his horse was killed and he was captured, but was later exchanged and rejoined his company. He was with Company F until the surrender and was paroled at Washington, Ga., on May 9, 1865.

"Returning to his home in Williamson County, he resumed his occupation as farmer. In 1868 he was married to Miss Mary Herbert, with whom he lived happily for over fifty years. After his marriage he removed to Brentwood and was a member of the old Smyrna congregation of the Methodist Church, South, there and had served as superintendent of the Sunday school for twenty-five years. He was a Christian gentleman, a good citizen and neighbor, a man who had many friends.

"Comrade Carmichael helped to organize Troop A in 1895 and was an honored member of the Troop until his death, which occurred on March 3, 1920, at his home, near Brentwood."[101]

CARNEY, JOHN L.: Capt. John L. Carney died in Clarksville, Tenn., October 28, 1904. He was born in Murfreesboro, Tenn., February 6, 1837, and was educated at Union University there. He loved his home and his people; their cause [conservatism] was his, and when war was declared he took up arms in defense of the South, and served to the end, surrendering with Forrest at Gainesville, Ala. He assisted in raising a company, of which he was made first lieutenant; and this company was D, of Douglas's Battalion, which, with Holman's Battalion, formed the Eleventh Tennessee Regiment of Cavalry, part of Forrest's old brigade. Lieut. Carney was appointed quartermaster of the regiment in 1864, and while serving in that capacity still continued with his company, never missing a battle. When Capt. John Lytle took charge of the private scouts Lieut. Carney became captain, and commanded the company in the rest of the battles, yet continuing to serve as quartermaster.

John L. Carney.

Brave and true, gentle yet firm, he was loved and honored by his comrades, for the ragged boys in gray had no hardships which he did not share. A few years after the war he removed from Murfreesboro to Lake Weir, Fla., which was his home at his death. His wife, who was Miss Amanda Turner, of Rutherford County, Tenn., survives him with five children. He was a

Christian, noted for his charity and generosity, and especially tender toward the poor and unfortunate. Death for him had no terror, and, resting upon the love and mercy of God, he felt: "Though from out our bound of time and place, the flood may hear me far, I hope to see my Pilot face to face, when I have crossed the bar."[102]

CARTER, JOE W.: Born under Southern skies, Maj. J. W. Carter, full-blooded Cherokee Indian and a veteran of the Confederacy, died at the age of one hundred and seven in his beloved Southland, at the Confederate Home of Alabama, on the night of March 3 [1927]. His death marks the passing of one of the most picturesque figures of the Confederacy.

This hardy old veteran saw service in the Texas war for independence under Gen. Zachary Taylor and served as chief scout under Gen. N. B. Forrest in the War between the States. The history of his life reads like fiction. Born in Floyd County, Ga., near what is now the city of Rome, in 1820, the "Wildcat" was taught the crafts of his tribe among the beautiful foothills of the Blue Ridge. But the day came when he must leave his native soil. Palefaces thronged into that section, and the Cherokees were driven into other lands. The "Wildcat" never forgot. . . . His people named that march across the Father of Waters as the "Trail of Tears." Hundreds died of starvation and fatigue; his journey ended in Oklahoma.

When the Mexican War broke out, Carter had established a reputation as a guide in the West, and General [Winfield] Scott sent for him; he refused to go, for Scott's soldiers, he said, were among those who had persecuted his people; but he joined Gen. Zachary Taylor and followed him through the war with Mexico. When the War between the States came on, Carter was living at Tahlequah, Okla. He joined the Confederate forces under Gen. Albert Pike and was made captain of scouts. He served in the Western campaign, including the battle of Red River and all the fights against the army of Franz Sigel, under General McCulloch. Later he was chief of scouts under General Forrest.

Shortly after the war, Major Carter went to Montgomery to spend the rest of his life in the "Cradle of the Confederacy," among his comrades in arms. Skilled in Indian lore, he set up a shop as "Herb Doctor" and enjoyed a wide trade, being held in high estimation. He was a member of Camp Lomax, U.C.V., of Montgomery, and never missed a reunion, where he was conspicuous in his broad-brimmed hat, a feather in the band, topping a mass of long black hair. Injured by a fall at his little home in Montgomery, he was sent to the hospital at the Confederate Home at Mountain Creek, where he died shortly afterwards and was laid by his comrades in the cemetery there.[103]

CASTLEBERRY, CHARLES C.: Charles C. Castleberry was born in Tishomingo County, Miss.; and died suddenly in New Albany, Miss., in September, 1909. He was very young when he enlisted in the Confederate service; but he was a brave soldier under Col. W. A. Johnson, and he surrendered with General Forrest at Gainesville, Ala. His six brothers were also in the Confederate army. At the close of the war he returned to Iuka Springs, where he made a good citizen, serving his county several times as sheriff.[104]

CHADICK, W. D.: [Rev. Dr. W. D. Chadick died in the 1890s. What follows are "some of his services and experiences during the war."] When he saw the war-cloud approaching he said he would rather die than see the Union dissolved, but when his state went out he went with it, heart and soul; he knew no half-measures in anything. He first went to Virginia as chaplain of the famous Fourth Alabama Regiment, from and about Huntsville, Ala. In the first battle of Manassas he shouldered a musket and fought with his soldiers. Col. Egbert Jones, of Huntsville, commander of the regiment, was severely wounded. After the battle Dr. Chadick took him to Warrenton and nursed him for six weeks until his death, and then attended the body to Huntsville for burial. After a short stay at home he was appointed major of a battalion, which went into camp near Huntsville, but was soon ordered to Mobile, and from there to Corinth, Miss., just before the battle of Shiloh. He went into that battle, and at the first fire all his officers were wounded and sent to the rear, and he had to fight the battle alone; besides, his horse was wounded, so that he had to dismount and fight on foot. His clothing on his right shoulder was pierced by a Minie ball, but he was not hurt. He was wonderfully preserved.

W. D. Chadick.

During this battle his command, in conjunction with Gen. Forrest's, captured the Prentiss (Kentucky) Brigade [U.S.A.]. As the [Yankee] prisoners filed past him to the rear he stood on a stump looking at them, and remarked, "You are a fine-looking set of fellows," when one of them replied, "Yes, and you fight damned well."

The night after the battle he stood on picket-duty in a hard rain, to spare his soldiers, many of whom were wounded. He was soon attacked by rheumatism, and lay at Tupelo, Miss., six weeks, unable to move hand or foot. As soon as able, he joined his command in Kentucky; but, as he was still suffering, a furlough was sent to him from Richmond, and he went home. Soon afterward he was appointed chief of staff to the Governor of Alabama, with the rank of colonel, and operated between Montgomery and the Tennessee River, making his headquarters at Whitesburg. He remained in this capacity until the close of the war.[105]

CHALMERS, JAMES RONALD: James R. Chalmers was born January 11, 1831, in Halifax County, Va. He practiced law in Mississippi and was a member of the state's secession convention. During Lincoln's War he began as colonel of the 9th Mississippi Infantry out of Pensacola, Fla. On February 13, 1862, he was promoted to brigadier general, fighting at Shiloh under General Withers. He then led a brigade under Bragg, and later under Forrest.

After the War Chalmers played an important role in the politics of Reconstruction, eventually removing to Memphis, Tenn., where he worked as an attorney until his death on April 9, 1898. Though his relationship with Forrest was often rancorous, his soldierly reputation as a brave and fearless Confederate officer will stand the test of time.[106]

James Ronald Chalmers.

CHEAIRS, THOMAS GORMAN: On September 15, 1909, Thomas G. Cheairs died at his home near Spring Hill, Tenn. He was born April 11, 1843, in Maury County, Tenn.

He enlisted in Forrest's escort in February, 1863, and served until he was paroled May 18, 1865. He was General Forrest's ideal of a good soldier. Ever near his chief, he was ready to go and do whatever ordered, however dangerous it might be.

Comrade Cheairs joined Leonidas Polk Bivouac and William Henry Trousdale Camp in 1897, and was a most faithful member, always at the meetings of the Bivouac and Camp, and he never failed to attend the Reunions unless sick. He was charitable and liberal to all the Confederate associations. The Church and the community will miss him; but it was in his home and immediate family where he served best and did most. He was the companion of his aged father, Maj. Nathaniel F. Cheairs [founder of Rippavilla, Spring Hill, Tenn.], and cared for him in declining years most beautifully. No one had more friends with the old comrades. We laid him to rest in Rose Hill Cemetery [Columbia, Tenn.] on September 17, after performing the Confederate burial service.[107]

Rippavilla Plantation, Spring Hill, Tenn. (Photo Lochlainn Seabrook)

CLAYBROOKE, SAMUEL PERKINS: Samuel Perkins Claybrooke died February 23, 1910, at St. Petersburg, Fla., where he had gone for a change of climate, not being in good health. When taken sick, his four sisters went to his bedside, and were with him during his last illness. He was born near Triune,

Tenn., the son of Col. John S. and Mary A. Claybrooke. His father was one of the foremost citizens of the State, giving much of his time and thought to promoting its best interests, and his mother by her unselfish devotion to duty and gentle dignity represented the highest type of Southern womanhood. Both were of the best families of Virginia and Tennessee (his ancestors came from Virginia to Tennessee) and held positions of trust and responsibility.

While a mere boy at school in Murfreesboro, under fifteen years of age, he enlisted in Starnes's cavalry company [eventually serving under Forrest]. He always took a deep interest in whatever pertained to the Confederacy and the cause [conservatism] for which he so bravely fought, and he rarely failed to attend the U.C.V. Reunions. In his last hours he was back with the boys who wore the gray, calling them by name and encouraging them to stand firm, saying: "Boys, don't let them get the best of us."

He was a brother of Frederick Claybrooke, major of the 20th Tennessee Regiment, who lost his life at Hoover's Gap while gallantly leading his men. After the war he engaged in agricultural pursuits, and for some years had resided on his farm near Brentwood. He was a public-spirited citizen, and by his integrity and generosity won the esteem of a large circle of friends. He was widely known.

Samuel Perkins Claybrooke.

The funeral services were held in Franklin at the Episcopal Church, of which he was a member, conducted by Revs. John B. Cannon and Arthur L. Seiter, where a large number gathered to pay the last tribute of love. The procession of veteran comrades was especially large. Representatives of Frank Cheatham Bivouac, Nashville, of which he was a member, as well as of McEwen Bivouac, of Franklin, were in the procession. He was laid to rest in Mount Hope Cemetery, and the services at the grave were conducted by Rev. R. Lin Cave, Chaplain General of the United Confederate Veterans, using the ritual of the Bivouac.[108]

CLAYTON, SOLOMON SMITH: There were many to deplore the passing of Solomon Smith Clayton, who died at Camden, Tenn., on August 21 [1932?], aged eighty-eight years, for his purity and goodness were felt by all with whom he came in contact. Always cheerful, calm, patient, resigned, his passing was as peaceful as the life that he lived.

Solomon Clayton was a sixteen-year-old boy when the War between the States came on, living on a farm near Camden. His father went into the service of the Confederacy, and after the battle of Shiloh, in April, 1862, the boy took his father's place as a soldier and served out the term of enlistment, returning home on New Year's Day of 1863. He re-entered the service in 1864, joining an independent company of the 20th Tennessee, Forrest's command, and took part in the battles of Franklin and Nashville, and was with Forrest in guarding the disastrous retreat from Nashville. He served to the end of the war, reaching home in a ragged uniform which he had to wear until his mother could spin and weave cloth for a suit.

For several years after the war, Comrade Clayton was a tobacco manufacturer in Tennessee, then went to Missouri, where he married in 1881. Some years later he returned to Tennessee and again went into the tobacco business. In 1901, he was married to Mrs. Leona Steele McDaniel, of Camden, daughter of W. A. Steele, Confederate soldier, and she survives him.[109]

CLAYTON, WILEY M.: Lieut. Wiley M. Clayton served in Forrest's Cavalry and died in Nashville November 5, 1911. [His last known address may have been] 723 Market Street, Nashville, Tenn.[110]

CLEMENTS, G. D.: Dr. G. D. Clements was born on a farm near Atwood, Carroll County, Tenn., December 17, 1844. He enlisted in Company B, 7th Kentucky Regiment, Forrest's Cavalry, and was a gallant, brave, and true Confederate soldier. He was paroled in Tennessee in 1865. In Memphis, Tenn., he met Mr. Hooker and family, friends and neighbors from Atwood, who were moving by wagon and carriage to Texas, so he joined them. On the trip he was married to Miss Sallie C. Hooker near Forrest City, Ark; and they all settled near White Church, in Woodruff County. This was in May, 1869, and in September Mr. Hooker and family went on to Texas. Dr. Clements practiced medicine and ran a farm until 1876,

G. D. Clements.

when he removed to his farm in Jackson County, Ark., near Shoffner, and from there in 1885 to Auvergne. He was a man of wealth, having large landed estates and a big mercantile business. In late years he was not actively in business, but traveled for his health.

Dr. Clements was a devoted member of the Methodist Church, liberal in his contributions to all its interests as well as to other benevolent enterprises and giving aid to many people. All who knew him loved him. He was a prominent member of Tom Hindman Camp, No. 318, U.C.V., of Newport, Ark., and helped to build the Confederate monument there. He is survived by three daughters.[111]

CLIFT, MOSES H.: There are elements in a man that draw men to him quite independent of his intellectual force or power of achievement. This rare power of inspiring personal attachment with that of diffusing the impression of independent force in thought and action is possessed by few men. Such a man was Col. Moses H. Clift, of Chattanooga, Tenn., who departed this life at St. Thomas Hospital, Nashville, on Sunday morning, December 3, 1911.

He was beloved beyond most men. That was illustrated in the remarkable tribute paid him by his fellow lawyers in Chattanooga December 4. A prominent attorney said: "Over along period of residence in Chattanooga I have attended many such meetings, but in genuine sorrow and uncontrolled emotion I never witnessed anything to compare with this." Another writes: "I have never been so impressed with the sincerity of every word uttered. When the speakers endeavored to tell of his integrity, his big heart, and unfailing kindness, their emotion almost prevented utterance, and there were none but tearful eyes among the listeners. I am confirmed in what I had long believed that no man held the love of his brother members of the bar as completely as Major Clift."

The mark of a gentleman is a keen sense of the feelings and susceptibilities of others. One of Major Clift's chief characteristics was kindness—kindness to everybody of every station in life. Humanity appealed to him. Out of the greatness of his heart he was heard often to say: "I am sorry for everybody." Verily he loved his fellow man. His hand was ever open to the needy, and he gave of himself with his alms.

Moses H. Clift.

Another distinguishing element in Major Clift's character was his fearlessness. This is the record of his life in peace as well as in war. Whatever he did resulted from an independence that none could fail to admire. He was too brave, too independent, and too noble to pander to anybody, and withal he was too gentle and too kind to offend willingly. This rare combination of qualities, coupled with a strong intellect, an integrity that was never questioned, and a nature most unselfish, justly placed him "a man among men" and drew them to him with bonds of immutable affection and confidence.

These forces in Major Clift's character must have received an impetus from a noble line of ancestry. For seven generations through the Brooks and Irwins on his mother's side and the Clifts, Campbells, [and] Hitchcocks in his father's line there is an array of soldiers, scientists, statesmen, teachers, preachers. With the exception of the Spanish-American War, some of this family have participated with distinction in every war fought in the United States and were of historical note in Scotland and England. In the Confederate army Major Clift was made a captain in the battle of Fort Donelson, major at Kennesaw Mountain, and colonel at Waynesboro, Ga., in 1865. He served under General Forrest and later under Gen. George G. Dibrell; was in twenty-five battles and was thrice wounded.

Colonel Clift's valor was so marked that General Wheeler wrote of him: "Major Clift served with me during the war, and probably won greater distinction than any other officer of his grade."

Lieut. Gen. A. P. Stewart once wrote a mutual friend: "Major Clift served with distinction and great credit in both Forrest's and Wheeler's Cavalry. He is a lawyer of long and excellent standing at the bar, a man of great ability, efficiency, and is thoroughly honest."

An ex-supreme judge of Tennessee wrote of him: "I heard from one of the most gallant generals of the Confederacy, General Dibrell, with whom Major Clift served for years and fought in many battles, that the South had no better soldier. He won his rank by gallantry and retained it by the preservation of a character of which all his friends are proud, and he is one of the few who have always since the war carried its honors in a private station."

Major Clift fought the battle of life as bravely as he had faced the enemy in war. No man ever saw him other than cheerful and helpful, and none ever heard him murmur or complain. He had an abiding faith in God; and when the last enemy was to be overcome, he exhibited the same characteristics that had ever distinguished him and that had made association with him so great a blessing—an unfaltering faith in his Maker, a calm courage, little consideration of his own suffering, putting forth his last efforts to comfort those about him whom he had loved best in life.

Major Clift was born at Soddy, Tenn., August 25, 1836. He was the son of Col. William Clift, one of the pioneers of this county and a man of remarkably rugged character and sterling worth. His wife, Arwin, was a daughter of Gen. Moses Brooks, of Knox County, Tenn., a soldier of the Revolution. Major Clift was the last survivor of this family of seven children. Others of them were well known and beloved. He read law in the office of Judge L. Hopkins, now of Atlanta, Ga., a brother-in-law, and he was admitted to the bar in 1861. But the call of his country took him from the office to the field, and he raised Company H of the 36th Tennessee, C.S.A., and enlisted as a soldier in the cause he decided was right, while his father became a colonel in the Union army.

Major Clift was twice married. His first wife was Miss Ataline Cooke, the daughter of Dr. Robert F. Cooke, a brother of the late Judge J. B. Cooke. To this union were born three children—Arwin (who married P. A. Brauner, Jr., and died some years ago), Roberta (the wife of T. R. Preston, President of the Hamilton National Bank), and Moses H. (who died in infancy).

His second marriage took place in Cartersville, Ga., in 1883 with Miss Florence V. Parrott, a daughter of Judge Josiah Rhoton Parrott, a distinguished jurist of Georgia, Solicitor General, President of the Constitutional Convention of 1867-68, and an able and fearless judge of the superior court, Cherokee Circuit, until his death, in 1872. [The wife of Dr. Robert Pillow, of Columbia, Tenn., is a sister of Mrs. Clift.]

In a crisis of Streight's raid, when General Forrest's brother had been wounded and he had lost two cannon, captured by the enemy, he rushed up to two of his regiments "in quite a passion," ordered Major Clift to duty on his staff, and moved forward in the lead. His selection of Major Clift for staff duty then was a great tribute to his valor and judgment.

Lieut. Gen. Alexander P. Stewart wrote a statement in 1904 showing the extraordinary efficiency of Major Clift at Bentonville: "At Bentonville, N.C., in 1865 General Johnston was informed by his cavalry commander that there was no road leading round Johnston's left to his rear. But there was such a road. A Federal division found it and came very near getting into our rear, which would have led to the capture or the utter rout of Johnston's little army. Cummins's small infantry brigade and Dibrell's small cavalry force (the latter being led by Maj. M. H. Clift) made a bold charge—one in front, the other on the flank—of this Federal division, threw it into a panic, and routed it. This alone saved the day."[112]

CLINTON, SAMUEL H.: Samuel H. Clinton, born and reared in Hardeman County, Tenn., gave four years to the service of the South. He was in the cavalry under Forrest, and was twice wounded. He removed to Bolivar a few years ago, where he died suddenly of apoplexy. He was a man of wonderful energy and industry, good judgment, conservative in his views, honorable and generous.[113]

COBB, THOMAS WILLIAM: Thomas W. Cobb was born June 12, 1844; and died December 11, 1911, at his home, in Union, Ala.

In the summer of 1862 he joined Company C, 43rd Alabama, Gracie's Brigade, and served in the Army of Tennessee until disabled by a long spell of typhoid fever, which prostrated him for more than a year. He afterwards joined Forrest's Cavalry, with which he served till the close of the war. He was a member of Camp Sanders, U.C.V., at Union, and almost invariably attended the reunions.

When the war was over, Comrade Cobb returned home, and after several years of close application to his books he taught school. Later he engaged in agricultural pursuits, whereby he successfully demonstrated the dignity of farm life, and from which he gathered a competency. He took a deep interest in State and county matters, serving nearly twenty years as County Commissioner. He was a member of the Church and was deeply interested in Christian service. His wife, who was Miss Dora Steele, and one daughter survive.[114]

Thomas William Cobb.

COKER, GEORGE W.: On Monday, May 12, 1929, George W. Coker died at his home near Tallassee, Ala., on the old Indian land known as Tukabachie, at the age of eighty-four years. He was buried at his old home, Mount Willing, Ala., in Lowndes County. He was born at Benton, Ala., and spent the greater part of his life in Lowndes County.

At the early age of sixteen years, George Coker enlisted for the Confederacy, serving with Company D, 7th Alabama Cavalry, Forrest's Brigade. Though just a lad, he was soon made sergeant, and none served more gallantly or loved the Southern cause more devotedly than he.

After the war, he reared a large family, whose members contributed much to the stable citizenship of Alabama. His devotion to his family, his loyalty to his friends, and his unflagging zeal in the service of his Church were the outward expression of the inward reality of a noble character, built upon the basic principles of justice and truth.

His death marks the passing of a great man, great because he was good. He was a most devout member of the Baptist Church, and his influence will long be felt in the Church he served so faithfully and well.[115]

COLEMAN, PRESTON B.: Preston B. Coleman died at his home in Union County, Ky., January 21, 1902, aged seventy-nine years. He enlisted in the Confederate service in 1862, Company F, organized by Capt. J. J. Barnett at White Sulphur Spring, of the First Kentucky Cavalry. Sometime in 1863, in reorganization, Company F was merged into Company G, and Capt. John Howell was elected to command of the company until the surrender on the 11th day of April, 1865, to Wilson of Illinois at Washington, Ga. He was in front of Sherman's Army from the beginning of his march to the sea, and was at Chickamauga and Murfreesboro. The First Kentucky was commanded by Col. Thomas Harrison, of Texas, at the close of the war. The brigade commander was Gen. "Cerro Gordo" Williams.

While under Forrest, Comrade Coleman was wounded in a stockade fight in Tennessee, the ball entering the front of thigh and passing through same. He rode in the ranks a whole day by placing one hand on pommel of saddle and the other on back part of same. Reaching McMinnville, Tenn., (where Forrest lost his negro boy and baggage wagon in the charge) he insisted on keeping his place in line of charging column, although unable to handle a weapon, but was finally persuaded from doing so. In any perilous detail work he was usually one of the number selected. After the war was over he returned to his home in Union County, Ky., and engaged in farming. He was a man of strong impulses, a stanch [meaning staunch] friend, true as steel. He left his wife and daughter a good farm.[116]

COLEY, WILLIAM H.: In March, 1863, when only fifteen years old, Comrade Coley joined the Tenth Tennessee Cavalry, then of Starnes's Brigade, but afterwards commanded by Gen. Dibrell under Forrest. He served as courier until the army fell back to Chattanooga. At Chickamauga he received his first wound during a charge with his regiment, near Gordon's Mill, on a Federal battery. He afterwards was attached to Longstreet's command, and served with it for eight months; but was transferred back to the Army of Tennessee, which he joined at Dalton, and participated in all the battles of

William H. Coley.

Johnston's army from Dalton to Atlanta. He served in the Tennessee campaign, was in the battles of Franklin and Nashville, and surrendered, under Forrest, at Gainesville, Ala., in 1865.

Since the war, Comrade Coley, while successful in business, has never permitted his business affairs to lessen his enthusiasm or abate his love and admiration for his old army comrades and friends. He was chiefly instrumental in organizing recently Bivouac No. 39 and Camp No. 1443, of which he was chosen President, and having them named in honor of his old comrade, Capt. John W. Morton, chief of Forrest's Artillery. Comrade Coley's family consists of two accomplished daughters and an only son, Robert Lee.[17]

COLLIER, WILLIAM ARMISTEAD: The familiar presence of Gen. W. A. Collier, Commander of Forrest's Cavalry Association, will be sadly missed from future gatherings of his Confederate comrades, for the beloved Commander has passed to his eternal reward. He died at Memphis, Tenn., on August 18, after a short illness, and his going has left a wide gap in the ever-thinning gray line.

William Armistead Collier, son of Thomas Barksdale and Catherine Page Nelson Collier, was born in Haywood County, Tenn., February 12, 1847. His parents were Virginians, of English descent, and sprung from the oldest and most prominent families of that State. He was related to the great English divine, Jeremy Collier, and Admiral Collier of the English Navy. Three great-grandfathers were officers and heroes in the Revolutionary War. The father of William Armistead Collier, a large and successful planter, died when his son was yet a child, leaving a widow and several children. When the neighborhood in which his mother lived was evacuated by the Confederates, she had on her plantation a large amount of cotton. True to the blood of her Revolutionary sires, she ordered this cotton burned rather than have it fall into the hands of the enemy. Being an invalid, she had her bed rolled to the window so that she could see the order executed.

Thus descended, it was but natural that young Collier, though little over fourteen years of age, should join one of the first companies organized for the Confederacy of Tennessee in 1861; but he was rejected on account of his youth. His family then sent him to Memphis, hoping to keep him out of the army. He was in Memphis but a short while when he joined a company, which afterwards became Company I, of the 1st Confederate Cavalry. This regiment served throughout the campaigns of 1862 and 1863 in Tennessee and Kentucky, under Generals Wheeler and Bragg.

In the spring of 1863 young Collier was discharged near Columbia, Tenn., because of ill health. The enemy was then advancing. It was necessary for him to retreat or become a prisoner. He determined, if his strength permitted, to go to his home in West Tennessee, then in the Federal lines. He was advised that it would be impossible for him to cross the Federal lines, not only because of the regular troops, but because of the bushwhackers and guerrillas that were infesting the country. Being so often warned of the danger, he attempted to ally himself with three other Confederates who were going his way, urging them that the four could make a strong fight if necessary; but they refused to permit him to accompany them.

This proved most fortunate for young Collier, as the three men were killed that night. After eighteen months of active service, he was still so frail and young that, disguised as a girl, he successfully passed the Federal lines, and reached his home in safety. During his stay at home he was often pursued by the Federal raiding parties, and was once captured and detained for a short while as a prisoner.

In the fall of 1863, his health being restored, Collier went south and joined Company B of the famous 7th Tennessee Cavalry, under General Forrest, the company that he had attempted to join early in 1861. He served until the end of the war in this command, and participated in the principal engagements, some of them the most brilliant in the history of our great struggle. He was never wounded, although he had a horse shot under him at West Point, and his clothes shot and his flesh burned at Tishomingo Creek.

When informed at Gainesville, Ala., that General Lee had surrendered, and that his command was expecting orders to do likewise, young Collier and his messmates, W. E. and John S. Maclin, determined that they would not surrender; so, with their servants [African-American Confederates], they left their command with the intention of crossing the Mississippi River and joining the Trans-Mississippi Department. Hearing of their departure, their colonel sent for them and advised and urged the young men to remain and surrender with the command, saying that if Lee and Forrest surrendered, they could afford to do so, too. Collier promised his colonel that he would remain provided he could know the terms of surrender in time to leave, if desired, as he would never surrender to any foe to be searched, insulted, and humiliated. The terms as given by the Federals were liberal, and he surrendered with the command.

After the war, Mr. Collier returned to his home and devoted several years to the reclaiming and upbuilding of the old family homestead and retrieving the ruins of the war. He studied law at Lebanon, Tenn., and located in Memphis in 1870, where he had since resided and become prominent at the bar, in business, and in politics. In 1872, he was married to Miss

William Armistead Collier.

Alice Trezevant, daughter of Nathaniel Macon and Amanda Avery Trezevant, of Memphis, who survives him with their four children, a daughter and three sons.

General Collier was always true, loyal, and active in maintaining the righteousness of the Confederate cause [conservatism], of instilling its history into his children, and of preserving the traditions of the Old South. A regular and prominent figure at all reunions, he had many years served as Commander of the Forrest Cavalry Corps; and at the Charlotte reunion, he was unanimously elected for the twelfth time to that honor he considered the highest he had ever received.

He was laid to rest in the gray uniform that he devotedly loved, his casket covered with the Confederate colors that he had so gallantly defended.[118]

Elijah Conklin.

CONKLIN, ELIJAH: Elijah Conklin, whose death occurred at Omaha, Nebr., on July 18, 1911, was born in Grand Gulf, Miss., in 1847. He joined the Confederate army at the age of sixteen, served in the Mississippi cavalry during the last two years of the war, and was paroled at Gainesville, Ala., in May, 1865, under General Forrest. He was borne to his last resting place in a casket of Confederate gray upon which were entwined Confederate and American flags. He wore the highly prized cross of honor, and his pallbearers were old veterans of both the Confederate and Union armies. Comrade Conklin was a member of Camp J. J. Whitney, U.C.V., of Fayette, Miss.[119]

COOK, BARNETT M.: Barnett M. Cook entered the Confederate army April 20, 1864, when in his eighteenth year, in Company G, 12th Kentucky Cavalry, Forrest's Corps (composed of Graves and Calloway County men), commanded by the ever-gallant Capt. James F. Melton, now deceased.

In the fighting on July 14, 1864, in front of Harrisburg, Miss., Barnett M. Cook was of the one hundred and fifty skirmishers covering the front of the Kentucky brigade and participated in the famous charge of that brigade on that fatal day. These skirmishers were commanded by the redoubtable Irish captain, J. J. Kelleher, of Company H (killed at Duck River on Hood's retreat from Nashville), and Lieut. William J. Mathis, of Company G, same regiment. They attained the nearest proximity to the Federal breastworks of any of the Confederate troops, but lost more than fifty percent of their number.

Barnett M. Cook was a soldier wholly without venditation, and did his full duty on all occasions and with an alacrity characteristic of the gallant men of that company and regiment, and he still lives in the memory and in the hearts of his surviving comrades. His parole, dated May 16, 1865, which he kept inviolate, attested his adherence to the waning cause of the Confederacy.

He was born at Boydville, Graves County, Ky., September 18, 1846; and died at Elmo, Independence County, Ark., October 18, 1911, of complications superinduced by a stroke of paralysis. He was a faithful soldier of the cross, of the Baptist persuasion, and an active Mason.[120]

COOK, VIRGIL Y.: Virgil Y. Cook, born at Boydsville, Graves County, Ky., November 14, 1848, entered the Confederate army while in his fifteenth year, serving in the Kentucky Brigade of Forrest's Cavalry Corps.

Virgil Y. Cook.

In 1866 he moved to Arkansas and engaged in merchandising at Grand Glaise, on White River. His firm. V . Y. Cook and Co., did an extensive business until 1874, when he removed to a point on the St. Louis and Iron Mountain railroad, and founded the town of Oliphant, and conducted a large and lucrative business there for ten years. After that he located at "Midland Holm," his country site of 5,000 acres, of which 3,200 acres are in a high state of cultivation, near Elmo, in the famous Oil Trough Valley, on Upper White River. He is a member of the Board of Trustees of the University of Arkansas, and a director of the Band of Newport.

At the beginning of the present Spanish-American war he was a Major General of the Arkansas National Guard and reserve militia, commanding the northern division, composed of eight brigades of reserve militia, two regiments of national guards, a squadron of cavalry, and a light battery. President [William] McKinley, having called upon Arkansas for its quota of troops (two regiments), Gov. Jones on April 20, 1898, appointed Comrade Cook Colonel of the Second Arkansas Volunteer Infantry, the highest office within his gift. After visiting Chickamauga Park, where the regiment is now stationed, in July, and seeing the efficiency of the regiment, Gov. Jones went to Washington and urged President McKinley to appoint Col. Cook a brigadier general in the volunteer army of the United States, which the President agreed to do in the near future. Col. Cook's regiment is brigaded with the Sixty-Ninth New York and Fifth Missouri, constituting the Second Brigade of the Second Division of the Third Corps.[121]

CORMAN, J. W.: J. W. Corman was born in Carlisle, Pa., in January, 1839; and died in Brooksville, Fla., in December, 1909. In 1861 he enlisted in the 3rd Kentucky Volunteer Infantry, under Col. A. P. Thompson, and served in the Western campaign under Generals Bragg and Johnston, being part of the time under Gen. N. B. Forrest. He was in the battles of Shiloh, Vicksburg, Baton Rouge, Port Hudson, Corinth, Harrisburg, Guntown, Murfreesboro, and a number of minor engagements, and was wounded in the breast at Shiloh and in the thigh at Sulphur Springs, Tenn. He engaged in the tinner's trade.[122]

CORNWALL, RICHARD OWEN: Richard Owen Cornwall, eighty-four years of age, died at his home in Dallas, Tex., on November 23, 1929. For the last forty years he had been an employee of the city of Dallas, and his honorary pallbearers were city employees, in addition to his comrades of the gray and Sons of Confederate Veterans. He is survived by his wife, three daughters, a son, and eleven grandchildren.

Born in Lexington, Ky., March 2, 1846, his service for the South began in 1862, when he ran away to join the Confederate army, becoming a courier boy under Gen. N. B. Forrest. He was later with John H. Morgan, and after the latter was killed, he served under Colonel Faulkner, of Morgan's Division. Although wounded, he served to the end of the war, never surrendered, and was never paroled; and he gave equally valiant service with the *original* Ku-Klux Klan [a non-racist, Conservative, pro-Constitution organization that is not connected to today's KKK][123] in correcting the evils following the war. His Cross of Honor, bestowed by the Bonnie Blue Flag Chapter, U.D.C., of Dallas, was a treasured memento of those days of service to the South, and for his unusual services to the Camp of Confederate Veterans, to the State Division and general organization of the United Confederate Veterans, the title of Major General was conferred upon him.[124]

COUCH, E.: Capt. E. Couch was born in Marshall County, Ala., on August 24, 1840, and enlisted in the Confederate army in 1861, under the command of Gen. Joe Wheeler, serving with distinction as escort to General Wheeler until he was captured in 1863. He was in prison in Chicago for eleven months. After being exchanged, he came back South and joined the army under Gen. N. B. Forrest, with whom he served until the close of the war. He was a brave and fearless soldier, true and tried, one of the great and noble patriots who shouldered a gun in defense of his country.

Captain Couch was sheriff of Marshall County, Ala., eight years. In 1806 he married Miss Elizabeth Carter and reared a family. His wife died some years ago, and he later married Mrs. Malvina Perry, who survives him with the children of the first marriage.

In 1881 he moved from Alabama to Arkansas, and soon afterwards located in Poinsett County, and lived on his farm near White Hall until his death, which occurred January 12, 1923, at the age of eighty-two years.

Captain Couch joined the Church in 1914, and lived a consistent Christian life. He was honored and loved as a good citizen, a kind and courteous neighbor and friend.[125]

COWAN, GEORGE LIMERICK: Capt. George L. Cowan, who died at his home, in Franklin, Tenn., on September 1, 1919, was born in County Derry, Ireland, on October 15, 1842, and came to this country in 1850 with his parents, who settled in Bedford County, Tenn.

He enlisted in the Confederate army in 1861 in Captain Boone's company of Shelbyville, which company was selected by Gen. N. B. Forrest as his personal escort. Comrade Cowan was with General Forrest in all the battles and skirmishes of his command and for quite a while, as first lieutenant, was in command of the company, surrendering with it at Gainesville, Ala., on May 9, 1865.

Any one acquainted with General Forrest's record will know that to hold the position held by Comrade Cowan he must have been a man of skill and address, of quick and sound judgment, and of undoubted courage. He was a soldier true and tried, giving to his country four years of the prime of life.

After the surrender Comrade Cowan returned home, but soon entered the wholesale mercantile business at Nashville, in which he continued several years. In 1884 he was married to Miss Hattie McGavock, daughter of Col. John McGavock, of Franklin, one of nature's noblemen and of the most prominent families of the whole Southland. [The McGavocks founded Franklin's famed Carnton Plantation and donated the land for the McGavock Confederate Cemetery located nearby.][126] Surviving him are his wife and five children.

George Limerick Cowan.

[From his bivouac:] "Whereas God in his providence has seen proper to call from among us Comrade Cowan, one of our best members, one who carried the Confederate soldier near to his heart, one who was instrumental in getting the headstones placed in McGavock Cemetery. In fact, at his own expense he visited the legislatures of Alabama and Mississippi while in session and procured a contribution from each of these States to help in this work and was at the time of his death President of the Board of Trustees of McGavock Cemetery Association. Comrade Cowan had been a Trustee of the Soldiers' Home since its foundation and did all he could to aid, relieve, and encourage the inmates. He served as President of our Bivouac a number of terms and was Secretary for years, until a short time back, when his eyesight failed—therefore be it

"Resolved, That in the death of Comrade Cowan our Bivouac has lost one of its most faithful and beloved members; that Masonry has lost one of the truest exponents of its doctrine, 'the brotherhood of man'; that his Church has lost a brother whose place will be hard to fill; that his community has lost an honorable, law-abiding, and respected citizen—yes, one of whom it can be truthfully said: 'In him there was no guile.'"[127]

COWAN, JAMES BENJAMIN: Dr. J. B. Cowan served as Medical Director for Forrest from the beginning to the close of his career, is a first cousin to Mrs. [Mary Ann Montgomery] Forrest. He is a native of Fayetteville, [Lincoln County,] Tennessee, was born in September [15th], 1831. His father was an eminent minister in the Cumberland Presbyterian Church for a half century.

Surgeon Cowan graduated in the New York Medical College in 1855. He gave his services to the Confederate Government, at Montgomery, early in 1861, and was first assigned to the Ninth Mississippi Regiment, then at Pensacola, Florida. In December, 1861, he was transferred to Forrest, at Hopkinsville, Kentucky, who had a Battalion of Cavalry. His promotion was continuous with Forrest until their surrender, May 12, 1865. In January previous Dr. Cowan was made Medical Director of Cavalry. He still lives, and is engaged in the practice of Medicine and Surgery at Tullahoma, Tenn.[128]

[From Dr. Cowan's obituary:] Dr. J. B. Cowan, chief surgeon of Forrest's Cavalry throughout the war and one of the best-known men of the great Confederate organization, his appearance being of high distinction and his service in the medical association ever being active at Reunions, died in Tullahoma, Tenn., July 24, 1909. He had never missed a general Reunion until the last, at Memphis. He had been in ill health for several months; but on the day of his death he was on the street with his youngest son, and remarked a little while before the end that he felt unusually well. A little later, however, he went into a drug store for some medicine; but the prescriptionist being busy, he went to another drug store, and ere he could be waited upon he fell on his face dead.

Dr. Cowan was a graduate of the medical colleges of Philadelphia and New York, and had attained a high rank in his profession. When the war began, he took an important place in the Confederate army. He was made chief surgeon of Chalmer's Regiment of Mississippi, and was later transferred to the command of N. B. Forrest, and under that notable chief served with distinction until the close of the war. He was on the staff of General Forrest nearly all the war, and he was the last survivor except Capt. John W. Morton, of Nashville, who was General Forrest's chief of artillery. Dr. Cowan took part in all the big battles of that famous command, winning great distinction for daring while attending to his duties as surgeon.

James Benjamin Cowan.

As "the bravest are the tenderest, the loving are the daring," Dr. Cowan was ever conspicuous by his courtly bearing and his courtesy, which marked him as one of nature's nobility.

He married Miss Lucy Robinson, and for fifty years lived with her in the holy ties of wedlock. He leaves his wife with seven children and many grandchildren, together with a large circle of friends, to mourn their loss.

The funeral of Dr. Cowan was largely attended, quite a number of army officers and personal friends going from a distance—the veterans and a large number of Odd Fellows attending and officiating. A large number of the townspeople were present also to show their sorrow and esteem for the most distinguished man of that section. The Cumberland Presbyterian Church could seat but little more than half of the attendants. Dr. Cowan was a loyal, devout member of that Church, while his father had been one of its eminent ministers for a half century or more. He was first cousin to General Forrest's wife [Mary Ann Montgomery], and was perhaps his most intimate friend for many years. Dr. Cowan was born in Lincoln County, and had resided in that section all of his life.[129]

COX, F. M.: On the 19th day of April, 1918, one of our most worthy comrades and citizens, F. M. Cox, passed away at his home, near Middleton, Tenn. He entered the Confederate army in 1861, volunteering in the first company of Middleton Tigers, one hundred and eighteen strong and one of the grandest companies that ever went on the battle field. It was a part of the 9th Tennessee Infantry. On April 6, 1862, the company was almost destroyed, Mr. Cox being one of the few who escaped death at that time, and his recent death removes the last survivor. After that battle he returned home and joined the 14th Tennessee Cavalry, Company A, under General Forrest, and remained with this company until the surrender. He was a true and faithful soldier, and Hardeman County knew no better law-abiding citizen. He was a Master Mason, having been a member of Adams Lodge, No. 264, something like forty years. He is survived by two daughters, both married.[130]

COYLE, BEN LEE: Ben Lee Coyle died at his home in Huntsville, Ala., on February 26, in his eighty-second year. He was born near Meridianville, Madison County, Ala., July 1845, and spent the larger part of his life in the country as a farmer, but had made his home in Huntsville for about nine years. His wife died some years ago, but their eleven children, seven sons and four daughters, all survive him.

Comrade Coyle served as a private of the 4th Alabama Regiment of Cavalry, under General Forrest, and made a gallant soldier. He was a valued and faithful member of the Egbert J. Jones Camp, No. 357, U.C.V., of Huntsville, and also a consistent member of the First Methodist Church there. He was laid to rest in Maple Hill Cemetery, at Huntsville, with the honors paid to a brave Confederate soldier.[131]

CRAWLEY, A. B.: A. B. Crawley, corporal of Company G, 8th Kentucky Infantry, died August 6, 1907, near Cadiz, Ky. He was a native of Charlotte County, Va., but enlisted in Kentucky in 1861. He was captured with his regiment at Fort Donelson, and was in prison seven months. After being exchanged, he was with his regiment at Coffeeville, Miss., Baker's Creek, Big Black River, around Vicksburg, Jackson, Paducah, Ky. Later, at Guntown, Miss., he was under Forrest; also at Tupelo, Harrisburg, Old Town Creek, Johnsonville, with Hood's advance into Tennessee, at Columbia, Spring Hill, Franklin, and Murfreesboro. He was of the reargaurd of Hood's army back to the Tennessee River, and was surrendered with his company and regiment at Columbus, Miss., May 15, 1865. Comrade Crawley made an ideal soldier, a splendid citizen, and died with the love and esteem of his neighbors.[132]

CRITZ, FRANK A.: Judge Critz enlisted in the Confederate service at the age of sixteen under Gen. Wirt Adams. He was afterwards transferred to the command of Gen. Forrest, and served to the end of the war in Company I, Sixth Mississippi Regiment, Forrest's Cavalry. He was sergeant of the company. Judge Critz was extolled for his gallantry and devotion to duty. He participated in all of the sanguinary engagements of Forrest's command. After the war Judge Critz prepared himself by teaching school, and reading law at night. He graduated at the University of Mississippi, has had a successful career as a lawyer and business man, and is now a leading candidate for Governor of Mississippi.[133]

Frank A. Critz.

CROFT, W. C.: W. C. Croft, one of the oldest and best-loved citizens of Fulton, Ky., died on July 20, 1925, after many months of illness, aged eighty-three years. He was born on March 6, 1842. He is survived by his wife, one son, five grandsons, and three great-grandchildren. He was a member of the Primitive Baptist Church, holding membership in Old Bethel Church for many years. He had served as justice of the peace in Weakley County and was also twice elected trustee of the same county, which office he filled in a very satisfactory manner. He served as director of the Confederate Home in Pewee Valley, Ky., until his death, and had been vice president of the City National Bank since it was organized. For more than forty years he served in some official capacity, and it was recognized that his word was as good as his bond under any and all circumstances.

As in time of peace, Mr. Croft was equally distinguished in time of war. He enlisted in the Confederate army at the age of nineteen, in Weakley County, Tenn., and was assigned to the 31st Tennessee Regiment. His first active engagement was at Belmont, Mo., and later on his regiment took part in the battles of Shiloh, Murfreesboro, Chickamauga, Chattanooga, Missionary Ridge, and Lookout Mountain. For months that regiment was in almost constant contact with the Federal forces. In 1864 he was given a furlough, and later found it impossible to rejoin his regiment. He then rode to Memphis and enlisted in Forrest's command, and with it had part in the fighting at Franklin and Nashville, Tenn. Comrade Croft had a vivid memory, and many interesting stories have been heard from his lips concerning those stirring days when North and South were at grips with each other.

"He left his impress upon his community, and his work will live after him."[134]

CROSSLAND, EDWARD: Col. Edward Crossland, of the 7th Kentucky Mounted Infantry, Forrest's Cavalry Corps, entered the Confederate service in May, 1861, as captain of the Alexander Guards, 1st Kentucky Infantry, C.S.A., and went immediately to Virginia with his regiment. This being a twelve months' organization, it was mustered out of the service at the expiration thereof, when both officers and men in nearly every instance joined other Kentucky Confederate regiments then serving in the Western armies.

In the meantime Captain Crossland had attained the rank of major and lieutenant colonel respectively in that organization.

The 7th Kentucky, then serving as infantry, having lost its colonel, Charles Wickliffe, killed at Shiloh April 6, 1861, was reorganized in June following, when Col. Edward Crossland was unanimously elected colonel thereof, and served in that capacity until the end in May, 1865. During the last fifteen months, however, he was in command of the Kentucky brigade of Forrest's Cavalry, constituted of the 3rd, 7th, and 8th Kentucky Mounted Infantry, and the 12th Kentucky Cavalry, Buford's Division. The first three regiments, having hitherto served as infantry, were on the 10th of March, 1864, mounted and assigned to General Forrest, thenceforth serving as "Soldiers on the Horse," but always dismounting and fighting as infantry, and their effectiveness was at all times highly satisfactory to General Forrest.

Edward Crossland.

Colonel Crossland was three times severely wounded: at Paducah, Ky., March 25, 1864; Harrisburg, Miss., July 14 following; and at Butler's Creek, just north of Florence, Ala., November 21, 1864. Brave, enterprising, kind, and considerate to his men, he was their idol at all times, and he never failed to lead them with conspicuous bravery, yet with such prudence and good judgment that all possible advantages were available to them; and doubtless no colonel serving under General Forrest at any time commanded at all times that general's confidence more thoroughly than did Colonel Crossland. Had there been a vacancy in the Kentucky brigade, Colonel Crossland would have been promoted to a brigadier generalcy, General Forrest often speaking of him in that connection.

Colonel Crossland began his public career as sheriff of Hickman County, Ky., his native county, in 1850; afterwards studied law and entered actively into the practice at Clinton, Ky., and later in 1857-59 represented his county in the Kentucky Legislature. On returning to Kentucky in the summer of 1865 he located at Mayfield, in Graves County, and again entered into the practice of law. In 1866 he was elected judge of the Court of Common Pleas, resigning therefrom in 1871 to take his seat in the Congress of the United States, in which he served brilliantly and effectively two terms as Representative from the First Kentucky District. On retiring from Congress, he was elected judge of the Circuit Court, which position he filled with distinguished ability and universal satisfaction until his death.

He was born in Hickman County, Ky., June 30, 1827; and died at Mayfield, Graves County, Ky., September 11, 1881.

A more extended tribute herein is due to this remarkable man. . . . This concise and fitting statement is made about him by Col. V. Y. Cook, of Batesville, Ark., who as a mere boy served under him for a time: "Crossland in many respects had no superior. He was as plain as the proverbial 'old shoe' and an accomplished gentleman."[135]

CRUMP, MARCUS V.: On the 15th of September, Marcus V. Crump died at the home of his daughter, Mrs. R. E. Bowen, in Memphis, Tenn., after a long illness, aged eighty-three years. He was one of the youngest of Confederate soldiers, having run away from home at the age of fourteen to fight for the South.

Marcus V. Crump was born in Purdy, McNairy County, Tenn., September 11, 1847, but the family moved to Williamson County, and in that county he joined a cavalry company under Capt. Thomas F. Perkins. However, his age and size were against him, and the captain would not enroll him, but he remained in rank. As he was so determined to be a soldier, his father secured the influence of Col. John F. House, of the 1st Tennessee Infantry, to suitably place him in the service, and young Crump was made courier at General Maney's headquarters, where he served until his uncle, Gen. Marcus V. Wright, commissioned him an aide on his staff. He so served until after the battle of Missionary Ridge, and when General Wright was withdrawn from field service and made commander of the post at Atlanta, Marcus Crump joined Forrest's Cavalry, and served with Barteau's 2nd Tennessee Regiment until captured near Columbia, Tenn., November, 1864, and sent to Camp Douglas. On February 28, 1865, with five hundred other prisoners, he was sent to Point Lookout, Md., and there remained until paroled June 10, 1865.

After the war, Comrade Crump entered the mercantile business, in which he was active for many years, and since his retirement he had served on the Pension Board of Tennessee, resigning as its President on account of ill health. He was also for many years Captain of Company A, a uniformed company of Confederate veterans of Memphis, Tenn. He was a gentleman of the old time Southern type of manners and courtesy. Two daughters and a son survive him.[136]

CULBREATH, J. M.: J. M. Culbreath, Company B, 7th Tennessee Cavalry, Forrest's Division, died in Arizona, January, 1924, aged eighty-six years. A true man, a good soldier, and faithful to every trust.[137]

George Dashiel.

DASHIEL, GEORGE: George Dashiel was born in Maryland January 10, 1828. The family removed to Tennessee in 1838. He was a merchant in Memphis at the commencement of the war, and enlisted in the Confederate army in April, 1861, as a private in Company B, One Hundred and Fifty-Fourth Tennessee Regiment. In October, 1861, he was appointed captain of cavalry by the [Confederate] War Department, and ordered to report to Gen. Leonidas Polk, and was assigned by him as paymaster of the Cheatham Division, he remained with that division until the spring of 1863, when he was transferred by the War Department, at the request of Gen. N. B. Forrest, to his corps as chief paymaster. He remained with Forrest until paroled at Gainesville, Ala., in 1865.[138]

DAVENPORT, Z. T.: Z. T. Davenport was born near Valley Head, Ala., November 17, 1845, and died January 6, 1922. Early in 1863 he enlisted in the service of his country and was a member of Company A, 1st Alabama Battalion Cavalry, in which he served faithfully to the end of the struggle. He was in the battle of Selma, Ala., under General Forrest, which was fought after the surrender at Appomattox.

He was married to Miss Amanda Alman, December 14, 1871. To this union were born two children, a son and daughter. The daughter, Mrs. Jesse Barnard, is still living. In 1883 Comrade Davenport joined the M. E. Church, South. He and the writer became attached to each other when small boys and had been lifelong friends. He was a man of veracity, industry, economy—true to his family, true to his Church, and true to his country. He was always cheerful and spread sunshine wherever he went. He was a member of Camp Estes No. 1659, U.C.V., was regular in his attendance, and was always the life of the occasion. For several months prior to his death he was a great sufferer, but he bore it all patiently and died peacefully and triumphantly.

He leaves a daughter, two grandsons, several brothers, and a host of friends to mourn his loss. Clothed in his Confederate uniform, he was laid to rest in the Valley Head Cemetery, there to await the resurrection morn.[139]

DAVIDSON, ELIJAH A.: Dr. Elijah A. Davidson was born seventy-six years ago in Bedford County, Tenn. At ten years of age he entered the home of his uncle, Dr. I. S. Davidson, at Richmond, Tenn., where he was reared and treated as one of the family. He was sixteen years old when the War between the States broke out.

He enlisted in October, 1861, in Captain Brown's company from Richmond, which became a part of the 41st Tennessee Regiment Volunteer Infantry, C.S.A. His first fight was at Fort Donelson, February, 1862, where he was captured and sent to prison at Indianapolis. After eight months' confinement he was exchanged at Vicksburg, Miss., in October, 1862, served with the 41st Tennessee Regiment in the campaign around Vicksburg. At Port Hudson he was discharged as under military age and returned home. In 1863 he reenlisted, this time with Company D, 4th Tennessee Cavalry (Starnes' Regiment), then under General Forrest. After the battle of Chickamauga his command was transferred to General Wheeler and served with him to the end, fighting Sherman through Georgia and surrendering at Washington, Ga., with his command in May, 1865. He was a brave, chivalrous, and faithful soldier.

After the war he studied medicine and practiced his profession at Richmond, loved, respected, and honored by all. Soon after the war he united with the Christian Church and had been a faithful member of it. For many years he had been an active elder, delighted in Sunday school work, being a fine teacher of the Bible class.

Dr. Davidson was married on February 18, 1885, to Miss Lizzie Marks, daughter of Rev. Y. B. Marks. Their home was a happy one and ever open to the preacher. Two children, Marks Davidson, of Petersburg, and Mrs. Nellie Shoffner, of Flat Creek, survive him. He died October 19 at his home at Richmond, Tenn., lamented by his loved ones and friends. He was laid to rest in the Old Orchard Cemetery, at Petersburg, Tenn. The grave must receive its own. Christ is our only Shield.[140]

DAVIS, BEN: One of the 65 African-Americans who served in Forrest's Cavalry, Ben Davis was a teamster under the great Rebel chieftain. Comrade Davis applied for a Confederate pension in 1921.[141]

DAVIS, CARROLL MAYHEW: Carroll Mayhew Davis, son of William R. and Elizabeth Keene Davis, was born in Clay County, Tenn., November 13, 1845; he died on January 19, 1927, at the home of his daughter, Mrs. Levi

Motley, in Vandalia, Mo., aged eighty-one years.

   Comrade Davis enlisted in the Confederate army at the age of sixteen years, serving with the 8th Tennessee Cavalry, for nearly three years and was then transferred to infantry; but the most of his service was under General Forrest. The last six months of the war he spent in prison at Camp Chase, Ohio, after his capture at the battle of Franklin, Tenn. Five brothers and three brothers-in-law also served the Southern army from this family. Young Davis was wounded and left for dead on the battle field of Franklin, and he carried that bullet near the hip to his grave. He was captured and taken as prisoner to Camp Chase, from which place he was discharged on June 15, 1865.

   The privations of war did not diminish his loyalty to the cause for which he fought, but with the coming of peace he made a true and loyal citizen of the united country. He went to Missouri shortly after the war and had been a distinguished citizen of Lincoln, Pike, and Adrian counties. He is survived by three sons and a daughter.[142]

DAVIS, COLUMBUS JACKSON: After an illness of several weeks, Capt. Columbus Jackson Davis died at his home, near Cookeville, Tenn., on February 17, 1917. He was seventy-six years old and had been a resident of Putnam County all his life, with the exception of the four years of service for the Confederacy. He was a man of splendid natural ability, a great student of history, a man of sound judgment and of the highest integrity and most charitable and unselfish nature, and he had always taken an active interest in public affairs.

   Although he had been lame from his childhood from an injury to his knee, in the fall of 1862 he enlisted as a private in Company C, 8th Tennessee Cavalry, Capt. I. G. Woolsey's company. In December he was captured in the fight at Parker's Crossroads and sent to Camp Chase Prison, where he was kept until his exchange, in June, 1863. Immediately afterwards he rejoined his command and served under General Forrest, until after the battle of Chickamauga. He was with Longstreet in all the fighting around Knoxville, was in the one hundred days' battle from Dalton to Atlanta, commanded the skirmish line at Saltville, Va., and was in all the engagements of his command from the day of his enlistment until the close of the war, except while he was in prison. Enlisting as a private, he was promoted step by step and had become captain of his company when the war closed. He was a man of distinguished and commanding appearance and a natural leader of men.

   Captain Davis served for many years as a member of the County Court of Putnam County and represented that county in the General Assemblies of 1895 and 1913. For about fifty years he had been a ruling elder in the Presbyterian Church and was no less zealous in the service of his Master than he had been in the service of his country. He loved the Southland with all the ardor of his being and was devoted to his State and the memory of its heroes and statesmen. He was one of the most active members of Pat Cleburne Bivouac at Cookeville. The *Confederate Veteran* had no stancher [meaning stauncher] friend than he.

From his young manhood he had been a devoted Mason; he was also a prominent Odd Fellow and was active in both of these orders.

In 1860 Captain Davis was married to Miss Almira Pendergrass, of Putnam County, who survives him. For fifty-seven years they journeyed happily through life. Four daughters and five sons are also left to mourn the loss of this loving and devoted father.[143]

DAVIS, J. A.: Dr. J. A. Davis was born in Green County, Ala., July 19, 1846, and died February 24, 1922. He enlisted as a private in the 7th Mississippi Cavalry, Duff's Regiment, and was assigned to Forrest's command, with which he served two years in Mississippi, Alabama, and Tennessee, participating in the raids for which that command became famous and taking part in the battles of Harrisburg, Oxford, and West Point, and was in the celebrated march to Nashville. Dr. Davis was an honored member of the John B. Gordon Camp, No. 200, U.C.V., of Norman, Okla. He had retired from active practice.[144]

J. K. Davis.

DAVIS, J. K.: "Taps" has sounded again, and J. K. Davis, a gallant Confederate soldier, answered to the call on Monday, February 13, 1899. At the age of sixteen he enlisted in the Confederate service, and, under the leadership of brave Gen. Forrest, he honored himself as a soldier. No braver man ever marched beneath the folds of the Stars and Bars or followed the strains of "Dixie." Since the war he had been a successful merchant, and always manifested interest in the welfare of his Confederate comrades. His hands, home, and purse were always open to an old comrade in need, and many deeds of charity were done of which the world knows nothing. He was one of the prime movers in the Bill Green Camp, at Dickson, Tenn. He was a liberal contributor to the Sam Davis Monument Fund, and the name of every member of his family appears on the list of contributors. . . . While he will meet his comrades no more at the camp fires on earth, he has joined his great leader and many comrades "across the river."[145]

DAVIS, ROBERT N.: Robert N. Davis passed away peacefully September 25, 1901, at his home in Trenton, Tenn., at the age of seventy-one years. Bob Davis, as he was familiarly called, was at his place of business until after nine o'clock Tuesday night in his usual health and cheerful spirits, but before five o'clock Wednesday morning he had gone from among us into the great beyond. Comrade Davis was born near Trenton, in June, 1830, and has lived in Gibson County all of his life. He was a prosperous merchant in Trenton for forty years. In 1859 he was married to Miss Belle McCleland. His wife, three sons, and three daughters feel their great loss keenly. He was a faithful member and a deacon of the Baptist Church and was a Knight of Honor. He was a member of the O. F. Strahl Bivouac and R. M. Russell Camp, of Trenton. He volunteered in Hill's Company, Forty-Seventh Tennessee Infantry, and was elected Lieutenant at the reorganization. He was afterwards transferred to the cavalry service, becoming a member of Capt. Shane's Company, of Russell's Cavalry Regiment. When on the raid with Forrest into Memphis, he was surrounded by the Federals, but fought his way out, and was with his command until the final surrender, in Alabama, in 1865.[146]

DAVIS, WILLIAM HUNTER: Friends will regret to learn of the death of William Hunter Davis, which occurred February 23, 1917, in Cuero, Tex. Mr. Davis was born and reared near La Guardo, Tenn., the son of Hon. John K. and Caroline Hunter Davis and a grandson of Thomas and Betsy Williamson Davis, pioneer residents of that neighborhood. In the spring of 1861, at the age of sixteen, he enlisted in the company commanded by his father, who subsequently was elected major of Starnes's cavalry regiment, which constituted a part of Gen. N. B. Forrest's command. When his term of enlistment expired, William H. Davis, with others, reenlisted for three years, or during the war, and in the reorganization of his command he became a member of Capt. J. R. Lester's company (F), 4th Tennessee Cavalry Regiment, Lieut. Col. Paul Anderson commanding for the most part, following the capture of Col. Baxter Smith. The 4th Tennessee ("Paul's People"), 3rd Arkansas, and 8th and 11th Texas Regiments composed Gen. Tom Harrison's brigade in Gen. T. C. Hines's division, under Gen. J. E. Johnston. Thus in the campaigns of the distinguished warriors, Forrest and Wheeler, William H. Davis fought for "God and his native land" wherever Generals Bragg and Johnston led their valiant hosts. No braver soldier ever stood in battle. Whether in camp or on the battle field, the same equanimity of mind was dominant; and fatigue of the march, privations, hunger, and thirst were borne without murmuring. Comrade Davis was accorded Confederate honors when borne to his last resting place. A Confederate flag was lowered into the grave, and a silken emblem crowned the flower-laden mount. Of his immediate family, one sister, Miss Alice Davis, of Cuero, Tex., survives him.[147]

DAWSON, W. A.: Col. W. A. Dawson, of the Fifteenth Tennessee Regiment, Rucker's Brigade, Jackson's Division, Forrest's Cavalry, was killed near Columbia, Tenn., on the morning of November 28, 1864. His regiment was in advance of the army, and ran into the camp of a brigade of mounted infantry about dark at Henryville, west of Mt. Pleasant, on the 1st of November, and stampeded them. Forrest and his escort were with them in the Henryville fight, and the Federals were pushed right along through the night, reaching Mt. Pleasant about four o'clock on

W. A. Dawson.

the morning of November 2. They moved on toward Columbia, fighting almost constantly until about ten o'clock, when Col. Dawson was killed. He had just crossed a bridge near Columbia in advance of his command. In fact he and two of his men from Company I (Capt. Williams) were the only men that crossed the bridge. On the 3rd Gen. Strahl detailed two men to find his body, and it was buried in the cemetery at Columbia.

In a personal letter Mr. J. H. Dawson, a son of Col. Dawson, who was flag bearer of the regiment, writes: "Bennie Butterworth jumped off his horse, got my father's saddlebags and his own pistols, which he had loaned my father in the charge. He had emptied the pistols and broken his saber. His horse ran on into the Federal lines."[148]

DEAN, MARCUS LAFAYETTE: At his home, in Centerville, Tenn., Marcus Lafayette Dean died December 25, 1917, after a long illness. He was born in the second district of Hickman County, Tenn., September 22, 1846. He enlisted in the Confederate army in September, 1864, in Company D, Tennessee Cavalry. Tom Easley was his captain, under General Forrest. He remained in the service until the close of the war and was paroled at Gainesville, Ala., May 10, 1865. He returned to Hickman County, where he engaged in farming. In 1886 he sold his farm and moved to Centerville, where he engaged in the sawmill business under the firm name of Dean and McFarland, later selling his interest in the mill and entering the retail grocery and hardware business, which he followed until 1910.

As a husband and father, where could his equal be found? His whole heart was in the Southern cause, and he loved it to the end of his life. Mr. Dean was married three times, his first wife being Miss Martha Bratton, of Little Lot. Three children were born to this union. His second wife was Miss Atlantic Anderson, of this county; and his third wife was Miss Mollie J. Thompson, also of this county. Four children of this union survive. He joined the M. E. Church several years ago, and his funeral was conducted from that church. A platoon of Confederate soldiers with flag draped with black acted as honorary pallbearers.[149]

DEATON, JOHN WESLEY: John Wesley Deaton was born near Raleigh, N.C., February 24, 1839. Fifty-seven years ago he was married to Miss Mary Tedford at Sulphur Springs, Tex. He died at Enid, Okla., May 9, 1928 and was buried at Sentinel by the side of his wife, who passed away four years ago.

He served the Confederate army with Moland's Battalion at Iuka, Miss., and was later attached to Gen. N. B. Forrest's brigade, and was in Company I, of an Alabama regiment, serving in all four years.

He was a man of the old school and possessed that courtly manner which has been the distinction of Southern civilization. He leaves a career of duty performed to God and country, a high example of splendid citizenship, imbued with intense patriotism and devotion to the best interests of his State and reunited country. He was a loyal Confederate, loving the "old boys," as he called them, and holding in sacred remembrance "the storm-cradled nation that fell."

The summons came suddenly, was merged into death so gently, and the transition into that "blessed sleep from which none ever wake to weep" was very peaceful. For this Confederate veteran we break the alabaster box of our affection, and in its fragrance embalm his memory.[150]

William R. DeLoach.

DELOACH, WILLIAM R.: Comrade William R. DeLoach was born June 4, 1842, and reared in Sumter County, Ala.; and died in Memphis August 5, 1910.

At the age of eighteen DeLoach enlisted as a private in the 5th Alabama Regiment, commanded by Col. (afterwards Maj. Gen.) R. E. Rodes. His service throughout the war was of the very best type. An old comrade once pointed to him as the only man he ever knew who was absolutely devoid of personal fear. This statement is not literally true. DeLoach's intelligence recognized the hazard of battle, but his true moral courage rose above it. To him "duty" to himself and family and love of country were higher than all else, and made him bear himself as if ignorant of fear.

He served with honor in Virginia, being badly wounded at Sharpsburg while climbing over the Federal breastworks, and later on was shot down at Mine Run while voluntarily leading a charge which was the duty of superior officers. He fell at the head of his men, with a jagged hole in the neck, which kept him out of the service for three months. Receiving his promotion at his return, he was assigned to Forrest's Cavalry and made captain of a company of independent scouts. Near Decatur, Ala., he was captured and kept on Johnson's Island until July, 1865.

The hardships of war bore lightly upon the youthful soldiers of the South. Their courage was inherited, the strength and joy of comradeship were theirs, and, like their ancestors, they met the foes of their country with inborn steadfastness. It was natural for DeLoach to fight; he had a knowledge of the questions at issue.

But it was after he returned home in 1865 that the real test of manhood came to DeLoach and to the men of his class. How he met this trial is known only to those who touched shoulders and divided counsel with him at that time. From that day till 1873, when the white people of Sumter came into their own again, was the time that tried men's souls in the Southland. From the town of Livingston, DeLoach's home, to the northern boundary of the county the proportion of blacks to whites was larger than in any other county in Alabama. The negroes almost from the first were under the control of aliens [Yankees] and renegades [Liberals], and the struggle for existence was on in earnest.

Reconstruction, with its deliberate plan to subject the native white people to their former slaves, was an unspeakable horror, to be resisted to the death. If the true story of reconstruction in the Black Belt of Alabama should ever be told, DeLoach's name would be written high up on the roll of honor. His judgment and courage were with him under all conditions. When the struggle was over, his kindliness made him resist any cruelty to, or oppression of, the negroes, when control was absolutely in the hands of the whites. He acted steadily upon this principle during his long service as judge, and no court was ever administered more fairly than his. His reelection time after time, making his term of office thirty-four years, was a tribute to his integrity and intelligence.

The writer of this sketch states: "Of all the men whom I have known and of all the comrades I have loved, DeLoach came nearest the right life, and his surviving friends will join me in this judgment of his character."

In 1867 Capt. W. R. DeLoach was married to Miss Susan Gibbs, a daughter of Col. Charles R. Gibbs, an officer of the War of 1812. Theirs was an ideal union. Will DeLoach and Sue Gibbs loved each other from youth through a long life, and parted only through that inevitable decree which "happeneth to all." Four children survive Captain DeLoach: Mrs. McLelland, Miss Rosa DeLoach, Dr. DeLoach, of Memphis, Tenn., and Mrs. R. G. Ennis, of Livingston, Ala.[151]

DEVAUGHN, JAMES ELIJAH: James Elijah DeVaughn was born near Jonesboro, Ga., December 20, 1840.

He attended school at Jonesboro and in Abbeville, S.C. From his native county he responded to his country's call for defenders against invasion. Enlisting as a private in October, 1861, in Company F, 2nd Georgia Cavalry Regiment, he rose through the various grades of promotion to the rank of captain, and was in command of his company when captured. His command was assigned to the Army of Tennessee, under General Forrest, and was later under Generals Wharton and Wheeler, being with the latter in the battles of Murfreesboro in 1862.

James Elijah DeVaughn.

The 2nd Georgia Cavalry made an admirable record as a fighting command, and Comrade DeVaughn remained with it to the close of the war, taking part in many notable battles, including Perryville, Stone's River, and Chickamauga. He was taken prisoner at Sugar Creek, Ala., while with General Wheeler, and remained a prisoner to the close of the war, being released June 12, 1865, after nearly two years on Johnson's Island.

In 1866 Colonel DeVaughn removed to Montezuma, Ga., where he married Miss Sallie V. McClendon, and to them were born nine children, five of whom survive him. He was happily married the second time in 1884 to Miss Mary E. Porter, of Griffin, Ga., who survives him.

Colonel DeVaughn was for many years the beloved Commander of Camp No. 65, U.C.V., at Oglethorpe, Ga., and two years ago was made Brigadier General of the Western Division, U.C.V., of Georgia, and was also a member of Gov. Hoke Smith's military staff.

After the war Colonel DeVaughn was a leader in the great work of restoration and rehabilitation, and overcame all obstacles by oppressive Federal [Liberal Yankee] laws and Federal [Liberal Yankee] interference. He turned disaster into triumph. He possessed a genius for business, and was successful in his undertakings.

He contracted a violent cold while at the Birmingham Reunion, from the effects of which he never recovered. His pallbearers were his old comrades in arms, and he was buried in his new uniform of Confederate gray, while over his flower-covered coffin was draped a beautiful Confederate flag.

He was a man of exalted character, generous in his benefactions, charitable in thought, and firm in religious principles. His well-spent life is over; and . . . so he went to rest, his work well done, his career complete, beloved by family and friends.[152]

DEW, ARTHUR T.: Arthur T. Dew was born in Wilson County, Tenn., March 23, 1844; but his parents removed to Weakley County, near Dresden, while he was a child, and there he grew to manhood.

He entered the Confederate army in 1863 as a member of Company I, 20th Tennessee Cavalry, Bell's Brigade, under Forrest, and served to the close of the war, surrendering at Gainesville, Ala. He was a splendid soldier. The day before the battle of Harrisburg he was left behind with a sick horse, but he procured another mount and joined the command that night and participated in the battle next day, in which he was slightly wounded.

After the war he married and settled near Sharon, Tenn., where he died on June 4, 1911. He was a brother of Col. R. J. Dew, of Trenton, Tenn.[153]

DEWOODY, WILLIAM LAWRENCE: William L. DeWoody, born December 30, 1847, at Athens, Ala., died June 30, 1918, at Pine Bluff, Ark., of which city he was a prominent business man and honored citizen for nearly fifty years. At the time of his death he was Dean of Arkansas Pharmacists, Honorary President of the American Pharmaceutical Association, and, besides, had many commercial interests. He was a member of the J. Ed Murray Camp, U.C.V.

He enlisted at the age of sixteen years in John J. Akers's Company, Simonton's Regiment, Mississippi State Militia. After this command disbanded he served as a guide and courier for Henderson's Scouts under General Forrest.

In May, 1870, Mr. DeWoody embarked in the drug business in Pine Bluff, Ark., in which he continued until his death. He was the son of Samuel DeWoody and Louisa Ann Comon and a grandson of William DeWoody and

Hannah Alexander, of Pennsylvania. On the maternal line he was descended from Col. Thomas Wade, a Revolutionary soldier from Anson County, N.C.

Mr. DeWoody was married in May, 1875, to Miss Mary M. Sorrells, of Warren, Ark., daughter of the late Judge T. F. Sorrells.

There was no man more loyal in his citizenship, more worthy the regard of his personal friends, or more deserving the high esteem of his fellow citizens at large than William Lawrence DeWoody.[154]

George Gibbs Dibrell.

DIBRELL, GEORGE GIBBS: George G. Dibrell was born on April 12, 1822, at Sparta, Tenn. A farmer and merchant, at the start of Lincoln's War he enlisted as a private, soon recruiting the 8th Tennessee Cavalry, of which he was made colonel. The unit was attached to Forrest's command, with which Dibrell served until he was assigned to combine with Gen. Joseph E. Johnston at Dalton. After service with Gen. Wheeler, Dibrell was promoted to the rank of brigadier general, and was paroled at Washington, Ga., May 9, 1865.

Following the War he became a Congressman, president of the Southwestern Railroad, and a coal mine developer. He died on May 9, 1888, and was buried at Sparta, Tenn., where he was living at the time. His numerous mentions in these pages attest to his patriotism, bravery, and integrity.[155]

DICKENSON, R. D.: R. D. Dickenson . . . was with Captains Craig and Nelson under Generals Forrest and Bell. His duty was to gather up the cattle and deliver to the commissary department.[156]

DILBECK, J. D.: The angel of death has visited our home and taken from us our husband and father, J. D. Dilbeck. He was born in Selma, Ala., March 4, 1840, and departed this life at Kellyville, Okla., where he had gone for a visit, August 28, 1916. The body was laid to rest in the Kellyville Cemetery.

He was a member of Company F, 1st Mississippi Cavalry, Forrest's Corps, Jackson's Brigade, Armstrong's Division, Army of Tennessee, having enlisted in 1861 and served to the close of the war. He was wounded three times during his service, but was never captured.

At the close of the war he went to Mississippi and lived three years, then moved to North Arkansas and lived there until 1907, when he removed to Oklahoma.

His happiest hours were spent in relating incidents of war times. He leaves a wife and six children—five daughters and a son—to mourn their loss.[157]

DINKINS, JAMES: James Dinkins was born April 18, 1845 in Madison Co., Mississippi. After finishing his schooling at the North Carolina Military Institute, he entered the Confederate army as a private in the 18th Mississippi Regiment. By 1863 he had been promoted to first lieutenant, afterward serving as aid-de-camp to Gen Chalmers, under Forrest. He ended the War as captain of the 18th Mississippi, then turned to writing, penning a number of interesting pro-South books on Lincoln's War and American history. He also worked as a railroad agent, passing away at Saluds, N.C., on July 19, 1939, at the age of 94. He was buried at New Orleans, La.[158]

James Dinkins.

DISMUKES, JOHN L.: John L. Dismukes, prominent citizen of Nashville, Tenn., died in that city on the morning of September 30 [1927], following a brief illness. He was born in Davidson County, March 4, 1844, at the place on the Gallatin Pike where his father settled when he went to Tennessee from Virginia.

In April, 1861, at the age of seventeen years, young Dismukes enlisted as a private in Company B, 18th Tennessee Regiment, with which he participated in the fighting at Fort Donelson, and was there surrendered. He was sent to the prison at Camp Butler, Ill., but escaped some six weeks later and returned to Tennessee. On the way to rejoin his regiment at Iuka, Miss., he joined fortunes with Morgan's cavalry command, until the disaster at Lebanon, after which he got back to his regiment, under General Bragg, in time to take part in the battle of Murfreesboro, where the 18th Tennessee was distinguished in the charge with Breckinridge's Division on January 2, 1863. At Chickamauga, for heroism in saving the flag as it fell from the hands of the wounded color bearer and carrying it forward, he was promoted to ensign of the regiment, with rank of first lieutenant.

In the official report of Brown's Brigade on the battle of Chickamauga, it is stated that "on Sunday morning, September 20, when the brigade was ordered forward, but forced to fall back by a most galling fire from the enemy's artillery, Sergt. Isaac A. Looney and Private John L. Dismukes continued to advance some hundred yards to a house within fifty yards of the enemy's guns and fired at the gunners until the next brigade came up." He served with the 18th Tennessee at Missionary Ridge, Dalton, Resaca, New Hope Church, and to the close of the Atlanta campaign, after which he was transferred to the 1st Tennessee Cavalry, under Col. Samuel P. Carter, with which he served as second lieutenant until wounded in the leg at the battle of Franklin. He surrendered with Forrest's command at Gainesville, Ala.

Returning to his home at Nashville, Lieutenant Dismukes engaged in the wholesale hat business in 1870, which became one of the most prominent and successful wholesale establishments of the city. He was actively connected with it to the end. Comrade Dismukes was married to Miss Andrea Russell Humes, of Knoxville, who died last June. Two daughters and a son survive him. He was a vestryman of Christ Episcopal Church at Nashville, and for many years junior warden there; was chairman of the building committee when the new church was erected.[159]

DODGE, D. F.: Commander D. F. Dodge, now eighty-seven years old, served with the 7th Tennessee Cavalry under Forrest, and took part in the famous engagements at Fort Pillow and Brice's Crossroads.[160]

DOERNER, GEORGE W.: Capt. George W. Doerner, born in Brooklyn, Ala., August 1, 1846, was the son of George H. and Sarah A. Doerner. He became a Mississippian by adoption and served in the Confederate army as a member of Company B, 5th Mississippi Cavalry (under Col. J. Z. George), Ferguson's Brigade, Forrest's Division. He died at his home, in Collinsville, Miss., on November 22, 1917, honored and respected by all who knew him.

While the Federal army was in Meridian, Miss., and vicinity in February, 1864, Major Reed was placed in command of a small detachment of cavalry to go in search of the Yankees. Five miles east of Marion they sighted a regiment of Yankee cavalry. Major Reed and his boys dismounted, hitching their horses some two hundred yards in the rear, and went in the direction of the Yankees. They took refuge behind a little shop within twenty yards of the public road, and when the Federal column got within forty yards of the hiding place a volley was fired into the front ranks, killing the colonel's horse. The little party of Confederates then ran to their horses; and of the two boys who mounted first, one turned to the east. The other's horse took fright and ran to the head of the regiment, then down the open column, continuing the wild race until he reached the provost guard, where both horse and rider were captured. The Yankees rushed up the road and captured the squad of scouts except the one who went eastward. The latter lingered in sight long enough to see the fate of his comrades, then rode away, and in less than an hour he came to my father's home, five miles east of where this occurred. He took dinner with us and related the fate of his comrades, all of which made a very deep impression on my mind, young as I was. I joined General Forrest's command in April, 1864, and was paroled in May, 1865. I never knew until some three years ago that the young hero whose horse ran down the open column was Captain Doerner, who told me of his capture.[161]

DOUGLAS, EDWIN H.: The death of Capt. Edwin H. Douglas, of Franklin, Tenn., which occurred recently, was a painful shock to his multitude of friends. He was of fine constitution, and by his active out-of-door life was strong and splendidly developed. The picture herewith presented represents him as he appeared in war times.

Edwin H. Douglas was born at Fayetteville, Tenn., May, 1840, son of Byrd and Mary Bright Douglas. They removed to Nashville in 1847, and Edwin received his education under Edwin Paschal at Kimberly and at the Western Military School at Nashville, graduating in 1859. He then entered promptly into business life. In 1861 he enlisted for the South in Capt. Ed Baxter's Battery, and was appointed gun sergeant. That battery was the first in action at Fishing Creek, under Zollicoffer, and took part at Iuka, Miss., and in the battle of Shiloh. Douglas was elected lieutenant when Freeman became captain. The battery was transferred to Bragg's command at Chattanooga; was afterwards attached to Murray's Brigade, which crossed the Tennessee River at Bridgeport and captured Stevenson, Ala. The battery was next transferred to Wheeler's Cavalry at Columbia, Tenn., and attached to Forrest's command. It participated in the battle of Parker's Cross Roads and in the severe fight near Thompson's Station, where it was captured by the Fourth United States Regulars and Capt. Freeman was killed, together with others of his battery who could not keep up with retreating Federals guarding them. Lieut. Douglas and other members of it escaped. The battery was with Forrest at the battle of Chickamauga, and was afterwards in most of his raids until the close of the war.

Edwin H. Douglas.

After the war Capt. Douglas entered the commission business in Nashville with Douglas, Sons & Co. In the early seventies he married Miss Bessie McGavock [full name, Elizabeth Harding McGavock], of Franklin, Tenn.,[162] and in 1875 began the life of farmer and stock raiser on the McGavock farm, which he purchased. His wife died after two years of married life, and several years later he married Mrs. Electra Woodfin, who survives him with two daughters. He was brave, and famously generous and kind-hearted. Gen. Forrest paid to him the high honor to say that he had no braver or more determined soldier in his command than Ed Douglas.

His generous nature caused ardent devotion by his friends. He died at the residence of his brother, Dr. Richard Douglas, in Nashville, to whom he came for consultation. Mr. Byrd Douglas, of Nashville, a brother, was part of the time a member of his battery.[163]

DOUGLASS, THOMAS J.: The death of Thomas J. Douglass in a collision of trains near Wheelerton, Ala., on May 19, 1917, removed another from the fast-thinning ranks of Confederate veterans and the oldest employee of the Louisville and Nashville Railroad at Nashville. He had been in railroad work continuously since 1867; and had he lived until June 1, he would have rounded out fifty years as a locomotive engineer.

Thomas Douglass was born in Wayne County, Tenn., February 23, 1843, but the family removed to Maury County when he was still a child, and he was reared at Columbia. He entered railroad service as a boy, his first work being with the old Tennessee and Alabama Railroad, a division of the Nashville and Decatur [Railroad]. In 1859 he was made fireman on the N. & D., but when the war came on he resigned to take up arms for the Confederacy. In May, 1862, he joined Company A, 9th Tennessee Cavalry, Colonel Biffle's regiment. He was captured in November, 1863, and imprisoned until March, 1865, when he was sent to Virginia for exchange; and he was paroled on May 3, 1865, with the Army of Tennessee. He was wounded in some fighting near Nashville, but escaped any serious injury during his service.

Comrade Douglass was held in the highest esteem by all who knew him. He was a man of high character, gentle and courteous, and a devout Christian. He was a member of Troop A, Forrest Veteran Cavalry, of Nashville, and a Mason of high standing, a member of Claiborne Lodge, No. 293, F. and A.M. He is survived by his wife, three sons, and two daughters. In his suit of gray he was laid to rest in Rose Hill Cemetery, at Columbia.[164]

DOUTHIT, THOMAS E.: Thomas E. Douthit was born in Maury County, Tenn., January 8, 1841; and died on March 10, 1914, at Houston, Tex. He was buried in the Angleton Cemetery, Brazoria County, having lived in the county for eighteen years. He was living in Farmington, St. Francis County, Mo., in 1861; and enlisted in the Confederate service as a private in Company E. 2nd Missouri Cavalry, Robert McCullough's regiment, on the 17th of November, 1862, serving under General Forrest until his regiment was paroled at Columbus, Miss., May 17, 1865. Comrade Douthit was Adjutant of A. P. Hill Camp. U.C.V., of Angleton, Tex. He was a chivalrous soldier, a noble citizen, a devoted husband and father.[165]

Thomas E. Douthit.

DOWDY, JESSE L.: [Jesse L. Dowdy] was a member of Company F, 9th Tennessee Cavalry, Biffle's Regiment, Forrest's Command, and . . . lived at Clifton, Tenn. [at the time].[166]

DOZIER, NATHANIEL BELL: One of the representative citizens of Franklin, Tenn., was lost to that community in the death of Nathaniel Bell Dozier, after a few hours' illness, on January 9, 1918. He was born at Lebanon, Tenn., May 13, 1846, the son of Joseph and Martha Caroline Bell Dozier. His father was of French Huguenot descent, his grandfather having come from Virginia to Tennessee in 1820, while his mother was of Scotch ancestry. When the war began he wished to enlist with his father in the Confederate army, but, being the oldest of six children, was told to remain at home and help his mother. In November, 1862, he piloted General Morgan across the river at Lebanon; and since he could no longer remain at home in safety, his mother consented for him to go. He enlisted in the company with his father, Company G, 4th Tennessee Cavalry, Starnes's Regiment, Forrest's Brigade, on November 6, 1862, at the age of sixteen. Soon afterwards he was made bugler of Capt. John W. Morton's battery. At his father's death he succeeded him as bugler of Starnes's Regiment and later was brigade bugler. He was proud of his record as a Confederate soldier and was ever in sympathy with the cause [conservatism] for which he had fought. His comrades of McEwen Bivouac, at Franklin, feel the loss of his loyal membership.

Nathaniel Bell Dozier.

Returning home when the war was over, Nathaniel Dozier assisted his mother in rearing the younger members of the family and was ever to her a devoted son. As a business man he was unusually successful. In his young manhood he became connected with the Wrought-Iron Range Company of St. Louis, and at the time of his death was Vice President and General Manager of its Southern Department. He was also a director of the Harpeth National Bank at Franklin and was serving the government as a member of the local Exemption Board. He was always actively interested in local enterprises, rendering his full duty in every capacity.

Mr. Dozier was twice married, his first wife being Miss Sallie Lanius, who left two sons and a daughter. In 1895 he was married to Miss Tennie Pinkerton, of Franklin, whose death followed his within three weeks, leaving two young daughters doubly bereaved. Their home was one of true hospitality. He was a ruling elder in the Presbyterian Church, to which he gave his loyal support in all its interests, spiritual and temporal. In his death the community lost one of its most public-spirited citizens and his family a devoted husband and father.[167]

DRY, MICHAEL ALFRED: Michael A. Dry was born at Mount Vernon, N.C., near Salisbury in June, 1829; died at Colorado, Tex., in May, 1910.

Michael Dry early became a man of promise in his community. He was made a Mason in 1854, and in 1856 was one of the delegates who helped to pass the free school laws for North Carolina. In 1860 he started overland with a party of friends to Arkansas. In Arkansas he taught a summer school. In the fall of that year he enlisted in the Confederate army as a member of Company D,

45th Arkansas Scouting Cavalry (Colonel Neblit commanding), Army of Tennessee, Western Army, under General Price, and also under Forrest and Cabell. He participated in the different battles and skirmishes of his command, through which he passed without a wound, and surrendered under Price. He taught school and was a merchant after the war. In 1873 he removed to Texas and located at Sipe Springs. In 1895 he went with his wife and two daughters to Colorado, Tex., where his wife died in 1896. He was a member of Albert Sidney Johnston Camp, U.C.V., at that place.[168]

Michael Alfred Dry.

DUDLEY, RICHARD HOUSTON: Maj. R. H. Dudley, a gallant Confederate soldier and one of the most prominent citizens of Nashville, Tenn., died in this city on the 30th of August, 1914, at the age of seventy-eight years. He was a man of great public spirit; and though his tastes inclined to commercial pursuits, he was always interested in the material and civic welfare of his State and community, lending his influence to the betterment of conditions as needed. He served one term as Mayor of Nashville and in other ways had taken prominent part in the life of the city.

Richard H. Dudley was born near Shelbyville, in Bedford County, Tenn., July 29, 1836, and was educated in the county schools. Upon reaching his majority he engaged in the general merchandise business at Smyrna, in Rutherford County, until the outbreak of war. After the war he went back to his business at Smyrna, but in 1873 he removed to Nashville and became one of the firm of Ordway, Dudley & McGuire, wholesale cotton and grocery dealers, and later went into the hardware firm of Dudley Brothers & Lipscomb, which was succeeded by Dudley Bros., and in 1895 by the large wholesale and retail firm of Gray & Dudley Hardware Company. Although he had given up active business for several years, he remained in the firm as a director and stockholder.

As a Confederate soldier Major Dudley made a gallant record. In May, 1861, he enlisted in Company I, Maney's 1st Tennessee Infantry, with which command he served three years as a private. In the summer of 1864 he and others of similar spirit organized a cavalry command in Middle Tennessee, inside the Federal lines, enlisting over a thousand men, and he was made captain of Company K of the command, known as the 21st Tennessee Cavalry, under Colonel Carter, and later he was elected major of the regiment. In the battle of Nashville Colonel Carter was wounded; and as Lieutenant Colonel Withers was absent on detached service, Major Dudley commanded the regiment on the retreat of Hood's army from Tennessee and surrendered with Forrest's Corps at Gainesville, Ala., in 1865. The 21st Cavalry saw most of its service under General Wheeler, but was attached to Forrest's command at the last.

The operations in which he participated included the campaigns of Cheat Mountain and Romney, W.Va.; the battles of Shiloh, Murfreesboro, Chickamauga, and Missionary Ridge; the numerous engagements during the hundred days' campaign in Georgia; the raid into Tennessee (September, 1864) with General Forrest, including the battles at Athens, Sulphur Trestle, and Pulaski; the campaign with Hood and the fights at Lawrenceburg, Franklin, and Shelbyville, and finally Forrest's campaign against Wilson's Raiders. Amidst all these dangers he escaped with only one wound, at Murfreesboro, by a piece of shell.

Major Dudley was one of the original members of Cheatham Bivouac, at Nashville, and had served as its President. He took active interest in the organization of the Confederate Soldiers' Home of Tennessee and made the first subscription, a substantial amount, toward its construction, and for many years he was one of its board of trustees. In accordance with his wish, he was buried with Confederate military honors. A detachment of veterans from Troop A, Forrest's Cavalry, stood guard until the funeral, and Frank Cheatham Bivouac conducted the burial services.

Richard Houston Dudley.

Major Dudley was thrice married. His first wife was Miss Mattie Ross, of Rutherford County, who lived but a few months. A few years later he was married to Miss Mary E. Beasley, of the same county, of whom he was bereft in 1907. His third wife was Mrs. Mollie Beasley, who survives him, as also three brothers and two sisters. No children were born to him, but he was a father to his younger brothers and sisters, and he also educated a number of his nephews and nieces.

Major Dudley was a long-time friend of [*Confederate Veteran* founder Sumner A. Cunningham] . . . by whom he was highly esteemed and loved, and by the will of Mr. Cunningham he was appointed a member of the Board of Trust under which the *Veteran* was to be continued for the benefit of all Confederate organizations.[169]

DUFFY, J. W.: J. W. Duffy was born in Dixon Springs, Tenn., March 12, 1844; and died at his home, in Nashville, January 11, 1910. Early in 1862 he enlisted in Company G, Starnes's 4th Tennessee Regiment of Cavalry. He served under Gen. Bedford Forrest until that commander was transferred to Mississippi, and afterwards gallantly followed General Wheeler in his campaign till the last few months of the war, when he became one of Yorke's scouts. He surrendered in Washington, Ga., May 9, 1865. After the war he returned to Dixon Springs, and remained there till about two years ago, when the family moved to Nashville. Mr. Duffy was a true-hearted man, and beloved by all who knew him.[170]

DUGAN, GEORGE M.: Colonel George M. Dugan was a member of Forrest's Cavalry. He followed Forrest in all the daring and desperate enterprises that made Forrest's Cavalry the wonder of the world.

I [Capt. James Dinkins] knew Colonel Dugan. We were in touch with each other during his service, except for three months when he was in prison at St. Louis in the winter of 1863-64. He was a man of enduring, sterling qualities, calm, dignified, courageous, and refined, splendid, never demonstrative; but as a faithful friend, he was supreme. His attitude at all times was to go forward and be unafraid. In emergencies he was like a volcano, and he would stand out in any company, more than holding his own, in all the qualities that make a man. He could always show high courage in the face of danger, and it was reassuring to feel the contact of his strong and capable presence.

Thinking of Colonel Dugan makes the dreams of youth come back again, but that cannot be, cannot be! I shall never be able to express my appreciation of him, but I shall maintain intact, as long as I live, the sacred memory of him. Whatever it is that makes a man matter, George Dugan had it in full measure. He had the gift of making friends, and that is one of God's gifts. My friendship for him is undimmed in the long retrospect of years and the imperishable past.[171]

DUNCAN, GREEN C.: In the death of Lieut. G. C. Duncan his personal friends and the veterans of the Southern army who knew him will feel poignant sorrow. He was born October 10, 1841, near Bloomfield, Ky., and died August 5, 1910, in New York City from a surgical operation.

He enlisted in Capt. W. D. McKay's company of Kentucky infantry in August, 1861, which joined Col. Marsh Walker's regiment of Alabama, Tennessee, and Arkansas troops, stationed at Island No. 10. With the fall of that port he was sent North with his company as prisoners of war. In September, 1862, he was exchanged at Vicksburg, and his company was transferred to the 8th Kentucky Regiment of Infantry, Col. H. B. Lyon, he being made first lieutenant.

He was with his company at Coffeeville, Baker's Creek, Big Black, Vicksburg, Jackson, Brice's Crossroads, Harrisburg, Tupelo, Miss., Johnsonville, with the advance of Hood into Tennessee, Columbia, Spring Hill, Franklin, Murfreesboro, and in all the engagements covering the retreat from Nashville across the Tennessee, at Montevallo and Selma, Ala., and finally surrendered with his company and regiment at Columbus, Miss., May 15, 1865. He returned to Kentucky, but shortly after went to Texas, settling at Egypt, in Wharton County, where he married and made a useful citizen.

Mr. Duncan was a model soldier, firm and exacting to duty, ever alert and prompt to secure all needful supplies for the comfort and efficiency of his men. As a citizen, public officer, and neighbor he was successful in business, efficient and popular, true and firm in his conviction of public polity.

[From a sketch by F. G. Terry, Cadiz, Ky., who writes: "He and I were the last known living of the staff of Gen. A. Buford, commander of the second division of Forrest's Cavalry. We served also in the Kentucky brigade of the same division, and shared many dangers and privations, making him dear to me."]

His friend, W. H. Bemiss, of Shelbyville, Ky., writes: "We were from the same place, Bloomfield, Ky., and went to school together in the long ago, though he was older than I. Green Duncan came from a prominent family and was one of the first to enlist in the Confederate army from that county, going out with Capt. W. D. McKay's company from Bloomfield in 1861. This company was later assigned to the 8th Kentucky Infantry. In the fall of 1863, when it was mounted and put with Forrest, serving with him under General Lyon to the end, Duncan became a lieutenant in his company, and was conspicuous for gallantry on many occasions. He was an honorable gentleman and a true friend."[172]

Thomas D. Duncan.

DUNCAN, THOMAS D.: In April, 1861, at Corinth, Miss., Thomas D. Duncan enlisted in the Confederate army, being then of "a very tender age." He was first enrolled in the Corinth Rifles, but later was transferred to the cavalry and became an active participant in the wonderful campaigns of Gen. Nathan B. Forrest. He took part in the battles around Forts Henry and Donelson and was present on the field of Shiloh, at the battle of Corinth, of which he gives a graphic description, in the various cavalry raids in West Tennessee, and in the battle of Chickamauga. He [spoke often] . . . of the sufferings of the Southern soldiers, unused to the privations of camp life; of his own narrow escape from death in battle; of the horrors of reconstruction . . .[173] [Duncan's photo] shows him at age fourteen, "two years before he rode with Forrest's famous troop."[174]

DUNCAN, W. D. L.: W. D. L. ("Bill") Duncan . . . was in Buford's Regiment of Cavalry, Cheatham's Division [Forrest's command].[175]

DUNLAP, R. A. D.: Col. R. A. D. Dunlap, of Gadsden, Ala., died at the home of his daughter, Mrs. Robert Cowan, at Cleveland, Tenn., on August 5 [1924]. He led an active life to the day before his death.

Colonel Dunlap was a native Tennessean, the son of Samuel C. and Angeline C. Dunlap, and was born in Henry County, October, 18, 1843. His parents came from the Carolinas. At the age of twenty he entered the Confederate army, though he had seen active service at Shiloh previous to this time. He enlisted with Forrest's Cavalry Corps and took part in many of Forrest's engagements in Mississippi and Tennessee. He was wounded at Guntown, Miss., later surrendering at Gainesville, Ala. After the war he taught school, then studied law, being admitted to the bar in DeKalb County, Ala., where he took up his residence soon after the war. Later he moved to Chattanooga, Tenn., then to Gadsden, where the greater part of his life was spent. He served as register in chancery many years after giving up his practice. He was a member of the Presbyterian Church, also a member of Emma Sansom Camp, U.C.V., and always took an active part in reunions of the Camp.

He was married in July, 1868, to Miss Susan G. Jacoway, of DeKalb County, who survives him with three daughters and three sons.

The following is taken from an editorial tribute: "In the death of Col. R. A. D. Dunlap, Gadsden and the country have sustained an irreparable loss. He was a pioneer of this city. Coming here as a young lawyer m 1875, he immediately identified himself with all that was worthy and, although tried in many difficult situations, he always stood firm for the right. There was never any doubt as to his position where decent citizenship was concerned. Of irreproachable integrity and stainless character in all relations of life, tolerant of opposition, yet tenacious of his own convictions; of an open nature, pleasing address, and a great kindliness of heart, he long enjoyed, in full measure, the confidence and good will of his fellow men."[176]

DUNLAP, W. N. L.: W. N. L. Dunlap died in Humboldt, Tenn., February 12, 1909. He was Commander of Camp No. 974, Bivouac No. 35, U.C.V., and was so devoted to the Confederate cause that he never missed one of the Reunions of his old comrades.

At the age of eighteen he enlisted in Company G, 47th Regiment Tennessee Infantry, and no braver soldier ever fought for his country. He was severely wounded in the battles of Franklin and Murfreesboro, and received a slighter wound during the Georgia campaign.

His life as a soldier was typical of his life as a private citizen, for he gave his State and fellow-men the same warm devotion and clear-minded service that he did his regiment. He was Master of Chancery for twenty-five years in the same county (Gibson, Tenn.) in which he was born.

He was especially strong in his assistance and counsel to the Nathan Bedford Forrest Chapter, U.D.C., Humboldt, Tenn., and they unite with a wide circle of friends in sorrow over their loss.

At a meeting of the Humboldt Camp, No. 974, U.C.V., April 3, 1909, the following committee was appointed to prepare resolutions touching the death of Comrade W. N. L. Dunlap: C. H. Ferrell, L. K. Gillespie, and N. A. Senter. The committee submitted the following report: "The death of our esteemed friend and comrade, W. N. L. Dunlap, fills us with a sadness that words cannot express. In every sphere of life he was the same true friend, the same brave man, the same honorable, upright citizen, whether in the domestic circle, where he was a true husband, a tender father, and a wise counselor, or in the Church, which he loved and served from his young boyhood, loyal to his Master, true to his vows, leading a life of true piety and setting a worthy example to others. On the field of carnage he was a brave soldier and a stanch [staunch] comrade, always ready to do his part. In civic life he filled main positions of honor and trust with satisfaction to his constituents and credit to himself. He was born October 5, 1843, in Gibson County, Tenn. He was the son of F. and Mary L. Dunlap."[177]

DUNNING, LEVI S.: Died, at Princeton, Ky., January 15, 1924, Levi S. Dunning, a prominent citizen, formerly of Trigg County, Ky. In January, 1863, he enlisted in Company B, 8th Regiment of Kentucky Infantry, going out of Kentucky to a point near Grenada, Miss., where the regiment was at the time, to enlist. He made a faithful and useful soldier, ever ready when duty called. He was in the battles of Baker's Creek, Big Black, and Jackson, Miss. In February, 1864, the 8th Regiment, with the 3rd, 7th, and 12th Kentucky, was assigned to the Corps of Major General Forrest, and from that time to the close of the war served in the mounted service. Comrade Dunning was with this command in the battles of Paducah, Brice's Crossroads, and all the engagements around Tupelo and Old Town Creek, and around Johnsonville and with Hood's advance into Tennessee, and was finally surrendered at Columbus, Miss., May 15, 1865, with his company and regiment.

Levi Dunning was the ninth in a family of thirteen children. He was born December 25, 1839, and thus had passed into his eighty-fifth year. But six of his regiment are now left, so far as known.[178]

DYE, SHELBY: W. P. Brown, Commander of Marion Cogbill Camp, No. 1316, U.C.V., of Wynne, Ark., reports the death of a member, Shelby Dye, at the great age of ninety-four years. He served with General Forrest in the 4th Mississippi Regiment and was in [a Yankee] prison for seven months.[179]

EAVES, JOSEPH C.: Dr. J. C. Eaves was born July 17, 1836; and quietly fell asleep in the presence of his children on February 19, 1912. He read medicine under Dr. Miller at Manchester, Tenn., attended the medical lectures at Nashville in 1859, and received his diploma in 1860. He volunteered in the Confederate army at the beginning of the war in Starnes's 4th Tennessee, Forrest's Cavalry, and served till the close of the war. His record as a soldier was to get there first and stay till the last. After the war he located at Spencer, Tenn., and began the practice of medicine, but later moved to White County, and continued the practice of his profession until a few years ago.

Kind and courteous in his disposition . . . [he had countless friends]. His life was devoted to charity, and whenever called ministered to the sick, no matter how poor. He was honored and loved by all who knew him. He was laid to rest in the cemetery near Quebeck, Tenn., where his friends gathered to pay their last tribute of love and respect.

From a tribute by O. V. Anderson, Tullahoma, Tenn.: "After the war Dr. Eaves located at Spencer, Tenn., and engaged in the practice of medicine. Later he removed to White County, where he continued to practice until a few years before his death.

His record as a soldier was to get there first and stay till the last. His life's work was charity. He visited the sick regardless of their ability to pay. He was ever loyal to the cause for which he fought. Kind and courteous in his disposition, his friends were legion; to know him was to love him. He quietly fell asleep surrounded by his children. The large assemblage which gathered to pay him last tribute testified to his worth. He is survived by three daughters and their families and a son, Robert, now in business in Chattanooga."[180]

EDGMAN, JOHN L.: I desire to bear testimony to the gallantry of John L. Edgman, who met his death leading the advance guard during the second day's fight at Brice's Crossroads. He was a native of Arkansas, enlisted in infantry service early in the war, but was discharged on account of ill health. He then made his way on foot to Southern Kentucky and joined Company I, Faulkner's 12th Kentucky Cavalry Regiment, Forrest's Cavalry. He was my messmate until he was shot from his horse on June 11, 1864. I loved him as a brother, and am very desirous that any of his family who are living may know how he died among strangers.[181]

EDMONDSON, HENRY C.: Among the papers left by the late Henry C. Edmondson, who died at his home, near Brentwood, Tenn., was the following sketch of his military career: "I enlisted in April, 1862, in Dick McCann's squadron. We acted as scouts in Bragg's army till the fall of 1862, and then were scouts for Forrest until the battle of Murfreesboro. While in camp at Lavergne we were detached and put in the commissary department, under Major Bridgewater, of Martin's Division.

"After the battle of Murfreesboro we were pickets for four months for Bragg's army, during which time we had control of all the mills between Shelbyville and Columbia. A few days before Bragg fell back we were ordered to Columbia to recruit the command, and after a few days we were ordered to report at Tullahoma. The command advanced and left me in charge of the cattle with no orders.

"Leaving Columbia, I went to Fayetteville. and from there to New Market, and crossed the Tennessee River at Fort Deposit with one hundred and seventy-five head of cattle. These I left and reported to my command at Chattanooga, which I found destitute of food and the cattle one hundred miles away. I went up on Lookout Mountain and found the finest lot of cattle we had during the war. The command left me at Bridgeport, and I returned for the cattle, taking them to Alexandria, Va., where they became diseased and all died.

"We had a hard time to feed the army at Alexandria. From there we went to Cartersville, Ga., for a few days until ordered to the front. We were in the battle of Chattanooga, after which we were ordered to Knoxville with Longstreet to capture Burnside, who, however, was reenforced, and made our way through the mountains to North Carolina and Virginia with Burnside in pursuit.

"Later from Cartersville, Ga., we became rearguard for Bragg's army back to Kennesaw Mountain. Major Bridgewater died while there, and Captain Bird took command. Then I was transferred to Hume's command, and we were ordered to Mississippi, remaining but a short time, and were then ordered to report to Coffeeville to get out ties from the Mississippi bottoms. Shortly afterwards the war closed. I was sent to Senatobia, and from there to Memphis, where I was paroled and given transportation home."[182]

ELCAN, ARCHIBALD LIEBIG: Dr. Archibald Liebig Elcan, a former prominent practicing physician of Memphis and who was also well known throughout West Tennessee, died at his home, in Los Angeles, Cal., in February, 1916. He went to California about ten years ago on account of the poor health of himself and a daughter, leaving one of the foremost practices in Memphis.

Dr. Elcan was born October 20, 1844, in Fayette County, near Belmont, now known as Mason. He joined the Confederate army in 1862 before he was eighteen years of age, serving first with Capt. Sam T. Taylor's company and later with Major General Loring in a secretarial and aid-de-camp capacity until February 24, 1864, when he joined Company B, 7th Tennessee Cavalry, of Forrest's command.

He was wounded while charging beside General Forrest at Prairie Mound, Miss., where Forrest led on foot, his horse having been shot from under him. He was again wounded in the retreat from Nashville near Richland Creek. At the close of the war he was first sergeant in Company B. Dr. Elcan was an honorary member of Company A, the crack Confederate company of Memphis.

After the war Dr. Elcan read medicine, took a full college course, and practiced medicine in Tipton County. He also served as a member of the legislature and as a justice of the peace in that county. He was well known as a writer for several leading medical journals and as a contributor to the daily and weekly press of this section.

He moved to Memphis in 1888 and devoted himself exclusively to his practice. He was married on November 4, 1869, to Miss Bettie Taylor, daughter of Dr. Joshua Swayne, of Carroll County, Tenn. Three daughters and a son survive him.[183]

M. A. L. Enochs.

ENOCHS, M. A. L.: Dr. M. A. L. Enochs was born in Lincoln County (now Moore County), Tenn., on December 19, 1843, and died on March 17, 1918, at his home, in Bedford County.

In 1861 he was of the age at which so many typical Confederate soldiers were made. He was just a boy; he was ambitious, not for promotion in office, but to make a soldier, and was admirably successful. Turney's 1st Tennessee Regiment came from the southern counties of the middle division of the State and went to Virginia before the State seceded and was for this reason in the beginning called the 1st Confederate Regiment. At that time the need for the services of young Enochs on the farm was so great that he could not be spared; but when corn was laid by he left his plow in the field and joined the company of that regiment which was composed of his playmates and schoolmates.

In the battle of Seven Pines, the first fought after he joined the regiment, he was wounded by a Minie ball in the right leg. He was received in the home of a Mr. English at Richmond, where he was tenderly and kindly nursed until he had recovered sufficiently to be able to walk. Then he received a furlough and of course started at once to see the folks at home. By rail he reached Chattanooga and then limped over the mountain and through the byways, so as to avoid Federal pickets, until he was at home, where he was welcomed and kept hidden by his parents. He remained there under the care of his loving mother until he was restored to health and strength.

He did not forget the people in Richmond who received him into their home and nursed him when he was wounded. On a visit to Richmond some years ago he found that his war time host had passed over the river, but he was cordially received and entertained by the son, who still owned the old English home.

Rejoining his regiment, still in Virginia, in the battle of Gettysburg, he took part in Pickett's charge, where he was again wounded, this time a Minie ball entering his temple and lodging in the back of his neck. While lying on the battle field he was wounded again and yet again, making in all four wounds he had received in battle. He was captured, and upon being exchanged he again made his way through the lines to his home and was again by that loving mother nursed back to health and partial strength. He then made his way on horseback through the lines and joined the cavalry and there remained a member of Forrest's escort until the end of the war, surrendering at Gainesville, Ala.

He was associated from his youth with an uncle who was a successful physician and from childhood was his uncle's student. When he came home from the war, both training and temperament inclined him to the medical profession, and he chose it as his life work. He chose also to become a humble follower of the lowly Nazarene, and to the end of life's battle he was a faithful physician and a faithful Christian soldier. He was of the Tribe of Abou Ben Adhem, loved by his fellow men. His beautiful character was that of the country doctor so vividly portrayed by Ian Maclaren in *Beside the Bonnie Brier Bush*.[184]

G. W. Evans.

EVANS, G. W.: After a short but acute attack of pneumonia, Dr. G. W. Evans died at his home, in Memphis, Tenn., on the 19th of December, 1905. He was born March 7, 1837, in Davidson County, Tenn., and graduated from the Medical Department of the University of Nashville in 1860.

He served the Confederacy for four years under General Forrest as assistant surgeon, Huggins's Battery of Horse Artillery. Dr. Evans is survived by his wife, three sons, and a daughter. He was a Mason of forty years' standing, and lived its principles. To his family is left a heritage of honesty and integrity.[185]

EVANS, THOMAS: Thomas Evans, familiarly known as "Uncle Tom," died at his home in Alamo, Tenn., on March 3 [1930?]. He was born in Faulkner County, Ark., his parents removing to Crockett County, Tenn., when he was four years old. He enlisted, in 1863, in the 12th Tennessee Cavalry, which later consolidated with Forrest's command, in which he served with honor the duration of the war. He was mustered out from Gainesville, Ga., at the close of the war, and went back to Crockett County to live with his family.

He was married to Miss Margaret Norville, of Alamo, and to this union ten children were born, of whom four daughters and a son survive him, with twenty-one grandchildren and twenty-eight great-grandchildren. Comrade Evans was associated with his son in business, and despite his advanced age, he had remained unusually active into his eighty-sixth year.[186]

Robert Hamilton Evins.

EVINS, ROBERT HAMILTON: Robert Hamilton Evins, Confederate veteran and Christian gentleman, departed this life on October 25, 1919, in his seventy-fourth year. He left the University of Alabama to enter the military service of the Confederate States in June, 1863, and became a member of Capt. Charles P. Storr's Company, of the Cadet Troops, which was organized at the University and which united on July 22, 1863, as Company F, with the 7th Alabama Cavalry. This organization, first stationed at Pollard and Mobile in 1863 and 1864, was transferred in October, 1864, to the command of Gen. N. B. Forrest, in the Army of Tennessee, and was assigned to Gen. E. W. Rucker as escort, serving with that gallant officer until he was wounded in 1864. Comrade Evins was engaged with his command at Johnsonville, Heneyville, Mt. Pleasant, Columbia, Spring Hill, Franklin, and Nashville, and rendered gallant service in practically all of its engagements, and participating at Columbus, Ga., on April 14, 1865, in one of the last engagements of the war. He laid down his arms at Gainesville, Ala., on May 14, 1865.

To designate him as "Confederate veteran and Christian gentleman" is briefly to describe him, for to honor these two estates was the dominating aim of his daily existence. That he served in the Armies of the Confederacy was his life-long pride.

In January, 1874, he was married to Miss Martha Amelia Thompson, of Marion, Ala. For some years he lived on his farm in Perry County, Ala., where two sons and a daughter were born. In 1887 he was appointed by Governor Thomas Seay as Clerk of the Circuit Court of Perry County, to which office he was repeatedly reelected. In 1904 he retired from active business, and in 1908, after the death of his wife, he removed to Greensboro, Ala., to reside with his son until the day of his death.

For seven years he was lay reader at St. Wilfrid's Church by appointment of Bishop Wilmer, of Alabama, by whom he had been confirmed.

He is greatly missed by all who knew him, for his life was passed in the service of God and man. His fellow veterans especially miss him, for he never failed to be present at any reunion possible for him to attend, and he was the favorite orator on many memorial occasions.

His universal charity and good will, which assembled every Church pastor of the town at his burial, elicited the statement: "Here is one who illustrated in his heart and in his life that Church unity so much hoped for by the Christian world."

Kindly and upright in all his relations with his fellow men, noble and generous in all his impulses, "he did justice, loved mercy, and walked humbly with his God."[187]

EWING, BENJAMIN DAVID: Benjamin D. Ewing was born in 1831 in Wilson County, Tenn., where he was reared to manhood, receiving a moderate education. He went to Texas in 1856; but upon the breaking out of the war, in 1861, he returned to Tennessee and enlisted as a private in the 1st Tennessee Cavalry, commanded by Col. Frank McNairy, which command was organized by special act of the Tennessee Legislature before the secession of the State. After about a year's service the 1st Battalion of Tennessee Cavalry was consolidated with the 7th and formed the 2nd Tennessee Cavalry. Comrade Ewing was with his command under Gen. F. K. Zollicoffer at Fishing Creek, and was in Forrest's Cavalry command for a long while, and in all the battles fought from Fishing Creek to the surrender of Forrest in Alabama. He was an active soldier from start to finish, as brave as the bravest, but with a heart as tender as a girl's. It is said that "he and his horse, a fine iron-gray called Mack, could be seen in the front in every battle." He was often placed in charge of a squad of soldiers on important duty, and exemplified thoroughly that a brave man in power is ever merciful. He was made a Mason during the war, and it was with Masonic honors that he was laid to rest at his old home, Lane, in Hunt County, Tex., on Christmas day of 1906. His devoted wife and five children survive him to bless his memory.[188]

FAIL, W. E.: W. E. Fail, [of] Hattiesburg, Miss., Station A, [was] seventy-four years old [in 1919]. . . . [He] served under General Forrest as a member of the 24th Mississippi Battalion, surrendering in the Bigbee River Swamp, above Gainesville, Ala.[189]

FARIS, CHARLES A. D.: On October 31, 1923, the spirit of Charles A. D. Faris passed into rest at his home in Chattanooga, Tenn. He was born in Rutherford County, Tenn., August 11, 1846, the son of the Rev. Charles Blackman and Mary Ransom Faris. His father was for many years an honored and beloved minister of the Methodist Episcopal Church, South.

He had three older brothers—John, Richard, and William serving in the Confederate army, and so great was his patriotism that in spite of parental opposition on account of his youth he slipped away from home and became one of Forrest's boy soldiers, being assigned to Company D, Bell's Brigade, 11th Tennessee Volunteer Cavalry, Jackson's Division.

He was a true and faithful soldier, ever ready for any duty, and his war experiences were many and interesting. He surrendered in April, 1865, at Gainesville, Ala., with his company and regiment. Stanch [meaning staunch] in his devotion to the cause for which he fought, he never failed, to champion the traditions and ideals of the Old South, and on his grave among the flowers was placed the Confederate flag he loved so well.

In early life he joined the Methodist Church and lived a consecrated Christian life, serving long as Sunday school superintendent and as steward for more than thirty years.

In all walks of life he was true, faithful to religious principles, conscientious to a marked degree, a good citizen, esteemed and honored by a host of friends for his fine qualities of mind and heart, and a devoted husband and father.

After the war he was engaged in the lumber business in Rutherford County, later moving to South Pittsburg, Tenn., where he had large lumber interests and was prominently identified with the city's business and social life until removing a few years ago to Chattanooga.

He was twice married; in 1894 to Miss Sallie Rogers, of Franklin, Tenn., who preceded him to the home beyond. In 1902 he was married to Miss Mary Hubbard, of Birmingham, Ala. He is survived by his wife and one son.[190]

FARROW, G. FERD: On October 29, 1907, at Whitehaven, Tenn., died G. Ferd Farrow, one of the noblest survivors of Forrest's Cavalry.

Comrade Farrow was born in Marshall County, Miss., of an old and respected family; but was brought to Tennessee when four years of age by his parents, who settled at Germantown, near Memphis. On April 20, 1861, he enlisted in Company C, 13th Tennessee Regiment. While a member of this command he participated in the battle of Belmont, in which his brother, John P. Farrow, was killed in the first volley fired by the enemy. The noble character of John Farrow, his great gallantry, the prominence of his family, and the fact that he was the first of the sons of the Confederacy to offer up his life upon the altar of his country in the Department of the West created a profound impression. His remains were sent home and buried with the greatest possible civic and military honors.

The death of this brother under such melancholy circumstances gave Ferd Farrow deeper reason than ever to render the very best possible account of himself in battle, which he did throughout four years of bloody strife. Soon after this he was transferred to McDonald's Battalion of Forrest's old regiment, with which he was connected until the end of the war. He was in all the important engagements which immortalized the "Wizard of the Saddle" and his heroic men. He was captured at Britton's Lane; but was exchanged ten days later and returned to his command, where he remained until he was surrendered, at Gainesville, Ala., in May, 1865.

He was in active service of the Confederate army for more than four years, enlisting when less than nineteen and surrendering at twenty-three years of age. Having been trained in such a strenuous school, he met every test of civil life after peace had returned. His record in peace was indeed typical of the career of thousands of others who had received the same stern discipline in war. Their splendid and successful struggle to build up the waste places of the South, which had been devastated by the contending armies, entitles them to a still higher niche in the temple of fame than their matchless deeds in battle.

G. Ferd Farrow.

He engaged in planting, and made a gratifying success. He always kept up an active interest in his old comrades, and in every effort made to preserve the annals of the Confederate soldiers from oblivion. He was a member of the Confederate Historical Society, and was ever zealous in its purposes. He was a member of the Whitehaven Baptist Church and a consistent Christian, passing to his future reward with an unfaltering trust. He fought a good fight.[191]

FATHEREE, L. L.: In memorial resolutions passed in tribute to a beloved comrade, L. L. Fatheree, who died February 16, 1929, the R. A. Smith Camp, No. 24, U.C.V., of Jackson, Miss., expressed a sense of loss in the going of this faithful and worthy member, and gave his Confederate record, as follows:

L. L. Fatheree was born in Hinds County, Miss., in that section between Bear Creek Church and Utica, in May, 1845; and was educated in the county schools and at Hazlehurst. When about eighteen years of age, he ran away from home and enlisted for service in Company C, of the 3rd Mississippi Cavalry, Forrest's command, in which he remained to the close of the war.

After the war, Comrade Fatheree engaged in merchandising, and later held town offices in Hazlehurst and Jackson. He was married in December, 1876, to Miss Mary Alice Thompson, at Jessamine Hill, in Copiah County. He had confessed Christ in early life and united with the Methodist Church.[192]

FAY, R. EMMETT: R. Emmet Fay, a member of Forrest's escort, died at Shelbyville [Tenn.] a few days ago [early 1900?]. He was a good soldier, and surrendered at Gainesville, Ala., with Forrest.[193]

FERGUSON, LON: Lon Ferguson joined, when sixteen years of age, with Forrest's Cavalry, under General Wheeler; was captured about the close of the war and kept a long time in Camp Chase, where he suffered everything possible, but finally escaped. He enlisted from Jacksonville, Ala.[194]

FERRELL, LUCILLIUS S.: Lucillius S. Ferrell died at his residence in Cage's Bend, near Gallatin, Tenn., November 11, 1901. His death was the result of an accident, he having fallen to the cellar of one of the farm buildings and sustained injuries which proved fatal a few hours later. He was living on the farm on which he was born seventy-two years before, and was laid to rest in the old family burying ground, where four generations of his kindred are sleeping.

Lucillius S. Ferrell.

In every relation of life Comrade Ferrell measured up to the full stature of a man. He was a member of Donaldson Bivouac and of Camp A. Wheeler's Cavalry U.C.V., having served from start to finish in the Confederate army, and his record is that of a gallant soldier. He belonged to Company K, Fourth Tennessee Cavalry, Harrison's Brigade, Wheeler's Corps, and his company for a time acted as escort for Gen. N. B. Forrest.

Comrade Ferrell was a consistent member of the Methodist Church, and for a number of years superintendent of Sunday school. He was a Mason, and lived up to the motto, "We meet upon the level and part upon the square." He left a wife, three sons, and two orphan grandchildren. . . . We will miss our comrade, but our grief is not without hope.[195]

FIELD, H. C.: H. C. Field died at the home of his daughter in Wellesley Hills, Mass., on April 14 [1930?], in his ninety-first year. He was born in Montague, Mass., but as a young man he went to Tennessee. His sympathies being with the Southern cause [conservatism], he enlisted in the Confederate army at Nashville, Tenn., in May, 1861, in Col. Geo. Maney's Regiment, being discharged in December of the same year on account of disability. According to the records, in July, 1863, he enlisted in Capt. John W. Morton's Company, Tennessee Artillery, C.S.A., attached to General Forrest's command, and served until the end of the war, which was a matter of personal pride with him.

It is interesting to know that Mr. Field was one of five brothers, the other four having served in the Union army. He was an honorary member of the Boston Chapter, U.D.C., and the Cross of Honor was bestowed upon him at the annual luncheon in honor of Gen. Robert E. Lee, on January 21, 1930. Mr. Field was exceptionally active and alert for his years, and thoroughly enjoyed attending the regular meetings of the Boston Chapter.

Through the good offices of Mrs. O. F. Wiley, Comrade Field was made an Honorary Member of the Boston Chapter, U.D.C., and he was deeply touched by the attention paid him and appreciative of this contact with the South and Southern interests. Alert of mind, active in body to a marked degree, being unattended in and out of Boston to his last illness, he was often welcomed to the meetings of the Chapter. With him was buried the Confederate flag, memorial of the cause he loved so well.[196]

FISHER, WILLIAM HICKORY: William Hickory Fisher was born in Arkansas in 1832, and came to Tennessee when only ten years old. He joined the Confederate cavalry, Tenth Tennessee, under Col. Cox in Gen. N. B. Forrest's command. He was elected lieutenant of his company, but acted as captain and took part, it is said, in every battle fought by Forrest. In his death Decatur County loses one of her best citizens, and his family and friends a kind and loving associate. He died at his home near Decaturville, Tenn., on November 27 [1901?], and was buried with Masonic honor on Thanksgiving Day.[197]

FLETCHER, JOHN DAVIDSON: John D. Fletcher was born in Neshoba County, Miss., in 1846. At the beginning of the war he was attending college at La Grange, Tenn. In 1863 he enlisted with Forrest's escort, just before the fight at Fort Pillow, and was ever at his post to the end of the war. Although in many hard battles and close places, he was never captured nor wounded.

In 1868 Comrade Fletcher removed to Arkansas, and located at Lonoke. He was one of the first settlers in that section. Consistent with his soldier life,

Comrade Fletcher entered the ministry of the Baptist Church. He preached as pastor at Shiloh, New Hope, Gum Woods, Lonoke, Pecan Grove, Little Elm, Prairie Grove, and Liberty, previous to 1895, after which he was in the mission field.

In 1875 Comrade Fletcher married Miss Ida Graves, of Clinton, Miss. They reared several children, all of whom survived the husband and father, who went to his reward February 2, 1900.[198]

FORD, CORNELIUS Y.: Capt. Cornelius Y. Ford, of Odessa, Mo., died at his home there on February 20, after an extended illness. At the funeral service in the Christian Church, of which he was a member, the Confederate ritual was read by an old friend, a Confederate chaplain, ninety years old, who was one of three Confederate comrades attending from Kansas City. Only about a half dozen veterans are now left at Odessa.

C. Y. Ford was born in Danville, Ky., April 12, 1843, from which place his parents removed to Missouri when he was about fourteen years old. They located in Pettis County, and that was his home until he went out to fight in defense of it. With eight of his schoolmates, young Ford enlisted with the Missouri troops under Sterling Price, and after one year they were mustered into the Confederate service at Memphis, Tenn., as the 2nd Missouri, under Gen. Earl Van Dorn, and remained with him until he was killed,[199] when they were transferred to the cavalry of Gen. N. B. Forrest, and served under him to the surrender at Columbus, Miss. He was in many hard-fought battles and skirmishes—Elk Horn, Holly Springs, Iuka, Corinth, Bratton's Lane, Fort Pillow—and he was the last of the eight comrades who enlisted in 1861.

After his marriage to Miss Sallie Beatty, in 1870, they made their home on a farm in the Greenton Valley until locating in Odessa some ten years ago. There was no man of the community better known or more highly esteemed than Captain Ford, and he was an acknowledged leader wherever he lived. He was a member of the Masonic Lodge for many years. Always deeply interested in the Confederate Veterans' organization, he had served it locally and in official appointments in the Missouri Division, attending every general convention until ill health prevented.

Kind and courteous, public spirited, and generous in his dealings with his fellow men, Captain Ford will be long remembered.[200]

FORREST, CAR: The death of Capt. Car Forrest at Waxahachie, Tex., on May 5 has removed one of Ellis County's most highly respected pioneer citizens. He was born in Marshall County, Tenn., in 1826, and removed to Texas in 1855, settling in Ellis County, near where is now the town of Forreston. The first court ever held in Ellis County was under a pecan tree on his farm, Judge John H. Reagan presiding. In 1861 he assisted in organizing Company C, of the 19th Texas Cavalry, enlisting as a private, but was soon advanced to the command. His company saw service in Louisiana, Arkansas, and Missouri. He was with Marmaduke in his raid through Missouri, where for six weeks the saddles were never taken from the horses, and he was also in the Red River raid after General Banks. Returning to Texas, the regiment was disbanded and all returned home. After the war Captain Forrest turned his attention to agriculture and invested largely in real estate. His wife was Miss Virginia Sims, whose father was also a Texas pioneer. A son and a daughter of their five children survive him. Captain Forrest had a most attractive personality, and in his death the State has lost a noble citizen. He was a cousin of Gen. N. B. Forrest.[201]

FORREST, WILLIAM MONTGOMERY: . . . Capt. William Montgomery Forrest was born in Hernando, Miss., in September [26th], 1846. He died in Memphis, Tenn., in February [8th], 1909. He was the only son of Gen. Nathan Bedford and Mary [Ann] Montgomery Forrest, their other child, a girl [Francis], having died in infancy. Early in 1861 William Forrest applied for admission to the company of which his father had been a member, but was rejected on account of age and size. Later, his father seeing he was determined to join the army, he was accepted, and served on the staff of General Forrest to the end of the war. William Forrest was a quiet but fearless soldier. He was sent on many dangerous missions, enduring many hardships.

When the war closed, Captain Forrest entered at Oxford, Miss., where he graduated from the literary and law schools; but he never practiced law. He joined his father as a railroad contractor, in which they were mainly successful. He was married twice. A wife and four children, a daughter and three sons by the first marriage, survive him. As soldier and citizen his service was without blemish.[202]

FOSTER, GEORGE W.: George W. Foster, born and reared in Marshall County, Tenn., died at Fayetteville, Tenn., on September 6, 1922, and was laid to rest in the cemetery at Belfast, where he was born seventy-nine years ago. He was married twice, and is survived by his wife and thirteen of the fifteen children which blessed his home.

Enlisting in 1861 in the 8th Tennessee Regiment, George W. Foster served with this regiment until he was severely wounded. A Minie ball passed through his neck, and came near making a fatal wound; in fact, he never fully recovered from it. When partially recovered, he was offered a discharge on account of the disability, but he refused it and asked for a transfer to Forrest's Escort, with which command he served until the surrender at Gainesville, Ala., in May, 1865. He was one of the bravest of Forrest's men. Always interested in what pertained to our Confederate organizations, he was President of the Shackleford Fulton Bivouac, of Fayetteville, at the time of his death.

Comrade Foster was an honest upright citizen, a brave soldier, a true, loyal, and devoted husband, father, and friend, a faithful member of the Christian Church.

It is sorrowful to see our comrades dropping out of the ranks so fast, yet it is sweet to know that when the roll is called up yonder, they'll be there.[203]

FOWLKES, JOHN ABNER: Capt. J. A. Fowlkes, one of the oldest and most beloved citizens of his county, passed away at his home in Schulenburg, Tex., on October 19, 1924, at the age of eighty-two years. He is survived by his wife, three daughters, and four sons.

John Abner Fowlkes was a native of Texas when it was a republic, born within a few miles of his late home, on February 14, 1843. He was of Scotch-Irish descent, his forefathers going into Ireland after the reign of Cromwell, and later coming to America. His grandfather, E. B. Fowlkes, of Culpeper County, Va., moved to Arkansas in 1839, and his father, of the same name, went on to Texas and located in Fayette County, and during the first years of the republic he was chiefly engaged in fighting Indians. He also taught school, being a man of liberal education, a graduate of Georgetown College, Washington, D.C. He later engaged in farming, and had a plantation in Colorado County, and during the sixties served the Confederacy in the militia.

He married Miss Mary McClelland, of Arkansas, and the second son was John Abner Fowlkes, who grew up on the plantation, but he was at school in Lavaca County when the war came on in 1861, and volunteered there in a company under Capt. Fred Malone. This was soon disbanded, and he then enlisted in Company C, of Willis's Battalion, which left for the front with more than seven hundred men, sustaining heavy losses during the war. In October, 1862, this command crossed the Mississippi River to assist General Van Dorn's army, and during 1863 took part in the Vicksburg campaign. After the fall of Vicksburg, Willis's Battalion was under General Forrest until the fighting at Harrisburg, and afterwards was under General Maury at Mobile, later returning to Mississippi, where a half of the Texas troops were furloughed. Comrade Fowlkes got one of these furloughs, and made his way home, walking from army headquarters to Beaumont, and by rail and horseback for the rest of his journey. As soon as some order had been restored, he took up farming and so continued throughout life, accumulating a handsome acreage. He was married in 1869 to Miss Mary McKinnon, whose father went from McNairy County, Tenn., to Texas in 1850.[204]

FRANCIS, JOHN: John Francis was born in Monroe County, Miss., November 12, 1841; and died in Lee County, Miss., in May, 1909. He enlisted in Captain Armstrong's company, 10th Mississippi Infantry, in April, 1861, serving in that regiment, then in Chalmers's Brigade, until after the battle of Shiloh. At the expiration of twelve months he reenlisted in Warren's Alabama Battalion of Cavalry, where he remained a faithful soldier until the end. He was with Forrest in many raids, and was one of the five hundred who rode with Col. W. A. Johnson from North Alabama to take part in the bloody battle of Brice's Cross Roads, and he was also at Hattiesburg.[205]

FRANCIS, JOSEPH H.: There is peculiar sorrow in the death of Mr. J. H. Francis, who had been so stanch [meaning staunch] a supporter of the *Confederate Veteran* for several years. He died at a hotel, having no family.

Comrade Francis was an efficient scout, serving Gens. Wheeler and Forrest as such in the war. He was a successful man in business, having a fine estate in Alabama. He was a member of Southern organizations in New York. His remains were sent to Jacksonville, Ala., for burial.[206]

FRANKLIN, L. C.: At the outbreak of the Civil War L. C. Franklin resided in Noxubee County, Miss. He helped to raise Company D, of the Eleventh Mississippi Infantry, under Col. Liddell, and was elected second lieutenant. He served in this gallant regiment through the Peninsular campaign and from Yorktown on to the close of the war. At the reorganization of the regiment he left the service for the sheriff's office in his county, but after the term expired went to the front again in Harrison's Sixth Mississippi Cavalry (a part of Forrest's command) and remained in this corps till the end. Comrade Franklin was a native of Georgia, born in November, 1828. After the war he came to Chicot County, Ark., and lived a valued citizen until his death, in October, 1902. He was a generous man, and none appealed to him in vain. He was our Commander at the Memphis reunion.[207]

H. M. Freeman.

FREEMAN, H. M.: Comrade Freeman was born sixty-seven years ago, in Lunenberg County, Va. He moved to Henry County, Tenn., when quite young; was reared on a farm, and married Miss Margaret Julian in 1856. Having no one to whom he could intrust the care of his wife and three little children, he was prevented from going out at the beginning of the great conflict between the States; but in the spring of 1863 he could not withstand the impulses that had been torturing him to cast his lot with his fellow-countrymen, so he raised a company of cavalry which became Company K, Twentieth Tennessee Regiment, in Forrest's Cavalry.

Capt. Freeman proved himself a superb soldier in the first engagement, Okolola, when he led the charge with his company, and at once won distinction as one of the most fearless officers in Forrest's Cavalry. He participated in every battle from that time to the close of the war; was on the Paducah raid, at Fort Pillow, Memphis, and at Forrest's greatest victory, Brice's Cross Roads. He had his men in the thickest of the fight from the beginning to the end. At Athens, Ala., Freeman's men helped to dislodge the enemy from their works, and either killed or captured the entire Federal command.

Capt. Freeman surrendered at the close of the war with the remnant of Forrest's Cavalry, and came home and took charge of his farm, which had been desolated by the ravages of war. In 1876 he was made deputy sheriff of Henry County, serving four years in that capacity; then, in 1880, was elected sheriff, and served three consecutive terms.

When Capt. Freeman retired from office he engaged in the hardware business in Paris, continuing in the same up to the time of his death, which occurred August 20, 1900. He always believed in the right of secession.[208] He was a man of decided political views. He loved his friends, and hated his enemies. His noble wife, who survives him, sacrificed everything for her loved one. One instance of her pluck and courage, while her husband was away following the knightly Forrest, was when her house was burned, leaving her and her children homeless. She took some men, went to the woods, hewed out logs, and soon had a good, comfortable house built.

Capt. Freeman never lost an opportunity to lend a helping hand to an old comrade. He was a member of Fitzgerald Camp, U.C.V., and took an active interest in everything relating to his old comrades. He seldom spoke of the war without paying a tribute to Gen. Forrest.[209]

FRENSLEY, HARRISON M.: [H. M. Frensley] served under Forrest in the 12th Kentucky Regiment.[210]

FRIZZELL, SAMUEL W.: Bob Gaston Camp, of Frankston, Tex., lost one of its leading members in the death of First Lieut. S. W. Frizzell on September 23, 1910. He enlisted for the Confederacy from his home in Kentucky early in 1861 as a member of the 3rd Kentucky Cavalry, and for the last two years of the war he was with General Forrest. He was a man loved and respected by all. He was in his sixty-ninth year. His wife survives him, and is living at Frankston; while his daughter, Mrs. Glasscock, is in Washington, D.C., and the son, Prof. L. T. Frizzell, at Groveton, Tex.[211]

FUQUA, JOHN FRANKLIN: On December 31, 1907, near Fountain Head, Tenn., occurred the death of John Fuqua, in his seventy-eighth year. He reared a family of eight sons and a daughter, three of whom were with him at the last. He was a consistent member of the Methodist Church, having joined with six of his sons about thirty years ago at Old Oak Grove. Death resulted from a stroke of paralysis in November. He and his brother, Joel Fuqua, whose death occurred seven months before, were both Confederate soldiers, joining in 1861 the company of Captain Lytle, Col. D. W. Holman's Regiment, 11th Tennessee Cavalry. He was afterwards in Company B, Forrest's Cavalry, and was released as a prisoner of war by Andrew Johnson at Nashville in 1865. His life as patriot, soldier, citizen, and Christian was without blemish. His wife, two sons, and a daughter preceded him to the better land.[212]

FUSSELL, JOSEPH H.: Capt. Joseph H. Fussell, prominent lawyer, Confederate veteran, and citizen of Columbia, Tenn., died there on November 4, 1915, having been in failing health for some time.

Captain Fussell was born in Maury County in January, 1836, and had nearly reached fourscore years of age. He is survived by his wife and several nieces and nephews. He was highly educated and exceptionally intellectual and was a lawyer of profound ability. He was one of the best-known Confederate veterans in the State and was at one time prominent in politics.

A desire to do something for his country was manifested early in life; for he enlisted at the age of eleven years as an American soldier to fight the Mexicans, but was rejected on account of his youth. At the beginning of the War between the States he enlisted in Forrest's cavalry as a private, but was soon promoted to the command of a troop of soldiers. His war experience included participation in seventy battles without losing a drop of blood. At the battle of Franklin he was shot through the beard, but was not injured. He was mustered out at Charlotte, N.C., on May 3, 1865, being under General Wheeler at that time. He returned to his home, in Columbia; and on January 23, 1873, he was married to Miss Margarete Roberts, a daughter of Capt. William Tate Roberts and granddaughter of Gen. Isaac Roberts, who was a general under [George] Washington in the [American] Revolution. He acquired his education at Jackson College, of Columbia, and received a law degree. After graduation he began the practice of law and soon entered politics.

In 1870 Captain Fussell was elected attorney-general of his district and served creditably until 1886. No public officer ever discharged his duties with more courage, fidelity, and ability. All his life Captain Fussell had been an ardent prohibitionist. He was a ruling elder in the Cumberland Presbyterian Church, having devoted most of the latter years of his life to the cause of that Church. He was a member of the Board of Publication, President of the Legal Board, and State Clerk of the Tennessee Synod. In 1910 he was unanimously elected Moderator of the General Assembly which convened at Dickson, where the Cumberland Presbyterian Church had been organized a hundred years before.

Captain Fussell was a man of sterling honesty and of high moral standards. He was a sincere and unselfish friend, a devoted husband, a strong patriot, and a high-class citizen. He was prominent in fraternal circles, having been a Mason, a Knight Templar, and a Knight of Pythias. He was looked upon as a leader among the Confederate veterans of his county and was always interested in the annual reunions.[213]

GALBRAITH, T. J.: An esteemed and honored as well as public-spirited citizen was lost to Henderson, Tenn., in August, 1905, in the death of T. J. Galbraith, who was nearing his seventy-first year. At the outbreak of the war he joined the command of Gen. N. B. Forrest and became first lieutenant of Company C, 21st Tennessee Cavalry. He remained in the service till the close of the war under this illustrious leader. Comrade Galbraith was married in 1864 to Miss Anne E. Barham, daughter of Robert Barham, who was the head of one of the pioneer families of that section. He was a man of faith—faith in the Confederate cause and faith in the men who espoused it.[214]

T. J. Galbraith.

GARDNER, W. M.: W. M. Gardner was born in Tennessee July 30, 1844, and died in Waxahachie, Tex., December 30, 1914. He was a member of Capt. James Rivers's company, 11th Tennessee Cavalry, and served under Forrest and Wheeler.[215]

GARRETT, ELIJAH: [Elijah Garrett served in] Morphis's Company, Kelley's Regiment, Forrest's Cavalry.[216]

GARRETT, WILLIAM ROBERTSON: Capt. William Robertson Garrett was born at Williamsburg, Va., April 12, 1839; and died in Nashville, Tenn., February 12, 1904. His father, Dr. Robert M. Garrett, and Mrs. Susan Winder Garrett, his mother, were members of the most prominent families of Virginia.

Capt. Garrett graduated with the degree of A.M. at William and Mary

College, and afterwards took a law course at the University of Virginia. In April, 1861, he entered the Confederate service as a private in the Thirty-Second Regiment, but a short time afterwards was elected captain of artillery, with which he served through the Peninsular campaign with such marked ability that at the expiration of the enlistment of his company, May, 1862, he was offered several staff positions, all of which he declined [in order] to accept a commission to raise a battalion of partisan cavalry for service in Tennessee. These troops, with Holman's Battalion, were consolidated and formed the Eleventh Tennessee Cavalry, with Capt. Garrett as adjutant, and became a part of Dibrell's Brigade under Forrest, until after the battle of Chickamauga, when they became a part of Gen. Wheeler's Division under Gen. Joe Johnston.

William Robertson Garrett.

When Hood retreated from Tennessee they again became a part of Forrest's Command, Bell's Brigade, and surrendered with it at Gainesville, Ala.

Soon after the war Capt. Garrett married Miss Flournoy Batts, of Pulaski, Tenn., and afterwards devoted his entire time to educational matters, for which by taste and study he was so eminently qualified, as evidenced by the many important positions he has filled. He was President of Giles College, Principal of Cornersville Academy, Superintendent of Public Schools for Giles County, Professor of Mathematics in the Montgomery Bell Academy, also of the University of Nashville, Principal of the Nashville Military Academy, State Superintendent of Public Schools, and at the time of his death, was Professor of American History in the Peabody Normal College for Teachers, and editor of the *American Historical Magazine*.

Capt. Garrett always took an active interest in the U.C.V. Association, and at the time of his death was a member of the Historical Committee of the Association and a trustee of the Confederate Memorial Association.[217]

GAY, A. T.: Capt. A. T. Gay, the founder of the Young County Camp of United Confederate Veterans, has been transferred to the great beyond, and now rests under the sod and the dew, awaiting the sound of the trumpet which shall call him to his everlasting reward.

Capt. Gay was a native of Tennessee, and when his State sounded the alarm and beat the long roll early in 1861, he enlisted as a private soldier in April, 1861, and in five months time was, by promotion, the captain of Company E, Thirty-First Tennessee Regiment. He served with this regiment until after Gen. Bragg's defeat at Chattanooga, when he was transferred to the cavalry service, and was captain of Company E, Twentieth Tennessee Cavalry, until the close of the war, when he surrendered with Forrest at Gainesville, Ala.

Like thousands of others, at the time of enlisting in the army, Comrade Gay went forth willingly and cheerfully to battle for [conservative] principles he then believed, and died believing they were just, honorable, and right. He was one of those patriotic and chivalrous spirits who made the name of Forrest so famous in American history.²¹⁸

GEE, JAMES L.: James L. Gee, a well-known photographer, died in the Baker Hotel September 25, 1911, after a brief illness, aged 72 years.

He served the Confederacy from the beginning of the war to the end in Company B, Seventh Tennessee Cavalry, Forrest's Corps, surrendered at Gainesville, Ala., on May 10, 1865, and ever retained his parole.

He went to Batesville some eight years ago, engaging in photography, and lived at the Baker Hotel the entire period, where he was a special favorite of all, and of whom Mr. Baker speaks in the highest eulogy, as well as all others with whom he came in business relations. The burial was in Oaklawn Cemetery, Batesville, Ark.²¹⁹

GEORGE, HENRY: In the death of Col. Henry George, which occurred in the city of Mayfield, Ky., on the 31st of May, 1919, the South has lost another distinguished citizen and patriot. He died suddenly of heart failure, and the next day he was laid to rest beside his beloved wife in Maplewood Cemetery. The Confederate veterans of Graves County attended the funeral, and at the grave Capt. J. T. Daughaday spoke with great earnestness and feeling of his companion in arms and lifelong friend. Colonel George left surviving him three children: Edwin George, of Louisville; Harry George, of Graves County, Ky.; and an only daughter, Mrs. Elizabeth Griffin, of Cynthiana, Ky.

He was a man of strong and robust physique, stately in appearance, most lovable in disposition, and was noted for his rugged honesty and steadfast friendship. He was possessed of a discriminating mind, and his judgment of men and measures was usually accurate and sound.

He was born in Graves County, Ky., in 1847 and entered the Confederate service in November, 1861, as a private in Company A, 7th Kentucky Infantry, and served with that command throughout the War between the States, participating in many engagements, among them Shiloh, Baker's Creek, Corinth, Jackson, Brice's Crossroads, Harrisburg, Tupelo, Old Town Creek, Paducah, Franklin, Nashville, Murfreesboro, Montevallo, and Selma. This regiment was mounted March 15, 1864, and assigned, along with the 3rd, 8th, and 12th Kentucky, to General Forrest, with whom they served until the end, surrendering May 16, 1865, at Columbus, Miss. He was shot in the knee at Harrisburg and cut in the arm with a saber at Selma, Ala., April 2, 1865 (General Forrest's last battle), and was captured by Wilson's forces.

After his return to Kentucky, he attended the public schools, taught school for a while, and then engaged in the mercantile business for several years. After serving as deputy clerk of Graves County, he was elected to the Lower House of the General Assembly of Kentucky in 1876 and to the Senate in 1878. In

1888-1891 he was Indian Agent in Arizona and California and then resigned and was reelected to the State Senate. After his term as Senator expired, he served two and a half years as warden of the Kentucky penitentiary, where he instituted many reforms in the prison. In 1898 he was appointed a State commissioner of the penitentiary. For about ten years he was commandant of the Kentucky Confederate Home at Pewee Valley, Ky., voluntarily retiring about two years ago on account of ill health.

Henry George.

Colonel George was the author of *History of the 3rd, 7th, 8th, and 12th Kentucky, C.S.A.*, which was published in 1911. It had an extensive sale and excited most favorable comment throughout the country. Gen. Bennett H. Young, former Commander in Chief of the Confederate Veterans, wrote a preface to this work, in which, among other things, he said: "Little is known by Confederates at large of the heroism of these Kentuckians who served under General Forrest. To give them their proper place in history has been the highest ambition of Col. Henry George. Forty-six years is a long period to await vindication, but through these years Colonel George has nursed his purpose to tell the world of what his associates did in the great war.

"Almost a child in 1861, he enlisted in the 7th Kentucky Infantry. He saw all that splendid regiment did, and in its battles and marches he followed its fortunes to the end, when in May, 1865, he furled its guerdons and laid down its arms, so gloriously borne, and accepted the results Fate decreed should come to the Confederate cause.

"Painstaking, candid, just, and, above all, scrupulously careful of truth, no man could bring himself to the task of putting these Kentuckians in proper historical setting better than the author of this book. Modest, he says but little of himself, and yet in the story of the dangers, privations, and triumphs of his beloved companions in arms he finds ample compensation for the labor, love, and energy that come to book-making. All those who love the Confederate cause, who cherish its heroic memories, will thank the author for what he has written in these pages, and the volume will be greatly valued by those who shall hereafter aid in writing a true history of the deeds of those who wore the gray and followed the Stars and Bars, some to death, but all who survived to the sad end of the Southland's illustrious effort for national life."[220]

GEORGE, J. H.: Capt. J. H. George was born July 4, 1827, in Iredell County, N.C. When he was five years of age his parents removed to Georgia, remaining there two years, thence to South Carolina, and after several years came to Lincoln County, Tenn. He attended the common schools of his section, and when a man held several minor offices.

In 1861 he volunteered and was made captain of Company D, Forty-First Tennessee Infantry; was mustered into service on November 4, 1861, at Camp Trousdale. He returned home soon after, on leave of absence, and was married, November 26, 1861, to Miss M. J. Halbert. He reported to his command soon afterwards. It was ordered to Bowling Green, Ky., under Gen. A. S. Johnston, hence to Russellville, Ky., and on to Fort Donelson under General Buckner. The regiment was surrendered with the army there February 16, 1862. With other officers, he was sent to Camp Chase, Ohio, thence to Johnson's Island, where he remained as prisoner of war until September 1 of the same year. His men were held at Camp Morton. The officers and soldiers were sent to Vicksburg, Miss., at the same time and exchanged. He saw service in Mississippi and Louisiana up to May, 1863, when, on account of bad health, he was discharged and returned to Tennessee.

After regaining his health, Captain George reentered the service as captain of a cavalry company, part of a regiment which was organized near the Tennessee River by Col. W. N. Nixon (?), of Lawrenceburg, Tenn., and known as Nixon's Regiment, and was soon attached to Col. Bell's brigade under Gen. N. B. Forrest.

Captain George was in command of the regiment at the time General Forrest made that notable raid in West Tennessee on the Tennessee River, capturing a large number of Federal transports, in which he did active service. He was also with the command on General Woods's raid into Middle Tennessee, and on the retreat to Corinth. From that time on he saw service through Mississippi and Alabama up to the close of the war. He was paroled with General Forrest at Gainesville, Ala., May 12, 1865. Returning home to Lincoln County, Tenn., he engaged in farming up to 1900, when he removed to Hunt County, Tex.[221]

GEORGE, J. T.: The last roll call sounded for Col. J. T. George, on September 20, 1929, in Mayfield, Ky. He was born in a log cabin in the south part of Graves County, near the historic church of Mt. Zion, August 28, 1847. When a small boy, he was left an orphan, his father and mother dying about twenty-four hours apart.

At the age of sixteen he joined the Confederate forces in Mississippi, early in the war, enlisting in Company C, 7th Tennessee Cavalry, under Gen. N. B. Forrest. He was in every battle in which Forrest's forces were engaged, including three of the fiercest battles of the war—Harrisburg, Guntown, and Brice's Crossroads. On account of his youth and gallantry, he became the favorite of the entire company. His record as a soldier was of the very best, for when duty called he was ever ready to go into the thickest of the fight.

J. T. George.

While on a scouting expedition at Johnsonville, Tenn., he was captured and taken to Paducah, Ky., where, with others, he was asked to take the [U.S.] oath of allegiance, but refused. He was then sent to Camp Morton, where he remained a prisoner for seven months, being released June 15, 1865, some two months after the close of the war, of which he had not been apprised.

Colonel George again took up his residence in South Graves, near his old home, and became an esteemed and honored citizen. In 1890, his popularity led to his election to the office of county clerk; four years later he was reelected. In 1923, he was honored with the appointment of State pension commissioner, which office he held to the satisfaction of all until 1927, when he retired and returned to his home in Mayfield, on the Paris Highway.

In the death of Colonel George our town and county lost a splendid man, one who, from a homeless youth, developed into the highest type soldier, friend, neighbor, and citizen.[222]

GHOLSON, SAMUEL JAMESON: Samuel J. Gholson was born May 19, 1808, in Madison County, Ky. After studying law he became a Mississippi Congressman and later a U.S. district judge.

Upon the start of Lincoln's War he enlisted in the Confederate army as a private. Soon promoted to brigadier general, he fought at Fort Donelson, Iuka, and Corinth. During operations in Alabama, Mississippi, and Louisiana, his cavalry was attached to Chalmer's Division of Forrest's Corps. He lost an arm at Egypt, Miss., in 1864.

After the War he was elected to the state legislature in 1865, and again in 1878. He died at his home in Aberdeen, Miss., on October 16, 1883, and was buried in Odd Fellows Cemetery.[223]

GIBBS, GEORGE R.: G. R. Gibbs was born September 23, 1843, at Brownsville, Tenn.; and died May 1, 1914, at Covington, Tenn. His father was one of the early settlers in West Tennessee and was extensively engaged in the river traffic on the Hatchie River.

He established the Brownsville Landing, and in 1854 moved to his farm, in Tipton County, where he lived until his death, in 1874. His son, George R. Gibbs, made for himself a name that will be prized by those who were near and dear to him.

When only a lad of seventeen years George R. Gibbs enlisted in the service of his country, and for four long years served under the leadership of General Forrest. In the camp, on the march, and on the red field of battle George Gibbs was at all times ready to perform his duty, courageous and brave. Surrendering with Forrest at Gainesville, Ala., he returned to his home to rebuild the waste places, and his success in life is evidence that the same courage and fortitude shown in war was manifest in his peaceful pursuits.

In February, 1874, he was married to Miss Martha B. Owen, of North Carolina. His wife and their two children, Thomas Owen Gibbs, of Chicago, and Mrs. Mary Owen Wilson, survive.[224]

James Wright Gillespie.

GILLESPIE, JAMES WRIGHT: James W. Gillespie, whose death occurred at his home in San Antonio, Tex., on July 9, 1910, was a native of Tennessee. He was born on the old family plantation in Fayette County on November 2, 1844, a son of Andrew Jackson and Julia Wright Gillespie. The Gillespies were an old and prominent Tennessee family, well known in the early history of that State. On his father's side he was descended from the Virginia Edmondsons, Gen. Edmondson Jones, of Confederate fame, being a cousin. On the maternal side William Gillespie was descended from the Wrights of North Carolina and the Philpotts. During the war he served with distinction as a member of the 7th Tennessee Cavalry, under Forrest.

After the war he completed his education in Europe, spending some time at Heidelberg, Germany, and Oxford, England. Upon returning to America he went with his family to Texas and settled in Colorado County. Later he removed to Dallas, and there married Miss Fannie McGary in 1873. In 1895 he became a resident of San Antonio, and had been one of the most active members of the Albert Sidney Johnston Camp. U.C.V., of that place. He had been interested for years in the land and mining business. Surviving him are his three daughters and two sons, five brothers and two sisters.

Comrade Gillespie was known extensively over Texas and loved for his genial, kindly personality. He was a true type of the courteous Southern gentleman, a consistent Christian. His friends were numbered among all classes.[225]

GIRTMAN, J. W. D.: J. W. D. Girtman . . . entered the [Confederate] service October 1, 1861, as a private in Company K, 2nd Georgia Regiment of Cavalry (Colonel Lawton), Forrest's Brigade, and was afterwards transferred to Wheeler's command.[226]

GLOSTER, A. W.: Maj. A. W. Gloster, Aid-de-Camp to Maj. Gen. A. J. Vaughan, commanding Tennessee Division, U.C.V., is a native of Fayette County, Tenn., and comes of substantial North Carolina parentage. Early in life he adopted civil engineering. He promptly responded to the call to arms for the South in 1861, and was sworn into the Army of Tennessee in May, at Randolph, a small town on the Mississippi River. He and N. B. Forrest were sworn into the cavalry company of Capt. White, of Memphis, together, their hands being on the same Bible. This was a few days before Forrest was commissioned by Gov. Harris to raise a battalion of cavalry.

Comrade Gloster was commissioned by Gov. Harris as lieutenant of engineers, and assigned to duty on Brig. Gen. John L. T. Sneed's staff, where he remained until the Army of Tennessee was transferred to the Confederate government. Subsequently he was assigned to duty with Maj. Minor Meriwether, acting chief engineer of the army at Columbus, Ky., remaining with him in active engineering service at Island No. 10, Fort Pillow, and Shiloh, and building fortifications in and around Corinth, from which place they went to Tupelo, Miss. He was in active engineering service until the fall of Vicksburg, when he was captured, and remained in parole camp at Demopolis, Ala., until October, when he was exchanged. He was then ordered to report to the army at Missionary Ridge, and was put in command of Company C, Third Regiment Engineers, and ordered to Atlanta to build wagons and boats for the pontoon trains of the army. This selection was without his knowledge or solicitation.

A. W. Gloster.

He remained in command of this train, building necessary bridges over the streams crossed by the Army of Tennessee, until the close of the war. Since the war Maj. Gloster has been engaged in locating and constructing some of the most important railroad lines in the South, both east and west of the Mississippi River. His home is at Gallatin.[227]

GOODMAN, JOHN: John Goodman, born in 1841, died in 1928, aged eighty-seven years. He was a member of the 10th Tennessee, Forrest's Cavalry.[228]

GRABER, HENRY W.: Henry W. Graber, of Dallas, is a veteran of the famous Terry's Texas Rangers, a cavalry regiment that achieved fame on so many battlefields of the Middle South, from Kentucky to the Carolinas.

Mr. Graber is a native of Germany, born in the city of Bremen in 1841, where his father conducted a large manufacturing and exporting business. In 1853 the family moved to Houston, Tex., where both parents and a brother died the same year. Young Henry was employed in business there, and afterwards in Waxahachie, Cypress City, and Hempstead. In 1860 he became the junior partner of the firm of Faddis & Graber at Hempstead, and was engaged in prosperous general merchandising at the beginning of the war. From this place he promptly joined the State troops in expeditions to Brazos, Santiago, and Indianola, where the garrisons soon surrendered. In September, 1861, he enlisted for the war as a private in Company B, Eighth Texas Cavalry, familiarly known as Terry's Texas Rangers, under the command of Col. B. F. Terry.

When elected second lieutenant in the first company organization at Hempstead he declined the honor, having no ambition to gratify, save to do his duty in a humble capacity. He served with his regiment in Kentucky in the fall and winter of 1861, fought at Woodsonville, the regiment's first engagement, where the gallant Terry fell, and at Shiloh under Col. Wharton. He was in the first battle and capture of Murfreesboro under Gen. Forrest; then with his regiment went into Kentucky with Bragg's army, and was in the battles of Mumfordsville, Bardstown, Perryville, and many minor engagements.

Early in 1863, while on a scouting expedition in Kentucky in an engagement near Bowling Green with an infantry force many times their number, he was severely wounded and six of his comrades killed. Unable to ride and make his escape, he was left near Woodburn, and the second night was captured by the Eleventh Kentucky Mounted Infantry [U.S.A.]. He was held at Bowling Green for several months awaiting court-martial, but, having attempted his escape, was sent to Louisville for safe-keeping, and there placed in irons for resenting an insult by Black, a [Yankee] negro captain. Subsequently, on the demand of Gen. Bragg, he was treated as a prisoner of war and sent to Camp Chase, Ohio.

After several months he was sent to Fort Delaware, from whence he escaped after four mouths' detention by assuming a sick man's name at roll call, going out with a party of Marylanders that were expecting to be paroled at Washington, but instead they were sent to Point Lookout, Md., from where, after several months' detention, again assuming the name of a dead Louisianian, he was sent with a part of Hay's Brigade of Louisianians to City Point for exchange. Arriving at Richmond, he immediately left for and rejoined his command in East Tennessee.

His next active service was in the Georgia campaign of 1864, participating in numerous engagements from Dalton to Atlanta and Jonesboro. He served under Gen. Joe Wheeler against Sherman during the latter's march to Savannah, wherein they fought daily. Near Savannah his company was detached for duty as scouts with Gen. McLaws, with whom he remained until the surrender in North Carolina. He was in the battle of Averasboro, Bentonville, and other smaller engagements.

At the close of this active military career, never having missed a duty on account of sickness or otherwise save during his twelve months' imprisonment, Mr. Graber returned to Texas, and resumed business at Hempstead, and was later at Courtney, Rusk, and Waxahachie. He has lived at Dallas since 1885. He has always been active and prominent in the work of the United Confederate Veterans, and was honored with a position as Quartermaster General on the staff of Lieut. Gen. W. L. Cabell, commanding the Trans-Mississippi Department U.C.V., at the time of its organization, which position he still holds. He is a member of Sterling Price Camp. He was its Commander in 1898, fully enjoying the confidence of his comrades. Mr.

Henry W. Graber.

Graber is now a member of the Board of Directors of the Texas Reunion Association, organized for the purpose of entertaining the General Reunion in April next at Dallas, and to build a monument to Gen. Robert E. Lee at the State capital. As President of the Graber Machinery Company and in all social and business relations he is highly regarded among the people of Dallas.[229]

GRANBERY, J. L.: Capt. J. L. Granbery, aged sixty-five years, died on January 31, 1902, at his home in Collierville, Tenn. He was a graduate of Chapel Hill College, N.C., and read law under the eminent and lamented Judge Calvin Jones, of Somerville, Tenn. Born in Fayette County, Tenn., of Southern blood and naturally of a sensitive and highly strung organization, when the Civil War broke out he was among the first to respond to his country's call, and organized a company known as the "Macon Grays." His command was mustered in as Company B, Thirteenth Regiment Tennessee Infantry, Col. A. J. Vaughn commanding. He received a wound at Shiloh, and owing to ill health resigned. After a short rest he reenlisted as a private in Company E, Twelfth Tennessee Cavalry, Forrest's command.

He won the esteem and confidence of his company and was soon made captain. W. M. S. writes a beautiful tribute to Capt. Granbery in which it is stated that he served and fought gallantly upon many battlefields, leading his men from victory to victory. No truer, braver hero ever marched under the flag or kept step to the wild, grand music. He needs no eulogy from any man; his life in war and peace was a better eulogy than any pen can write. As a citizen he was most prominent, always ready with means and brains to advance the interests of his own.

For twelve years he had been cashier of the bank at Collierville, filling the position with credit to himself and satisfaction to others concerned. About a year ago his beloved wife was taken from him, and only two weeks after his death, his youngest daughter, wife of J. E. Jesse, of Collierville, passed away. Only one member of his family now survives, Mrs. H. P. Davis, of Memphis, who shares the sympathies of many friends.[230]

GRAY, H. T.: H. T. Gray, member of Breckinridge Camp, U.C.V., Danville, Ky., passed to his reward February 3, 1907. He was born in Harrodsburg County in 1837, and enlisted in Company K, Forrest's Regiment, at Memphis, Tenn., in October, 1861. After the battle of Perryville, he was transferred to Morgan's command, 3rd Kentucky Regiment, under Col. Dick Gano. He was captured in Ohio in 1863, exchanged, and at the close of the war received his honorable discharge.[231]

GREEN, THOMAS WALLACE: Thomas W. Green was born near Hopkinsville, Ky., on February 22, 1842. His parents were John R. Green and Elizabeth Nelson, and he was the second son of a large family. He joined Hill's Confederate Cavalry in Tipton County and served throughout the war as a scout. He was never wounded. He was elected captain several times, but preferred the most dangerous position and was a brave soldier to the end. He was under Gen. N. B. Forrest in 1862 and 1863 and had pleasant recollections of that great leader.

Mr. Green was reared a Presbyterian, but on April 21, 1886, he was confirmed by Bishop T. F. Gailor. In October, 1869, he married Miss Katherine Taylor Somerville, of Tipton County, and leaves a daughter and a son—Mrs. Edward Tarry and John W. Green—also two grandchildren. Mr. Green passed away at his home, at Keeling, Tenn., on October 24, 1920, and was laid to rest at Old Trinity Chapel, in Tipton County.[232]

GREER, B. T.: The last taps of the drum of life's battles resounded for B. T. Greer on January 31, 1926, in his eighty-first year.

B. T. Greer was the youngest son of Henry and Essie Nash Greer, early pioneers of North Mississippi, of Scotch and Irish descent. His father was one of the commissioners who helped to lay off the county site of Lowndes County, Columbus, Miss. Young Greer enlisted at the age of sixteen in Company G, of the 16th Mississippi Cavalry Regiment, under the command of Nathan Bedford Forrest.

Shortly after the war, he married Miss Carrie Carlisle, of Aberdeen, Miss., who lived only a short time. He was married again to Miss Mary Jackie Parker, and from this union were born four sons and two daughters.

He joined the Methodist Church soon after the war, and all of his family are members of the same Church. His life of stable habits, integrity, honor, and Christian virtues furnish a living example to the younger generation; a man of few words, simple, unassuming, good-natured, respected, and loved by all who knew him.

His body was laid to rest in the family square in the cemetery at Luling, Tex., where he lived prior to going to Austin to place his youngest son in the State University. Many lovely flowers covered the mound where soon will be seen the verdant grass of a Texas spring.[233]

GREER, JONES: Jones Greer was one of the 65 African-Americans who served in Forrest's Cavalry. Greer distinguished himself on and off the field as the servant of Lieut. George L. Cowan, who was General Forrest's personal escort.[234]

GRIFFITH, JOSEPH DICKSON: Joseph Dickson Griffith, one of the most prominent citizens and best-loved Confederate veterans of Madison County, Tenn., died at his home in Jackson on August 17 [1929?], following a lengthy illness.

He was born, September 6, 1846, in the Cotton Grove neighborhood of this county, son of the late Daniel and Elizabeth Dickson Griffith, pioneer residents of the county. When a youth, he moved with his family to Gibson County. There, in 1863, he ran away from home and affiliated himself with the Confederate forces, being in the company with his elder brother, Lieut. W. R.

Griffith. On account of his youth and enthusiasm for the cause which he so nobly served, he was frequently used as a courier, and throughout his career in the Confederate army he was devoted to the South and the cause which he served.

At the close of the war, he was with forces that surrendered at Gainesville, Ala., being a member of Company A, 115th Tennessee Regiment, under General Forrest, and throughout his life Comrade Griffith remained a loyal and devoted Southerner, and gave his best efforts to the reconstruction of the land which he loved so well.

Following the war, he returned to his native county and was engaged in farming for many years. In November, 1879, he was married to Miss Anna Bell Morgan, who survives him with two daughters and three grandchildren. A brother, John D. Griffith, of Lockney, Tex., is also a survivor.

Though he never sought public office, Mr. Griffith served frequently on the equalization board, election boards, etc., in the city and in the county, and for many years was president of the John Ingram Bivouac of the Confederate Veterans. He was often called on by the U.D.C. Chapter of Jackson for information. He loved to discuss the glories of the old South, yet he never lost step with the present-day trend of affairs.

He was a member of the First Baptist Church, of Jackson, and was regarded as one of the most loyal members of the congregation and deeply interested in its Sunday school work.

Members of John Ingram Bivouac acted as honorary pallbearers and escort to his last resting place in the Pleasant Plain Cemetery.[235]

GRIZZARD, R. E.: R. E. Grizzard, of Camp R. M. Russell at Trenton, Tenn., died on August 8 [1901?]. . . . Of Comrade Grizzard, the Strahl Bivouac gave the following report: He was born at Nashville in December, 1839, and at an early age removed to Tullahoma, where his childhood was passed. He was a student at Andrew College, Trenton, and then returned to Nashville to live. When the war broke out he enlisted in Company A, Rock City Guards, Maney's Regiment, First Tennessee Volunteers. He served through the first year of the war in West Virginia in the Cheat Mountain campaign. He was then [honorably] discharged, and, returning to Tennessee, enlisted in Company A, Bluff City Grays, part of Forrest's command. He served with this company till the close of the war, making a true and faithful soldier, always ready to discharge any duty assigned him.[236]

GRIZZLE, ROBERT A.: [Robert A. Grizzle] was a teamster under Captain Rice in Forrest's command.[237]

GUERRANT, P. M.: P. M. Guerrant, son of Rev. Peter D. Guerrant, was born in North Carolina in 1863. When a small boy his family moved to Danville, Va. He was married to Miss Mariah Cole in 1855, and moved to Kentucky in 1887. Up to the time of Mr. Guerrant's death, February 12, 1903, at Fulton, Ky., he lived a consistent life as a Christian, and as a husband, father, and neighbor. He was faithful in the discharge of every duty in life. He served for three years under Gens. Wheeler and Forrest, Second Kentucky Regiment, and was noted for his bravery.[238]

Lundie Bird Gunn.

GUNN, LUNDIE BIRD: Lundie Bird Gunn died at the home of his daughter, Mrs. E. L. Wetherbee, at Shubuta, Miss., on April 21, and his body was taken back to the old home, Waynesboro, Miss., and laid beside that of his wife, who died many years ago. He was born in Tuscaloosa County, Ala., November 17, 1841, and thus had passed into his eighty-third year. He was a faithful member of the Primitive Baptist Church.

At the beginning of the war Comrade Gunn enlisted as a member of the Buena Vista Rifles, which company was mustered into service at Corinth, becoming Company A, of the 17th Mississippi Infantry. The command was at once sent to Virginia and took part in the first battle of Manassas, and was also in the engagement at Leesburg and the seven days fighting around Richmond, Sharpsburg, Harper's Ferry, Cold Harbor, Spotsylvania, and in the Gettysburg campaign. He was later transferred to the command of General Forrest, under whom he continued to serve to the close of the war. He received many slight wounds in different battles, but no serious injury. He rose to the rank of lieutenant, and was found ready to perform every duty devolving upon him, while his fidelity and valor are indicated by many commendatory letters of leading men of the day. Col. W. D. Holder said of him: "He has no superior in the Confederate or any other army."

In October, 1865, Comrade Gunn was married to Miss Bettie Brandon. Thirteen children were born to them, eight of whom, with twenty-five grandchildren and six great-grandchildren, survive him.[239]

GURLEY, FRANK BALLOU: In the death of Capt. Frank Ballou Gurley the Confederate Veteran Association has lost a loyal and patriotic member, than whom the Confederacy had no braver nor truer soldier.

At the very incipiency of the war, when in his young manhood, he enlisted as a private in the company commanded by the renowned fighting preacher, Rev. D. C. Kelley, who afterwards became General Forrest's confidential and able assistant. This company went to Memphis, where it was mustered into service and assigned to the battalion of which General Forrest was then lieutenant colonel.

During Private Gurley's service with Forrest's Battalion he participated in many spirited skirmishes and was personally known by the great wizard, for he never failed to perfectly satisfy the exactions of that great leader, for even then Private Gurley possessed attributes worthy of all praise.

Soon after the battle of Fort Donelson Gurley was ordered home to recruit a company, which he did of one hundred and fifteen of as gallant soldiers as ever fought for a glorious cause. He was elected captain of this company, which was assigned to the 4th Alabama Cavalry, Col. A. A. Russell, and became Company C thereof.

Captain Gurley commanded his company with his regiment on General Forrest's first expedition into West Tennessee in December, 1862.

Late in the afternoon of December 17, 1862, General Forrest, then near Lexington, West Tenn., knowing that on the morrow he would engage the enemy, called for Captain Gurley and gave him specific instructions, with orders to take the advance with four companies of his regiment early the following morning. Some eight miles east of Lexington he clashed with the 3rd Battalion of the 5th Ohio Cavalry, commanded by Capt. J. C. Harrison, which Captain Gurley promptly defeated, and in a running fight from there to Lexington he made many captures.

At Lexington General Forrest speedily came up with the balance of his command and with an eye and judgment equal to any emergency assigned Captain Gurley, with the four companies under his command, to a position on the left of the Confederate line. In the fight which followed, Captain Gurley in person captured the great Robert G. Ingersoll [noted Yankee atheist], then colonel of the 11th Illinois Volunteer Cavalry and in command of the expedition sent forth with instructions to whip and capture General Forrest, who was known to have crossed into West Tennessee.

Frank Ballou Gurley.

Captain Gurley also captured all of Colonel Ingersoll's artillery, consisting of two three-inch steel Rodman guns of Kidd's 14th Indiana Battery, commanded by the gallant Lieut. John W. H. McGuire. These guns formed the nucleus for the famous Morton's Battery, used thenceforth and effectively by General Forrest until the end in May, 1865.

In the summer of 1863 Captain Gurley, in command of an expedition, encountered the Federals near Huntsville, Ala., commanded by Brig. Gen. Robert L. McCook, who was killed in the spirited skirmish which followed. That skirmish almost proved fatal to Captain Gurley, for later he was captured and identified as the man who killed General McCook and by suborned evidence was convicted and sentenced to be hanged. He was sent North for safe-keeping, was threatened by mobs at several places, and was subjected to great exposure and all kinds of brutal treatment. At one place the leader of the mob threatened dire punishment to all the prisoners in the party if Captain Gurley was not pointed out to them. Thus it was that death looked him in the eye, but found no blinking. In the meantime General Forrest in his blunt and positive way notified the Federal authorities that if Captain Gurley was executed he would exact a heavy toll therefor.

Finally the Federals decided that General McCook's death was only one of the fortunes of war, and Captain Gurley in February, 1865, was sent to Acres Landing, on the James River, twenty miles below Richmond, and exchanged.

Captain Gurley was born in Maury County, Tenn., August 8, 1834, and passed to his great reward at Gurley, Ala., March 29, 1920.[240]

GUSTAVAS, W. V.: W. V. Gustavus, aged eighty-four years, died in Madison County in December 1901. He served in Company G, Thirty-Sixth Mississippi Cavalry, under Forrest, and came to Texas in the fall of 1865.[241]

GWYN, JAMES: Capt. James Gwyn died very suddenly of paralysis at the home of his son, Mr. John Gwyn in Bartlett, Texas, December 1st, 1896. He had gone into his room when he was heard to fall, which attracted the attention of the family, and upon entering, they found him upon the floor in a dying condition, and he passed peacefully a way shortly afterwards.

Captain Gwyn was born in Walton County, Ga., April 8, 1833. In 1836 his parents moved to Fayette County, Tennessee, where he enlisted in the Confederate service, and was Captain of Company D, Fourteenth Tennessee Cavalry, under General Forrest until the surrender at Selma, May 11, 1865.

Captain Gwyn was a gallant soldier, an honorable citizen. At the funeral there were a number of his comrades.[242]

HAILS, GEORGE WILLOUGHBY: Col. George Willoughby Hails, one of the best-known Confederate veterans of Alabama and a public official who counted his friends literally by the thousand, died at his home in Montgomery on January 25, 1925, following a long illness.

George Willoughby Hails was born January 20, 1847, in Montgomery County, and, with the exception of the years he spent in the Confederate army, lived there all his life. He was a student at the University of Alabama when the War between the States broke out and joined the cadet company which was organized at the university and which became part of the 7th Alabama Cavalry. He served first on the coast and was then transferred to Gen. N. B. Forrest's command in North Mississippi, where his company was detailed for escort duty to General Rucker. He saw active fighting as a courier and sharpshooter at Paris Landing, Johnsonville, Henryville, Columbia, Spring Hill, Franklin, and Nashville. The cadet company saved the wagon train for General Hood after the disastrous fight at Nashville by great heroism and received honorable mention in general orders, also in Jordan's history of Forrest's command. The death of Colonel Hails leaves Capt. W. B. Whiting, of Montgomery, the sole survivor of the famous University of Alabama Company.

At the close of the war Colonel Hails returned to Montgomery and became a planter. He was active in the overthrow of "carpetbag" rule [that is, the postwar Liberal-socialistic government illegally installed across the South by Liberal Yanks] and the restoration of the [Conservative] government of Alabama to the white citizenship. In 1900 he was elected tax collector, and he remained chief clerk in the tax office during several administrations to the time of his fatal illness.

Capt. W. T. Sheehan, of Montgomery, paid this tribute to his friend of many years: "Colonel Hails had a rigid sense of integrity and honor, and he held the old-time Southern ideals of personal responsibility and absolute honor in public and private service in greater degree than any other man I have ever known. He knew every one in the county, and he was always at their service. When the people from the country came to the courthouse to transact business, no matter what that business was, he would help them, go out of his way to show little kindnesses to them, introduce them to the proper departments for the completion of their business, and make them feel that he was there for that purpose. His allegiance to the Confederate soldiers, his old comrades, was something beautiful to witness. He spent a large part of his time caring for them and working out their difficulties."

Colonel Hails was married, December 10, 1874, to Miss Susan Tyler Nesbitt, of South Carolina and Virginia parentage, with a distinguished line of ancestors, including representatives in Congress and Supreme Court judges. She was a great-granddaughter of Gen. John Scott, one of the founders of Montgomery.

Surviving him are six daughters, one son, George W. Hails, Jr.; and one brother, Charles E. Hails.

Colonel Hails was first lieutenant commander of Camp Lomax, U.C.V., of Montgomery, and adjutant of the First Brigade, Alabama Division, on the staff of Gen. Hal. T. Walker. He was a notable figure at State and general reunions and one of the most enthusiastic members of Camp Lomax from the time of its organization.

The funeral was held from St. John's Episcopal Church, of which he was a member, and comrades of Camp Lomax attended in a body conducting the final rites at the grave in Oakwood Cemetery.[243]

HALBERT, P. W.: Dr. P. W. Halbert died at his home, in Lincoln County, Tenn., on April 4 [1907], in his sixty-fourth year. At the age of eighteen he enlisted in the Confederate army in April, 1861, as a member of Captain Ramsey's company of Fayetteville, Tenn., which was a part of Col. Peter Turney's regiment, the first regiment that left Tennessee for the seat of war in Virginia. He was in the battle of Bull Run, and was badly wounded in the lungs at Seven Pines. After recovering from that, he was attached to Company F, 12th Regiment of Cavalry, better known as Nixon's Regiment, Bell's Brigade, under General Forrest. He was wounded again in a skirmish at Campbellsville, Tenn., a Minie ball in his wrist disabling him for a short time, and he was with the army and saw the stars and bars go down at Gainesville, Ala., on May 12, 1865. After the war he studied medicine, and practiced his profession until his health failed. He made many friends as a physician and citizen, and always took an active interest in the welfare of his county and State.[244]

HALE, HENRY STEPHENSON: Henry S. Hale was born in Warren County, Ky., May 4, 1836. In September of 1861 he enlisted in Company H, Seventh Kentucky Regiment. He made up a company in Graves County, Ky., and was elected its captain, as which he served till after the battle of Shiloh, when, at the reorganization, he was elected major of the regiment.

Maj. Hale took part in many important battles—Shiloh, Corinth, siege of

Henry Stephenson Hale.

Vicksburg, Baker's Creek, Jackson, Miss., Brice's Cross Roads, Harrisburg, and Old Town Creek, Miss. He was severely wounded in the latter engagement, but through the careful nursing and motherly attention of Mrs. James Sykes, of Columbus, Miss., one of the devoted Southern mothers of the time, he was restored to health and rejoined his command at West Point, Miss. He was then promoted by Gen. Forrest to the rank of lieutenant colonel for gallant conduct in the battle of Baker's Creek, June 10, 1864, and assigned to duty with the Third and Seventh Kentucky Regiments, then mounted infantry. He surrendered with this command at Columbus, Miss., in April, 1865.

Col. Hale was never a prisoner of war, but he surrendered to the captivating smiles and graceful accomplishments of one of the South's fairest daughters—a graduate of the once famous Institute for Mutes, at Columbus—a daughter of Mrs. Eliza Gregory, of DeKalb, Miss., to whom he was married in November of 1865.

The uniform of which the old coat was a part was bought in Mobile, Ala., in the early part of the year 1864, at a cost of $800. It has been preserved, and is now held as a relic of war and love by the fair lady who has been the life companion and the inspiration of the purposes and achievements of his life, humble though they be, and who is now the President of the Mayfield Chapter, Daughters of the Confederacy. Though overpowered in war and a willing victim in love, he came out of it all a victor in the end, and is thankful to the great Commander for continued health and prosperity.[245]

HALL, G. H.: G. H. Hall was born July 24, 1843, near Nashville, Davidson County, Tenn., and died at Fort Smith, Ark., June 13, 1929. During his early manhood he worked in several of the Southern States, but came back to Nashville and was engaged in truck farming when the War between the States broke out. He volunteered, with his two brothers, in the Confederate service under General Forrest, and they made valiant soldiers until the close of the war in 1865. He took active part in several noted battles—Franklin, Murfreesboro, Gettysburg, and Shiloh.

After the war, Comrade Hall returned home and resumed farming. In 1868, he was married to Miss Serena Smith, of the same county. In 1881, he took his wife and children to Sebastian County, Ark., where he remained until his death. His loving wife died more than a year ago, and two sons and two daughters survive him.

"Uncle Green," as we called him, was a Southerner and a true Democrat [then a Conservative].[246] In early manhood, he and his wife identified themselves with the Missionary Baptist Church, which they held in highest esteem. He was a cripple for twenty years, and for over ten years was totally blind, but these afflictions he bore with patience. For several years their home was with their children, Mr. and Mrs. Ode Looper, proprietors of the Arlington Hotel at Fort Smith. Rev. H. E. Marsh, of Fort Smith, conducted the funeral of this good man who had "fought a good fight and kept the faith."[247]

HALL, J. P.: J. P. Hall was born in Maury County, Tenn., May 4, 1844; and died at Town Creek, Ala., January 26, 1911. In his young manhood J. P. Hall became a soldier of the Confederacy, becoming a member in 1862 of Company C, 9th Tennessee Regiment, Forrest's Cavalry. The record of Forrest's men is indelibly written in the memory of men and the annals of war, and to say that Comrade Hall was one of them is sufficient record as a soldier. After the conflict was over, he engaged in mercantile pursuits at Town Creek, Ala., in which he continued through life with commendable success. He made many friends who miss him from the familiar walks of life. His fellow-members of Camp Fred A. Ashford, U.C.V., passed resolutions expressing the esteem in which he was held and their loss in his going.[248]

HALL, JOHN W.: John W. Hall was born April 8, 1827, in Hickman County, Tenn., and was reared in Alabama. He went to Gonzales County, Tex., in 1846. In April, 1846, he joined Capt. Ben McCullough's Company of Texas Rangers, and arrived at Point Isabel, where Gen. Taylor's army was in camp, just in time to take part in the battle of Palo Alto and Resaca de la Palma on the 8th and 9th of May, 1846. Afterwards, in September, 1846, the Rangers were discharged, and with other comrades he returned to Gonzales County.

On June 3, 1847, he married Miss Mary Mauldin, daughter of Dr. William P. Mauldin. He engaged in stock-raising successfully.

In 1862 he volunteered in Willis's Battalion, Waul's Legion, and went east of the Mississippi River, where he served under Gens. Van Dorn and Forrest until the close of the war. He lost his wife in 1875, and went to the Pacific Coast, where he remained for eighteen years, engaged in mining. He was assistant sergeant at arms of the Nevada Legislature, and held other places of trust and responsibility. A resolution offered in the Nevada Legislature concerning Col. Hall is as follows: "Col. Hall is a true type of the Southern gentleman of the old school, with a record of kind deeds, enriched by devout Christian faith, exemplified by daily practice, and gentlemanly deportment, endearing him to all the members and attaches. I hope that some one will present to posterity an elaborate account of his bravery on the frontier of Texas, in Mexico, and a full description of the twenty-nine battles in which he was engaged during the civil war. Col. Hall will leave to his children the greatest legacy ever bequeathed by any father: a pure and spotless name."[249]

HALL, LAFAYETTE BENTON: In the death of Judge L. B. Hall, of Dixon, Ky., that community has lost one of its most prominent and enterprising citizens, and his family is bereft of a loving husband and father. Death came to him suddenly in his sixty-second year. Lafayette Benton Hall enlisted in the Confederate army in 1861, joining the Eighth Kentucky Infantry and serving under Capt. Jones, Gens. N. B. Forrest, Buford, and Lyon, as he was transferred from time to time. He was First Sergeant during the greater part of his service, and went through the war without getting wounded. He was a brave soldier and always true to the cause he served. This is also said of him: "The official career of Judge Hall was one of the most successful and remarkable of any man in his county. In 1874 he became a member of the fiscal court of Webster County and served four years, and in 1879 was elected county judge, and so well did he serve the people that he was indorsed for that position every time he asked it, serving as judge for twenty-three years—till January, 1902. His name was synonymous with justice and right. He was married in 1874 to Miss Martha Williams, and of the eleven children born of this union ten survive."

Judge Hall was a member of the order of Masons from 1866; and after the usual religious services at the funeral, the remains were taken in charge by the Masons and interred according to their rites.[250]

Lafayette Benton Hall.

HAMBLETT, JAMES G.: Col. James G. Hamblett, formerly of Mason, Tenn., died at his home, in Houston, Tex., on March 11, 1920. He had gone to that city about a year ago in search of health.

Colonel Hamblett was a well-known figure in the State of Tennessee, where he had lived for more than sixty years, and his loss was keenly felt, particularly in Confederate circles, as he was closely affiliated with many Confederate organizations. A gentleman of the old school, he bore the stamp of the Southland's true aristocracy and met the last foe in the same fearless way he marched into battle back in the sixties. He served the Confederacy as a member of Company B, Forrest's command. In 1907 he was made colonel and assistant commissary general on the staff of Gen. George W. Gordon, commanding the United Confederate Veterans. After the war he was still a Confederate in heart, soul, and purse, devoted to his country's need and always faithful to the cause for which he fought. He was the proud father of a veteran of the Spanish-American War and of three veterans of the great World War, and at his own request he was laid away in the uniform he so proudly wore as a Confederate.

After the simple but beautiful services at the family residence by the pastor of the First Presbyterian Church, to which he belonged, the burial services were concluded by the Masons, of which he was a lifelong member.

Colonel Hamblett is survived by his wife, six sons, and three daughters, also a sister and a brother.[251]

HANCOCK, RICHARD R.: Richard R. Hancock, private in Company C, 2nd Tennessee Regiment Cavalry, Bell's Brigade, Forrest's Command, has passed over the river and now rests under the shade of the trees in God's glorious haven of rest. Comrade Hancock died August 11, 1906, at his home, near Auburn, Tenn. He enlisted at the age of twenty on the 26th of June, 1861, and was honorably paroled on May 10, 1865, date of surrender of Forrest's Cavalry at Gainesville, Ala.

He was a typical Southern soldier. He participated in all the engagements of his command up to October, 1864, when he was seriously wounded at Paris Landing, on the Tennessee River, disabling him from active duty until about the close of the war. A braver, more gallant, and faithful soldier was not to be found in the army. His was a courage which nothing could daunt—a bravery which feared no danger. He was modest and full of honor, faithful to every performance of duty. Whether in camp, on the march, or on the firing line, his superior officers and comrades alike honored him for his loyalty to duty. His patriotism knew no bounds; he was a true Southern man in every respect, a soldier by instinct, with implicit confidence in the righteousness of his cause [constitutional conservatism].

He was the author of *Hancock's Diary of the 2nd Regiment Tennessee Cavalry* and the contributor of many facts of history and parts taken by Forrest's Cavalry. His writings contained the data kept by himself during the entire war, giving each day's movements of the command, his dates of engagements and important movements, and were therefore absolutely correct; hence his "Diary" is invaluable to the future historian, who will seek facts of the world's greatest cavalry leader.

After the close of the war, Comrade Hancock returned to his home, and applied the same devotion to duty in making a useful citizen and the upbuilding of his country as he practiced as a soldier. On September 27, 1871, he was happily married to Miss Sue Lester, who died some five years ago [1902?]. He was an active member of the Baptist Church, of which he was a member from 1856 and in which he was ordained a deacon in 1877. His final sleep is near the spot that gave him birth, among the hills and valleys that he loved so well.

Though the winter's blast may chill and deaden the surrounding verdure of the hills and valleys and make it sad and desolate, yet the springtime in all its glory and life will return annually and bring to life the roses and lilies to brighten and beautify the little mounds of buried chivalry. When friends and patriots seek for the resting places of the South's heroes, the little swelling mound of R. R. Hancock in Cannon County, Tenn., will not be forgotten.[252]

HANNER, JAMES PARK: Dr. Hanner was born in Nashville, Tenn., July 4, 1835; graduated at the Western Military Institute, Drennon Springs, Ky., in June, 1853, as first lieutenant of the corps of cadets. He received the degree of M.D. in the University of Pennsylvania in March, 1857, and was mustered into the Confederate service in May, 1861, as captain of Company D, First Regiment of Tennessee (Maney's). Was invalided and resigned his commission in December, 1861; commissioned as captain and assistant surgeon of Morton's Battery, Forrest's Cavalry, in May, 1863; paroled at Greenville, Ala., May 10, 1865; commissioned as a Major and Assistant Surgeon General on the staff of Maj. Gen. A. J. Vaughan, commanding Tennessee Division, U.C.V., in 1897.[253]

James Park Hanner.

HARDISON, W. T.: Capt. W. T. Hardison, a paroled Confederate veteran, died at his home, in Nashville, Tenn., on Sunday, July 20, 1919. He was a native of Maury County, Tenn., born on March 20, 1839, being the sixth child of a family of ten, six boys and four girls. His grandfather, James Hardison, a native of North Carolina, was a soldier in the American Revolution, and his name is engraved on a tablet in the courthouse yard of Davidson County, Tenn. James Hardison moved to Maury County, Tenn., and was granted a pension as a Revolutionary soldier in 1832. He died in 1842.

Captain Hardison's father, Humphrey Hardison, was born in North Carolina in 1804, and after moving to Tennessee he lived in the eastern part of Maury County on a large farm and was known as one of the most successful farmers in that part of the State.

W. T. Hardison attended the common schools of the neighborhood until he was sixteen years of age, when he was sent to a high school for one year, after which he taught school for a year and then finished his education at New Hope Academy. In an autobiography, written by him in 1913 for the benefit of his immediate family, he states that he was elected valedictorian of the high school and also was elected valedictorian of his class at the academy, and that after he had written his valedictory speech in English the principal of the school insisted that he should put it into Latin, which he did, and gave it in Latin the last day of the school.

In October, 1860, Mr. Hardison started to Texas with a party moving from Maury County, and they were thirty-seven days on the road. He remained in Texas until June, 1861, when he started home, traveling by stage until he reached the first railroad. Returning to his father's place, near Hardison Mills, Tenn., he and his brother, R. C. Hardison, joined a cavalry company on July 5, 1861, and were mustered into the Confederate States service near Mount Pleasant, Tenn., as members of Capt. Andrew Polk's company. After drilling about one month in Maury County, the company was ordered to Camp Trousdale, in Sumner County, near the Kentucky line. Before that time the company went into a battalion, of which Col. Nick Cox was elected major, and it was known as the 2nd Battalion of Tennessee Cavalry.

In writing about the march from Maury County to Camp Trousdale, Captain Hardison says: "We were three days on the road to Camp Trousdale,

I am inclined to think that when we left Mount Pleasant we had more cooking vessels, camping supplies, tents, wagons, etc., to move than Gen. Joseph E. Johnston's entire army had when it surrendered at or near Charlotte, N.C."

He has told the writer that at the beginning of the war the captain of his company used a fine carriage and span of horses, having a carriage driver and extra horses.

Later a regiment was organized, and Jake Biffle was elected colonel. After the battle of Fort Donelson his regiment retreated to Nashville, where he saw the old wire bridge across the Cumberland River destroyed. They then fell back to Corinth, Miss., and his brother, R. C. Hardison, was elected second lieutenant. After the battle of Shiloh his regiment was left at Corinth for some time and had a number of engagements with the Federals. After the evacuation of Corinth they fell back to Tupelo, Miss., where the regiment was reorganized by consolidating the 2nd Battalion with the 4th Battalion, and the consolidated command was known as the 1st Tennessee Cavalry Regiment, James T. Wheeler, of Giles County, being elected colonel, and the regiment from that time to the close of the war was known as Wheeler's 1st Tennessee Cavalry.

On October 22, 1862, Generals Van Dorn and Price attacked Corinth and captured the breastworks, but could not hold them, and later in the year they fell back to Holly Springs, on the Mississippi Central Railroad. General Grant, having failed to capture Vicksburg with his gunboats, left Memphis to move with his army by land down the Mississippi Valley Railroad, and when he reached Holly Springs he made that his base of supplies.

About that time Gen. Van Dorn, who had been operating west of the Mississippi River, was put in command of the cavalry, and on December 22, 1862, his command went around the flank of General Grant's army and captured Holly Springs. Captain Hardison says he was told by Capt. H. B. Douglas, of Aurora, Ill., who was one of General Grant's engineers at that time, that General Grant had over a million dollars' worth of supplies which were captured, together with quite a lot of greenback money in sheets which had not been separated. After that the 1st Tennessee Cavalry went to Thompson's Station, Tenn., and, with the other members of the command, captured a regiment of Federals on March 4, 1863, and another regiment at Brentwood on March 25.

After Gen. Van Dorn's death, in 1863,[254] the regiment was under Gen. N. B. Forrest for some time, and in the second battle of Thompson's Station they captured Major (afterwards Major General) Shafter, who was in command of the American army in Cuba in the Spanish-American War. This regiment participated in the battle of Chickamauga and after that was with General Wheeler and under

W. T. Hardison.

him until the close of the war. The regiment was in a number of hard-fought battles and many skirmishes, and Captain Hardison was with it all the time.

About the 1st of September, 1864, the commissary of his brigade was relieved. The assistant commissary was in very delicate health, and Mr. Hardison was detailed to act as commissary for the brigade, which he did from then until the surrender in May, 1865, that being a position held by a major, but he filled it while still a private.

. . . When Captain Hardison left Columbia to go home he had a negro man who had been given to him in Georgia, and he had only two dollars in greenbacks. He gave one to the negro man and kept one for himself. In his autobiography he says: "Four years before this, when I left home, there must have been one hundred and fifty mules, horses, and cattle on the place, and thirty or forty negroes; but when we arrived at home things looked very gloomy."

He says that the stock had all been taken except a couple of old mules and an old lame horse, and they had no way to make a crop. He was not accustomed to manual labor, but his father had a fine field of timothy and orchard grass, and he and his brother cut and housed this hay, and then, beginning the 1st of August, 1865, he taught school for five months. After that, as there were very few horses in the neighborhood, he made two or three trips North and bought horses, bringing them down to sell to the neighbors.

On October 20, 1867, he was married to Miss Martha G. McLean, one of the grandest women in the country, and they lived happily together until her death, on December 29, 1911. He left surviving him a daughter, Mrs. Mackie Hardison Montgomery, and a son, Humphrey Hardison. Another son, W. T. Hardison, Jr., died April 1, 1905, soon after arriving at the age of twenty-one years.

Mr. Hardison moved to Obion County, where he bought land and ran a store from the latter part of 1868 until about 1872, when he moved to Nashville. He was in the family grocery business until 1890, being with the firm of McLean & Hardison and later Hardison & White. In July, 1890, he bought an interest in the firm of Ireland & Phillips, and the name was changed to Ireland & Hardison. Afterwards he bought out Mr. Ireland, and from that time until his death he was the senior member of the firm of W. T. Hardison & Co., dealing in lime, cement, sand, etc.

Mr. Hardison was an honest, capable, and successful businessman. He professed religion and joined the Cumberland Presbyterian Church when about twenty-six years of age. He was made a ruling elder in 1866 and was an active elder in his Church until it united with the Presbyterian Church of the United States of America in 1907, and he continued a ruling elder in this congregation until his death. He was also a member of the Board of Publication of the Cumberland Presbyterian Church for a number of years and of the Presbyterian Church, U.S.A., until the Nashville branch was removed to Philadelphia. He was largely instrumental in the building of Grace Presbyterian Church in Nashville, being by far the most liberal contributor, Mr. Hardison was one of the most thoroughly charitable men I ever knew, but he never spoke of his good works. In his autobiography he says: "I never ran for any office. I never wrote or received a letter that I was not willing for my wife and daughter to read. I never went to any place that I was not willing they should go with me."

. . . Capt. W. T. Hardison was truly one of the purest and best men I ever knew and one who had thousands of friends who loved him dearly and mourn his death.[255]

HARDMAN, CHARLES T.: Capt. Charles T. Hardman died at his residence in Birmingham, Ala., on February 21, in his seventy-second year. He was one of the oldest residents of the city, having removed there in 1871, shortly after the site of the city had been surveyed. He was a native of Morgan County, Ga., but in his childhood his parents removed to Pike County, Ala.

At the outset of the war he organized a company, of which he was chosen lieutenant, and which became Company B, of the First Regiment Alabama Infantry. He served with this regiment at the battle of Shiloh and in various minor engagements. Owing to severe physical disability, he was compelled to return home in June, 1862. In the autumn of that year he organized Company B, of the Sixth Alabama Cavalry, and was elected captain. In this rank he served with James H. Clanton's Brigade till the end, frequently being in command of the regiment and occasionally of the brigade. His military service was mainly in Alabama and Georgia. In 1865 the regiment fought with Steel's advance against Mobile, and with Wilson's raiders through central Alabama. Prior to this the regiment had been active between Dalton and Atlanta. After the surrender of the forces under Forrest, Capt. Hardman went to Montgomery and was paroled. Capt. Hardman was widely known for his daring, gallantry, and skill in leading troops.

Old in years and virtues, but young to the last in human love and sympathy; old in war, old in peace, but young in love and death—this old soldier of the young heart was laid away by battle-scarred comrades to sleep on death's eternal camping ground, where no sound of battle shall be heard, where there shall be no more strife.[256]

HARGIS, J. H.: J. H. Hargis, Commander of Albert Sidney Johnston Camp, of Taylor, Tex., was born in Sequatchie Valley, near Chattanooga, Tenn., July 7, 1844, and died at his home near Taylor, Tex., October 11, 1923, in his eightieth year. In his seventeenth year he entered the Confederate service as a private of Company H, 4th Tennessee Cavalry, Forrest's Brigade, Dibrell's Division, Wheeler's Corps, and participated in all the actions of his command throughout the four years of war. He was once in prison at Johnson's Island, but was never wounded. He was with Forrest when General Streight was captured and when the patriotic young girl, Emma Sansom, rendered such valuable aid.

Comrade Hargis was never married, but made his home with his brother, D. Hargis, at the splendid residence owned jointly by them. He was ever devoted to the cause for which he had fought, and contributed liberally to the work of the U.C.V., organization, as well as to every other good cause. He was commanding his Camp at the time of his death, and was a regular attendant on reunions of his comrades until his health failed.[257]

HARPER, W. B.: Col. W. B. Harper was living in New York City when the Civil War broke out. He came South and joined a company which was formed at Reelfoot Lake, Tenn. The name of the company is not known. He was under Jeff Thompson, General Buckner, and Forrest. In 1864 he resigned and ran a blockade on the steamer *Blenheim* from Wilmington to Nassau. At the close of the war he went to Alabama, where he remained until his death, in 1907.[258]

HARRELL, REUBEN G.: Reuben G. Harrell, a pioneer resident and land attorney of Fresno, Cal., died at his home there on February 19, 1920, of pneumonia. He was born in Gallatin, Tenn., where he spent his boyhood days, the family removing to Dyer County in 1858. He entered the Confederate army in his seventeenth year and served on the staff of Gen. Tyree H. Bell, of Forrest's command, to the close of the war.

Comrade Harrell was married to Susan Bell, a daughter of Gen. T. H. Bell, and went with other members of that family to California in 1876, settling in Fresno County, where he engaged in stock-raising for several years, until his health failed. In 1886 he took up his residence in Fresno City and served as deputy county assessor for eight years. There being much United States land business in this section of California at that time, he qualified as a land law specialist and had his office in the Temple Bar Building for more than twenty-five years, doing much work for the government, as well as private clients, up to the time of his illness. He was an active member of the Methodist Church, South, serving as trustee at the time of his death, and he was always actively interested in the Democratic party [which was the Conservative party until 1896].[259] He is survived by his wife and four daughters.[260]

HARRIS, C. C.: Capt. C. C. Harris, a faithful member of Sterling Price Camp, of Fresno, Cal., died in Fresno on November 16, 1906, aged sixty-six years. He was born near Gallatin, Tenn., in 1840. He enlisted in the Newbern Blues, Capt. W. M. Harrell's company of Colonel Russell's Regiment Tennessee Infantry, at Newbern, Tenn., in May, 1861, and was afterwards promoted to chief of ordnance, Bell's Brigade, Forrest's Cavalry. He participated in all the campaigns and battles of the Army of Tennessee, and was mustered out of service at Gainesville, Ala., May 10, 1865.[261]

HARRIS, GIDEON DOUSE: Gideon Douse Harris was born on the 9th of June, 1846. On the 3rd of September, 1919, while working in his garden, he was stricken with apoplexy, dying almost instantly.

At the early age of sixteen years Gid D. Harris entered the Confederate service as a messenger boy, but in 1863 he became an enlisted member of Company H (Capt. John H. Richards), 6th Mississippi Cavalry (Col. Isham Harrison), Mabry's Brigade, Forrest's Cavalry Corps, and as such he was honorably discharged from the service on the close of the war. He was wounded in one of the battles of his command and carried to his grave the fearsome marks of a Minie ball which crashed through his left elbow joint.

For more than twenty-six years Gid D. Harris was superintendent of the Methodist Sunday school in Columbus, Miss., and was ever faithful, intelligent, cheerful, and a living example to the young of an active Christian, claiming God's promises and obeying his mandates as dictated by the still small voice of an active conscience. Prominent in business and civic affairs as well as in Church affiliations, he will be missed as a splendid example of indefatigable energy, wise business judgment, safe counselor and friend, having for seventy-three years gone in and out before this community with no stain upon his upright character.

He was laid to rest in the Odd Fellows Cemetery on September 4, 1919, where he waits with no fear the coming of his Lord.[262]

HARRIS, JOHN W.: John W. Harris is a Tennessean, born November 24, 1848. He ran away from home in 1863 and joined the army at Jackson and served with the 20th Tennessee Regiment, Bell's Brigade, Buford's Division, Forrest's Cavalry. He was on courier duty most of the time, but took part in the battle of Harrisburg and a number of skirmishes. In January, 1870, he married Miss Susan Corilla Wall, and they had three children, but none are living [as of Autumn 1920].[263]

HARRIS, W. W. S.: On the morning of the last day of the old year 1906, after a lingering illness and much but patient suffering, the soul of W. W. S. ["Billie"] Harris returned to God, who gave it. His death, daily expected for weeks, caused general regret.

Comrade Harris was born in Humphreys County, Tenn., November 17, 1841, where he had lived all his life except the time spent in the Confederate army. No man was better known or more highly respected. He practiced the golden rule by every one. He was loyal to all that was good, great, and noble. His life was like the days, more beautiful in the evening, and like the autumn, rich with golden sheaves when good works and deeds have appeared in the field. He was the last of five brothers and three sisters to "cross the river." His youngest sister (Mrs. Sallie Short, wife of Capt. W. A. Short, who died about four years ago), who was living with him, was found dead sitting in her chair in her room about three hours before his death. It was peculiarly sad—the two funerals and burials of the same family at the same time.

Comrade Harris was a member of Company F, 10th Tennessee Cavalry, which joined Gen. N. B. Forrest during his raid in West Tennessee in 1862, and was in the battle at Parker's Crossroads, where Colonel Napier was killed. He followed the "Wizard of the Saddle" in all of his principal battles and skirmishes until after the battle of Chickamauga, in 1863. During the fall and winter of 1863-64 his command was with General Longstreet's army in East Tennessee. He was with Joseph E. Johnston's army at Dalton, and was under Gen. Joseph Wheeler in all of that famous retreat to Atlanta and until General Hood's raid into Tennessee, when his regiment joined Forrest's command at Florence, Va., and remained with him until the surrender of his army at Gainesville, Ala., where the men were paroled by Major General Canby on May 10, 1865.

After the surrender Comrade Harris returned home to his father's farm, afterwards began merchandising, and was one of the firm of Harris, Rogers & Co., whose business was destroyed in the fire at Waverly November 26, 1883. He was afterwards appointed Clerk and Master of Chancery Court by Judge Seay in 1887, and reappointed by Judges Gribble and Stout, which office he filled until his death.

He was married to Mrs. Tennie Drummond Berglund April 5, 1888, who, with two sons, survives him. A few weeks before his death, while confined to his bed, the Cross of Honor was conferred upon him by the Daughters of the Confederacy. No one could have appreciated the honor more highly or have worn it more worthily. His dying request, that he be buried with Masonic honors (of which he was a member and a long-time treasurer of the Waverly Lodge, No. 304) and that his body be lowered in the grave by old Confederates, was strictly complied with. He was a consistent member of the M. E. Church, South. He was a good soldier, a useful citizen, a true friend, a tender father, a devoted husband, a faithful civil officer, and a Christian gentleman.[264]

Needham Fayette Harrison.

HARRISON, NEEDHAM FAYETTE: Capt. Needham Fayette Harrison, of Germantown, Tenn., died January 10, 1924, at the home of his daughter, Mrs. James Britt, Memphis, Tenn., after a lingering illness. Captain Harrison was eighty-eight years "young" on September 13, as he himself wrote in a short sketch of his life a few days before his death. He was born in Fayette County, Tenn., and moved to Shelby County when eight years of age. In 1861 he enlisted in the Confederate army as a private in Company C, 13th Tennessee, serving throughout the entire four years. He received a serious wound at the battle of Chickamauga, was commissioned first lieutenant after being wounded, and later made captain. He was appointed by Gen. W. A. Collier as brigadier general of the Western Division of Forrest's Cavalry Corps, U.C.V. Captain Harrison was prominent in public affairs for years, and in 1886 he was elected county register. He was also prominent in Masonic circles, and was Grand High Priest of the Royal Arch Chapter of Tennessee. Captain Harrison was a most lovable character, the typical Southern gentleman. After the war he married Miss Fannie E. Neely, sister of the late Col. J. C. and H. M. Neely of Memphis. He is survived by three daughters and two sons.[265]

HATFIELD, JOHN H.: Capt. John H. Hatfield, a member of St. Louis Camp, No. 731, U.C.V., died at the Confederate Home of Missouri, at Higginsville, on February 10 [1932?], at the age of eighty-nine years. He was born in Mesopotamia, Ala., and enlisted in the Confederate army at Aliceville, Ala., in 1861, being one of the original members of Captain McCaa's Rangers, and served with Generals Forrest and Wheeler. He took part in the battle of Missionary Ridge, Shiloh, Brice's Cross Roads, and other bloody engagements, until the close in 1865.

Captain Hatfield came to St. Louis in 1870, and was associated with Samuel C. Davis in a dry-goods company. He was a former Commander of the St. Louis Camp, U.C.V., in a day when the Camp boasted a membership of hundreds, the majority of them being Missourians and citizens of St. Louis who had served the most glorious cause. More recently he was a member of the staff of Gen. William A. Wall, present State Commander of Missouri Confederate Veterans. He was a staunch Democrat [until 1896, a Conservative], the kind most popular in Missouri. The passing of Captain Hatfield is much lamented by his comrades and the members of the Southern Society of St. Louis. He is survived by his wife, three sons, and a daughter.[266]

HAWKINS, A. G.: Hon. A. G. Hawkins, Judge of the Ninth Chancery Division of Tennessee, died at his residence, in Huntingdon, Tenn., May 17, 1906. His son, Clarence M. Hawkins, Private Secretary to Gov. John I. Cox, was with him at the end. His other sons . . . [Prince and Leslie] had been wired of his illness, but did not arrive before his death.

Hon. Albert G. Hawkins was born near Huntingdon April 24, 1841. His father was John M. Hawkins. He was one of thirteen sons, all of whom have held prominent positions. One brother, Ex-Gov. Alvin Hawkins, died last year.

Chancellor Hawkins was reared to manhood on a farm and was educated in the country schools and at the Huntingdon Male Academy. In January, 1861, he went to Shreveport, La., and for five months engaged in teaching school. After his return to his native county, he enlisted in Captain Bryant's company, 55th Tennessee Infantry, C.S.A., and served until 1862, when he came home on account of illness. Recovering, he joined Forrest's Cavalry, and served in that capacity until the close of the war, surrendering at Gainesville, Ala., on May 11, 1865. He was wounded at Brice's Crossroads.

He began to study law in 1861, and resumed it in 1865. He was admitted to the bar in 1866, and practiced for a number of years. He was elected Chancellor of the Ninth District in 1886, and held the office until his death. He was one of the ablest lawyers in Tennessee. In politics he was a Democrat [then a Conservative]. In 1876 he was elected to the Tennessee Senate. In 1880 he was the Democratic elector for the Eighth Congressional District. He was a Mason and a K. of H.

In 1869 Comrade Hawkins married Miss Ellen Prince. To them were born four children, three of whom are living—Prince A. Hawkins, a prominent attorney of Boulder, Colo., Clarence M. Hawkins, Private Secretary to Governor Cox, and Leslie O. Hawkins, who is in school at Ann Arbor, Mich. Judge Hawkins's wife died several years ago, and in 1900 he was married to Miss Kate Van Horn, of Paris, Tenn., who survives him.[267]

HAWKINS, BENJAMIN FRANKLIN: On August 15, 1924, a gallant soldier laid down his arms and went to rest on the other shore. The call came suddenly, but there was no need for Benjamin Franklin Hawkins to make a last peace with God, he so lived his life—gentle, sweet, kindly, God-fearing—that at whatever hour the summons came he was ready to answer: "Here."

Benjamin Franklin Hawkins was born September 5, 1845, at Raleigh, Shelby County, Tenn. When but a lad of sixteen years he enlisted in the Confederate army at Cuba, Tenn. He was taken to Memphis and sworn in for Confederate service June 11, 1861. From 1861 to 1862 he was a member of Company A, 21st Tennessee Infantry, Pillow's Brigade, Polk's Division, Army of the West. In 1862, being under age, and having completed the one year of service for which he enlisted, he was honorably discharged at Tupelo, Miss. He immediately entered the service again, and served on the Confederate government transport, *The Cotton Plant*, from 1862 to 1863. In the winter of 1863, he joined Forrest's Cavalry, Company C, 7th Tennessee Cavalry, Rucker's Brigade, Chalmer's Division, and served with Forrest until the surrender, receiving his parole at Gainesville, Ala., May 11, 1865.

A letter from Comrade J. T. George, Mayfield, Ky., reads: "There was no better soldier in our company than Ben Hawkins; there was no better companion in camp and on the march than Ben Hawkins. He was a great gentleman under all conditions and circumstances."

In 1870 Comrade Hawkins married Miss Nancy Ward. She died some twelve years ago, but he cherished her memory fondly, and each day found him doing some act of kindness because "It would please Nannie." Three sons and two daughters are left to sorrow, and their grief will be the deeper for the memory of his ever-loving indulgence.

A devoted father, a kindly neighbor, a loyal citizen; he will be sadly missed.[268]

HAWKINS, HIRAM PRESTON: As morning dawned on June 6, 1924, Hiram Preston Hawkins, soldier and honored citizen, passed from among us. So reticent and retiring was he in his daily life that many did not know that he was as brave a soldier as ever charged a foe, a follower of the fearless Forrest.

Born near Jordan, Fulton County, Ky., on September 22, 1844, he grew to young manhood in that vicinity and in early life located at Buckskull, Ark. There, in August, 1861, he enlisted in Company A, White's Battalion, Jeff Thompson's Brigade, and served with this command until he was given a furlough to recuperate from a wounded shoulder. During this leave of absence he was with his brother at the old home near Jordan, Ky., and was soon cut off from his Trans-Mississippi Command. Eager to return to the front, he availed himself of a horse which a Federal soldier had "hitched to the rack" in front of a store in Jordan, a saddle was proffered by a friend, and he rode away to join Company B, 12th Kentucky Cavalry. Assigned to scout duty, for which his splendid horsemanship admirably fitted him, he served with Forrest's Cavalry until he received his parole at Paducah, Ky., May 6, 1865.

After the war Mr. Hawkins located in Union City, Tenn., where he resided until he removed to Paducah, Ky., in 1893. On December 8, 1875, he married Miss Lucy E. Jenkins, of Obion County, Tenn., who survives him. One daughter, Mrs. Weightman Smith, of Berkeley, Calif.; two sons, H. P. Hawkins and Edward Carr Hawkins, and one grandson, H. P. Hawkins III, all of Paducah, Ky., are heirs to his record of valor.[269]

HAYNIE, HOUSTON: Houston Haynie was born in Pontotoc County, Miss., November 7, 1845, and spent most of his life there. His father was Elijah B. Haynie, who settled in Mississippi, from Anderson District, S.C., and died in 1846, soon after going to Mississippi.

Houston Haynie grew up in the home of his grandfather Caldwell, and his early career was on a farm, during which time he attended the country schools. In 1862, at seventeen years of age, he enlisted in Company G, of the 48th Mississippi Infantry, under Capt. John N. Sloan and Col. A. B. Hardcastle. Later he was under the command of Col. W. H. H. Tyson, in Lowrey's Brigade, Pat Cleburne's Division, Hardee's Corps, Army of Tennessee. His regiment joined the army at Tullahoma, Tenn., and took part in the famous Atlanta campaign. He was at Chickamauga, Mission Ridge, Ringgold Gap, Resaca, New Hope Church, Kennesaw Mountain, Atlanta, Jonesboro, and was in the big engagement of the 22nd of July, 1864, before Atlanta. With Hood's army, he went back into Tennessee, and captured many Federal prisoners on the way to Franklin. He was engaged in detail duty at the time of the battle of Franklin, and immediately thereafter his company was disbanded, and its members secured horses and many of them joined Forrest's Cavalry. With that famous command, Mr. Haynie engaged in desultory fighting and skirmishing until his surrender at Meridian, Miss.

Only once was he wounded, and that was at New Hope Church. His health was good throughout the service, and when mustered out he was ready to take up the battle of civic life at once. His possessions consisted of the clothes he wore home and a dollar bill on an Atlanta bank. At twenty years of age, he took up farming on his grandfather's place for three years. He then got married, and set up for himself in Union County, which was then a part of Pontotoc County.

The prospect of making a better living for his increasing family induced him to migrate to Texas, a brother having already moved to the Lone Star State. He took his wife and two children to Texas, in 1885, and located in Kaufman County. Two years later he built a home in Kemp, but continued farming and accumulated large acreage, which he sold at a good profit, and invested in land adjoining the town site of Kemp. In 1901 the family became identified with mercantile enterprise, the sons engaging as general merchants under the title of

Haynie Brothers. They are still connected with merchandising there, and among the other family connections are large interests in land in Kaufman and Henderson Counties.

Some years ago, Comrade Haynie organized the First National Bank of Kemp, and was a director and vice president from its organization. He died on the morning of September 2, 1924, having almost completed his seventy-nine years. He was buried in the Kemp Cemetery, by the Odd Fellows, of which order he was a Past Noble Grand.[270]

HENDRICKS, JAMES A.: J. A. Hendricks was born in Simpson County, Ky., in 1833, and when thirteen years old his parents moved to Missouri. In the summer of 1861 he enlisted in Company E, Gilroy's Scouts, Shelby's Brigade, Missouri Volunteers. He rose to the rank of first lieutenant and served to the close of the war. He was in Texas at the surrender, and went with his command into Mexico, returning to Missouri in 1866. He went to Montana in 1884 and engaged in mercantile pursuits. He was one of the organizers of N. B. Forrest Camp of Helena, and was an active and devoted member. His death occurred on April 11 [1904], after a lingering illness. He leaves a wife, five sons, and three daughters.[271]

HIBBLER, JAMES EDMUND: James Edmund Hibbler, son of James L. and Mary A. Hibbler, of Sumter County, Ala., was born on September 20, 1847. His parents, who were people of wealth and culture, removed prior to the War between the States to Noxubee County, Miss., where he was reared.

In the spring of 1863, when scarcely sixteen years of age, he left college to answer his country's call to arms. He joined the 1st Mississippi Cavalry and was a member of Company G, which, with Company F, was known as the Noxubee Squadron, of which Col. R. A. Pinson, their commander, was so justly proud.

There are two survivors of Company G, Mr. A. D. Binion, of Macon, Miss., and Mr. M. J. Clark, of Mobile, Ala. The only survivor of Company F of whom the writer knows is Mr. W. G. White, of West Point, Miss. This gentleman, in writing of Colonel Hibbler, says: "A soldier who was in the 1st Mississippi Cavalry and followed such men as General Ross, of Texas, General Armstrong, of Missouri, Van Dorn, of Louisiana, Gen. Stephen D. Lee through the campaign of Georgia, and Gen. N. B. Forrest in the last campaign in Mississippi and Tennessee were men who were doing their whole duty. Ed Hibbler and I were right together,

James Edmund Hibbler.

marched, fought, and camped together, and we had no better soldier in our regiment than he."

In 1864 Ed Hibbler, in company with three recruits for the 1st Mississippi Cavalry, rode across Alabama and into Georgia just after Hood's army evacuated Atlanta. They were with General Wheeler at first, but after going into Tennessee joined Forrest's Cavalry and were with him until the close of the war.

M. J. Clark pays tribute to his comrade: "Ed was as brave and fearless a soldier as ever served in the army. He was ready to go where duty called him, always at his post, always anxious to go on scouts where he might be able to capture the enemy. He was always full of fun and had a kind word for the boys as he passed them on the march."

The last service he rendered the "boys" was in 1920, when he made arrangements with all of the banks in the county in which he lived to pay the old veterans their pensions, so they could have it before the new year.

Colonel Hibbler's optimism was a great asset. He said he did not mind the reverses of fortune, because his life had been happy. . . .[272]

HIGHT, J. P.: The death of Dr. J. P. Hight, at his home in Fayetteville, Ark., removed one of the prominent and most esteemed residents of that community. His death occurred on January 19, after a short illness, and on the same day he had been presented with the Cross of Honor.

Dr. Hight was born in Bedford County, Tenn., July 7, 1843. His parents were also natives of Tennessee. His maternal grandfather, John Patterson, was a native of Scotland and a descendant of the Patterson who founded the Bank of England. He was educated in the Unionville University, Tennessee, and St. Louis University. With the outbreak of the war in the sixties, he joined the 23rd Tennessee Infantry, with which he served for two years. He was wounded five times and captured four times, escaping three times and being released the fourth. At Chickamauga, he was badly wounded, and was afterwards transferred for scout duty under Forrest.

He was also at Murfreesboro, where he was again wounded. Altogether his service was for more than four years.

After the war, Dr. Hight went to Washington County, Ark., from Tennessee, on foot, giving his only team of horses to his father. He started his career with a capital of two dollars, but within a comparatively few years he built up a considerable fortune. After establishing a home in Arkansas, Dr. Hight engaged in road building, and next in school teaching, later entering a medical college in Missouri. He built up a wide practice, which he followed until his retirement in 1900. He also found time for farming and business dealings, acquiring large holdings in farm and town property. A number of years ago he made a division of his property to his family, desiring to see all his children established in life.

In 1873 Dr. Hight was married to Miss Mary Cladonia Cummings, a native of this county, and six children were born to them. He was a member of the

Knights of Pythias Lodge, and both he and his wife were members of the Christian Church. She survives him with their three sons and three daughters. There are also two brothers and three sisters left of his family.

Working hard in his youth and middle years, he earned, as he said, "a period of quiet in the evening of one's days," taking enjoyment in his retirement, but keeping up his interest in life in general.[273]

HINDMAN, JOSEPH: Joseph Hindman, of Graham, Tex., . . . served under Forrest in the 7th Tennessee Cavalry, Company B. [In 1914 he was eighty-six years old and in feeble health].[274]

Addison D. Holland.

HOLLAND, ADDISON D.: Dr. Addison D. Holland was a Kentuckian, but resided in Arkansas since 1878. He entered the Confederate service at Hopkinsville, Ky., October 6, 1862, in Company G, Woodward's 2nd Kentucky Cavalry, and served under Forrest and Wheeler respectively until the sounding of taps. He was one of the immortal guards to President Davis in the latter's movements southward after the surrender of Gen. J. E. Johnston's army. Dr. Holland was born in Christian County, Ky., July 24, 1843; and died July 11, 1907, at Newport, Ark., where he had practiced dentistry successfully for nearly thirty years.[275]

HOLLEMAN, L. F. A.: L. F. A. Holleman was born in Smith County, Tenn., October 15, 1831, and died at the home of his daughter, Mrs. J. R. Mathis, in Stigler, Okla., on November 4, 1916. At the age of seven years he was converted and joined the Methodist Episcopal Church, South, and was elected a steward at the age of seventeen. Comrade Holleman was a Confederate soldier, brave and true, and his heart was always loyal to the Confederacy. He served with Cheatham's Brigade during the first years of the War between the States; but when General Forrest turned westward on his notable campaign he asked of General Bragg that young Holleman, with the latter's consent, be allowed to go with him, and with this division of the army he remained until the close of the war. He was never wounded.

After the war he went from Alabama to Arkansas, and then some years ago he went to Oklahoma and made his home with his daughter at Stigler.[276]

L. F. A. Holleman.

HOLLOWELL, THOMAS R.: Thomas R. Hollowell was born in Rutherford County, Tenn., September 16, 1839; and died January 9, 1904. On May 28, 1861, at Jackson, Tenn., he enlisted in Company H, Twelfth Tennessee Regiment. He was in the battle of Belmont, Tenn.; also in the two days' fight at Shiloh, where, on the second day and in the last charge his regiment made, he was almost in reach of the flag he was striving to capture, when he was shot three times and fell, with what was supposed to be fatal wounds, with the coveted prize waving directly over his head. He was left on the field for dead, but after recovering consciousness was taken prisoner and sent to Cincinnati, Ohio, then to Camp Dennison. He was offered the privilege but refused to sign the oath of allegiance to the United States. He was from there transferred to Camp Chase, Ohio. After recovering from his wounds, he was exchanged at Vicksburg, Miss., March, 1863, and was then assigned to duty in the purchasing Commissary Department of Cheatham's Division. In March, 1864, he was commissioned to raise Company I, Twenty-First Tennessee Cavalry, which was done, and surrendered at Gainesville, Ala., under Gen. Forrest, at the close of the war.

He was elected trustee of Rutherford County in 1878, and reelected in 1880, and had been in the general merchandise business since 1882.[277]

HOLMAN, JESSE AUSTIN: After a brief illness, Jesse Austin Holman answered the last roll call on May 27, 1922, at his home in Comanche, Tex. He was born in Fayette County, Tex., June 4, 1842, a son of George T. and Nancy Burnam Holman, and a grandson of Capt. Jesse Burnam, of Texas history fame. He graduated from the school at Independence, Tex., in June, 1861, and in August enlisted as a private in Company F, 8th Texas Cavalry, and was reported present at the last roll call of the company, February 28, 1864, as a sergeant. With thirteen others of the 8th Texas Cavalry, he was captured on December 31, 1862, at the battle of Murfreesboro, Tenn., and confined in Camp Douglas, Chicago, Barracks No. 1, White Oak Square. He was exchanged at City Point, Va., April, 1863. His company was first under General Terry and then under General Forrest through all his campaigns, yet Comrade Holman was never on sick leave or in a hospital. Some of his company were not present when Gen. Joseph E. Johnston surrendered at Greensboro, N.C., and afterwards they started to Texas, but, upon learning that the Mississippi was very high, they went before an officer at Tuscaloosa and asked to be paroled. His company was captured by the 2nd Regiment Illinois Cavalry, and paroled, May, 1865.

Returning to Texas, Comrade Holman took charge of the old plantation, his father having died shortly before the close of the war.

He married Miss Mary Folts, and moved his family to Comanche, Tex., in the fall of 1882, where he engaged in the real estate business. Retiring from business a few years ago, he took much interest in building his home. He was one of the best-informed men of the town, a true type of the Southern gentleman, a devout Episcopalian. He leaves his wife, four daughters, and three sons.[278]

HOLT, JOSEPH DANIEL: Dr. Joseph Daniel Holt died at his home near McDade, Tex., November, 1901, and was laid to rest with Masonic honors. He was born in Bedford County, Tenn., graduated from the Medical Department University of Nashville in 1858, and soon after removed to Benton, Ark., where at the beginning of the great war he enlisted in Company F, First Arkansas Mounted Rifles.

Was in first battle at Oak Hills, Mo. He was afterwards transferred to artillery service, Capt. Thrall's Battery, and during the last two years of the war served as surgeon with field hospital corps. At different times he was under Gens. . . . Kirby Smith and Forrest, and was in numerous engagements, including the battle of Chickamauga. He lost four brothers in the Confederate service.

Dr. Holt was made a Master Mason at Tullahoma, Tenn., in 1858, and received Royal Arch Degree, Rupell Chapter No. 65, Stevenson, Ala., June, 1863. After the war he returned to Tullahoma, but went to Texas in 1877 and spent the greater part of his time afterward in Bastrop County practicing medicine.[279]

HOOD, BYNUM H.: Maj. Bynum H. Hood died at his home, in Dawson, Ga., on December 6, 1905, after many months of feeble health.

He was sixty-nine years of age, was born in Meriwether County, and was educated under Morgan H. and George C. Looney in Fayetteville. He enlisted in April, 1861, in Forrest's Brigade, under his teacher, Capt. George C. Looney, and was with him through the Western campaign, in the famous raid on Murfreesboro July 23, 1862, in the battles of Perryville, Chickamauga, and around Atlanta.

Failing health caused his discharge in 1863, but he continued with the army and was detailed by General Hood on his return to Tennessee to get up supplies. He served in this capacity until the surrender, and was mustered out in May, 1865.

He went to Dawson in 1866 to teach school, but soon after became identified with the business interests of that place, and in 1889 was prominently connected with the building of the Columbus Southern Railroad through Dawson.[280]

HOOPER, CHARLES WORD: Gen. Charles Word Hooper, Commander of the Alabama Division, U.C.V., who died at Selma, Ala., on September 6, 1919, was born at Lafayette, Ga., near Rome, the son of Charles Jefferson and Jane Byrd Word. His record as a Confederate soldier was a brilliant one, and the bestowal upon him of the highest honor in the Alabama Confederate Veterans' organization was highly merited and was discharged with credit.

Elected Brigadier General of the Alabama Division, U.C.V., in 1913, General Hooper was two years later, in October, 1915, elected to head the State Division as Commander and was reelected three successive terms by acclamation. Among the achievements credited to his regime is the securing of an appropriation of $1,000 from the State to be used at the yearly Reunions. For the past three years General Hooper devoted his efforts to obtaining a pension of $12.50 per month for every Alabama veteran, a plan which had much opposition at first, even among the ranks of the veterans.

Charles W. Hooper entered the Confederate army as a private in the 8th Georgia Infantry May 17, 1861. He was promoted to the rank of lieutenant in the 21st Georgia Infantry the next year. It was while he was recuperating at his home, near Rome, from wounds received that Streight made his raid on that city. An interesting bit of history is related by Gen. D. E. Scott, adjutant to General Hooper in the U.C.V. organization, who had the story from General Forrest some years ago.

Young Hooper, although still suffering from his wound, organized a company of young men and those exempt from military duty for the defense of Rome. Each man furnished his own equipment, and Hooper was chosen captain. The gallant little company made a juncture with Gen. N. B. Forrest and without the formality of being mustered into the Confederate army.

Streight was captured with their help, and afterwards General Forrest asked Captain Hooper to what command his company belonged.

"None, sir," answered the young captain.

"Will you join my command as an escort?" asked General Forrest.

The matter was favorably voted on by the company, which thenceforth was known as Forrest's Escort, No. 2.

Captain Hooper served as a scout for General Forrest and spent much time within the enemy's lines. His services were dashing and brilliant, and General Forrest years afterwards characterized him as one of the most reliable of that picturesque band of men who were eyes and ears for the army.

When General Forrest surrendered at Gainesville, Ala., May 11, 1865, Captain Hooper was with him and received his parole at the same place.

General Hooper was a man of wide charities and for years past had been one of the most prominent citizens of Selma. As merchant, banker, city builder, his work has been of the enduring and lasting quality which leaves Selma better than when he found it.

Surviving him are two sons and four daughters. The funeral services were very simple, and he was laid to rest attended by many friends.[281]

HOSKINS, JAMES: James Hoskins, who was only fifteen years of age when he left his home in Mississippi and served under Forrest to the end of the war, died on October 22, 1925, at the age of eighty years. He was buried at Atoka.[282]

HOUSE, SAM J.: On the morning of January 16, 1923, Sam J. House died at his home in Sentobia, Miss.

He was born near Huntsville, Ala., April 7, 1841, and moved to Mississippi in the fall of 1859. He enlisted in the Confederate army in 1861, in the first company that was formed in his county, and which was part of the 9th

Mississippi Infantry, commanded by Col. James R. Chalmers. This regiment served twelve months at Pensacola, Fla., and, after being mustered out, reenlisted in different commands, Mr. House going into the cavalry and served through the war as orderly sergeant of General Armstrong's escort company. He was wounded at Thompson's Station, Tenn., while serving under General Van Dorn, and again wounded in the battle around Jonesboro, Ga., while serving under General Forrest. He never lost a day from the beginning to the end of the war, except when wounded, and surrendered with Forrest's Cavalry at Gainesville, Ala., 1865. A more patriotic soldier never donned the gray.

He served as a deputy sheriff for several years after the war, then was elected Chancery Clerk for four consecutive terms of four years each. No official ever kept the records better or was paid more compliments by the judge than he, and no man had more friends. He was not a member of any Church, though he was a believer of the doctrine as taught by the Primitive Baptist Church.

His funeral was conducted by the Baptist and Presbyterian ministers of the town, and he was buried with Masonic honors. Comrade House had been a subscriber of the *Confederate Veteran* since its beginning and looked forward every month to the day when it would arrive. He was the best posted man in the county on Confederate records.[283]

HOWARD, LUTHER M.: Luther M. Howard was born in Columbus, Miss., June 26, 1846; and in April, 1863, at the age of seventeen years, he enlisted in the Confederate army as a member of Company I, 6th Mississippi Regiment, Col. Isham Harrison commanding. Immediately afterwards he marched with the regiment to Big Black River, where the command remained several months.

He was then transferred at Okolona to Forrest's troops, and to Rice's Battery of Artillery just before the battle of Harrisburg. Shortly after this he was sent from Jackson, Tenn., to the Tennessee River to oppose the enemy's gunboats. He served throughout the Tennessee Campaign with Hood's army, and at the end of the retreat was sent to Fort Sidney Johnston, at Mobile, and later to Meridian, Miss.

Returning to Columbus, Comrade Howard resumed his occupation as a stonemason. In 1878 he was married to Mrs. Anna K. Oden. In 1880 he removed to Florida, settling on a small lake in Sumter County. Losing his orange grove in the freeze, he again resumed his trade. In 1890 he moved to West Palm Beach to assist in building the Flagler residence, remaining there sixteen months. He then went to Miami, where he passed the remaining years of his life.

Comrade Howard became a member of Camp Tige Anderson, U.C.V., as soon as it was organized, and was greatly esteemed. He had been a member of the Cumberland Presbyterian Church since December, 1878. He passed quietly away on August 30, 1912, and was buried in Confederate gray, his coffin draped with the flag he loved so well. His wife, a son, and a daughter survive him.[284]

F. A. Howell.

HOWELL, F. A.: [F. A. Howell of Durant, Miss., was a] Brigadier General 1st Brigade Mississippi Division U.C.V.

Enlisted in Company F, 11th Mississippi Regiment, August 16, 1861; was severely wounded at Gettysburg, and on that account entered the cavalry service, joining Company A, 6th Mississippi Cavalry, Mabry's Brigade, Chalmer's Division, under General Forrest, and serving with that command to the surrender at Gainesville, Ala., May 19, 1865. He was one of four brothers in the service who survived the war.[285]

HOWS, STEPHEN H.: Stephen H. Hows, a gallant Confederate soldier and a highly esteemed and beloved citizen, died on April 21 at his home on the Memphis-to-Bristol Highway, near Newsom Station, Tenn., after an illness of several weeks. He was eighty-four years of age.

He was the son of Rasa and Nancy Lovell Hows, born March 15, 1844, at the Hows homestead near the farm where he died. He was the last surviving member of his family.

Young Hows entered the service of the Confederacy during the first year of the war, and was a member of General Forrest's command. He served throughout the war in the 10th Tennessee Regiment, and was paroled at Gainesville, Ala., May 10, 1865.

It is told that he returned home after the war just about election time. A friend, who had been a Union sympathizer, secured for him a voter's certificate and he resumed the right of his ballot at once. Since that time he has voted the straight Democratic [before 1896, the Conservative] ticket in every election for more than sixty years.[286] He always wore the Confederate cross of honor on election day.

Stephen Hows was married, in 1877, to Miss Nancy Lovell, of Pond Creek, who survives him with one daughter. He was a member of the county court for twenty-four years, a charter member of the Davidson county board of education, a Mason for forty years, and a consistent member of the Methodist Church.[287]

HOWSE, AMBROSE: Comrade A. Howse, a native of Rutherford County, Tenn., died at his adopted home, Leger, O.T. [Oklahoma Territory], on March 14, 1903, in his sixty-seventh year. In 1861 Comrade Howse enlisted in the Forty-Seventh Tennessee Regiment. He served in the battles of Shiloh and Corinth, and for gallant service was promoted to the rank of captain, and commanded Company G, Twelfth Tennessee Cavalry, sharing the hardships with Forrest's men to the close of the war. In 1865 he returned to his devastated home in Gibson County, Tenn., where he remained until 1871, when he removed to Johnson County, Tex. In 1891 he moved to Greer

County, O.T., where his family still reside.

Comrade Howse was elected captain of Altus Camp, No. 1417, U.C.V., at its first meeting, and was reelected annually up to the time of his death. Quoting the language of G. H. Kennedy, adjutant of Altus Camp: "Greer County has lost a good citizen, the Methodist Church a zealous worker, and the U.C.V. a faithful comrade."[288]

HOWSE, L. C.: I am grateful that I have lived all these years since the war and am permitted to read the good articles in the *Confederate Veteran* written by the noble men who took part in the struggles of the sixties. I am also thankful that I served nearly three years under Gen. N. B. Forrest in the 14th Tennessee Regiment, and was in such battles as West Point, Harrisburg, Hurricane Creek, the raid into Memphis, and others that showed the [Conservative constitutional] principles of my comrades to be valued more than life itself.

I am also thankful that through it all I was never wounded, although I had one horse killed under me. I was paroled at Gainesville, Ala., in May, 1865. I am also thankful I have reared a family of useful men and women.[289]

HUBBARD, DAVID: David Hubbard was born in North Alabama, but after the war had lived in Louisiana and Mississippi until his death, at Terry, Miss., November 5, 1904. His father, Maj. David Hubbard, was a gallant soldier under Gen. [Andrew] Jackson in the war of 1812, and during the War between the States was Commissioner of Indian Affairs. His son, Maj. David Hubbard, organized a battalion of cavalry early in 1861.

After the battle of Shiloh, in which his battalion served with gallantry, at the suggestion of his friend, Gen. Leonidas Polk, he returned to Alabama and recruited additional companies to make a regiment of his battalion; but the Confederate government, needing more infantry at that time than cavalry, had them mustered into that branch of service, and Maj. Hubbard resumed command of his battalion with just a sufficient number of his new recruits to make it full. Soon after this, in a sharp little engagement with the enemy, a shell exploded near his head, injuring his hearing so that it incapacitated him for a time from service. As soon as his hearing was sufficiently restored he organized a company of scouts and reported to Gen. Forrest, with whom he served until the surrender.

His wife and three children, a son and two daughters, survive him. Maj. Hubbard's two brothers were in the Confederate army. Duncan C. Hubbard served on the staff of Gen. Beauregard and George Hubbard was killed in the severe battle at Baker's Creek.[290]

HUDSON, C. T.: C. T. Hudson, who died at the age of eighty-four years, was born and reared near his late home, and held the highest esteem of the people of that section. During the sixties he followed the fortunes of the Confederacy under Bedford Forrest, and was true to his colors. He was twice married, and is survived by six children, three of each marriage.[291]

HUDSON, THOMAS: In the death of Thomas Hudson, aged eighty-two, during November, 1923, the last survivor of the famous Canebrake Rifle Guards has passed. He was born at Uniontown, Ala., and had lived there nearly all of his life, being at one time an enterprising newspaper man. He had owned and edited the Marion Standard, and also established two other papers.

Comrade Hudson was a charter member of the Masonic Lodge and the Knights of Pythias, of Uniontown, and an active member of the Presbyterian Church. He was an alumnus of the University of Alabama and of the University of Virginia. Leaving the latter institution when Alabama seceded from the Union, he returned to Uniontown and joined the Canebrake Rifle Guards in the spring of 1861, and surrendered with General Forrest's command at Gainesville, Ala., in the spring of 1865. Surviving him are four sons and a daughter.[292]

HUDSON, WILLIAM: At the age of eighty-one, Comrade Will Hudson has passed over the river. He enlisted in April, 1862, in Company A, 14th Tennessee Cavalry, under Bedford Forrest, and was with him until the retreat from Nashville, when he was cut off from his command and could not get back. Only four of this company made it through with the command to Gainesville, Ala., out of the one hundred and twenty-five in the battle of Franklin. The survivors of the company never got together any more.

Comrade Hudson was only a private, always ready to answer to his name. He was of the Primitive Baptist faith and is sadly missed in the councils of his Church. Only a short while, and we will all be "tenting on the other shore."[293]

James H. Hughen.

HUGHEN, JAMES H.: James H. Hughen died at the home of his daughter, Mrs. C. B. Gentry, in Saline County, Ark., on January 18, 1922. He was born in South Carolina, July 21, 1826, but his parents moved to Georgia while he was young. He united with the Methodist Church at the age of eighteen, and was teacher and superintendent of a Methodist Sunday school sixty-one years. He was living in Jackson County, Ala., when the War between the States came on. He loved the Southland, and bared his breast against the invading foe. Joining the 4th Alabama Regiment under Captain Smyth, he followed General Forrest in many of his campaigns. When the war ended he returned to his home to find it almost completely destroyed. In 1871 he took his family to Arkansas and there made his home until the summons came calling him away from the trials of life. Slowly and peacefully he sank to rest. He was nearly blind for two years, but, during the last year his eye sight returned. He read the *Confederate Veteran*, and read the Testament through six times.[294]

HUGHES, C. B.: C. B. Hughes [served in] . . . the 2nd Company F, 12th (10) Mississippi Cavalry, which was under General Forrest . . .^{295}

HUGHES, JAMES DOUGLAS: James Douglas Hughes, born January 15, 1847, in Jackson, Miss., died June 24, 1929, at San Diego, Calif.

At the beginning of the war in 1861, James Douglas Hughes ran away from home to join the Confederate army. His ambition was to join Col. John H. Morgan's command in Tennessee, and, boylike, he succeeded, traveling most of the way on foot from Jackson to Memphis, then to Nashville in an ox-cart. Going to Morgan's camp, he was placed in Captain Crutchfield's company, later being transferred to Company A, Forrest's 5th Cavalry Regiment; and after the battle of Shiloh, he was placed in the 1st Alabama Regiment, Company I. At Altoona, Ga., his last battle, he was wounded in the left hip and his right eye was also injured by the explosion of a shell. He was then taken to Alabama and put in the enrolling department, under Major Stone and Capt. Henry J. Beebe, later being transferred to the medical examining board.

Mr. Hughes came to California about forty years ago. He was the last member of the Maj. Hugh Gwyn Camp, U.C.V., of San Diego, and after it went out of existence, he was made an honorary member of the Stonewall Jackson Chapter, U.D.C., of San Diego, and the Daughters cared for him in his declining years. He was totally blind, the injury to his eye having caused complete loss of sight in time. He was a Mason and a member of the Methodist Church.

Mr. Hughes was laid to rest beside his wife in the Chapter's Confederate Plot in Mount Hope Cemetery, San Diego. The Confederate flag was draped over the casket, and red and white flowers were banked about it as a last tribute to our beloved soldier of the Confederacy.^{296}

HUMPHRIES, JOHN PITTMAN: The death of John Pittman Humphreys, on August 20, 1924, in Collierville, Tenn., removed from our community one of the few remaining Confederate veterans.

He was born in Marshall County, Miss., August 23, 1847, being the eldest son of John W. and Ann Turner Humphreys. His education was received in Chalmers Institute, of Holly Springs, Miss., and, finishing his academic course, he was preparing for the study of law when he entered the Confederate army. In May, 1863, not being quite sixteen, he enlisted in Company C, 18th Mississippi Cavalry, and served under General Forrest throughout the remainder of the war. During Forrest's campaign in Middle Tennessee, he acted as courier to General [E. W.] Rucker, a position of trust.

On January 23, 1872, he was married to Miss Margaret Emily Canon, of Holly Springs, Miss. Five children blessed this happy union, all of whom survive, with four grandchildren and two great-grandchildren. Mrs. Humphreys died in 1910, and during the latter years of his life he had the devoted care of his daughter, Ann Turner Humphreys, who was his companion in the home.

Mr. Humphreys was a devoted member of the Presbyterian Church and a Mason. He came to Collierville in 1876, and to the time of his death remained actively interested in the upbuilding of his town and community. He served many terms as mayor and vice mayor, was a member of the Shelby County Court for fifteen years, and chairman for one term.

The Louisa Bedford Chapter, U.D.C., loses a loyal friend. He was a devoted husband and father, a brave soldier, a good citizen, a Christian. "God's finger touched him and he slept."[297]

HUNT, THOMAS WINN: Captain Hunt, a son of Abijah Hunt and Mary Walton, of Jefferson County, Miss., born February 21, 1842, died September 30, 1895, in St. Paul, Minn. He was the grandson of David Hunt, one of the grand characters of long ago, who was a power in his community, always giving liberally to the advancement of religion and education, a boon to his friends and neighbors in times of stress, and deeply mourned by them at his death in 1861.

On April 1, 1861, Thomas Winn Hunt was commissioned adjutant and second lieutenant in the Confederate States army and ordered to report to General Bragg at Pensacola, Fla.; and about September, 1861, he was ordered to report to Gen. A. S. Johnston, at Columbus, Ky. In January, 1862, he was ordered to report to Gen. William J. Hardee, at Bowling Green, Ky., and acted as A.D.C. to that officer until December 31, 1862, when he was commissioned as captain and acting adjutant inspector general, P.A.C.S., until December 1864. He was then ordered, by request, to report as Assistant Inspector General to General Jackson, commanding division of Gen. N. B. Forrest's Cavalry Corps. He was paroled May 18, 1865, at Columbus, Miss. He was with General Hardee from January, 1862, until 1865.[298]

HUNTER, THOMAS: R. W. Macpherson, "an unreconstructed old Rebel" of Toronto, Canada, writes of the death of [a] good friend up there, Thomas Hunter, who gave four years of his life to the Southern Confederacy. Comrade Macpherson says: "Poor Tom cashed in [died] in February 1922. He joined Forrest's Cavalry from Glasgow, Ky.; was for many years a prominent citizen and alderman here, and an ardent Confederate. There was a sprinkling here of irreconcilable 'Confeds'—Dr. Oliphant, of New Orleans; Ovenden, of Hood's Texans; and a number of others, all fallen out by command except myself and first Sergeant Sutherland, of Forrest's Cavalry, groggy, but still in the ring at eighty-eight, and able to tackle a Yankee of his age. Colonel Mosby visited me in 1914, just before the trouble in Europe began [World War I]. He lectured at the Military Institute here to several hundred Canadian officers, most of whom were later wiped off at Ypres and other places. Toronto, with a population of over 600,000, sent to the big war 60,000 men...."[299]

IJAMS, J. C.: Capt. J. C. Ijams was born near Corinth, Miss., on May 26, 1844, and died at his home, in Marietta, Okla., on December 17, 1918, after a brief illness of influenza. In 1863, at Tuscumbia, Ala., he enlisted in the Confederate army, serving in W. Y. Baker's company (A), Baxter's Battalion, Forrest's Regiment, 19th Tennessee Cavalry.

He participated in the battles of Jackson, Tenn., Athens, Pulaski, Franklin, Brice's Crossroads, and Harrisburg, Miss. He surrendered on May 11, 1865, at Gainesville, Ala. After the war he returned to his home in Mississippi, and on February 25, 1873, he was married to Miss Julia M. Smith. Four children survive this union.

J. C. Ijams.

Captain Ijams was prominent as a Confederate veteran, having served one term as Superintendent of the Confederate Home at Ardmore, Okla. No one enjoyed more the companionship of his veteran comrades, and one of his chief pleasures was attending the Confederate Reunions.

He was a consistent member of the Baptist Church and was ever identified with the best interests of his community, having served as mayor and holding other positions of trust. At the time of his death he was Commander of Camp Rice, U.C.V., of Marietta.

A daughter of Captain Ijams, Mrs. Mary L. Haydon, served as matron of the Confederate Home at the time he was superintendent. Only six days after his death she also died of influenza. Mrs. Haydon was a member of the Chickasaw Chapter, No. 299, Oklahoma Division, U.D.C.[300]

IRELAND, RUFUS MORGAN: Rufus Morgan Ireland, member of a pioneer Tennessee family, and one of the few surviving members of Forrest's Cavalry, died at his home in Nashville, Tenn., on November 2 [1930?], after many months of failing health, aged eighty-six years.

Mr. Ireland's forebears settled in Tennessee in the period preceding the War of the Revolution, and for generations his family had taken an active part in the life of the State. He was born on the plantation of his father in Sumner County, where he spent his early boyhood. The son of Benjamin R. Ireland and Fanny Stratton, he lived on the Sumner County plantation until the outbreak of the War between the States, when he enlisted in Forrest's Cavalry, serving throughout the conflict under that famous general. At the close of the war, he returned to his home, later moving to Nashville, where he was connected with the Nashville, Chattanooga, and St. Louis Railway, and later he represented the railway company in the capacity of agent at Lebanon, Tenn.

For many years he has made Nashville his home, being actively engaged in business here until his advanced age forced his retirement.

In 1878, he married Miss Addie Frances Kelly, of New Orleans, and for fifty-two years he and his wife, who survives him, were an example of lifelong devotion. All who knew him were strongly impressed by the kindliness of his character. In addition to his wife, two sons and two daughters survive him, also a foster-daughter and several grandchildren.[301]

IRVINE, ADAM COLEMAN: After several weeks of illness, Capt. A. C. Irvine passed away January 12, 1908, at his home, in Gainesville, Tex.

Adam Coleman Irvine came from a long line of distinguished citizens of Virginia and Kentucky. His grandfather was a hero of the early struggles in the "Dark and Bloody Ground." His uncle was a major in the War of 1812, and became a prisoner of the English when General Winchester was defeated at the battle of River Raisin, on January 22, 1813. After the war he served as a member of the Kentucky Legislature. Another uncle, David Irvine, was County Clerk of Madison County for forty years.

His father, Albert G. Irvine, removed to Missouri in 1835, and in 1837 married Mrs. Ann Howell Brown, who had returned from Texas as the widow of Capt. John Brown, who came to Texas in 1824. (Captain Brown was a prisoner among the Indians for eighteen months, and was afterwards a merchant in San Antonio.) The father of Captain Irvine was a pious man and filled a local Methodist pulpit in Kentucky; but he was game, and would brook no insult. He was once insulted in Cincinnati by a burly policeman; and quickly throwing off his ministerial coat, he administered a good thrashing to the minion of the law.

At the age of twenty Adam C. Irvine enlisted in Troop K, 3rd Texas Cavalry, and served throughout the war without ever returning home. Of his Texas commanders were Whitfield and Ross. Later he was with W. H. Jackson, while in the latter part of the war he was with Forrest. His first battle was Oak Hills, Mo. In 1862 he was in the battle of Elkhorn, where Generals McCulloch and McIntosh fell. He crossed the Mississippi with Gen. Van Dorn.

In the reorganization at Corinth he was elected lieutenant, and soon afterwards became first lieutenant. He was with Beauregard in the retreat from Tupelo, and was in the battle of Iuka. In Van Dorn's great raid on Holly Springs he commanded the scouts. In the fight at Middleburg he was highly complimented for his work and was promoted to a captaincy.

As captain of scouts at Yazoo and at Thompson's (?), his company faced such a terrible fire that three-fourths of his men were killed or wounded. On that field, it will be remembered, Gen. Van Dorn was shortly afterwards murdered,[302] and on that field Captain Irvine met Miss Mary Moss, who now survives him as his widow. As a captain in Ross's Brigade, he saw service day and night for four weeks on picket duty, as his command covered the retreat to Jackson. The hard service in sandy bottoms caused Captain Irvine to lose his sight, and he was in the hospital for some time; but recovered in time to lead the raid on Bolton Depot and the capture of the place with many prisoners. He next encountered seventy-four [Yankee] negroes while in a flanking party near Vicksburg, and it is stated that only two of them and one of their white officers escaped alive.

Under General Forrest Captain Irvine participated in the battles at Franklin and Murfreesboro. Later he went West with Ross, and his command surrendered at Clinton, La., on June 22, 1865.

After the war he returned to Texas, and in 1870 returned to Tennessee, where he again met Miss Moss; and on October 11, 1870, they were married. They lived for ten years in Pulaski, and then returned to Texas. He had been in Gainesville for many years, and was a man who was loved by all who knew him. At the time of his death he was Quartermaster General of the Third Division of Forrest's Cavalry, United Confederate Veterans. Captain Irvine is survived by a widow and one daughter, Mrs. Oscar F. Scott, of Gainesville.[303]

IRWIN, JAMES W.: Captain James W. Irwin, of McMinnville, Tenn., appointed by the Secretary of War, Mr. Lamont, United States Agent for the purchase of the battlefield of Shiloh for a National Military Park is native of Hardin county, and was reared in the vicinity of this historic place. He enlisted in the army in '61, and served in the First Confederate Cavalry Regiment to the close of the war. He is a member of Cheatham Bivouac, Nashville.

Captain Irwin was in the battle of Shiloh. His regiment served under Gen. Joe Wheeler after his transfer to cavalry, and afterward was with that gallant command which "participated in nearly one hundred battles and skirmishes." After the battle of Nashville the First Confederate was transferred to Gen. Forrest, and served under him to the end of the war. At the surrender it was in the Division of Gen. William H.

James W. Irwin.

Jackson—"Old Red"—at Gainesville, Ala., May 11th, 1865.

Capt. Irwin is of Revolutionary patriots on both sides. His father came at an early day from Pennsylvania to Tennessee. His mother was Nancy Sevier, born and reared in Green County, East Tenn., a member of that illustrious family. Capt. Irwin is a practical business man, and this selection is wise and safe for the government.[304]

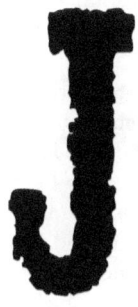

JACKSON, WILLIAM HICKS: Surrounded by his devoted children and other nearest relatives, Gen. W. H. Jackson fell peacefully asleep on the night of March 31 [1903], at historic Belle Meade, the fairest of all the Southland's fair homes, made beautiful by a combination of early traditions and nature's choicest endowments.

Gen. Jackson was born in Paris, Tenn., October 1, 1835. Both his father and his mother (Dr. A. Jackson and Mrs. Mary Hurt Jackson) were Virginians, who removed to West Tennessee in 1830. As a boy he was manly and courageous, and by nature endowed for the stirring scenes in which he was to participate. While a member of the senior class of the West Tennessee College he received an appointment to West Point, entering the academy in 1852. He graduated with credit in the large class of 1856, and the following year joined the Mounted Rifles on the Mexican border and learned stern lessons of soldiering in Indian fighting. From 1857 to 1861 he was second lieutenant under Col. W. W. Loring. When the great conflict came, he was in the field against the Apaches near Fort Staunton, N. Mex. His record had been enviable. For faithfulness in the performance of duty and gallantry in the field he had been highly complimented by the War

William Hicks Jackson.

Department. Such was his record in the United States army when the Civil War became inevitable. Squaring his accounts with the government, he tendered his resignation, and with Col. Crittenden, of Kentucky, made his way to New Orleans.

Through Maj. Longstreet he tendered his services to the South, being at once commissioned a captain of artillery by the Governor of Tennessee. As an officer of the Confederate States he won his claim to military distinction by the brilliancy of his achievements on many fields. At Belmont he led a brilliant charge of infantry, which nearly cost him his life, the minie ball that entered his side remaining there. Holly Springs and Lovejoy Station, against the dashing Kilpatrick, were steps by which he rose to recognition as a cavalry leader. Then, in company with Forrest leading the Confederate advance into Tennessee and covering the retreat of Hood, his services again were of a nature to be considered worthy of higher command, and he was assigned to a division, leading it to the end of the war. At the close of the war he was assigned as commissioner for the parole of troops at Guntersville, Ala., and Columbus, Miss.

Gen. Jackson brought with him from the great war, in addition to the Federal bullet, a reputation as a gallant soldier which survived the forty years of peace. But it was as proprietor of beautiful Belle Meade [Plantation] that he was best known in the middle and later years of his life. So intimately was his name associated with the superb establishment, the cradle of so many of the racing traditions of the country, that his retirement and dispersal in May last were spoken of as the end of an era in the Southern country. With the close of the war he had returned to his father's plantation and taken up the latter's interests, superintending them with profitable results.

Belle Meade Plantation, Nashville, Tenn. (Photo Lochlainn Seabrook)

In 1868 he married Miss Selene Harding, daughter of Gen. W. G. Harding, of Belle Meade, and became intimately associated with his father-in-law in the latter's varied interests. These interests involved not only the extensive management of the various departments of a plantation and stock farm, but broadened into a deep, humanitarian sympathy and affection for generation after generation of faithful negroes employed, whose comfortable homes, in the shadow of "the house," felt the influence of its genial kindliness.

Gen. Jackson's brother, the late Howell E. Jackson, of the United States Supreme Court, married Miss Mary Harding, a daughter of Gen. W. G. Harding, the two families sharing the magnificent estate near Nashville.

Up to the time of his death Gen. Jackson kept alive the spirit of ante-bellum days, and white and black alike, from the President of the United States down to the humblest negro, appreciated the quality of welcome that went with his firm grasp of the hand and deep-voiced assurance, "I am glad to see you!" There must be glad welcome from the shores of eternity for the spirit of one who has cheered the stranger within his gates and given shelter to those who have craved his bounty and with confidence sought his help.

The funeral of Gen. Jackson was conducted by his warm personal friend and associate in arms, Col. D. C. Kelley, now an eminent minister of the Methodist Church and at the head of Forrest Cavalry Corps of Veterans.[305]

JAMES, JOHN A.: John A. James died at his home, in Hattiesburg, Miss., February 20, 1905. He was born in Arkansas in 1840, was reared in Tennessee, and during the war served in Company G, 4th Regiment Tennessee Cavalry, under Forrest. He was married in Nashville, Tenn., in 1868, and spent many years of his life in that city. His wife and eight children survive him. Hattiesburg Camp, No. 21, U.C.V., adopted resolutions in his honor.[306]

JARVIS, RICHARD ABNER: On October 22, 1918, Richard Abner Jarvis, of Hansford, Tex., answered the last roll call on earth. Born February 7, 1845, near DeKalb, Miss., he enlisted in the Confederate army at that place in September, 1862, as a private in Company I, 5th Mississippi Cavalry, Harris's Brigade, Chalmers's Division, Forrest's Corps. He was in the siege of Vicksburg, serving as sharpshooter most of the time, and with his company was quartered in the courthouse at the time it was blown up by a mortar shell, killing many of the company. He was in the fighting at Harrisburg, Selma, and several smaller battles; was wounded several times. He was captured on July 4 and afterwards paroled, but reenlisted later in the 6th Mississippi Cavalry. At Harrisburg his cartridge box was cut from his belt and his gun knocked from his hand by grapeshot. He was near his colonel, Isham D. Harrison, at the time he was wounded. As a comrade, Henry Edwards, raised the colonel in his arms, a bullet pierced the arm of Edwards, causing him to drop the body of Colonel Harrison.

Richard Abner Jarvis and wife.

Comrade Jarvis surrendered with his command at Gainesville, Ala. He then returned to Mississippi, locating near DeKalb, and in December, 1869, he was married to Miss Martha L. Murray, a descendant of the Adamses of historic fame. To this union were born seven children, three sons and four daughters, all of whom survive, with their mother.

In 1872 Mr. Jarvis removed to Texas and settled near the line of Fannin and Grayson Counties, later going to Bolivar, in Denton County, and in 1902 he removed to Hansford County, where he died. He was buried in the Lieb

Cemetery, near his home, attended by a large concourse of people, many from other counties. His Confederate comrades were among the pallbearers, while Sons of Confederate Veterans marched in front, with Confederate *and United States flags* at half-mast, to the soft beat of the drum. Thus in the midst of his sorrowing family—wife, children, grandchildren, and friends—the body of this brave Southern soldier was borne to the grave. Devoted to his family, a loving and tender husband and father, a loyal, patriotic citizen, a faithful friend and neighbor, a consistent and devout Christian, an honorable, upright man, he leaves a rich heritage in character and a strong witness to Christianity in his life and death.[307]

W. B. Jennings.

JENNINGS, W. B.: Col. W. B. Jennings, one of the best-known and most highly esteemed Christian gentlemen of Moberly, Mo., died from an operation on May 1, 1911.

Comrade Jennings served throughout the war in Clark's Battery, afterwards Kings and then Farris's, most of the time in Forrest's command, until the close of the war. He was a good and faithful member of Marmaduke Camp, U.C.V., and he was in the service of the Wabash Railroad Company for forty years in the freight department. He was a noble soldier, true to any trust imposed in him, and as a citizen commanded the respect of all with whom he came in contact. A good comrade is gone. Peace to his ashes.[308]

JETTON, CHARLES WESLEY: Capt. Charles Wesley Jetton died at his home, in Murray, Calloway County, Ky., August 19, 1913, aged seventy-five years. He was born and reared in Calloway County, and lived there all his life, excepting four years spent in the Confederate army.

He entered the army in October, 1861, in Company H, 7th Kentucky Infantry, as a private, but soon thereafter was made first sergeant, which position he resigned a few weeks later in deference to an old friend recently recruited.

In May, 1862, he was elected first lieutenant, and a few weeks later was elected captain, which position he held until February, 1865, when the 3rd and 7th Kentucky, then mounted infantry serving with General Forrest, were consolidated.

Captain Jetton was then elected captain of Company F, of the consolidated 3rd and 7th Kentucky Mounted Infantry. This compliment was the more pronounced because Captain Jetton was at that time absent on detached service; for there were several splendid senior officers displaced by the consolidation of the two regiments, and these consolidated offices were much sought.

Captain Jetton fought at Shiloh, Corinth, Hatchie Bridge, Vicksburg, Baker's Creek, Big Black River, Raymond, Jackson, Paducah, Brice's Crossroads, Harrisburg, Old Town Creek, Athens, Sulphur Trestle, Tarpley's Shop, Pulaski, Tenn., and in all the battles incident to Hood's Nashville Campaign. He was wounded at Tarpley's Shop, near Pulaski, Tenn., September 27, 1864, when temporarily in command of the regiment.

He was always a conspicuous figure on the battle field, for he was brave almost to a fault, yet wholly without ostentation or flurry. He was quiet and considerate of those under his command. In his death the regiment loses a link with the past, and the battle line that knew him so well then (he never missed a battle) will know him here no more; but when the roll is called up yonder he will be there. He was always benign, to the fullest extremity, to the men of the company, and his goodness to them at all times was beyond the power of eulogy.

Charles Wesley Jetton and wife.

Captain Jetton was mentioned in regimental orders at Baton Rouge for burning the Federal cantonments there on August 5, 1862, under orders with a small detachment and in the presence of both armies and under a tremendous enfilading Federal fire of musketry and artillery. He did the work well and with much alacrity, eliciting the applause of the Confederates who witnessed the achievement.

He was the father of the late Charles Jetton, an eminent young lawyer of Murray, Ky., and leaves an aged widow, the wife of war days, who shared the many vicissitudes common to the women of the South during the war period, two married daughters, and several grandchildren.[309]

JOBE, WILLIAM L.: [William L. Jobe was a member of the 15-man squad which made up Morton's Battery, of Forrest's Cavalry.][310]

JOHNSON, ADAM RANKIN: Kentucky has produced many remarkable characters, but few of them, however, will be found more worthy of honorable mention than Gen. Adam Rankin Johnson. He was a distinguished brigadier, and doubtless many old Kentuckians who knew of the fearful wound he sustained will be surprised to learn that he is still alive. Gen. Johnson lost his sight from a wound received in battle during the Confederate war, and for more than thirty years night and day have been alike to him. During all these years of darkness he has been alive to every impulse that moves an active citizen and a restless, energetic business man.

He resides in the town of Marble Falls, Tex., a little city of his own making. He selected the location, and the town had its conception in a brain that can only picture its streets and public buildings and its picturesque beauty in imagination. He was the prime mover and energetic central figure of the great enterprise which resulted in the erection of a gigantic cotton mill building at the great falls of the Colorado. (This building is three stories high and 300 x 100 feet, and grew in the brain of this blind man long before a dollar had ever been raised to pay for its construction.) He is the father of the town, and through his untiring energy and the donation of grading the road (which cost $40,000) he induced the Austin and Northwestern Railway Company to construct a branch from Burnet.

Gen. Johnson can be seen upon the streets almost every day during business hours. He walks with his head erect, much faster than many younger men who possess all their faculties, and no one would ever dream that the man was pushing along in darkness were it not that he is usually accompanied by a little boy who holds one of his hands. He seems to be perfectly familiar with the step and voice of every human being in the town, and seldom makes a mistake in calling the names of persons who pass or address him. He has recently been engaged in constructing a mill and harnessing a water power to furnish the city with water. Everything has been done according to his plans and under his direct supervision. He closely examines every piece of machinery, every rock, and every wall.

Adam Rankin Johnson.

Gen Johnson is one of the pioneers of Texas. He went there in 1854, and settled on the extreme frontier, where people herded their stock and cultivated their fields with weapons at their belts. He was personally acquainted with many noted Indian fighters, and he participated in many of the battles and stirring scenes that are now regarded with thrilling interest by the rising generation.

During the civil war he was one of the confidential scouts of Gen. Forrest until after the evacuation of Corinth.[311] He was ordered into Kentucky on the night of the evacuation on secret service, and with only one tried friend he flanked the great Federal armies and reached safely his destination in Kentucky, and there, isolated from any aid from the Confederacy, raised, mounted, and equipped over two thousand men, drawing his arms and ammunition from the enemy. With the aid of only two men, Col. R. M. Martin, now of Louisville, and Capt. F. A. Owen, of Evansville, Ind., he attacked the [Yankee] provost guard in the town of Henderson, killing and wounding the captain and lieutenant and eight or nine soldiers. With twenty-seven men he crossed the Ohio River and made the first capture during the war north of the Mason and Dixon line (Newburg, Ind.), carrying off over five hundred stands of arms and paroling one hundred and seventy men. This gave him the sobriquet of "Stovepipe Johnson," as he used stovepipes to imitate cannon, and threatened to shell the town, thus causing the surrender. The capture of Henderson, Hopkinsville, Clarksville, and Uniontown, with their garrisons, and many other desperate engagements of his, are worthy of record.

He commanded one of Morgan's brigades on the Ohio raid, and afterwards reorganized that command and commanded it during the Battle of Chickamauga. Later, on his second expedition, which was a forlorn hope, he entered Kentucky with fifty-five men and officers, issuing his conscript order that caused Burbridge and Hobson to suspend their secret expedition into Virginia and turn their forces against him. This has been considered one of the most daring and successful feats of the war, and President Davis himself said that it did as much to prolong the war as any other movement. It was in this expedition that he lost his sight, August 20, 1864. He was the only blind man on either side that was confined in prison, and when solicited by Attorney-General Speed and Gov. Powell, of Kentucky, to release him, Lincoln replied "that he thought he was worth swapping," and he was exchanged. When he returned to Texas he took his place on the frontier, which was then being harassed by Comanche Indians, and did much to check them.[312]

JOHNSON, DANIEL SARTOR: On the 16th of January, 1919, the gentle spirit of Comrade Daniel S. Johnson passed from earth. He had reached the advanced age of eighty-seven years.

He was a Confederate soldier, having served from April, 1864, to May, 1865, as a member of Company E, 8th Mississippi Cavalry, Stark's Brigade, Ricker's (later Chalmer's) Division, Forrest's Corps. He was captured by Wilson's troops at the fall of Selma, Ala. A month or so later he was paroled and returned to his home, in Chickasaw County, Miss., and resumed his occupation as a farmer.

As an ante-bellum slave owner he was such a kind and indulgent master that most of his slaves continued on the plantation of "Mars Dan" many years after being freed [a widespread but seldom discussed occurrence across postbellum Dixie].[313]

Comrade Johnson was so highly esteemed by his community that he was elected Supervisor for two or more terms. Then for 1890 he was chosen as a delegate to Mississippi's great Constitutional Convention. It was at this convention that statutory laws were changed and new ones enacted to conform to the then existing conditions brought about by misrule of carpetbaggers, scalawags, and negroes from 1870 to 1876.[314]

He was a member of Houston Lodge, A. F. and A. M., and was for many years a member of the Chickasaw County Board of Education. He was a steward of the Methodist Church, South, for more than fifty years and was superintendent of his Sunday school for thirty-five years before his death.

His wife, who was Miss Cornelia Tucker, died many years ago, and of their six children five survive him. One son, Dr. Daniel S. Johnson, is now in the Medical Reserve, A.E.F., in Germany.

Our comrade truly lived a life of sacrifice for his country and his family. A good man has gone to his reward.[315]

JOHNSON, JOHN N.: After a brief illness, Gen. John N. Johnson, Commander of the Forrest Cavalry Association, and President of the Pension Board of Tennessee, died in Nashville in the early morning of February 4, in his eighty-fifth year. He had also been Commander of the Camp at Bristol, Tenn., where he lived at one time, and of the Forrest Camp of Chattanooga, which city had been his home just before coming to Nashville. Forrest Camp once numbered a membership of 558 veterans of the Confederacy, now reduced to seventeen.

General Johnson was given a military burial in the Confederate Circle of Mount Olivet Cemetery, with the Confederate Ritual, after lying in state two days at the State Capitol.

Although a mere lad when the war came on in 1861, John N. Johnson twice ran away from home to fight, and was brought back each time; but in 1864 he was allowed to enlist, and entered the ranks of Company C, 1st Battalion, Kentucky Cavalry, and thus became one of Morgan's men. Cut off from his command during a battle at Cynthiana, Ky., he and his companions wandered for days through enemy territory. Finally, after swimming their horses across the river at Paducah, the party made its way to Corinth, Miss., and there became attached to Forrest's command.

At Harrisburg, Miss., this young soldier was left for dead on the field of battle, and, when peace did come, found himself in a hospital at Jonesboro, Tenn., not many miles from his birthplace in Bedford County, Virginia.

John N. Johnson was born August 18, 1847, his parents being descendants of English nobility. The family removed to Bristol, Va.-Tenn., while he was still young, and there he attended private schools, later going to Emory and Henry College and then studying under tutors here and abroad.

In 1882, General Johnson was married to Miss Lucy Herndon Botts, of Savannah, Ga., where he was then in business, and three children were born to them, a son and two daughters. Ten years after marriage, he bought a large farm near Bristol, Tenn., where he lived for some years, dealing in real estate. He located in Chattanooga in 1912.

General Johnson recently became a member of the 109th Calvary, Tennessee National Guard, with the honorary rank of Colonel. He held the rank of Major General in the United Confederate Veteran Association.[316]

JOHNSON, SIDNEY SMITH: Sidney Smith Johnson was born in Choctaw County, Miss., April 19, 1840. His father moved to Texas and settled in Cherokee County in 1849, and came to Tyler in 1854. He died in Tyler, Tex., January 26, 1910, and was buried by his old comrades in Oakwood Cemetery, where his body will remain until the "roll is called up yonder."

On June 9, 1861, young Johnson enlisted at Tyler in Capt. D. Y. Gaines's company, K, 3rd Texas Cavalry, and was elected third lieutenant of this company. After twelve months' service, he was elected captain, and served with this rank until the close of the war. He was in many of the fierce battles for which Forrest's Cavalry was noted. He was severely wounded at Lovejoy

Sidney Smith Johnson.

Station, and at other times received slight wounds. In the latter part of 1864 he campaigned in Tennessee under General Forrest, and finally closed a worthy and gallant career as a soldier in the spring of 1865. When the war ended, his company disbanded without surrender. He returned to his old home, and on October 15, 1867, he was married to Miss Zelda Smith, daughter of Dr. L. W. Smith. To this union was born eight children, seven of whom survive him. The eldest son, Sidney S. Johnson, Jr., is a leading lawyer and Mayor of the city of Tillamook, Oregon. The other children live in Texas.[317]

JOHNSON, WILLIAM: While the race problem [instigated at that time, as today, by Liberals, then the Republican Party] creates serious concern for the welfare of both races and for the country, it behooves the [white] Southern people, who are, and ever have been, their best friends [i.e., blacks], to be on the alert for opportunities to influence all classes for the general good. [The white South] . . . improves its opportunities to pay tribute to faithful slaves, and it bespeaks the cooperation of our people in sending concise contributions to the honor of those who have ever been faithful. [One illustration is] here given.

William Johnson (colored) lives by Nolensville, Tenn., near his birthplace. He was a slave, and the property of Mr. Ben Johnson, as was also his mother.

In 1862 a part of the army commanded by Gen. Forrest was stationed at Nolensville, and young William Johnson (fifteen years old) drove one of the wagons with provisions for the army. Capt. B. F. White, who had been assistant adjutant general on the staff of Gen. Forrest, had been detached, and was in command of a battery of artillery captured at Murfreesboro. Seeing the boy William, he liked him, and proposed to buy him. Mr. Johnson sold him to Capt. White for $1,200 [$50,000 in today's currency], and *he went with Capt. White in the regular field service.*

Soon after his purchase of William, the great battle of Murfreesboro was fought; and while on the battlefield, during the battle, Capt. White was attacked suddenly with inflammatory rheumatism. His servant William was with the wagon train, and did not reach him until the next day. The day following, the Confederates retreated, and the Federals, who also had been falling back, retraced their movements and occupied the area in which Capt White was left in that painful and awful predicament, attended only by his servant William. For three months Capt. White was guarded by the Federals in a house on Thomas Butler's plantation, near the village of Salem. One bitter cold night the [Yankee] guard went to his camp some distance away, when the Captain [White] asked William if he couldn't get him away from there. It was soon arranged for him to take a spring wagon and a broken-down army horse on the Butler farm. He put his charge in the wagon, and by a circuitous route got away without apprehension. Late in the night the horse so nearly gave out that William walked in water and ice over his boots, and would lift the wheels of the vehicle out of the mire, and moved on until they were safe in the Confederate lines. A better horse was procured, and the afflicted officer was taken to Shelbyville, and from there he was permitted to visit Mobile, where he recuperated, William of course going with him. This faithful servant remained with Capt. White, who went back into field service, but his health failed, and when his constitution gave down he was put on post duty, and at the end of the war he was paroled at Albany, Ga. He brought William back to Nashville, leaving him with an uncle when he left to reside in Memphis. He afterwards moved to California. They never met again.

William Johnson.

When the notice of Capt. White's death appeared in the December *Veteran* for 1899, William saw it, and asked to pay tribute to his memory. That desire becomes the occasion for the *Veteran* to pay just and well-merited tribute to William Johnson.

. . . William has lived all these years in the neighborhood of his birthplace, and has maintained a reputation as an honest, upright man—such as *will ever have the devoted friendship of the white people, and who will prove it if later in life misfortunes should render him unable to support himself.*

During the time of Capt. White's confinement in the Federal lines he allowed William to carry three young ladies through the lines to Shelbyville. They were Misses Sallie J. McLean and Lizzie and Julia Lillard. After his return from that trip, Capt. White gave him [William] permission to visit his mother, at Nolensville, before they escaped to the South.[318]

JOHNSTON, WILLIAM ALSTON: William Alston Johnston died in Fort Worth, Tex., on February 20, 1923, following a short illness. He and his wife went to Fort Worth about a year ago to make their home with their sons.

Mr. Johnston was born in Haywood County, Tenn., near Brownsville, February 8, 1840. When the war broke out between the States, he enlisted in Forrest's Cavalry and served throughout the conflict. In 1878 Mr. Johnston came to Lee County, Ark., and for many years taught school in Spring Creek Township, at Oak Forest and La Grange. He was also a civil engineer, and practically all the surveying done in Lee County in the early days was done by him. He served as county surveyor many years.

Mr. Johnston's first wife was Mrs. Fannie Sullivan, whose maiden name was Burford. One son, John, of Forrest City, Ark., survives this union. After the death of his first wife, he married her sister, Miss Sallie Burford, who survives him, with three sons and one daughter.

For many years "Uncle Buck" had been a familiar figure in Marianna. He was keenly interested in current events, political and otherwise, always kept himself well informed, and was possessed of a great fund of rare information and interesting experiences that made him a good entertainer. His going has created a vacancy that only "Uncle Buck" could fill.

Mr. Johnston was a descendant of Col. Philip Alston, John Ramsey, and John Johnston, all of whom fought in the Revolutionary War.[319]

JONES, A. M.: A. M. Jones, of Trenton, Tenn., is doubtless the oldest soldier in Gibson County, if not in West Tennessee, having celebrated his eighty-fourth birthday in December last. Though growing quite feeble, he is cheerful and full of song. He belonged to the 4th Brigade, 12th Tennessee Cavalry, under D. C. Kelley, Forrest, and Hood. Committing his wife and several small children to the care of his Heavenly Father, as well as to that of his earthly father, Rev. John W. Jones, he joined the Confederate army, and was ever a faithful soldier, whose veracity and efficiency were never questioned. The hardships he endured were borne patiently.[320]

James Chamberlayne Jones.

JONES, JAMES CHAMBERLAYNE: Few more popular men than Capt. Jones have ever lived in Shelby County, Tenn., and his death in June, 1907, removed one who had established himself worthily in the regard of his people. He was born in Lebanon, Tenn., in 1844, the son of Hon. Jones, who served Tennessee both as Governor and in the United States Senate. The family came from Virginia to Tennessee, and in 1849 removed to Memphis. Comrade Jones left college to bear arms for the Confederate cause [conservatism], enlisting as a private in Company A, 7th Tennessee Cavalry, under W. F. Taylor, afterwards colonel. Efficient service won for him a lieutenancy, and later he was an adjutant general on the staff of Gen. W. H. Jackson, of Forrest's Cavalry.

After the surrender, Captain Jones returned to Memphis, where he was in business until 1878, when his health failed and for some time he was an invalid; but undiscouraged, he established a school and devoted his energies to the work of teaching. Closing his school in 1901, he became a private tutor in Mississippi. He was elected to the office of County Register of Shelby County, Tenn., in 1902, and reelected to the same office in 1906, being the only man who ever succeeded himself to this office. He was married in 1878 to Miss Alice Tait.

In the business life of the city of Memphis Mr. Jones held an honored place.

He was intensely public-spirited, honestly and actively interested in the development and prosperity of his city. He graduated hundreds of young men from his school, most of whom have done him honor.[321]

JONES, JAMES MONROE: James Monroe Jones, who died November 22, 1925, at Somerville, Tenn., was born December 2, 1846, the son of the late Chancellor Calvin Jones and Mildred Williamson, both natives of North Carolina. The Jones family was of old colonial stock, with a distinguished Revolutionary record, and many of its members have held high military and political office in North Carolina and Tennessee. His early education was principally at Phillips's Academy, but after the war he attended the University of Mississippi and there completed the classical course.

In 1863, when but sixteen years of age, James M. Jones joined Forrest's Cavalry and followed that gallant leader to the close of the war, being paroled in Alabama in May, 1865. He was not only a gallant and faithful soldier, but was given to deeds of reckless daring beyond the call of duty. After the war he took an active part in restoring . . . [the South's traditional Conservative government] and was an early member of the *original* Ku-Klux Klan—[a Conservative non-racist organization with no connection to today's KKK][322]—one of its organizers having been his cousin, Calvin Jones, of Pulaski, Tenn.

In 1874, Comrade Jones was married to Miss Anna Hortense Moody, and of their eleven children six sons and three daughters survive him. His second marriage, in 1908, was to Mrs. Laura B. Stainback, who survives him. After funeral services at the home, he was laid in the family lot in the Somerville Cemetery, the pallbearers being his six sons and two grandsons.

Much could be said of the admirable characteristics of this comrade. *He was a friend of all* classes, *colors*, and conditions; kindly and charitable in speech as well as deed; always genial and of good cheer, always courteous, tolerant, and forbearing with others; a man of culture, widely read in the classics, and he kept abreast of modern thought to the last. He had been an advanced farmer, probably of the first to extensively diversify along the lines of horticulture. He had orchards, vineyards, and berry fields in which he found diversion and recreation. With these and the blooming shrubs about him, he lived serene and content upon the plantation where he was born. His affection for the old home grew with the years.[323]

JONES, JOHN M.: Dr. John M. Jones was born July 3, 1846, in Weakley County, Tenn., and entered the Confederate army at the very incipiency of the war in Company H, Forrest's old regiment, participating in the battles and campaigns of that command, which were many, and surrendered at Gainesville, Ala., May 11,

John M. Jones.

1865. He was a member of Tom Hindman Camp, U.C.V., Newport, Ark. He had lived at Newport for thirty-one years, where he practiced medicine successfully the entire time, dying February 13, 1908, aged sixty-two years—an excellent soldier and an eminent physician. Dr. Jones survived his wife, who was Miss Callie Patterson, of Weakley County, Tenn., but five days, she having been an invalid for ten years.[324]

JONES, TIMOTHY PICKERING: At the age of ninety years, Col. Timothy P. Jones died at Seguin, Tex., on the 18th of October [1904]. He was born in North Carolina, but the family removed to Jackson, Tenn., when he was a small boy. That was his home till 1882, when he went to Seguin, Tex., residing there afterwards. He was a roommate of Edgar Allan Poe while a cadet at West Point. Col. Jones crossed the Sabine River into Texas the day he was twenty-one years old as a soldier, and served that republic for two years. He was captain of the Second Tennessee in the war with Mexico, and as lieutenant colonel commanded the Sixth Tennessee Infantry at Shiloh. After that battle the Sixth and Ninth Tennessee were consolidated, and Col. Jones served with Forrest. He was a personal friend of David Crockett, and knew nearly all the leaders in the Texas republic.[325]

William B. Jones.

JONES, WILLIAM B.: After a long period of ill health, Capt. William B. Jones died at the home of his daughter, Mrs. J. E. Wilson, at Flora, Miss., on the 8th of April, 1925.

Captain Jones was a pioneer citizen of Madison County, public spirited and progressive, one of the most outstanding men of the State, whose deeds are a monument to his memory.

He was born at the old home near Robinson Springs on September 24, 1847, the son of James M. and Marie Wiggins Jones. His father was from South Carolina, his mother a native of the Old North State. She died when he was three years old. He was reared on the plantation in Madison County, but was a student at the township school at Mount Olympus in March, 1862, when he joined Company C of the 39th Mississippi Regiment, C.S.A. After serving with that command for about a year, in 1863 he joined Company M, of Wirt Adams's Cavalry Regiment, with which he was paroled at Gainesville, Ala., as a part of Forrest's Cavalry. He had participated in the battles of Corinth, Franklin, and other engagements of that famous command.

After the war, he finished his education at the Summerville Institute, at Gholson, Noxubee County, Miss., graduating in 1868. Returning home, he took up life on the farm which his father had turned over to him. In November,

1870, he was married to Miss Flora Mann, and her name was given to the station located on the Yazoo and Mississippi Valley Railroad, for which he had given a third of the right of way through Madison County. Captain Jones built a residence and several stores at Flora and began merchandising there in 1885 in connection with his farming interests. He had become the largest land owner in the county and produced more cotton than any other planter. He organized the Bank of Flora in 1909, and was made its president, from which he resigned in 1917 on account of the ill health of his wife, who died in November of that year. He also turned over his mercantile interests to his son, Hal J. Jones, and son-in-law, J. E. Wilson, retiring from all business.

Captain Jones was a member of the Baptist Church, to which he ever contributed generously, as well as to educational funds. He was a trustee of the Mississippi College at Clinton for about ten years, of the Baptist Hospital at Jackson, and of the Baptist Orphanage there, and to all of these his contributions were liberal, and his interest in their support never wavered. His contribution to the Orphanage included a barrel of flour each month for twenty-two years, and his trusteeship of that institution continued through twenty-five years. He was ever true and loyal to his God, to his Church, to his family and friends, to his community and country. At the age of seventy-seven years, his life here was ended, and his body was laid by the side of that of the beloved wife in the cemetery at Flora. A son and daughter survive him.[326]

JORDAN, M. D. L.: Dr. M. D. L. Jordan, born near Milan, Tenn., November, 1833, died in Nashville, February 29, 1896. He was attended by his war-time comrade, Dr. J. R. Buist. The minister present asked how it was with him, when, raising his hand to his brow, he gave the soldier's salute, and said: "Ready for marching orders." He was "every inch a soldier," whether on the field of battle administering to the comfort of the wounded and dying, or in the devastation that surrounded him after the war.

Dr. Jordan graduated at Union University, Murfreesboro, Tenn., in 1850, and in the Jefferson Medical College, Philadelphia, Pa., in 1855. He was Surgeon in Gen. Forrest's Cavalry. Having been taken prisoner at Murfreesboro, he was retained there for several months on hospital duty, attending, the wounded of both Armies. Later he was sent to Fort McHenry, and held six months as hostage for a Federal surgeon, in a close narrow cell, with but one aperture.

M. D. L. Jordan.

He was elected to the State Senate in 1874. He was also Surgeon for the Illinois Central Railroad, during an epidemic of yellow fever, and as Medical

Inspector of trains was greatly exposed to the disease. Dr. Jordan was a Knight Templar. In 1890 he moved from Milan to Nashville, and engaged in the practice of medicine here until his death.

He was twice married; first, Miss Martha Hillsman, of Trezevant, Tenn., in 1856. She died in 1876. In 1877 he married Josephine E. Perry, of Nashville, great granddaughter of Maj. John Buchanan, a pioneer of the Volunteer State. Two sons and daughters, together with the wife, survive him. Dr. Jordan was a member of Cheatham Biouvac, and was surgeon of the Veteran C. A. Cavalry, commanded by Capt. George F. Hager. Dr. Jordan was a true "Soldier of the Cross."[327]

James Warren Juniel.

JUNIEL, JAMES WARREN: James Warren Juniel was born in Halifax County, Va., April 22, 1844, and died November 14, 1918, at Bearden, Ark.

He was the son of John and Julia Wilkins Juniel, natives of Virginia, who went to Arkansas in 1850 and engaged in farming. Young Juniel was educated at McKenzie College, Texas, leaving school when the war broke out in 1861. He enlisted in Company G, 12th Arkansas Infantry, where he served with distinction until disabled at Belmont and discharged. After recovering he again enlisted in Company G, 12th Arkansas Cavalry, and served under Generals Forrest and Wheeler until December, 1863, when he was placed in the secret service on account of his success as a scout, acting under Capt. A. M. Shannon and operating in Tennessee, Georgia, and North and South Carolina until the close of the war. He was wounded twice at Murfreesboro and was captured three times, but made his escape each time.

Returning home in August, 1865, he began merchandising and farming. He was elected to the legislature in 1888; had been an active and efficient member of the Ouachita County Quorum Court and a justice of the peace for more than forty years. He was recently chosen Commander for life of Hugh McCollum Camp, U.C.V., and was appointed Brigadier General of the 2nd Arkansas Brigade, U.C.V. He seldom failed to attend the reunions and was very loyal and enthusiastic in everything pertaining to the U.C.V. He had long been an active member of the Masonic fraternity and was a consistent member of the Baptist Church, having served many years as deacon.

Comrade Juniel was married in November, 1866, to Miss Mary McDaniel, daughter of Judge James McDaniel, of New Edinburg, Ark. He is survived by his wife and two children, a son and a daughter. He was laid beside his father in the family cemetery with Masonic honors.[328]

David Campbell Kelley.

KELLEY, DAVID CAMPBELL: D. C. Kelley entered the Confederate army in 1861 with N. B. Forrest, and was paroled at Gainesville, Ala., at the close of the war, his parole registering his rank as "colonel commanding Forrest's old regiment of cavalry." This regiment was regarded by Forrest as his "right arm of power" from first to last. Its commander is spoken of by Lord Wolseley, in a sketch of Forrest, thus: "His second in command, D. C. Kelley, was as brave a man as ever smelled gunpowder."

Col. Kelley participated in seven great battles, beginning with Fort Donelson and ending with the battle of Nashville. He was under fire in more than sixty skirmishes, in seven of which, as brigade commander, he handled with eminent success artillery, cavalry, and infantry. Only once was he unsuccessful in fourteen engagements when in independent command.

Perhaps his most important service was at the close of the battle of Nashville. The soldiers under his command had been engaged in the first day of battle on the extreme left of the Confederate line constantly and successfully from 9 a.m. to 8 p.m. The line had been broken between his right and the left flank of the infantry, so that the night was spent in a most difficult march. Daylight dawned as he made good his connection with the left of Hood's infantry on the Hillsboro pike. The command was actively engaged during the greater part of the day.

About 4 p.m. an order from Gen. Hood was handed him, which read: "The army is in full retreat: hold the enemy off my flank at all hazard."

The brigade which Col. Kelley commanded had by this time been reduced to less than one thousand men. Dismounting all but two squadrons, which he placed on either flank, he threw his command across the Granny White pike just in time to meet and repel the fierce charge of the enemy's cavalry. For three fateful hours, until night had closed in, he held this position, rolling back onset after onset of the opposing force, until he found his command nearly surrounded in the darkness. Then, mounting his men, by a rapid gallop he threw himself between the Federal cavalry and the rear of the army, then passing Brentwood. The Federal authorities vary as to the number of cavalry thus held in check. Some estimate the number as high as fourteen thousand. Had this body struck Hood's flank at the hour his command was received by Col. Kelley, half Hood's army would never have crossed [the] Harpeth River [at Franklin].

Col. Kelley preached every Sunday when in camp, and while a member of Forrest's military family blessing was always invoked. In absence of Maj.-Gen. Lyons, First Brigadier-General D. C. Kelley [was put] . . . in command of Forrest's cavalry organization in the C.S.A. reunion at Atlanta.[329]

[From Col. Rev. Kelley's obituary:] Rev. D. C. Kelley, D.D., was born in Leesville, Wilson County, Tenn., in 1833 ; and died in Nashville in 1909. He was sent as a missionary to China by the M. E. Church, South, and for years did very noble work in propagating Christianity in that far-off land. On his return to America he organized a company of cavalry which was called Kelley's Troop and which served under Gen. N. B. Forrest, and was with that gallant commander during the war.

D. C. Kelley so distinguished himself for coolness in action and bravery in face of danger that he was rapidly promoted, being made major of battalion. He was elected lieutenant colonel of Forrest's Regiment the day before the battle of Shiloh, and took the duty of colonel in the battle of Murfreesboro. He was on Forrest's staff as chaplain and aid. Afterwards he commanded a regiment, then a brigade till the end of the war, winning a brilliant reputation as "Forrest's fighting preacher."

At the end of the war he was made pastor of several of the largest Methodist Churches in Tennessee. Here his influence for good was widely felt, as in his upright life and true Christianity he was an example of what a noble man should be.[330]

KELLY, J. O.: J. O. Kelly passed from this life at his home in Jeff, Ala., March 8, 1897, in his seventy-first year. Comrade Kelly was an old soldier, a true Confederate veteran. He enlisted under Gen. Forrest March 10, 1862, in Company K, Fourth Alabama, and remained to the end. He was a member of Egbert J. Jones Camp No. 357, U.C.V., Hoy, Ala. He attended all the reunions, going out to Houston, Tex., Richmond, Va., and expected to be at Nashville in June. He did all that he could to promote its extension, not only answering for himself, but for many others. Noble in war and pure in all the paths of life, he has "fought the good fight," and is now enjoying the Christian's rest. "There is no death; what seems so is transition."[331]

KELLY, WILLIAM CHARLES: William C. Kelly, a native of Alabama, born in Russell County, October 17, 1843, died at the home of his daughter in Houston, Tex., on November 22, 1922, after a short illness. His father was John William Kelly, of a Scotch-Irish family which came to this country in 1800 and settled in Pennsylvania; he came South and married Miss Sarah Carolina Martin, of Georgia, in 1840.

William C. Kelly was a soldier of the Confederacy, serving with Company C, Tuskegee Light Infantry, which command was in the Army of Northern Virginia, and took part in the battle of Seven Pines and in the seven days' fighting around Richmond. In November, 1862, Comrade Kelly was transferred to the cavalry under Forrest, with whom he served until the close of the war, surrendering at Gainesville, Ala.

After the war he was married to Miss Addie Moore, of Tuskegee, Ala., and settled in Chambers County, removing in 1868 to Texas and locating in San Saba County. In Texas he had a long and notable career as a railroad agent, closing his service of thirty-five years in the claim department at Austin, retiring with the respect and friendship of all with whom he had been associated and the public which he had served. After the death of his wife, in 1905, he made his home with his children in different parts of the country. Eight children survive him—four sons and four daughters—twenty-seven grandchildren, and five great-grandchildren.

He was a devoted father, a loyal friend, and an earnest Christian; simple in his habits, conscientious and painstaking in his work. He counted his friends from the general public to the highest railway officials. Comrade Kelly was buried at Ledbetter by the side of his wife, many friends from Houston and other places attending the funeral.[332]

KEMP, JOHN R.: John R. Kemp, whose death occurred at Clinton, Ky., July 9, 1911, was the son of William T. and Sallie Emerson Kemp, and was born at Burkesville, Ky., May 18, 1844. His parents moved to Hickman County when he was eight years old, and the greater part of his life was spent there. At the age of seventeen he enlisted in the Confederate Army, first joining the 12th Tennessee Regiment, and he was in that "first battle" at Belmont, Mo.

After the battle of Shiloh his company was placed with the 3rd Kentucky. In 1864 it was mounted and assigned to General Forrest. He was in active and hard service for four years, and was believed to be fatally wounded in the battle near Franklin. He was carried to the McLemore

John R. Kemp.

home, where he was nursed back to life. Miss McLemore made him her special charge, and to her unremitting attentions was due his ultimate recovery. The friendship thus cemented was dissolved only by death, and the younger generations of both families still cherish it. Mr. T. M. Rogers, of Florence, Ala., a son of the former Miss McLemore, journeyed to Clinton to lend the comfort of his presence to the family in their bereavement.

After the war Mr. Kemp was in Mississippi and Louisiana for several years. In 1870 he was married at Byhalia, Miss., to Miss Julia Raiford, who, with two daughters and a son, survives him.

In 1880 Mr. Kemp was elected circuit clerk of Hickman County, serving for six years, and was then elected to the State Senate. He was publisher and editor of the old *Clinton Democrat* for several years. In 1897 he was elected circuit Clerk for the second time, and was filling that office most efficiently at the time of his death.

Mr. Kemp was a faithful member of the Church, also a Mason, and for years had been Commandant of Ed Crossland Camp U.C.V. at Clinton. He possessed a most delightful personality. No appeal to him for charity or sympathy was ever made in vain. He was the friend and counselor of many.[333]

KENNEDY, T. J.: Capt. T. J. Kennedy was born September 27, 1828; and died April 19, 1909, having attained the ripe age of eighty years.

He was born in Tennessee, but was living in Pontotoc County, Miss., in April, 1861, when he entered the Confederate service as captain of a company which made a part of the 41st Mississippi Infantry, and which served under General Bragg. He was in the great battles of Murfreesboro and Perryville. His brother, Capt. William Kennedy, was killed in the former, while he himself was wounded in the latter. After going home to recuperate, he resigned his position in the infantry, raised another company, and again entered the service as captain of Company H, 28th Mississippi Cavalry. Under the gallant Forrest he was in the bloody battles of Brice's Crossroads, Harrisburg, and Fort Pillow.

Made penniless by the war, and thinking he could do better in a new land, in 1871 he removed to Texas and settled in Fannin County, near Red River, where he opened a new farm and prospered. He had married in 1859 while living at Pontotoc, Miss., Miss Josephine Johnson, who survives him with their six children and twenty-seven grandchildren, who cherish the memory of him who has fallen asleep at the end of a long and useful life.[334]

KIMBRO, JOHN: John Kimbro was a scout under Forrest.[335]

KING, B. F.: B. F. King, a gallant Confederate soldier, of Kemper County, Miss., is resting from all the cares of life. Death came to him suddenly on October 23, 1915. He was born in Kemper County, March 12, 1845, and enlisted in the Confederate army when eighteen years old as a member of Company C, 2nd Mississippi Regiment, serving under Captain Rogers in Armstrong's Brigade, Forrest's Cavalry. He was with Johnston from Resaca to Atlanta and with Hood from Atlanta to Jonesboro, to Nashville, and then by way of Columbus, Miss., to Selma, Ala., where he was in his last battle. In all

B. F. King.

the trying ordeals of that arduous service he never failed to answer roll call or to perform faithfully any duty assigned to him.

He was a devoted member of the Baptist Church and a Democrat [up until 1896, a Conservative] of the old school; but it was in his home and community that his life shone brightest. He was a kind husband and devoted father, an example for anyone to follow. As a citizen he was modest and retiring; a safe counselor for those who came to him for advice. He was as loyal to friends as he was to principles. He was twice married and is survived by his second wife, with her two daughters, Misses Alma Kate and Eileen King, and son, Lamar King, all of Battlefield, Miss., and by the children of his first marriage, who are: R. C. King, of Greenwood, Miss.; M. D. King, of Hattiesburg, Miss.; Mrs. Maggie Hester, of Lytle, Tex.; and Miss Vestry King, of Greenwood, Miss. A brother and sister, of Burley, Miss., also survive him.

He was tenderly laid to rest near his old home in Zion Cemetery, Kemper County, surrounded by many sorrowing friends and relatives.[336]

KING, JAMES W.: James W. King died at his home near Lynnville, Graves County, Ky., July 3, 1911, aged 72 years.

He entered the Confederate Army September 18, 1861, as a private in Company H, 7th Kentucky Infantry, which regiment was afterwards mounted and served under General Forrest to the end of the war. James King was one of those few soldiers who never missed a roll call nor a battle nor was he ever wounded. Shiloh, Bolivar, Davis's Mill, Corinth, Hatchie Bridge, Coffeeville, Baton Rouge, Baker's Creek, Big Black, Raymond, Edward's Depot, Jackson, Paducah, Brice's Cross Roads, Harrisburg, Athens, Sulphur Trestle, Pulaski, Paris Landing, Johnsonville, Spring Hill, Franklin, Nashville, and Selma were some of the battles in which he participated, and he did in each, without ostentation, deeds of gallantry beyond the normal.

On August 25, 1864, when the Federal General Hatch, who commanded the cavalry under A. J. Smith, occupied and burned Oxford, Miss., the Confederate line of battle was some four hundred yards eastward of the eastern limits of Oxford, from which the Federals could be heard talking, but could not be seen. James King and a comrade were ordered to reconnoiter the Federal position and, in order to get the needed information, penetrated too far the enemy's lines. When they were beset on all sides by Federal cavalrymen attempting their capture, four stalwart Federal cavalrymen in a hand to hand combat with King failed to kill or capture him, but got his horse, a valuable roan. This was one of the many daring adventures which revealed the distinctive traits of the gallant King, who was rated as one of the very best all-round soldiers in the regiment, a regiment than which the Confederacy could boast no better. In battle, mounted or on foot, on the skirmish line, in the trenches, on picket, or anywhere else where danger was rife and duty demanded the risk, Jim King, the ideal soldier, was always to be found there. Never flinching, never grumbling, never shirking, he was loved by the entire company, and we were all proud to claim him as our comrade. Untutored and without much worldly chattels, but with a citizenship unsullied, he loyally kept the faith unto the end.

James W. King.

His brother, Rice B. King, killed on July 14, 1864, at Harrisburg, Miss., was also an excellent soldier and his brother's equal in some respects. Gallant comrades, may your intrepid spirits rest in peace.[337]

KINSOLVING, WILLIAM CAREY: [The following is from] resolutions passed by Tom Green Camp, No. 72, U.C.V., of Abilene, Tex., in tribute to the loved Commander and comrade, W. C. Kinsolving who died on July 11 [1925], at his home at Lytle Lake, near Abilene, at the ripe age of eighty-four years:

His life as a citizen and soldier was one of activity and usefulness, beginning and ending in the Southland. He was born at Charlotte, Va., in 1840, spending his boyhood in Princeton, Ky., and there, on July 4, 1861, joining Company C, 3rd Kentucky Infantry, C.S.A.; was wounded at the battle of Shiloh, and also at the second battle of Corinth and captured, escaping the seventeenth day and tramping through the Mississippi woods and swamps, rejoining his command at Vicksburg. He was at the siege of Vicksburg when the *Arkansas* ram went through the Federal fleet; had charge of the guard where she landed. At Baton Rouge he had charge of the Guard of the Fatigue Corps that started the fortifications at Port Hudson. Was at the bombardment of this port when the flagship was burned and Admiral Farragut and Lieut. George Dewey, barely escaped capture.

Was at the Battle of Baker's Creek and Jackson, Miss. Was counted at Canton, Miss., and, under Gen. John Adams, made numerous raids on Grant's army investing Vicksburg. Was afterwards transferred to Gen. N. B. Forrest and served as commander of a special scout squad under Forrest and Buford. Was with Forrest during his raid into Kentucky, Tennessee and Alabama, participating in the battles of Athens, Fort Pillow, and Johnsonville. Was in the advance guard for General Hood at Franklin, Nashville, and Murfreesboro, and covered the rearguard on Gen. Hood's retreat back to Mississippi, participating in the battles of Brice's Crossroads, Baldwin, and numerous small engagements. Paroled in May, 1865, at Columbus, Miss., ten days after the department surrendered, having been on a scouting raid in North Alabama.

He had held the following honorary positions in the U.C.V. Association: Lieutenant Colonel on General Van Zandt's staff; Brigadier General on General Carr's staff; the same rank on General Halderman's staff, extending into General Thomas's staff, and had received notice of appointment by General Freeman on his staff; had also been appointed by General Sneed as Chief of Artillery of the Trans-Mississippi Department.

Comrade Kinsolving moved to Palo Pinto County, Tex., in the early days, and there, fifty-four years ago, married Miss Mattie Brown, the daughter of a pioneer cattle raiser and, so far as known, the first white child born in that county.

His wife, four daughters, and two sons survive him. Our worthy comrade had served the Southern cause with bravery and distinction, and thereafter served his country with no less distinction; he had been a kind and loving husband and devoted father, having reared a splendid Christian family. His daily life was one worthy of emulation.[338]

KITTRELL, ROBERT H.: The long and active life of Robert H. Kittrell came to an end in the early morning of April 1, at his home near Thompson Station, Tenn., in his ninety-first year. He was born November 30, 1839, near Mount Pleasant, Tenn., the son of George Kittrell, who came from Kittrell, N.C., and Elizabeth Rutherford Kittrell, of Sumner County, Tenn.

As a Confederate soldier, Robert H. Kittrell enlisted in the 2nd Battalion Tennessee Cavalry, in July, 1861, at Mount Pleasant, under N. N. Cox, captain. Later, the 2nd and 9th Battalions consolidated, forming the 1st Tennessee Regiment, with which he served as a member of Company I. His service was throughout the war, and on many occasions he fought with Gen. N. B. Forrest, and he was on picket before the battle of Shiloh.

For the past forty-seven years, he had resided on his farm near Thompson Station, in which he was actively interested until his last illness. He was a member of the Christian Church, and always interested in the Church work. He was twice married, both wives having preceded him many years. Two daughters survive him.[339]

KLYCE, H. C.: The Christian soldier, Capt. H. C. Klyce, passed into the great beyond on the morning of December 15, 1915, aged seventy-seven years. He was born in Maury County, Tenn., in 1838, but removed to Mississippi in 1855 and continued to make his home in that State.

His life was that of a Christian gentleman. For forty years he was a member of the Methodist Episcopal Church, and for twenty years he was superintendent of its Sunday school.

Captain Klyce enlisted as a private in the first company organized in his section of the State, and at the close of the war he was captain of Company I, 19th Tennessee Regiment, Bell's Brigade, Forrest's command. He was with Forrest in most of his campaigns and was at Fort Pillow, on the raid into Memphis, at Brice's Crossroads, Harrisburg, Sulphur Trestle, Athens,

Johnsonville. He was also with him in Hood's campaign into Tennessee and helped to cover Hood's retreat out of the State, then on to Selma and the finish, surrendering with Forrest at Gainesville, Ala.[340]

KNOEDLER, LEWIS P.: Lewis P. Knoedler, late of Chicago, formerly of Augusta, Ky., died on the 3rd of February, 1919, at his home, in Chicago, after a short illness, and was laid to rest in Augusta, Ky. He was born in New Jersey in 1839 and removed in boyhood to Kentucky, locating in Augusta. When the crisis came and the War between the States was on, from principle he elected to join with the cause of the South [conservatism and constitutionalism]. He was a firm believer in the doctrine of State rights and the right of the State to secede or withdraw from the Union. After entering the Confederate service he became a member of Morgan's Cavalry, and after its capture in the Ohio raid he, having escaped capture with a small remnant of the command, was placed in Forrest's escort, but subsequently was transferred to a Kentucky brigade commanded by Cerro Gordo Williams, with whom he served for over a year. Subsequently his battalion was transferred to the Army of Northern Virginia and placed in Duke's Brigade. After the close of hostilities his brigade was selected as part of the escort to President Davis to the Gulf.

Having been closely associated with Comrade Knoedler through this trying period of his life, I think I can speak advisedly of him as a man and soldier. He was awarded an honorable and responsible position by his comrades, and during the whole period of our service I can truthfully say that I never saw him deviate from what he believed to be right and just. Gallant and fearless in battle, honorable and just in camp, he merited and received the respect and affection of his comrades. And after the bloody tragedy closed when the Stars and Bars was forever folded,[341] he again took up the duties of citizenship in a reunited country and became a most exemplary citizen and lived a long, useful, and successful life. When I say successful I mean it in its broadest sense—a full rounded life, a devoted husband, a loving father, and a true friend. In all that makes up good citizenship he was supreme. As a comrade in arms and an associate in peace I gladly pay this tribute to his memory.[342]

KNOX, J. P.: J. P. Knox, the fifth son [and brother of John L. Knox above and Richard M. Knox below], was just eighteen years old when the war broke out. His company, Pettis's Flying Artillery, was mustered into service in May, 1861, at Eureka, Miss., and on June 28 they went to Memphis, thence to New Madrid, Mo., and soon afterwards were put in Bowen's Brigade, under Gen. Price. His captain, Hudson, was killed at Shiloh. The battery was known as Hudson's Battery, and later as Walton's. At Port Gibson, Miss., this battery fired the first gun on Gen. Grant's Army after crossing the Mississippi River. They were captured at Vicksburg and paroled. He remained a few weeks at home, and then went to parole camp at Enterprise, Miss., where he was soon exchanged and assigned to Gen. Forrest. He was surrendered at Gainesville, Ala., and now lives at Houston, Tex.[343]

KNOX, JOHN L.: John L. Knox is a native of Gibson County, Tenn., and was born April 22, 1834. In his fifteenth year he went to Panola County, Miss., where he now resides. Although a "states' rights" Democrat [then a Conservative], he was opposed to secession and also to coercion.

As a member of the Panola Guards, he left for Pensacola, Fla., March 27, 1861, the day after enlisting. At the close of a year, the time of his enlistment, he was discharged. He then helped to organize "Yates's Battery," and was chosen first lieutenant. He did hard service with the battery, but resigned at Vicksburg in 1863.

Joining W. G. Middleton, who became captain of a cavalry company, he was given the same second position that he had in the battery. The company became a part of the Eighteenth Mississippi Cavalry and served under Forrest. Middleton was killed July 15, 1864, and Lieut. Knox succeeded him. He was paroled at Gainesville, Ala., late in May, 1865, having served four years and two months in actual service. He was never wounded, never a prisoner, never missed a roll call without a lawful reason, nor a battle in which his company was engaged.[344]

All six of the Knox brothers, sons of Absalom and Sarah Higgins Knox, served in the Confederate military, three of them with General Forrest. Left to Right: John L. Knox, Dr. N. C. Knox, W. H. Knox, J. P. Knox, S. Y. T. Knox, Richard M. Knox.

KNOX, RICHARD M.: Richard M. Knox [brother of John L. and J. P. Knox above] was born in March, 1838, and was the third son. He was ten years old when the family moved. When twenty years old he returned to Milan, Tenn., obtained a situation in the first dry goods store opened there, and remained until January, 1861. Going back to Mississippi, he clerked in a store at Batesville until June, when he enlisted with his brother in the First Mississippi Cavalry. He served under Van Dorn and Forrest and was in all the battles in which his command was engaged, including Shiloh, Holly Springs, and Corinth;

was at Atlanta, Franklin, and Nashville, and helped to cover Hood's retreat [south to Alabama]. At Selma, Ala., three-fourths of his command was captured, but he made his escape. He had two horses shot from under him, but was never wounded nor taken prisoner.

At the close of the war he made a corn crop on a piece of land bought during the war with Confederate money. After finishing his crop he went to Memphis, secured employment as salesman in a wholesale dry goods house, and remained there until July, 1871, having saved enough money to go into business for himself. He went west to Pine Bluff, Ark., engaging in a general merchandise business, and has ever been successful. He has always taken great interest in the reunions of veterans, and was at Birmingham, Houston, and Richmond. His daughter, Miss Sue, was chosen maid of honor for her state at the latter reunion.

He is one of the founders of the Confederate Home in Little Rock. In the beginning he, Col. J. B. Trulock, and the late Capt. John P. Murphy spent a week at the state capitol, urging the Legislature to make an appropriation, and finally got them to levy one-fourth of a mill for pensioning indigent soldiers and the building of a [Confederate Rest] Home, each of them contributing one hundred dollars personally. While commander of the J. Ed Murry Camp at Pine Bluff, he is also brigadier-general of the Second Arkansas Division, U.C.V. Having been a private during the entire war, he selects his staff from those who served as privates.[345]

James Lachlison.

LACHLISON, JAMES: "'Tis never right to say a good man dies." On Monday, November 1 [1920], the spirit of Capt. James Lachlison passed away peacefully and bravely, as he had lived. He was born in Charleston, S.C., on April 18, 1837, but spent all his boyhood in Savannah until he went to Philadelphia to the Polytechnic College, where he graduated. In 1858 he was married in Philadelphia to Miss Sarah Thompson, of that city. She preceded him to the "great beyond" about fifteen years.

In August, 1861, he entered the Confederate service as second lieutenant of the Oglethorpe Light Infantry and was the last of the charter members of the company. In the battle of Fort Pulaski he was taken prisoner and confined on Governor's Island, N.Y., then transferred to Johnson's Island, Ohio. He was exchanged, and in September, 1862, was made first lieutenant. He served several months around Savannah and was promoted to captain of his company. He was in the first attack upon Fort Wagner, Charleston Harbor. He was in the battles of Kennesaw Mountain, Jonesboro, and Atlanta, and was wounded in front of Atlanta. He was with Forrest covering Hood's retreat at Nashville. In April, 1865, he surrendered with his company at Macon. He has ever been a loyal son of the Confederacy and true to the best traditions of his native South.

He moved to Darien, Ga., in 1869 and engaged in the lumber business, and until his retirement, a few years ago, he was with the Hilton, Dodge Lumber Company. He was a faithful and consistent member of the Methodist Church, serving for many years as steward. He was the oldest Past Grand Master of the

Odd Fellows in Georgia and was also a prominent Mason.

For several months his health had been failing, but his interest in local and public affairs was truly remarkable. His intellect and character were of the highest order, and he has left the priceless heritage of a stainless name. He is survived by a sister (Mrs. James Foster, of Savannah), two daughters (Mrs. P. S. Clark, of Darien, Ga., and Mrs. T. H. Thomson, of Dawson, Ga.), eight grandchildren, and two great-grandchildren.[346]

LANDMAN, J. HENRY: On June 24, 1915, at his home, in Huntsville, Ala., J. Henry Landman died at the age of eighty years. In his death there was lost to his State a man whose high and lofty ideals of duty and responsibility made his life that of an honorable and patriotic Confederate soldier and citizen.

J. Henry Landman was born in the year 1835 near Huntsville, Madison County, Ala., where he lived with his parents until about nine years of age, when the family removed to Demopolis. There his father died in less than a year, and shortly afterwards his mother took her children back to Madison County.

J. Henry Landman.

During the three years just preceding the outbreak of the war Henry Landman was cashier for Bradley, Wilson & Co., one of the largest merchandise and cotton houses in the whole South. The home office of this company was located at Huntsville, with branches at New Orleans, La., and Charleston, S.C. As cashier for this company Mr. Landman was sent to Charleston on horseback upon a mission of unusual trust and confidence, and on returning he brought with him to his employers in his saddlebags $1,250,000.

Henry Landman enlisted at Huntsville on September 16, 1862, as a Confederate soldier "for the war" under Capt. J. M. Hambrick in Company F, Forrest's Regiment of Cavalry. Later this regiment was reorganized, and Comrade Landman became a member of Company K, 4th Alabama Cavalry Regiment, Col. A. A. Russell's command, serving as high private in this company till October 20, 1862, when he was detailed by order of Brig. Gen. N. B. Forrest to report for duty to Maj. C. S. Severson, brigade quartermaster of Forrest's command. Later, on July 17, 1863, by order of General Bragg, whose headquarters were then at Chattanooga, Tenn., Mr. Landman was again detailed to report for duty to Maj. C. S. Severson, and he served as his assistant until the surrender.

So competent and efficient was he in this branch of the Confederate army that his services were indispensable to Major Severson, who on May 15, 1864, made direct application to the Secretary of War of the Confederacy at Richmond, Va., to have Mr. Landman appointed his first assistant, saying: "I earnestly recommend and solicit the appointment of Mr. J. Henry Landman, of Huntsville, Ala., as assistant quartermaster with the rank of captain, and ask that he be ordered to report to me for the following reasons—to wit: In the interest of the government I require an assistant. . . . I want a commissioned and bonded officer as an assistant, so that when I am compelled to leave the command to get up supplies I can leave my business in charge of an officer responsible to the government and qualified to attend to any business that may come up during my absence. . . . He can give the required bond and is in every way worthy and deserving of the appointment."

Gen. N. B. Forrest also wrote the department, giving his indorsement of this application, and said of Mr. Landman: "Mr. Landman is an excellent businessman, an excellent accountant, and one whose habits, experience, and reliability would, aside from the considerations urged by Major Severson, render his appointment an acquisition to the quartermaster's department."

Mr. Landman never received the appointment, however, for Brig. Gen. A. R. Lawton, quartermaster general at Richmond, in making his reply to Major Severson's application, said: "No new appointments are necessary, as there are officers available for assignment."

Mr. Landman continued to serve in the quartermaster's department as assistant to Major Severson until the surrender at Gainesville, Ala., on May 10, 1865, when he was paroled by E. S. Dennis, brigadier general U.S.A. After being paroled he returned to Huntsville, where he was in the dry goods business for two years, and then with his brother, George P. Landman, he established the cotton firm of Landman & Co., of which he was the active head until his death.

Mr. Landman was the second son among five brothers, all of whom served in the Confederate army. His elder brother, William B. Landman, served in Company I, 4th Alabama Infantry, and lost his life in the battle of First Manassas. His parents, George P. and Eliza (Griffin) Landman, were among the first settlers of this section of Alabama. His father was a native of Virginia and his mother of Kentucky. Mr. Landman was twice married, first to Miss Frances M. Kelly, of Madison County, on November 28, 1861. His second wife was Miss Fannie B. Caruthers, of Huntsville, whom he married in 1885. He is survived by one brother and five sons.[347]

LANKFORD, PETER L.: Peter L. Lankford, pioneer settler of Lauderdale County, Tenn., died at the home of his daughter, Mrs. M. A. Loyd, near Henning, on June 19, at the age of ninety years. He was born April 11, 1838, near Brownsville, in Haywood County, the son of J. D. and Patty Lankford. "Uncle Peter," as he was known, was loved wherever known. He was a son of the Old South, and no truer son ever gave allegiance to section, State, and county. He was a gentleman and scholar, an honorable, sincere man, his life dedicated to the principles which stood for the best in manhood.

Enlisting at the beginning of the War between the States, Peter Lankford served with Company K, 9th Tennessee Infantry, Cheatham's Division, Army of Tennessee, under Forrest and Joe Johnston, throughout the war, an honorable and valiant soldier of the Confederacy. He was wounded at the battle of Shiloh. The war over, he returned to his home and had been active in the progress of his community, his county, and State ever since. While in his teens, Lauderdale County had become his home and there he became one of the most prominent citizens of the county, ever devoted to its interests and advancement.

In December, 1865, he was married to Miss Mary Elizabeth Thun, who died in 1907. To them were born a son and seven daughters, and five daughters survive him, with a number of grandchildren and great-grandchildren. "Uncle Peter" was converted early in youth and joined the Baptist Church, and was active in its work until his death. He will be remembered as a quiet, unassuming, Christian gentleman, and his going was widely felt. Henning and Lauderdale County will miss this noble character, his kindly words and gentle deeds.[348]

John C. Latham.

LATHAM, JOHN C.: John C. Latham was born in Hopkinsville, Ky., in 1844; and died in New York City, August 18, 1909.

At the age of seventeen he enlisted with Gen. N. B. Forrest, and received his baptism of fire at Fort Donelson, where he proved his worth as a soldier. Later he was transferred to General Beauregard's command, in which he served with distinction. After the war he went into business in Memphis; but moved first to Hopkinsville, then to New York, where he organized the Wall Street banking firm of Latham, Alexander & Co.

Being a natural financier, and conducting his business with unswerving honor and on the highest principles, he rapidly acquired great wealth, which he used as a vehicle for doing good or giving pleasure to others. He ever retained his love for his native city, and in Hopkinsville he kept up the family homestead in princely style. His many donations to the welfare of this city caused him almost to be regarded as its patron saint. When the good roads movement in Christian County began, Mr. Latham subscribed fifty thousand dollars. Later he caused the bodies of about a hundred and twenty-five Confederate soldiers who were interred in various parts of the graveyard to be reinterred in a triangle in the center of the cemetery, and had a ten-thousand-dollar shaft erected over them.

Mr. Latham invested twenty-five thousand dollars in the first tobacco warehouse of Hopkinsville, thus establishing the beginning of an industry that has made that city famous. He gave five thousand dollars to the Episcopal Church for an organ and seven thousand dollars to the Methodists for a church. He fitted out the military company with arms and accouterments, and erected at the cost of fifty thousand dollars a family mausoleum, where he will be buried. His private charities were numerous and far-reaching. His first wife was Miss Mary Allen, of Memphis, and his second wife, who survives him, was Miss Elsie Gaylor, one of Louisville's social favorites and a reigning beauty. Of this marriage two children were born, a girl and a boy, of whom the girl alone survives.[349]

LAUDERDALE, JOHN M.: John M. Lauderdale died at Glasgow, Ky., on November 26, 1907, aged seventy-three years. He enlisted in May, 1861, in the 2nd Tennessee Regiment, and his company was the first to leave Hartsville, Tenn. After service of one year in Virginia, his regiment was transferred to the Army of Tennessee. Comrade Lauderdale went into the battle of Shiloh with a thirty-day furlough in his pocket. After that battle his company was transferred to Forrest's Cavalry, and served with that command to the end. Comrade Lauderdale was a devoted Christian. His wife and two daughters have the consolation of a life well spent, an honor to his name and country.[350]

John M. Lauderdale.

LAWRENCE, JAMES J.: James J. Lawrence, a veteran of two wars, died at his home in Springfield, Mo., on March 24, 1911, aged seventy-eight years. He was born near Nashville Tenn., in 1833, his parents going there from Norfolk. Va. He grew to manhood in his native State, then went to Texas, where, during the winter of 1856, he enlisted with a company of men to join the forces of Gen. William Walker, who was at that time conducting a filibustering campaign down in Nicaragua. After his experiences as a cavalryman in Central America, he returned to Nashville, and in January, 1858, was married to Miss Martha S. Duncan. Of this marriage two daughters survive.

At the outbreak of the War between the States Mr. Lawrence enlisted as a private in the regular service; but was soon promoted to second lieutenant of Company G, 2nd Tennessee Cavalry, under Forrest. He participated in many fierce engagements and had several horses killed under him, but went through the entire war without receiving an injury. His company was disbanded at Okolona, Miss., in May, 1865; and he returned to his native State, locating at

James J. Lawrence.

Hartsville and engaging in the saddlery business. He was married in 1870 to Miss Mary E. Hager, who, with six children, survives him. In 1880 he removed his family to Missouri, and for the past twenty-four years had been a resident of Springfield. He was a member of Campbell Camp, U.C.V., of Springfield, and his fellow members rendered him the last sad services.[351]

LEE, JAMES C.: James C. Lee died January 29, 1917, at the residence of his son, S. Y. Lee, Waco, Tex., after an illness of less than a week. He was born July 5, 1837, near Greensboro, Ala. On January 6, 1862, he joined the Confederate army over the protest of his home doctor, who said it would be like committing suicide for him to join, as he would not last a month on account of his health. The regimental surgeon said: "Young man, you had better go home." But he served until the close of the war under General Forrest, belonging to Company F, 3rd Alabama Cavalry.

After the war he settled in Marengo County, Ala., and lived there till 1896, when he went to Texas and located at Cameron, Milam County. In 1901 he went to Waco, which was his home until the time of his death. In 1875 he joined the Baptist Church in Marengo County, Ala.; and in 1901 he placed his membership with the Columbus Street Baptist Church, of Waco, and was a member of that Church until his death. He was also a member of Pat Cleburne Camp, No. 222, of Waco. He is survived by two children, S. Y. Lee and Miss Mary E. Lee, of Waco, and four grandchildren, Misses Myrtle, Lois, Mildred, and Master James E. Lee, of Waco.[352]

LEIPER, JOHN: John Leiper, a prominent citizen of Weatherford, Tex., for the past forty-four years, died there on May 20, 1924, aged seventy-eight years.

He was born in Murfreesboro, Tenn., January 6, 1846. He served the Confederacy three years as a member of the famous Forrest Cavalry and did valiant duty for the Southland in the long and bitter struggle of 1861. He was a cousin of Gen. E. W. Rucker, who was aid to General Forrest, and they served in the same command.

Comrade Leiper went to Texas in 1876, settling in Parker County. He was married to Miss Susan Norton, and to them five children were born, one son only surviving him. He was many years in the general mercantile business in Weatherford, later engaging in other business there, retiring some eight months ago.

John Leiper was always known to the people of Weatherford and Parker County as an honest, upright man, with whom it was a pleasure to do business and a delight to make acquaintance and friendship. A man of sterling worth and character, he numbered his friends by his acquaintances.

In addition to his son, he is survived by a sister and one brother, William K. Leiper, of McMinnville, Tenn.

He was a member of the Methodist Church, also a member of Tom Green Camp U.C.V., of Weatherford. The honorary pallbearers were from his Confederate comrades.[353]

LEWIS, THOMAS WILSON: Maj. Thomas Wilson Lewis was born September 10, 1840, and departed this life June 27, 1915. He was one of eight children born to the marriage of Thomas W. Lewis, Sr., and Miss Sophronia Nolen Lewis. They came from Rockingham County, Va., and settled in Stewart County, Tenn., in the year 1802; and when the stirring events of the War of 1812 came, he went to New Orleans as the lieutenant of his company, and for courage and daring in that memorable battle General Jackson promoted him to the command of his company.

Maj. T. W. Lewis, Jr., came from this splendid ancestry. His parents were of English and Irish descent. He was reared on a farm, but was given an academic education. When the War between the States came on, he joined Company B, 14th Tennessee Volunteer Infantry, as a private soldier. After three months he was promoted to second lieutenant of his company. In July, 1862, he resigned on account of his health and went home; but being of a restless spirit, he raised a company of cavalry and joined Col. T. G. Woodward's regiment, 2nd Kentucky Cavalry, at Clarksville, Tenn. The regiment was afterwards assigned to Gen. Van Dorn, but when Van Dorn was killed it was placed under Gen. N. B. Forrest.

Thomas Wilson Lewis.

In 1863 he was commissioned major of his regiment. The original number of his old company was sixty-five men, and of that number forty-three were either killed or wounded. After the battle of Chickamauga, the regiment was transferred, by order of General Bragg, to Gen. Cerro Gordo Williams, under whom he served until the surrender. Colonel Woodward being suspended from office in 1864, Major Lewis took charge of the regiment. He had many narrow escapes. In the second battle of Fort Donelson he had seven bullet holes shot in his clothes, and during his service he had three horses shot from under him. While the regiment was in South Carolina General Beauregard called Major Lewis to Charleston. He had him to select picked men to go with him to Lexington, Ky., for a secret purpose, but before he reached that place General Lee surrendered. Four of the men selected were Lieut. Frank Buckner, Capt. Since Bell, C. W. Tyler, and Emmett Gilbert. No more daring men ever lived. Major Lewis was one of the most beloved men of his regiment.

After the war he was a prominent farmer of his county. He served as a member of the State legislature one term and was the first man who made a plea for the pensioning of Confederate soldiers by the State of Tennessee. He was a Royal Arch Mason and a member of the Methodist Church for forty-six years. He leaves a wife, four daughters (Mrs. Will Lewis, Mrs. Robert McFall, Mrs. Ewing Richardson, and Miss Rena B. Lewis), one step-son (Mr. Will West), and one son (Joe Lewis), all of whom live near Cumberland City, Tenn. He was laid to rest at his home, near Cumberland City, funeral services being conducted by his pastor, Rev. S. C. Coke, of Indian Mound. The large concourse of friends and acquaintances which gathered to pay tribute to this great soldier evidenced the love, respect, and devotion in which he was held in his community.[354]

LINDSEY, LIVINGSTON: Dr. Livingston Lindsey, Commander of Lloyd Tilghman Camp No. 965, U.C.V., died January 3, 1898. Dr. Lindsey was born in Christian County, Ky., and moved with his father to Cadiz, Ky., when a boy, where he was reared and educated. In 1852 he settled in Clarksville, Tenn., and practised medicine. In October, 1861, he enlisted as a private in Company F, Forty-Ninth Tennessee Regiment; was appointed assistant surgeon December 27, 1861, and was captured at Fort Donelson in 1862. He was promoted to surgeon August 27, 1862, and served with McDonald's Battalion, Forrest's Cavalry; was captured at Farmington, Tenn., in October, 1863, and paroled at Grenada, Miss., May 18, 1865. His record as a soldier and loyal friend of the South is without a flaw. He was a gentleman by birth and education, and his life as a husband, father, and citizen illustrated all that is true and noble.[355]

LINN, J. Z.: J. Z. Linn, captain Company E, 12th Kentucky Cavalry, died October 11, 1911. He was born in Calhoun County, Ky., in 1836. He was a railroad conductor at the beginning of the war, and was elected captain of his company while away in charge of his train. He served under General Forrest.[356]

LINTON, JOHN WESLEY: The end of a useful life came with the death of John Wesley Linton on July 4, 1930, at the home of his brother, Ben T. Linton, near Russellville, Ky.

He was born in Muhlenberg County, Ky., in November, 1843. Entered the Confederate Army at age of seventeen, enlisting in Company D, Kentucky Cavalry, N. B. Forrest Command; was captured and imprisoned at Camp Chase, Columbus, Ohio; was exchanged near the close of the war, rejoined his command, and served to the end.

He was a lifelong member of the Methodist Church, ever loyal to all that was good and true.

He is survived by one brother, three sisters and four manly sons. A loving father and brother and a friend to all in need might fittingly be inscribed as his epitaph.[357]

LIPSCOMB, THOMAS C.: Col. Thomas C. Lipscomb, of Denison, Tex., died April 3, 1901, after a short illness. He had nearly reached his seventieth year, and had long been a resident of that section, having settled there before the town was thought of.

He served in the Fourteenth Mississippi with rank of corporal, and was stationed at Pensacola, Fla., for twelve months. He then reenlisted for the war in the Second Mississippi Battalion, serving two years in Virginia. After the battle of Antietam he was commissioned lieutenant colonel, and returned to

Columbus, Miss., where he raised a company of cavalry and joined Gen. Forrest's command. At the battle of Harrodsburg both colonel and major were killed, and he was promoted to colonel, and served with Gen. Forrest to the end of the war. He removed to Grayson County, Tex., in 1868.[358]

T. C. Little.

LITTLE, T. C.: Gen. T. C. Little, who was elected to command the Tennessee Division, U.C.V., at the annual reunion in Fayetteville, Tenn., October 10-11, was born in Bedford County, Tenn., March 17, 1848, [and] therefore, is one of the "young" Confederates. He enlisted in the Confederate army in September, 1864, at Shelbyville, Tenn., and was in the fight at the salt works in Virginia. He also helped to fight Sherman on the way to the sea; was with General Forrest after the battle of Franklin to the surrender; fought with Forrest's Escort during Wilson's raid, and was paroled with the Escort, May 9, 1865. He is one of the leading citizens of Fayetteville and devoted to the principles [conservatism and constitutionalism] for which he fought in the sixties.[359]

LITTLETON, ISAAC FRANKLIN: Prominent in the affairs of his section for three quarters of a century, was Ike F. Littleton, who died at his home at Puryear, Tenn., in his ninety-fourth year. He was the last of his father's family of five sons and four daughters. After funeral rites at the Baptist Church, burial was in the family cemetery at Puryear.

Isaac Franklin Littleton, familiarly known as "Uncle Ike," was born in Sumner County, Tenn., September 24, 1837, going to Henry County seventy-three years ago with his parents, who were of prominent English ancestry. Two years later he was married to Miss Emily Catherine Fitts, who died some twenty years ago. Four daughters were born to them, three surviving him, with six grandchildren and three great-grandchildren.

Comrade Littleton was one of Forrest's cavalrymen, serving with Captain Stocks' Company G, 7th Tennessee Cavalry, and he was one of the thirty present at the surrender. He was a faithful soldier throughout the war, and since had been actively interested in the welfare of his comrades and the organization of veterans, also the United Daughters of the Confederacy and kindred associations; he was the oldest member of the Fitzgerald-Kendall Camp, U.C.V., of Paris, and a comrade much beloved.

After the war, Comrade Littleton became a successful farmer and stockman, active in his farming interests until his last illness, and especially giving attention to the shrubbery and plants about his comfortable farm home. He was known as a man loyal to home and family, gentle in manner, kind and considerate to all with whom he came in contact, ever ready to lend assistance where needed.[360]

LIVINGSTON, JAMES L.: Comrade Livingston was born in Orangeburg District, S.C., February 22, 1831, and moved with his parents to Haywood County, Tenn., in 1847, near Lebanon Church, which was his home until his death, September 30, 1904. On December 12, 1860, he was married to Miss Ann W. Carlton, who, with a large family of children and grandchildren, survives him. On April 12, 1862, at the call of his country and with the blessing and tears of his devoted young wife, he entered the Confederate army as a member of the Seventh Tennessee Cavalry. He was elected sergeant and later lieutenant of the company, serving gallantly under Forrest until the surrender, at Gainesville, Ala., May 10, 1865. Lieut. Livingston was an active member of Hiram S. Bradford Bivouac until his death, and in the resolutions passed expressive of their sorrow and esteem they say: "Those who were never within the circle of his influence and never felt the blessings of his presence can realize only in an imperfect degree the loss we have sustained in the death of Comrade Livingston. This Bivouac has lost the active service and wise counsel of a devoted and able comrade, whose life as a soldier, a citizen, and a Christian gentleman is a worthy example to the living; whose death was a victory and whose memory is a benediction."[361]

LOGGINS, WILLIAM EASLEY: William Easley Loggins, who died January 14, 1916, in Reedley, Fresno County, Cal., was a veteran of the Confederacy and a member of Sterling Price Camp, U.C.V., of Fresno. Born in Centerville, Tenn., September 5, 1845, he enlisted at the age of sixteen years and served for over three years in Company D, 9th Battalion, Tennessee Cavalry, General Forrest commanding. This battalion saw hard service and engaged in many encounters with Sherman's army in the march through Georgia, surrendering at Charlotte, N.C., May 3, 1865, under General Johnston. While still but a boy in years, the hard life of the army had not deterred his development; and he was at this time a man of remarkable physique, standing six feet four inches in height and weighing two hundred and eight pounds.

Returning to his old home, Mr. Loggins met and assisted in combating the terrors of the Reconstruction period, being among the first to join that brave and historic band known as the Ku-Klux Klan [a Conservative non-racist organization with no connection to today's KKK].[362] After a few years he went to Obion County, Tennessee, where, in 1875, he married Miss Nannie Curie, of Lynchburg, Va. In 1884 Mr. Loggins removed his family to Fresno County, Cal., where he resided for thirty-one years, establishing a reputation for absolute honesty and integrity. He was a brave soldier, a self-sacrificing comrade, a merciful adversary to those in his power, a kind and loving husband, an almost worshiped father, and an honest, upright, clean-minded man. What better record can be left?[363]

LOLLAR, D. F.: On the 26th of October, 1915, there was laid to rest in the cemetery at Blair, Okla., the soldier, patriot, and Christian gentleman, D. F. Lollar. He was born in Kentucky August 31, 1841, and when but an infant went with his parents to Dade County, Mo. At the breaking out of the War between the States young Lollar cast his lot with the then organizing cavalry troop known as Forrest's Cavalry, afterwards so famous. It is needless to say that many fine steeds fell under his saddle during that eventful period.

Comrade Lollar had married Mary C. Albert before the war, their two families then living north of the historic Mason and Dixon Line. When excitement began to run so high, the Alberts decided to leave that country. So, leaving most of their possessions behind, they went through Arkansas and Indian Territory to Texas and there remained till the close of the war and the return to wife and child of the brave and devoted soldier husband.

Some years later Comrade Lollar located at the thrifty little village of Blair and carried on a successful mercantile business at that place and at Warren, on the Red River, until he sold out the business, a few weeks before his death. To him and his devoted wife were born three sons and five daughters, all surviving him. He was a member of the Church of Christ for over forty years.[364]

LONG, B. R.: At the age of eighty-eight years B. R. Long, former commissioner of Grayson County, Tex., died at his home, in Sherman, on New Year's morning, after a long illness. He was one of the pioneers of his county and was one of the best-known and best-beloved citizens of Sherman. He is survived by his wife, two daughters, and a son.

Comrade Long was a native of Marshall County, Tenn., where he was born on June 21, 1830. He lived for a number of years in Mississippi and served a term in the Mississippi State Legislature. He went to Texas some thirty-nine years ago and, with the exception of three years in Austin, made his home in Sherman all the while. He gave four years of his life to service in the Confederate army under Forrest and since early boyhood had been a stanch [meaning staunch] member of the Methodist Church. Wherever he was known he was regarded as a sincere Christian, faithful in the performance of his duties, loyal in his trusts, and ever ready to lend a hand to those less fortunate. He had long been prominent in county affairs, and his loss will be deeply felt.[365]

LONG, LEMUEL: Near Mt. Pleasant, Tenn., on August 19, 1906, the soul of Lemuel Long passed suddenly but quietly into eternity. A man fitly "formed for deeds of high resolve!" Worth, courage, and honor were his birthright. His genial, hearty companionship, his generous sympathy, kindly courtesy, high principles, and worthy citizenship are sadly missed.

He was a native of Maury County, Tenn., having been born January 11, 1827, within a mile of Mt. Pleasant. Old Jackson College was his Alma Mater. He served the Confederacy under Generals Pillow and Forrest during the four years of fratricidal war. It was under Gen. G. J. Pillow's leadership that Major Long distinguished himself and won the rank of major. He was serving as aid-de-camp until General Pillow was made chief of conscripts in the Western Department; then Major Long was transferred to the 9th Tennessee Cavalry, under Gen. N. B. Forrest, in which he served till the close of the war. His ardent love for the Southern cause never waned. He was a member of the Leonidas Polk Bivouac, U.C.V., of Columbia, and a subscriber to the *Confederate Veteran* from the beginning and the tenets of its faith in the Southland. He was also a faithful soldier of the cross of Christ.

Through his mother Major Long was descended from the Lawrence, Willis, and Boddie families of Virginia and North Carolina which figured in early Colonial and Revolutionary times. He married in the later fifties Miss Martha Woodson Pillow, the second daughter of Jerome B. Pillow, one of the foremost men of Maury County—a woman beautiful in person and attainments, saintly in character, and in every sense a helpmeet to her husband, who was loverlike in devotion and chivalrous courtesy throughout their long companionship of more than half a century. Their home life was ideal, their children worthy scions of a worthy ancestry (both were descended from the cavalier settlers of Virginia).

Lemuel Long.

No man stood higher in the esteem of his fellows than Maj. Lemuel Long. His sudden death occurred while on a visit to the summer home of his daughter, Mrs. E. A. Orr, near Summertown. A vigorous constitution had been his blessing through life; but when he began to decline, a faulty action of the heart gave anxiety to friends. When the Master's summons came, he "fell like autumn fruit that, mellowed long," had waited for the garnering. His body was brought back to the home for the last sad rites, and then borne in the midst of friends and laid to rest in historic old St. John's Churchyard at Ashwood beside his wife, who died a few years ago.

Five children are left with the memory of his life as a benediction: Miss Maude Long, Mrs. E. A. Orr, Mr. Jerome Pillow Long, of Memphis, Rev. Lemuel Long, of Centerville, and Hon. William Bethell Long, of Mt. Pleasant.[366]

LOVING, A. B.: Dr. A. B. Loving, a splendid physician, died at his home, in Pine Bluff, Ark., February 8, 1913, after a long illness. Dr. Loving became a member of Company C, 7th Tennessee Cavalry, at the beginning of the War of the States, and he followed Gen. N. B. Forrest to the close of the war. He leaves a widow and two children to mourn his death. Dr. Loving stood high with the medical fraternity, and was truly a Christian gentleman.[367]

LUCKETT, H. C.: Comrade H. C. Luckett, who died on January 5, 1930, was born in Madison County, Miss., on the 9th day of April, 1848. He joined the Confederate army on the 9th day of April, 1864, serving in Armstrong's Brigade under Gen. N. B. Forrest. He was active to the time of his death as a member of Camp No. 17, of Baton Rouge, and had served as Assistant Quartermaster General, ranking as Colonel, on the staff of Commander in Chief J. C. Foster, in 1927, later being placed on the staff of Commander R. A. Sneed, ranking as Major General.

Comrade Luckett was one of the oldest real estate dealers in the South, for many years running a car on the Illinois Central Railroad from Champaign, Ill., to points in the South, taking prospective buyers from the North. He was also for many years connected with the American Book Company. The last fifteen years of his life were passed in Baton Rouge, during which time he had given undivided attention to his comrades of the Southern cause, working in and out of season to get legislative measures in their behalf. He was very active in getting through the late pension bill which increased the pensions for veterans and widows in Louisiana. His unfailing courtesy and cheerful manner made him a favorite personage in Baton Rouge, and he had friends and admirers among the people of all ages. He is survived by two daughters and a number of grandchildren and great-grandchildren.[368]

LUNSFORD, T. A.: My brother and comrade, T. A. Lunsford, was born in Russell County, Ala., May 19, 1839. Our parents removed to Holmes County, Miss, in 1844, and he was educated in the schools of the county. Responding to the call of the South in 1861, he joined Capt. Josh McBee's cavalry company, made up in Lexington, Holmes County, Miss., which was sent into the Western Department under command of General Forrest.

T. A. Lunsford served in Company A, 28th Mississippi Cavalry, and continued in the cavalry service throughout the war, bringing out with him the same horse with which he entered. His command was in front of Sherman from Vicksburg to Greensboro, N.C. After following Hood into Tennessee and out, he was with the command, retreating slowly and fighting hard all the way to Greensboro, N.C., where Johnston's army surrendered May 1, 1865. He was never wounded.

He returned home after the war to begin life anew. On February 5, 1867, he was married to Miss India Wells, and together they lived a long and useful life and reared a large family of children. He was a devoted member of the Methodist Church. He answered the last roll call and "crossed over the river" on the morning of February 1, 1915.[369]

LYERLY, CHARLES ABNER: Capt. Charles A. Lyerly, one of the best-known citizens of Chattanooga, Tenn., and a leading financier, died in that city on August 9, 1925, after some years of failing health. He was seventy-eight years old, one of the youngest of Confederate veterans.

Charles Abner Lyerly was born in Enterprise, Miss., on March 29, 1847, and enlisted from that place in the Confederate army on April 16, 1864, becoming a member of Company A, Captain Berry, 1st Mississippi Battalion Infantry Reserve forces, and he was made ordnance sergeant of his company. This battalion, which was to have been the 1st Mississippi Regiment but was put into action before the regiment was formed, was intended for provost duty, such as patrolling the trains, guarding military stores and Federal prisoners, and was made up mainly of youngsters who could not be kept out of the war. It was under Gens. S. D. Lee and Forrest in the battle of Harrisburg, Miss., July 14, 15, 1864, and was later sent to Memphis to meet the Federal forces under Canby. It was also in skirmishes during Wilson's raid on Selma and later was paroled at Meridian on May 11, 1865. Sergeant Lyerly was a member of the Mississippi State Guard in the seventies, and was captain of the company.

Comrade Lyerly was educated in the schools of his native place, but at the age of fifteen went into business in order to help the family. He was a merchant at Enterprise until 1880, when he removed to New Orleans, then to Jackson, Miss., in 1884, where he organized the First National Bank of that city and was also interested in the cotton business. He located in Chattanooga in 1887 and organized the First National Bank there, serving as president of that and the First Trust and Savings Bank and was also prominently connected with other banking interests there and in Alabama, cotton mills, express company, and a director in the Alabama Great Southern Railway and the Tennessee Electric Power Company. He was also interested in agriculture, owning a large fruit farm in Georgia and had invested in real estate at Chattanooga. He took a keen interest in political and civic affairs, and was actively interested in the advancement of his adopted city. He served as president of the Chamber of Commerce and was a member of the Mountain City Club. He and his family were communicants of the Episcopal Church, and he was a beloved member of N. B. Forrest Camp, U.C.V.

With many enduring monuments to his work at Chattanooga in a material way, Captain Lyerly will also be remembered for his understanding sympathy and the little acts of kindness which reflected the heart of the man. He is survived by two daughters and two sons, four grandchildren, also a sister and brother living in Mississippi.[370]

LYNN, L. C.: L. C. Lynn, a comrade of Joe Shelby Camp, No. 975, U.C.V., of Chickasha, Okla., was born on November 18, 1844, in Craig County, Ky., and died at Chickasha on July 18, 1920. He volunteered for the Confederate army at Murray, in Callaway County, Ky., in July, 1861, as a member of Company H, 3rd Kentucky Regiment, and was mustered into service at Camp Brooks, Clarksville, Tenn., under Breckinridge, Hardee, and Albert Sidney Johnston. He was wounded twice at Shiloh, in the right arm and left leg. He was promoted to company sergeant in 1863 and was later transferred to Forrest's Cavalry Corps, where he served to the end of the war.

Comrade Lynn was a man of sterling worth, and his influence was felt in his community; he was widely known and highly esteemed. His attractive and genial personality made him a charming companion and loyal friend. He is survived by his wife, who was Miss L. S. Thornton, and eight children. Two of his sons are serving as judges in the courts of Oklahoma. His body was taken back to Kentucky and laid to rest in the cemetery at Murray.[371]

LYON, HYLAN BENTON: [The following is] . . . a tribute to the memory of Gen. H. B. Lyon, who died quite suddenly on his farm, near Eddyville, Ky., on April 25, 1907.

Hylan Benton Lyon.

General Lyon was a graduate of West Point; and when the War between the States was declared, he was a lieutenant in the United States army and out on the Indian reservation. At the very beginning of the war he resigned his position there and hastened home to offer his services to the Confederacy. He at once raised and organized a company for a battery of field artillery. He was soon thereafter elected lieutenant colonel of the 8th Kentucky Infantry, and in that capacity commanded that regiment in the battle of Fort Donelson, where he made himself conspicuous for his cool courage and the intelligent manner in which he handled his regiment. He surrendered there with the army, and was taken as a prisoner of war to Johnson's Island. He was held for seven months, at the expiration of which time (an agreement between the North and South for an exchange of prisoners having been made) he, with his regiment, was sent South. He entered into active service again, and ere long he was engaged in battle at Baker's Creek, Miss. He was sent to Vicksburg with his regiment, and was there shut in with Pemberton's army. His regiment having been mounted, he was granted permission to fight his way through General Grant's lines, and in this he was successful without the loss of a man. For several weeks he operated in the rear of General Grant's army, and did valiant service for the Confederacy; and when Vicksburg was forced to surrender, he went to Jackson, Miss., and was in the severe battle fought there on the 11th and 12th of July, 1863.

Comrades will recall the cool, undaunted courage of General Lyon on this occasion, and where he charged the enemy, losing half of his regiment in a few minutes. Notwithstanding his loss was so great, he forced the enemy to retreat, leaving in front of his command forty-five or fifty, more of the enemy dead than his regiment numbered when the fight began.

In March, 1864, the 3rd, 7th, 8th, and 12th Kentucky Regiments were brigaded together, and General Lyon was given the command. Lyon's Brigade was with Forrest during his memorable campaign into Middle Tennessee. He fought at Athens, Sulphur, Pulaski, and all other battles under General Forrest. He brought on that fearful engagement at Brice's Crossroads, or Tishomingo Creek, as some call it, where General Forrest gained his most signal victory, one of the most complete victories gained by any general during the war, and which General Forrest himself afterwards said was largely due to the undaunted courage of Gen. H. B. Lyon and his Kentuckians.

After this he was given a detached command, and with it made a raid into Kentucky in the rear of General Thomas. That raid demonstrated the fact that he was fully competent to lead an independent command; and had he been given an opportunity, he could and would have written his name high up on the walls of fame as a general and leader of men.

General Lyon was a true, courageous man in all the walks of life. As soldier, legislator, and citizen, he was without hypocrisy or guile. A blunt, honest man, and totally without fear, he spoke his mind on all occasions. Whether it was to applaud a good deed or to denounce infamy, it was no trouble to secure his opinion of men or measures; and we all can truthfully say that in his death the State has lost one of its truest and best citizens, the United Confederate Veterans one of their most courageous comrades, and his family a true husband and loving father.[372]

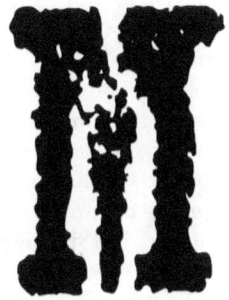

MABRY, HINCHIE P.: Hinchie P. Mabry, listed as a brigadier general in the OR,[373] was born in Georgia, educated at the University of Tennessee, at Knoxville, and came to Jefferson, Tex., when only twenty-one years old and entered upon the practice of law. He was a member of the Texas Legislature, 1859-60, and opposed secession, but believed of course in allegiance to his State, and followed her fortunes. In May, 1861, he served in the expedition that captured Forts Washita and Arbuckle in the Indian Territory. In June, 1861, he became captain of Company G, 3rd Texas Cavalry, commanded by Col. E. Greer, and was in the battle of Oak Hills August 10.

Hinchie P. Mabry.

In the following autumn, under orders of Gen. Ben McCulloch, he and Capt. Alfred Johnson went on a scout as far as Springfield, Mo. Leaving their commands after night, they entered the town on foot while General Fremont [U.S.] held it with over fifty thousand men. They entered the house of a widow whom they knew in search of information. A Federal officer discovered their presence and sent a squad of twenty men to capture them. Going a step into the yard to see that all was well, Captain Mabry was confronted by seven of this squad, who demanded his surrender. Knowing that as a prisoner his fate would be that of a spy, he promptly took the hazard of resistance. With his Bowie knife he cut down two and wounded a third. Captain Johnson sprang from the back door and with his revolver opened on the thirteen remaining in the back yard. The result, all the work of a few seconds, was seven Federals killed and several others wounded. They escaped and, eluding pursuit, rejoined their little command.

Johnson was severely wounded, and Mabry had his hand and arm terribly shattered. He bore this crippled arm and hand the rest of his life, but he recovered in time to lead his company in the battle of Elk Horn. After this battle, he, with the entire regiment, was transferred to Corinth, Miss. In April, 1862, he became lieutenant colonel, and a month later colonel of Johnson's (afterwards Hawthorn's) 6th Arkansas Regiment. He commanded the regiment in the battle of Iuka, where he was severely wounded in three places and captured. Too badly hurt to be moved, he was paroled, and later, in 1862, exchanged at Vicksburg, reassuming command of his regiment, then a part of Whitefield's Brigade. In the summer of 1863 General Whitfield went west of the Mississippi River, and Colonel Mabry then took command of the brigade, then composed of Whitefield's Legion, 3rd and 9th Texas Cavalry, and Craft's Georgia Battery. He commanded the brigade till March, 1864, when Gen. Sul P. Ross, with his old regiment, 6th Texas, added, took command. "At the same time Colonel Mabry was raised to the rank of brigadier general and assigned to the command of a brigade consisting of the 4th, 6th, and 38th Mississippi Regiments, the 14th Confederate, the 14th and 16th consolidated Arkansas Regiments, and an Arkansas battery."

General Mabry was placed in command at Yazoo City and surrounding country, and with his cavalry captured the gunboat *Petrel*, the first incident of the kind on record. He next served with Forrest in all his subsequent campaigns, but was left behind on the campaign into Tennessee. During General Hood's campaign north General Mabry commanded in West Tennessee and North Mississippi. He victoriously fought a severe battle and preserved Hood's connections. He was offered a command under Gen. Stephen D. Lee, but preferred to keep his old command. In March, 1865, Gen. Dick Taylor sent him to Louisiana to conduct troops to the east side of the Mississippi River, but before anything could be accomplished the surrender by Taylor occurred.

The order of Forrest's assistant adjutant general, J. P. Strange . . . was made in March, 1864. . . .

And now a word personally. I want to show how this scribe knows so much about Judge Mabry (I having been until the battle of Mansfield, in 1864, in Hood's Brigade, A.N.V.). We lived in the same town, Jefferson, where I still live, and General Mabry's mortal remains lie in our beautiful Oakwood Cemetery. At the first election in Texas after the war (1866), before *the colored brother* had been enfranchised by the Reconstruction Acts of 1867, General Mabry ran for district Judge and I for district attorney. We were both elected in a large district comprising eleven counties in Northeast Texas, and held our offices until we were officially decapitated by the "carpetbag" [Liberal Yankee] rulers under "Reconstruction." The boys all called General Mabry "old auger eye," owing to a peculiar cast of his eyes which seemed to see everything. For three years we drove together over our district in a double buggy, as it was ten years before we got a railroad, and autos were undreamed of. Invariably the Judge would start to drive every morning, but within the first half hour he never failed to strike a stump, and would coolly inform me (who was ten years his junior) that if I could do any better to drive myself, throwing me the lines. Of course I drove. There was little we did not tell each other on these journeys, and we were very intimate. The lawyers of each county generally drove or rode with us on the circuit. There is nothing set down here but what came from himself, and might almost be considered a part of his autobiography. There are many anecdotes that might be told showing his noble and amiable disposition and his popularity as a judge and a citizen, but I refrain.[374]

MACKEY, BENJAMIN F.: Benjamin F. Mackey died at Center, Ala., on July 28, 1924, aged seventy-eight years. He was born August 14, 1846, in DeKalb County, Ala., and, as a boy of seventeen, enlisted in the army of the Confederacy, serving the last fifteen months of the conflict with Company B, 4th Alabama Cavalry, Morgan's Brigade, Martin's Division, and with Forrest.

After the surrender at Gainesville, Ala., he went to Cherokee County, where he resided until the end. On January 8, 1872, he married Mrs. Sara Hale, of Virginia, and six children were born of this union, of whom four survive him—Leonard E. Mackey, of Mackey, Ala.; Joe A. Mackey, of McAlester, Okla.; Mrs. Etta E. Trotter of Chattanooga, Tenn.; and Mrs. Marie E. Hale, of Leesburg, Ala. Also a stepson, William I. Hale, of Sweetwater, Tenn.

Benjamin F. Mackey.

In 1881, Comrade Mackey embarked in the general merchandise business, and established the post office, Mackey, Ala., at his place of business, which he served as postmaster for over thirty-five years, being the oldest postmaster in Alabama. During his entire business career he never allowed any bills to run past due and never had a claim against him in a lawyer's hands. By integrity and long, steady, conscientious dealing he acquired a competency. He was Scotch-Irish, and naturally a Presbyterian, being a devoted member of the Cumberland Presbyterian Church. He was also a prominent Mason, the oldest member of Sam Dixon Lodge at Center, Ala. An outstanding Democrat [at the time a Conservative],[375] he was a member of the Executive Committee for forty years, and was one of the most earnest, potential units of the party, desiring nothing but to see his friends and Democracy succeed—an unselfish Democrat. He was first lieutenant of Stonewall Jackson Camp No. 658, U.C.V., and was fond of his comrades, enjoying the meeting with them at all reunions.

He was not a man to advertise his deeds, but was always ready to help a good cause—honest, upright, and true in every relation of life. Attended by Confederate comrades and many friends and relatives, he was laid to rest in the family cemetery at Mackey, Ala., by members of his Masonic Order.[376]

MACMURRY, JAMES ALLEN: From memorial resolutions adopted by Camp Sterling Price, No. 31, U.C.V., Dallas, Tex., on December 26, 1920:

"James Allen MacMurry was born in Smith County, Tenn., on November 14, 1842, and died at his home, in Dallas, Tex., on December 6, 1920.

"Comrade MacMurry enlisted in the Southern army in the spring of 1862 in the company known as 'Ward's Ducks,' 9th Tennessee Cavalry, Basil Duke's brigade. He was with Morgan in his Ohio raid and a part of the time in Kip Bennett's battalion. He did scout work for Forrest and was with him at Chickamauga and Missionary Ridge. He was still with Forrest from Dalton to near Atlanta and was captured and thrown into Rock Island Prison, where he was when the war closed.

James Allen MacMurry.

"Comrade MacMurry was married in 1870 to Miss Emily Turner, of Sumner County, Tenn. She survives him, with their six children, two sons and four daughters. The daughters are married and live in Dallas; one son is married and living at Cisco and one is at San Antonio.

"Mr. MacMurry moved to Dallas in 1874 and was a brick contractor. But the last five years he has been in bad health and for two years confined to his home, much of the time to his bed.

"Our comrade was faithful to his country, made a good soldier, and loved to talk with his old friends of the sixties. He was a good neighbor, loving father, and loved our Southern country. Therefore

"Resolved, That we, the Camp, have lost a true man and will miss him. His family has lost a loving father and his wife a kind, trusted husband."[377]

MAHON, JAMES NORFLEET: After an illness of two weeks, James N. Mahon passed away at his home three miles west of Columbus, Tex., on April 14, 1926, aged eighty-nine years. He was a native of Kentucky, his parents going to Texas when he was four years old, first to Fayette County, and, after the war, to Colorado County, where he lived till his death, an honored and much loved citizen.

Comrade Mahon entered the Confederate service in 1861 at Fayetteville, Tex., enlisting in Company D, Nichol's Regiment, Sibley's Brigade, Waul's Texas Legion. He served with his regiment under Forrest in the memorable campaigns which made the cavalry of that period famous, seeing hard service in Louisiana, Mississippi, and Tennessee, including the siege of Vicksburg. After his surrender in May, 1865, Mr. Mahon returned to his home in Fayette County, and, in 1866, was married to Miss Phynetta Gregory, who survives him with one daughter, one grandson, and a great-grandson.

So passes a gentleman of the Old South, a veteran true to his comrades, an honorary member of Shropshire-Upton Chapter, U.D.C., who, with loving hands, placed the evergreen wreath and Confederate flag on his last resting place.[378]

MARSHALL, F. L.: One of the old-time citizens of Weatherford, Tex., passed with the death of F. L. Marshall at his home there on January 16, at the age of eighty-two years. He was born in the State of Tennessee, February 3, 1846, and as a lad of fifteen years he enlisted in the Confederate army, served out his time, then returned home and after a year reenlisted with Forrest's Cavalry and served to the end.

Comrade Marshall went to Texas in 1879, and to Weatherford, in Parker County, about 1884. Then he removed to South Texas and lived there some twenty years, returning to Weatherford a few months ago. He was an active member of the Methodist Church, and it was a matter of pride to him that during his long life he had organized and conducted many Sunday schools. He was a strong believer in education, and gave his children the benefit of the best instruction available that they might be well prepared for their work in life. In his active years he was engaged in the nursery business and had a large nursery and orchard near Weatherford. He is survived by his wife, three sons, and three daughters. Interment was in Greenwood Cemetery at Weatherford.[379]

Jacob T. Martin.

MARTIN, JACOB T.: Among the hosts of brave men who upheld our glorious cause through those years of sacrifice and suffering not one was braver or more devoted than Capt. Jacob T. Martin, of the Eleventh Tennessee Cavalry, who died at his home near Thompson's Station, Tenn., November 12, 1897. It was my [Rev. James H. McNeilly] privilege at one time to be thrown with him quite intimately. I was so impressed with his sterling integrity, his absolute truthfulness, his transparent sincerity, and withal his remarkable modesty, that my heart went out to him at once. He represented some of the noblest characteristics of the old-time Southern gentleman. He was a patriot incorruptible; a knightly soldier "without fear and without reproach"; a friend and neighbor delighting in kindness; a husband and father devoted to his family—above all, an earnest, humble Christian, a worthy example for his generation. It may gratify his old comrades to have a slight sketch of the man whom they so often saw tested and who always stood the test, whom they all loved and respected.

Jacob T. Martin was born near Dixon Springs, in Smith County, Tenn., July 17, 1829. He received a common school education, but his father's death while he was yet a boy made it necessary for him to help in the support of the family. In 1852 he came to Nashville and secured employment. In 1856 he was married to Miss Sue E. Drake, of Williamson County, Tenn., and it was a singularly happy marriage. His devotion to his wife and children for more than forty years was the most powerful earthly influence in forming his character. In 1859 they moved to a farm near Thompson's Station, which his wife inherited.

When the civil war came on, in 1861, Mr. Martin with enthusiasm espoused the cause of the South. He raised a company of cavalry in his neighborhood numbering one hundred and forty. He was elected captain of the company, which afterwards became a part of the Eleventh Tennessee Regiment. Capt. Martin's military service was arduous and brilliant. For a considerable time he served under Gen. Forrest, and he won the confidence of the great cavalryman. He took part in the celebrated capture of Col. Streight and his raiders. He was intrusted sometimes with difficult and dangerous missions which required not only courage, but coolness, prudence, and skill. He never failed to discharge them to the satisfaction of his superior officers.

In June, 1863, to the north of Shelbyville, Tenn., he was cut off from the main army, and extricated his command with such military skill that he gained the admiration of his chiefs and his fellow officers. He served with distinction in the desperate battle of Chickamauga, in September, 1863. His regiment was then on service under Gen. Longstreet in East Tennessee. In that severe campaign they suffered intensely from cold, being poorly provided with clothes; yet he set an example of uncomplaining faithfulness and unselfish modesty. The brigadier general had been wounded; the colonel of his regiment was in command of the brigade, and he was urgently recommended by the officers of the brigade for a commission as colonel, but he refused to accept it. He would not agree to be separated from the boys of his company, who were devotedly attached to him. While as senior captain he commanded the regiment much of the time, and did it with notable skill, yet he refused promotion. He, with his regiment, was under Gen. Wheeler during the campaign of 1864 in North Georgia.

When Gen. Hood undertook his disastrous expedition into Middle Tennessee the Eleventh Tennessee was again under Gen. Forrest. They participated in the hard fighting of that campaign in the advance upon and retreat from Nashville. They made the last desperate stand under their great leader around Selma, Ala.; and then when strength was gone and hope was dead they surrendered the remnant of their magnificent regiment, having done everything that brave and honorable men could do.

Capt. Martin came back to a desolate home. Although he had never done a cruel act to the enemy nor allowed any violation of private rights by his men, yet in the fall of 1864 a Federal force turned his wife and children out of doors and burned their house and destroyed all the supplies they had. He set himself to repair the ruin as best he could, determined to fulfill every obligation of good citizenship. He built a log cabin for his family, and without a murmur went to work. He subsequently came to Nashville, and was here able to make a living and educate his children.

In his later years the family went back to "Happy Valley," where the infirmities of age came upon him, and he also suffered from the results of exposure during the war. But he enjoyed the kindly ministrations of his loved ones and the social intercourse of his neighbors and the consolations of religion until the final summons came.

His letters written to his wife during the war are models of pure English, of lofty sentiment, and manly devotion to his loved ones. A cause which could command the loyal and enthusiastic service of such a man as Capt. Martin was worthy of success, even though success did not crown it.[380]

MARTIN, JONATHAN MCCALEB: In the death of Jonathan McCaleb Martin, of Port Gibson, Miss., one of the prominent men of Claiborne County and Mississippi, and a historical character has passed away. Born on the Talbot Plantation, his father a Marylander, his mother of Mississippi, he early imbibed the cardinal virtues of patriotism and religion. He was educated in private schools and at the University of Virginia, and early in the War between the States he enlisted under Gen. N. B. Forrest, and his distinguished gallantry on the battle field of Harrisburg, as elsewhere, is a part of historic record.

When the South stacked its arms, he turned to complete his academic education and study law in New Orleans, during which time he joined with Capt. Frank McCloin, as a private in that memorable battle of the 14th of September on the levee front of New Orleans to overthrow the hordes of radicalism [that is, Liberalism and its close cousin socialism], and from this experience he helped to establish law and order in the revolution of 1875 in his State.[381]

Mr. Martin was preeminently a lawyer and gave the best of his legal talent in many important cases that came before the Mississippi bar. He was a practical Christian, and his charity of good deeds and words to high and low, rich and poor, cannot be measured. The summary of his life is well expressed in this: Born a Southern gentleman, serving as a gallant soldier of the Southern cause, a leader in reconstruction days, a constructive legislator, an advocate of agricultural supremacy, faithful Christian, devoted husband, a stanch [meaning staunch] friend.

The work of his life was well and amply done, and his services had the appreciation of his fellow men while he was with them, as attested in resolutions by civic committees and clubs from the days of reconstruction. His life was an inspiration and an example to those who follow on.[382]

MARTIN, P. T.: An appreciated honor was bestowed upon Rev. P. T. Martin, of Franklin, Tenn., Chaplain of the Tennessee Division, U.C.V., by making him Chaplain for Life. This beloved veteran enlisted April 7, 1861, becoming a member of Company F, 17th Tennessee Regiment, under Captain Miller, of Chapel Hill, Marshall County, Tenn., and his first battle was at Fishing Creek, Ky., where General Zollicoffer was killed. He and his wounded brother were

P. T. Martin.

among the prisoners taken there, and they spent eight months in prison, being exchanged at Vicksburg. They got back to their command in time to fight Yankees again at Murfreesboro.

He met them again at Chickamauga, and there, on Saturday, he was shot and taken to the hospital, but was able to get back in the battle early Sunday morning, and that was his hardest day's fighting during the war. He says: "When Colonel Floyd formed our regiment and counted us, he said, 'Well, boys, we have lost heavily, but I have yet seventy-six as brave men as ever fired a gun,' my boyish pride welled up in my heart indescribably. From there my command went to East Tennessee with General Longstreet and had a fight at Knoxville, and the next engagement was at Bean Station, where a 'careless Yankee' put a Minie ball into my thigh, where it has been ever since.

"After being disabled for six months, I got back to my command at Petersburg, Va., finding it in the ditches. When we were ordered out for battle, I found that I could not endure the marching and was given a transfer to Forrest's Cavalry [note: believing it a waste of time, Forrest did not march his men], with whom I surrendered at Gainesville, Ala."[383]

MARTIN, RICHARD WALTER: Dr. Richard Walter Martin was a member of John Sutherland Camp, No. 890, of Ripley, Tenn. He was born July 25, 1841, in Chesterfield County, Va., of French-Huguenot descent. He died in July, 1903. He graduated from the University of Virginia in 1860. Responding to the call of Virginia for army surgeons in 1861, he served as a member of the First Virginia Infantry, enlisting at Richmond under Stonewall Jackson, and later with N. B. Forrest. He also served with J. C. Johnson's "Special Regiment" in the siege before Charleston in 1864, and was given an honorable discharge for faithful service rendered during that memorable time; but he reenlisted and came farther south. He was sent to Memphis under a flag of truce to attend wounded Confederate soldiers, and was there captured and imprisoned in the Irving Block, where he contracted typhoid fever. Through the influence of Mrs. E. R. Davis, of 247 Madison Street, he was liberated, and by her gentle ministering restored to health and strength.

Richard Walter Martin.

He was in North Mississippi at the close of the war, and came to Henning, Tenn., and settled in the practice of his profession. Some years later he was married to Miss Dora Posey, which union was blessed with a daughter, now Mrs. J. B. Alston, of Henning. He was actively engaged in the practice of medicine for more than thirty years. He held a membership in the Masonic Lodge and the I.O.O.F. Lodge, of Ripley. He was a good and charitable citizen, a kind and affectionate husband and father, a zealous Christian, a true Mason and Odd Fellow, and a brave and fearless soldier. His remains were interred in Bethlehem cemetery on July 17, 1903, under the direction of the I.O.O.F. and Confederate Veterans. No more fitting tribute may be paid his memory than the unconscious influence of his life, which still lives.[384]

MARTIN, WILLIAM PITTS: William Pitts Martin was born in Columbia, Tenn., May 11, 1848, and was the youngest of six brothers who served in the Confederate army. He ran away from school three times to join the army, but his father was successful in getting him back twice. The last time he was followed to the battle field. His father consented to his remaining, but told him if he ever showed the "white feather" not to return home. He was then fifteen years of age. He served two years with General Forrest in the 9th Tennessee Cavalry. His parole was signed by General Dibrell.

Mr. Martin was married twice, and of the first union three sons survive. His second wife was Miss Mai Oliver, who is left with one daughter. For the past quarter of a century he had made his home in Arkansas, mainly in Searcy, where he was actively connected with Church work. A few years ago he moved to Weatherford, Tex., where his death occurred shortly after the Reunion at Little Rock, which he had attended with much enjoyment. He was believed to be the youngest veteran in attendance. His body was carried back to the old home at Searcy, and there in his uniform of Confederate gray and with the flag about him he sleeps well.[385]

MASENGILL, JOHN D.: Dr. John D. Masengill, who died on January 8 at Blountville, Tenn., was born in Sullivan County, Tenn., May 11, 1844. He served the entire four years as a Confederate soldier, having volunteered at the age of sixteen, and enrolled as a private in the 4th Tennessee Cavalry, Company B. The first two years of the war he was under General Forrest, and in the last two under General Wheeler. During this time he participated in nearly all of the important battles in which the Western Army engaged, including Perryville, Shiloh, Missionary Ridge, and Chickamauga.

After the war he reentered school and later took up the study of medicine, graduating at the Baltimore College of Physicians and Surgeons in 1874. Since that time he had been engaged in practicing medicine and farming near Blountville. In October, 1868, he married Miss Josephine Evans, daughter of Maj. Samuel Evans. He joined the Methodist Church, South, in 1866, and remained a consistent member. Dr. Masengill is survived by his wife and two sons, the latter of Bristol, Tenn.[386]

James M. Mason.

MASON, JAMES M.: Rev. James M. Mason, D.D., a member of Camp Lomax, U.C.V., at Montgomery, died in Opelika, Ala., on February 3, after only a few hours of illness. When but a boy Dr. Mason enlisted in the 4th Alabama Cavalry. The regiment was at an early day attached to Forrest's command, and followed that great leader to the end of the war. Young Mason shared in all the exploits of his command, and deported himself with such gallantry that he was soon promoted to a lieutenancy. He had many thrilling adventures when on detail. More than once he with a few of his comrades crossed the Tennessee River to scout in the rear of the Federal army.

After the war, being convinced that his duty lay that way, he became a Methodist minister, and was as gallant and true a soldier of the cross as he had been of the Confederacy. He rose to eminence in his Church, and filled many of her most responsible positions, among others being a member of six General Conferences. He was loved and honored in Alabama as a good citizen, a faithful and able minister, and a man without reproach.

He was for several years Chaplain General of the Alabama Division, United Confederate Veterans. Gen. George P. Harrison, who had been his intimate personal friend for many years, issued the following General Order as Circular No. 1: "Headquarters Alabama Division, U.C.V., Opelika, Ala., February 3, 1909. It is with profound grief and heartfelt sorrow that the Commanding General announces the death of Col. J. M. Mason, the Chaplain General of this Division, which sad event occurred in this city at 6:30 this morning.

"Suddenly and with little warning he was called by the God he loved and served so well to the better world above. In his departure the Confederate veterans of Alabama have lost a comrade that all loved who knew him. As a follower of the gallant Forrest he won honors that endeared him to all who served with him. He was devoted to our cause next to the service of his God, and always loved to meet with the 'boys who wore the gray.' We will all miss him at our Reunions, where his prayers and benedictions were so comforting to us. In his death the Commanding General has lost a member of his staff whom he loved like a brother and to whom he always looked for counsel and advice.

"While we shall never shake his genial hand again on earth, let us try to emulate his Christian example and meet him when we too 'shall have passed over the river.'"

A delegation from Camp Lomax attended his funeral at Auburn, Ala., and with the reading of their ritual, following the solemn burial service of the Church, his body was laid to rest in the sure hope of a glorious resurrection.[387]

MAY, AUGUSTUS MCCONNICO: [Comrade May] enlisted at Selma, Ala., as one of General Forrest's bodyguards. [He had passed away by June 1914.][388]

MAYS, SAMUEL T.: Samuel T. Mays was born in Davidson County, Tenn., August 12, 1837; died at Baton Rouge, La., October 2, 1909.

Samuel Mays was reared on a farm and was educated at private local schools, finishing at Chapel Hill College, in Williamson County, Tenn. In the fall of 1861 he enlisted in the Confederate army at Nashville, Tenn., and became a lieutenant of Company G, 5th Tennessee, Wills Gould being the captain. His regiment was in the battle of Fort Donelson, in 1862, and in the surrender of General Buckner to General Grant. The privates and noncommissioned officers were sent to Camp Douglass and Alton, Ill., while all officers above the rank of captain were sent to Fort Delaware. The line officers were sent to Camp Chase, Ohio, and later on were removed to Johnson's Island. They were exchanged at Vicksburg in September, 1862, and from there went by rail to Jackson, Miss., where the companies and regiments reorganized, when Samuel Mays was made captain of Company G and C. A. Sugg was made colonel of the regiment. The regiment served in Gen. Lloyd Tilghman's brigade and later in Gregg's Brigade. Captain Mays continued with his command to the end, participating in many battles—with Van Dorn at Holly Springs, at Vicksburg, Port Hudson, and Chickamauga, where nearly all the officers of the regiment were killed or wounded.

Another reorganization took place after this battle, and Gregg's Brigade was assigned to different commands, the 50th, 41st, and 1st Tennessee going to Gen. George Maney's Tennessee brigade. Later his regiment was in the battle of Missionary Ridge, under General Cleburne, Maney's Brigade supporting Granbury's Texans on Sherman Heights. The regiment was almost exterminated here, and

Samuel T. Mays.

this battle ended Captain Mays's career as a soldier. He was the last man shot down, quite in the enemy's line, receiving four shots, three of them severe, which disabled him for further service. He returned home in May, 1865, a cripple, after having been paroled with Forrest's forces at Gainesville, Ala.

After the war Captain Mays rebuilt Riverside to something of its former beauty and bounty. In 1866 he was married to Miss Carrie Taliaferro Hill, of an old Tennessee family, and to this union were born two sons and a daughter, the second son only surviving. After the loss of his wife, in 1874, he spent many years in Nashville, and married a second time in 1882. He removed finally to Ennis, Tex., and thence to Baton Rouge, La., where he died at the home of his son Robert.

Captain Mays kept up his interest in Confederate matters, and was an honored member of Cheatham Bivouac, of Nashville. In 1895 he was elected captain of Company B, a Confederate organization, and commissioned as such by Gov. Peter Turney in the National Guards.[389]

MCCLERKIN, LUTHER CALVIN: Luther Calvin McClerkin, born near Lexington, Tenn., died at his home in Dyersburg, Tenn., on January 23, 1901. When nineteen years of age he enlisted as a private in Company I, Twenty-Seventh Tennessee Infantry. By devotion to duty and conspicuous bravery, he was made captain of his company. On the reorganization of the army, he joined the Thirteenth Tennessee Cavalry, Col. Wilson, which was a part of Bell's Brigade, Forrest's Division. Here, as well as in the infantry, he performed his part so faithfully and well as to gain the plaudits of comrades and the confidence and esteem of his superior officers. Only when the "stars and bars" were furled in the sad surrender did Capt. McClerkin leave his post of duty. He made Dyersburg his home since the war, and was a member of Dawson Bivouac, by which he was buried. A wife and six children survive him.[390]

Baker W. McClure.

MCCLURE, BAKER W.: Baker W. McClure was born November 27, 1841, in Ballard County, Ky. He entered the Confederate army in June, 1861, in Company B, 3rd Kentucky Infantry, and participated with that regiment in the battles of Shiloh, Corinth, Hatchie Bridge, Vicksburg, Baker's Creek, Jackson, Edwards's Depot, Raymond, and Port Hudson. In July, 1863, he was elected second lieutenant in Company E, of the newly organized 12th Kentucky Cavalry, and at the reorganization of this company in November following he was promoted to first lieutenant, thenceforth serving with General Forrest, and from March 15, 1864, with the Kentucky brigade of Forrest's Cavalry. This brigade was composed of the following regiments: 3rd, 7th, and 8th Kentucky Mounted Infantry, and the 12th Kentucky Cavalry, and was commanded respectively by Brig. Gen. H. B. Lyon, formerly of the 8th, and Col. Ed Crossland, of the 7th.

Lieutenant McClure, with this brigade, was engaged in all the battles and campaigns in which Forrest's Cavalry participated: Okolona, Union City, Second Paducah, Brice's Crossroads, Harrisburg, Old Town Creek, Athens, Sulphur Trestle, Tarpley's Shop, Pulaski, Columbia, Johnsonville, and all the battles incident to Hood's Nashville campaign, covering the rear in Hood's disastrous retreat from Nashville, in which diurnal engagements took place. He participated with the brigade in the Selma (Ala.) campaign in the spring of

1865, which terminated April 2. He surrendered at Columbus, Miss., May 16, 1865. He was married March 24, 1872, at Clinton, Ky., to Elizabeth Todd, who died June 22, 1891. He died on December 4, 1912, in Hickman County, Ky.[391]

MCCONNELL, W. M.: W. M. McConnell... is a native of Hartsville, Tenn., was born January 7, 1833. He was raised in Fulton County, Ky., and joined Henderson's Scouts, under Gen. Forrest, where he served during the war, surrendering at Gainesville, Ala. Maj. Charles W. Anderson, a confidential staff officer to Gen. Forrest, in a letter to Capt. J. W. Morton, chief of Forrest's Artillery, pays fine tribute to Capt. McConnell's efficiency as an officer of Henderson's Scouts. He says: "When sent on missions of great importance, the execution of which required energy, intelligence, and nerve, they were ever faithfully executed, and I know he was highly appreciated by Gen. Forrest as a reliable, efficient, and brave officer of that department in the service."[392]

W. M. McConnell.

MCCULLOCH, ROBERT: Col. McCulloch was one of the first sons of Missouri to respond to the call of Gen. Sterling Price, in 1861, for troops to defend the State from Federal invasion. He reported promptly with a full company at Jefferson City, and from there followed the fortunes of Gen. Price's command through the Missouri campaign of 1861.

Early in 1862 he raised and organized the Second Missouri Cavalry, was made colonel of the regiment, and after the battle of Pea Ridge, or Elkhorn, was transferred with Price's troop east of the Mississippi and joined Gen. Bragg's army at Corinth. After the battle of Corinth Col. McCulloch and his regiment were assigned to Gen. Forrest, with whom he served until the close of the war, winning the rank of brigadier general.

Col. McCulloch, although a man of strong personality and a strict disciplinarian, was as gentle and tender as a woman. He knew personally every man in his regiment, and when in camp made their comfort his first consideration; but he would lead them with fierce and reckless daring into the very thickest of the fray. He was badly wounded twice, and much of the time confined to his ambulance while on the march; but he never gave up the

Robert McCulloch.

active command of his brigade. The Second Missouri Cavalry was composed almost entirely of young men and boys of the best families in the State. It is believed that a majority of them were killed or wounded and their bones bleached on the fields of battle fought over by Forrest in West Tennessee, Mississippi, and Alabama.

Col. McCulloch is yet living at his old home in Boonville, Mo., at the ripe old age of eighty-four. The other officers of this gallant old regiment yet living are: Lieut. Col. Robert. A. McCulloch, a kinsman of Col. Robert; Maj. P. A. Savery, of Tupelo, Miss.; Capt. Gus Zallinger, of Otterville, Mo.; Lieut. George M. Buchanan, of Holly Springs, Miss.; Capt. Ed Aldrich, of Collierville, Tenn.; and Lieut. Zack Jennings, of Water Valley, Miss.[393]

MCCUTCHAN, A. C.: Comrade McCutchan died at his home in Victoria, Marshall County, Miss., on May 27, 1901. A. C. McCutchan was a member of Company F, Second Missouri Cavalry, McCulloch's Regiment, Forrest's Cavalry. Survivors of this grand old command will not fail to remember Ab McCutchan, the bold and daring scout, in which capacity he had but few equals. He was a true and courageous soldier on all occasions, utterly unselfish, always ready to help the helpless. He was a great favorite with the whole command. At the close of the war Comrade McCutchan married and located near Byhalia, Miss., where he reared a family of four daughters and three sons, all of whom are now grown. His wife and children all survive him. For a long number of years he was an active and useful citizen. Many years ago he became a zealous member of the Methodist Church, and was always faithful in the discharge of his religious duties.[394]

MCDANIEL, TUBAL E.: Tubal E. McDaniel, one of the few Confederate veterans of Warren County, Ky., died at his home in Smith's Grove on September 10, 1923. He was born near what is now that town on December 6, 1841, and thus had nearly completed his eighty-second year.

He joined the Buckner Guards at Bowling, Ky., the last of December, 1861, commanded by Captain Ridley. This company was disbanded at Corinth, Miss., and he was then transferred to Morgan's Squadron as a member of Company D, Captain Brown, of Louisiana, commanding.

Tubal E. McDaniel.

On Morgan's first raid into Kentucky he was taken prisoner at Lebanon, Tenn., and sent to Camp Chase, Ohio. He reached Vicksburg, Miss., September 10, 1862, on exchange, and in November he was placed in the 9th Kentucky Cavalry, under Col. W. C. P. Breckinridge, as a member of Company I, Capt. William Roberts. He was with Morgan on his raid to Kentucky, Christmas, 1862; in the battle of Milton, April

20, 1863; Missionary Ridge, November 27, 1863; was wounded in the right shoulder at Dud Gap, on Rocky Face Mountain, near Dalton, Ga., May 8, 1864, and was sent to the hospital at Oxford, Ga., but stayed only twenty-five days, reporting to his company before the wound had healed.

He was in the battle of Atlanta, July 22, 1864; was in front of Sherman, and with General Wheeler on his march into Middle Tennessee. He was also with Forrest in Middle Tennessee in October, 1864, reporting back to his command in November. He was wounded severely in the knee in a skirmish near Macon, Ga., November 24, 1864, and was paroled at Macon, April 28, 1865, on crutches. He carried with him through life a stiff knee.

When he returned from the war, he accepted the situation philosophically and devoted himself loyally to his government, but never for a single moment doubting the rectitude of the fight he made for the South. He was a lifelong member of the Methodist Church, an earnest Christian, and was ready with abundant sheaves to answer the last roll call of his great Commander.

He leaves a wife, his companion for fifty-six years, and three daughters, and to these loved ones he has left a heritage of lasting qualities far more precious than many jewels.[395]

MCDOWELL, LUCIEN: Dr. Lucien McDowell died at Flemingsburg, Ky., December 4, 1902, in the seventy-third year of his age. The grave has closed over a good citizen, a Christian gentleman, a comrade tried and true. He was warmhearted and generous, always ready to help where help was needed, and especially where the needy ones were Confederates or their families. He died as he had lived—loyal to his comrades and to the principles for which he had fought and bled.

Comrade McDowell was born in Fleming County, Ky.; graduated at the University of Louisville in 1849, and married the following year. He practiced medicine in Kentucky seven years, and moved to Chillicothe, Mo., in 1856. He enlisted in the Confederate service as surgeon of a regiment under Gen. Jeff Thompson, Price's army, in 1861; served faithfully and well with the gallant Missourians, and was wounded in the battle of Pea Ridge. He was subsequently transferred to the department east of the Mississippi River; had charge of a hospital at Vicksburg during the siege of that city, and was there wounded. He remained in the city to care for the Confederate sick and wounded two months after the surrender. After that he was transferred to the cavalry under Gen. N. B. Forrest, and followed that peerless chieftain through all his trying campaigns. He was at Fort Pillow, at Brice's Cross Roads, and in nearly all subsequent engagements, acting as Gen. Chalmers's division surgeon a portion of the time.

Dr. McDowell stayed till all was over, till the starry cross went down forever;[396] but he did not surrender, he was not paroled, did not take the oath of allegiance to the United States Government, but, bidding adieu to his comrades who were waiting to be paroled, he rode away, with his face toward his "Old Kentucky Home," where he met the wife and children from whom he had been separated for four long years.

At Flemingsburg, the home of his childhood, he began anew the battle of life. He was penniless but not friendless. For thirty-seven years he practiced his profession with success, but never neglected the poor.[397]

William Wallace McDowell.

MCDOWELL, WILLIAM WALLACE: Judge William Wallace McDowell was born near Ironton, Tenn., on June 26, 1833; and died April 30, 1894, and was buried in Elwood Cemetery, Memphis, Tenn.

Judge McDowell was the eldest son of John Davis McDowell, who moved from Mecklenburg County, N.C., and settled in Gibson County, Tenn., in 1832. Judge McDowell was reared on a farm, and educated in the country schools and at Andrew College, Ironton, Tenn., after which he attended the Lebanon Law School, graduating with honors. While attending this school he professed religion and joined the Cumberland Presbyterian Church, of which he was a consistent and devoted member until his death. He returned to Ironton and commenced the practice of law.

When the War between the States broke out, he was one of the first to tender his services to *defend the constitutional rights* of the Southern States. He enlisted in Capt. W. B. Russell's Company, 12th Regiment Tennessee Infantry, on May 10, 1861, and was elected first lieutenant. In the battle of Belmont, Mo., while leading a charge, he was shot down and supposed to be mortally wounded by a Minie ball, which lodged in his body and remained there to his death. He recovered in a few months, however, and returned to his command.

In the battle of Shiloh his captain (B. H. Sanford) was killed and Judge McDowell was elected in his place, which position he held until a consolidation of his regiment with the 22nd Tennessee, which necessitated the discharge of one-half of all the company and regimental officers. He, with officers thus discharged and boys under eighteen years, went to Tippah County, Miss., and, adding to these discharged Tennesseans, raised a company of cavalry, joined Col. J. G. Ballentine's regiment and served under Gen. W. H. Jackson and Gen. Earl Van Dorn until the latter's death, after which he and the Tennesseans with him were transferred to Gen. Tyree Bell's escort, Forrest Cavalry, Capt. McDowell commanding the escort until the army surrendered, at Gainesville, Ala., May 11, 1865—having served four years and one day.

Capt. McDowell was wounded by a piece of a shell which struck him on the breast during the Hood campaign into Tennessee, but refused to leave the command. He was again struck on the breast by another piece of shell in a subsequent battle; but it being slight, he continued with the command. He always entered a battle at the head of his men, apparently fearless of consequences. As commander of his company, he was uniformly kind to his men, all of whom were devoted to him.

Shortly after the war he moved to Memphis, Tenn., and resumed the practice of law, forming a partnership with George Gantt and Josiah Patterson. In a short time he was elected county attorney, and was reelected for three successive terms, after which he was elected chancellor, which position he held for eight years. In 1888 he was elected a member of the State Senate, which position he most worthily filled.

Judge McDowell was married twice: first to Miss Annie E. Jones, on March 27, 1867. Of this union three children were born—W. W. McDowell, Eula Ewing, and John Overton McDowell. His second wife was Mrs. Lizzie Freeman, daughter of Capt. Joseph Lenow. One daughter (Edith) and two boys (Neely and Francis) were born of this marriage.

Although Judge McDowell was a lifelong Democrat [until 1896, a Conservative], a worker in every campaign, he had few, if any, enemies and a host of friends. He was of Scotch-Irish descent, both of his great-grandfathers performing gallant service in the Revolutionary War. His maternal great-grandfather, Gen. Robert Irwin, was one of the twenty-four signers of the Mecklenburg Declaration of Independence. His brother. Col. J. H. McDowell, of Union City, Tenn., is noted for his Confederate valor and his devotion to his comrades.

Dr. A. H. McAllister writes from Blue Mountain, Miss., of Capt. McDowell's high qualities: "He was truly patriotic and brave, and as daring as a thoughtless boy. In camp to talk of close places and noble and brave deeds of his boys to him was a joy. He was a gentleman of the highest type; he was social and kind to all good and faithful soldiers, while a coward he despised. He was so high-minded that his Christian influence over me (then a small, timid boy) was elevating and inspiring, and it has done me good through life."[398]

MCGANN, JAMES L.: It is my sad privilege to announce to the remnant of that gallant throng who once marched so proudly beneath the Stars and Bars that another of their comrades has dropped from the ranks and joined the colors in the march triumphant on the other shore. The bugle has sounded its requiem, and the drum has beat its last tattoo over all that was mortal of James L. McGann.

He was born on the 17th of January, 1840, and died October 12, 1915. He celebrated his majority by enlisting as a soldier in the Confederate army and served as a member of Barteau's 2nd Tennessee Regiment, Morton's Battery, Bell's Brigade, Jackson's Division, Forrest's Cavalry. He was personally engaged in the battles of Parker's Crossroads, Okolona, Fort Pillow, Memphis, Brice's Crossroads, Harrisburg, Johnsonville, Franklin, Athens, Sulphur Trestle, Iuka, Corinth, Bay Springs, Hood's Raid, Scottsville, and Gainesville. No soldier who followed the dauntless Forrest through his campaigns needs any one to attest to his courage or vouch for his loyalty. To be of Forrest's command was to laugh at danger and defy privations.

To the end of his life James McGann was true to the principles for which he fought. The Confederacy [an ancient, Conservative form of government][399] was a cause sacred to him, and its memories were among his most cherished recollections. In politics he was a Democrat [then a Conservative] of the old time variety. He went astray after no new fads, no modern inventions of the catch-vote kind. As a citizen he was modest and retiring, as chivalrous and courteous as a Bayard, demanding that respect from all which he extended to all. He was a truthful man, scrupulously honest, loyal to friends as he was to principles. Having lived a life of seventy-five years in this community, he left it without a reproach upon his name. As a husband and father he was an example that all

James L. McGann.

might follow. For years before her death his wife was an invalid, and during this time he waited upon her with a tenderness and devotion that was the admiration of all who saw it.

Captain McGann lived his life without ever having been confined to his bed by sickness, and when his end came he died without pain or fear of the future. He laid him down to his last sleep like "one who wraps the drapery of his couch about him and lies down to pleasant dreams."

With sincere regard for the friendship that existed between us, it is in sadness that I place this humble tribute to his memory.[400]

MCGAUGHY, J. B.: He was born September 26, 1834. He married at the age of nineteen, and of this union there were born six sons and one daughter. All but one son survive him. He moved to Texas in 1873, and to Brownwood in 1889. In recent years his home was with his daughter, Mrs. Charles [O'Connor] Blakeney,[401] at Stephenville, where he had been city health officer and a consulting physician, having retired from active practice.

Dr. McGaughey was a Royal Arch Mason of many years' standing and a member of the Cumberland Presbyterian Church, a Christian gentleman whose character was worthy of emulation.

During the war he was surgeon of the 4th Alabama Regiment under General Forrest, with whom he was personally and intimately acquainted. Throughout the long struggle he gave his skill and best service to the Southern cause. At Brownwood he was a member of the Stonewall Jackson Camp, and at the time of his death he was an honorary member of the Camp at Stephenville.[402]

MCGLATHERY, JAMES MIKAJAH: James M. McGlathery entered into rest in his beautiful home, "Miramir," in Pass Christian, Miss., on November 3, 1918, after a brief illness, in his seventy-third year.

James Mikajah McGlathery.

Born in Corinth, Miss., November 25, 1845, Comrade McGlathery was but sixteen years of age when the State of Mississippi seceded from the Federal Union. Two years later he joined Forrest's Cavalry and remained in the service of the Confederate States until the close of the war, a gallant soldier of the Southern cause. He enlisted first in Company A, 19th Tenn. Cavalry, Col. John A. Newsom, Bell's Brigade, Buford's Division, Forrest's Cavalry. In March, 1865, when the 19th and 25th Regiments were consolidated, Company J was formed of what was left of Company A and parts of other companies under Capt. H. C. Klyce, and young McGlathery was made corporal. He was paroled at Gainesville, Ala., on May 8, 1865.

Comrade McGlathery was a member of Camp 120, U.C.V., of Mississippi and represented his camp at most of the Confederate reunions. He received the Cross of Honor from Pass Christian Chapter, U.D.C., and regarded it as one of his cherished possessions.

Most of his useful life was spent in railroad service in Tennessee and Louisiana; but in 1899 he removed to Pass Christian, Miss., where he engaged most successfully in the hotel business until the time of his lamented death.

Captain McGlathery, as he was commonly called, was a member of the Protestant Episcopal Church and was Senior Warden of Trinity Church at Pass Christian, from which he was buried in the beautiful Lone Oak Cemetery, with full Masonic honors at the grave.

Faithful in the discharge of every duty which came to him to perform, our comrade was a valuable member of the community, a devoted husband, a loving father, and a loyal friend. His memory will be cherished by all who knew him. He was married November 3, 1873, to Miss Georgia Campbell, of Shuqualak, Miss., and is survived by his wife, a daughter, and three sons, one of whom, Capt. Samuel L. McGlathery, is with the 312th Engineers, U.S. Army, American Expeditionary Force, in France.[403]

MCGOWAN, JOHN L.: H. H. Stevens, Adjutant Sam Benton Camp, U.C.V., at Byhalia, Miss., December 15, 1900, reports that "the Silent Reaper has again invaded the ranks of our Camp, and a noble Mississippian (Capt. John L. McGowan) was gathered in the harvest of death on Friday, December 7. A brave soldier, a patriotic citizen, and a good man has crossed over to where he will again enjoy the companionship of his immortal comrades who had preceded him into eternity. History is eloquently told in the annals of his State and of the Confederacy. The Sam Benton Camp, U.C.V., pay tribute to the memory of their deceased comrade.

Capt. McGowan was born in Union District, S.C., in 1840, and came with his father's family to Marshall County, Miss., in 1848. He enlisted in the Confederate army March 27, 1861, and, after serving one year at Pensacola as first lieutenant in Company F of the Ninth Regiment Mississippi Volunteers, he was made captain in Ballentine's cavalry, and was a most efficient officer. He was frequently detailed by our gallant Gen. Forrest to perform perilous duty. He surrendered with his command at Grenada, Miss., in May, 1865. He was a Presbyterian and a Mason. Two brothers, one son, and five daughters survive him.[404]

MCGREGOR, AUGUSTUS SILAS: On October 29, 1914, The Florida State Reunion at Lakeland was saddened by the death in their midst of Comrade A. S. McGregor, of Tampa, Fla. His remains were taken to Tampa for burial.

Augustus S. McGregor was born near Rockmart, Polk County, Ga., on April 28, 1842, the youngest of seven children. In September, 1861, before he was of age, he enlisted under Capt. John Crabb in Company A, 7th Georgia Cavalry, serving at first in Forrest's Brigade and Martin's Division, Army of Tennessee. The first battle of importance in which he took part was at Murfreesboro, Tenn., July 30, 1862. Like others, he had many very close calls. Once while in the enemy's camps near Chickamauga he was discovered as a spy, but managed to make good his escape. Again, in June, 1864, while at home on a brief visit, the house was surrounded by forty-two Federal soldiers. Escape seemed impossible, as he had to cross a twelve-hundred-acre farm in his dash for safety, but this he accomplished safely.

After serving a while under Forrest, he was transferred to Wheeler's command. During his four years of service he took part in over a hundred engagements, the last one being near Raleigh, N.C. He was paroled at Greensboro, N.C., on April 28, 1865. He was wounded twice during his service, once at Somerset, Ky., in March, 1863, and again at Atlanta, Ga., in July, 1864.

After returning home he attended school until 1868, when he was elected sheriff of Polk County. He served thus until 1874. On December 15, 1870, he was married to Miss Dora Burge at Stilesboro, Ga., and lived on his farm until 1884, when he moved to Florida. In 1889 his life was saddened by the death of his wife. He is survived by five children, one brother, and two sisters.[405]

MCINTOSH, W. D.: The summons so anxiously awaited came to one of God's noblemen at the close of January 23 [1916?] when the gentle spirit of W. D. McIntosh passed into the great beyond. His earthly pilgrimage was over fourscore years. He died at the home of his son in Hereford, Tex., and was buried at Rosebud on the 26th.

W. D. McIntosh was born July 18, 1843, in Darlington, S.C., but moved to Mississippi, and from that State he enlisted in the 20th Mississippi Regiment under General Forrest and did gallant service throughout the War between the

States, receiving a wound in the battle of Corinth.

In October, 1865, he was married to Miss Marian Hardy, of Hardyville, near Newton, Miss., and twelve years later they went to Texas, locating in Robertson County, later living in Milan and Falls Counties. He united with the Baptist Church in 1866 and lived a loyal, consistent Christian life. His chief characteristics were honesty, truthfulness, loyalty to his friends and to his convictions. He is survived by four sons.[406]

MCKISSACK, A. C.: Capt. A. C. McKissack, of Holly Springs, Miss., died in Memphis, Tenn., September 28, 1898. From a memorial prepared by a committee of fellow-members of Camp Kitt Mott No. 23, U.C.V., the following is taken:

He was a native of Pulaski, Tenn., and a graduate of Yale College. He made Marshall County, Miss., his home in 1856. When the call to arms was made, in 1861, he was among the first to respond, enlisting as a member of the noted Jeff Davis Rifles, commanded by Col. Sam Benton, and upon the organization of the Ninth Mississippi regiment he became its color bearer. Afterwards, when the term of service of the Ninth regiment had expired, Capt. McKissack was called to the command of a company of cavalry under the immortal Forrest, in which capacity he served until the close of the war.

Having done his full duty, Capt. McKissack again sought quiet in his country home, a peaceful citizen ever; a patriot, whose highest aim was his country's welfare; a philanthropist, whose creed was based on the immaculate law of fraternal love and charity. The committee was composed of J. B. Mattison, Addison Craft, and S. H. Pryor.[407]

MCKNIGHT, MOSES WADDELL: Col. M. W. McKnight, distinguished as an officer of Forrest's Cavalry, was born in Cannon County, Tenn., June 22, 1833, son of Alexander and Anna P. McKnight and great-grandson of Moses Waddell, the famous educator, founder, and President of North Carolina University.

Comrade McKnight was graduated at Irving College, near the Cumberland Mountains, in 1853. He taught school and read law with Maj. J. L. Fare and Charles Ready, gaining admission to the bar at Woodbury, Tenn., in 1858. In 1855 he was married to Mary A. Fare. He engaged in the practice of law until after the formation of the Confederacy. Being of old Whig stock [the American Liberals of the day], he opposed secession, and on the night before the election which decided the withdrawal of Tennessee he made the last Union speech in the city of Nashville, in which he stated, however, that whatever the result might be he would go with his State, enlist in her army, and fight to the end.

He enlisted as a private in Capt. T. M. Allison's company of the 1st Battalion, Tennessee Cavalry, June 28, 1861. He was soon elected sergeant major of the battalion. At Jacinto, Miss., on May 14, 1862, his company reenlisted for three years or during the war, and he was elected captain. His battalion and the seventh were consolidated, his company becoming Col. the

2nd Regiment Tennessee Cavalry, under Col. C. R. Barteau. This regiment was in Bell's Brigade under Nathan B. Forrest, distinguished in many famous victories.

Captain McKnight gallantly led the regiment as its temporary commander in the battle of Okolona, Miss., in February, 1864, and was badly wounded in the left breast late in the afternoon, but did not leave the field. In the fight at Paducah, Ky., March 25, 1864, he again commanded the regiment, and was stricken down and his head fearfully crushed by a falling chimney which had been hit by a shell. Though he still suffered from the injury, he participated in the great victory at Brice's Crossroads, June 10, 1864, and the exciting pursuit of the enemy back to Memphis. On July 13, the day before the battle of Harrisburg, he was again wounded, the bones of his left leg being shattered between the knee and ankle. He was sent to the home of Col. J. D. MacAlister, near Aberdeen, Miss., and in August while there he received notice of his promotion to colonel of cavalry by General Forrest; but he could not accept the position, and was never again in the field. When General Forrest surrendered his command in May, 1865, he sent Colonel McKnight his parole in care of General Bell.

Colonel McKnight, returning to Tennessee, was elected President of the Woodbury College, a position he held for three years, at the same time looking after his law practice. In 1870 he was elected Attorney-General of the Seventh Judicial Circuit of Tennessee, and he filled this office most ably until 1878. In 1880 he moved to Waxahachie, Tex., and prominently began the practice of law. He was an elder in the Presbyterian Church, a high Mason, and a Democrat [a Conservative at the time]. His wife, a loving and devoted companion and mother, died in Chicago, Ill., September 25, 1894, and was buried at Lebanon, Tenn. There are two children living, Sarah A., wife of Dixon C. Williams, of Chicago, Ill., and Alex J., of Commerce, Tex.

Colonel McKnight was a faithful and devoted member of Camp Winnie Davis, of Waxahachie, Tex., and we, the members of this Camp, do hereby express our deep sorrow in the loss of our beloved comrade, friend, and associate, a man of honor, veracity, and integrity and much loved.[408]

MCLAUGHLIN, JAMES WHARTON: Dr. J. W. McLaughlin, one of the leading physicians of Austin, Tex., and Regent of the University of Texas, died at his home on the 13th of November, 1909. He was born near Springfield, Ohio, in 1840. On the death of his father he studied medicine with his uncle, C. D. McLaughlin, with whom he lived until the breaking out of the War between the States. Being an ardent supporter of States' Rights [that is, a Conservative], young McLaughlin was soon convinced that south of Mason and Dixon's line was the safest place for him; so he quietly disappeared from his home early in April, 1861. Reaching Louisville, Ky., he enlisted in Company D, 1st Kentucky Infantry, and at Harper's Ferry, Va., was sworn into the Confederate service for one year, but remained in the service unto the end, serving at various times under Johnston, Jackson, Morgan, and Forrest.

Unreconstructed, McLaughlin and A. H. Cross, an army comrade, started for South America [in 1866]; but on reaching Texas McLaughlin began the practice of medicine with Dr. McLeary near Columbus, and the next spring, 1867, he graduated in medicine at the University of Louisiana.

He was married in September, 1867, to Miss Tabitha Bird Moore, and located in Fayette County; but in 1869 he removed to Austin, where he had become one of the most widely known physicians of Texas. His intellectual and spiritual characteristics were such as to make him an ideal physician, whose great heart gave comfort to many ills of the spirit and of the flesh. His work was his joy, as the love he inspired was his comfort. Dr. McLaughlin was always a student of medicine and the allied sciences, and worked earnestly to the advancement of medicine along scientific lines. His numerous contributions are scattered widely through current medical literature. He served as President of the District Medical Society, the Travis County Medical Society, the Texas State Medical Association, and as President of the Texas Academy of Science. From 1897 to 1905 he was professor of medicine in the University of Texas, and in 1907 he was made Regent of that institution through the appointment of Governor Campbell. Though greatly beloved by his students, his greatest work was as physician and friend.[409]

James Wharton McLaughlin.

MCLEAN, WILLIAM HEWLETT: William Hewlett McLean, a native of Winston County, Ala., was at La Grange in 1860-61 as a State cadet. From 1862 to the close of the war he served in Company A, 11th Alabama Cavalry, under Forrest. He was wounded at Harrisburg, Miss., in July, 1864, and again in Hood's Tennessee campaign in December of the same year. He died in Alabama on the 6th of August, 1915, in his seventy-second year.[410]

MCMURRAY, W. J.: . . . It would not be extravagant to state that [Dr. W. J. McMurray, of Nashville] was the most useful Confederate in Tennessee. Impaired by the loss of an arm in the service and an education which was kept back by the four years of war, still he began the uphill of life with courage undaunted. Soon after beginning his educational course as a physician reconstruction methods were such as to compel renewal of strife in a more complicated way than open war for the defense of home and morality, and young McMurray organized the Ku Klux [a Conservative non-racist organization with no connection to the modern KKK][411] in a large area extending south of Nashville for fifty miles.[412] Two deserters from the Klan reported its secrets to the military authorities in Nashville, and the determination to have him executed was quickly ascertained. It was believed that summary methods would be adopted, so in a few hours' time the traitors disappeared from the face of the earth and no other witnesses could be found to condemn him. He remained about home during that perilous period. Dr. McMurray began to write the history of the Ku Klux operations just before the attack of his fatal illness, but had gone far enough with his notes to enable his friends to complete it.

W. J. McMurray was born in Williamson County, Tenn., September 22, 1842, the son of John McMurray, a noted teacher of young men in that county. When but ten years of age, his mother was left a widow with seven children. As a child he had often heard his father speak of the war that would take place between the North and South; and when the first bugle blast swept over the hills of old Williamson, young McMurray was among the first to respond to its call, and joined a company that was being raised by Capt. Joel A Battle at Nolensville in April, 1861, which afterwards became Company B, 20th Tennessee Infantry Regiment. Devotion to duty and bravery on the field won him promotions as corporal, orderly sergeant, and to first lieutenant. Some marvelously heroic deeds were performed by this young lieutenant, one of which was the capture of a party of Federal soldiers in the basement of a house by his bold demand that they surrender. An incident of his cool courage is told by his comrades of his going into the battle at Resaca, Ga., with a rallying song on his lips. He was wounded several times. At Murfreesboro he was wounded in the breast, and lay all night in the rain; at bloody Chickamauga he was thought to have been mortally wounded, and was again left on the field through the night; at Resaca he was wounded in the left leg; and on the 5th of August, 1864, he lost his left arm in front of Atlanta. When he had recovered from this wound, he again reported for duty, and surrendered with General Forrest at Marion, Ala., May 17, 1865.

W. J. McMurray.

After the war was over, he returned home and went to work in the field to get money for his living and to finish his education, graduating as valedictorian of his class at the Nolensville Academy in 1867. He then read medicine with two physicians there, and graduated in medicine from the University of Nashville two years later, receiving the unanimous vote of his class of seventy-two graduates to deliver the valedictory address. He began the practice of medicine in 1869, and became noted in his profession and for his liberality toward his patients, and especially for his charity practice. His first prominence in this latter respect was attained by his charity practice for the Tennessee Industrial School, which he served for twelve years.

The crowning work of Dr. McMurray, however, was in his service for the Tennessee Confederate Soldiers' Home, eleven miles from the city. In selecting a Board of Managers some twenty years ago, Dr. McMurray, Capt. M. S. Cockrill, and Maj. R. H. Dudley, all of Nashville, were made an Executive Board, and for several years the three practically managed the Home. Captain Cockrill looked after the farm (the Hermitage), Dr. McMurray looked specially to the sick (a physician was employed later), and Major Dudley, merchant, looked after the finances. Upon his election as Mayor of Nashville, Major Dudley resigned, and Mr. Joseph B. O'Bryan was chosen his successor, continuing till his death, when Mr. J. B. Richardson succeeded him, and Mr. Tim Johnson succeeded Dr. McMurray. In all these years Dr. McMurray continued his oversight of the sick, traveling a distance in the aggregate of perhaps more than eight thousand miles, at a sacrifice of at least ten thousand dollars. With all these detractions from business he was successful, and he procured a fine estate.

Dr. McMurray was a charter member of Frank Cheatham Bivouac, of Nashville; was one of its presidents, and also President of the State Association. He was President of the State Board of Health at the time of his death, and for a number of years he had been Surgeon General on the staff of Gen. S. D. Lee, Commander in Chief U.C.V. His loyalty and devotion to the cause will be best appreciated by comrades of the South in being recalled as the Commissary for both the Nashville Reunions. His "Confederate Hotel" was always mentioned with pride and satisfaction by the committee. When the second Reunion for Nashville was suggested, he was of the first to say, "No; we have an established reputation and do not want to risk it again"; but when it was decided to entertain the Confederates the second time, Dr. McMurray told his family that he would have to give up home again, and he practically worked night and day until every visiting comrade had left the city.

Dr. McMurray was an enthusiast for the 20th Tennessee Infantry, and with the assistance of Dr. Deering J. Roberts he issued a most authentic history of the regiment a year or so ago. He wrote the sketch of that regiment for Lindsley's *Military Annals of Tennessee.* He was married in 1873 to Miss Francis M. McCampbell, daughter of Hon. Thomas C. McCampbell, State Senator from the Knoxville District in 1845. She and their only child, Mrs. Charles L. Ridley, with three grandchildren, survive him.[413]

MCNEILL, MALCOLM: Sergt. Malcolm McNeill passed away March 28, 1917, aged seventy, at the home of his son, in Estill, Miss., and was buried in his suit of gray in Elmwood Cemetery, Memphis, Tenn. He was born in Christian County, Ky., and grew up in that State and in Mississippi. At the age of sixteen he enlisted in Forrest's Cavalry, Company L, 18th Mississippi Regiment, and with this command he fought till the close of the war and was then paroled.

Leaving Mississippi soon after the war, he went to Chicago, where he was quite successful in business until the financial depression of 1893-95 caused him to lose all of his previous gains. In 1901 he moved to Georgia, where he remained until failing health caused his retirement from business, and in 1916 he went to the home of his son Tom, who gave his father most loving care until death.

The love of Malcolm McNeill is one of the treasures of my memory. Without fear, he was as loving and tender as a woman. His generosity was without limit. He could not be content unless he was giving to those he loved, and his wife received from him a love that amounted almost to idolatry. As a climax to all of his noble qualities, he was a devoted follower of the Saviour. Brave he was, yet tender; of noble lineage, he was humble; a daring Confederate soldier, he had no hate. True to every trust, loyal to his friends, his was the full measure of manhood. His wife, Mrs. Willie Gilmore McNeill, and five children survive him. I thank God that it was my privilege to be his friend.[414]

MCNEILLY, FELIX C.: Felix C. McNeilly, aged eighty-one years, died on January 28, 1924, at the home of his son, Charles M. McNeilly, in Miami, Fla., where he had gone to spend the winter. He was born in Dickson County, Tenn., March 19, 1843, and his boyhood was spent in Charlotte, Tenn., where he received his education at Tracy Academy. He was engaged in mercantile pursuits until forced to retire on account of the infirmities of age.

With the death of Mr. McNeilly there comes to a close the career of one of the well-known heroes of the War between the States. Upon the secession of Mississippi, he enlisted as a soldier in the 28th Mississippi Regiment, Armstrong's Brigade, W. H. Jackson's Division, under the command of Gen. Joseph E. Johnston. He held the rank of sergeant

The cotton ginhouse, located at the epicenter of the Battle of Franklin (II), November 30, 1864.

and served throughout the war. During a portion of the war he served in General Forrest's command. He and his two brothers, Thomas Lucien and the late Rev. James H. McNeilly, participated in the battle of Franklin, when the brother T. L. met his death in the attack at the ginhouse. He was a soldier of unflinching courage, and was conspicuously faithful to duty in the most trying circumstances. He was twice desperately wounded in battle.

Mr. McNeilly was a man of handsome appearance and of fine mind. He was absolutely true and dependable in all the relationships of life. A very positive character, fearless and outspoken in his views, yet a person of great generosity and kindness. He was greatly respected by all who knew him, and his sterling qualities of character won to him many friends.

He was an earnest, devoted, and consistent Christian, being a member of the Presbyterian Church, in which he was reared. His religious interests and activities were not restricted to his own denomination, but he was active in aiding and upbuilding the Churches of the other denominations in any community where he resided.

On October 15, 1873, he was married to Miss Ella E. Bagwell, of Montgomery County, Tenn., who died October 14, 1909.

Mr. McNeilly's body was taken to Ashland, Ky., his former home, for burial beside his wife. He leaves three children—Mrs. Sam Chesnut, of Elkton, Ky.; G. W. McNeilly, Ashland, Ky.; and Charles M. McNeilly, Miami, Fla.; also six grandchildren.[415]

MCREA, JESSE WORK: Jesse Work McRea, joined [the Confederate army] in Montgomery, Ala., under Bedford Forrest, Company F, 21st Alabama Regiment; attended to the horses for General Forrest.[416]

MCREE, F. M.: F. M. McRee, born August, 1845, died July 25, 1928, aged eighty-three years. He was a member of the 10th Tennessee, Forrest's Cavalry.[417]

MCREE, N. L.: Comrade N. L. McRee was born in Gibson County, Tenn., September 16, 1846; and died in Trenton September 4, 1912. He was a Confederate soldier in Capt. Tom Gay's company of Col. R. M. Russell's regiment, Bell's Brigade, Buford's Division, Forrest's Cavalry Corps, with which he served until surrendered and paroled at Gainesville, Ala., May 9, 1865. He became a member of the Presbyterian Church in 1863, and was a deacon and treasurer from that time until his death. He was a druggist by profession, and remained in the business all his life. He was widely known and dearly beloved, a good soldier and a good citizen.[418]

John Metcalf.

METCALF, JOHN: John Metcalfe died at his home in Montgomery, Ala., on April 3, 1924, at the age of seventy-eight years.

He was born in Washington, D.C., and was taken by his parents, to Montgomery when he was seven years of age. In 1863 he entered the Confederate army, the 7th Alabama Cavalry, under Capt. C. P. Stone and Col. James Hodgson. He has served on the staff of the Commander of Alabama U.C.V., and was a member of Camp Lomax, of Montgomery.

His life in the business world was spent in railroad work, which began with the Louisville and Nashville. In 1889 he formed connection with the Southern Railway and remained with that company until his death, serving for a time as district passenger agent.

His last position was that of special passenger agent. He ever had the confidence of his superiors.

He is survived by his wife, who was Miss Cora Annulette Farley, two daughters, and three sons, also by two sisters.

Comrade Metcalfe was a brave son of Alabama during the War between the States. He and his devoted friend, George W. Hails, of Montgomery, entered the war together and fought side by side throughout the struggle. Young Metcalfe volunteered at the age of sixteen, enlisting in the Tuscaloosa Cadets in 1863. In 1864 his cavalry outfit was placed under the command of Nathan B. Forrest. It was in the battles in Tennessee that he saw the greatest service. He was in the thick of the fighting at Nashville. Gen. E. W. Rucker, whose death is just reported, was his commander at that battle. One of his daring acts during the war was near Columbia, Tenn., when he captured a flag of the enemy.[419]

MICHIE, ROBERT WASHINGTON: At Stantonville, Tenn., on September 1, 1931, Robert W. Michie, one of the boys in gray who engaged in that valiant struggle of the Confederacy for a great cause, passed peacefully into rest. The passing years having taken from his eyes vision of the fallen dead, and Time's sweet healing having removed from his hearing the noise and strife of mortal combat, this good old man, eighty-six years of age, heard the peaceful blasts of the Great Bugler, and now "no blaring horn nor screaming fife" that warrior's dreams alarm.

Mr. Michie was one of ten Confederate veterans remaining in McNairy County, and was Commander of the Albert Sidney Johnston Camp, U.C.V., at Shiloh. He always enjoyed the interest of people in "Old Soldiers Day," and liked to meet his comrades in reunion and commune with them on the days of war, living over those long marches, the many privations, the battles, the comrades lost, Appomattox, and the return to a land of woe and desolation, and the rehabilitation of a devastated section.

Now he has joined his comrades in that sinless, summerland where there will be no more tattoo and no more reveille. He was a brave and gallant soldier of Company E, 18th Tennessee, the "Shiloh Regiment," following the intrepid Forrest for four long years. In times of peace he was no less renowned in his efforts to make the county a better place in which to live.

Mr. Michie was laid to rest in Carter's Cemetery in the 9th District of McNairy County. He is survived by his wife and seven children, a host of relatives and friends. All honor to his memory.[420]

MILLS, JOHN RICHARD: John Richard Mills, one of the best and most beloved citizens of Madisonville, Ky., died on July 31, 1910, at the age of sixty-six. He was born at Roaring Spring, Ky., February 14, 1844, and was a member of one of Trigg County's (Ky) oldest and best families.

At the first call to arms in 1861, although only seventeen years of age, he left his home and school, near Providence, Ky., and, in company with several schoolmates, went to Hopkinsville, Ky., and joined a company organized by Capt. J. K. Huey, of Smithland, Ky., which became Company H, 1st Kentucky Cavalry, and became a part of General Forrest's regiment. He followed the fortunes of the Confederacy until the battle at Fort Donelson, where he was captured. He was sent to prison at Indianapolis, Ind., and after eight months was exchanged at Vicksburg, Miss. He was a man of unbending integrity, yet gentle as a woman; of dauntless courage, yet modest and retiring. He was genial, kind, charitable, generous, the very soul of honor, and a humble Christian.

As a soldier John Richard Mills was brave, prudent, faithful. He never shirked a duty or sought an easy place; he cherished fondly the memory of those glorious days. He enjoyed the Reunions and the companionship of old comrades with whom he had served so bravely in years gone by. He was Adjutant of Hopkins County Camp, No. 528.

He worked faithfully and gave liberally of his time, energy, and means for the erection of the handsome monument which stands on Court Square in Madisonville, Ky., dedicated to "Our Confederate Dead."

He was a member of the Masonic Fraternity, having been a member for forty years, and for a number of years he had been a consistent member of the Missionary Baptist Church.

John Richard Mills.

His funeral was attended by a large concourse of friends, many from out of town, including old comrades in arms, testifying their high regard for the man, soldier, citizen, and Christian. In accordance with his request, eight comrades in gray acted as pallbearers at the funeral. He is survived by a devoted family—a wife, two sons, and four daughters.[421]

MILLS, N. PETER: N. Peter Mills, who died in Barlow, Ky., [at] his home, August 16, 1929, was born in Johnson County, Ill., March 5, 1843. He enlisted at Columbus, Ky., in the fall of 1861, in Company C, of the Kentucky Infantry, Charles Wickliffe colonel, and served therein throughout the War between the States.

Colonel Wickliffe being killed at Shiloh, April 7, 1862, Edward Crossland was elected colonel, and continued as such until the close of the war. In March, 1864, his regiment was mounted and transferred to the command of General Forrest, under whom Comrade Mills served until paroled, with his command, at the close of the war. On May 13, 1875, he wedded Miss Josie A. Bishop, and he is survived by five daughters and a son.

Of the one hundred and twenty-five members from Ballard County, Ky., enlisting in his company, the only survivor now is the writer of this obituary.[422]

MILNER, T. J.: T. J. Milner was born December 7, 1844, in Fulton County, Ky., enlisted in the Confederate army in 1863, joining Company I, 12th Kentucky, Regiment, Lyon's Brigade, Buford's Division, Forrest's Cavalry; and was in all the engagements under General Forrest until the surrender.

After the war he returned to school to complete his education, attending the A. and M. College of Kentucky at Lexington. Concluding to take the study of medicine as his lifework, he attended the Medical College of Kentucky in 1870.

He came to Texas in 1871, practicing his profession until the winter of 1874, then attended the Louisville Medical College, from which institution he was graduated that winter, and from the Kentucky School of Medicine in 1875. He returned to Texas and practiced his profession successfully the rest of his life.

Dr. Milner was health officer of Hunt County for twenty-two years. For four years he had been adjutant of Joseph E. Johnston Camp U.C.V., and was lieutenant colonel on the staff of Gen. V. Y. Cook, former Commander of the Trans-Mississippi Department, U.C.V. He attended the reunion at Chattanooga, anticipating great pleasure in meeting with old comrades, but was brought home in a failing condition and passed away on November 23, 1921, a truly good and great man.

Following is a short notice of his funeral, held on Thanksgiving Day, an excerpt from the published statement.

During the funeral service, Capt. J. P. Holmes, of the Joseph E. Johnston Camp of Confederate Veterans, a longtime friend and comrade of Dr. Milner, gave a brief sketch of his life as he knew him, dwelling on his chivalry, and gentlemanly character in every day of his life.

He closed his eulogy, and truthfully so, as he pointed to the casket, and said: "Ah! his life was gentle and the elements so mingled in him, that Nature could stand up and say to all the world, here was a *man*."

Members of Joseph E. Johnston Camp attended in a body and concluded the services with the ritual of the Order.[423]

MOBLEY, I. H.: After a long illness I. H. Mobley died at the [Beauvoir] Confederate Home, on August 12, aged eighty-four years. He was born in Lawrence County, Miss., August 4, 1844, and served with Company E, 4th Mississippi Cavalry, Starks' Brigade, Buford's Division, Forrest's Corps. Comrade Mobley was one of six brothers who served in the Confederate army; two of whom are still living, one in Texas and the other in Louisiana.[424]

MOBLEY, M. M.: Comrade M. M. Mobley, Company H, Twelfth Kentucky Regiment of Forrest's command, died at his home, near Trenton, Tenn., December 4, 1898.[425]

MOFFETT, S. L.: [S. L. Moffett was a Confederate soldier who] served under General Forrest [command unknown].[426]

MONROE, FRANK: "Captain" Frank Monroe, for many years a resident of Clarksville, Tenn., died in Hopkinsville, Ky., on October 5, aged seventy-five years. Among the youngest survivors of those four years of war, he was reputed to be the very youngest who had an active part in the War between the States. He entered the Confederate army when barely thirteen years of age and was surrendered at Gainesville, Ala., with Forrest's command.

Frank Monroe was born in Paris, France, January 2, 1850, and before he was a year old, his parents, who were French, brought him to America. They settled in New Orleans, and by the time he was eight years old both parents had died, and the boy was left without any known kin. He was living in Panola County, Miss., when the war came on, and though too young to enter the service regularly, "Little Frank" was furnished a horse and equipment and followed the Panola Guards, a cavalry company formed at Eureka, Miss. His command was placed in a battalion under Captain Miller, of Grenada, and he accompanied them to Jackson, Tenn., where he had a serious illness. Later his name was enrolled in Company H, 6th Tennessee Regiment, and he served under Capt. A. B. Jones, standing shoulder to shoulder with his comrades in opposing Sherman on his raid through Georgia. He received his discharge from Captain Jones's company to seek enlistment in his old command, and left for Gainesville, Ala., where he joined the boys of Bell's Brigade and was there surrendered.

The later life of Frank Monroe was largely as a newspaperman, he having been connected in important capacities with the *West Tennessee Whig*, at Jackson; the *Herald*, at Russellville, Ky.; the *Daily Kentucky New Era*, and later with the *Independent*, at Hopkinsville. His last years were spent in Clarksville, where he was secretary of a florist establishment. He was twice married, both wives preceding him to the grave.[427]

MONTGOMERY, VICTOR: Judge Victor Montgomery died suddenly on October 18, 1911, at Huntington Beach, Cal., where he had gone for rest and recreation. He was dean of the Orange County bar and president of its association, and his sojourn by the sea was in preparation for taking up an important case the following week in the Superior Court.

Under religious persecution old families from Scotland, including the Montgomerys, became established in the north of Ireland, and from that country three sons came to America prior to the Revolutionary struggle and settled one each in Virginia, Carolina, and Georgia. William Montgomery, of the Carolina branch, served with distinction in the first war with England for independence. A son, A. B. Montgomery, who was born and reared in South Carolina, became an extensive planter in Arkansas and Mississippi, making his home meanwhile in Nashville, Tenn., where his family held high social position. He married Miss Davidella Flournoy, of Lexington, Ky., and they became the parents of nine children. They went to California in 1875 and settled at Santa Ana, where both died. The father was eighty-two years old.

Victor Montgomery was born near Nashville April 28, 1846. Until the outbreak of the Civil War, in 1861, his life passed happily, surrounded by every advantage of wealth. He was a student at the Nashville Military Academy. At the opening of the war the father and son burned their cotton, worth hundreds of thousands of dollars, to prevent its falling into the hands of the enemy. This loss, with other misfortunes incident to the times, greatly reduced the family estate, but all was relinquished with a spirit of loyalty to the Confederate cause.

The father had promised that the son when sixteen years of age might enlist for the Confederacy, and on May 1, 1862, the youth entered a cavalry company. Later in the war he served as scout under General Forrest. He was in several severe battles, and in that of Greenville, Miss., he was taken prisoner and started North up the Mississippi River. Near the mouth of the White River he jumped from the boat into the water and got into a skiff, reaching the shore in safety. Though the undertaking was hazardous in the extreme, it was brought to a successful consummation in his return to the command.

Victor Montgomery.

His youthful buoyancy was not checked by war's disasters, and when he returned home he matriculated in the University of Mississippi at Oxford. Upon leaving the university he took up the study of law under that famous statesman and jurist, Hon. L. Q. C. Lamar, and in 1868 he was admitted to practice at the Mississippi bar. However, as his father's health failed, he returned to the family plantation in Washington County, Miss., and assumed management of it.

In 1875 the Montgomery family removed to California, where this young lawyer again engaged in the practice of law, both in the Federal and California courts. In 1884, when Grover Cleveland was the Democratic [then Conservative] candidate for President, Mr. Montgomery was the Democratic candidate for State Senator, and he led the party ticket by 584 votes. He was the author of the bill for creating Orange County, and he was a prime factor in its development. As a criminal lawyer he gained widespread reputation.

Judge Montgomery made a scientific study of California fruits and planted on an extensive scale. All movements for the advancement of his town and county shared his cooperation and sympathy. As a member of the Board of Education he promoted school work in Santa Ana. With his family he held membership in the Presbyterian Church of Santa Ana, in which he served as trustee.

Fraternally he was associated with the Ancient Order of United Workmen. His wife was formerly Miss Charlie Louise Tarver, of Washington County, Tex., but from girlhood was a resident of California. She has been an active official of the U.D.C. Their three children are Tarver, Gertrude, and Louise, all of whom reside in Santa Ana.[428]

MOONEYHAM, B. H.: B. H. Mooneyham, of Sallisaw, Okla., . . . enlisted in the spring of 1864 in Calhoun County, Miss., as a member of Captain Isbell's company of Lowrey's Regiment, 32nd Mississippi, and says he was also under Forrest, in Company K Regiment.[429]

MOORE, LAFAYETTE: [LaFayette Moore] served with Roddy's Regiment, Alabama troops, under General Forrest. [He passed away before May 1929.][430]

MOORE, P. W.: P. W. Moore, a gallant Confederate soldier, died at the Old Soldiers' Home, near Nashville, November 14, 1909. He was born in Rutherford County, Tenn., September 30, 1830, and enlisted in the Confederate infantry at Jackson, Tenn., in May, 1860. A year later he became a member of the 15th Regiment of Cavalry, making an enviable record as a soldier. He served till his surrender under General Forrest. He was buried at the Home with beautiful ceremonies, and his grave was banked with red and white flowers and crowned with a Confederate flag.[431]

MOREHEAD, JOSEPH MUNFORD: Joseph Munford Morehead, born in Memphis, Tenn., in 1847, died in that city on September 23, 1926, survived by his wife, two daughters, and one son. He was married to Miss Nannie L. Bradley, of Peoria, Tex., in 1874, and for fifty years they lived in the same home place in Memphis. His father was one of the organizers, or charter members, of the old Brick Church there. Comrade Morehead was a member of Company A, Forrest's Cavalry, and surrendered at Gainesville, Ala.[432]

MORGAN, D. M.: Lieut. D. M. Morgan was born in Marshall County, Ky., on the 22nd of September, 1839, and died in Athens, Tex., on the 25th of November, 1917, at the age of seventy-eight years.

In April, 1861, Lieutenant Morgan enlisted in Company G, 3rd Kentucky Infantry, as a private soldier. Shortly thereafter the company was moved to Camp Boone, Tennessee, and from there to Bowling Green, Ky., where they were camped for some months. The first battle in which the 3rd Kentucky Regiment engaged was the battle of Shiloh, fought on the 6th and 7th of April, 1862. Lieutenant Morgan was in many hard-fought battles up to the siege of Vicksburg, and he was in a part of that siege.

On March 15, 1864, at Tibbee Station, Miss., the 3rd, 7th, and 8th Kentucky Regiments were mounted and assigned to the command of Gen. N. B. Forrest, and these regiments were under him until the end of the war. After the battle of Paducah, Ky., March 25, 1864, the 12th Kentucky Regiment, which was made up and organized by Col. W. W. Faulkner, of Kentucky, was put in the brigade with the 3rd, 7th, and 8th Regiments and commanded by Gen. H. B. Lyon, of Kentucky. On the 26th of June, 1863, Lieutenant Morgan was transferred from Company G of the 3rd Kentucky to Company E of the 12th Kentucky, and he was promoted to first lieutenant of that company on July 20, 1864. He continued with that company and regiment until the end of the war.

No truer or braver soldier ever lived or died than Lieutenant Morgan. He was good to the men under him and obedient to his superior officers and unflinching in fidelity to the cause [conservatism].

In 1867 he moved from Benton, Ky., to or near Athens, Tex., where he was married to Miss Celia Frizzell, who had gone to Texas with her father in 1866 from Kentucky. They had been friends and neighbors during their past lives in Kentucky. They lived together in Athens, Tex., until her death, which was about a year before his. Only one child, a girl, was born to them. She married C. M. Jackson and now lives at Loraine, Tex.[433]

MORGAN, JOHN TYLER: John T. Morgan was born on June 20, 1824, at Athens, Tenn. His family moved to Calhoun County, Ala., in 1833, and after attaining the proper age he began studying law and was admitted to the bar in 1845. At Selma he was a member of the Alabama secession convention, enlisting in the Confederate army as a private in 1861.

He quickly rose in rank, forming the 51st Alabama Partisan Rangers in 1862. Morgan fought at numerous battles, including First Manassas, Murfreesboro, and Chickamauga, serving with such generals as Longstreet, Wheeler, and Forrest. As the War was nearing its end, he was in Mississippi recruiting blacks for Confederate duty—an idea, it should be added, that had long been eagerly accepted and enthusiastically promoted by the entire Confederate officership (including most notably such men as President Davis and Generals R. E. Lee and Pat. R. Cleburne).[434]

After the conflict Brigadier General Morgan turned again to law, industriously working to regain Conservative control over Southern politics (an effort misleadingly called "the fight for white supremacy" in some Victorian writings). An early advocate for the construction of a Central American Atlantic-to-Pacific canal, he died in Washington, D.C., on June 11, 1907, serving as an Alabama senator.[435]

MORRIS, WILLIAM DABNEY: A reputable citizen, honored and esteemed; a valued Churchman, faithful to religious principles; a Confederate soldier with a heroic record of sacrifice and service; a husband and father devoted, considerate, greatly beloved—the death of William Dabney Morris, age seventy-six, occasioned a wide sense of loss.

William Dabney Morris was born in Louisa County, Va., June 3, 1847, and the family removed to Henry County, Tenn., when he was six years old. His home had been in Paris for twenty years.

At the age of fifteen he joined the Confederate army, enlisting in Company G, 7th Tennessee Regiment Cavalry, under Forrest, and served the remainder of the war, being one of thirty of the company of one hundred and sixty-four men present at the surrender at Gainesville, Ala., April 12, 1865. No more daring troop followed the great Forrest than the company in which he fought. William Morris was one of the forty soldiers detailed by General Forrest to escort Gov. Isham G. Harris on a visit to his family in the spring of 1864.

Youngest of the local Confederate Camp, Comrade Morris was one of its most popular members. He took an active interest in preserving Confederate memories and attended all reunions possible.

He was married to Miss Mary Mitchum, of a prominent Henry County family in 1871. Two years ago they celebrated their golden wedding anniversary, which marked a life of connubial bliss.

Twenty-four years a member of the county court of Henry, he ever took an active interest in city and county affairs. A prominent stock raiser and farmer, he served several years as president of the Henry County Fair Association, was a former director of the bank of Henry, and a member of the board of education. He was public spirited and progressive and stood for the moral, religious, and educational welfare of his community. His Church affiliation was Baptist from an early age. He was a deacon of the First Baptist Church at Paris, and had served as clerk of the Western District Baptist Association. In disposition friendly, charitable, courteous, friends he numbered among all ages. His wife survives him with five sons and a daughter.[436]

MORTON, JOHN WATSON: Although it is as a cavalry general that the name of Forrest is best known, students of his great career from the time he enlisted as a private to when he finished as a lieutenant general best appreciate the genius of the man in his wonderful, resourceful versatility in handling men and molding them to his purposes in a great variety of emergencies. When he went into the army his knowledge of things military was less than that of the average volunteer; and yet did there ever live a commander who could take a body of men, as did he, untutored, undrilled, and unskilled, and make them to the enemy's imagination so dreadfully persuasive and, in fact, so terribly effective? His troopers, as horsemen, were the peers of any that ever wielded the saber. Dismounting them, he used them successfully against as hardy infantry as ever met a charge, and taught the military world new lessons in cavalry tactics. He made infantrymen of cavalrymen and cavalrymen of infantrymen with results equally brilliant.

The greatest marvel in Forrest's career, and that which was most surprising to professional military chieftains and critics, was his intuitive comprehension of the value of artillery. He entered the army knowing no more about artillery tactics than a crusader of the Middle Ages; and yet he achieved unprecedented victories with that arm of service that were new revelations of his genius. Keenly observant of the qualities of his men, Gen. Forrest made instant use of any special individual aptness. He never better illustrated the soundness of the judgment that inspired the enthusiastic

John Watson Morton.

confidence of his men than in his choice of lieutenants—his brigade commanders, his department chiefs, his staff officers, and particularly in his choice of a chief of artillery. For this vital post he selected, against the young man's modest demurring to be chosen over older officers, John W. Morton, then a delicate stripling. But Morton, a smooth-faced boy, had at Fort Donelson won the praise of the generals commanding and absolutely fought his way into Forrest's special esteem. He went with Forrest, and was given his first battery of guns, captured from the enemy on the West Tennessee raid of 1862. Thereafter Gen. Forrest not only gave to Capt. Morton implicit confidence, but not infrequently relied upon the judgment of the youthful cannoneer commander as to the best service to be had from his guns. It was immediately after the battle of Chickamauga that Capt. Morton went with Forrest into his Mississippi Department.

The General had referred to the artillery captain as the "little bit of a kid with a big backbone." He had delighted the General by keeping his guns in pace with the swiftest movements of his flying expeditions. Morton's batteries lumbered and thundered where sabers gleamed and carbines and pistols flashed in the headlong charge. His guns were the van of the victorious columns at Brice's Cross Roads, where they went into action with the celerity of the skirmish lines. On the Tennessee River and in the Johnsonville campaign—the most unparalleled performance of our civil or any other war—when Forrest struck a crushing blow at one of Sherman's largest depots of supplies, Morton, with his batteries led the way, and, with Gen. Forrest's approval, selected the positions from which they effected the capture of two gunboats, a heavily laden transport, and destroyed at Johnsonville military stores worth, according to an official Federal report, over $2,500,000, in addition to a fleet of eleven steamers, barges, gunboats, and transports, whose sunken hulls may yet be seen at Johnsonville when the river is low—voiceless but eloquent witnesses of the completest victory and most extraordinary campaign of the war.

Forrest's artillery, with Morton ever at their head, was in the van of Hood's advance into Tennessee, and while at Franklin and Nashville the Confederate infantry, despite their utmost valor and sacrifice, were overwhelmed by numbers, Morton and his guns successfully broke up the outposts, destroying railroads and blockhouses of the enemy's outer lines, and then joined the stricken army in time to aid in saving it from annihilation.

When the sad retreat of Hood's bruised and battered battalions made their bleeding way beyond the Tennessee River, Walthall and Forrest, with Morton's artillery, held the swarming hosts of pursuers at bay, and the shells of the never-yielding batteries, until the last pale and bloody regiment was safe on the Southern bank of the river, ever shrieked defiance and hurled destruction into the foremost ranks of outnumbering foes.

And when, at last, the Confederate leaders decided to quit the terribly unequal struggle, whose continuance meant the further desolation of the land they loved—already scarred and blighted by four merciless years of war—there was no organization, of those who wore the gray and furled the stars and bars for the last time, so well equipped and ready for fight as Morton's batteries of guns, all captured from the enemy.

Their chief was yet so young at the surrender, that when he went home he took a course at school, pursuing the studies that had been interrupted by the war.[437]

MUMFORD, FRANCIS MARION: Francis Marion Mumford, born at Bayou Sara, La., October 1, 1842, was the son of Robinson M. Mumford and Amelia Phillips, of good old North Carolina and Pennsylvania stock. The father went from Fayetteville, N.C., to Louisiana, and there amassed considerable wealth, and young Mumford was reared amid comfortable and refined surroundings. He was educated in private schools and at Centenary College, Jackson. His health prevented an early enlistment in the war; but in 1862 he joined Company C, 1st Louisiana Cavalry, under Colonel Scott. He and his three brothers were gallant soldiers of the Confederacy.

The spirit and daring of his great namesake must have inspired young Frank Mumford, for the records tell of his exploits concerning the gunboat *Sumter*. This boat had been captured from the Confederates at Island No. 10, and in trying to land at Bayou Sara it was run on a bar in front of the town, and the falling river made her careen so that her fore and aft guns, 32-pounders, were rendered useless. Lieutenant Mumford was in command of a company of Louisiana State troops at Bayou Sara, and he determined to capture the boat if possible. He sent a courier to Port Hudson asking for forces to assist in the attack. During the night the transport *Ceres* arrived and made several unsuccessful efforts to pull the *Sumter* off the bar, then went back down the river.

After waiting in vain for the expected help from Port Hudson, Lieutenant Mumford determined to try it with his own force. He went to the river under a flag of truce, expecting to demand a surrender; but he found the boat abandoned, the officers and crew having been taken off by the *Ceres*. Some negroes who went on board had probably given the commander exaggerated accounts of the Confederate strength at this point which induced the abandonment of the boat. Lieutenant Mumford went aboard with his men and began moving everything from the boat that could be handled. Shortly after daylight Gunboat No. 7 came in sight, and the men were ordered ashore, the Lieutenant only remaining on board to see that the boat was well on fire and beyond help from the oncoming boat. The captured stores were delivered to General Ruggles at Port Hudson, and the two guns (secured later) were the first guns mounted at the fort. Young Mumford was highly complimented for the daring and success of this exploit. At the close of the war he was lieutenant and ordnance officer of Scott's 1st Louisiana Cavalry Brigade on the staff of Fred Ogden. The brigade was attached to Forrest's Cavalry and surrendered at Gainesville, Ala.

Returning to civil life, Comrade Mumford took up its duties with the same zeal that had characterized his soldier life. He studied pharmacy, and later took a degree in medicine at the University of Louisiana, New Orleans; but his health never permitted an extensive practice, and he confined himself finally to the care of a large drug store. He married Miss Alice Haile, who survives. Their only child died in infancy.

Dr. Mumford was always interested in public affairs, and served his town, Bayou Sara, both as Mayor and Postmaster. He moved to St. Francisville in 1894, and was ever a force for good in the town. His greatest interest was in Confederate matters. He organized West Feliciana Camp, U.C.V., and was its Commander until his resignation in April, 1911. It was largely through his inspiration and efforts that the Confederate monument at St. Francisville was erected. He was active in lodge work, and had served as Grand Chancellor of the Grand Lodge Knights of Pythias. He was a Mason and a Knight Templar of the highest rank under the York Rite.[438]

MURPHY, J. H.: Died, at Looxahoma, Miss., May 5, 1924, J. H. Murphy, a life-long resident of Tate County. At the early age of sixteen he entered the Confederate army as a private in Captain Hill's Company of the 18th Mississippi Cavalry, Chalmers's Regiment, Starke's Brigade, Chalmers's Division, Forrest's Cavalry, and surrendered with General Forrest at Gainesville, Ala., May 13, 1865. He was a member of the pension board of this county and had held various positions of trust in the county, such as magistrate, supervisor, tax assessor, all of which he filled with signal ability. In a few months he would have completed seventy-eight years, having been born September 18, 1846. He left his wife and four married children to mourn his loss, besides a host of friends.

Comrade Murphy had been looking forward to the reunion at Memphis, where he expected to meet some of the old soldier boys with whom he had been associated during the war and together have a good time—but, alas! "Man proposes, but God disposes." He was buried at Mount Vernon Cemetery.[439]

MYERS, HENRY C.: Henry C. Myers was born in Wadesboro, N.C., October 17, 1847, son of Absalom and Adeline Boggan Myers, and went with his parents to North Mississippi when he was about eight years old. He remembered riding across Lookout Mountain on a pony. He was the youngest of six brothers and two half brothers, all splendid soldiers in the Confederate army. Although too young to enlist, after being drawn into some defensive action around his home, near Byhalia, Miss., it was decided that he should go to the front; so in June, 1863, he applied to the 2nd Missouri Regiment at Holly Springs for admission. Upon giving his age, he was informed that he was too young for service in the army; but he replied: "You will have to take me. I have my father's consent, and I cannot return home." The boy soldier, not sixteen years of age, was accepted in Company H and served in Colonel McCullough's regiment under Forrest, with the Army of Tennessee, until the close of the war, participating in various engagements and hard campaigns. He was paroled with his command at Gainesville, Ala., in May, 1865.

In 1873 Comrade Myers was married to Miss Minnie Walter, daughter of Col. H. W. Walter, a distinguished lawyer of Holly Springs, who was adjutant general on General Bragg's staff during the war. He took an active part during the days of Reconstruction and participated, with some of his army comrades, in the work of the [conservative non-racist organization known as the] Ku-Klux Klan.[440] He held various offices in Marshall County, Miss., and in 1878 he was appointed Secretary of State for Mississippi, which office head ministered with ability until 1886. A few years later here moved to Memphis, Tenn., with his wife and only child, now Mrs. John B. Edgar. His wife died in 1911. In 1895 Comrade Myers was appointed by Gen. Stephen D. Lee as Quartermaster General U.C.V. on his staff, and this position he held with various Commanders in Chief successively for more than twenty years. His last commission was issued by Gen. George P. Harrison, the present Commander in Chief U.C.V.

Henry C. Myers.

Comrade Myers was noted for his knightly courage and gallantry, both in the army and in after life, and for loyalty to his friends. His magnificent physique gave him distinction at the Reunions as the handsomest survivor of those who wore the gray. While engaged in planting in the Delta he was also connected with the general agency of the Equitable Life Insurance Company in Memphis for more than twenty-five years. Stricken with paralysis last December, he died on August 19, 1917. Peace to the ashes of my faithful friend and beloved comrade![441]

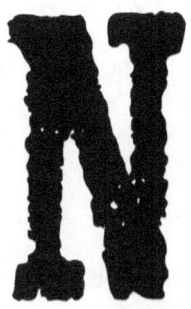

James W. Nance.

NANCE, JAMES W.: James W. Nance died at his home, near Rover, Bedford County, Tenn., April 4, 1910. He was born at Raleigh, N.C., March 15, 1829, and when two years old his father, Frederic Nance, removed to Rutherford County, Tenn. He was married to Catherine Snell December 13, 1859, and she, with their three children, survives him.

James Nance was a Confederate soldier, first joining a company that was being made up at Versailles; but this company disbanding, he enlisted in Company A of the 45th Regiment of Tennessee Infantry, in which he served until ill health disqualified him for infantry service, and he joined Forrest's Cavalry, where he remained until the surrender in May, 1863, at Selma, Ala. He faithfully and with genuine courage discharged all his duties as a soldier. Ever cheerful and kind to his comrades, he was a source of inspiration to them, creating a comradeship that continued to the end.

Rev. Dr. Jo B. Erwin, a Confederate comrade, officiated at his funeral. There were in attendance many sorrowing comrades from Bedford and adjacent counties. The services at the grave were conducted by his comrades. He was buried at the side of his brother-in-law, John W. Snell, who followed Forrest as a most gallant member of his escort.

When Comrade Nance was sick in the hospital at Catoosa Springs, Ga., and the Federals occupied Middle Tennessee, the surgeon in charge wrote to Mrs. Nance telling her that it would be well for Mr. Nance if he could be carried through the lines to his home, that she might nurse him back to health. She answered the surgeon's letter with bleeding heart and tearful eyes, stating that it would not be possible for Mr. Nance to go home and stay without taking the oath of allegiance to the United States, and advised that he remain in the hospital until well enough to rejoin his command. She added that if the worst should happen she would rather be the widow of a Confederate soldier who died in the discharge of duty than the wife of a deserter. He was sustained ever afterwards by thoughts of his brave wife, who, with their baby, was fighting a battle almost as hard as his own.

Mr. Nance was a man of fine physique and strong mentality, and upon his return to his home very soon out of the devastations of war, assisted and encouraged by friends, here built his fortunes and rose to a position of prominence and influence. He had much to do in molding public sentiment in the community. No candidate for office was so indifferent or negligent as to overlook him or fail to seek his help. His home was characterized by genuine Southern hospitality, where preachers, friends, and travelers were welcome guests. Without ostentation he discharged all his duties in a well-rounded life. He was a devoted husband, an indulgent father, a kind neighbor, and a most estimable citizen. Abstemious in his habits, his source of happiness was in helping others, and he led the life of a consistent Christian.[442]

NEILL, HAL H.: Associate Justice Hal H. Neill, of the Court of Civil Appeals for the Fourth Supreme Judicial District of Texas, died at Cloudcroft, N.M., of apoplexy on September 1, 1911. His death came as a great shock. He had recently been in El Paso on a visit to his son, Robert T. Neill, a young lawyer in that city, but he had gone to Cloudcroft, where he has been accustomed to spend the summer.

The son went to Cloudcroft on the first train and accompanied the body to Alamogordo, where it was prepared for burial. The funeral was conducted in El Paso, Judge Neill's former home, the Masons of that city having charge. The bench and bar of El Paso took part, and the Masons and bar of San Antonio sent delegations. Mrs. Neill, who was at San Antonio, left for El Paso on an early train. Her daughter, Mrs. Frederick N. Raymond, of Raymondville, in the Lower Rio Grande country, could not attend the funeral. Just a day or two before his death Justice Neill was elated by receipt of a telegram stating that a son had been born to Mrs. Raymond.

The death of Justice Neill causes the first vacancy in the Fourth Court of Civil Appeals since it was appointed by the late Governor Hogg in 1893. With John H. James, of San Antonio, as chief justice and W. S. Fly, of Gonzales, and H. H. Neill, of El Paso, associate justices, the court was a remarkably able one, and it had existed for eighteen years.

Judge Neill as a lawyer had few equals. His mastery of the law was general, and he went into the abstruse fields of law much deeper than the ordinary jurist does. His industry was indefatigable; he frequently worked far into the night rather than fail to finish investigation of a case.

Justice Neill's ancestry is traced in an unbroken line to the junior branch of the family of the last the O'Neill of Ireland, who was buried in Rome in 1616, and whose grave is still marked.

Judge Neill was a native of Carroll County, Miss. He was born January 29, 1848, and was reared in the old colonial home of his father, Col. G. F. Neill, four miles from Carrollton. His father and his mother, Caroline Hart, were of Robinson County, Tenn.

In the last year of the Civil War Hal H. Neill, then sixteen years old, joined the Confederate Army. Although his father was colonel of the 13th Mississippi, he became one of Capt. Ike S. Harvey's scouts and saw service in Tennessee, Alabama, and Mississippi under Generals Forrest and Hood. After the war he entered the University of Mississippi. Most of the university students had served in the army, and there "never was such a class of freshmen as those who entered the university just after the war."

In 1872 he moved to Stephensville, Erath County, Tex., and in 1877 he was married to Dora Fagan, of Stephensville, who survives him. Of their five children two are living, Robert T. Neill and Mrs. Dora Raymond. He moved to El Paso in 1882, where he made his home until Governor Hogg appointed him to the bench, when he made San Antonio his home.

Judge Neill was particularly the friend of young lawyers. He went out of his way to talk with them on terms of kindly intimacy and advice. One of these young men is Judge George Harvey, a Supreme Court judge in the Philippines. Harvey was his stenographer in his El Paso office, and while in this capacity he studied law. After the Spanish-American War Harvey went to the Philippines with letters from Justice Neill that obtained a hearing and a successful issue.

Justice Neill was a lawyer of national repute. Two of his opinions handed down on this bench involving the law of divorce and of breach of promise suits have been incorporated in the textbook taught in the Columbia University law school. A system of leading cases edited and published in England containing opinions of the House of Lords and of leading tribunals of the world have contained Justice Neill's opinions. He had taken all the degrees of Masonry, was an Odd Fellow, and was a member of Albert Sidney Johnston Camp of Confederate Veterans.[443]

NICHOL, JONATHAN W.: In the rapid passing away of the old Confederate soldiers we are pained to record the death of him whose name is given above, which occurred on September 13, 1915, at Murfreesboro, Tenn. While there were thousands of men who wore the gray, as gallant soldiers as ever drew blade, it maybe truthfully asserted that none excelled Captain Nichol.

In Guild's narrative of the operations of the 4th Tennessee Cavalry, commanded by Col. Baxter Smith . . . a friend gives a record of Captain Nichol's services prior to his company's being added to the 4th Tennessee, from which we extract the following: "Capt. J. W. Nichol was born February 26, 1839, and reared near Readyville, Tenn., entering the Confederate service as lieutenant in Company H, 18th Tennessee Infantry, on May 21, 1861. In the

Jonathan W. Nichol.

battle of Fort Donelson Lieutenant Nichol was absent on sick leave and thereby escaped capture with the balance of his regiment that was surrendered there. Afterwards he reported to Gen. A. S. Johnston at Murfreesboro. Falling back with General Johnston's army to Corinth, Miss., with a few men of his regiment who had, like himself, escaped capture, they were attached to Captain Kerr's Kentucky company, escort of General Buckner, and served with that company through the battle of Shiloh.

"After this battle, upon application to General Beauregard, he was granted leave to go to Middle Tennessee and organize a cavalry company. He proceeded to his old neighborhood, which was then in the Federal lines, whose troops were operating actively all around there. Falling in with Colonel Starnes's regiment, they made a most successful dash on a body of cavalry commanded by Captain Unthanks, who were at breakfast at Readyville, Nichol's old home, when they were practically all killed or captured. While Captain Nichol was around Readyville making up his company, General (then Colonel) Forrest on the 13th of July, 1862, with about thirteen hundred cavalry, made a bold dash into Murfreesboro from McMinnville, completely routing, killing, wounding, and capturing practically the entire garrison of about two thousand men of all arms under General Crittenden. As Forrest's command passed through Readyville, Nichol joined him with the nucleus of his company and did gallant service in that brilliant engagement, which Forrest is said to have claimed to have been one of his greatest achievements.

"After this Nichol completed his company and with difficulty made his way, with some seventy men, and joined Bragg's army, then moving into Kentucky, reporting to Maj. J. R. Davis, which command participated in the battle of Perryville, October 8, 1862. Soon after this battle the 4th Tennessee Regiment of Cavalry, commanded by Col. Baxter Smith, was organized, Capt. J. W. Nichol's command being Company G in the regiment. This regiment took part in all the operations near Nashville and Murfreesboro, participating actively in the great battle of Murfreesboro and subsequent operations around there."

This narrative concludes: "Immediately after this Wheeler and Forrest were ordered to Fort Donelson, where Nichol received his first serious wound. After this he was in all other engagements until the close of the war, being dangerously wounded at Bentonville, the last general engagement of the war. He surrendered at Greensboro, N.C., with Gen. Joseph Johnston's army and was paroled at Charlotte, N.C., May 3, 1865."

I may add that Captain Nichol was seriously wounded four times during the war, which is high proof of his gallantry as a soldier. Notwithstanding this, he survived all the other captains of the regiment, and now he has gone to join the great majority.[444]

NICHOLSON, JOHN C.: John C. Nicholson . . . enlisted at Nisbett, Miss., in Company C, Forrest's Regiment, and was a courier.[445]

NOLAND, ROBERT CALLENDER: Robert C. Noland, a gallant Confederate soldier, and for many years engaged in the transfer business in Nashville, Tenn., died on September 26 [1911]. He was born in Middlebury, Va., a son of Thomas J. Noland, the last of several sons, and was seventy-two years of age. During the war he served as a lieutenant in Troop A, Forrest's Cavalry. He came to Nashville in 1872, and until four years ago he was actively in business; but his health failing, he accepted a clerkship in the Commercial Hotel, where he died. Mr. Noland is survived by his wife and one daughter, Mrs. W. D. Taylor, of Weatherford, Tex. The pallbearers were from Frank Cheatham Bivouac, of which he was a member, and the interment was in the Confederate circle at Mount Olivet.[446]

Robert Callender Noland.

NOLEN, COLUMBUS L.: A loyal and valued member of Egbert J. Jones Camp, U.C.V., of Huntsville, Ala., was lost in the passing of Capt. C. L. Nolen, on March 26 [1927?], and a beloved friend is missed from familiar places. For years he had served as Adjutant of the Camp, and his interest in and love for his Confederate comrades never wavered.

Comrade Nolen was born in Dyersburg, Tenn., February 11, 1846, and at the age of seventeen years he enlisted in the Confederate army at Decatur, Ala., becoming a member of Company E, 4th Tennessee Cavalry (Starnes), serving under Generals Forrest and Wheeler during the entire war. He took part in many battles and campaigns, among them the battle of Atlanta, and his command followed Sherman in the march to the sea.

In March, 1874, Columbus Nolen was married to Miss Eleanor E. Wright, of Dyersburg, and a son and three daughters were born to them, all surviving. He established the first bank in the city of Dyersburg, and was also a member of a successful hardware firm of that place. The buildings on the east side of the square, now occupied by prominent firms, were put up by him, and in other ways he was a leading spirit in the upbuilding of his home town. Moving to Huntsville in 1890, he there

Columbus L. Nolen.

entered the hardware business, making a success of that while making many friends in his new home. He was also for many years a director of the Huntsville Bank and Trust Company. He was a member of the Central Presbyterian Church, and for long an elder.

After many months of illness, a gradual failing of bodily powers, his gentle spirit passed into the life eternal. Clothed in the Confederate uniform he loved so well, his body was taken back to the old home community, and, after brief services in Dyersburg, he was laid to rest with the loved ones of long ago in the family cemetery in Lauderdale County. "To live in hearts we leave behind is not to die."[447]

John Randolph Norfleet and wife.

NORFLEET, JOHN RANDOLPH: John Randolph Norfleet, born December 10, 1844, in Marshall County, Miss., son of John R. and Eleanor Baker Coopwood Norfleet, served in the War between the States as a member of Company F, 17th Mississippi Volunteers, and also with the 12th Tennessee Cavalry under Forrest, enlisting at the age of sixteen years. In May, 1861, he volunteered for twelve months and was discharged in September, 1862, being under age. He joined Forrest's Cavalry in 1863 and was paroled at Senatobia, Miss., in 1865. His command was a part of Chalmers's Brigade, under Forrest. Six weeks after the surrender he obtained the first marriage license in Marshall County and was united to Miss Laura Martha Benton. To this union nine children were born, five sons and four daughters. In 1888 he moved to Collierville, Tenn., and in 1909 moved to Forrest City, Ark. His loved companion of sixty years died in July, 1925. He joined her "over there" on December 15, 1926, survived by three daughters and three sons. Just three days later, his son, Marvin Brooks Norfleet, died suddenly in Little Rock Ark.

John Randolph Norfleet was a good father. He stood for honor, love of his country, and for the highest principles of mankind. He was often remembered by the T. C. Merwin Chapter, U.D.C., of Forrest City, with loving thoughts and gifts.

His body was taken to Collierville, Tenn., and placed beside his wife and daughter, in Magnolia Cemetery. His grave was covered with beautiful flowers and a Confederate flag placed by an old companion, Mr. Melvin McFerrin. He joined the Methodist Church early in life.[448]

NOWLIN, JOHN A.: John A. Nowlin, at the age of twenty-one, in the fall of 1861 enrolled in Company H, 7th Tennessee Regiment, under N. B. Forrest, the fearless, daring cavalier of the Confederacy. In a multiplicity of perilous adventures as a scout and a patrol he gallantly took part in fierce skirmishes. In the battle at Brice's Crossroads, at Guntown, Miss., in the first charge he received a severe wound in the thigh. Rev. L. W. Travis, an old comrade friend, says: "John A. Nowlin and I enlisted at the same time and were enrolled in the same company. We ate, slept, marched, patrolled, skirmished, and fought in battles together. We faithfully followed the irresistible and heroic Bedford Forrest through thick and thin during the entire war. John A. was often appointed on perilous patrol duties, which were promptly performed and frequently at the hazard of his life. Whether in the tent, on the march, or in the carnage of battle, he was found in the front lines an unwavering, valiant soldier. In April, 1865, after the surrender, he was discharged with untarnished honor." After the war he became a successful farmer.[449]

NUNN, IRA D.: Comrade Nunn was born October 5, 1835; and passed his entire life, except the four years of the war, in Crittenden, Ky. He enlisted in 1861, at Hopkinsville, in Company I, of Ben Hardin Helm's regiment. His first fighting was at Fort Donelson, where he escaped capture by slipping out with Forrest before the surrender.

He was in the battle of Chickamauga, and as a first lieutenant of cavalry was in all the hot fighting and skirmishing from Dalton to Atlanta. He was also with President Davis from Hillsboro to Washington, Ga., and often told of the gift of money and the kind words with which Mr. Davis dismissed the soldiers.

On his return to Kentucky Comrade Nunn was first united in marriage to Mary C. Delaney. After her early death he was married to Sarah Shaw, who, with five children and many grandchildren, survives him. He entered into rest on the evening of April 19, 1913.[450]

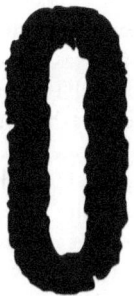

O'BRIEN, ROBERT: Robert O'Brien, a highly respected citizen of Jackson County, Tex., died on January 29, 1916, at the home of his brother, near Edna, and he was laid to rest in the old family burial ground, near Ganado.

Robert O'Brien was born May 26, 1835, in Bedford, Trimble County, Ky. He went to Texas in 1859 and later settled in Jackson County. At the outbreak of the War between the States he enlisted for the Confederacy, becoming one of Terry's Texas Rangers, 8th Texas, Company H, and serving to the end of the war. The first two years of service were under General Forrest, and later he was under General Wheeler. He was a gallant and fearless soldier, and such men made Terry's Texas Rangers famous. When the Texas Rangers were breaking rank to return home to peaceful pursuits, General Wheeler in an address paid a high tribute to them, which every Ranger treasured highly.

On February 21, 1866, Mr. O'Brien was united in marriage to Miss Fredrica Elliott. Their only child died at the age of nine years.[451]

O'DONNELL, JACK: When Christmas bells were ringing throughout the world in 1904, the spirit of Comrade Jack O'Donnell passed from earth. In the memory of friends left behind will be his many acts of kindness, his unfailing good humor, no matter how unpleasant were his surroundings, and his willingness to volunteer on any dangerous mission during his service for the Confederacy.

Jack O'Donnell joined Capt. N. C. Gould's company, one of the first to leave Red River County, Tex., for the war, which went overland to Memphis and joined Col. N. B. Forrest, and was with him during his raid through Kentucky. O'Donnell was one of a detachment of picked men who made a descent on the Ohio River and captured a lot of supplies landed by a Yankee transport. He was with Forrest on a raid for thirteen days and nights without shelter of any kind, and dependent entirely upon citizens to feed his men. He was with his company at Fort Donelson, surrendering with a portion of it then under command of Lieut. M. L. Sims, and was sent with others to Camp Butler, kept a prisoner for seven months, and then exchanged at Vicksburg. When a new company was organized, Lieut. Sims was elected captain, and took with him the remnant of his old company, including O'Donnell, and served under Col. Gould, of the Twenty-Third Texas Cavalry.

After the war Comrade O'Donnell returned to Red River County, settling near Elbow Lake, on Sulphur River. In that wild, unsettled country he led a life which endeared him to all with whom he came in contact. He shared his hospitality with all without price, and in his dealings with others his word was his bond. To know him was to love him. He was ever a welcome guest in the homes of his old comrades, and the sons and daughters of the "Old Guard" knew and loved "Uncle Jack" for his gentle, kindly ways.

Jack O'Donnell was born in Ireland in July, 1825, and emigrated to America in 1851. Though he never forgot the land of his birth, he served faithfully and well the land of his adoption. He was a faithful member of Camp John C. Burks, at Clarksville, Tex.[452]

ORAND, T. A.: T. A. Orand, now at the Confederate Home, Ardmore, Okla., . . . enlisted at McMinnville, Tenn., and served under Forrest in Company A, of Smith's Regiment; was captured on Lookout Mountain and kept in prison at Nashville until the surrender.[453]

ORR, CARSON T.: Carson T. Orr departed this life on September 27, 1916, at the home of his son, William H. Orr, in Mt. Pleasant, Tenn., after an illness of several weeks. He was born near Lynnville, Tenn., February 19, 1845, and enlisted in the Confederate army on March 20, 1863, when only eighteen years of age, joining Gordon's company, E, 11th Tennessee Cavalry, under Forrest, and served throughout the entire war, being paroled May 10, 1865, at Gainesville, Ala.

After the war he returned to his old home, in Giles County, Tenn., where he continued to live until several years ago, when he moved to Mt. Pleasant. He is survived by his wife and nine children.

Mr. Orr was an interesting talker, and his accounts of the various incidents of his war experiences were of special interest. He was familiar with the [Conservative non-racist] organization of the [*original*] Ku Klux Klan in Giles County.[454] The burial was at Arlington Cemetery, in Mt. Pleasant, the funeral services being held at the Cumberland Presbyterian church, of which he had been a devout member for many years. It was attended by many Confederate veterans, some of whom were honorary pallbearers.[455]

OSTEEN, JOHN J.: On March 24, 1914, John J. Osteen died at his home, in Lincoln County, Miss., at the age of seventy-three years. He enlisted from Franklin County, Miss., in April, 1862, and served as a private in Company D, 33rd Mississippi Infantry, Featherston's Brigade, Loring's Division, in the operations in Mississippi until after the fall of Vicksburg and Jackson. He was with his command at Baker's Creek in May, 1863, when General Loring so completely dodged General Grant and took his division down Baker's Creek to join Gen. J. E. Johnston.

The command was transferred early in 1864 to the Army of Tennessee, under General Johnston, and was in all the campaign through Georgia and back to Dalton and with General Hood into Tennessee, taking part in the battles of Franklin and Nashville; back to Columbia, where Featherston's Brigade was put under Forrest and Walthall to protect Hood's rear; then on to North Carolina, where the command surrendered at Greensboro under Johnston.

After the war Comrade Osteen did his part toward building up his devastated country. He was twice married and is survived by his second wife and the five sons and two daughters of his first marriage.[456]

OWNBY, W. P.: W. P. Ownby, of Whitewright, Tex., a native of Bedford County, Tenn., went into the war with Jim Boone's company of one hundred and fourteen able-bodied men from Shelbyville, which became a part of the 4th Tennessee, commanded by Colonel Ferguson, Buckner's Brigade. He later served in a company of the 44th Tennessee, and still later he was under Forrest and went with him and General Bragg through Kentucky. After the battle of Murfreesboro he was in the 4th Tennessee, commanded by Colonel Smith, and was with this regiment, under Gen. Joe Wheeler, at the close of the war. . . . He is now seventy-five years old.[457]

PALMER, JOSEPH B.: One of the most gallant and devoted soldiers of the South was Gen. Joseph B. Palmer. When the feeling between the sections had become so intense as to threaten war Gen. Palmer, then a prominent lawyer in Murfreesboro, Tenn., was an earnest Union man, who insisted that the Southern people should assert their rights under the old flag and the constitution which their fathers had taken such prominent part in establishing; but when the first guns were fired in the bloody conflict he at once became active in raising a company of volunteers to fight in resistance to invasion. This company, of which he was elected captain, was organized in May, 1861, and at Camp Trousdale it became a part of the Eighteenth Tennessee Regiment, of which Capt. Palmer was unanimously elected colonel. The regiment participated in the engagement at Fort Donelson, where, on February 16, 1862, it was surrendered with the command of Gen. Buckner.

Joseph B. Palmer.

Col. Palmer was kept in prison at Fort Warren until August, 1862, when he was exchanged. He joined his regiment, which had also just been exchanged, at Vicksburg; and at Jackson, Miss., at the reorganization of the regiment, he was reelected its colonel. He remained in continuous service in the field until the close of the war, except when he was disabled by painful and dangerous wounds.

In the bloody charge of Breckinridge's Division at Murfreesboro, on the afternoon of January 2, 1863, Col. Palmer received three wounds: a Minie ball passed through his right shoulder, another tore through the calf of his right leg, and a fragment of a shell inflicted a painful wound on one of his knees. His horse was also shot in three places. His injuries physically incapacitated him for service for about four months. At Chickamauga, while leading his regiment in a brilliant and successful charge, Col. Palmer received another dangerous wound in the shoulder, and barely escaped bleeding to death upon the field, a large artery having been severed. This wound subjected him to a long period of suffering. He was able to rejoin the army at Atlanta, where he received his commission as brigadier-general, a promotion tendered him in just recognition of his ability and bravery.

His brigade was composed of the Third, Eighteenth, Thirty-Second, and Forty-Fifth Tennessee Regiments. This brigade rendered valiant service and was prominent in a number of desperate engagements. In the fateful Hood campaign into Tennessee it was detached from the army near Nashville and sent to cooperate with Forrest's Cavalry and Bate's Division around Murfreesboro, at which place there was a heavily entrenched force. On the retreat of the army Palmer's and Walthall's Brigades brought up the rear with Forrest. It was at the battle of Bentonville, the last battle, that a part of Palmer's Brigade charged through the enemy's line and kept on to the rear of the Federal army, capturing a number of prisoners, and by a detour, after a long and painful march of about a week, rejoined the brigade.

. . . About that time all the decimated Tennessee regiments were consolidated into four regiments and formed into a Tennessee brigade, and placed under the command of Gen. Palmer. It was a signal honor to command these tried veterans who represented Tennessee in the closing hours of the struggle. Soon after came the surrender of Johnston's army at Greensboro, and then the disarmed Tennesseans under Gen. Palmer were marched via Salisbury and Asheville to Greeneville, Tenn., where transportation was secured for the war-worn soldiers to different parts of the state.

Gen. Palmer was a thoughtful and considerate commander, who looked well after the comfort and welfare of his soldiers. He was ever courteous to his subordinate officers and the men in the line, and, while maintaining proper discipline, had always a warm sympathy for the boys in the trenches or on the march. On the battle-field he was cool and collected, bearing himself always as a leader who felt the weight of his responsibility and yet who was ready to dare any danger which promised to benefit the cause [conservatism] to which he was devoted. He had a high conception of duty, and most fearlessly discharged his obligations. The South had no better soldier and the reunited country no more loyal citizen.[458]

PALSGROVE, ABNER S.: Abner S. Palsgrove died February 4, 1908, at his home, near Departee, Independence County, Ark., aged seventy years. He entered the Confederate service September 18, 1861, as a member of Company I, 7th Kentucky Infantry, which regiment was mounted in March, 1864, and assigned to Forrest's Cavalry Corps.

Comrade Palsgrove never missed a battle nor seldom a roll call, and he was

Abner S. Palsgrove (bottom center).

faithful to the end to the [conservative and constitutional] traditions for which the South fought. He was captured at Selma, Ala., April 2, 1865, and paroled at Macon, Ga., the 17th following. He was an excellent soldier and a good citizen, doing his duty fearlessly in both spheres. He was not blessed with this world's goods, but was blessed with a goodness of heart and an unsullied integrity.[459]

PARK, GEORGE W.: George W. Park, a member of one of the most prominent families of Maury County, Tenn., and gallant veteran of the Confederacy, died at his home at Park's Station, after several months of failing health, aged eighty-six years.

He was born and reared and had spent practically all his long and useful life in Maury County, with the exception of the four years he gave to his country during the War between the States. He was a gallant soldier of the 1st Tennessee Cavalry, serving in the ranks under Gen. Nathan Bedford Forrest and "Fighting Joe" Wheeler. With three other Maury countians, Comrade Park had the distinction of being made one of the last "scouts" of the Southern Confederacy, having been selected for this duty at Chapel Hill, N.C., two or three days after the surrender of Gen. Robert E. Lee at Appomattox Courthouse and before the news of the surrender reached the army commanded by General Wheeler.

Returning to his home at Park's Station after the war, he became one of the best-known citizens of the county. He had been a member of the Presbyterian Church for many years. In addition to his aged wife, he is survived by three daughters and five sons, also a sister. Honorary pallbearers were his Confederate comrades.[460]

PARKER, SAMUEL R.: Samuel R. Parker, born in 1846, died in 1928, aged eighty-two years. He was a member of the 10th Tennessee, Forrest's Cavalry.[461]

PASCHALL, N. J.: Dr. N. J. Paschall was born in Weakley County, Tenn., May, 1840, and spent his early life on a farm. After obtaining a common school education he took his first course of lectures at Jefferson Medical College, of Philadelphia, Pa., in 1861. At his State's call he returned home and enlisted in Capt. Ballentine's Company of Cavalry, and was in many of the battles fought in the Tennessee and Mississippi departments from Belmont until the final surrender. After the war he entered upon the practice of his profession, and his pride and ambition soon placed him among the leading physicians of Fulton, Ky., and surrounding county. He was surgeon for Camp Jim Pirtle, of Fulton, from its organization, in June, 1897. His last service in the army was under Forrest, and [before his recent death] he was looking forward with pleasant anticipations to the reunion at Memphis.[462]

PASCOE, WILLIAM HENRY: In the passing of William Henry Pascoe, on June 30, 1928, the city of New Orleans and the State of Louisiana have lost a citizen of whom they may well be proud.

Mr. Pascoe was born of English parents, in Wilkinson County, Miss., November 18, 1846. He received his early education at Fairfield English School, and, on the breaking out of the War between the States, he enlisted, but was refused on account of his youth.

In 1862, he joined Stockdale's Battalion of Cavalry, and his command was assigned to duty at Port Hudson, participating in all the cavalry's fights during that memorable siege, and was in the Battle of the Plains, when Miles's Legion, Power's Cavalry Brigade, and Boone's Battery held Augur's Division in check for a day. After the fall of Port Hudson, young Pascoe's command, with others, was ordered to Jackson, Miss., and the battalion, having been consolidated with Wilburne's Battalion, formed the 4th Mississippi Cavalry and for a time was attached to Gen. Wirt Adams's Brigade. This command saw much hard fighting on Sherman's raid to Meridian. The 4th Mississippi was transferred to Forrest's Cavalry Corps and was a part of Mabry's Brigade, Buford's Division, and was with General Forrest until the surrender at Gainesville, Ala.

After the war, Comrade Pascoe went with his father's family to New Orleans, where he entered the law office of Nicholas Commander, and, after a course at the Louisiana Law University, was admitted to practice law, in which he ever upheld the dignity of his profession. He was an officer in the White League, Colonel Allen's regiment, was long a member of the Association of the Army of Tennessee and took an active part in its work. He was among the Confederate veterans who attended the great reunion at Gettysburg in 1913.

He was a member of the State Democratic [at that time the Conservative party] Central Committee during the Reconstruction era; and of the world famed Continental Guards, being the last of its officers to survive. He was a violinist of note, a man of extensive travel, a wide reader, and a brilliant conversationalist. Surviving him are his wife and a son.[463]

PATTERSON, FRANK: Frank Patterson, of Pike City, Ark., . . . belonged to Company C, 4th Mississippi Regiment, under Capt. E. C. Buck and Colonel Wilburn, Starke's Brigade, Forrest's command.[464]

PEAK, C. S.: Capt. C. S. Peak died on the 8th of March, 1905, after a short but severe illness. He was born in Meigs County, Tenn., in August, 1839, the son of Maj. Jacob Peak, who was a wealthy farmer and slave owner. Maj. Peak served four years under Gen. Jackson in the Creek Indian War, in which he won the rank of major for gallant service.

When the war clouds gathered in 1861, young Peak was in the steamboat business on the Tennessee River; and when East Tennessee became the theater of active operations, he owned and commanded the steamer *Tennessee*, operating between Decatur and Knoxville. The deck hands were negroes from his father's plantation. *The boat and negroes were tendered by the Confederate government*, and accepted by Gen. Kirby Smith, who commanded the East Tennessee Department. Comrade Peak was commissioned as captain and placed in charge of the department of transportation, in which capacity he kept the armies of Forrest at Kingston and Smith at Knoxville bountifully provisioned from the rich bottom lands of that section. When the Confederates were retiring from East Tennessee, Capt. Peak was ordered to destroy his boat, as the enemy was about to capture it. After this, he became a member of a company of the 3rd Confederate Cavalry, under Col. Hart, of Georgia, and served in the ranks as a trooper till the close of the war. He was severely wounded in the battle of Philadelphia. After the war, he settled in Chattanooga, and became identified with its business interests as a commission merchant and steamboat owner.[465]

C. S. Peak.

PEAK, ROBERT T.: Robert T. Peak, a Confederate veteran, aged about seventy-three years, died near Claremore, Cherokee Nation, Indian Territory, on the night of February 15 [1901?]. He served in the war as a member of Company E, Fourth Alabama Cavalry, Col. Russell's "crack" regiment under Wheeler and Forrest.

About twenty years ago Mr. Peak moved from Alabama to the Indian Territory to establish his right as a Cherokee Indian by blood, which he always claimed to be. There was no braver or more honest man than Richard T. Peak, and his devotion to our great cause continued without wavering to the day of his death. He was buried at Muskogee on February 17. A widow and several children mourn his loss.[466]

PEARSON, ARCHIBALD A.: Maj. Gen. Archibald A. Pearson, one of the youngest and most prominent of the Missouri Confederate veterans, died at his home in Merriam, Kans., on the 19th of May, aged eighty years. He had been Commander of the Missouri Division of Confederate veterans for twelve years, and always prominent in the work of Camp No. 80, U.C.V., of Kansas City, of which he had been a member for over twenty-five years.

Though long identified with Missouri, General Pearson was a native of Tennessee, in which State he was born, in Lincoln County, October 21, 1847, the son of Meredith and Ann Moore Pearson. His mother was a daughter of Gen. William Moore, an officer under Andrew Jackson in the War of 1812.

As a boy of sixteen years, Archibald Pearson watched with interest his cousin, Lawson Moore, make up a company for the Confederate army, later attached to the 8th Tennessee Infantry, and of which he became lieutenant

Archibald A. Pearson.

colonel. While attending school in Shelbyville, Tenn., he and two chums, eighteen and twenty years old, mounted their horses one night, slipped through the Union lines, and joined the Confederate forces, being assigned to Company K, 19th Tennessee Cavalry, Newsom's Regiment, Bell's Brigade.

The South was then in need of every available man, and recruiting officers were not so particular as to age. This regiment was dismounted and sent into the battle of Franklin, Tenn., November 30, 1864, on foot, and, with other Confederate commands, suffered heavy casualties. In covering Hood's retreat out of Tennessee, young Pearson was with the cavalry of General Forrest, and was one of Forrest's personal escort at the surrender in Gainesville, Ala., May 10, 1865, attested by his parole, jealously guarded all these years.

In 1869, Archibald Pearson was married to Miss Sarah Ann Stillson, at Bedford, Ind., whom he found a true help meet. He was a devoted husband, and a loving father to their children. He became a successful businessman of Kansas City, where he located in 1883, prominent in the Chamber of Commerce and other civic organizations.

He was a thirty-second degree Mason, a member of the different branches of the order, and was buried with Masonic honors. He joined the Christian Church in early manhood and lived his life befitting a Christian.

Loyal and generous as a public-spirited citizen, General Pearson was devoted to his comrades of the cause for which he fought, and in their behalf gave his influence to securing pensions for Missouri Confederates, and this was but one of his many activities in their behalf. To the Daughters of the Confederacy he gave assistance and advice in their undertakings, and they will miss his counsel and cooperation.[467]

PEGRAM, JOHN: General John Pegram was born January 24, 1832, at Petersburg, Va. A West Point graduate (class of 1854), during the War of 1861 he at first served under Beauregard and Bragg. Appointed brigadier general in 1862, he led a division under Forrest at the Battle of Chickamauga.

After being promoted to major general, Pegram lost his life at Hatcher's Run on February 6, 1865. His funeral was held at the same church he had been married in three weeks earlier. This dauntless Confederate-American patriot was buried in Hollywood Cemetery, Richmond, Va.[468]

John Pegram.

PETERS, THOMAS H.: . . . Thomas H. Peters [died] on the night of Christmas Eve, 1905, in Columbus, Miss., where he was born and reared and where he had been a brilliant factor in the upbuilding of the community. He died in his fifty-ninth year.

While yet a boy at a military school, and before the war was half over, Thomas Peters left his books and enlisted in Company E, 6th Mississippi Cavalry Regiment, Mabry's Brigade, Chalmers's Division, and was one of those youthful soldiers who made the legions of Forrest famous the world over for their brilliant victories. His first duty as a soldier, having had military training, was to drill raw recruits, among them men old enough to be his father; but while still a boy in his teens he became a regular soldier. He was in more than twenty-five battles and skirmishes, and was always found in front on the firing line, never shrinking from duty, and he carried with him the scars of battle to the end. As a leader of true and brave patriots during the dark day of reconstruction, he helped to wrest his State from the hands of [the Northern Liberal] usurpers in 1875 and restored her to her present prosperity. A wife and three sons, with a host of relatives and friends, mourn his loss.[469]

PETTUS, W. G.: Dr. W. G. Pettus . . . was born in Lunenberg County, Va., on February 28, 1844. He served in the Confederate army under Generals Van Dorn, Chalmers, Forrest, and Stephen D. Lee, seeing service in Alabama, Mississippi, and Tennessee.

Of his days with Forrest's cavalry, he speaks with great pride. Before the war, he attended Baylor University, at Independence, Tex., under the Presidency of Rufus Burleson. Of his old teacher he speaks to-day with the enthusiasm of a boy. Following the war, he took a medical course in the Universities of Virginia and Maryland, receiving his diploma from the latter. He practiced medicine for a number of years in Fort Bend County, Tex.

Now, however, for more than half a century he has been with us, the people of Georgetown, Tex., a beloved ambassador of the "Old South," sweet and gracious, ever revealing that fine sense which men call courtesy; bringing to us in the nobility of his life, the lofty [Conservative and constitutional] principles for which we trust the South will ever stand. Truly, he is the embodiment of the highest Christian ideals of the old Southern aristocracy.[470]

PIERCE, RICE A.: Gen. Rice A. Pierce, the new Commander of the Tennessee Division, U.C.V., is one of the young veterans of the Confederacy, having enlisted as a boy of fifteen in 1862. He was born July 3, 1847, on a farm in Weakley County, Tenn., and was reared on a farm at Pierce's Station in Obion County, Tenn. In November, 1862, he joined Dibrell's Regiment, the 8th Tennessee, of Forrest's old Brigade, and he served in Forrest's campaigns in West Tennessee, Mississippi, Georgia, and Alabama, and in Middle Tennessee; was surrendered at Gainesville, Ala., May 9, 1865.

At the reunion in Charlotte, N.C., June, 1929, he was made major general in Forrest's Cavalry Association, and at the annual reunion of the Tennessee

Rice A. Pierce.

Division, October, 1929, was unanimously elected Commander of the Tennessee Division.

From a tribute by former Governor Patterson the following is taken: "For fifty years or more, General Pierce has been before the people as a member of Congress back in the seventies and eighties or as taking a prominent part in State politics, . . . and at the bar his voice has been heard in a thousand battles in the legal forum. Few have excelled him as a trial lawyer, . . . and, though now past eighty years of age, he is still active in his profession. His mind is clear, his step elastic, and his voice yet fresh and resonant. Like an old tree sound in body and limb that bears abundant fruit, General Pierce lives on, enjoying life, helping others, and splendidly fulfilling the duties of citizenship."[471]

PITMAN, R. W.: Col. R. W. Pitman . . . served in the 13th Tennessee Regiment under General Forrest.[472]

PITTS, JAMES MONROE: James Monroe Pitts was born in Pontotoc, Miss., October 21, 1847, and gave his services to the South in the War between the States when he was but sixteen years old, serving until the end. He was a member of Captain Bailey's company, of the 1st Mississippi Regiment of Cavalry, commanded by R. A. Pinson, Armstrong's Brigade, Chalmers's Division, Forrest's Corps. He was severely wounded in the right side, also in each arm, in the battle of Selma, Ala., on April 2, 1865, and was left on the field for dead, where he lay for more than twenty-four hours, suffering untold agonies.

After being taken to the hospital and given proper care, he recovered and, the war being over, started to his home, something over three hundred miles away. The railroads were in such bad condition that it took him four days to make the trip, and he then had a long walk before him. Painfully making his way, he at last reached home, where his return brought great joy, as he had been reported dead.

In 1870 Mr. Pitts was married to Miss Eleanor Wilson and soon thereafter removed to California, settling in the San Gabriel Valley, which he helped to develop.

From 1899 the home was in Redlands, where he died on August 19, 1917, survived by his wife and eight children, six daughters and two sons. His venerable mother is also living at the age of ninety-four years.

Mr. Pitts was a kind husband and a loving father. In a last message to his children he asked that they would not let his going lessen their joys, but to keep his memory green by making the world a sweeter place to live in; to love and be kind to one another.[473]

POOL, JAMES MONROE: J. M. Pool was born in Christian County, Ky., in 1825. He enlisted early in 1861 in Capt. Ben D. Terry's Company of Cavalry. J. M. Hollingsworth and T. J. Johnston, a committee, paid tribute from which the following is copied: His company was one in the organization that composed the famous First Kentucky Cavalry, commanded by Col. Ben. Hardin Helm, and said by Gen. Albert S. Johnston to be the finest regiment of cavalry he ever saw.

Comrade Pool served in the western army all the time under Gens. A. S. Johnston, Beauregard, Bragg, Joe Johnston, and Hood, but immediately under Gens. Wheeler and Forrest. He was in all the battles these generals fought, except while in prison at Camp Morton. He was wounded and captured at Fort Donelson and never entirely recovered from that wound; but as soon as he was exchanged he went to his command, which was then with Gen. Morgan, and remained with him and Gen. Duke until the surrender. He and Joe Boytnott made the trip to Princeton together muleback, where he spent the remainder of his days.

He was a successful farmer for many years, but on account of his popularity his friends would not let him remain on his farm. In January, 1877, he was elected jailor, and held that office twenty consecutive years, when he retired from office with competency and spent his declining years with a large and devoted family. [He died on March 1, 1902.][474]

POPE, WILLIAM HENRY: William H. Pope died at his home, in Macon, Ga., on July 25, 1908. Bravely he fought during those historic years of his country's struggles and bravely he lived after the smoke of battle cleared away.

Although he had been in ill health for a year or more, pneumonia caused his death. That dread disease laid hold upon him July 19, 1908, and he died on the 25th. The sorrowing members of his beloved family were with him. His casket was draped with an old Confederate flag, a fitting tribute to this noble soldier. Many floral tributes were sent by friends and admirers. The body was taken to Butler, Ga., the family cemetery, for interment.

William Henry Pope.

William Henry Pope, named for his father, was born in Huntsville, Ala., on December 18, 1844. His mother was Frances Anne Erwin, of Bedford County, Tenn. The senior W. H. Pope, a large slave owner and planter, was killed by being thrown from a horse in 1847. His widow later married Gen. Lucius J. Polk, of Maury County, Tenn. The junior W. H. Pope spent much time in his early life with his grandfather, Col. Andrew Erwin, at Beechwood, his famous country home near Wartrace, Tenn.

In 1859 he entered Lagrange Military Academy, North Alabama, and was a member of the famous cadet corps of that college up to 1862. When camps of instruction for volunteers were established by the Governor of Alabama in 1861, he was detailed from the academy as drillmaster for the camp at Decatur, Ala. In this capacity he served for several months.

In 1862 when the 35th Alabama Infantry was organized young Pope's company became a part of the regiment. He served with this regiment until the army returned from Corinth to Tupelo, Miss. Attacked by typhoid fever, he was taken to a hospital at Columbus, Miss.

Mr. Pope was with Bragg's army on its Kentucky campaign, serving on General Hardee's staff in the battle of Perryville, Ky. After the fight at Murfreesboro and the army fell back to Tullahoma he joined Capt. Ed P. Byrnes's battery of Gen. Basil Duke's brigade in Gen. John H. Morgan's command. He served with this battery until after the fatal Ohio raid, and was one of the few who escaped capture at Buffington, Ohio.

After his return to Chattanooga, through the influence of Gen. Leonidas Polk, Mr. Pope was made a special scout. His operations for the next year were principally in Tennessee and North Alabama. He also served for a short while under General Forrest. He was in the entire campaign in Hood's advance into and retreat from Tennessee. Mr. Pope was wounded three times during the war—in the breast on the skirmish line near Corinth, Miss., in the right leg in Tennessee in a fight between Gen. John H. Morgan's command and General Wilder's brigade of the Federal army, and again while scouting in Tennessee he was wounded in his right side. He surrendered at Gainesville, Ala.

After the war he entered the mining business in Tennessee. In 1869 he engaged in the wholesale tobacco business in Atlanta, Ga. In 1873 he went to Macon, where he lived until his death, being then engaged in the wholesale grocery business, milling, and brokerage.

Mr. Pope was married three times. His first wife was Miss Annie Brock, of Lafayette, Ala., and one child of this union (Mrs. James Timmons, of Atlanta, Ga.) survives him. His second wife was Miss Elizabeth Patton, of Columbus, Ga., and of this marriage one child (W. H. Pope, Jr., of Waco, Tex.) survives him. On June 9, 1881, he was married to Miss Olivia J. Montfort, of Butler, Ga., who survives him with four children, Misses Matebil, Tatum, Erwin, and Edgar.[475]

PORTER, DAVID CORNELIUS: David Cornelius Porter, of Houston, Tex., ... enlisted with the 1st and 7th Alabama Volunteers from Decatur, Ala., under Hatchel Cochran and Forrest, and after eighteen months he went with the 1st Tennessee Scouts, under Captain Shaw. He was a companion of [Confederate boy-hero] Sam Davis, whom he had known before the war, being in the same military school.[476]

PORTER, WILLIAM NEWTON: At his home in Aransas Pass, Tex., Gen. William Newton Porter died suddenly on the morning of May 5, in his eighty-ninth year. Thus was a career of rich experiences brought to a close—a life enriched by the joy of giving happiness to others, for his presence radiated cheer, and his passing brings sadness to all who knew him.

William Newton Porter was born in Gibson County, Tenn., August 1, 1844, and while still in his teens, he enlisted for the Southern cause, joining Forrest's Cavalry as a member of Company D, 20th Tennessee Cavalry, under Colonel Russell. He was one of the few remaining veterans of that famous cavalry command, and was Commander of the Western Department of Forrest's Cavalry Corps Association. He had hoped to attend the Richmond Reunion.

General Porter located in Aransas Pass in 1912, but moved away and returned a few years ago to spend his remaining years there. That he was recognized for his fine citizenship was shown by the closing of business houses during his funeral, and his fellow-citizens and members of the civic associations spoke of him in terms of highest praise and affection. In his Confederate uniform, which represented the beloved cause for which he had fought in his young manhood, he was laid to rest until reveille shall sound again for the hosts in gray. General Porter was twice married, and is survived by his wife and relatives in different States.[477]

POWELL, B. C.: Comrade B. C. Powell [of U.C.V. Camp James Adams], Company F, Fifteenth Tennessee Cavalry, under Forrest, died March 19, 1898.[478]

J. Green Powell.

POWELL, J. GREEN: In the death of J. G. Powell, on July 14, 1922, New Orleans lost one of its most valuable citizens. He was one of the pioneers of the State, and during his long and useful life of eighty-one years he had built up a large lumber business in Louisiana.

When the call to arms was sounded in 1861, he and two younger brothers were among the first to volunteer in the service of the Confederacy, joining the Beaver Creek Riflemen, Company E, of the 4th Louisiana Regiment, with which he served until after the battle of Shiloh, where he was under Colonel Allen. The regiment was then ordered to Vicksburg, where his company was transferred to Winnfield's 3rd Louisiana Cavalry and ordered to Louisiana to join that regiment. It was not mounted at the time, but was attached to the 10th Arkansas Regiment and went into the battle at Baton Rouge with Boyd's Battalion; and it was this battalion, with Company E and one section of Simms's Battery that opened the battle. Simms's battery was commanded by Captain Fauntleroy. At the siege of Port Hudson the company served as infantry with the 10th Arkansas, and after the surrender there it was ordered into camp, when J. G. (Green) Powell was made first lieutenant of the company; the men were then mounted and served with the 3rd Louisiana Cavalry. Powell was captured shortly afterwards in a skirmish near Port Hudson, but made his escape; he was captured again and taken to New Orleans and held in prison for six months, when he and two others made their escape. He was taken care of by friends in New Orleans, among whom was a Miss Kate Watkins, who gave him financial aid, enabling him to rejoin his company. He surrendered at Gainesville, Ala., under General Forrest.

Comrade Powell was twice married, and is survived by four daughters, who are active members of the United Daughters of the Confederacy, doing what they can to perpetuate the service of the Confederate soldiers. Four brothers and two sisters also survive him.[479]

PRICE, GEORGE W.: Gen. George W. Price died at his beautiful home in Water Valley, Miss., on the 6th of July, 1921. He was seventy-nine years of age, having been born in Pontotoc County, Miss., in 1842. He enlisted on the 15th of April, 1861, in Company K, 17th Regiment Mississippi Volunteers, commanded by Colonel Featherstone. At the reorganization of his company in January, 1862, he was elected second lieutenant. He was in the battle of First Manassas, July 21, 1861, also in the battles of Balls Bluff, the Yorktown campaign, the Seven Days' Battles around Richmond, the battle of Second Manassas with Longstreet's command, in the Maryland campaign at South Mountain and Harper's Ferry, in the bloody battle of Sharpsburg in September, 1862, and was finally in the severe campaign that ended at Fredericksburg in December, 1862, losing his leg defending that city. As soon as his wound healed after the amputation of his leg, he had a cork leg adjusted and, until the close of the war, he did valuable service as a scout in Forrest's Cavalry in North Mississippi.

Returning home at the close of the war without any financial resources, he at once went to work to make his way in the world. He won the confidence of the business world, and for many years was a successful merchant. He removed to Water Valley many years ago and was afterwards elected sheriff of Yalobusha County; was also treasurer of his county for four years. He and his friends were proud of the record he made in both offices, and the county never had a more faithful and efficient officer. He was elected Brigadier General of the Third Brigade of United Confederate Veterans in North Mississippi and filled the office for two terms; was afterwards elected for two terms as Commander of the Mississippi Division, U.C.V., filling both positions with great efficiency.

His life was as stainless as that of a pure woman. He was cast in a heroic mold, and from the lofty heights where such spirits are at home he looked down with scorn upon all that was base and mean. He was one of the bravest and truest soldiers that ever served the Confederate cause, always ready, willing, and anxious to do his full duty. The passing of such a splendid soldier and citizen is a loss to the world, and especially to the community in which he lived.

I was his close comrade during his service in the Virginia Army and was his schoolmate from my very earliest remembrance; was with him in the operating room when his leg was amputated, was with him in the dreadful Peninsula campaign and battles around Yorktown, and amid all the trials and difficulties of a Confederate soldier's life he never lost his nerve or gave way to despondency.

He left surviving him his wife, Mrs. Virginia Price, and several children. His body was laid to rest in the cemetery at Water Valley, Miss., in the evening of July 6, 1921, amid the sorrow and tears of a large number of citizens and friends. With sincere appreciation of the friendship that existed between us from our earliest schoolboy days and through the days of bloodshed and carnage of war when we slept under the same blanket and shared the same trials and hardships it is with sadness and sorrow that I pay this humble tribute to his memory. All's well with my friend. Peace to his soul![480]

PRICE, JOHN HENRY: Rev. John Henry Price, well-known Methodist minister and Confederate veteran, died suddenly on the morning of September 23 [1923?], at the home of his daughter, Mrs. Lulu Nelson, in Jackson, Tenn., where he and his wife were on a visit. He was taken back to the old home at Bowling Green, Ky., and laid to rest in Fairview Cemetery.

John Henry Price was born May 1, 1847, and in November, 1862, he enlisted for the Confederacy, joining Company D, 4th Tennessee Cavalry, serving under Colonels Starnes and Dibrell, Forrest's command. He was captured near Franklin, Tenn., and paroled during the latter part of January, 1865, a few days after his capture. A faithful soldier of the Confederacy, there was none more interested in the preservation of Confederate memories. At the time of his death he was Commander of the Kentucky Division of Forrest's Cavalry Association and a member of General Collier's staff. The only survivors of his old command left in Warren County, Ky., are: James Bemiss, William M. Cox, James Choate, William Cole, Dr. William M. Baily, Beverly Thomas, E. C. Brown, B. W. Atkinson, Dr. Ward, and William S. Overstreet.

Comrade Price was twice married, his first wife being Miss Helen Potts, who died many years ago. Six children were born to them, two daughters only surviving him. In January, 1890, he was married to Miss Addie Edwards, and in November of that year he located at Bowling Green, Ky. He had been a member of the Methodist Church since he was eight years old, and had also served the Church as minister in different localities. For forty-one years he was connected with the L. & N. Railroad Company, having been retired on August 1 [1923?].[481]

PRICE, SIDNEY T.: Maj. Sidney T. Price was born at Bladen Springs, Ala.; and died in Atlanta January 8, 1910, aged sixty-three years. He served during the entire war in Forrest's Cavalry. He leaves a sister and five children.[482]

PRIEST, T. R.: Comrade T. R. Priest enlisted in the Maury Artillery at Columbia in the summer of 1861, was captured at Fort Donelson in February,

1862, and sent to prison at Camp Douglas. After being exchanged at Vicksburg he was sent to Port Hudson, on the Mississippi River, and after the capture of that place the Maury Artillery was disbanded, and he joined Forrest's Escort. He was wounded near Selma, Ala., in April, 1865, and was paroled from the hospital in June, 1865. His death occurred on July 22, 1920.[483]

PRYOR, J. P.: [J. P. Pryor] enlisted from Missouri and belonged to General Forrest's cavalry.[484]

PTOMEY, JOHN W.: John W. Ptomey died near Pine Apple, Ala., June 4, 1905, aged seventy years. He was born in Wilcox County, Ala., March 27, 1835, and always lived in the same neighborhood. He was twice married, and leaves a large family to mourn his death. He was firm in his convictions for the right. He was a good neighbor. J. F. Fore, of Pine Apple, writes that when the war broke out between the States Mr. Ptomey was one of the first men in his section to volunteer. He left Pine Apple September 3, 1861, marched to Montgomery, Ala., under Capt. Harper, and was mustered into the Confederate service there on September 15, 1861. Soon afterwards he was ordered to Memphis, Tenn., where he met Col. N. Bedford Forrest, who had orders from the Governor of Tennessee to raise a regiment of cavalry. He joined Capt. W. C. Bacot's company, which was Company B of that regiment. Mr. Ptomey was made a sergeant. He was with Forrest at Fort Donelson and in many other dangerous conflicts. His funeral was largely attended, conducted by his pastor, Dr. David Adams, assisted by Rev. P. M. Jones.[485]

PULLEN, J. B.: J. B. Pullen died at his home near Covington, Tenn., on May 18, 1923, after a long illness. Funeral services were conducted at the Methodist Church, with burial in the Clopton Cemetery. Comrade Pullen had reached the venerable age of eighty-four years. He served as a Confederate soldier under General Forrest, in the 7th Tennessee Cavalry. He was a consistent member of the Methodist Church for many years, and was most highly esteemed in his community. In accordance with his wish, he was buried in his Confederate uniform. He is survived by one son and a number of grandchildren.[486]

PURDON, S. H.: S. H. Purdon, member of Camp Townsend, Calvert, Tex., died some time since [1898], and was buried with military honors. He was from Mississippi, and served under Forrest.[487]

PUTCH, WILLIAM: On Wednesday, March 15, 1922, we paid our last rites to our deceased comrade, William Putch, who lived to the ripe age of more than ninety years, in good health almost to the end of his exemplary and eventful life.

He was born in Westphalia, Prussia, in 1831, and at an early age came to Missouri, settling in Arrow Rock, Saline County, engaging in the banking business.

In 1861, feeling that the cause of the South was just, he cast his lot with us and endured the many hardships incident to four years of active service in the second Missouri Cavalry. After the battles of Elk Horn, Iuka, and Corinth, he served under General Van Dorn,[488] and when he was killed we were placed under that matchless soldier, Gen. N. B. Forrest.

Comrade Putch took part in all the battles fought by that wonderful soldier, in all these cavalry battles in the prairies of Mississippi—West Point, Okolona, Soochatonia Bridge, Fort Pillow, Harrisburg, and many others. He rode from the Missouri River to the Gulf of Mexico (Mobile), and return, on horseback during the four years.

His life was quiet and unostentatious, but in every way exemplary and worthy to be followed. He served Saline County several years as treasurer. He leaves a wife, four sons, a daughter, and a host of friends to mourn his loss.[489]

PYROM, S. B.: S. B. Pyrom in his life presented a splendid example of true Southern manhood. He began early in life to establish that high character which ever guided him to a coveted position in the minds of thinking men. His rugged integrity, his devotion to family, the moral purity of his life, his exhaustless energy in varied useful and unselfish undertakings, and his loyalty to his friends, combined with the shirking modesty peculiar to refined natures, placed him near the head of the column of his fellows, fighting the battles of life always manfully and well.

S. B. Pyrom, with his wife, daughter, and son.

He was a member of Company G, 2nd Regiment Tennessee Cavalry, Bell's Brigade, Forrest's Command. His record as a soldier stands untarnished by a single unworthy deed and characterized throughout by the same fidelity and loyalty of purpose as exhibited in his daily walks of life as a citizen. At the final roll call he will gladly greet his old comrades.[490]

QUINN, W. S.: This veteran passed away at West Point, Miss., in November, 1902. He was born in Lincoln County, N.C., eighty-two years ago, and was a sergeant in a battalion of cavalry from Georgia in the Mexican war. He served in the militia of Mississippi, and surrendered at Vicksburg after that terrible siege. Though not liable to military duty, he afterwards joined Harrison's Mississippi Regiment of Cavalry, and fought to the end under Forrest.

After the war he returned to his farm, some twelve miles west of West Point. He was a model citizen and successful. He served his country later in the State Legislature; also his county as its public treasurer. He was worthily honored, a patriotic citizen and consistent Christian.[491]

RAMSEY, CHARLES A.: Charles A. Ramsey died at his home, in Greensboro, Ala., March 1, 1908, in his sixty-first year. When a youth of sixteen he joined the forces of the Confederacy as a member of a company commanded by Capt. James Winston, of Sumter. He was of Forrest's escort, and a valiant soldier.[492]

RANDLE, E. H.: E. H. Randle, A.M., LL.D., educator, scientific writer, and Christian gentleman, a typical representative of the Old South, died at his home, in Hernando, Miss., on September 27, 1916.

He was born in Tennessee in 1830; hence he had reached the ripe age of eighty-six years. His active life was devoted to school work, except while serving his Southland under that great cavalry leader, Bedford Forrest. Nearly fifty years of his life were devoted to school work in such places as McKenzie and Ripley, Tenn., Paducah, Ky., and Byhalia and Hernando, Miss.

He was not only a successful educator, but an author well known in the scientific world. The books published by him are: *Plurality of the Human Race*, *Characteristics of the Southern Negro*, and *Antagonism of Forces in Nature*.

He was a contributor to the *Memphis Commercial-Appeal*, also to religious, medical, and legal magazines, and was a member of the American Society for Scientific Research.

Professor Randle was a member of the Methodist Church and was always ready to advance the cause of Christ, and by his daily walk and conversation he was a benediction to those with whom he came in contact. His students had forceful evidence of his goodness of heart and his constant effort to lead them in the right paths. He leaves a wife, daughter, and three sons, the latter being residents of Paducah, Ky., Yazoo City, Miss., and Chattanooga, Tenn.[493]

RANDOLPH, GEORGE W.: George W. Randolph enlisted near Houston, Miss., in November, 1862, in Company D, Ballentine's Regiment. He was provost marshal at West Point, Miss., part of the time and also a scout for General Forrest.[494]

REAGAN, WILLIAM BALLARD LENOIR: William Ballard Lenoir Reagan was born in McMinn County, Tenn., at what is now Reagan's Station, on May 31, 1838; and died at Terrell, Tex., September 1, 1913. He was a son of Gen. James H. Reagan and Ann Lenoir Reagan, of Lenoir City, Tenn.

The son was given such an education as the public schools afforded at that time, and when a mere boy he served as assistant cashier and bookkeeper of the branch Bank of Tennessee, located at Athens, of which his father was president. Here he remained until the beginning of the war, when he enlisted with Col. John C. Vaughn's 3rd Tennessee Regiment, serving first as a member of the Cornet Band; but wishing to be in the thick of the fight, he served later as first lieutenant and adjutant in Col. John R. Neal's 16th Battalion, Tennessee Cavalry, Rucker's Legion, Pegram's Brigade, under General Bragg, in Kentucky and Tennessee.

He was with Vaughn's Regiment in Virginia. He was under Forrest in the battle of Chickamauga, was afterwards with Vaughn's Cavalry Brigade in the Valley of Virginia and Maryland campaigns, and was in all the engagements of his command up to the time he was wounded near Winchester, Va., July 24, 1864, when he lost his leg. Soon afterwards he was captured by the Federals and placed in Old Capitol Prison, at Washington, and then removed to Fort Delaware, where he remained until June, 1865.

He was a faithful and gallant soldier. Until his removal to Texas, a few years ago, Comrade Reagan lived at the old homestead, in McMinn County, Tenn.[495]

REED, THOMAS CLARK: Capt. Thomas Clark Reed, a long-time resident and deeply revered and esteemed citizen of Ladonia, Tex., passed away at the family home thereon March 24, 1923, following a general breakdown in health that confined him to his bed several weeks.

Capt. Tom Reed was born March 16, 1843, in Lawrence County, Ala., and had just passed the eightieth milestone along life's highway. He moved from Alabama with his father's family to Tennessee, later going with them to Texas about fifty-six years ago, and had been a resident of Ladonia forty-eight years.

Thomas Clark Reed.

At the age of nineteen, on March 1, 1862, he felt the call of his beloved Southland and enlisted in Whitefield's Legion, Company K, near the Texas line. He was in Arkansas at the time, in the home of his brother-in-law and sister, having gone there to recover his health. Later his command was a part of the brigade under Gen. Sul Ross, where he remained until he was captured near

Corinth, Miss. He was sick at the time, but through the influence of a cousin, Capt. Jim Reed, of the Northern army, he was sent to his father's home on Jack's Creek, Tenn., and, being in bad health, he remained there several months. Then, Ross's Brigade being away over in Georgia, he went to Clifton on the Tennessee River and joined Gen. N. B. Forrest's Cavalry, Company H, in Colonel A. N. Wilson's 16th Tennessee Regiment, Bell's Brigade, serving under Capt. "Billy" Bray. He was with Forrest until he surrendered at Gainesville Ala., in May, 1865.

To Captain and Mrs. Reed were born seven children, four of whom, with the heartbroken mother, survive him. These children are: Forrest T., John M., and Miss Pansy Reed, of Dallas; and Paul C. Reed, of Burkburnett.

Courteous, kind and loyal, a splendid type of Southern gentleman, a gallant member of the Confederate army, Captain Reed had always been an active member of Robert E. Lee Camp, No. 126, U.C.V., and his passing leaves a sad gap in the ranks of this camp's membership, and marks the slow, but sure, depletion of the number of those old heroes who fought for the loved principles represented by the Stars and Bars [conservatism and constitutionalism]; and though they will all soon be only memories, it will be a sad day for this dear old Southland when mention of their chivalrous deeds fails to bring to Southern hearts a sensation of pride and a throb of sadness.

For over fifty years Captain Reed had been a member of the Baptist Church, and his funeral services were held at the First Baptist Church in the presence of a large throng of friends, among whom was the entire membership of Robert E. Lee Camp, and by these comrades he was laid to rest with the ritual ceremony, the last rite being the placing of a Confederate flag on the casket.[496]

REESE, DAVID NELSON: David Nelson Reese, who died January 1, 1931, at his home in Watauga, Tenn., was born in Harrison County, Ky., near Cynthiana, on October 13, 1839, and had thus passed into his ninety-second year. His youth was spent in the Reese neighborhood near Cynthiana, and he attended school at Mt. Zion, his last school days being spent at Millersburg, Ky.

He was the son of George and Minerva Bailey Reese. The Reeses came from Wales to America some time before the American Revolution. Isaac Reese married Sarah Harcourt, who came from New Jersey with her brother, Richard Harcourt, to Kentucky. They were descendants of Richard Bard Harcourt, of Great Berkhampstead, Hertfordshire, England. His grandfather, Benaiah Bailey, born and reared at Norwich, Conn., graduated from Yale College as a physician and surgeon, was appointed assistant surgeon of the 29th Regiment in the War of 1812, and was at the Battle of Lundy's Lane. He married Ellen Yates in New Jersey, and soon afterwards they went to Kentucky.

When the War between the States came on in 1861, David Nelson Reese joined Captain Joe Desha's company, which joined with several other companies, making the First Kentucky Regiment, under Col. Blanton Duncan. This regiment went to Nashville, Tenn., and from there they went direct to

Harper's Ferry, Va., where Gen. Thomas J. ["Stonewall"] Jackson was in command. When the regiment was mustered out after twelve months service, David Nelson Reese went to General Marshall in Kentucky, and then was at home a while. He then joined Marshall's and Morgan's command and was sent down to Chickamauga under Gen. Joe Wheeler and Forrest and was at the siege of Knoxville. He was in Morgan's last raid into Kentucky, and was at Greeneville when General Morgan was killed. On the night of April 9, 1865, Reese was with Capt. John B. Castleman's company on Wolfe Creek in Bland County, Va., which intended to continue east, but learned that General Lee had surrendered.

In December, 1864, Reese was married to Anna Margaret Johnson, a niece of Andrew Johnson, later president. He had been an active member of the Southern Methodist Church since his early boyhood. He taught school in Kentucky and Tennessee. He was the oldest citizen in the little village of Watauga, Tenn., and was loved by everyone. He was laid to rest in Highland Cemetery at Elizabethton, Tenn. Surviving him are a daughter and two sons, ten grandchildren, four great-grandchildren and one sister.[497]

REYNOLDS, ALFRED C.: Alfred C. Reynolds was a member of the 21st Alabama Infantry and enlisted in 1861. He was appointed ordnance sergeant and located at Corinth, Miss. He was in most of the fights around Atlanta and was wounded there. He was promoted to first lieutenant and transferred to Forrest's Cavalry and paroled at Gainesville, Ala.

Comrade Reynolds removed to St. Louis soon after the war ended and lived there for many years. He was an active and interested member of Camp St. Louis, No. 731, U.C.V., and until his health failed he usually attended the Reunions. He was a good soldier and a good citizen, a Christian gentleman, and had the respect and esteem of all who knew him. He recently removed to Livingston, Ala., where he passed away on April 24, 1915. By his special request he was buried with a large Confederate flag around his coffin.[498]

Robert J. Rhodes.

RHODES, ROBERT J.: Robert J. Rhodes, one of the most prominent men of Whiteville, Tenn., and an honored Confederate veteran, passed into eternal rest February 29, 1916.

Mr. Rhodes was born in Fayette County August 11, 1844, and was married to Miss Martha Neville April 15, 1865. He leaves this loyal, noble wife, a devoted daughter, Mrs. Roberts, of Hot Springs, Ark., and a faithful son, Festers Rhodes, cashier of the People's Bank, Whiteville, Tenn.

At the age of seventeen Robert Rhodes enlisted with Capt. C. S. Schuyler, Company E, Forrest's old regiment, at New Castle, March 12, 1862. Soon after he was sworn into service at

Somerville and fought faithfully and bravely throughout the war. A faithful Confederate to the end, he missed but one Reunion in his life. He loved the gray and treasured the small bronze cross. He was ever thoughtful of the old veterans and in many ways added to their happiness. At any public meeting it was his great pleasure to have his old comrades share the very best. He loved to entertain them. He was a patriot; he loved his country; he loved his State; he loved his kind. Clad in his gray uniform and resting in a casket of gray, the "clay tenement" of the grand old Christian soldier was lowered by loving hands into the bosom of mother earth, there to await the glorious dawn of the resurrection morn.[499]

[A few years before his death patriot Rhodes wrote the following:] "Comrades, when I begin to think of what I should be thankful for, I am overwhelmed, and then think of the things for which I am not thankful. The good Lord in his loving-kindness has gently led me through life. I don't know the taste of that awful enemy to mankind, whisky; neither that of coffee nor tobacco. Yes, I am thankful that I am at peace with our Heavenly Father. I served thirty-two months in the cruel war under General Forrest. In one of our charges in the battle of Iuka, Miss., my horse threw me. Our captain, Rufus Brooks, was wounded and captured with others. I am thankful that the enemy thought I was dead and left me on the field, so I was never a prisoner. To all comrades who wore the gray and the blue I am thankful to have a heart full of good wishes."[500]

RICE, ROBERT H.: The long roll has again been beaten and another comrade has answered "Present." Robert H. Rice, an estimable man, sincere friend, and gallant Confederate soldier, one who rode with the mighty Forrest in the War of the States, has joined that mighty host of heroes who since the day of Appomattox have been "passing over" in review by our great dead commanders.

Robert H. Rice.

Comrade Rice was born in Copiah County, Miss., and served in Company F, 4th Regiment of Mississippi Cavalry. Although but fourteen years old, his comrades testify that "he was a good soldier and did his duty to State and cause manfully," a consoling eulogy to sorrowing relatives and friends. When the last one of us who wore the gray has closed the circuit, let this epitaph appear: "He was a good soldier."[501]

RICHARDS, DANIEL R.: It is not my purpose to testify as to the qualities of Daniel R. Richards as a Confederate soldier, for his comrades need not be told of that, but it is to tell them of his life and character after that great struggle that I write. In October, 1862, he left his pleasant home, devoted wife, and prattling children to become a target for the leaden hail of an army which was being organized to take from him his property. He enlisted in Capt. James McRunnell's Company of the Eighth Tennessee Cavalry, commanded at first by Col. G. G. Dibrell, and which was afterwards under Gen. N. B. Forrest. When the stern decree of fate as to the war was settled, he returned to his family in White County, Tenn., and began civil life anew on the farm. Brave and true as a soldier in the army, he became a citizen faithful in all of life's duties.

Born in June, 1832, he was married to Miss Mary J. Taylor in April, 1855, entered the Christian army in 1857, and died May 22, 1901. He was gentle, kind, and good. It is said of him that "he was one of God's great men." The relentless messenger came as gently as a springtime zephyr, and without a sigh this grand old veteran "passed over the river to rest under the shade of the trees." There are no words too strong, too tender, or too delicate to be modeled by some master into a beautiful epitaph to perpetuate the memory of this noble man who delighted to serve and honor God.[502]

RICHARDSON, ROBERT VINKLER: Robert Vinkler Richardson was born on November 4, 1820, in Granville County, N.C., after which his parents moved the family to Hardeman County, Tenn. He later worked as a lawyer in Memphis, where he became a business associate of Nathan Bedford Forrest.

During Lincoln's War Richardson eventually came to serve in Forrest's command, recruiting the 12th Tennessee Cavalry. He fought gallantly at Corinth and Shiloh, was appointed brigadier general on December 3, 1863, and served out his enlistment under General Chalmers.

After the War, Comrade Richardson returned to Memphis, once again partnering up with General Forrest, this time in the railroad business. During a trip concerning a proposed road, he was seriously injured on January 5, 1870, at Clarkton, Mo., by a mysterious stranger who fired a shotgun at him. He passed away the next day from his wound, and was laid to rest in Elmwood Cemetery, Memphis.[503]

RICHMOND, B.: The parole of B. Richmond, a brother of W. B. Richmond, whose family now resides in Nashville with his daughter, Mrs. C. M. Morford, is dated Augusta, Ga., May 10, 1865, as a private in the 2nd Kentucky Regiment, Col. T. G. Woodward. A parole for twenty days was given B. Richmond on March 21, 1864, as assistant paymaster of Forrest's Division.[504]

ROANE, ARCHIBALD T.: Judge Archibald T. Roane, who died at his home in Grenada, Miss., on April 27, 1923, came of a long line of ancestors notable in affairs of statesmanship and war. His grandmother was a "Campbell of Argyle," and his grandfather, Governor Archibald Roane, of Tennessee, was a soldier of the Revolution; his father, Andrew Roane, was an officer in the Mexican war. When the War between the States came on, Archibald Roane enlisted in the Confederate army and served his loved Southern cause in Virginia with the 17th Mississippi Regiment, Longstreet's Brigade, and was then with Forrest's Cavalry until after the battle of Selma, Ala. Entering the service as second lieutenant, he was later made captain, and just as the war was closing he was recommended for a major's commission by General Forrest, who had seen him handle a difficult situation.

With the close of the war there were still other battles for him where hard issues were to be decided. In the "Black-and-Tan" Legislature of Mississippi in Reconstruction days [in which uneducated racist blacks had been given political positions that allowed them to freely oppress and terrorize Southern whites], he worked tirelessly [against the carpetbag regime (that is, the Left-wing government that had been forced upon Dixie after the War)] . . . and was one of the notable "thirteen" who delivered the State from radical [that is, Liberal and socialist] domination.[505] [The writer is speaking here of the far left members of the Republican Party, which was the Liberal Party up until the election 1896.][506]

Throughout the years since he was ever awake to the best interests of his country and people, taking pride in his position and the service he could render. He lived through hard times. Coming back from the war, he found his home burned, his father, a practicing physician, broken in health; so upon him devolved the support of the four sisters and two younger brothers. He gave them his best, and sought to inspire them to a life worthwhile. He studied law while working hard as a merchant, was admitted to the bar, and in his profession attained eminent success, a number of times being honored by his fellow men with public trust. He served three terms in the lower house of the State legislature, and two in the Senate, and one six-year term as Circuit Judge.

The motto of his Scotch ancestors, "Faithful," was fully exemplified in every relationship of life, even "unto death," and he looked forward joyfully to the promised "crown of life."[507]

ROARK, W. H.: W. H. Roark [served in] Forrest's Cavalry, 7th Tennessee, Bell's Brigade; [he died in 1924] aged eighty-three.[508]

ROBERTS, PRESTON: Preston Roberts was an African-American member of Forrest's cavalry; head of mess, he was in charge of 75 cooks, and was the purchaser of food not provided by the commissary. After the War the United Daughters of the Confederacy awarded Roberts the Southern Cross of Honor.[509]

ROBERTSON, GEORGE MURRAY: George Murray Robertson passed away on October 17, 1923, at his home in Deerbrook, Miss. He was born and reared in Huntsville, Ala., descended from two prominent Southern families, his father being Rev. John Murray Robertson, of Maryland, and his mother, Rebecca Lowrie Robertson, of North Carolina.

As a youth of eighteen years in 1861, he joined the 4th Alabama Cavalry, Colonel Russell, Company C, Captain Gurley [under Forrest]. . . . Captain Gurley time and again said he could always depend on Murray in any contingency. There were four Robertson brothers in Russell's regiment, three with Gurley.

George Murray Robertson.

Murray Robertson was with us at the reunion in October looking well, strong, and handsome.

He was all that a son, brother, husband, and father should be—thoughtful of others, kind and generous to all.

His family still cherish a beautiful little silk flag presented to him on September 1, 1862, at Mooresville, Ala., by Molly Hussey, on which is written these words: "Receive this flag as an emblem of friendship, and may it fan thy noble brow to victory."

He leaves a wife, four children, and a sister to mourn his loss. Wherever he went he made lasting friends. His faith was that of his forefathers, trusting and true, and those near and dear to him, while mourning, feel that to some it will not be a long parting.[510]

RODDEY, PHILIP DALE: Philip D. Roddey was born April 2, 1826, at Moulton, Ala. Though lacking a traditional education, he worked his way through early life, eventually becoming sheriff of Lawrence County. Upon the start of Lincoln's War, he founded a cavalry unit that worked independently, scouting for the Confederacy. In 1862, now a colonel, he organized the 4th Alabama Cavalry, serving under both Wheeler and Forrest. At the Battle of Selma he and Forrest managed to evade capture by swimming across the Alabama River in the dark of night. After the War, Comrade Roddey took up the pump business in New York. On July 20, 1897, while in England discussing the sale of a patent, he passed away from uremia at Westminster Hospital in London. His body was returned to Tuscaloosa, Ala. for burial. Another stalwart patriot has passed from our midst.[511]

ROGERS, BENJAMIN ARMSTEAD: On July 18, past [1902], in Florence, Ala., the knightly spirit of Benjamin Armstead Rogers left earth to join his comrades in the bivouac of heaven. As husband, father, friend, and soldier he did well his part. He was a native of the grand old "Volunteer State," having been born near Clarksville sixty-seven years ago. He was a graduate of the college of that city, afterwards taking a full course in the Lebanon Law-School, and graduating with distinction there. He stood gallantly for the "bars and stars" during the entire period of the war. A wealthy Kentucky relative

Benjamin Armstead Rogers.

offered to make him heir to a large estate if he would not enter the Confederate service, but to no avail. He was too true to his inherited principles of right to shirk when duty called.

His father was a distinguished soldier under Andrew Jackson, and his grandfather served in the Continental army. He was made provost marshal of Clarksville, and afterwards captain of Company H, Second Kentucky Cavalry, under Col. Woodard. His company saw service under Forrest and Wheeler, and so well did he perform his part that he was promoted to major for distinguished gallantry. His health failing, he was changed from field service to the secret service of the government, where he did still more valued service by his courage and skill.

He was a true representative Southerner of the old school. Manhood is elevated by the record he made. He was a man of superior intelligence, an advanced thinker. He reared his children to believe in the justice of the cause for which he fought [conservatism], and his dearest possession was his Southern Cross of Honor. He was gently laid away by forty old veterans of Camp O'Neal, of which he was a member, with the dear old Southern flag enshrouding him.[512]

ROGERS, R. E.: R. E. Rogers died at his home near Belmont, Tenn., in February [1923], in his eighty-third year. He was a member of Company B, 7th Tennessee Cavalry, Forrest's Division, and was mustered into service on May 31, 1861, surrendering at Gainesville, Ala., 1865. He was as brave a soldier as ever rode with Forrest.[513]

ROGERS, WILLIAM JAMES: On the 9th of January [1908] William J. Rogers breathed his last at the home of his son, Charles P. Rogers, at DeLong Terrace, Lexington, Ky., aged sixty-five years. The interment was at Cave Hill Cemetery, Louisville, Ky. He is survived by two sons, Messrs. Charles P. and J. Will Rogers, of Lexington.

Comrade Rogers was a soldier of the Civil War, he and a younger brother, John (now Judge Rogers, of the Federal court in Arkansas), having enlisted in March, 1862, at Canton, Miss., in the Semmes Rifles, commanded by Capt. Hugh Love. This company soon after became Company H, 9th Mississippi Regiment Infantry, Chalmers's Brigade, Army of Tennessee. Both brothers were wounded at Munfordville, Ky., and W. J. Rogers was sent North to prison.

After being exchanged, though disabled for infantry service and discharged, he immediately joined the 1st Mississippi Cavalry, in Armstrong's Brigade, was made orderly sergeant of his company, and served through the war under Wheeler and Forrest.

The romance of his life occurred near the spot where he was wounded and captured. The deadly missiles of battle passed over the country home of the "girl he left behind him," Miss Martha L. Lewis, who afterwards became his wife and the mother of his children. Though bereft of her by death for more than thirty years, his last thoughts were of this beloved companion of his early manhood, and her name was among the last on his lips.

The death of this good man is a loss deeply felt in his community, where, though known only in the quiet walks of life, he had endeared himself through his kind and lovable nature.[514]

ROSE, T. A.: T. A. Rose was born in Lawrence County, Ala., October 10, 1844, and died at his home, in Cisco, Tex., on April 10, 1918, after a long illness, having been confined to his home some eight months.

Comrade Rose volunteered his services to the Confederacy during the War between the States and served at Galveston, Tex., six months on the gunboats. He then entered the cavalry and served in one of the Texas legions of Ross's Brigade under General McCulloch; and while his service as a soldier extended throughout the full four years, it is not clearly known just when and where he was under Price and Forrest, though it seems that he was at Corinth and Iuka; and he also served in Mississippi, Tennessee, Georgia, and Alabama under Capt. B. H. Norsworthy. He was in the battle at Thompson's Station, Tenn., at Jonesboro, Ga., and in another hard-fought battle at Middleburg, Tenn., in which he was wounded.

He surrendered in Mississippi and remained in that State until his marriage, in November, 1867, to Miss Louisa P. Davis. Two children were born to this union and survive him—Walter Rose, of Fort Stockton, Tex., and Mrs. W. R. L. Williams, of Merincea [Morenci?], Ariz. Mr. Rose was a member of the Methodist Church, a devoted Christian, and a loving husband and father.[515]

ROSS, EDWARD BARKER: Capt. Edward Barker Ross was born in Todd County, Ky., March 5, 1840; and died December 7, 1911. His father, James Ross, was one of the most scholarly men of the time, being well educated in both Latin and Greek, and he was conversant with the general literature of his day. His book, *The Life and Times of Elder Reuben Ross*, is a faithful history of his father, a pioneer Baptist preacher of that country, and it is also an excellent interpretation of the men and women of those early times. This truly great book is in style and quaintness of humor charmingly original.

Though born in Kentucky, Captain Ross was reared on a farm near the State line in Tennessee, where he lived and died. He received his education on the farm at his father's school for boys, his college period occurring while he was a Confederate soldier. He and his three brothers all enlisted in the army and served to the close of the war, save Col. Reuben Ross, who was killed early in the service at

Edward Barker Ross during the War.

Hopkinsville, Ky. So distinguished was the latter's service at Fort Donelson that the Confederate authorities requested his promotion to brigadier general, but owing to his early death the commission was not executed.

Captain Ross enlisted July 20, 1861, in Company K, 3rd Kentucky Infantry, organized by Col. Lloyd Tilghman. He was third lieutenant in Captain Barnett's company, and made a fine record as a soldier. Gentle and brave, he won both the admiration and the affection of his men, who always followed his lead. His regiment was at Bowling Green under Gen. Albert Sidney Johnston, following in the retreat, and was in the carnage at Shiloh. Early Sunday morning, the first day of that battle, he was wounded, had his wound dressed, and went back at once to the front and fought to the end of the second day. Again in the first siege of Vicksburg he showed the same fighting spirit. After the *Arkansas* ram had successfully executed its daring feat in breaking through the Federal chain of forty vessels, disabling three or four of them and losing ten or twelve of her men, a call for volunteers was made to take the places of her killed and wounded. Captain Ross was among the first to step forward as a volunteer for this dangerous service.

In April, 1863, after General Grierson had made the most successful raid ever made by the Federals, marching through Tennessee and Mississippi to Baton Rouge, several companies of the 3rd Kentucky were mounted in order to intercept similar raids. As mounted infantry Captain Ross's company covered the retreat of Gregg's Brigade from the battle of Raymond, Miss., where this brigade had fought one of Grant's army corps practically from sunrise to sunset. Not the charge of the Light Brigade nor Pickett's still more famous charge at Gettysburg is more glorious than the heroic fighting of Gregg's Brigade at Raymond.

Some two months later this mounted infantry were ordered to give up their horses and take their places in the infantry service. About fifty men refused to be dismounted and left for their homes in Western Kentucky. General Buford selected Captain Ross as the man best suited to send after these men with instructions to persuade them to return to their commands or to hold them together and act independently, reporting to him once a month. These men were brave soldiers, but they claimed that as the term of their enlistment had expired they had the right to reenlist where they pleased. The authorities thought differently, hence the trouble. Captain Ross did not succeed in persuading them to come back, but he held them together and added new recruits and made it so uncomfortable for the Federal forces at Paducah that they dared not send out small raiding forces in the adjacent country. In this way Captain Ross was of great service to all the country between Paducah and Mayfield, besides aiding our armies in procuring supplies from that rich farming section.

After he had accomplished all that could be done on this mission, he returned to his company at Paris, Tenn. He was with Forrest at the capture of Johnsonville, and it was he, Capt. H. Clay Horn, and the gallant Capt. Frank Gracey, of Clarksville, Tenn., who first attempted the crossing of the river on an improvised raft to capture and bring over the Federal transport, the *Mazeppa*, which had been disabled by the Confederate batteries. The raft breaking to pieces, immersing all three, the gallant Gracey stripped his clothes and, tying them and his pistols around his neck, threw one arm over one log of the raft, and thus got across the river and captured the vessel.

When General Hood was on his way to Franklin, Tenn., General Lyon was sent to make a diversion on a raid into Kentucky, and Captain Ross went on this raid. General Lyon went as far north as Elizabethtown and captured there a whole train of provisions. But finding himself completely surrounded by the enemy, he gave orders to his men to get back South as best they could. Captain Ross and four of his men were captured by a large force of the enemy just as he was pushing off from the bank of Green River. This was about December 24, 1864. He was carried to Camp Chase Prison, where he suffered terribly from cold and hunger until he was exchanged about the middle of March, 1865.

Edward Barker Ross in later years.

As soon as Captain Ross was exchanged at Richmond he went back to his regiment, and remained with it until the surrender at Gainesville, Ala., on May 9, 1865. A comrade has written of him: "When I saw him after his captivity, he was just as hopeful and determined to continue fighting as at the beginning of the war. He never gave up, and would have fought all his life had the war continued so long."

Returning home from the war, Captain Ross was not cast down nor disheartened by defeat, but with tireless energy and with that buoyant hopefulness which never deserted him he took the management of his father's farm and assisted him in teaching. He soon became a successful farmer.

In October, 1870, Captain Ross married Dorothea Crouch, a refined and cultured lady, who survives him. To this union were born six children, four daughters and two sons, all of whom are living and are worthy sons and daughters of their honored father.

In 1880 Captain Ross engaged in the tobacco business in connection with his farm, building a stemming factory and putting up strips for the English market. So careful and so honest was he in all his work in this business that when he visited England to look after his tobacco business, those merchant princes, the Giliots and the Babingtons, one a member of Parliament and governor of the Bank of England, entertained him in their homes during his entire stay.

He took a deep interest in all that concerned his neighborhood. He got up a Good Roads Club and induced all his neighbors to join in building one to the Clarksville Pike.

While stationed at Holly Springs during the war he became a member of the Episcopal Church, and from that time was ever a true follower of Christ. There being no church near enough for the family to attend, he threw his whole energy into the matter of having one built, interesting the community in the enterprise, and within a few months had built the little country church which is a lasting monument to his name. For several years he taught in the Sunday school, never failing to attend, and doing everything in the capacity of a layman that he could. His little church being too poor to employ a minister, he took orders in the Episcopal Church and became a regular minister, although against his inclination; but it was an emergency. Though burdened with large business activity, he always had time to visit the sick, to console the distressed, and to cheer the despondent.

Stricken by a fatal malady eight years before he died, he was still the same cheerful, self-denying man, lightening his own heavy burdens by sharing those of others. He never was a truer soldier of the cross than when he was an invalid and waiting for his end.

In reviewing the life of this masterful and yet loving and tender man, it can truly be said that he was a faithful son, a devoted husband and father, a courageous and victorious soldier of his country and of the cross.[516]

ROSS, LAWRENCE SULLIVAN: The immensely popular Lawrence S. "Sul" Ross was born September 27, 1838, at Bentonsport, Iowa, after which his family removed to Texas. After graduating from Wesleyan University, he served as captain of a unit of Texas Rangers against the Comanches. During this dangerous employment he was responsible for the rescue of the famous Cynthia Ann Parker, and also for the killing of Chief Peta Necona, ensuring his fame upon entering the Confederate army in 1861.

A brigadier general by 1863, he served under, and was highly commended by, General N. B. Forrest, among many other Confederate chieftains. The War ended with Ross having been in 135 conflicts, and he returned to Texas, like Forrest, bankrupt. Entering the political arena, he served as both a Texas senator and governor, before becoming president of the Agricultural and Mechanical College of Texas, a position he held up to his death on January 3, 1898. There is a state university in Alpine, Tex., named after him.[517]

RUCKER, EDMUND WINCHESTER: The death of Gen. E. W. Rucker, at his home in Birmingham, Ala., on the night of Sunday, April 13, 1924, takes another from the fast-dwindling list of gallant Confederate leaders and one of the patriotic upbuilders of the South since the war. He had reached the advanced age of eighty-eight years, but was still an outstanding figure in the business and social life of that city. After the war, and before removing from his native Tennessee, he built a forty-mile stretch of the Memphis and Little Rock Railroad. Later he was president of the Salem, Marion and Memphis Railroad following his removal to Birmingham, and had also been prominently connected with large manufacturing interests of that city.

Edmund Winchester Rucker was born July 22, 1835, at Murfreesboro,

Tenn., the son of Edmund and Louisa Winchester Rucker, and a grandson of Gen. James Winchester, a noted Tennessean, and commander on the disastrous field of Frenchtown in the War of 1812. The family removed to Wilson County in his childhood, where he was educated. In his early life he went to Memphis and entered the engineering business, in which he was engaged when the war came on.

Enlisting for the South, "he was appointed a first lieutenant in the regular army of the Confederate States in November, 1861, and assigned to duty at Columbus, Ky. In the spring of 1862 he was at Island No. 10 commanding a battery, and on March 17, made a gallant fight against the Federal gunboats, lasting from noon until dark, and in which the enemy was repulsed. His gallantry won him the commendation of his general (Trudeau), who brought up his name for promotion, and just before the campaign in Kentucky he was commissioned major and led the 16th Tennessee Battalion, Scott's Cavalry Brigade, which was in the advance on the day of victory at Richmond, Ky.

Edmund Winchester Rucker.

"In the spring of 1863 he was promoted to colonel, commanding Rucker's 1st Tennessee Legion, the 12th and 16th Battalions. In the Chickamauga campaign he led his legion in Davidson's Brigade, of Pegram's Division, Forrest's Cavalry Corps. Later he was attached to Grigsby's Brigade, Kelly's Division, Wheeler's Cavalry Corps, and participated in the cavalry operations of Longstreet's campaign in East Tennessee.

"Transferred to Mississippi and assigned to command the 6th Brigade of Forrest's Cavalry, May, 1864, he was put in charge of operations in northwest Mississippi, taking an important part in the following famous campaigns of Forrest. He served with distinction at the battle of Harrisburg, under General Chalmers, and was severely wounded, but again led his brigade with gallantry and soldiership during the raid into West Tennessee, October and November, 1864, taking a leading part in the achievements at Paris Landing and Johnsonville. In Hood's Tennessee campaign he commanded a brigade composed of the 7th, 12th, 14th, 15th, and Forrest's Tennessee Cavalry, the 7th Alabama, and 5th Mississippi. He defeated Capron's cavalry near Henryville, November 23, pursued the enemy to within seven miles of Columbia, and skirmished about there until the Federals evacuated the town on the 28th.

"Still pursuing, he fought at Spring Hill and Franklin, and after the investment of Nashville, his command was posted so as to blockade the Cumberland River, and was engaged with the Federal gunboats. He was forced to abandon this position on the 15th of December, and after the battle of Nashville his brigade was stationed at Brentwood, to hold the pike at all hazards.

In the desperate hand-to-hand fighting at night he was wounded losing his left arm and captured, but he was back with the army in time for the surrender in North Carolina."[518]

After the War, Forrest hired General Rucker to serve as the superintendent of his railroad company, a position he kept even after Forrest resigned his presidency in 1874.[519] Rucker is survived by his wife, two daughters, and a son, Dr. E. W. Rucker.[520]

RUCKER, J. M.: J. M. Rucker, who went to Texas some thirty years ago from Franklin County, Ala., was another soldier of the South who helped to build up that great State. He died at his home in the "Caps Community" at the age of eighty-two years. He is survived by his wife, five sons, and two daughters, also thirty grandchildren and seven great-grandchildren. He had been a leading citizen of Taylor County for the past quarter of a century.

Comrade Rucker was the youngest of nine brothers who fought for the South. He served in the 4th Alabama Regiment, under Gen. N. B. Forrest, and took part in many important battles during three and a half years. He had been a member of the Baptist Church for fifty-seven years, and served forty years as deacon. [He was a member of Tom Green Camp No. 7, U.C.V., of Abilene, Tex.][521]

RUTLEDGE, WADE PRESLY: Wade Presly Rutledge, of Vance, Tenn., died June 22 [1903]. Comrade Rutledge left school and entered the Confederate army early in 1861, joining Capt. Gammon's company in the Nineteenth Tennessee Infantry. He was later with Forrest, and then with Wheeler as a member of Company B, Fourth Tennessee Cavalry, and was paroled at the close of the war in North Carolina.[522]

John Sampson.

SAMPSON, JOHN: At the age of eighty-nine years, John Sampson died at his home in Kaufman, Tex., on February 1 [1928]. He was born and reared at Carthage, Tenn., and enlisted in the Confederate army in April, 1861, serving as a member of Company G, 2nd Tennessee Cavalry. He took part in many battles during the war, among which were Shiloh, Iuka, and Farmington, Miss. Capt. H. B. Moore commanded his company, which was surrendered at Gainesville, Ala., on May 10, 1865, and he served under General Forrest through the war.

Surviving Comrade Sampson are several sons and daughters living in different parts of Texas. One daughter, Mrs. Tolbert, lives at Kaufman. He was a splendid citizen, and his life was that of a Christian from youth up, his religious affiliations being with the Baptist Church. He is now with his comrades in the heavenly reunion.[523]

SANDERS, HARVEY C.: Harvey C. Sanders, a native son of Trigg County, Ky., but for many years a citizen of Texas, died on September 30 [1925], at the home of his son in Bowie County. He was born November 24, 1837, and had thus nearly completed his eighty-eighth year.

At the breaking out of war between the States, Harvey Sanders joined Company B, 2nd Kentucky Volunteers, C.S.A., and served under General Forrest until he was transferred to the West. He was then attached to General Wheeler's command, with which he served to the close of the war. He was in many important battles, among them Chickamauga, Missionary Ridge, Shiloh,

Vicksburg, Lookout Mountain, Petersburg, Fort Donelson, Perryville, and Murfreesboro. He was twice wounded—by a saber thrust, and again by a gunshot. He was one of the bodyguard of President Davis, and was captured in Washington County, Ga.

After a year in prison, Comrade Sanders returned to his home in Trigg County; and in December, 1867, he was married to Miss Alice Baker, of that place, who died in 1869, leaving a son, who died in his young manhood. In 1872, he married Miss Elizabeth Jones, of Caldwell County, Ky., and four of their five children survive him—three sons and a daughter. A brother also is left, Joshua Sanders, of Trigg County.

Comrade Sanders went to Texas in 1882, locating in Coryell County, but in 1887 he removed his family to Bowie County, which was his home until death. The funeral was from the Christian Church, of which he had been a member for more than sixty years. The Odd Fellows Lodge officiated at the burial service in Red Bayou Cemetery, he having been a member of this order for more than fifty years and was Past Grand Master.[524]

SANDERS, J. A.: J. A. Sanders [was with the] 7th Tennessee Regiment, Forrest's Cavalry; [he died in 1924] aged seventy-nine.[525]

SANDERS, JAMES W.: James W. Sanders died at the age of eighty-two years, at his home near Camden [Tenn.], December 26, 1929. He had been a lifelong Democrat [before 1896, a Conservative] and served as night watchman of the capitol under the administration of Governors Benton McMillin and M. R. Patterson. "Uncle Jim," as he was known, was a member of Forrest's Cavalry, and took a great interest in all the reunions of the Confederate soldiers.

He was buried at Camden Cemetery after services at the Methodist Church, of which he was a devoted attendant until his infirmities kept him away. He is survived by one daughter and three brothers.[526]

SANFORD, J. B.: J. B. Sanford was born January 16, 1844, near Gurley, Ala. He enlisted in Gurley's Company C, 4th Alabama Cavalry, in November, 1862, and served with that company under Forrest and Wheeler at different times until the close of the war. After the war he moved to Mississippi and engaged in farming up to the time of his death, September 16, 1909. He leaves a sorrowing wife and many friends.[527]

SANFORD, WILLIAM: William Sanford, born February 15, 1846, in Tipton County, died at his home in Covington, April 7, 1923. His parents were of a well-known family of Tennessee, and of strong and Christian character. He left the schoolroom early in 1862, at the tender age of sixteen, and enlisted in Company I, 7th Tennessee Cavalry, under Forrest, taking part in the battles of West Point, Okolona, Tishomingo Creek, Harrisburg, East Point, Franklin, Nashville, and was in the rearguard of Hood's retreat, when he was captured and sent to prison near Chicago. There he was detained until long after the surrender, when he was paroled, and walked from Alabama to his home near Covington. He first worked in the field and raised a crop, then went back to school, studied law, was admitted to the bar, and was eminently successful as a lawyer. He retired from practice some years ago.[528]

SAUNDERS, FRANCIS MONTGOMERY: Francis M. Saunders enlisted as a musician in Forrest's Regiment at Saundersville, Tenn., early in the war and served through the four years.[529]

SCALES, DAVID CAMPBELL: David Campbell Scales, a comrade of Cheatham Bivouac of Confederate Veterans at Nashville, Tenn., died in that city on the night of October 1 [1927?], at the age of eighty-four years. He had been a dominant figure in affairs of the Methodist Church, of which he had been a member for more than fifty years, serving in an official capacity each Church with which he was connected.

He was born at Triune, Tenn., April 14, 1843, and received his education at the Hardeman Academy there and at the Campbell Academy in Lebanon, until his studies were interrupted by the call to arms. In April, 1861, he enlisted with patriotic fervor in Company B, of the 20th Tennessee Infantry. He was at the battle of Fishing Creek, after which he was detailed for service under the division quartermaster, which he accepted with the understanding that when his regiment went into battle, he was to return to the ranks. When the army moved against Grant at Corinth, he was stationed at Iuka, but by riding all night he was able to reach his regiment for the battle of Shiloh, in which he took an active part and was thrice wounded. While a comrade was bandaging the second wound, a shell burst between them, killing the comrade and knocking him senseless. From this wound he was disabled until November, 1862, when he reenlisted in the 11th Tennessee Cavalry and began a gallant career under Forrest and Wheeler. He was captured at Franklin, Tenn., in 1863, and sent to Fort Delaware for eighteen months. After being exchanged, he was transferred to Col. D. C. Kelley's regiment under Forrest, with which he served to the end, surrendering at Sumterville, Ala.

After the war, Comrade Scales was engaged in business in Arkansas until 1874, when he located in Nashville, and was in active business until his retirement some twenty years ago. He was married in 1880 to Miss Grace Hillman, and five children were born to them. She survives him with a son and a daughter.

Captain Scales was ever loyal to the cause for which he had fought and interested in the welfare of his comrades in arms. Each year he met with the survivors of the old Twentieth Regiment at their annual reunion in Nashville, and for their picnic dinner he furnished the famous "Dalton pies," which were in high favor with the Confederates while at Dalton, Ga. His was the moving spirit of these gatherings, and he will be sadly missed when they come together again, and by his comrades everywhere. He was a Mason for over a half century, a Knight Templar, and a Shriner.[530]

William Henry Scanland.

SCANLAND, WILLIAM HENRY: Maj. William Henry Scanland died August 30, 1916, in Shreveport, La., survived by his wife and seven children, also one brother. He was born at Grand Gulf, Miss., January 7, 1842. His grandfather was a Virginian, his father a Kentuckian, and his mother a Mississippian. He lost both parents at an early age, and in his eleventh year he and his brother began work in the printing office of the *Caddo Gazette*. The *Bossier Banner* was established by him at Bellevue on July 1, 1859, and, with the exception of the four years of war, he never missed an issue. His editorials were classics of the highest order. His paper never compromised with evil, and in his fifty-seven years of newspaper work he exerted an influence for good over three generations. In 1861 young Scanland was among the first to volunteer in defense of his country, first with the "Bossier Boys" and later serving with the Bossier Cavalry from April, 1862, to May, 1865, when he was paroled. His service was under Generals Marmaduke, Hardee, Van Dorn, Hebert, Armstrong, Cosby, and Forrest.

After the war he resumed publication of the *Bossier Banner*, removing it in 1891 from Bellevue to Benton, La., and during the ten years of the South's darkest history [that is, "Reconstruction"] he fought as well and as wisely for his State as he had fought for his country. He was honored by the citizens of his parish, having represented them in both houses of the legislature, as parish treasurer for sixteen years, and as superintendent of public education for twelve years.

In Confederate circles he was honored by being on the staffs of succeeding Commanders of the Louisiana Division, U.C.V. He was also Assistant Quartermaster General on the staffs of Commanders in Chief Gordon and Young and had just received an appointment on the staff of Gen. George P. Harrison, ranking as major.[531]

SCOTT, BURGESS HENRY: A sad loss to his family, his city, and his country occurred in the death of Burgess H. Scott, of Paducah, Ky. He was prominent in business affairs of his generation until his health failed, a few years ago.

Burgess Scott was born at Eddyville, Ky., September 28, 1843. He was the son of William Henry Scott and Mary Greenfield Scott, the latter of Madisonville, Ky. At the beginning of the Civil War he joined the Confederate army, and served to the end. He was slightly wounded in the leg. He enlisted in the service from Hopkinsville, Ky., in Forrest's old regiment in the early part of the war, and was with that regiment in all of its rounds until he was transferred in the fall of 1862 to the 2nd Kentucky Cavalry. He remained with this regiment until the close of the war.

His brother-in-law, W. R. Bringhurst, of Clarksville, Tenn., writes of him: "We served under Forrest from the fall of 1862 until after the battle of Chickamauga, when the 2nd Kentucky Regiment was transferred to Wheeler, and we were with that commander until the close of the war. Immediately after the surrender of Lee, Dibrell's Division was ordered to Greensboro, N.C., as a special escort to President Davis—who was still with the Confederate Cabinet and Treasury—and acted in this capacity from Greensboro to Washington, Ga. There Mr. Davis left the main body of the escort with only a few men . . . . Johnston had surrendered. The war was then over, and after paying the men $26 each in coin, President Davis left the main command with only a small escort, and was captured a few days afterwards. The command proceeded homeward in a body, but upon reaching Chattanooga their horses and side arms were taken from them (in violation of their paroles). However, after vigorous protests from the officers in the command, their property was restored to them."

Mr. Bringhurst adds: "I would like to be equal to the task of writing a history of both the personal and soldier life of Burgess Scott that he deserves. I was intimately associated with him during the war and up to the time of his death, and always found him to be a man fearless in the discharge of duty, of strict integrity, and just to all men." [The intimacy of these two men was fraternal—each married the other's sister.]

At the close of the war Mr. Scott went to Alabama, and after engaging in the cotton business for several years went to Clarksville, Tenn. There he met and was later married to Miss Julia Bringhurst in 1873. From Clarksville they removed to Dyersburg, Tenn. About twenty years ago, however, they moved to Paducah, where they afterwards lived.

He and E. W. Smith founded the Smith & Scott Tobacco Company at Paducah, and he was president of the company until his health gave way. He was founder of the Mechanics' and Farmers' Bank of Paducah, and was President of the Hardy Buggy Company. He was one of the

Burgess Henry Scott.

prime movers in building the present Broadway Methodist edifice, and was chairman of the board of stewards for about fifteen years, resigning only when his health failed. He held official Conference relations, even as a delegate to the General Conference.

He was a member of the Plain City Lodge of Masons and of the James T. Walbert Camp, U.C.V. He was a gentleman of the old school, chivalrous, with an old-time courtesy, ever sympathetic and generous. Surviving him are his wife (Mrs. Julia Scott), two daughters (Julia Scott and Mary Scott), and three sons (Robert and Edward, of Paducah, and William H. Scott, editor and publisher of the *Third District Review*). Mr. Scott is also survived by a sister (Mrs. W. R. Bringhurst, of Clarksville), and a brother (Mr. Walter Scott, of Montgomery, Ala.). The funeral services were conducted in the Broadway Methodist Church by the pastor, Rev. G. T. Sullivan. The honorary pallbearers were of the Walbert Camp, U.C.V.[532]

SCOTT, FRANK T.: "As loyal as a Confederate soldier" might well pass into a proverb, and among the most loyal was our friend Capt. Frank T. Scott, of Camden, Ark. He was born in Gainesville, Ala., January 4, 1835, a son of Hon. C. C. Scott, who afterwards moved to Arkansas and became judge of the supreme court.

Captain Scott joined the Confederate army among the earliest volunteers and was a member of Company B, Camden Knights, 1st Arkansas Regiment. This company left Camden on June 21, 1861, and shortly afterwards became a part of the 11th Arkansas Regiment. They fought gallantly at Memphis, Fort Pillow, New Madrid, and Island No. 10, where on April 8, 1862, the regiment was captured, and Captain Scott, with other officers, was sent to Johnson's Island as a prisoner of war.

After being exchanged, the regiment was reorganized at Jackson, Miss., and Captain Scott was placed in command of Company G. Under his leadership the company did valiant service in battles at Clinton and Jackson, Miss., and at Port Hudson. At the time of the surrender they were under the command of General Forrest.

In 1863 Captain Scott spent a furlough with relatives in Gainesville, Ala., his birthplace, and there renewed his early acquaintance with Miss Leila McMahon, who became his wife in 1868. They spent their married life almost entirely in the old Scott home, near Camden. Theirs was a beautiful home life. A charming atmosphere of parental care and filial devotion between the parents, two sons, and three daughters always prevailed.

Frank T. Scott.

Captain Scott was a devoted member of the Presbyterian Church and left with his family many precious testimonials of the strength and comfort to be found in the service of God. He fell asleep quietly on March 19, 1918, and was buried with Masonic honors by Whitfield Chapter, F. and A. Masons.

The last time he signed his name it was to the Confederate record of one of his comrades, and among the last lines he wrote we find these words: "Most of the Camden knights are gone. Those living are past threescore years and ten; but we hope to meet again under Gens. Leonidas Polk, Stonewall Jackson, and Robert E. Lee in the spirit land."[533]

SEA, ANDREW M.: Amongst the survivors of the Confederate soldiers death of late is stalking with reckless footsteps. With increasing years the death rate makes rapid advances.

On the 5th of December, 1917, in the line of duty, while proceeding in the street cars to Pewee Valley to assume temporary charge of the Kentucky Confederate Home to oblige its Board of Trustees, Capt. Andrew M. Sea was suddenly stricken and died before the help of a physician could be obtained. He fell while responding to the call of duty and on the firing line. This is doubtless the way this valiant soldier would have preferred to go.

Captain Sea was born in Anderson County, Ky., and through his veins flowed the blood of distinguished families, the Seas and the McBrayers, Whites and Blackwells. Carefully reared, of distinguished ancestry, just graduating from a great college, life was opening before him with many attractions and charms. His grandfather, Leonard Sea, had been with General Wayne and was one of his most trusted lieutenants; other ancestors fought in the Revolution. Soldier visions and dreams were a part of his make-up; and when the gauge of battle was thrown down by the North to the South, Captain Sea with the inborn courage of a hero said: "I will give my life, if need be, to the cause of Southern independence." He sought artillery service. He rode with Forrest and Wheeler, and the artillery of these generals was always in the front.

During the four years in the Army of Tennessee he fought in many battles and always with splendid courage. He met every demand of even the exacting Forrest; and those who fought with Forrest know that he not only got what he requested, but the best that was in the men. He participated in the battles of Shiloh, Chickamauga, Resaca, Peach Tree Creek, Columbia, and in the campaign from Dalton to Atlanta in front of Sherman. For a time he was assistant ordnance officer of Wheeler's Corps. He destroyed the Broad River bridge at Columbia, S.C., after Wheeler had withdrawn his troops and thus forced Sherman to go eight miles up the river to the ford. For the last nineteen months of the war he commanded Wiggins's Battery, and when this was finally surrendered it was probably the last battery under arms east of the Mississippi River.

Andrew M. Sea.

In his sphere no man did more than Captain Sea for the Southland. He always fought without fear and never hesitated in the face of any danger. When the trying end came, he, with his battery, was designated to accompany Jefferson Davis and members of his cabinet in their attempt to escape from the pursuit of those who had crushed Lee and Johnston, and he left Mr. Davis only when he was bidden.

At the end of hostilities he returned to Kentucky and began a long, active, and honorable business career. He was prominent as an officer in the Presbyterian Church. He was a public officer honored and trusted by all who knew him. His loyalty to the cause of the history and principles of the South was without break. He gloried in what the men and women of the South did to win liberty, and he never regretted the four years of danger and sacrifice that he gave to the Confederacy.

Captain Sea was prominent in the work and mission of the United Confederate Veteran Association. For more than twenty years he served the Association in various offices, more than a third of which was as Commander of the George B. Eastin Camp, U.C.V., of Louisville, one of the great Camps of the Association.

For thirteen years he was a member of the Board of Trustees of the Kentucky Confederate Home. He was during all this period Secretary of the institution, and his cotrustees are of one voice in declaring that no one ever did better service to any such institution. His tenderness toward the inmates and his unceasing solicitude for their welfare will long remain a beautiful and cherished memory.

Shortly after the war Captain Sea married one of the most beautiful, accomplished, and talented of Kentucky's daughters, Miss Sophie Irvine Fox, of Danville, Ky., and they lived as models of conjugal devotion until the great enemy tore him away from his home and his friends.

No Confederate in Kentucky more thoroughly commanded the respect and regard of his comrades, and they all unite in expression of sorrow that Captain Sea has been called to the home prepared for those who through faith have won the crown of eternal life and joy.[534]

SEARCY, JOHN NEILL: John Neill Searcy answered the last roll call on October 27, 1926, at his residence in Longwood, Fla., aged eighty-four years. After services of the Episcopal Church, the Masonic burial service was conducted by the Longwood Masonic Lodge, of which he was a Past Master.

John N. Searcy was born March 15, 1842, near the village of Fairfield, Bedford County, Tenn. His grandfather, Robert Searcy, was clerk of the Federal Court in Nashville, and the second Grand Master of Masons in Tennessee. His father, Dr. James Searcy, was born in Nashville, December 8, 1812, and moved to Panola, Panola County, Miss., in 1855, where the family resided until the War between the States began. John Neill Searcy and his oldest brother, in May, 1861, joined the Pettus Artillery, Mississippi Volunteers, commanded by Capt. Alfred B.

John Neill Searcy.

Hudson, who was killed at the battle of Shiloh. The name of the company was then changed to the Hudson Battery, which name was retained until the end of the war. After the siege of Vicksburg, the battery was placed in Gen. N. B. Forrest's Corps. John Neill Searcy was paroled as sergeant of the Hudson Battery at Gainesville, Ala., on May 12, 1865.[535]

SEXTON, H. M.: H. M. Sexton joined Company G, 12th Kentucky Cavalry, at Springfield, Tenn., in 1863, under a Captain Melton, and in Forrest's command. He was paroled May 15, 1865.[536]

SHEARER, JOHN: John Shearer, who died at his home in McCrory, Ark., on November 23, 1923, was born in Edinburgh, Scotland, and was brought to America when he was about four years old and placed in an orphan's home at Montreal, Canada. His only relative then was an old grandmother, who lived to be one hundred and five years of age. Calamity seemed to follow the family. His grandfather was killed in the battle of Waterloo, his father was drowned at sea, and his mother died from injuries received during a hotel fire.

He was living in Arkansas when the war came on in the sixties and went to Augusta to join Captain Mattocks's company of cavalry, but he had no horse, and no money with which to buy one; so he walked thirty-five miles to Jacksonport, where an artillery company was being organized. James C. Thrall was captain; Robert Anderson, first lieutenant; J. C. Barlow, second lieutenant; J. C. Myers, orderly sergeant; John Shearer was second sergeant. This company was moved to Memphis, and was initiated in war during the two days' battle of Shiloh. Thrall's Battery did some of the deadliest work in that battle, being on the front line for two days.

After our move to Tupelo, Thrall's artillery was sent to Mobile, but later it was attached to Forrest's Cavalry and was with it to the last—after the battle of Franklin and covering the retreat from Nashville—surrendering at Meridian, Miss. This company was from my old town of Jacksonport. John Shearer was a brave soldier.

After the war he came back to Woodruff County, Ark., worked hard, and had a fine estate in McCrory. His first wife was Miss H. E. Brown, whom he married in 1871; his second marriage was in April, 1903, and his wife survives him.

Comrade Shearer had a room in his home devoted to his war relics and pictures—Lee, Jackson, Joseph E. Johnston, Forrest—and this he called his "Confederate Den." Governor Brough, of Arkansas, visited this room and wanted to move its contents to the State Historian's room at the Capitol, but Shearer said it could not be done while he lived. He was a devoted attendant on reunions, a subscriber to *Confederate Veteran* for twenty years, and read it as we all do—every word in it. Unwavering was his devotion to the cause for which he fought, and over his casket was draped the Confederate flag he loved so well. He was a Scottish Rite Mason, and his funeral was conducted by the Scottish Rite and Blue Lodge Masons.[537]

SHELDON, CHARLES A.: Capt. Charles A. Sheldon was born in Gaston, Ala., June 11, 1846, and died March 3, 1920, at his home, in Abbeville, Ga. He left the University of Alabama and enlisted among the first volunteers C.S.A. and had the distinction of serving under two of the war's greatest generals, Stonewall Jackson and N. B. Forrest. He was wounded in the battle of Seven Pines. Returning to Alabama in July, 1862, he raised a cavalry company and joined the Western Army under General Forrest, with whom he served for the remainder of the war and surrendered with him on May 14, 1865, as captain of Company D, 8th Alabama Regiment.

In 1869 Captain Sheldon removed to Florida, and in 1870 he married Miss Elizabeth Coffee, daughter of Capt. Hill Bryan Coffee, of the War between the States, and granddaughter of Gen. John Coffee, of the War of 1812.

Captain Sheldon was an elder in the Presbyterian Church for forty-six years, and his Church duties were his first consideration. He was an ardent Confederate veteran, attending all U.C.V. reunions, and at his request he was buried in his gray uniform at Brunswick, Ga. The Veterans of Camp Jackson, of which he was a member, served as military escort, and the pallbearers were the officers of his Church. Many floral offerings bore testimony of the esteem in which he was held. The laurel wreath and Confederate flag by the Daughters of the Confederacy remained on his gray casket.

He is survived by his wife, three daughters, and a son, an older son having died some years ago. There are also five grandchildren and one great-grandson.[538]

SHEPHERD, JAMES MARTIN: James Martin Shepherd was among the youngest of that splendid manhood of the South which offered all on the altar of patriotism, enlisting at the age of fifteen under General Forrest and serving as a member of Company A, 10th Alabama Regiment, which he joined at Huntsville, Ala. He was also with other divisions of Forrest's command, serving in Mississippi, Tennessee, Georgia, and finally in Forrest's last battle at Selma, Ala. He escaped capture there, but had some thrilling experiences before reaching home.

He was paroled at Columbus, Miss., and suffered the humiliation of being guarded by negro troops [the most gullible and uneducated of whom had been indoctrinated by Liberal Yanks to hate and harass Conservative Southern whites—a divisive Left-wing ploy that continues to this day]. Returning to the place of his birth at Newtonville, Ala., Fayette County, he tried bravely to adjust himself to altered conditions, and he was a great factor in helping to restore order to that lawless community during the Reconstruction period.

At the age of twenty-one, he married Miss Mary Elizabeth Henry, daughter of Joseph E. Henry, who was also a hero of the sixties. He led an active life, living on the same farm for nearly fifty years, and reared a large family, every member of which is filling his sphere in life in an honorable, worth-while manner. He was known far and wide as an upright Christian and an honorable citizen. He never lost interest in the cause for which he had fought so valiantly, and looked forward to the Confederate reunions with fond anticipation. After an active and useful life, death came to him suddenly while at the home of his son in Tuscaloosa, Ala., and his body was taken back to the old home for burial on Easter Sunday in March, 1921. Friends from far and near came to pay their last tribute, and his old comrades of the gray were the honorary pallbearers. His wife survives him, with their sons and daughters.[539]

SHERRILL, RICHARD E.: Richard E. Sherrill, born near Covington, Tenn., June 12, 1846, died at his home at Stanton, Tenn., in his eighty-fourth year, on February 20, 1930. In 1862, he enlisted in Company C, 12th Tennessee Cavalry, under General Forrest. He was in several important battles, and a prisoner in the Irving Block, Memphis, for a few months.

In February, 1870, he was married to Miss Ann Virginia Smith, at Hickman, Ky., and three daughters were born to them. He is survived by his wife, his loved companion of sixty years, and one daughter, Mrs. T. S. Jackson, of Stanton. He was a devoted husband and father.

In early life, Comrade Sherrill joined Mount Carmel Presbyterian Church, and was a consistent member; he was a deacon there for a number of years. In January, 1915, he moved to Stanton, Tenn., and was elected an elder in Stanton Presbyterian Church; was honored and loved by all who knew him. Death came in the advancing weakness of old age, and he calmly waited for that clear call to a higher service in the "land beyond." He was laid to rest by loving hands in Mount Carmel Cemetery, February 21, 1930.[540]

Robert S. Shreve.

SHREVE, ROBERT S.: One of the youngest ex-Confederates of Kentucky, is Robert S. Shreve, of Louisville. He was born August 27, 1848, and enlisted with Forrest's Cavalry at Port Gibson, Miss., where he was then living, August 17, 1862, just ten days before he was fourteen years of age. Mr. Shreve served throughout the war, and was paroled on May 12, 1865, at Gainesville, Ala. During the Confederate reunion at Louisville he had charge of the Mississippi headquarters, where he "lived over again the old times of the sixties" with old friends, many of whom he had not seen for over thirty years. In token of Mississippi's esteem for Mr. Shreve, the delegates from that State presented him with a gold-headed cane and a gold medal. Gen. Gordon, the Commander in Chief, appointed him a colonel on his staff. [The accompanying] picture was taken during the reunion, and the medal presented to Col. Shreve appears on his coat.

An official tribute was paid to Comrade Shreve by the Mississippi Division at Louisville, in which it was resolved that the "sincere and heartfelt thanks of that division of the United Confederate Veterans from the State of Mississippi be tendered our comrade, Robert S. Shreve, Chairman of the Mississippi Headquarters, and his First Lieutenant and Clerk, Mr. John Ropke, for their uniform courtesy and kindness extended us in providing for our care and comfort at this reunion." R. A. Owen, C. R. Nesmith, and Samuel Bridges comprised the committee.[541]

SIGMAN, T. F.: After several months of confinement in the hospital at Beauvior Confederate Home, T. F. Sigman, who served in the 13th Tennessee Infantry under that splendid cavalry officer Nathan Bedford Forrest, passed over to meet his comrades and relatives who had gone before him across the "Golden Strand."[542]

SIMMONS, JOHN S.: Capt. John S. Simmons died at his home, in Maitland, Fla., on November 6, 1913, after a long illness. He was born in North Carolina in 1836, and when he was but a small child the family removed to Mississippi, in which State he was reared and educated. He graduated from the University of Mississippi with honor in 1854 and was engaged in teaching for some years before the war came on. At the outbreak of hostilities he dismissed his school and enlisted in the 1[st.] Mississippi Cavalry. His company was ordered to Kentucky and was in some of the battles there under Generals Van Dorn and Forrest.

Comrade Simmons was elected captain of his company in a short time and took part in some of the hard fought battles of Tennessee and Georgia. He was a brave and fearless soldier and held the esteem of all his men. He was captured at Selma, Ala., by General Wilson's command and sent to Macon, Ga., about the time of the surrender and from there was sent home to Carroll County. He resumed his vocation of teaching and helped to educate many of the sons of Mississippi who have been actively connected with the State's interests. In 1876 he removed to Florida and settled at Maitland, in Orange County, and soon went into orange culture. He was also treasurer of the county for fifteen years.

Major Simmons had married Miss Margaret Elliott, of Jackson, Miss., before the war, and while he was away fighting for his country she stayed at La Grange, Tenn., with her father's family and was a faithful nurse in the hospital there. When the Federals invaded the town she returned to Mississippi. She survives her husband with their four children—two sons and two daughters.[543]

SIMS, W. E.: W. E. Sims died suddenly at his home in Shelbyville, Tenn., February 19, 1902. His father, Richard Sims, was one of the most prominent men in that section, and, although reared in wealth, Ed Sims was unpretentious and thoroughly genial. He was kind and universally popular in his section.

He rode with Forrest in the great war, and afterwards wooed and won for his companion Miss Lucy Burt, widely

W. E. Sims.

known and popular among Confederates. Of their three children, the younger son enlisted in the Spanish-American War [1898] at a very early age.

A. D. Adair, of Atlanta, expressed the opinion entertained by his friends generally in which he stated: "Your husband was a good soldier, a loyal friend, an honest man. He was my friend and comrade in the old escort of General Forrest." He held an appointment in the United States Internal Revenue Service under an appointment by President [Grover] Cleveland, having been favored in this matter by his personal friend, Senator Isham G. Harris.[544]

SMITH, BAXTER: In the death of Col. Baxter Smith at Chattanooga, Tenn., on June 25, 1919, there passed one of the most prominent of the surviving officers of the Confederate army. He served as captain, major, and colonel of the 4th Tennessee Cavalry under Forrest and was commanding a brigade of cavalry at the close of the war, and for some years he had been commander of the survivors of Forrest's Cavalry Association, having succeeded the late H. H. Tyler, of Kentucky. Since 1910 he had been Assistant Secretary of the Chattanooga and Chickamauga Park Commission and to the last took an active part in the affairs pertaining to the reservation.

Baxter Smith.

Colonel Smith was born in Davidson County, Tenn., March 10, 1832, and was thus in his eighty-eighth year. He was the son of Dr. Edmond Byars Smith, a native of Kentucky, and Miss Sallie Baxter, of Georgia. He was educated in law at the Cumberland University, of Lebanon, Tenn., and had begun the practice of that profession at Gallatin when the war came on. He promptly enlisted, and with the 4th Tennessee Cavalry he followed Forrest from Shiloh to Chickamauga, was with Joseph E. Johnston in his operations from Dalton to Atlanta, and surrendered with Johnston at Charlotte, N.C. His record as a soldier is written in blood and glory.

After the war Colonel Smith removed to Nashville and resumed his law practice, in which he became very prominent. His only public service was in the State Senate of 1881, and he attained considerable note as a member of that body. He was a member of the Presbyterian Church and of the Royal Arcanum.

Colonel Smith came of distinguished ancestry, and he inherited the indomitable spirit of his race and the charm of his Southern parentage. His wife was Miss Bettie Guild, of Nashville.

He is survived by a son and three daughters. He was laid to rest in the cemetery at Nashville, in which city his most active and successful years had been spent.[545]

SMITH, J. D.: This heroic soldier in war and model citizen in peace passed away at his home, in Houston, Miss., on June 28, 1905. He deserves a place in the gallery of dead [Confederate] heroes . . ., that modest temple of fame where privates as well as generals are admitted. Captain Smith organized Company C, Twenty-Fourth Mississippi Infantry, at the outset of the war, and afterwards commanded it with signal gallantry till, from wounds and ill health just after the battle of Chickamauga, he was transferred to the cavalry, in command of Company E, Sixth Mississippi Regiment, Stark's Brigade. To the end of the war thereafter he fought under the lead of Forrest, and was one of his favorite and bravest officers.

At Chickamauga, on the second day, the last of the field officers of the Twenty-Fourth Mississippi fell, and the command of the regiment devolved on Captain Smith. He led it in all its desperate charges that followed, and the terrible onsets against it, till he fell wounded. On the third and last day, though suffering from wounds, he resumed command of the shattered remnant of the Twenty-Fourth and fought it to the glorious finish which ended in the utter rout of Rosecrans's command. A large number of the company officers of the regiment had also fallen, and hardly forty per cent of that gallant regiment was left to answer roll call. At one time for an hour three Federal batteries, combined with small arms, poured in a concentrated fire on this regiment where it seemed that nothing could live. This regiment was in Walthall's famous Mississippi Brigade, which lost fully fifty per cent of its men in that battle. General Walthall speaks in the highest terms of Captain Smith in his official report of that bloody battle; and praise from Walthall was praise indeed!

The official report of the part the Twenty-Fourth Mississippi took in that battle, made by Captain Smith, discloses the most frightful losses. The writer of this brief memorial, O. C. Brothers, and Captain Smith were as brothers during the war—not only brothers in arms but as brothers by blood. We ate, slept, marched together, constant companions and chums, till Captain Smith was transferred to the cavalry; and amid the fierce onset and the roar of battle the writer's thoughts followed with intense anxiety his chivalrous friend and messmate, because he always led where the fight was hottest and most desperate. Around the camp fire he was a noble companion—bright, joyous, genial, gentle as a woman, and as loving as a child, he was indeed a most lovable man; but in battle he knew not fear, and seemed to court death itself by his heroic dash and superb bravery.

After the war Captain Smith was called by the people of Chickasaw County to many important offices of trust, such as chancery clerk, assessor, treasurer. In all he served with honor and credit, and *all the people, both white and black, mourned his loss.* He was seventy-two years old. May he sleep in peace![546]

SMITH, JOHN PRYOR: John Pryor Smith, born near Bolivar, Tenn., July 10, 1845, volunteered as a boy of sixteen, and served throughout the war under Forrest as a gallant soldier of the Confederacy. After the war he went to Mississippi, locating near Holly Spring, and in 1874 he was married to Miss

Emma Crum, at Hickory Flat. In 1886 he removed to Memphis, Tenn., which had since been his home. He is survived by his wife, three daughters, and six sons, fifteen grandchildren, and one great-grandchild. He was a devout Christian, a member of the Methodist Church, which he had joined in early manhood. He was a devoted husband and father and a citizen of the highest type.[547]

SMITH, JOSEPH P.: Joseph P. Smith . . . enlisted with Forrest from Monticello, Mo., Lewis County, and served until captured some time before the battle of Missionary Ridge; was a prisoner at Alton, Ill., for the rest of the war, and was paroled at Richmond, Va. [He may have been] with the 15th Tennessee Regiment.[548]

SMITHSON, GEORGE W.: Capt. George W. Smithson (senior member of the firm of Smithson & Kennedy), widely known and generally beloved, died at his home, Franklin, Tenn., on Monday, October 1, 1900, in his sixty-third year. The announcement of his death was a shock to the community.

George W. Smithson.

Capt. Smithson's life was an epistle worthy to be read of all men. In it were the attributes that make up that noblest work of God—an honest man. In his young manhood he laid his all upon the altar of his country, and for four years of fire and blood he did his full part to crown with undying honor the brightest character on the page of history—the Confederate soldier. He was a member of Company B, Second Tennessee Regiment, Bell's Brigade of Forrest's Cavalry. Surviving comrades at his grave bore testimony to his gallantry in those brave old days. The McEwen Bivouac and Starnes Camp attended the funeral and officiated in a last tribute of affection and honor to their departed comrade. He was wounded on Gen. Hood's retreat. Sad loss was sustained to the business and social circles of Franklin in his death, and the deep sorrow of the community was everywhere manifested. As a special mark of respect, the dry goods stores of the city were closed during his funeral.

Capt. Smithson was married in 1871 to Miss Sallie Henderson, whom he survived scarcely one year. He left four children: Mrs. W. J. Bruce, George H. Smithson, Mrs. N. C. Perkins, and Miss Sallie Smithson.[549]

SMOOT, JOHN NEFFE: John Neffe Smoot, M.D., son of John N. and Elizabeth H. Smoot, was born July, 1840, in Huntingdon, Tenn., and was educated there. He enlisted in the Confederate army at Camp Beauregard, Ky., October, 1861, in Company C, Twenty-Second Tennessee Regiment. In the battle of Belmont, Mo., November 6, 1 861, he did faithful service; and in the fight at Shiloh, or Pittsburg Landing, Tenn., April 6, 1862, he was severely wounded and carried from the field by an older brother. He was conveyed to his home in Huntingdon, where he was cared for by his widowed mother for several months. During this time the Federal soldiers frequently entered the town, and on one occasion came very near capturing young Smoot. Fortunately, he saw them at the gate, and, though unable to walk, he jumped out of a window, falling about eight feet into high grass and weeds. He escaped by crawling on hands and knees (dragging his wounded leg) at least three-fourths of a mile, part of the time in a ditch containing much mud and water.

As soon as practicable, he reported to Col. T. A. Napier, who commanded a regiment of cavalry under Gen. Forrest and operated in Humphreys County, on the Tennessee River. This command did much to annoy and harass the Federal transports as they ascended the river. While connected with this work young Smoot was commissioned lieutenant, and assigned command in the Second Tennessee Cavalry under Gen. Lyon. In a fight at Hopkinsville, Ky., his horse was killed under him, and he was captured, carried to Bowling Green, Ky., and put in jail. From there he was taken to Louisville, Ky., put in prison, and adjudged a guerrilla, or bushwhacker, notwithstanding he showed his commission, which proved he was a regular officer in the Confederate army. While Lieut. Smoot was at Bowling Green the weather was intensely cold, and the prisoners suffered for lack of clothing and bedding. Fortunately for him, his oldest brother, Rev. R. K. Smoot, of the Southern Presbyterian Church, resided there, and was permitted to supply him with these necessities. When he was sent to Louisville Dr. Smoot was allowed to follow him, and was ordered to "report at the Federal prison." When he arrived there he found personal friends to aid him in averting the terrible fate which threatened his brother.

John Neffe Smoot.

Vice President Elect Andrew Johnson had been a warm personal friend of the Smoot family before the breaking out of the war on account of certain favors shown him by them during his contest for the governorship of Tennessee. Having expressed himself as anxious to reciprocate this friendship a hasty interview with him was sought, which resulted in the final release of Lieut. Smoot on a parole. He left Louisville, and spent some time with a friend in Indiana. The severity of the campaign through which he had passed, and exposure and suffering during his imprisonment, aggravated the old wound received at Shiloh, and by the time he was able to return to duty the war had closed.

He took up new duties after the war with a brave heart. He opened a drug store in Huntingdon, and while engaged there he read medicine and subsequently graduated at the Jefferson Medical College, in Philadelphia. He practiced his profession in Huntingdon for several years, and then moved to Fulton, Ky., where he was married to Miss Alice M., daughter of Rev. Dr. Patterson, of that place. A few years later his health failed, and he went to Austin, Tex., in the hope of recovering; but he died soon after reaching Austin. He was a brave and faithful Confederate soldier, a consistent and honorable Christian gentleman.[550]

SNEED, JOHN H.: John H. Sneed died on November 3, 1920, a veteran known for his splendid war record, and no man ever left a better record of citizenship. He entered the service of the Confederacy in October, 1862, at the age of nineteen, and served the rest of the war, always able to report for duty. He entered as a private and remained a private, being too humble and modest to accept an office had it been ever so earnestly urged upon him. He served with Company C, Capt. M. W. McKnight, Clark R. Barteau's Regiment. He was with Forrest at Fort Pillow and remained with Forrest to the end. He was a devout Christian, a stanch [meaning staunch] believer in the Baptist faith. He loved the Confederacy and talked it to his last day. He was the last member of a large family and was never married.[551]

SNELL, JOHN A.: John A. Snell, of Columbus, Miss., died at his home, in Columbus, on October 12, 1015. He was born in Lowndes County in 1846 and spent his boyhood days on the farm. His parents were of the old-fashioned type and reared their children to fear and love God and to be kind to their brother man. In the early part of 1863, while a boy of only sixteen years, he left school and responded to the call of his country, enlisting in Company I, 6th Mississippi Cavalry Regiment, Forrest's command. From that date he was in active service until July 14, 1864, when he was wounded in the battle of Harrisburg, near Tupelo, Miss., losing a leg, which was shot away by a shell while his command was charging the enemy's breastworks. When quite a young man he was united in marriage to Miss Mattie Bryant, of Lowndes County. They moved to Columbus, and for many years he was engaged in the mercantile business there. His life was an honorable and useful one. He was a consistent member of the Presbyterian Church and was loved and respected by all who knew him. Several times he was chosen by his fellow citizens to positions of honor and trust, and at the time of his death he was a member of the city council. He died, as he had lived, a Christian gentleman, at peace with God and man. I offer this tribute to the memory of the friend of my youth, my comrade in arms, and my associate day by day for the past forty years.[552]

SOMERVILLE, WILLIAM B.: William B. Somerville, one of the leading citizens of the Aliceville community in Pickens County, Ala., and an esteemed Confederate veteran, passed away at his home near that city on July 9, 1927, being in his eightieth year. He had lived all his life in this community, was well known throughout Pickens County, and had served the people of the county as tax collector for one term.

At the early age of sixteen years he enlisted in the ranks of the Confederate army and served from his enlistment throughout the remainder of the war in the company of Captain Baskins, under the command of General Forrest. After the cessation of hostilities, he returned to his father's home to assist in the rehabilitation of the Southland. He was married in 1875 to Miss Mollie Archibald, and to them were born several children, who, with their mother, still survive. Soon after marriage he removed to Franconia, Ala., where the family still resides.

Mr. Somerville, when but a lad, identified himself with the Presbyterian Church and was an honored officer of his Church and clerk of its Session for years, and it was in the Church which he loved so well that his friends gathered in large concourse to pay their last respects to his memory. His body now rests in Oak Grove Cemetery.[553]

STAFFORD, JOHN: Marion Cogbill Camp, No. 1216, U.C.V., of Wynne, Ark., mourns the loss of a loved comrade in the death of John Stafford. He was born in Fayette County, Tenn., November 25, 1846, and died in Cherry Valley, Ark., May 3, 1924. He served with General Forrest. The writer was with him at the Chattanooga reunion in 1913 and visited the battlefield of Chickamauga, and this comrade pointed out the places where he had fought.

Comrade Stafford leaves a wife, three sons, and a daughter. He was a noble man, loved by all who knew him. Though in feeble health for several years, he was always cheerful and ever met his friends with a smile. There was large attendance at his burial on a beautiful Sabbath evening, and the grave was covered with flowers.[554]

STANDFIELD, N. B.: N. B. Stanfield was born December 4, 1847, and enlisted in the Confederate service in 1861 at Brandenburg, Ky., when hardly fifteen years old. He was a member of Forrest's 1st Kentucky Cavalry; but later was with Morgan's command, and was captured during the famous Ohio raid. Some will yet remember the little boy with his "flag of truce" who "hailed and captured" the Yankee gunboats on the Ohio River, ever after bearing the name of "White Pigeon." He escaped from prison twice, but was recaptured; and when he finally emerged from prison walls, within which he had suffered injuries, cold, and starvation, he was but a shadow of himself. Whether within prison walls or on the forced march, hungry and footsore, he was always

N. B. Stanfield.

cheerful; and in the memorable fights in which he participated he was among the bravest. When the end came, the same courage which animated him to deeds of valor on the field of battle nerved and sustained him during the dark days of reconstruction and on to the end.

Subsequent to the war Mr. Stanfield resided in Henderson, Ky.; but removed to Hopkinsville, and in 1878 was married there to Miss Gabe Hamill. He came to Nashville in 1808, and died in this city on the 11th of October, 1905, leaving a widow and four children. He was a consistent Christian, a member of the Presbyterian Church, and ever strove to do his duty. His great simplicity and sincerity of character had endeared him to a host of friends, who honor his memory.[555]

STARKE, PETER BURWELL: Peter B. Starke was born in 1815 in Brunswick County, Va., where and his family ran a stage coach line. He entered Mississippi politics in the 1840s, occupying several positions from legislator to senator. During Lincoln's War, Comrade Starke, a brother of celebrated Confederate General William Edwin Starke, was named colonel of the 28th Mississippi Cavalry, fighting at Vicksburg. Serving under Joseph E. Johnston and Frank C. Armstrong, after being promoted to brigadier general he was attached to General Forrest and finally General Chalmers. After the War he returned to Mississippi, then back to Va., where he died on July 13, 1888, and was buried in an unmarked grave.[556]

STEELE, WILLIAM A.: Camden and Benton County lost one of its most influential citizens in the death of William A. Steele, on December 21, 1927, at the age of eighty-four years.

"Uncle Bill," as he was known by the young and old alike, was a favorite with the entire population of Benton County. He was born and reared in Camden, and had always lived in Camden with the exception of the four years that he spent in the Confederate army under the leadership of Gen. Nathan Bedford Forrest, as a member of Company L, 20th Tennessee Regiment.

He was captured and placed in prison at Rock Island, Ill., during the latter part of the war. Following the war he was county court clerk of Benton County, and for several years served as county surveyor, and he was one of the pioneer school-teachers. He was postmaster of Camden during the Grover Cleveland administration. He was a member of the Cumberland Presbyterian Church and served as an elder for about forty years.

Comrade Steele was married to Miss Mary Viola Willis in 1868, and is survived by two daughters and three sons, also a brother.[557]

STEGER, JOHN C. W.: The death of Dr. John C. W. Steger, of Madison County, Ala., on November 19, 1922, brought sorrow to many friends to whom he was endeared by a life of active kindliness. He was a member of Camp Egbert Jones, U.C.V., of Huntsville, Ala., but his home was at Gurley for many years.

John C. W. Steger was born in Madison County, Ala., February 28, 1834, and graduated in medicine at the Nashville Medical College, 1857. During the War between the States, Dr. Steger served as a surgeon in the 4th Alabama Cavalry, Russell's Regiment, Forrest's command. He was captured at Fort Donelson, and released in March, 1863, at Petersburg, Va.; paroled May 9, 1865. With the exception of his term of imprisonment, his service as a soldier was continuous, having only eight days' leave of absence, on account of sickness. Of his service, he wrote: "I did what I could to sustain the cause, and regret I could not do more."

A friend and comrade, J. E. Hewlett, pays this tribute: " I am proud that I can claim the honor of having been with him in the service of the Confederacy from 1862 to 1865, and can say of him that I never knew a braver, truer soldier. He was always where duty called attending the sick and looking after the wounded in time of battle. He and I surrendered and were paroled at Gainesville, Ala., one month after Lee had surrendered in Virginia. . . . We started out on horseback for Hunstville, Ala., our home, and on the way spent one night at Governor Chatman's home at Tuscaloosa. The next day we rode sixty miles and spent the night in a farmhouse where the Avondale Library now is in Avondale Park, Birmingham. Then all around where the springs now are was a willow swamp.

"For several years after the war Dr. Steger was connected with an iron company at Dover, Tenn., on the Cumberland River, as physician, and later on had charge of and settled up the business of the company. . . . After spending many years in Tennessee, he decided to retire from active business and come back to his native heath and take life easy. . . . He built a summer home on Sharp's Mountain, about twenty miles east of Huntsville, and often spent the winter there as well, sometimes with friends around and with him. . . .

"His Camp will miss him, his hosts of friends will miss him, the birds of the mountain that often sang him to sleep will miss him. He has answered the last roll call, has crossed over the river, and I hope some sweet day we will meet him again 'over there.'"[558]

STEWART, JAMES TURNER: In the death of Maj. James Turner Stewart, of Savannah, Ga., another of the "Old Guard" has passed into the new life, leaving only to those who knew him the memory of a faithful, valued friend. Maj. Stewart was born at Greenock, Scotland, June 7, 1834. His family was a prominent one. He was the youngest of five children. Maj. Stewart was educated at the University of Glasgow, and was one of the most popular of its many students. He received his degree in 1850. After his graduation followed a long sea voyage, going around the world. In 1853 he settled in New Orleans, engaging in the cotton business with his brother John. He went to Savannah in 1857. He married before the war a daughter of his friend and partner, Frank Reid.

When the tocsin of war was sounded in 1861, and though still a British subject, he answered promptly the call of the people with whom he had cast his lot, volunteering as a private in the Savannah Artillery. He was made a sergeant and saw duty with that command at Fort Pulaski. A few months later he was detailed as drill master, performing such duty on the forts around Savannah and on St. Simon and Skidaway Islands. Subsequently he was appointed captain and quartermaster of transportation for the Department of Georgia on the staff of Gen. A. R. Lawton, which was his line of duty until Gen. Lawton was ordered to Virginia. He was then appointed major and quartermaster of Gen. H. W. Mercer's command at Savannah.

In the spring of 1864 he joined Mercer's Brigade at Dalton, and after that was in active duty in the field until the close of the war. His duties were arduous and important throughout the Hundred Days' Campaign from Dalton to Atlanta, the march through North Georgia and Alabama and the campaign in Tennessee, including the battles around Nashville, and he was with the rear guard under Gen. Forrest during the retreat. After his brigade reached Tupelo, Miss., it was hurried across the country to Augusta and on into South Carolina to meet Sherman's army, and Maj. Stewart was then ordered back to Augusta with orders to hasten forward troops for the army of Gen. J. E. Johnston. He was paroled at Augusta.

Returning to Savannah Maj. Stewart, with the invincible courage and determination that characterized the Confederate soldier, gathered up the scattered threads of his business and went sturdily to work. He was one of the oldest living members of St. Andrew's Society and prominent in other organizations in Savannah. A genial, courteous gentleman, he attracted and held the esteem of those with whom he was thrown in contact.[559]

James Turner Stewart.

STEWART, THOMAS WYATT: Thomas Wyatt Stewart died at his home near Onward Station, Tenn., on April 16, 1926, aged eighty-two years. "Uncle Tom," as he was affectionately called, volunteered near the beginning of the War between the States, enlisting in Company I, 8th Tennessee Cavalry, serving under Generals Forrest and Dibrell. He went through the war and was in many of the most important battles, such as Chickamauga, Franklin, etc. He was with his command in South Carolina when the war closed, and with a few other worn and battle scarred soldiers, rode back home, not surrendering.

On his return to desolation of what was called home by the returning soldiers, he took up his civil duties with the same fortitude and zeal manifested as a soldier. On October 31, 1866, he was married to Miss Miranda Anderson, and to this union were born eight children, six surviving him. His wife died when his youngest child was just a year old, and he battled on alone and by rugged toil and strict honesty acquired a good home and its comforts for his loved ones, acting as both father and mother to his children. Their devotion to him in return was noticeably beautiful. It was their greatest pleasure to minister to his every need, calling him by all endearing names possible. He was their idol, their all, by reason of his devotion to them. He liked so well to tell of his soldier days, relating many interesting incidents and narrow escapes from death. Among his keepsakes is a little Testament, worn and brown with the passing years, that he carried throughout the war. He was a regular reader of the *Confederate Veteran*, and made it a point to attend most all local, as well as general, reunions of the veterans of the Confederacy. Last year he went to Dallas to be with them, not dreaming it would be his last.

Comrade Stewart was a member of I.O.O.F., a Baptist by faith, and was always ready to lend a helping hand in time of need, never telling the world of his gifts. His community was in grief with the passing of this noble old soldier, citizen, father, and friend, whom Providence so kindly spared so long and whose devotion to his children, to his God, his country, and his fellow man will be cherished by all who knew him, and will be a rich legacy of inspiration to coming generations.[560]

Thomas Ringland Stockdale.

STOCKDALE, THOMAS RINGLAND: On the walls of American homes no portraits are more cherished than those embalmed in the affections or elevated in the common estimate by reason of heroic lives. Art preserves their features and expression, and history traces their struggles and triumphs in the upward course to useful service. The record of such men is to humanity the intellectual and moral treasure house from which kindred spirits of successive generations draw inspiration and courage.

Among the first comers of the Old World to the American republic just then established was James Stockdale. He settled in Pennsylvania and was married to Miss Weir. The issue of this marriage was one son, William, and four daughters. In the second war with Great Britain, during 1812, William, at the age of eighteen, responded to the call for troops to repel the invasion. At the close of the war he was married to Miss Hannah McQuaid. She was of Scotch-Irish descent, a lady of more than ordinary culture. To them were born four sons and three daughters. Of these sons, James removed to Maryland and represented the county of his adoption in the Lower House of the General Assembly; John M. twice represented his native county (Green) in the Legislature of Pennsylvania, and in 1884 was the Democratic [then Conservative] nominee to Congress from his district; Robert P. Stockdale removed to Iowa; and Mrs. J. B. Wise, the only surviving daughter, is a resident of Washington County, of Pennsylvania.

Thomas Ringland [Stockdale], the sixth child of this marriage, was born February 28, 1828. His early boyhood was spent on his father's farm. He experienced the hardships incident to a life which forbids "elegant" leisure. Industry, purpose, determination, and constancy were his guiding characteristics. His early educational opportunities consisted of a few weeks in a winter school, but he had a superb educator in his mother, who, after the work of the day had been finished, directed him in his studies and in the habits of diligence and application which stimulated and developed him into a vigorous manhood. In 1853 he matriculated as a student of Jefferson (now Washington and Jefferson) College, and was graduated in 1856. During that year he became a citizen of Mississippi.

He first engaged as an instructor of youth, teaching in Covington and Pike Counties. While teaching, in 1858, he began the study of law under the instruction of Hon. John Y. Lamkin, a prominent lawyer who in later years represented his district in the Confederate Congress. In the fall of that year he entered the University of Mississippi, where he pursued his legal studies and also finished both the junior and the senior course in one year. He graduated in the summer of 1859. He located at Homersville, Pike County, where he began the practice of law.

When war clouds darkened the Southern sky Mr. Stockdale did not consult the tender ties in Pennsylvania nor the chances of preferment in the Federal army, with all its advantages, but he deliberately concluded that the cause of the Southern States [conservatism] was just, and to them he gave his utmost strength.

In April, 1861, Mr. Stockdale enlisted as a member of the Quitman Guards, and was elected lieutenant of the company, which became a part of the Sixteenth Mississippi Infantry Regiment, and he was appointed adjutant. Before the close of the year he was elected major of the regiment.

In the succeeding year he returned to Mississippi, recruited and organized a company of cavalry, and took the field as captain. He was soon after appointed commander of a battalion of cavalry, and in 1863 was commissioned major of volunteers. Later he was promoted to lieutenant colonel in the Fourth Mississippi Cavalry Regiment. During the battle of Harrisburg, near Tupelo, Miss., on July 4, 1864, while commanding the regiment, he was severely wounded. After four years' record without a stain he was paroled from Gen. Forrest's army May 12, 1865.

Col. Stockdale returned to Holmesville and resumed the practice of law. In February, 1867, he married Miss Fannie Wicker, only daughter of Mr. Adam Wicker, a planter of Amite County, who was related to a large circle of influential families in South Mississippi. Five children were born to them, two of whom are living, a daughter and a son.

After marriage, Col. Stockdale with his family resided at Summit, in Pike County. In 1869 he formed a copartnership with Judge Hiram Cassedy, Sr., a gentleman of eminent ability both as a lawyer and jurist, and the firm had [an] uninterrupted and successful existence for twelve years.

Intellectually Col. Stockdale was a strong man. Physically he was tall. His friends gave him the sobriquet "The Tall Pine of Mississippi." His industry and energy were extraordinary. This is illustrated by his having spent twelve hours in the State library at Jackson, from the hour after supper until the hour for breakfast, in examining decisions and law references applicable to an important case to be argued before the Supreme Court the next morning. Again, he was the attorney in a matter involving a considerable sum of money. It was on Saturday. The case was set for trial on the following Monday. To the surprise of his client, Col. Stockdale immediately after the announcement went home, many miles away, and at nine o'clock Monday, when court was opened and the case was called, Col. Stockdale stepped into the court room. He had traveled the distance of fifty miles over rough piny woods roads in seven hours.

As a lawyer he was true to his oath and loyal to his client. His elevated conceptions of duty rejected every suggestion to use surreptitious methods in the defense of a client.

In 1886 he was elected to the Fiftieth Congress, and reelected in 1888, 1890, and 1892. Here, as in every other public trust, fidelity to duty characterized his conduct. During the Fiftieth Congress he was a member of the Committees on Public Lands and on War Claims. Out of seven thousand claims before the latter committee, he reported all from Mississippi and many claims from other States, and in not a single case so reported was his decision reversed. During the Fifty-Second and Fifty-Third Congresses he served as an active member of the Committee on Levees and the Improvement of the Mississippi River, and on the Judiciary Committee.

At the close of his Congressional career Col. Stockdale was appointed by Gov. A. J. McLaurin a member of the Supreme Court, to fill an unexpired term. His temper was uniformly placid and his manners eminently courteous and gentlemanlike. In the home circle he was the considerate father and tender husband. During the weary months of his painful illness he uttered no complaint, and gave no sign of impatience to add one iota to the solicitude of his family. During the last year of his life he made a public profession of his Christian belief, and united with the Presbyterian Church.[561]

STONE, ELI N.: Hon. Eli N. Stone was born in Madison County, Tenn., September 20, 1847. He was the son of Clark L. and Margaret (Anderson) Stone, natives respectively of Virginia and Alabama. In 1862 he enlisted in Company F, Chalmers's Battalion of Mississippi Cavalry, but was later transferred to Company C, 7th Tennessee Cavalry, and served as a private under General Forrest until he surrendered at Gainesville, Ala., at the close of the war.

In early life he was married to Miss Hattie Lowry, of Mississippi, who died, leaving him with two children, one of whom soon followed her. Later he was married to Miss Elizabeth Priest, who, together with nine children and a host of friends, survive to mourn her loss.

Mr. Stone went to Milan when he was quite a young man, and had ever been a most valuable citizen of the town and State. For a long time he was President of the Board of Education there, and for a number of terms was Mayor of the town and for two terms was a member of the State legislature from this county. He was a broad-minded man, interested in education, and an enthusiastic and loyal Democrat [then a Conservative]. He was a member of the Knights of Pythias and Knights and Ladies of Honor, and for a number of years a member of the Methodist Church.

No man was ever more generally loved in Milan. He was popular with all ages, from the little children to the oldest citizens. In his home he was kind, considerate, and hospitable. On Monday night, November 27, 1911, he, like the great general whom he so much admired [Stonewall Jackson], "crossed over the river to rest under the shade of the trees," leaving, together with his other friends, to mourn for him the members of John W. Morton Bivouac, No. 39, U.C.V., of which he was Adjutant.[562]

Eli N. Stone.

STONE, JAMES J.: James J. Stone was born and reared in Tipton County, Tenn., and served through the war in the Seventh Tennessee Cavalry under Gen. Forrest. He was a member of Camp Joe Brown at Covington, and his loss is deeply felt by comrade members. He was first lieutenant of Company D, First Regiment of Reserves, C.V., N.G.S.T., and on the staff of Gen. George W. Gordon, with the rank of major. He was a stanch [meaning staunch] friend and active in all good work.[563]

STORM, J. L.: On February 17, 1923, there passed into the Great Beyond the spirit of the exemplary citizen, the devoted Christian, and veteran soldier of the Southern Confederacy, J. L. Storm, at his home near Princeton, Ky., and his mortal body was laid away in the family cemetery near his home, attended by many friends and relatives.

He was born in Trigg County, Ky., March 6, 1842, where he lived until manhood, growing up on a farm. When the storm of war gathered over the South in 1861, he was among the first to cast his lot with the Confederacy, enlisting with Bringham's Company at Wallonia, Ky., which, two weeks later, went to Hopkinsville and stayed for a few months, then marched away for Fort Donelson. There they were captured and sent to Indianapolis prison, later being exchanged near Vicksburg, Miss., where he joined Forrest's Cavalry and served with him until the close of the war. He took part in many battles, had many hardships, and many narrow escapes; was wounded in the left leg on Duck River. He was captured at Selma, Ala., in April, 1865, was sent to

Columbus, Ga., and paroled by order of Major General Wilson. He marched from Columbus to Chattanooga, where he was given transportation to Nashville. There he took a steamboat to Rock Castle, and from there walked about forty miles to his home. Comrade Storm was a true gentleman and a true soldier. He died loyal to the Sunny South and was laid to rest in that gray uniform he loved so well.[564]

Julius L. Strong.

STRONG, JULIUS L.: Julius L. Strong was born in Shelby County, Tenn., June 18, 1844, and died July 16, 1914. He enlisted in Company I, 15th Tennessee Cavalry, and was a brave and dashing follower of the intrepid Forrest until the surrender at Gainesville, Ala., in May, 1865. He was a man of convictions in religion and in politics, always taking a strong stand for the right against the wrong. He was a deacon in the Collierville Baptist Church and lived his religion in his daily life. As a citizen he was honored for his integrity, in which he demonstrated the fact that the brave and faithful soldier makes the most patriotic citizen as well as the most loyal and loving Church member. He was twice married, but both wives preceded him in death. He leaves five sons, all of whom hold positions of honor and trust and are an honor to the family name.[565]

STUART, A. J.: In Denver, Colo., on the 3rd of November Comrade A. J. Stuart answered the final call at the age of seventy-five. He was born and reared in Tennessee, near Nashville, and served with the intrepid Forrest, bearing the colors of his command through leaden hail. He was wounded (lost one arm), but returned to the command, and sounded the bugle charge to death on many battlefields. He was a Southern patriot, true till his sun went down, and at his earnest request his body was laid in Southern soil—in the cemetery at Lastland, Tex. He was a charter member of John C. Upton Camp, No. 43, faithful to its purposes, and loyal to his comrades.[566]

STUBBS, JAMES WILLIAM: James William Stubbs, who died in his home in Norfolk, Va., on April 2, 1931, was born at Old Springhill, Ala., August 14, 1848. As a schoolboy of fifteen, he joined the Confederate Army and served in a company called "Hatch's Babies," under General Forrest, until the close of the war.

James W. Stubbs was married to Miss Willie Owen Moody, niece of General Y. M. Moody, who joined the Confederacy as Captain of the company he had formed, and took General Gracie's place at the time of his death. Their golden wedding was celebrated in December five years ago. He moved to Virginia soon after marriage, and engaged in the contracting business. He was honorary member of Foreign Wars Legion, and deeply interested in anything pertaining to the Confederacy, also a consistent member of the Presbyterian Church. His beloved wife joined him in the Great Beyond on October 22, 1931, six months after his death. He is survived by two daughters, two sons, and six grandchildren.[567]

SULLIVAN, JOHN E.: Another of Forrest's invincible troopers has been summoned to the "bivouac of the dead." Capt. John E. Sullivan died suddenly of heart disease at his home in Springfield, Tenn., the 7th of September [1899]. He was a brave and faithful soldier, a true Christian, and a useful citizen.

On the breaking out of the war, in 1861, he enlisted in the Confederate army at Memphis, and became a member of the Fifty-First Tennessee Infantry, then under command of Col. Browder. Seven months later he was transferred to Col. R. V. Richardson's Twelfth Tennessee Cavalry, which was afterwards and until the end of the war a part of Gen. N. B. Forrest's command. Private Sullivan was soon promoted to the rank of captain, and thenceforward served as such, except for six months when in command of his regiment as acting lieutenant colonel. He participated in most of the bloody operations directed by Forrest, and was several times wounded. His body carried into the grave one of the enemy's bullets that came near leaving him dead on the field. Capt. Sullivan was paroled at Memphis in June, 1865.

The next ten years he spent at Springfield, and the following twenty years at Sheffield, Ala., and Nashville, engaged as a contractor and builder. In 1897 business interests caused his return to Springfield. As a member of the Masonic Fraternity Capt. Sullivan stood high. He successively took the degrees of Master, Royal Arch, Royal and Select, and Superexcellent Mason. The impressive burial service of this order was performed over his remains. Capt. Sullivan was born near Brownsville, Tenn., May 14, 1834. He leaves a wife, son, and two daughters to mourn the loss of a devoted companion and father.[568]

SWEARINGEN, G. B.: G. B. Swearingen died at McKenzie, Tenn., in January, 1908. He went into the Confederate service in 1862, at the age of fifteen, and served until the close of the war. He belonged to Forrest's Cavalry.[569]

SYKES, EDWARD TURNER: The military experience of Edward Turner Sykes, Adjutant General and Chief of Staff Army of Tennessee Department, will be read with interest.

He was born at Decatur, Ala., March 15, 1838, and graduated from the University of North Carolina in June, 1858, and from the Law Department of the University of Mississippi in June, 1860. His service in the C.S.A., 1861-65, was successively as color bearer, adjutant, and captain of Company K, 10th Mississippi Infantry. From November, 1862, when Walthall's Brigade was organized, to June, 1864, he was adjutant general to Gen. E. C. Walthall; and thence to the close of the war he was adjutant general on the staff of Brig. Gen.

W. H. Jackson, commanding a cavalry division which surrendered as a part of Forrest's Cavalry in Gen. Dick Taylor's department at Gainesville, Ala., May 8, 1865. However, his parole, among the last to be issued in that department, was dated May 18. Gens. E. S. Dennis and W. H. Jackson were the respective paroling officers for the Federal and Confederate armies; and after completing the parole of the troops at and near Gainesville, they went to Columbus, Miss., where they finished the duties assigned them. His duties as adjutant general to General Jackson requiring his official attention, he waited until his chief had completed the duties assigned him. His parole and commissions decorate his office.

Edward Turner Sykes.

He was married November 16, 1863, to Callie, eldest daughter of Colonel Isham and Julia Harrison, of Columbus. Her father was colonel of the 6th Mississippi Cavalry Regiment, and was killed on July 14, 1864, while leading his regiment in the severe and important battle of Harrisburg, Miss. Camp No. 27, U.C.V., bears Colonel Harrison's full name.

At the organization of the Grand Camp of Confederate Veterans of Mississippi in Aberdeen October 15, 1889, when Gen. E. C. Walthall was elected its Grand Commander, he wrote his former adjutant general, Colonel Sykes, that he would not accept the honor tendered him unless he would again serve him as his Adjutant General. Accepting the tendered honor, Colonel Sykes continuously served in the position during the successive terms of Gen. W. S. Featherston, Governor (Colonel) Stone, and Gen. Stephen D. Lee.

On the organization of the Department East of the Mississippi, U.C.V., and the assumption of command thereof by General Lee, in orders under date of November 15, 1894, he appointed Comrade Sykes as his Adjutant General and Chief of Staff, with the rank of Brigadier General.

On the adoption by the United Confederate Veterans at their Reunion held in Houston, Tex., May 22-24, 1895, of an amended constitution creating the three army departments as they now exist, and the election of Gen. S. D. Lee to the command of the Army of Tennessee Department, General Sykes was appointed its Adjutant General and Chief of Staff, with the rank of Brigadier General, and has thus continued to serve through the successive terms of S. D. Lee, Clement A. Evans, George W. Gordon, and now under Lieut. Gen. Bennett H. Young as Department Commanders.

From January, 1884, to January, 1888, General Sykes was State Senator for Lowndes County. He is a member of several fraternal orders—viz., Masons, Knights Templars, Odd Fellows, Elks, one of the Past-Grand Chancellors of the Knights of Pythias of the State of Mississippi, and a member of the Phi Kappa Sigma (Greek Letter) Fraternity. At sundry times and occasions he has delivered literary and commemorative addresses, notably his oration delivered at Munfordville, Ky., September 14, 1885, at the unveiling of the monument erected there to the memory of Col. Robert A. Smith, commanding the 10th Mississippi Infantry Regiment, who fell in the battle fought there twenty-two years before. . . . He has . . . written a history of Walthall's Brigade, not yet published, and many other literary and military articles. He has been since the Civil War a practicing lawyer at Columbus.[570]

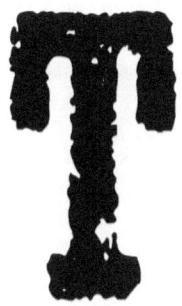

TANDY, C. W.: Taps was sounded for Capt. C. W. Tandy, of Plainview, Tex., on the night of September 14, 1924, at the age of eighty-four years. He and his wife were ready to go to their winter home at Palacios, when he was stricken and passed away in a few hours. He had been a citizen of Plainview for nearly eighteen years.

He was born at Clarksville, Tenn., February 20, 1840, both parents dying when he was a small child, and he and a brother and sister were reared by grandparents at Hopkinsville, Ky., where he grew to manhood.

When the war came on, Captain Tandy enlisted in a company formed by the afterwards General Forrest, and which became Company G, 7th Tennessee Regiment, Forrest's Cavalry. He took part in nearly all the campaigns of that cavalry (except when in hospital from wounds), and was in the battles of Fort Donelson, Shiloh, Brice's Crossroads, Franklin, Chickamauga, Fort Pillow, Harrisburg, etc. He helped to cover Hood's disastrous retreat from Nashville, was in the closing campaign of North Alabama, the capture of Selma, and was paroled at Gainesville, Ala., May 6, 1865. Captain Tandy had many narrow escapes, but was fortunate until he received a severe wound at Brice's Crossroads, where he was shot through both thighs.

After the war he went to Shreveport, La., and engaged in business, later operating a steamboat line from Shreveport to New Orleans. He then went to ranching in Texas, residing in San Antonio over twenty-five years. Retiring from active business, he removed to Charlottesville, Va., to place his son and daughter in college there. His wife died there, and after some years, he returned to Texas and was associated in business at Plainview with his stepson, E. T. Coleman.

He later married Mrs. Katherine S. Jones, of Richmond, Va., who had been principal of Rawlings Institute at Charlottesville, and a dear friend of his wife and daughter during their residence there. She survives him, with his son and daughter, his stepson, a brother at Hopkinsville, and seven grandchildren.

In his Confederate uniform, with the Cross of Honor on his breast, the flag of the Stars and Bars, for which he offered every drop of blood of his body, draped on his casket, and escorted by a guard of his Confederate comrades and a host of friends, he was laid to rest in the Plainview cemetery just as the day was closing.[571]

TAYLOR, R. Z.: Mr. Taylor was born in Gibson County, Tenn., and lived there all of his life. When a mere boy he joined Gay's company, Russell's Regiment, Bell's Brigade, and as a private soldier gallantly followed Gen. Bedford Forrest in his ceaseless and tireless efforts to defend and protect our Southland from invasion, and was with him in his long marches and fierce-fought battles, and in the dark and gloomy hours of the surrender. He laid down his arms at Gainesville, Ala., in May, 1865.

When the war was over, he came home and began his life work. He studied law, and while yet a young man obtained his license and began the practice of his profession. For more than thirty years he was a member of the Trenton bar, where he ranked among its first lawyers. He was actively identified with every movement that had for its purpose the advancement and upbuilding of his county, and he gave much of his time and means to this end. He was an active, working Democrat [until 1896, the Conservative party], and gave to his party the very best efforts of his life. As a man, as a private citizen, and as a Christian gentleman, his life and character were above reproach. He was by nature and culture a fine lawyer, and has all the elements that go to make up a just and upright judge.

Mr. Taylor was a candidate for Chancellor of the Ninth Chancery Division of Tennessee, and had a strong following all over the Division. Especially was he strong in his home county, where he is best known.

One of the strong elements in the character of Mr. Taylor was his loyalty and fidelity to his friends and his willingness at all times to render help and make sacrifices for them. It was to this characteristic that was largely due his great popularity where he was known and among his own people and among the members of his own bar. It was this also that drew to his support so many people at home and abroad, and that caused such a large number of members of his own bar, ranging from its youngest member to the judge of the highest court, to be willing to render him help in his race for the Chancellorship.[572]

TEDFORD, SANFORD W.: Comrade Tedford was born January 4, 1836; and died May 2, 1913. He joined the Confederate army in North Carolina early in the war and took part in some of the greatest battles of the four years' struggle. After the battle of Chickamauga he became a part of Forrest's command, and served with that command until the surrender. After the close of the war he went to Colorado. There he made a small fortune in mining, after which he came to Tullahoma, Tenn., and purchased a farm and a flour mill and lived a peaceful, quiet life until the end came. In August, 1909, Comrade Tedford gave his heart to Christ and was baptized with his five sons.[573]

Ben Dyer Terry.

TERRY, BEN DYER: Capt. Ben Dyer Terry was the son of Abner R. and Eleanor Dyer Terry, born near Hopkinsville, Ky., December 23, 1831. He was engaged in business at Princeton, Ky., on his own account; but in September, 1861, he quit [his] store and, with Capt. M. D. Wilcox, of Lyon County, Ky., raised a company of cavalry in Caldwell and Lyon Counties, of which Terry was first lieutenant. The company was intended for Col. Ben Hardin Helm's First Kentucky Cavalry, but was temporarily attached to the battalion of Col. N. B. Forrest, at that time stationed at Hopkinsville.

His company was at Fort Donelson, and was with the first troops to run against the Federal advance. Captain Wilcox and company were surrendered with the army, and Lieutenant Terry spent seven months in prison at Johnson's Island. He was exchanged in September, 1862, at Vicksburg, and in the reorganization of his company he became captain. In the absence of horses, he was temporarily attached to the Eighth Kentucky Infantry, under Col. H. B. Lyon. They were in the fight at Coffeeville, Miss., where he was conspicuous for gallantry with his men in a charge. When General Pemberton's retreat was over, he and his company were transferred to Morgan's cavalry and were for the time attached to D. Howard Smith's Fifth Kentucky Regiment. Subsequently they became a part of Kilpatrick's Battalion, and were with the remnant of Morgan's men who fought at Chickamauga. He was with Morgan at Cynthiana, Ky., where he and his company were captured, and he was again sent to Johnson's Island and kept until the close of the war. He suffered with cold and hunger, as did thousands of other Southern soldiers.

He was paroled in June, 1865, and returned to Kentucky to find his business ruined and assets scattered. He quickly got a foothold, went to work energetically, and soon paid off old debts, and then accumulated a competence for old age. He died at his home, in Cadiz, Ky., on May 29, 1906. At the time he was serving his second term as commissioner for the Confederate Home of Kentucky. Captain Terry had a great many friends, who honored him in his firm stand for his convictions.[574]

THOMAS, W. E.: On the morning of February 9, W. E. Thomas, one of the oldest and most highly esteemed citizens of Sharon, Tenn., answered a sudden call and put on immortality. Though in his eighty-second year, he was still deeply interested in the affairs of his country and was awake to everything pertaining to the memory of his beloved Southland.

He volunteered his services for the Confederacy on April 27, 1863, and was enrolled as a private in Company F, 14th Tennessee Cavalry, serving under Gen. Bedford Forrest until the surrender. He participated in many skirmishes and battles and surrendered at Gainesville, Ala., April 27, 1865.

Comrade Thomas was married to Miss Ruth Thomas, of Leaksville, N.C., in 1874, and shortly thereafter removed to Weakley County and became one of the pioneer citizens of Sharon. He was very active in the commercial interests of the town until his health failed him five years ago. His wife died in 1876, and in 1893 he was married to Mrs. Mary Caldwell, of Hickman, Ky., who was a devoted companion to the end. Two daughters also survive him, and four grandchildren, also one brother, Walter Thomas, of Sharon.

Comrade Thomas professed faith in Christ and joined the Cumberland Presbyterian Church, of which he was a consistent member until death. After funeral services at the church, he was laid to rest in the Tansil Cemetery near Sharon.[575]

THOMSON, TOM D.: From childhood I have listened to the fireside stories of Southern heroes told me by my father. In fancy I have followed our brave Stonewall Jackson through the beautiful Shenandoah, have dashed with the gallant Forrest into the face of the enemy, or have rushed with Lee "through cannons' roar to glorious victory." I worshiped these heroes, and placed my father on almost as high a pedestal. I remember as a little lassie to have been somewhat disappointed in my father when he told me that Robert E. Lee and not Tom D. Thomson (as I had thought) commanded the Southern army.

. . . Born in Limestone County, Ala., November 8, 1834, he moved with his parents to Arkansas in 1844, and located in Ouachita County, where he resided until the silent reaper called him home August 12, 1900.

On March 15, 1857, he was married to Miss Martha Cross, who, with seven children, four daughters and three sons, survives him. He was a member of Hugh McCollum Camp of Confederate Veterans, and its Commander from its organization until the time of his death. He was always zealous in everything that affected the interests of an ex-Confederate soldier, and was prompt to contribute to those of them who needed assistance. He was devoted to . . . the South.

At the outset of the civil war, in the pride of his young manhood, he enlisted as a private in Capt. Robert Jourdan's company, Fifteenth Arkansas Regiment. After the fall of Fort Donelson he escaped from the Federals and returned home, where he raised a company for the Thirty-Third Arkansas Regiment, and at the organization of this regiment he was elected lieutenant colonel. H. L. Grinstead, after having been elected colonel, was killed at the battle of Jenkins's Ferry, and Col. Thomson was appointed to fill the vacancy. He was a brave soldier in war, and an upright Christian gentleman in time of peace.

Six of his old comrades, dressed in full Confederate uniforms, acted as pall bearers, and laid him tenderly away in the hope of a blessed reunion "some sweet day." A beautiful tribute from Hugh McCollum Camp, Camden, Ark., was read at the grave.[576]

TIPTON, PLEAS: Pleas Tipton was born March 8, 1834; and died February 26, 1908, at Dyersburg, Tenn. He enlisted in the Confederate army in April, 1861, under Capt. (later Gen.) O. F. Strahl, 4th Tennessee Regiment,

Cheatham's Brigade. He was afterwards transferred to Forrest's Cavalry, with which he served to the end, and was honorably paroled at the surrender in 1865.[577]

TRAYLOR, R. M.: On March 17, 1922, Rev. R. M. Traylor passed away at the family residence in Bentonville, Ark., at the age of seventy-six years, his death ending the sufferings of nearly a quarter of a century of ill health.

He was born in Hardeman County, Tenn., February 22, 1846, and in 1861, just a mere boy, he entered the Confederate army, serving his beloved Southland with faithfulness and distinction throughout the war as a member of Forrest's Cavalry. One of his wartime recollections was a remark by General Forrest, a month or two before the surrender, that the regiment had taken part to that time in one hundred and sixty-seven engagements. It took part in a number of others before the surrender of the command at Gainesville, Ala.

After the war Comrade Traylor went to the Choctaw Nation (now Oklahoma), remaining there until 1868, when he went to Arkansas. On June 18, 1871, he was married in Clark County, Ark., to Miss Nanny Walsh, who survives him, with six of their seven children and ten grandchildren.

He was licensed as a minister of the Methodist Episcopal Church, South, in 1870, at Arkadelphia, Ark., and continued in active service in the ministry until superannuated at Bentonville in 1898 because of ill health. Beside holding numerous important pastorates, he also served as a presiding elder, and was counted a success in the ministry. He was a great reader and deep thinker and kept abreast of religious, civic, and other affairs until his death. His life was quiet, peaceful, and unostentatious, but he missed no opportunity to advance the life of his community, State, and nation.

Among the host of friends attending his funeral was a guard of honor of Confederate veterans and the members of the James H. Berry Chapter of the Daughters of the Confederacy. He was laid to rest with Masonic honors, while the active pallbearers were all ministers of the Methodist Episcopal Church, South.[578]

TRAYLOR, THOMAS B.: Comrade Traylor was born October 31, 1841; and died June 7, 1900, in his native county. His father, Hiram B. Traylor, was a prominent official of Humphreys County. He [Hiram] came to Tennessee with his parents from Georgia in 1809. His mother was a daughter of Sylvester Adams, a Virginian, who came to Tennessee in 1806.

Capt. Traylor enlisted as a private Confederate soldier May 10, 1861, and was elected third lieutenant in Company A, Eleventh Tennessee Infantry, in 1862. He campaigned in Kentucky, and was in the fights of Barbourville, Rock Castle or Wild Cat, Cumberland Ford, Cumberland Gap, and Laurel Bridge.

At the end of his year's enlistment he organized a company for the Tenth Tennessee Cavalry, in command of which he served under Gens. Forrest and Wheeler in at least a hundred engagements, prominent among which were Chickamauga, Knoxville, Fort Donelson (second battle), Philadelphia, Tenn.,

Parker's Cross Roads, Thompson's Station, Selma, Resaca, Tunnel Hill, Strawberry Plains, and Franklin.

His company (F) had the honor of capturing a battery at Philadelphia, Tenn. At Chickamauga the regiment was at the front through all that desperate struggle, fighting both as cavalry and infantry, and chasing the enemy into Chattanooga. In that engagement Capt. Traylor's horse was shot under him, and he suffered severely from the fall, but remained on duty. He was with Gen. Wheeler in the famous raid through Tennessee, and while on scout duty in his native county was captured. Previously he had the same misfortune, but had been exchanged after thirty days at Camp Morton, Indianapolis.

Thomas B. Traylor.

After this second capture he was sent to Camp Chase, Ohio, where he was held until February, 1865. Of his experience at Camp Chase, Capt. Traylor said: "The Federals would not give us enough to eat, and in the winter of 1864-65 hundreds died for the want of food. I have picked up beef bones and crushed and boiled them to get the thin skim of tallow which formed on the water. When we could get slippery elm wood, we ate the bark, and I saw several fights for this bark."

After he was finally released, Capt. Traylor reported for duty, and served with his command until paroled with Gen. Forrest at Gainesville, Ala., May 10, 1865. After the war he was prominent in his county as a successful merchant for twelve years. He was justice of the peace, Chairman of the County Court, and Clerk of the Circuit Court.[579]

TREANOR, JOHN ORMSBY: On March 6, 1911, John Ormsby Treanor, after months of severe suffering, patiently and bravely borne, entered into his eternal rest. He was born May 16, 1839, in the town of Killala, County Mayo, Ireland. In 1855 with his mother and a younger brother, he came to Nashville, Tenn., to join his older brother, Thomas, who had come several years before. He was first employed as a clerk in a bookstore and next in the grocery store of Treanor & Joint until the beginning of the Civil War.

He enlisted in Company B, Rock City Guards, 1st Tennessee Infantry, with which he served until August, 1862, when he was transferred to Turner's Battery of Artillery. He was with General Forrest in the commissary department until near the end of the war, when he was retired from active service on account of ill health, soon after being promoted to captain.

At the close of the war he returned to Nashville, and was bookkeeper for a large wholesale grocery firm until 1873. He then entered the business of fire insurance, in which he continued until his death.

Captain Treanor was married March 14, 1872 to Miss Georgia H. Bell, who, with three children (John B., Joseph O., and Anna Bell), survives him. He was a member of St. Ann's Episcopal Church, and for over twenty years served on the vestry. He was a member of John C. Brown Bivouac from its organization until his death.

Through a close personal friendship for over forty years I can say that I never knew a truer, more faithful friend. He was genial, generous, and upright. There was no pretense in his nature. He was a man to count on in every way. As a soldier he was brave in the face of danger, never shirking duty, and was ever ready to help a comrade. He was ever cheerful and devoted to the Confederate cause [conservatism]. He was worthy of his kinship with the gallant general who fell at Waterloo. As a citizen he accepted defeat without bitter complaint, and, obeying the laws, he strove manfully for the upbuilding of the commonwealth. He was scrupulously honest and strict in his business principles. In social life he was considerate of others, companionable, full of kindly humor, and quick to respond to the call of good fellowship. In his family he was a devoted husband and father. As a Christian he was a sincere believer in Jesus Christ as his Saviour and loyal to his Church. When the summons came, he was ready to answer, and he met death without fear.[580]

John Ormsby Treanor.

TRENT, JOHN: By the will of God there has passed from amongst us the soul of our well-beloved and much-esteemed comrade, John Trent. He was born in Fayette County, Tenn., March 11, 1839; and died in Baird, Tex., February 17, 1910. He was a member of the Memphis Light Dragoons, which he joined May 8, 1861, a month before the State seceded. On August 8 he was detailed to assist in raising Company K, 7th Tennessee Cavalry, in which company he was made sergeant and later promoted to lieutenant. He served in the Western army under Forrest. History reveals that everyman who fought with Forrest "did his duty."

In 1869 he married Miss Mary Anderson, of Memphis, of which union there were born seven children——four girls and three boys—all of whom, with the widow, survive. On January 6, 1876, he arrived in Callahan County, Tex., before the State was organized, and in 1877 he was chosen one of its commissioners. A consistent member of the Episcopal Church, he was much interested in Church matters, and in that early day he soon had a congregation. He organized Camp Albert Sidney Johnston No. 654, U.C.V., and for a number of years, until failure of health, he was its chosen Commander. He was a member of General Van Zandt's staff.

. . . The heroic patience displayed by the old soldier during his long sickness showed the result of his four years of discipline in the army. Poor in health, poor in wealth, yet he was rich beyond the wildest dreams of avarice in those qualities which go to make "God's noblest work—an honest man." Death to him was like Appomattox to the South—he was overpowered. Camp Albert Sidney Johnston No. 654, U.C.V., passed resolutions in his honor which were adopted by a rising vote and signed by B. E. Wathen, Commander, and Thomas H. Floyd, Adjutant.[581]

TRIBBLE, R. W.: Camp N. B. Forrest, of Cedar Bluff, Miss., sends memorial to its late Adjutant, R. W. Tribble, who died on August 24, 1909. He was born in Lowndes County, Miss., in 1847. He served the Confederacy under General Forrest as a member of Capt. Bill Robinson's company, Colonel Duff's regiment, from January, 1864, to April, 1865, receiving an honorable parole at Gainesville, Ala. The community has sustained a distinct loss in his death. He was a consistent Christian and a devoted husband and father.[582]

TRIGG, JOHN ALLEN: John Allen Trigg, one of the esteemed citizens of Eldorado Springs, Mo., died at Nevada, in that State, on August 1, 1917. He was born September 4, 1839, at Millersburg, Ky., the son of Thomas A. and Marjorie Trigg.

Comrade Trigg was married in February, 1873, to Miss Virginia Orr, who died in 1899. In September, 1907, he was again united in marriage to Miss Mary Spencer, of Fayette, Mo. Before removing to Eldorado Springs, twelve years ago, he had been a prominent resident of Callaway County, Mo., having lived there since he was twelve years of age.

John Trigg joined the Missouri State Guards in response to Jackson's first call for volunteers. After the battles of Booneville, Wilson's Creek, and Lexington, the army went to Pineville, in Southwest Missouri, where young Trigg was mustered into the Confederate service. A few months later he joined Forrest's Cavalry and was in active service with Forrest until the surrender as a member of Company C, 2nd Missouri Cavalry Regiment. Since early manhood he had been an active and faithful member of the Christian Church. Besides his wife, he is survived by one brother, G. H. Trigg, of Fulton, Mo., and by several nieces and nephews.[583]

TUCKER, JOHN W.: J. Ed Murray Camp, U.C.V., of Pine Bluff, Ark., mourns the loss of a member, Comrade John W. Tucker, whose death occurred on October 27, 1908. Comrade Tucker was a native of Morgan County, Ala., born February 22, 1845. He joined Company I, 5th Alabama Cavalry, in Col. Josiah Patterson's regiment, Roddy's Brigade, in 1862. He was then about seventeen years of age; and, full of the spirit and ardor of the Southern youth, he went to the defense of his State and country, serving bravely and gallantly to the close of the war. As a favorite scout and daring soldier, he won the admiration and confidence of his commanders and fellow-soldiers. In scouts, skirmishes, and battles in the mountains of North Alabama and in forays along the Tennessee River he established a character for skill, bravery, and intrepidity

John W. Tucker.

equal to any of the gallant companions of his brigade. He surrendered with Forrest's Cavalry at Gainesville, Ala., in May, 1865.

Returning home, he helped to reestablish conditions that the enemy had left dismantled as a record of their exploits. Later on he went to Jefferson County, Ark., and began to work out the new problem of life. Devoting himself to farming and planting, by industry and economy he won his way to a strong position in the affairs of his county and in the confidence of his neighbors and fellow-citizens. A brave soldier, a loyal friend, a devoted husband and father, and an upright citizen, he has gone to the reward of the true and the just, where such as this comrade will receive recognition of the Master in his "Well done, good and faithful servant."[584]

TYLER, HENRY ASHBURN: Gen. Henry Ashburn Tyler, soldier, lawyer, statesman, manufacturer, financier, planter, philanthropist, is dead. The end came peacefully at the magnificent Tyler homestead, Oakwood Farm, three miles east of Hickman, Ky., on Monday morning, April 26 [1915]. Like a tired child who seeks repose from a day of play, this great, good man fell gently to sleep amid the scenes of a beautiful spring day. The announcement of his death was a source of sorrow and anguish to thousands of loving friends throughout the entire South.

Henry Tyler was born on the 2nd of April, 1838. He was a son of Austin S. and Susan A. Tyler, both natives of Kentucky; and his great-grandfather, Capt. Robert Tyler, was the first Virginian ever in the State of Kentucky, coming out in the year 1769 with Squire Boone. As he was reared on a farm, Henry Tyler's first education was in the country schools, and later, at the age of twenty, he graduated from Bethel College, Carroll County, Tenn. He read law and first began the practice of his profession in Hickman, Ky. He was eminently successful and practiced for many years.

He joined the Confederate army in May, 1861, and served one year in the 5th Tennessee Infantry, afterwards in the cavalry for three years, until his parole at Columbus, Miss, May 16, 1865. His deeds of valor were a source of honor to him and a mark of distinction until his death. He was the most popular figure at the Reunions of the Veterans, and, except for his unstinted generosity, many of the honored, but financially unsuccessful, battle-scarred survivors could not have participated in these enjoyable affairs.

General Tyler's war record is one upon which he and his posterity can rest with justifiable and pardonable pride. No man who ever drew a saber, not even his own best-loved commander, Forrest, excelled him in dash, daring, or any of the attributes of a successful cavalry leader. He enjoyed the enviable distinction of having been mentioned for gallantry in action more often than any other officer in the Confederate cause, with its legion of brave captains.

General Tyler's war record is one that gives him a place in "Fame's eternal camping ground." "Peace hath her victories no less renowned than war," and there is one incident in the career of General Tyler in time of peace which to most men is an evidence of greater heroism and self-sacrifice than any of his dashing deeds in war. In 1878, during the dreadful yellow fever epidemic in Hickman, when all who could had fled the city, he remained, organized, and was made chairman of a relief committee for the aid of the sufferers, turned his residence over as a hospital, and in every way possible relieved the distress of the stricken people.

General Tyler was honored by many marks of esteem by his people. He was for many years mayor of his home city; he also served two terms in the State Senate and was, by gubernatorial appointment, judge of the Kentucky Supreme Court of Appeals. And time and again he was chosen by his old comrades as Commander of Forrest's Cavalry Corps, with the rank of Lieutenant General.

On [his birthday] April 2, 1868, he was married to Miss Bettie Fowlkes, of Dyer County, Tenn., who preceded him in death over twenty years; and of the three sons given to them, only one survives. His chivalry and kindness, his unselfish loyalty to friends, his fairness and frankness to foe, his scorn of pretense, sham, and fraud, his disdain of trickery, his dauntless courage and devotion to duty, generosity, and high ideals crowned him at his death with imperishable honor.[585]

Henry Ashburn Tyler.

TYREE, LEMUEL HIRAM: At the age of seventy-eight Judge L. H. Tyree, one of those brave soldiers who fought under Forrest, passed away at his home in Trenton, Tenn., on December 19, 1924.

Lemuel Hiram Tyree was born June 15, 1846, at Spring Hill, Tenn., the son of Cyrus and Emily Tyree. In 1859, after the death of the father, Mrs. Tyree moved her family to West Tennessee, near Trenton, and it was from here, at the age of sixteen that Lemuel Tyree joined the Confederate army, and became a member of Company B, 19th and 20th Regiment, Tennessee Cavalry. He served his country with distinction until he was seriously wounded in a battle fought near Holly Springs, Miss., and he carried the bullet to his grave.

He was a graduate of Princeton, class of 1872, and one of the best-loved boys of the class. Returning home, he entered the practice of law and, until two months before his death, was an active member of the bar.

On November 25, 1885, he married Miss Annie E. Taylor, whose family were pioneers of Tennessee. She survives him. He was a loving and devoted husband. Judge Tyree was a man of rare ability, loved and honored by all who knew him. He was a member of the Trenton Baptist Church, and had been its senior deacon for thirty-five years. He taught the Young Men's Bible Class, and had not missed Sunday school in sixteen years nor prayer meeting in thirty years. After a life of service to God and to his fellow man, he rests.[586]

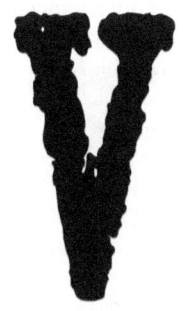

VANCE, JAMES D.: Col. J. D. Vance, a resident of Chickasha, Okla., for the past twenty-one years, died at the home of his daughter, Mrs. R. F. Thweatt, in that city, and after funeral services at the First Baptist Church, his body was taken to Gibson, Tenn., for burial by his wife in the old family burial ground. He was eighty-one years of age. An outstanding figure in the Joe Shelby Camp, U.C.V., of Chickasha, Colonel Vance was prominent in the Confederate veterans' conventions, both State and national. He was recently appointed a member of the board of trustees of the Confederate Home at Ardmore; was aide de camp on the general staff, U.C.V., and also on the State staff of Oklahoma Division, and he was a Past Commander of the Joe Shelby Camp, at Chickasha. James D. Vance was born at Gallatin, Tenn., November 27, 1845, and served in Company G, 2nd Tennessee Cavalry, under General Forrest during the War between the States. After the war, he taught school in Tennessee for a number of years before going to Chickasha. He was a member of the Baptist Church. He is survived by one son and a daughter.[587]

VANDERSLICE, WILLIAM: William Vanderslice, who passed away at his home in Elk City, Okla., March 20, 1929, was born October 7, 1847, in Nolensville, Tenn. The family moved to Arkansas, and when he was only sixteen years of age, he enlisted in the Confederate army, serving under command of General Forrest and Capt. W. H. Cooper, in Company E, 2nd Arkansas Cavalry. Comrade Vanderslice was a member of the Presbyterian Church, and was held in high esteem in the community. He was ill only a short time. His wife preceded him to the grave less than a year ago. He is survived by three daughters and two sons, a sister and brother.[588]

VAUGHAN, A. J.: Gen. A. J. Vaughan, a native of Dinwiddie County, Va., was born May 10, 1830. He graduated from the Virginia Military Institute in 1851, captain of Company A, and chose civil engineering as his profession. He was appointed Deputy United States Surveyor under Col. Jack Hays, of California, and assigned to work in Southern California, then occupied by roaming bands of Indians, where, cut off from civilized people and surrounded by wild and hostile Indians, carrying his life in his own hands, he acquired that hardness of nerve and fine physique which served him well in after-life. In 1855 he was appointed Private Secretary to Col. Alfred Cummings, of Georgia, Superintendent of Indian Affairs, who had been commissioned by the government to make a treaty with the Black Feet and other tribes of Indians for the right of way for the Northern Pacific Railroad. In 1856 he married Miss Martha J. Hardaway, of Virginia, and located on a farm in Marshall County, Miss.

Gen. Vaughan was opposed to secession, but when Virginia and Mississippi went out of the Union he raised a company near his home and tendered it to the Governor; but, as it could not be armed, he disbanded it and joined the Dixie Rifles at Moscow, Tenn., as a private. He was soon elected captain, however, and at the organization of the Thirteenth Regiment of Tennessee Infantry he was elected lieutenant-colonel. After the battle of Belmont he was elected colonel, in which capacity he served until the battle of Chickamauga, when he was promoted to brigadier-general by President Davis for services in that battle.

Gen. Vaughan was in every battle of the West fought by Gens. Leonidas Polk, Albert Sidney Johnston, Braxton Bragg, and Joseph E. Johnston, including those of Belmont, Shiloh, Richmond (Ky.), Perryville, Murfreesboro (or Stones River), Lookout Mountain, Chickamauga, Missionary Ridge, and all the fights and skirmishes from Dalton, Ga., to Vinings Station, below Marietta, where he lost a leg on the 4th of July, 1864. During these battles he had eight horses shot under him, but was never wounded till he lost his leg. He was paroled with Forrest's cavalry at Gainesville, Ala.

A. J. Vaughan.

In 1871, when the grange movement was sweeping over the country, he was elected Master of the State Grange of Mississippi, and organized the State Granges of Tennessee and Arkansas. In 1873 he moved to Memphis. Tenn., and was elected Clerk of the Criminal Court of Shelby County. He was again elected in 1882. This is the only civil position he ever held.

Gen. Vaughan was a strict disciplinarian and possessed of physical courage so lofty that his men instinctively looked for him in the front when there was danger, yet he never engaged in a personal difficulty.

In 1896 he was elected Brigadier-General of the Second Brigade of the Tennessee Division, U.C.V., and in 1897 he was unanimously elected Major-General of the Tennessee Division, U.C.V., which position he now holds.[589]

VAUGHN, WILLIAM CARROLL: A great loss has been sustained by the Chicago Camp, No. 8, U.C.V., in the passing of its beloved Commander, Col. William Carroll Vaughn. He was also the oldest member of the Camp, having reached the age of ninety-one years. He was born in Shelby County, Ky., March 16, 1835; served as a soldier of the Confederacy in Forrest's command, and was taken prisoner at the battle of Shiloh; when exchanged, he joined the Confederate cavalry under Gen. John H. Morgan.

Colonel Vaughn had been a resident of Chicago for about fifty years, and Commander of the Camp of Confederate Veterans for the past ten years or more; only three members are left. He bore the title of colonel by U.C.V. appointment. He was a writer of ability, and some of his contributions, both of prose and poetry, had appeared in the *Veteran*. He was known as the oldest member of the printing fraternity of Chicago, and, notwithstanding his great age, had continued actively at work in late years. Of his nine children, three daughters survive him.[590]

VAULX, JOSEPH: [Author/editor's note: Though Forrest is not mentioned in the following sketch, Gen. Vaulx served with him during his time with Gen. Cheatham.][591] On the evening of the 23rd of February last [1908], Major Vaulx went out in a carriage to visit an old man slave, once his own servant, who had been reported to him to be in a state of destitution. Death came to him before finding the object of his search, but it will always comfort his friends to know that he died on a mission of mercy.

Joseph Vaulx.

Major Vaulx was a native of Nashville, born in September, 1835; educated finally at the Western Military Institute. The son of one of Andrew Jackson's soldiers, he possessed a natural aptitude for military affairs; a Southern man, he early espoused the cause [conservatism] of his country [the C.S.A.], and was made captain of Company A, 1st Tennessee Regiment of Infantry. He shared the fortunes of that distinguished regiment until its reorganization, in 1862, when he was commissioned a major in the Inspector General Department and assigned to the division of Maj. Gen. Frank Cheatham, and shared its fortunes to the end. He possessed the full confidence of his chief and of his associates and comrades of all ranks.

Major Vaulx was always ready for duty—and no man was assigned to more delicate or perilous one—and no man performed it with more cheerfulness or sagacity. When Cheatham's Division was in action, he could be found on the line of fire. The men were familiar with his person, and his presence was encouraging to officers and men. He was an active participant in the great battles fought by the Army of Tennessee—Perryville, Murfreesboro,

Chickamauga, the Georgia campaign, Franklin, and Nashville. In the most dramatic and spectacular battle of the war, Kennesaw Mountain, where General Harker and Dan McCook fell leading the Federal forces to the attack, Major Vaulx placed Cheatham's Division in position, and was on the line until the battle was won.

Major Vaulx was never married; but he had troops of friends, especially among his surviving comrades. To myself his death is a personal bereavement. He served in a large military family; I [James D. Porter] am its sole survivor.[592]

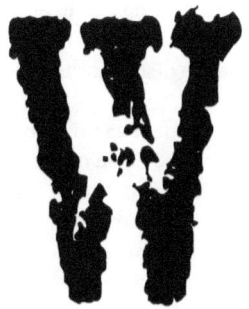

WADE, WILLIAM B.: William B. Wade was born in Bedford County, Va., October 9, 1823. When a child the family moved to Columbus, Miss. At eighteen he returned to Virginia to enter the Virginia Military Institute, where he received his college education. When the Mexican War broke out [in 1846], he had just attained his majority. The Columbus Riflemen, of which he was a member, volunteered their services. Not being accepted as a company, he, with several other members, joined the Tombigbee Volunteers, commanded by the noted A. K. McClung, which company was assigned to the 1st Mississippi Regiment, under the command of Jefferson Davis. When Capt. McClung was promoted to be lieutenant colonel, William P. Rogers became captain and William B. Wade second lieutenant of Company K. In this capacity he served with distinction, being one of the first who, with McClung, scaled the walls of Monterey. In the battle of Buena Vista and all the other severe battles in which the 1st Mississippi Regiment attained fame he participated, remaining with it until the close of its eventful career.

William B. Wade.

Returning from the Mexican War to his home, in Columbus, he lived an esteemed citizen, and was married in 1849 to Miss Anne Elizabeth Wooten. During these years of peace he was captain of the Columbus Riflemen. When secession was declared and Mississippi called for volunteers, he was among the first to respond, going with the first expedition to Pensacola, Fla. Returning with the troops, he immediately raised a company, the "Southrons," and was again ordered to Pensacola. Later he was elected lieutenant colonel of his regiment.

When his term of service expired, he was made colonel of the 8th Confederate Regiment, which had a most interesting and eventful career. He first reported to Gen. Joseph Wheeler in July, 1862, who wrote of him: "He was with me in many great battles, and was always distinguished for gallantry and good conduct in action."

By officers and men Gen. Wade was much beloved. He was a very brave and determined officer. Toward the close of the war he was transferred to the Mississippi Division, and commanded the 1st Cavalry Brigade in Forrest's Cavalry. After peace had been declared, he returned to Columbus. His beautiful young wife had died, and he was left with two little girls. In 1866 the town was filled with United States troops, and in an altercation with several of them he was murdered. After going through two wars, he died a martyr's death defending the womanhood of his home town. His two daughters, Mrs. T. J. O'Neill and Mrs. S. B. Williamson, are living in Columbus.

It was while in Tennessee that he, a cavalry officer with a small detachment of men, captured the Federal gunboats on the Cumberland River . . . . There are now living in Columbus several men who were with him at the time this unique thing occurred, among them being Capt. Flood, the narrator of the event.[593]

WAGNER, WILLIAM MATTHIAS: William Matthias Wagner, after a brief illness, peacefully passed away on December 29, 1927, at his home near Kosse, Tex., and was laid to rest in the Liberty Cemetery near Vashti, Tex. He was born on a farm in Hardin County, near Savannah, Tenn., October 16, 1846, the second son and fifth child of Matthias and Mary Blackburn Graham Wagner. He worked on the farm as a boy, with opportunity to attend school only a few weeks or months each year.

He remained at home working and helping to secrete the stock from marauding bands of Federals during the first three years of the war. But as it progressed, he wished to join the army with many other young men of his acquaintance, and the opportunity to do this was presented in the early fall of 1864, when he was about eighteen years old. His older brother Jim, later Dr. James D. Wagner, of Selma, Calif., who had been in the army since the first year of the war, came home to secure another mount, and Will at once began making preparations to go back with him. A short time before this his heart had been deeply stirred with indignation at seeing one of a band of Federal soldiers shove his mother down while she was begging him not to take a work animal which was needed on the place and which the soldier had just taken from the plow—both the soldier and his captain laughing as his mother fell. He needed no more to fix in his heart a firm resolution to join the Confederate army at the first opportunity, "determined to kill as many Yankees as he could."

They slipped out and reached his brother's command, which he at once joined, Company G, under command of Capt. Jim W. Irven, of the 1st Confederate Cavalry. This had been under Gen. Joe Wheeler up to this time, but was now stationed at Lexington, West Tennessee, under command of

General Forrest. They served together for the rest of the war under this indomitable leader, engaging in many hard marches, raids, and battles, and enduring all the attendant hardships during the winter and spring. Once his comrades thought he was killed when a shell hit the wall of a fort just below him and exploded; but he came out of the smoke unhurt. They surrendered to General Canby, at Gainesville, Ala., May 11, 1865.

Young Wagner returned home and to work, both witnessing and enduring the ills of reconstruction and carpetbag [that is, Liberal-socialist] rule in his [Conservative] community. But here again he manfully and bravely, with honor and self-restraint, bore his part in the "Invisible Empire,"[594] and in other ways seeking to ameliorate those intolerable conditions under which his community, and the whole South, suffered at that time.

In 1868, he went [by] horseback to Titus County, Tex., where he remained about two years. He returned to Tennessee on horseback, and, January 4, 1871, married Annie Josephine Walker. He engaged in farming until the fall of 1874, when he again went to Texas, this time driving through in a wagon part of the way. His young wife, with her two sons, soon joined him, by rail, at Bonham. They farmed four years in Hunt, Montague, and Parker counties, enduring the many hardships and privations incident to the life of pioneers. In 1879, they settled on a farm which he bought near Newport in Clay County, where they remained eight years. He then ran a mail hack line for a short time, after which he engaged in the mercantile business in Post Oak, Newport, and Vashti during the period from 1890 to 1905. His hearing having become impaired, he retired and lived at Bowie for over seven years, where he became an active member of John C. Pelham Camp, U.C.V. In January of 1913, he moved to a farm in Limestone County, near Kosse, where he lived till his death.

His first wife, a woman of fine Christian ideals and rare mental endowment, was called from his side in 1888. Ten children were born from this union, of whom five are living and present during his last illness. In 1890, he married Mrs. Ellen R. Spikes, who was a devoted Christian and wife, a faithful mother to his children, and who survives him.

He became a Christian in boyhood and joined the Methodist Church, but spent most of his life in the Presbyterian Church as a ruling elder. He was also a Mason, and from his youth up his life was one of singular purity in speech and morals. He always stood firmly for his convictions as to right, truth, and progress in community, Church, and State, yet was kind and considerate to all. The firm discipline which he maintained in his family was always tempered with love, and made effective by a good example and sincere religious instruction.

He was a patriotic and loyal citizen at all times, and ever true to the memories, ideals, and principles of the Southern cause [conservatism], and loved dearly to be with the old comrades in reunions, which he attended when possible. The most impressive sentiment he was ever heard to express was this: "The two things in my whole life that I remember with greatest satisfaction, apart from my family, are, first, that I became a Christian in my youth; and, second, that it was my privilege to serve as a Confederate soldier."[595]

WALKER, J. H.: J. H. Walker, aged eighty years, died it his home, near Springfield, Ky., after a long illness. He was a son of the late D. C. and Martha Grundy Walker, a prominent Kentucky family. His early youth was spent in Washington County, but while yet a mere boy he went to Canton, Miss., where he studied medicine under an older brother. While in that city the war broke out, and he enlisted in the Confederate army in 1862, serving with distinction under Colonel Adams in General Lee's division and General Forrest's corps.

At the close of the war he was mustered out of the army and returned to his native county, engaging in general farming, in which he was very successful.

On September 26, 1888, he was united in marriage with Miss Josephine Howe, of Washington County, which union was blessed with three children.

Few men bore a wider acquaintance or were more universally liked than Dr. Walker, as he was familiarly known, although he never engaged in active practice. He was a pleasant talker and delighted in relating his experiences during the War between the States. His wife, two sons, and a daughter survive him.[596]

WALKER, WILLIAM B.: Col. William B. Walker died at his home, in Brandon, Miss., on August 20, 1908, in the sixty-second year of his age. He was born in Canton, Miss., in 1846, his father being the Rev. Dr. J. R. Walker, a distinguished Methodist divine. At the age of seventeen years William Walker joined the 4th Mississippi Cavalry, and fought under Forrest till the close of the war as a private. He was a true and devoted soldier, never known to shirk a duty nor flinch under fire. He was an efficient soldier, besides doing the most arduous scout duty, for which he was admirably fitted.

After the war he went to New Orleans, engaging in reportorial work on the leading papers, becoming later editor in chief of the *Picayune*, which failing health forced him to resign, though he retained a position as correspondent for this journal up to his death. During the dark days of reconstruction his trenchant pen was a power in the land, and his influence was felt in the highest places. Here again did he render conspicuous service to his country.

In 1887 Comrade Walker married Miss Julia Jayne, of Brandon, Miss., a fitting companion for this brilliant writer. In 1889 he removed to Brandon, and had resided there since that time. He was honored and respected, and he was recognized as one of the most accomplished scholars of his State and a genial, loving gentleman "of the old school." Though possessed of a store of learning, he was not pedantic, but was modest and retiring. He was wholly unselfish, and wrought alone for his family, to whom he was devoted.[597]

WALL, ROBERT BRUCE: Robert Bruce Wall, a member of Stonewall Jackson Bivouac of McKenzie, Tenn., was born in Dover (Fort Donelson), Stewart County, Tenn.; and died January 27, 1909. He enlisted in Gould's company D, Forrest's Regiment, in 1861. By some mishap Gould's company failed to receive orders that General Forrest was going out, and the captain ordered his company to escape if possible and report to him in Texas. In the darkness and confusion this company had not received the order or failed to understand, and so were left behind and were being surrounded by the enemy.

Robert Wall looked about him with despair in his heart and with a prison in view. Looking to the right, he saw that the place was familiar from boyhood. He had new scenes, however. Long lines of glittering bayonets were rapidly approaching. He turned toward the river and saw the approach of the gunboats. Looking down the bank, he saw a flatboat containing Confederates pushing out into the river. With strength born of despair, he leaped far out, reached the boat, and escaped by crossing the river. At a farmhouse he found rest, food, and friends. Resting by day and traveling by night, he reached his home, in Henry County.

After a few days he mounted a splendid horse which had been presented to him by friends who knew his worth as a true soldier and started on his lonely journey to a distant Texas town to join those of his company who had escaped. A letter written at Atchafalaya, La., and dated July, 1864, states: "I am writing by the light of the camp fire, while my comrades lie sleeping around me. The first dawn of peace will see me on my way home. The thought of that time thrills me with feelings beyond description. Yet as long as a man remains in the field I too will be there."[598]

WALTHALL, EDWARD CAREY: Edward Carey Walthall, senior Senator from Mississippi and late major-general in Stewart's Corps, Army of Tennessee, C.S.A., died in Washington, D.C., at 5:30 p.m. April 21, 1898. This announcement will create much genuine sorrow. He was one of the most distinguished and best-beloved public men of the day.

He was born in Richmond, Va., April 4, 1831; received an academic education at Holly Springs, Miss.; studied law there, and was admitted to the bar in 1852. He commenced the practise the same year in Coffeeville, Miss. Was elected in 1856 District Attorney of the Tenth Judicial District, and was reelected in 1859. He resigned that office in the spring of 1861, and entered the Confederate service as a lieutenant in the Fifteenth Mississippi Regiment; was soon afterward elected lieutenant-colonel of that regiment. In the spring of 1862 he was elected colonel of the Twenty-Ninth Mississippi Regiment; was promoted to brigadier-general in December, 1862, and major-general in June, 1864.

Edward Carey Walthall.

After the war he practised law at Coffeeville until January, 1871, when he removed to Grenada, and continued the practise until March, 1885. He was a delegate at large to the National Democratic [then the Conservative party]

Convention in 1868, 1876, 1880, 1884, 1892, and 1896 [the latter year in which the Democrats became the Liberal party and the Republicans became the Conservative Party],[599] being chairman of the Mississippi delegation and one of the Vice-Presidents of the convention of 1868. He was appointed to the United States Senate as a Democrat to fill the vacancy caused by the resignation of Hon. L. Q. C. Lamar, who was appointed Secretary of the Interior, taking his seat March 12, 1885. He was elected by the Legislature in January, 1886, for the unexpired term; was reelected in January, 1888, and again in 1892. His present term of service will expire in 1901.

In the year 1839, while he was yet a lad, his family (of the old Virginia line), seeking to repair reverses of fortune, found a home in Holly Springs, Miss., then a frontier town, but settled by educated and refined people. With limited education, but with rare natural gifts and high purpose, he began the study of the law. Obtaining a license in 1852 and locating at Coffeeville, Miss., he at once entered upon a successful practise, in which he continued until the beginning of the war, in 1861. At the call to arms he enlisted as lieutenant in the Fifteenth Mississippi Infantry, but was soon after elected lieutenant-colonel, being in command. In the regiment's first bloody encounter, at the battle of Fishing Creek, where the fall, through treachery, of the lamented Zollicoffer threw the Confederate forces into confusion, they were only saved from disaster by the gallant stand of the Fifteenth under the rally and superior military ability of their leader.

In the spring of 1862 he was elected colonel of the Twenty-Ninth Mississippi Regiment, forming a part of the advance in Bragg's campaign into Kentucky, and taking part in Chalmers' desperate and much-criticized assault upon Munfordville, where so many valiant Mississippians found bloody graves, and sharing in all of the struggles of that swift and eventful march.

In December of that year (1862) he was promoted to the rank of brigadier-general, having assigned to him the Twenty-Fourth, Twenty-Seventh, Twenty-Ninth, Thirtieth, and Thirty-Fourth Mississippi Regiments, known to the end of the war as Walthall's Brigade, and having a fighting record unsurpassed by any other command of the Western army. With this brigade and one other Gen. Walthall held Lookout Mountain against Hooker's heavy corps during the whole day and far into the night, inflicting serious loss, as, rock by rock, he yielded a position untenable before such superior numbers. In like manner, when the Federal columns in successive lines charged the attenuated lines on Missionary Ridge, he did not withdraw until after support had been driven from right and left, and, although painfully wounded, being disabled for many weeks afterward, kept his saddle until after nightfall, when the army withdrew in an orderly manner.

It was in these trying moments that his conspicuous gallantry, his commanding presence, and his cool encouragement inspired deeds of valor that make up the matchless record of the men and their leader.

At Chickamauga, as part of what was organized as a reserve division under Walker, this brigade opened the fight at Alexander's Bridge, capturing a battery early in the engagement; and during the days of combat on this famous field no individual command contributed more in securing the victory than the Mississippians.

Promoted to major-general in June, 1864, Gen. Walthall was in active field service until the close of the war, his division forming a part of Hood's army when he hurried from Georgia into Tennessee, and being in the fateful charge upon the breastworks at Franklin, one of the deadliest of all the sad stories of the war.

When this campaign ended in disaster before Nashville, and the broken ranks turned in retreat toward a place of safety beyond the Tennessee River, Gen. Walthall was assigned to the command of a meager force of eight skeleton brigades, numbering scarcely three thousand men, charged with the duty of covering the retreat, but destined, as was supposed, to certain capture. It was when tendered this perilous post that he made the prompt and characteristic reply: "Make your order, Gen. Hood. I never sought a hard place for glory nor a soft place for comfort." With the assistance of Forrest and his cavalry, the pursuing force, largely preponderating in numbers, was successfully held in check through days of fierce encounter and nights of vigil, the shattered army, with all of its trains, and also the protecting rear-guard, with its trophies of several captured guns, reaching the south bank of the Tennessee in safety.

The hurry of events in the closing struggle speedily carried the remnant of Hood's forces to the assistance of Gen. Johnston, in the East, and in the early spring Gen. Walthall fought in his last battle at Cole's Farm, near Bentonville, N.C. In a letter written since his death his distinguished corps commander gives this vivid description of the engagement: "The enemy, in overwhelming numbers, was upon us. A cannon-shot struck the horse of Reynolds, of Arkansas, in the chest, plowed its way through his body, and took off the left leg of his rider, who could not repress an exclamation of pain. Immediately in our front lay Walthall's Division, at the edge of an open field, and it was my lot to send them forward to the encounter. It was an inspiring sight, witnessed by many brave men, some of high rank, to see the firm, steady lines, their intrepid commander, in whom all had unbounded confidence, towering above them on his own horse, advancing under a shower of bullets into the storm of battle. The enemy gave way before their invincible attack. I love to think of Gen. Walthall as he appeared on that occasion."

His sword sheathed, Gen. Walthall resumed the practise of his profession at Coffeeville, Miss., removing later to Grenada, accepting the position of General Attorney for the Mississippi Central Railroad Company and of the subsequent great system of which it became a part. In directing the legal department of these vast and valuable interests he took rank with the great corporation lawyers of the day.

Though never seeking or holding political office prior to 1885, he was a stanch [meaning staunch] party man of the Democratic [then Conservative] faith, prominent in council, as is shown by his attendance as chairman of his state delegation upon every National Democratic Convention from 1868 to

1896 inclusive. Upon the resignation of Hon. L. Q. C. Lamar, his intimate friend, to assume the duties of Secretary of the Interior in Mr. [Grover] Cleveland's cabinet, Gen. Walthall was appointed by Gov. Lowry to fill the unexpired term, taking his seat in the United States Senate on March 12, 1885. This seat he held by successive elections, without opposition, to the day of his death, with the exception of fourteen months of one term, when he resigned, because of ill health, but returned to his place the following year. His career in the Senate is a part of the current history of the nation, his standing and influence and the personal esteem in which he was held being evidenced by the fact that he was the first of the Senators from the South after the war to be honored with the appointment of chairman of the Senate Committee on Military Affairs.

Superb in his mental, moral, and physical endowments, he had no occasion for ambitions. With a cool head and a warm heart, fully equipped, when duties were laid upon him he discharged them with courage and promptness. When honors were bestowed he wore them with dignity and grace.

His garments are empty. He rests where his childhood and youth were spent, under the dews that make green the graves of his kindred. It may be permitted one who has stood near him through all the happenings of his days to say that he was a man who dwelt upon the summit of life, walking always in the light—that light under which no virtue fails to shine forth, no blemish fails to grow blacker. With him there was no blot to darken, no reflection that did not give back warmth and radiance. He was true to all the ties that make home sacred, to all the bonds that guard friendship as a treasure, to all the duties that in their fulfilment ennoble life. "He serves all who dares be true."[600]

WARD, FRANK F.: Frank F. Ward, born in Wadesborough, Ky., January 28, 1845, died on October 3, 1928, after a long illness, aged eighty-three years. He enlisted in the Confederate army under General Forrest, and the captain of his company was his brother, Rufus K. Ward. He was regularly discharged from the army after the surrender of General Lee and returned to his home. In July, 1873, he was married to Miss Lily Brown, formerly of Mississippi, and settled near Conyersville, Tenn. Twelve children were born to them, of whom four sons and two daughters survive him, also five grandchildren.

Comrade Ward joined the Methodist Church some forty years ago and remained a faithful member of the Church at Conyersville to his death. He was known throughout the whole country as an earnest Christian. He had long been a member of the Fitzgerald-Kendall Camp, U.C.V., at Paris, Tenn., though prevented by illness from participating in its activities for some years. He laid down the implements of war in 1865 and resumed the paths of peace, and after life's fitful journey, beset with numerous difficulties, he sleeps well.[601]

WARDLAW, ZACK: Gen. Zack Wardlaw, commanding the 3rd Brigade of the Mississippi Division, U.C.V., died on May 10, 1928, at Little Rock, Ark. He was born December 22, 1844, in Warren County, Miss., and in July, 1861, as a sixteen-year-old boy, he answered his country's call and enlisted in the Hinds County Guards, which was afterwards Company B, of the 22nd Mississippi Regiment. His company was in the terrible winter campaign of Kentucky when, for several months, measles, mumps, pneumonia, and the dread contagious spinal meningitis reduced the regiment to less than half its fighting force. The hardships at this time were more demoralizing than in the final campaign in Georgia, for there was not shelter from the intense cold of a Kentucky winter, not sufficiently warm clothing to protect them, and, in addition, they were not inured to hardships of any kind.

Zack Wardlaw.

From the battle of Shiloh, in which the company had a part, until the last gallant charge at Bentonville, N.C., March 19, 1865, the company was in as constant fighting as any Mississippi command in the Confederate service, and won as much renown. Perhaps the greatest compliment was in being selected as members of Featherston's Brigade, by General Walthall, when he picked his men at Columbia, Tenn., December 20, 1864, to act as rearguard infantry for the retreating army. With Forrest's Cavalry, this company remained in the face of the enemy until the rest of the army had gained two-days start. On the retreat they were in battle with their pursuers at Albany Hill and Sugar Creek. So close was the enemy that no time could be spent in cooking, so for three days they lived on hard-tack and raw bacon. Very little sleep was to be had, and each morning, when reveille sounded, the whole army was found covered with snow. Many of the soldiers were ragged, and some barefooted, yet they waded the Tennessee River. Zack Wardlaw used to say: "Forrest marched us just like we were horses, and we kept up with his horses, too."

No private ever more deserved the honor of being a brigadier general in the U.C.V. organization than did Zack Wardlaw, yet when he donned his uniform of general, he said to a friend: "I did not win these stars; I was only a private. They are just an honor."

Since the war his activities and relations had been many and varied. For years he was a member of the Board of Trustees of Mississippi College, faithful to attend every meeting possible. During the Whitfield administration, he served Hinds County in the legislature. He had been for many years a deacon in the Utica Baptist Church, and its interests were his delight.

The first impression he always made on strangers was his gentlemanly bearing. It was a delight to be in his home and enjoy his fellowship. Soon after the war, he married Miss Laura Cook, from the home of her sister, Mrs. W. T. Ratliff, at Raymond. To this union two daughters and a son were born, the latter dying several years ago. His second wife was Mrs. Mahan, of St. Louis,

Mo., a former resident of Utica, who preceded him in death less than a year.

While attending the Confederate reunion at Little Rock, Ark., in his office as Commander of the 3rd Mississippi Brigade, U.C.V., he slipped on the marble stairway at Hotel Marion, striking his head on the sharp edge of the step, from which injury he never regained consciousness, dying shortly afterwards.[602]

WARREN, WALTER M.: The committee appointed by W. B. Plemons Camp, No. 1451, U.C.V., to present memorial resolutions upon the death of Capt. Walter M. Warren, whose death occurred at his home, in Amarillo, Tex., on October 12, 1917, reported the following: "In May, 1861, Walter M. Warren enlisted in Company D, 3rd Tennessee Infantry, C.S.A., and after two years' service rose to the rank of first lieutenant. He was captured at Fort Donelson and taken to Camp Douglas Prison, but made his escape the following June, reached the South by rail, and joined Forrest. In the battle of Murfreesboro he was wounded by a Minie ball passing through the upper portion of the right lung and was again captured; but on his way from Triune to Nashville he again escaped and rejoined Forrest at Gainesville, Ala., where he first heard of the surrender.

Walter M. Warren.

"His first wife died in 1906, and in November, 1910, he was married at Wichita Falls, Tex., to Mrs. Nora Bynum, who survives him.

"The *Sunday Bulletin* of the Methodist Church, of which he was a member, contributed to his memory the following: 'We regret deeply to announce the death of Captain Warren. His passing came after along life of useful years, many of which were spent in Amarillo, and all of us have loved him as a father. 'And they shall see his face; and his name shalt be in their foreheads. And there shall be no night there; and they need no candle, neither light of the sun; for the Lord God giveth them light; and they shall reign forever and ever.'

"Whereas the all-wise Maker and Ruler of all things has taken from us our beloved comrade, as we bow in humble submission to the will of God we wish to leave upon record a testimonial of the love and esteem we held for him—his unswerving devotion to duty in all the walks of life, his fearless and undaunted bravery as a Confederate soldier *in defense of the Constitution and the rights of the States*, his loyalty to his Church, and his Christian virtues. All who knew him loved him. He was honorable, noble, true, and brave."[603]

WATKINS, GEORGE W.: George W. Watkins, of Rhome, Tex., died on the 15th of December [1907?]. He was born in Trigg County, Ky., in 1842. He volunteered in August, 1861, in Company B, 8th Kentucky Infantry, and was wounded twice at Baker's Creek, Miss. He was present and saw General

Tilghman killed in that battle. He was under General Forrest in mounted infantry at the battle of Harrisburg and Tupelo, Miss, where he was severely wounded. He was carried to the hospital at Lauderdale, Miss, thence to Gainesville, Ala., where he was discharged from the service on account of his wounds.[604]

WATSON, MACK G.: Mack G. Watson, who served through the war under Gen. Nathan Bedford Forrest, died in Nashville, Tenn., on March 11 [1931?]. He had reached the advanced age of ninety-one years in the enjoyment of good health to the last. Death came suddenly and his passing was peaceful.

Comrade Watson had been always interested in the activities of the United Confederate Veterans, and had attended many reunions. His erect soldierly bearing was a distinguishing characteristic. He was one of the last survivors of that famous fighting force immortalized in its service to the Confederacy as Forrest's command, and was widely known among the thinning ranks of Confederate veterans. He was born in Shelbyville in 1839, and was reared there. As a youth of twenty, he, with his older brother, ran away and enlisted in Forrest's forces at the outset of the war; he fought throughout the conflict.

He was a wood turner by trade and came to Nashville a few years after the war, and for many years was connected with a leading firm of this city dealing in wooden ware. Comrade Watson had never married, and lived with the family of his brother in the Watson home in Nashville. Surviving him are three nieces, four nephews, and a number of grand-nieces and nephews. Burial was in Mt. Olivet Cemetery, Nashville.[605]

WATSON, WILLIAM FONTAINE: William Fontaine Watson, son of Dr. Overton D. Watson, was born in Lauderdale County, Ala., on January 15, 1842, and died at the Kentucky Confederate Home on March 1, 1921. His mother was Miss Annie Dickson. A sister and a brother, Miss Sene W. Watson, of Richmond, Va., and L. D. Watson, of Nashville, Tenn., survive him. He became a member of the Christian Church shortly after the War between the States and was a faithful attendant on its services for many years.

William Watson enlisted in Company F, 4th Alabama Cavalry, in 1862—Col. W. C. Johnson's regiment of Roddy's Brigade—and served under General Forrest up to the surrender. His record as a soldier is without stain. He was faithful, brave, and true, never shirked a duty, and was ever ready to go when called upon. He loved the cause for which he so valiantly fought.

Comrade Watson was an inmate for many years of the Kentucky Confederate Home and was very popular with the comrades there. Everybody liked "Billy" Watson, as he was familiarly called, and he is greatly missed.[606]

WEAKLEY, RICHARD WATSON: R. W. Weakley was born July 24, 1841; and died March 29, 1910, at Nashville, Tenn. He was the son of Dr. B. F. and Mary E. Weakley. He was educated in the Davidson County schools. In 1858 he entered Wesleyan University, Florence, Ala., and graduated in June, 1860.

Soon after the War between the States came on he entered the company of Capt. H. J. Cheney, Company C, Bate's 2nd Tennessee Regiment, and was elected lieutenant of the company. The command was sent at once to Virginia, and served along the Potomac for the first year. The command reenlisted for the war, and was transferred to the Western Army and fought at Shiloh. He left his old command after going to the Western Army, and joined Capt. James Briton's "Cedar Snags," Col. Baxter Smith's 4th Cavalry Regiment, serving under Wheeler and Forrest until the surrender in North Carolina.

The war over, he returned to his home, in Nashville, Tenn., and assumed the duties of citizenship. For many years he was Superintendent of Education for Davidson County. Afterwards he was associated with Dr. John H. Callender at the Tennessee State Asylum for Insane. He was Deputy County Trustee under W. B. Clark.

After the death of his father, he returned to the old home to look after the farm and his mother and sisters. He spent the remainder of his life leading a gentle and quiet time in the bosom of his loved ones. He had no taste for political life, and was possessed of qualities and abilities that would have honored high positions of trust and honor. He was a man of splendid education, and took great pleasure in reading and literary pursuits. He was a true, brave, and loyal Confederate soldier, and has left a record worthy of imitation. He was a member of a large family of brothers and two sisters. He never married. In Mount Olivet Cemetery he rests among those of his family who have "crossed over."[607]

WEATHERLY, W. M.: W. M. Weatherley [died in 1925 and was] ninety years old; Tennessee, Forrest's command.[608]

WEEMS, ROBERT D.: Robert D. Weems, of Company F, 2nd Mississippi Cavalry, Armstrong's Brigade, Forrest's Cavalry, died at Shubuta, Miss., on January 22 [1908?], aged seventy-eight years. He served through the war and was paroled at Gainesville, Ala.[609]

WHARTON, JOHN AUSTIN: John A. Wharton was born July 3, 1828, outside the city of Nashville, Tenn. He and his father soon removed to Texas, where he attended school and practiced law until becoming a member of the state's secession convention in 1861.

He was made captain of a company in Terry's Texas Rangers, assuming full command after the death of Colonel B. F. Terry. Comrade Wharton fought at Shiloh and was in the Kentucky campaign of 1862. Promoted to brigadier general that year, he went on to serve under Wheeler and Forrest, and was present at the Battles of Murfreesboro and Chickamauga. Now a major general, he was moved to General Richard Taylor's command as head of cavalry, serving out the War in the Red River campaign, and finally in the department of the Trans-Mississippi.

General Wharton's death was tragic: on April 6, 1865, in a Houston hotel room, he became involved in a heated argument with Confederate Col. George W. Baylor. After slapping Baylor and calling him a "liar," Baylor drew his pistol and shot the unarmed Wharton, who was later buried at Austin.[610]

WHISENANT, JACOB W.: . . . Jacob W. Whisenant [was] captain of Company C, 2nd Alabama Cavalry, under Forrest. . .[611]

WHITAKER, WILLIAM BURTON: W. B. Whitaker, a prominent citizen of Meridian, Miss., died at his home there on July 8, 1916. Representatives of Walthall Camp, U.C.V., of Meridian, of which he was a member, and of both Chapters, U.D.C., were present at the funeral, and the red and white of the Confederacy was largely in evidence in the many beautiful floral tributes.

William Burton Whitaker was born in Orange County, near Raleigh, N.C., February 18, 1840. Later he went to Tennessee, and just at the close of the war he was married to Miss Mary Simpson, of Purdy, Tenn. His married life was spent in Tupelo, Miss., and the last twelve years in Meridian. He was mustered into the service of the Confederacy under Jefferson Forrest and after the death of the latter served under Gen. N. B. Forrest until the close of the war, being one of the advance guard of this noted cavalry leader. At one time, while stationed near a Northern regiment at Fort Pillow, one of the Northern soldiers dared young Whitaker to come and take the Stars and Stripes that was flying from the fort. Whitaker answered: "You wait, and I'll do it." When the fighting began, the daring soldier did capture the colors. President Davis wrote offering to make him a lieutenant for his bravery, but, ever modest and reserved, he declined the honor and told his chieftain that he preferred to remain in the ranks as a private soldier.

It is with pride that his family tells of their father's great love for General Forrest, and his record as a soldier under that great leader is a precious heritage to them.[612]

Benjamin Franklin White.

WHITE, BENJAMIN FRANKLIN: Benjamin Franklin White was born in New Berne, N.C., and finished his education at the Western Military Institute, at Nashville, Tenn. Immediately after the declaration of war, in May, 1861, he resigned his position as Assistant Secretary of the Memphis Gas Company and raised a company of infantry, the Tennessee Guards, by whom he was elected captain. This company left Memphis in Col. Neely's Regiment, of Gen. Pillow's command. After serving in the infantry for some time, Capt. White joined the cavalry under Gen. Forrest, who detailed him to raise a company of light artillery. This he did, and commanded it until the battle of Chickamauga, when he was promoted on the field and given command of a battalion of artillery in Gen. Wheeler's Cavalry. Capt. White took part in every fight in which his company was engaged, but was never wounded, though he had several horses shot under him and numerous bullet holes made in his clothes. He was captured at the battle of Murfreesboro, but was so ill from rheumatism that he was placed in a private house under guard. From this place, with the aid of *his faithful negro* servant, he made his escape.

When Gen. Stoneman was captured near Macon, Ga., Capt. White was in command of the artillery of Wheeler's Division, and was presented with a handsome pair of field glasses by the artillery officers under Stoneman. These glasses are now in possession of Mrs. Charles B. Ryland, his daughter, residing in San Jose, Cal. A few months before the final surrender Capt. White was so crippled from rheumatism that he was assigned to post duty and made commandant of the post at Albany, Ga.

He was married at Dalton, Ga., in January, 1864, to Miss Fannie Owings Ballard, of Memphis, Tenn., daughter of the late S. O. Ballard, collector of customs at that port at the time of his death. Capt. White returned to Memphis, where he lived a number of years, removing thence to San Francisco, Cal. His death occurred February 14, 1897. He left a widow and five children.[613]

WHITE, JOHN BENNETT: Dr. J. B. White, the son of William White, was born in 1844 at the old White homestead, near Franklin, Tenn. He was educated at the University of Tennessee. He practiced medicine for a time, but the greater part of his life was spent in the drug business. He was a member of the Presbyterian Church for nearly half of his life.

When a boy of sixteen he went to Mississippi and joined General Chalmers's escort, and he rode with Forrest, the "Wizard of the Saddle." He joined the Cheatham Bivouac in Nashville twenty-seven years ago and took an active interest in everything pertaining to the Confederacy. Loyal and faithful to the cause for which he fought, his last thoughts were of his comrades. He requested that he be buried in his uniform of gray. He died September 25, 1910. The funeral services were conducted at the residence by Rev. W. T. Haggard on Tuesday morning, the veterans taking charge of the remains at the grave.

Dr. White was married in 1877 to Miss Sue Webb, of College Grove, daughter of Dr. Samuel Webb and Adelaide Battle. His wife and their only children, Dr. Sam White and Mrs. James Henderson, survive.[614]

WHITE, R. L. C.: Dr. R. L. C. White was born in Lebanon, Tenn., in 1844; and died in Nashville in October, 1909. He began his education at Cumberland University in his native town. In 1862 he enlisted in the Confederate service under Col. Paul Anderson. His company, famous as the "Cedar Snags," served for a time as escort to Gen. N. B. Forrest and Gen. John B. Hood, and did some of the hard fighting of the war.

After the surrender Dr. White finished his literary course at Cumberland University and began the study of medicine, attending the University of Nashville and later the Jefferson Medical College at Philadelphia. He began the practice of medicine, but it was uncongenial to him.

Soon afterwards he began his career as a writer through contributions to the *Nashville Banner*, using the pen name of "Paul Crimson." He became editor of the *Lebanon Herald*, where his beautiful use of pure English and critical faculty won him high reputation which his subsequent work along literary lines increased. He was much interested in fraternal orders, was a Thirty-Second Degree Mason, a Shriner and Odd fellow, and was the Grand Keeper of Records and Seal for the Knights of Pythias for twenty-two years in succession.

He was the leading spirit of the Tennessee Press Association for many years. He was a charter member and wrote the Constitution of the Nashville Press Club. He was a trustee both of the Howard Library (afterwards the Carnegie) and the University of Nashville. He possessed so accurate a memory that he could detect the slightest divergence in a quotation. He had decided poetic gifts, and the small volume of verse he published for his friends possessed great merit. His wife and five children survive him.[615]

WHITE, WILLIAM HENRY: On December 20, 1929, Rev. William Henry White, veteran preacher and teacher, died at his home in Brownwood, Tex., aged eighty-five years. He was a native of Rutherford County, Tenn., born November 16, 1844.

His early years were spent in Tennessee, but the family removed to Kentucky before he had reached manhood's estate, and from that State he enlisted in the Confederate army, serving with Company E, 12th Kentucky Cavalry, commanded by N. B. Forrest. He was in several important battles and had many narrow escapes. In late years he was a prominent member of the U.C.V. Camp at Brownwood and a high officer in the Mountain Remnant Brigade.

In January, 1870, he was married to Miss Sarah C. Burns in Rutherford County, and of the three children born to them a son and a daughter survive him. His second wife was Miss Martha Adelaide Christopher, of Murfreesboro, Tenn., and of this union also a son and daughter survive. In 1924, he was married to Mrs. Mary Elizabeth Curtis, of Brownwood, Tex., who was his faithful companion to the end.

In early life, Comrade White joined the Cumberland Presbyterian Church, and for sixty years served it as minister. He was known for his outstanding scholarship. He was a graduate of Kentucky Teacher's Normal, Concord College, Southwestern University in Tennessee, and Cumberland University, holding degrees from these institutions. To secure this educational training, he worked his way through school, teaching, preaching, and doing night work.

He founded and served as President of Turrentine Academy in Bedford County, Tenn., and after going to Texas, about 1880, was the first president of the College at Buffalo Gap; he also taught in the public schools of this county.

Moving to Brownwood, in 1903, his life there was quietly spent in work and service for the Master. He had held a number of important pastorates for his Church over the State of Texas and in Tennessee, and devoted much time to outpost work in home mission territory.

Death came gently in the advancing weakness of age, and he calmly waited for that clear call to a higher service in the "land beyond."[616]

WHITTLE, R. M.: R. M Whittle, born in Alabama in 1845, was taken by his parents to Alcorn County, Miss., while a small child. When the War between the States began, he enlisted for the South, serving with the 11th Mississippi Cavalry under Gen. N. B. Forrest, making a fearless soldier, always at his post, always cheerful.

After the war, he removed to Van Alstyne, Tex., where he remained until his death, July 24, 1907. Comrade Whittle was never married.[617]

WILHOITE, WILLIAM MONROE: William Monroe Wilhoite, a prominent Confederate veteran of Jefferson County, Ky., died at his home near Buechel, Ky., on August 14, 1928, after a long illness. He celebrated his ninety-first birthday on July 9, having been born in Oldham County in 1837.

Young Wilhoite joined the Confederate army and fought throughout the War between the States, except for a brief interval when incapacitated from a wound he received in the battle of Perryville. During that memorable battle, he witnessed the death of a brother who was fighting by his side. His command served under Generals Forrest and Butler.

At the close of the war, Comrade Wilhoite returned to Oldham County, Ky., and engaged in farming. In October, 1866, he was married to Miss Louisiana Crum, and they made their home near Crestwood until 1878, when he purchased a tract of land near Buechel, to which he added from time to time, and at his death was one of the largest land owners in Jefferson County.

He is survived by two sons, a daughter, five grandchildren, and five great-grandchildren. He was buried in the Pleasant Hill Cemetery, near Crestwood, in Oldham County.[618]

WILKERSON, THOMAS O.: Thomas O. Wilkerson was born February 15, 1845, and died September 22, 1902.

In 1863 he enlisted in Company E, of Forrest's old regiment, and remained with it to the end, never missing a roll call or a duty. In 1865 only some seven or eight were left to return to their devastated homes.

Comrade Wilkerson was faithful to duty in all relations of life. He was buried by the Masons, of which he was a prominent member in his community. A wife and daughter survive him. His home was at Whiteville, Tenn.[619]

WILKES, NIM: Nim Wilkes was one of the 65 African-Americans who served in Forrest's Cavalry; he was a teamster. He applied for a Confederate pension in 1915.[620]

James Williams.

WILLIAMS, JAMES: James Williams, Assistant Secretary Shiloh Battlefield Association, lives at Savannah, Tenn. He enlisted as a private in Robertson's Cavalry, Nov., 1861, which company served in Col. R. H. Brewer's Battalion at Shiloh through the two days' battles. It was re-organized at Spring Creek, Tenn., and commanded by Col. Thomas Claiburne and other officers. It was known as the first Confederate Cavalry. Young Williams was appointed Ordinance Sergeant at Murfreesboro in 1863, and was afterwards commissioned as such by President Davis at Dalton, Ga., 1864. He served with the gallant Gen. Joseph Wheeler, in rear of the Federal lines, and was in the battles from Chattanooga to Atlanta, and with Gen. Hood in his march to Tennessee. Transferred to Gen. Forrest, January, 1865, and surrendered at Gainesville, Ala., May 11, 1865. Comrade Williams spent his last Confederate dollar, that would go, for a small fishhook.[621]

WILLINGHAM, WILLIAM J.: William J. Willingham entered the Confederate army at the beginning of the war in Company E, 12th Tennessee Infantry, and participated with that regiment in the battles of Belmont, Mo., and Shiloh, Tenn.

At the reorganization of the army in June, 1864, Company E, being composed entirely of Kentuckians, [he] was transferred to the 3rd Kentucky Infantry, and became Company L thereof, serving in the infantry until March 15, 1864, when the men were mounted and assigned to General Forrest's cavalry, with which it served until the end, in May, 1865. That regiment, with the 7th, 8th, and 12th Kentucky Regiments, constituted the Kentucky brigade of Forrest's Cavalry. This brigade participated thenceforth in all the battles of that command.

In addition to Belmont and Shiloh, Comrade Willingham was in the battles of Bolivar, Davis's Mill, Corinth, Hatchy Bridge, Coffeyville, Champion Hill, Jackson, Vicksburg, Paducah, Brice's Crossroads, Harrisburg, Old Tom Creek, the raid into Middle Tennessee during September, 1864, and all the battles incident to Hood's Nashville campaign in the winter of 1864, Lawrenceburg, Shoal Creek, Campbellville, Spring Hill, Franklin, Nashville, Murfreesboro, and in the rear of Hood's Infantry on that fearful retreat. Comrade Willingham seldom missed a roll call, and never

William J. Willingham.

missed a battle. He became first sergeant, and was esteemed by the entire regiment. He attended all the general Reunions, and cherished with felicitous pride the many achievements attained by Forrest's Cavalry.[622]

WILSON, WILLIAM HENRY: William H. Wilson died on August 21, 1922, at his home in Opelousas, La., after an illness of several months. He was born in New Orleans, March 19, 1846. His parents removed to Mississippi when the New Orleans and Jackson Great Northern Railroad was being built, and his father built the first store in Summit, Miss. Just after the War between the States they went to St. Landry Parish, La.

Comrade Wilson joined the Confederate army as a young boy, becoming a member of Company I, 4th Mississippi Cavalry, then in Wirt Adams's Brigade, afterwards Mabry's, then Stark's Brigade, Chalmer's Division, Forrest's Cavalry; and he was paroled at Gainesville, Ala., May 15, 1865. He participated in the battles of Johnsonville, Tenn., Brice's Crossroads, Batesville, Tupelo, Harrisonburg, Miss., and others.

"Uncle Billie," as he was called, led a consistent Christian life, a member of the Presbyterian Church, loved and respected by all who knew him. He was the last of my old comrades living in this section; we lived near each other in Mississippi. A good man has gone to rest under the shade of the trees, and we miss him from our midst.[623]

WINFREE, WILLIAM POWHATAN: Judge William Powhatan Winfree, who died at Hopkinsville, Ky., on March 8 [1923], was of French descent, his progenitors having sought refuge in America after the massacre of St. Bartholomew. They settled in Powhatan County, Va., about thirty miles from where Richmond now stands, and members of the family were in the Revolutionary ranks. On his mother's side he was of English blood, the Atkinson family. He was born January 28, 1843, the first of fourteen children. His father moved to Tennessee, and soon after to Christian County, Ky., where for the rest of their lives their interests have been identified with the public good.

William Powhatan Winfree.

At eighteen years of age, William Winfree joined Capt. Henry Leavell's Company, known as the Oak Grove Rangers, which was later a part of the 1st Kentucky Cavalry as Company H. This regiment was commanded by Ben Hardin Helm, brother-in-law to Mrs. [Abraham] Lincoln [Mary Todd], and her brother, Harry Todd, was the adjutant of the regiment. Helm was promoted to the command of a Kentucky brigade, and was killed in the first day's fight at Chickamauga. Judge Winfree was in command of General Forrest's bodyguard both days of that battle, and he regarded General Forrest, not only as a great and brave soldier, but as a great cavalry leader, second to none on either side. Young Winfree was wounded once.

After the war he studied law under Judge Henry Stiles, of the Appellate Court. His license to practice was signed by Judge R. I. Petree and Judge Ashur Graham. From 1882 to 1890 he was Judge of the County Circuit Court, and, on retirement from office, resumed practice, his service as lawyer extending over fifty-four years.

In 1868 he was married to Miss Carrie Bradshaw, member of a family as much identified with the county as his own. His wife survives him with five children. A devout Christian, a generous friend, a kind counsellor, the keynotes of his character were duty and loyalty. Now the family find their richest heritage and consolation for his loss are the honor and affection in which his memory is universally held.[624]

WINGO, THOMAS RUDD: Dr. Thomas Rudd Wingo was born October 12, 1826, in Nottoway County, Va. His father was a soldier in the war of 1812 with the troops stationed at Norfolk. Several of his uncles were also in that war, so the Wingos were of good old Virginia fighting stock.

In 1835 young Wingo removed with his parents to Middle Tennessee, living several years near [Andrew Jackson's home,] the Hermitage. Subsequently they located in Carroll County. In 1848 he entered Union University, Murfreesboro, Tenn., and was connected with that institution as student and teacher for nearly ten years. Deciding to make the profession of medicine his life work, he entered the Medical Department of the University of Nashville in 1859. In 1860 he went to Jefferson Medical College, Philadelphia, where he graduated in the spring of 1861. Returning to West Tennessee, he practiced medicine until the beginning of the war, when he was made assistant surgeon of the Twenty-Seventh Tennessee Regiment, which was first stationed at Trenton, Tenn. His first actual service was as a volunteer in caring for wounded in the battle of Belmont, Mo., although his regiment was not in it. Dr. Wingo was always at his post in time of battle, however furious it was. He did not lose an hour from duty except when on furlough during the four years.

Thomas Rudd Wingo.

While the army was encamped at Shelbyville, Tenn., in 1863, Dr. Wingo was promoted to full surgeon of his regiment. Toward the close of the war Gen. Tyree H. Bell, one of Forrest's most trusted brigade commanders, asked General Cheatham for a good surgeon from his division to act as his brigade surgeon, and Dr. Wingo was assigned to the place.

Dr. Wingo never gave down by the results of the war, but began life anew, and even now, at the good old age of seventy-six, is enthusiastic in every good work. He is a general favorite with his comrades and the younger generations, and at the large reunion in his section of the country is a magnetic delineator of the past, and a wise, comforting counselor of the future. The younger Wingos and the people generally are blessed by his example as a hero and a Christian.[625]

WINN, FRANCIS MARION: Francis Marion Winn, born in Sumner County, Tenn., February 15, 1847, died in Redlands, Calif., October 6, 1923. At the age of about sixteen he enlisted in the Confederate army, serving under General Forrest in Company D, 2nd and 21st Cavalry, Tennessee Volunteers, taking an active part in many hard-fought battles. He was paroled at Gainesville, Ala., May 11, 1865, returning at once to the home of his father, near Castalian Springs, Tenn. Soon after this he developed a substantial business as a contractor and builder and left many elegant buildings as monuments to his ability as a builder. One of the last services he rendered his native State in this capacity was that of being chief supervisor of the construction of the present courthouse at Hartsville, Trousdale County, Tenn.

In 1913 he removed to Redlands, Calif., and bought an orange grove, giving it his personal attention, but some three years ago he sold his grove and retired from business.

He was thrice married and is survived by his last wife and fourteen children, twenty-three grandchildren, and two great-grandchildren. All his children were with him during his last illness, and it was a notable incident that his eight sons were the active pallbearers at his funeral and burial, which was at beautiful Hillside Cemetery, adjacent to the world-renowned Smiley Heights, near Redlands.

Comrade Winn was ever loyal to his Church and its ordinances, and in civil life he was known universally as a man of excellent character, uncompromising as between right and wrong, true to everything Southern, the cause for which he fought so well and faithfully being always dear to him. He was the only Confederate veteran residing in Redlands, but the G.A.R. has an organization here, and because of his sterling traits of character he had so won their esteem and admiration that he was invited to participate in all their social activities, an exhibition of splendid spirit which resulted in much pleasure to all concerned.

Outside his own family relations, the best friend he had in Redlands was an old Union soldier, who sat with him in Sunday school class every Sunday. He has fought his last battle and won the glorious victory. Peace to his ashes.[626]

WINSTON, JAMES M.: Another one who wore the gray during that fearful period of 1861-65 has passed over the river to appear before the bar of eternal justice, where motives are not misjudged and acts are judged in love and mercy.

In April last, at his home, Ramsey Station, Sumter County, Ala., there died Capt. James M. Winston, who had reached the ripe age of seventy-eight years. Early in the war he entered the Confederate service as a member of the 36th

Alabama Regiment. In the spring of 1863 he was transferred to the cavalry service, becoming a member of a new company then being raised by Dr. D. H. Williams, of Gainesville, Ala., and was elected first lieutenant thereof at its organization. This company was attached to a regiment of which Col. Isham Harrison, of Mississippi, was commander. Subsequently it was transferred to the 16th Confederate Cavalry Regiment, which was then commanded by Col. Armstead, who was soon thereafter promoted brigadier general, and that brave and gallant cavalier, Col. Philip B. Spence, succeeded to the command, and continued till the close of the war.

James M. Winston.

Soon after this transfer Dr. D. H. Williams, then captain, was promoted to brigade surgeon, and Capt. Winston succeeded him as leader of Company A. This position he retained until surrendered by Gen. Forrest at Gainesville, Ala., in May, 1865.

As a soldier, Capt. Winston served his country faithfully and well. He participated in many battles, and was with his regiment in the last battle fought east of the Mississippi River.

As a commander, he was courageous and always at the head of his company in battle. He loved his men, looked after their interest, and always tempered his discipline with justice and charity. As a man, he was upright, honest, generous, and at all times ready to respond to the distress of the widow and the wail of the orphan; and as a citizen, he upheld the law and promoted the welfare of the community and State.

Capt. Winston married, in early manhood, Miss Broadway, who shared his joys and sorrows and ministered unto him even unto his departure. Five children survive him—four daughters and one son, worthy offsprings of a noble stock. After the war he returned to his home and resumed farming, which he continued till his death. Besides his family, he is mourned by a host of friends, and the country has lost one of its noblest sons. Peace to his soul.⁶²⁷

WISDOM, DEW MOORE: The late Col. D. M. Wisdom, who died in Muskogee, Ind. [Territory], was much of his life a resident of Western Tennessee. He served in the 13th Tennessee Infantry as captain of Company F. He was severely wounded in the battle of Belmont, Mo. He was in the battle of Shiloh. Later he served in cavalry, but under Gen. Roddy was soon transferred to Forrest's command. Referring to his military service, the Jackson (Tenn.) *Sun* states: "For two or three years he served under that 'Wizard of the Saddle.' In the battle of Harrisburg, near Tupelo, Miss., he was again wounded. In many engagements he manifested marked bravery, inspiring his men to deeds of valor by his own courage. By the timely arrival of his regiment he saved the day at Brice's Cross Roads. Col. Wisdom led the Tennessee troops in the storming of Fort Pillow, and was in many other engagements of importance. He was colonel of the 18th Tennessee Cavalry.

"In 1885 Col. Wisdom was appointed by [U.S.] President [Grover] Cleveland to the position of chief clerk at Union Agency, Muskogee, having jurisdiction over the nations. In 1893 he was appointed Indian agent of the Union Agency, and served in that capacity for six years. He then resigned on account of the change of the administration at Washington. In this position he made a national reputation by the wise, judicious, and efficient manner in which he discharged his duties. In May, 1900, he was elected mayor of Muskogee, his administration being businesslike and progressive."[628]

WISEMAN, W. J.: W. J. Wiseman, eighty-seven years old, served with Company I, 20th Tennessee Cavalry, under Forrest through the war. His parents dying when he was quite young, he became the guardian of two younger sisters and a brother, giving his life to their rearing and care afterwards. He and his sisters never married, but made their home together all these years. He is survived by one sister and the brother. The family was loved and respected by all who knew them.[629]

WITHERS, EMILE QUARLES: A soul valiant for honor and right passed on December 3, 1926, with the death of Col. E. Q. Withers, of Macon, Miss.

Emile Quarles Withers was born November 7, 1845, on his father's plantation near Holly Springs, Miss., in Marshall County, and was the eldest son of Albert Quarles and Matilda Jones Withers. He enlisted in Company G, 17th Mississippi Regiment, at Corinth, Miss., on May 27, 1861. Soon afterwards this company was sent to Virginia and was first inducted into the military life at a camp near Manassas Junction. Company G was detached and sent to Michell's Ford on Bull Run Creek, where it remained until July 18, 1861. There the company heard the first shell passing over its head. Company G rejoined the regiment at Elam's Ford on Saturday evening, July 21. The brigade of D. R. Jones, of which the 17th Mississippi was a part, made a futile attack on the enemy's right, and was repulsed. This regiment soon after the battle was moved to Leesburg, Va., and took part on October 21, 1861, in the battle of Leesburg with the 18th Mississippi and 8th Virginia Regiments. This was a signal victory for the Confederates.

In the early spring of 1862 the regiment was moved to the Peninsula near Yorktown, from which place there was a slow move toward the outskirts of Richmond, the various commands being organized into brigades and divisions. They occupied this line until the seven days' fight was commenced. The 17th Mississippi fought at Savage Station and at Malvern Hill, and some time in August or September, moved north with other commands and engaged in the first Maryland campaign.

Colonel Withers was discharged at Culpeper Courthouse while on the march north to Maryland, he being very ill at the time. He went home and remained until the spring of 1863, when he enlisted in the 3rd Mississippi Cavalry, which became a part of Forrest's command, and then participated in all of its engagements, serving until the end of the war as a lieutenant. He was discharged at Grenada, Miss. Colonel Withers is survived by his wife, two sons, one daughter, and three sisters. He was for many years a planter of North Mississippi and a cotton factor at Memphis, Tenn.[630]

WOOD, N. E.: Capt. N. E. Wood passed away on April 1 [1923], Easter Sunday, at his home four miles from Whiteville, Hardeman County, Tenn., lacking but ten days of reaching his eighty-fifth year. At his request, he was clothed in his suit of gray that he had worn at reunions in other days; in a gray casket borne to the family burying ground, where the funeral service was held by Rev. Jenkins, assisted by Rev. W. M. Moment, uncle of Captain Wood, now in his ninety-fourth year. The floral tributes spoke quietly of the true worth of the true-hearted, brave man, loved by all.

He was born and reared in Whiteville; educated at the once flourishing college at McLemoresville; joined the Cumberland Presbyterian Church in early life, and remained a consistent member. He joined the Confederate army in Captain Schuyler's company, and was made first lieutenant, later captain, which place he held during the war in Forrest's Cavalry. It was said when General Forrest had special work to be done or a message to be sent, he called for Captain Wood. His bravery and trustworthiness were known by all. He was greatly beloved by his comrades. Only one or two of his company are living.

Captain Wood married Miss Maggie Harvey just before the close of the war, and when the struggle was over came home and settled down in a country home; but the happy home was broken up by the early death of his wife. In 1878 he was married to Miss Maggie Tisdale, and four children were born to this union; two sons, a daughter, also several grandchildren, with his wife, surviving him. Many friends will cherish the memory of his many kindly deeds, [and] the truly modest, unassuming virtues of this good man.[631]

WOODS, CLAYTON ROGERS: Clayton Rogers Woods passed away at his home, in Savannah, Ga., on December 2, in his seventy-seventh year. He came to Savannah in 1866, immediately engaging in the cotton factorage business with his brothers, William Henry and S. A. Woods, continuing in the business for a great many years, retiring within late years on account of failing health. For over fifty years he was a member of the Cotton Exchange of this city, and his form has been a familiar sight on our streets even after he gave up active business.

As a lad of seventeen Clayton Rogers Woods enlisted in the Confederate army, joining the Eufaula (Ala.) Light Artillery on March 12, 1862, and serving with it until paroled on May 10, 1865, near Meridian, Miss. He saw service with Gens. E. Kirby Smith, Nathan Bedford Forrest, Joseph E. Johnston, John B. Hood, and Braxton Bragg. His battery was engaged in many battles and skirmishes, yet he received only one wound, and that was at New Hope

Church, Ga., while Gen. Joseph E. Johnston was leading Sherman on down toward Atlanta and by his wonderful strategy causing Sherman to lose many men and much supplies. Comrade Woods at one time was persuaded by his captain to accept the position of sergeant, but he shrank from all titles. In business life, however, he had been director in various banks and of the Central of Georgia Railway Company.

On December 27, 1870, he was married to Miss Cecelia E. Malone, of Mobile, Ala., and had he lived until the 27th inst. would have celebrated his fiftieth wedding anniversary. He is survived by his wife, one son (Rogers S. Woods), and one daughter (Mrs. William R. Dancy), both of Savannah. Comrade Woods was of a kindly, retiring disposition, altruistic by nature, and he did quietly what good he could to his fellow man.[632]

WRIGHT, WILFORD FERRIS: In San Antonio, Tex., April 16 [1905], Capt. Wilford Ferris Wright passed into eternal rest. He was born in Obion County, Tenn., in 1839, and was nearing his sixty-sixth year. Capt. Wright entered the Confederate service in the 22nd Tennessee Regiment, from which he was transferred to Forrest's Cavalry and commanded a company of scouts. He went to Texas in 1871, where he held the respect of all with whom he was associated in business and social life. The funeral was conducted by the Albert Sidney Johnston Camp, of which he was a member.[633]

WYETH, JOHN ALLAN: Dr. John A. Wyeth was born May 26, 1845, at Guntersville, Ala., to Louis (of Harrisburg, Pa.) and Euphemia Allan Wyeth (of Huntsville, Ala.). One of his ancestors, George Wythe, signed the Declaration of Independence.

John Allan Wyeth.

He served in Russell's Fourth Alabama Cavalry, Forrest's Brigade, experiencing the many vicissitudes of army life, including a miserable stay in a Yankee prison.

Wyeth was a surgeon of note, and at the fifty-second annual meeting of the American Medical Association, held at St. Paul, Minn., June 4-7 [1901?], he was elected President. This came soon after his election as President of the New York State Medical Association, and the receipt of the honorary degree of Doctor of Laws from the University of Alabama, his native State.

While practicing and reforming medicine in New York, he died of a heart attack on May 22, 1922. He was laid to rest at Greenwood Cemetery, Brooklyn, NY.

One of Gen. Forrest's greatest admirers, Dr. Wyeth is best known to Southerners as the author of *With Sabre and Sword: The Autobiography of a Soldier and Surgeon*, and *Life of General Nathan Bedford Forrest*.[634]

WYNN, J. A.: J. A. Wynn, of Cedartown, Ga., died on August 3, 1918. He was born in Dekalb County, Ga., February 6, 1846. While he was a small boy his father died, and his mother moved to Polk County, where some time in 1863 "Jule" Wynn, as he was familiarly known, entered the Confederate army as a member of Company A, 1st Georgia Cavalry, with which he remained until the surrender at Greensboro, N.C. He was in many hard-fought battles during that time, with many minor engagements while on scouting duty under Gen. Joe Wheeler, who had great confidence in the 1st and 6th Georgia Cavalry. It is on record by a marker that these two regiments opened the battle of Chickamauga early on Saturday morning under the command of General Forrest and held the ground occupied until they were relieved later in the day by infantry.

Early in 1869 Comrade Wynn joined the Methodist Church, in which he served as steward for a number of years. On December 23 he was united in marriage to Miss Olivia Borders, who survives him with four children, two daughters and two sons. Both daughters are married. One son, F. A. Wynn, is a captain with the American forces in France, while the other is a lieutenant in camp at Dallas, Tex.

More than twenty years ago the 1st and 6th Georgia Cavalry Regiments, which were very closely allied during the war, formed a reunion association, which meets the first Wednesday in August of every year. Comrade Wynn was adjutant, secretary, and treasurer of the organization until his death, which occurred three days before the time this year, and on this account the meeting was postponed two weeks. He was the main factor in keeping the association up to a high standard and was ever ready to defend *the cause for which the South so nobly fought [conservatism], always maintaining that the cause was not lost or dead, but more alive to-day than it was in 1861*. He will be sadly missed by his comrades when they meet hereafter in reunion.[635]

Abner Yarbrough.

YARBROUGH, ABNER: Abner Yarbrough was born in Hopkins County, Ky., March 26, 1844, and enlisted, October 5, 1861, in Company A, of the 8th Kentucky Infantry, serving under Capt. I. B. Jones. He went through the war and was wounded three times in battle; was mounted in March 1861, and became an attache of Forrest's Cavalry; was paroled May 16, 1865, and returned home, married, and removed to Paragould, Ark., where he died on November 25, 1927, and was laid to rest in Linwood Cemetery at Paragould. He was a member of the Methodist Church. Comrade Yarbrough is survived by his wife, two sons, five grandchildren, and five great-grandchildren, also one brother, Robert Yarbrough, of California. So far as records show, Abner Yarbrough's death leaves but one survivor of Captain Jones's company, George Wiley, of Hopkins County, Ky.[636]

YOUNG, G. WHIT: G. W. Young was born September 18, 1845, near Orysa, Lauderdale County, Tenn., and died at his home, in Ripley, Tenn., May 8, 1916. He was the son of Rev. G. W. Young, a pioneer Baptist preacher, whose vigorous intellect and pious life gave caste and character to the community in which he lived. Under the godly life of his father the son united with the Durhamville Baptist Church in early life, becoming an active, consistent Christian, prominent, though a meek and humble worker in his Church and a close student of the Bible.

He took an active part in the affairs of the town and county, serving as justice of the peace and coroner and as a member of the school boards for a number of years, proving faithful and efficient to every trust.

G. W. Young enlisted in Captain Davis's company of the 7th Tennessee Cavalry, Forrest's command, and was continuously in service until the close of the war; was in the surrender at Vicksburg. No braver nor more conscientious soldier ever flashed a saber or fired a gun. He was an active member of John Sutherland Camp, No. 890, U.C.V., having served as its Commander, and he was Adjutant of the Camp at the time of his death, always active in the annual reunions and work of the organization. His gentle demeanor, inflexible integrity, and consistent Christian life commanded the admiration of all.

G. Whit Young.

He was married in 1871 to Miss Emma Anthony, a descendant of the Lees of Westmoreland County, Va., and leaves surviving him his wife and three daughters, one brother, and two sisters.[637]

YOUNG, SAMUEL: Grandfather Samuel Young was born December 13, 1844, in Tishomingo County, Miss., and spent most of his childhood days in that State, removing to Arkansas in his early youth. Early in 1861 he volunteered in the Confederate army, becoming a member of Company C, 3rd Arkansas Cavalry. His service was in Northeastern Arkansas and Missouri until the spring of 1862, when he was transferred to the army east of the Mississippi. He was in the battle of Corinth and many others under Generals Van Dorn, Wheeler, and Forrest; was captured by the Federals in the winter of 1864-65, and was in prison at Fort Delaware when the war closed, being paroled at Little Rock, Ark., June 1, 1865.

Samuel Young.

Returning to his home in Benton, Ark., he was married to Mrs. Louisa Julian Thompson in 1866, and in the following year they made their home at Detonti, Ark. To this union were born eleven children, of whom eight survive him, also thirty-seven grandchildren and eight great-grandchildren. Losing his devoted wife and companion in 1890, he contracted a second marriage with Mrs. Rachel Holiman, who was a faithful companion in his declining years.

Soon after his marriage grandfather became a Master Mason in the Benton Lodge, No. 34, F. and A. M., of which he was a consistent member. At the age of thirty-eight years he had joined the New Friendship Baptist Church and was an honored and beloved deacon at the time of his death, which occurred on the 5th of October, 1919. He was laid to rest in the cemetery at New Friendship, with funeral services by his Church and Masonic Lodge.

Grandfather was always true to his convictions. As a soldier he was full of courage, unmindful of danger, and always at his post of duty. During the late war [World War I] in Europe his patriotism was no less fervent, and he gave seven of his grandsons to the cause of humanity. His greatest earthly desire was to live to see the close of the war and to have his grandsons return with the cause of right fully vindicated. As a companion and father he was kind and true, and his heart's desire was to rear his children in the fear and admonition of the Lord. As a Christian he was prayerful, administering to the poor and needy, visiting the sick and afflicted, giving words of counsel and comfort in distress. He spent a life of usefulness and service worthy of emulation.[638]

YOUNGBLOOD, G. W.: G. W. Youngblood died on November 7, 1907, at his home, in Stotts City, Mo., aged sixty-four years. He was born in Warren County, Tenn., in 1843, and in 1862 enlisted in the Confederate army under Gen. N. B. Forrest as a member of Company A, 11th Tennessee Cavalry, serving until the close of the war. He took part in many battles, some of which were Chickamauga, Vicksburg, and Lookout Mountain. At the close of the war he returned home without having received a wound or been a prisoner. He was married in 1870, and in 1874 removed his family to Arkansas, thence in 1876 to North Missouri, residing at Golden City until 1888, when he removed his family to Stotts City.[639]

ZOLLINGER, AUGUSTUS L.: Capt. A. L. Zollinger, who commanded Company A, 2nd Regiment Missouri Cavalry (Col. Robert A. McCulloch's regiment), died at his home, in Otterville, Mo., on March 30, 1914, in his eighty-ninth year.

Captain Zollinger joined the Confederate army in 1861 and served the entire war, following the fortunes of Price's army while in Missouri. After his command was transferred to Memphis, Tenn., he served the remainder of the war chiefly with Forrest's command.

Returning to his home after the war, Captain Zollinger became one of the most active men in his section as merchant and banker. He was a member of the "Missouri Fraternity" for fifty years and an Odd Fellow for sixty-seven years. To his efforts was largely due the early organization of the Confederate Soldiers' Home at Higginsville, Mo., of which he was a trustee for many years.

He was a most useful citizen and noted for his many acts of charity and assistance to the unfortunate and needy. From his earliest childhood Captain Zollinger was a member of the Church and died in faith of the resurrection. He leaves a family of four sons and two daughters.[640]

Historical marker between Columbia and Spring Hill, Tenn., concerning Gen. Forrest's engagement with Union Gen. James. H. Wilson. (Photo Lochlainn Seabrook)

APPENDICES

Additional interesting facts, information, lists, and articles related to General Nathan Bedford Forrest and his men.

"Surely no greater hero ever wore the gray than General N. B. Forrest."

A Confederate veteran

APPENDIX A

Forrest's Escort

THE FOLLOWING ROLL INCLUDES MEMBERS OF FORREST'S WORLD-RENOWNED ESCORT; MEN WHO SURRENDERED WITH THE FAMOUS GENERAL AT GAINESVILLE, ALA., MAY 5, 1865.

STAFF: Majs. J. P. Strange and C. W. Anderson; Lieuts. William M. Forrest, Sam Donelson, C. S. Severson, R. M. Mason, and G. V. Rambaut; Capts. George Dashields, Charles H. Hill, and J. G. Mann; Drs. J. B. Cowan and G. W. Jones.

OFFICERS: J. C. Jackson, captain; Nathan Boone, Math Cortner, and George L. Cowan, lieutenants; M. L. Parks, first sergeant; W. E. Sims, second sergeant; W. A. F. Rutledge, third sergeant; C. C. McLemore, fourth sergeant; W. H. Mathews, first corporal; H. J. Crenshaw, second corporal; W. T. H. Wharton, third corporal; P. C. Richardson, fourth corporal; R. C. Keeble, fifth corporal; W. F. Watson, bugler.

PRIVATES: J. N. Anderson, A. D. Adair, H. L. W. Boone, J. H. Bivins, P. P. Bennett, J. W. Bridges, W. A. Bailey, S. E. Batts, W. F. Buchanan, J. O. Crump, W. C. Cooper, Alex Cortner, Sam Carter, Joe Cunningham, Silas J. Clark, E. C. Clark, Thomas Childs, T. G. Chairs, S. W. Carmack, D. H. Call, C. A. Crenshaw, George R. Dismukes, W. R. Dyer, H. F. Dusenberry, Phil Dodd, L. A. Dwiggins, J. G. Davidson, G. W. Davidson, F. M. Dance, T. J. Eaton, John Eaton, W. D. Elder, S. W. Edens, M. M. Emmons, M. A. L. Enochs, A. Forrest, J. D. Fletcher, George W. Foster, George W. Felps, R. E. B. Floyd, R. C. Garrett, J. S. Garrett, George C. Gillespie, G. W. Hooper, H. A. Holland, D. C. Jackson, John F. Key, A. W. Key, W. S. Livingston, H. D. Lipscomb, C. T. Latimer, E. E. Linch, Thomas C. Little, W. T. McGehee, T. N. McCord, R. F. McKnight, B. F. Martin, J. O. Martin, R. H. Maxwell, O. W. McKissick, A. McEwin, T. H. Moore, J. M. McNabb, J. W. Newsom, F. C. Nolan, J. K. P. Neece, E. P. Oakly, D. C. Padgett, B. A. Pearson, J. B. Pearson, T. R. Priest, W. R. Poplin, D. G. Roland, C. H. Ruffin, R. Felix Renfro, J. K. Reaves, John W. Snell, Joel Reese, W. L. Shofner, J. K. Stephenson, G. W. Stevenson, C. Searback, W. R. Shofner, A. M. Spencer, Noah Scales, H. C. Troxler, J. N. Taylor, W. F. Taylor, L. E. Thompson, W. A. Thompson, J. R. Troop, E. F. Tucker, A. (Sandy) White, T. H. Wood, Mark G. Watson, W. A. Woodard, J. H. Womack, J. H. Word, W. D. Ward, Flinch Woodard, A. A. Pearson.

NOTE FROM ORIGINAL ARTICLE: L. H. Pass and W. H. Moon were both in prison at the time of the surrender, and there were other members of the company who were entitled to be paroled at Gainesville, who were unavoidably absent on detached duty or were sick in hospitals.[641]

APPENDIX B
Annual Reunion of Forrest's Escort
1906

Forrest's staff and escort held their annual reunion at Fayetteville, Tenn., September 6, 1906. Doubtless no company in the Army of Tennessee was more widely and favorably known or did more perilous service than Forrest's escort. It was organized in October, 1862, ninety strong, by Capt. Montgomery Little, of Bedford County, Tenn., who was killed at Thompson Station, Tenn., in March, 1863, and who was a warm personal friend of General Forrest before the war, and had been with him after the fall of Fort Donelson. Though often depleted, this company received many recruits, so that it numbered over one hundred men at the surrender at Gainesville, Ala., May 10, 1865. About thirty are still living.

Those present at Fayetteville were Dr. J. B. Cowan, Staff Chief Surgeon; Escort T. C. Little, President; W. L. Shofner, G. W. Foster, Joel Reese, O. W. McKissick, J. H. Pearson, Geo. Davidson, G. W. Enochs, H. T. Childs, E. M. McClure, E. G. Montgomery, and Col. D. C. Kelley, who commanded Forrest's old regiment.

The officers elected for next year are: O. W. McKissick, President; J. N. Taylor, Corresponding Secretary; G. L. Cowan, Recording Secretary; Tom Cheairs, Treasurer; T. C. Little, Chaplain.[642]

APPENDIX C
Confederate Generals of Tennessee

NATHAN BEDFORD FORREST WAS ONE OF 38 KNOWN CONFEDERATE GENERALS FROM OR ASSOCIATED WITH THE VOLUNTEER STATE. A NUMBER OF THESE MEN SERVED WITH FORREST.

1910

Alexander P. Stewart
Nathan Bedford Forrest
William B. Bate
John C. Brown
Benjamin F. Cheatham
Daniel S. Donaldson
W. Y. C. Humes
Bushrod R. Johnson
John P. McCown
Cadmus M. Wilcox
John Adams
Samuel R. Anderson
Frank C. Armstrong
Tyree H. Bell
Alexander W. Campbell
William H. Carroll
John C. Carter
H. B. Davidson
George G. Dibrell

George W. Gordon
Robert Hatton
Alfred E. Jackson
George Maney
William McComb
Joseph B. Palmer
Gideon J. Pillow
William A. Quarles
James E. Rains
Preston Smith
William H. Jackson
Thomas Benton Smith
Ortho F. Strahl
R. C. Tyler
A. J. Vaughan
John C. Vaughan
L. M. Walker
Marcus J. Wright
Felix K. Zollicoffer[643]

APPENDIX D
A Remarkable Group of Men

1913

The following-named six veterans rendered faithful service to the Confederacy: William Jerome Willingham, Mike Word, Pitts McMurray, Don Singleterry, D. J. Murphy, and Jap Nall. They enlisted at the beginning of the war in Company E, 12th Tennessee Infantry, and participated with that regiment in the battles of Belmont, Mo., and Shiloh.

Upon the reorganization of the army in June, 1862, this company, being composed entirely of Kentuckians, was transferred to the 3rd Kentucky Infantry and became Company L, so serving until March 15, 1864. Then they were mounted and assigned to General Forrest's cavalry, and with it served until the end, in May, 1865. The 3rd, 7th, 8th, and 12th Kentucky Regiments constituted the Kentucky brigade.

In addition to Belmont and Shiloh, they were in the battles of Bolivar, Davis's Mill, Corinth, Hatcher's Bridge, Coffeeville, Champion Hill, Jackson, Vicksburg, Paducah, Brice's Cross Roads, Harrisburg, and Old Town Creek. Then they were in the raid into Middle Tennessee during September, 1864, and in the battles generally incident to Hood's Nashville campaign in the winter of 1864. This included Lawrenceburg, Shoal Creek, Campbellville, Spring Hill, Franklin, Nashville, Murfreesboro, and the fights in the rear of Hood's Infantry on their fearful retreat.

"The Remarkable Group." Bottom: D. J. Murphy; middle row, left to right: Don Singleterry, Jap Nall; top row, left to right: Pitts McMurray, Mike Word, William J. Willingham.

They seldom missed a roll call. Willingham became first sergeant and was esteemed by the entire regiment. He has attended all the general Reunions.[644]

APPENDIX E
Where Forrest Surrendered

1916

An effort is being made to mark the place of the surrender of General Forrest's troops in Gainesville, Ala. The importance of this is made evident by a recent article in the *Birmingham Ledger* which [incorrectly] speaks of the "surrender of Forrest at Selma, Ala."

B. L. Roberts, of Gainesville, says there are five veterans living there who can locate the place of surrender, and they will be glad to cooperate with the Daughters of Alabama in placing a suitable marker at the place near the Public Square of the town. The U.D.C. Chapter at Livingston, Ala., is asked to take the initiative in this important movement and ask Mr. B. L. Roberts to act as temporary chairman. Any one interested may address him, giving ideas as to the kind of marker to be used.

An old Gainesville "girl" suggests a boulder taken from the Tombigbee River and a bronze tablet attached, the inscription to be decided upon by a selected committee, the chairman of which shall be the President of the Alabama Division, U.D.C.[645]

Gen. N. B. Forrest.

APPENDIX F
General Forrest's Grandson Vs. Public School

1920

Commander in Chief [of the Sons of Confederate Veterans] N. B. Forrest [II, General Forrest's grandson; son of his son William M. Forrest,] is making a strong fight to prevent the use in the public schools of Beard and Bagley's [anti-South, historically inaccurate] textbook, *The History of the American People.*

It is charged that this history is *socialistic,* is unfair in its treatment of the negro question, magnifies the Northern heroes in the War between the States, and is repugnant to the people of the South. It is also alleged that it slurs at the Constitution of the United States and should be rejected on that point alone.

In the topic of the Revolutionary period Comrade Forrest [II] stated that twenty-five pages are devoted to men of the North and only one page to Southern men. [This problem continues today, and is actually now far worse than it was in 1920. L.S.][646]

Nathan Bedford Forrest II (1872-1931), grandson of General Nathan Bedford Forrest (1821-1877).

APPENDIX G
Company G, Forrest's Cavalry

THE FOLLOWING IS A ROSTER OF COMPANY G, FORREST'S CAVALRY, WHICH SURRENDERED AT GAINESVILLE, ALA., IN 1865, MAY 11. IT CONTAINS THE NAMES OF MANY OF THE BOYS WHO WORE THE GRAY FROM GIBSON COUNTY. THE COMPANY WAS IN MOST OF THE FIGHTING THAT THE REGIMENT TOOK PART IN AND SERVED WELL THE CAUSE OF THE CONFEDERACY.

1923

W. T. Carmack, captain, Shelby County.
J. S. Appleberry, first lieutenant, Shelby County.
H. House, second lieutenant, Gibson County.
G. W. Frost, first sergeant, Gibson County.
E. R. Greer, second sergeant, Fayette County.
S. A. McDaniel, third sergeant, Gibson County.
T. B. Johnson, fourth sergeant, Fayette County.
J. A. Williams, first corporal, Fayette County.
J. S. Wood, second corporal, Gibson County.
H. G. Edwards, third corporal, Fayette County.
J. M. Leath, fourth corporal, Gibson County.

Privates (Shelby County)—R. G. Appleberry, J. M. Hannatt, R. N. McCalla, J. C. Thompson, L. W. Thompson, A. C. Taylor, G. M. Tucker, W. W. Wade, I. F. Wade, T. P. Wylie, W. C. Allen.

Privates (Gibson County)—W. A. Banks, J. B. Bowman, B. H. Bennett, J. C. Bessent, M. L. Crisp, O. G. Fitzgerald, W. T. Gleason, J. E. Johnson, E. B. Jones, A. M. Jones, J. D. McCutcheon, R. W. McCutcheon, A. C. McLeary, J. M. Moore, G. C. Maun, W. C. Robinson, J. M. [or J. W.?] Sappington, J. B. Jones.

Privates (Haywood County)—F. V. Baldwin, T. J. Evans, W. T. Bass, A. T. Edwards, E. R. Freeman, D. F. Griffin, N. W. Galloway, T. J. Flippin, W. J. Hodges, H. Harvel, W. T. McFadden, J. D. McCrow, J. P. Robinson.

Privates (Rutherford County)—-W. A. Cooper.

Privates (Lincoln County)—J. W. McClough, J. M. Strong, M. Walker.[647]

Street named after Gen. Forrest, Franklin, Tenn. (Photo Lochlainn Seabrook)

APPENDIX H
At the Birthplace of General Forrest

1928

The name and fame of Nathan Bedford Forrest have been further recorded for future generations by the erection of a monument at his birthplace, the little community of Chapel Hill, in Marshall County, Tenn. In a humble home [long since disappeared] there the great Wizard of the Saddle was born one hundred and seven years ago, and on July 13, 1928, his natal day was commemorated by the dedication of this monument which perpetuates the fame of a great soldier.

Site of Forrest's birthplace, Chapel Hill, Tenn. (Photo Lochlainn Seabrook)

Fitting exercises attended the dedication, beginning in the morning of the 13th and concluding in the afternoon, when the monument was unveiled in the presence of many hundreds of spectators, some of them special guests of the occasion, all of whom were welcomed to the community by Mayor W. T. Hurt, and on behalf of the county by J. N. McCord, of Lewisburg. Addresses were made by Hon. Ewin L. Davis, representative in Congress from this district, who was followed by Mrs. J. A. Hargrove, of Chapel Hill, on behalf of the U.D.C., in accepting the monument. Some of the other speakers were Gen. T. C. Little, for the Confederate Veterans; Col. Joel B. Fort, of Nashville; Scott Davis, a veteran of Forrest's Cavalry; and Charles Moss, of Lewisburg.

Special credit for the erection of this monument goes to Mrs. J. A. Hargrove, President of the U.D.C., Chapter at Chapel Hill, who started the movement some three years ago and had worked untiringly to its completion, ably assisted by other Daughters of the Confederacy there and friends. By their efforts the site was secured and an appropriation made by the State of Tennessee to thus honor a son who had honored his native State by his great services in time of war and in the days of peace. A splendid tribute was paid to Forrest in the address by Judge Davis, not only as a soldier, but as "a man of unimpeachable integrity, high moral courage, and constructive citizenship."

Music and readings appropriate to the occasion made the exercises complete, and the day was one of the most interesting that the old community of Chapel Hill has ever known. The tall granite shaft will ever cast its shadow over the place which once enshrined a little babe destined to immortality.[648]

NOTES

1. *Confederate Veteran*, March 1923, p. 117.
2. *Confederate Veteran*, February 1927, p. 76.
3. Woods, p. 47.
4. On Lincoln's socialistic, Marxist, and communist thoughts, ideas, and tendencies, see my books: 1) *Lincoln's War: The Real Cause, The Real Winner, the Real Loser*; 2) *Abraham Lincoln Was a Liberal, Jefferson Davis Was a Conservative: The Missing Key to Understanding the American Civil War*; 3) *Abraham Lincoln: The Southern View*. Also see McCarty, passim; Browder, passim; Benson and Kennedy, passim.
5. See J. W. Jones, TDMV, pp. 144, 200-201, 273.
6. See Seabrook, TAHSR, passim. See also, Pollard, LC, p. 178; J. H. Franklin, pp. 101, 111, 130, 149; Nicolay and Hay, ALCW, Vol. 1, p. 627.
7. BISG (the "Book Industry Study Group"), for example—a Left-wing organization which describes itself as "the leading book trade association for standardized best practices, research and information, and events"—gives its BISAC ("Book Industry Standards and Communications") listing for works on the War for Southern Independence under the heading "Civil War Period, 1850-1877." Nearly all books published in the U.S.A. today are under the categorizational control of this progressive group located in New York City.
8. See e.g., Seabrook, TQJD, pp. 30, 38, 76.
9. See e.g., J. Davis, RFCG, Vol. 1, pp. 55, 422; Vol. 2, pp. 4, 161, 454, 610. Besides using the term "Civil War" himself, President Davis cites numerous other individuals who use it as well.
10. See e.g., *Confederate Veteran*, March 1912, p. 122.
11. Minutes of the Eighth Annual Meeting, July 1898, p. 87.
12. For more on the nihilistic, atheistic, anti-life, anti-tradition, anti-American, anti-Constitution, anti-capitalism, anti-South agenda of the Victorian Republican Party (then the Liberal Party) and the modern Democrat Party (now the Liberal Party), otherwise known as "The Communist/Socialist Rules for Revolution," see Hasselberg, pp. 2350-2351; Lenin, passim; Marx and Engels, passim; B. Dodd, passim.
13. *Confederate Veteran*, July 1901, p. 318.
14. *Confederate Veteran*, April 1910, p. 170.
15. Seabrook, ARB, p. 557 (2011 paperback edition).
16. Seabrook, ARB, p. 542 (2011 paperback edition).
17. *Confederate Veteran*, December 1930, p. 452.
18. *Confederate Veteran*, February 1923, p. 77.
19. *Confederate Veteran*, August 1921, p. 304.
20. U.S.W.D., MRTTGO, p. 27; Warner, GIG, s.v. "William Wirt Adams."
21. *Confederate Veteran*, February 1921, p. 68.
22. *Confederate Veteran*, October 1901, pp. 449-450.
23. *Confederate Veteran*, May 1907, p. 240.
24. *Confederate Veteran*, March 1903, p. 125.
25. *Confederate Veteran*, June 1912, p. 289.
26. *Confederate Veteran*, July 1907, p. 327.
27. *Confederate Veteran*, March 1912, p. 124.
28. *Confederate Veteran*, February 1896, p. 62.
29. *Confederate Veteran*, May 1912, p. 231.
30. *Confederate Veteran*, March 1908, pp. 137-138.
31. *Confederate Veteran*, July 1896, p. 237.
32. *Confederate Veteran*, September 1896, p. 288.
33. *Confederate Veteran*, September 1902, p. 420.
34. U.S.W.D., MRTTGO, pp. 25, 30; *Confederate Veteran*, April 1910, p. 171.
35. *Confederate Veteran*, October 1915, p. 468.
36. *Confederate Veteran*, January 1898, p. 30.
37. *Confederate Veteran*, November 1932, p. 394.

38. *Confederate Veteran*, November 1923, p. 439.
39. *Confederate Veteran*, August 1915, p. 369.
40. *Confederate Veteran*, April 1930, p. 156.
41. *Confederate Veteran*, December 1898, p. 559.
42. *Confederate Veteran*, June 1931, p. 225.
43. *Confederate Veteran*, April 1907, p. 181.
44. *Confederate Veteran*, November 1920, p. 426.
45. *Confederate Veteran*, November-December, 1921, p. 433.
46. *Confederate Veteran*, June 1912, p. 284.
47. *Confederate Veteran*, November 1929, p. 427.
48. *Confederate Veteran*, January 1903, pp. 33-34.
49. *Confederate Veteran*, September 1914, pp. 420-421.
50. *Confederate Veteran*, November 1898, p. 529.
51. U.S.W.D., MRTTGO, p. 30; *Confederate Veteran*, October 1902, p. 464.
52. For more on the topic of Reconstruction, see Seabrook, AL; Seabrook, NBFATKKK.
53. *Confederate Veteran*, September 1920, p. 391.
54. *Confederate Veteran*, July 1903, pp. 368-369.
55. *Confederate Veteran*, February 1918, p. 79.
56. *Confederate Veteran*, August 1907, p. 373.
57. *Confederate Veteran*, August 1908, pp. 409-410.
58. *Confederate Veteran*, October 1918, p. 451.
59. *Confederate Veteran*, June 1911, p. 294.
60. *Confederate Veteran*, August 1923, p. 306.
61. There is no irrefutable evidence that General N. B. Forrest ever served as the Grand Wizard of the original KKK, or what I call the "Reconstruction KKK," a *temporary* aid-and-welfare society and protection organization set up by Conservative Southerners shortly after the War—and which endured for less than four years, from 1865-1869; a group that has no connection to today's *permanent* KKK (founded in 1915), except the name. For more on this topic, see Seabrook, NBFATKKK.
62. *Confederate Veteran*, August 1924, p. 314.
63. *Confederate Veteran*, September 1898, p. 435.
64. *Confederate Veteran*, September 1920, p. 349.
65. *Confederate Veteran*, November 1923, p. 426.
66. *Confederate Veteran*, October 1910, p. 481.
67. *Confederate Veteran*, March 1922, p. 107.
68. *Confederate Veteran*, October 1915, p. 468.
69. *Confederate Veteran*, September 1921, p. 346.
70. *Confederate Veteran*, December 1929, p. 469.
71. *Confederate Veteran*, January 1912, p. 36.
72. *Confederate Veteran*, May 1927, pp. 184-185.
73. *Confederate Veteran*, April 1899, p. 175.
74. *Confederate Veteran*, April 1899, p. 175.
75. *Confederate Veteran*, September 1901, p. 419.
76. *Confederate Veteran*, September 1900, p. 411.
77. *Confederate Veteran*, August 1928, p. 307.
78. *Confederate Veteran*, November 1913, p. 551.
79. *Confederate Veteran*, November 1920, p. 427.
80. *Confederate Veteran*, June 1909, p. 289.
81. *Confederate Veteran*, June 1923, p. 228.
82. *Confederate Veteran*, November 1918, p. 492.
83. *Confederate Veteran*, July 1898, p. 337.
84. *Confederate Veteran*, June 1909, p. 294.
85. *Confederate Veteran*, November 1924, p. 436.
86. *Confederate Veteran*, February 1918, p. 95.
87. *Confederate Veteran*, October 1905, p. 445.

88. *Confederate Veteran*, January 1913, pp. 36-37.
89. *Confederate Veteran*, August 1911, p. 391.
90. *Confederate Veteran*, February 1923, p. 68.
91. *Confederate Veteran*, March 1919, p. 105.
92. U.S.W.D., MRTTGO, p. 24; *Confederate Veteran*, November 1894, p. 326.
93. *Confederate Veteran*, March 1912, p. 130.
94. *Confederate Veteran*, August 1925, p. 286.
95. *Confederate Veteran*, December 1912, p. 576.
96. *Confederate Veteran*, November 1931, pp. 426-427.
97. *Confederate Veteran*, April 1910, p. 171.
98. U.S.W.D., MRTTGO, p. 30; Warner, GIG, s.v. "Alexander William Campbell."
99. *Confederate Veteran*, September 1909, p. 523.
100. *Confederate Veteran*, December 1909, pp. 612-613.
101. *Confederate Veteran*, December 1920, p. 470.
102. *Confederate Veteran*, January 1905, p. 38.
103. *Confederate Veteran*, June 1927, p. 227.
104. *Confederate Veteran*, December 1909, p. 609.
105. *Confederate Veteran*, July 1898, pp. 325-326.
106. U.S.W.D., MRTTGO, p. 18; Warner, GIG, s.v. "James Ronald Chalmers."
107. *Confederate Veteran*, December 1909, p. 609. Note: Some of the information in this entry was derived from my personal family tree: I am fourth cousins with Nathaniel F. Cheairs.
108. *Confederate Veteran*, May 1910, p. 238.
109. *Confederate Veteran*, November 1932, pp. 394-395.
110. *Confederate Veteran*, June 1912, p. 260.
111. *Confederate Veteran*, September 1915, p. 418.
112. *Confederate Veteran*, March 1912, pp. 131-132.
113. *Confederate Veteran*, November 1905, pp. 516-517.
114. *Confederate Veteran*, May 1912, p. 231.
115. *Confederate Veteran*, September 1929, p. 347.
116. *Confederate Veteran*, June 1902, p. 273.
117. *Confederate Veteran*, January 1904, p. 42.
118. *Confederate Veteran*, November 1929, pp. 412-413.
119. *Confederate Veteran*, October 1911, p. 492.
120. *Confederate Veteran*, February 1912, p. 81.
121. *Confederate Veteran*, August 1898, p. 365.
122. *Confederate Veteran*, April 1910, p. 175.
123. For an in-depth discussion of this topic, see Seabrook, NBFATKKK.
124. *Confederate Veteran*, January 1930, p. 26. My emphasis.
125. *Confederate Veteran*, June 1923, p. 227.
126. For more on the Confederate McGavocks and their celebrated home in Franklin, Tenn., see Seabrook, TMOCP; Seabrook, CPGS; Seabrook, EOTBOF.
127. *Confederate Veteran*, December 1919, p. 468.
128. *Confederate Veteran*, September 1896, p. 288.
129. *Confederate Veteran*, August 1909, p. 424.
130. *Confederate Veteran*, July 1918, p. 315.
131. *Confederate Veteran*, July 1927, p. 227.
132. *Confederate Veteran*, November 1907, p. 513.
133. *Confederate Veteran*, June 1903, p. 271.
134. *Confederate Veteran*, April 1926, p. 148.
135. *Confederate Veteran*, August 1911, p. 366.
136. *Confederate Veteran*, November 1930, pp. 436-437.
137. *Confederate Veteran*, June 1924, p. 232.
138. *Confederate Veteran*, August 1898, p. 379.
139. *Confederate Veteran*, March 1922, p. 109.

140. *Confederate Veteran*, January 1922, p. 28.
141. Seabrook, ARB, p. 277 (2011 paperback edition).
142. *Confederate Veteran*, May 1927, pp. 185-186.
143. *Confederate Veteran*, April 1917, p. 171.
144. *Confederate Veteran*, June 1922, p. 226.
145. *Confederate Veteran*, March 1899, p. 132.
146. *Confederate Veteran*, September 1901, p. 420.
147. *Confederate Veteran*, June 1917, p. 278.
148. *Confederate Veteran*, April 1901, p. 149.
149. *Confederate Veteran*, July 1918, p. 310.
150. *Confederate Veteran*, August 1928, p. 306.
151. *Confederate Veteran*, April 1911, p. 177.
152. *Confederate Veteran*, February 1909, p. 87.
153. *Confederate Veteran*, September 1911, pp. 438-439.
154. *Confederate Veteran*, March 1919, p. 106.
155. U.S.W.D., MRTTGO, p. 29; Warner, GIG, s.v. "George Gibbs Dibrell."
156. *Confederate Veteran*, February 1917, p. 99.
157. *Confederate Veteran*, January 1918, p. 31.
158. Information from my personal family tree. Also see Dinkins.
159. *Confederate Veteran*, December 1927, p. 429.
160. *Confederate Veteran*, December 1927, p. 435.
161. *Confederate Veteran*, September 1918, p. 405. The author of this entry was J. J. Hall.
162. Bessie was the granddaughter of Randal McGavock, the founder of famous Carnton Plantation, Franklin, TN. For a detailed study of the McGavocks of Franklin, see Seabrook, TMOCP.
163. *Confederate Veteran*, November 1899, p. 517.
164. *Confederate Veteran*, September 1917, p. 420.
165. *Confederate Veteran*, November 1914, p. 521.
166. *Confederate Veteran*, February 1919, p. 44.
167. *Confederate Veteran*, May 1918, p. 219.
168. *Confederate Veteran*, October 1910, p. 480.
169. *Confederate Veteran*, October 1914, p. 466.
170. *Confederate Veteran*, April 1910, p. 184.
171. *Confederate Veteran*, January 1929, p. 10.
172. *Confederate Veteran*, September 1910, p. 442.
173. *Confederate Veteran*, July 1923, p. 278.
174. Duncan, p. 160 a.
175. *Confederate Veteran*, January 1929, p. 2.
176. *Confederate Veteran*, September 1924, p. 354.
177. *Confederate Veteran*, June 1909, p. 287.
178. *Confederate Veteran*, March 1924, p. 108.
179. *Confederate Veteran*, September 1927, p. 345.
180. *Confederate Veteran*, June 1912, pp. 286-287.
181. *Confederate Veteran*, July 1911, p. 328.
182. *Confederate Veteran*, November 1909, p. 565.
183. *Confederate Veteran*, April 1916, p. 178.
184. *Confederate Veteran*, June 1906, p. 277.
185. *Confederate Veteran*, May 1918, p. 216.
186. *Confederate Veteran*, May 1930, p. 195.
187. *Confederate Veteran*, November-December, 1921, p. 431.
188. *Confederate Veteran*, April 1907, pp. 181-182.
189. *Confederate Veteran*, January 1919, p. 38.
190. *Confederate Veteran*, June 1924, p. 232.
191. *Confederate Veteran*, March 1908, p. 131.
192. *Confederate Veteran*, July 1929, p. 267.

193. *Confederate Veteran*, March 1900, p. 130.
194. *Confederate Veteran*, November 1928, p. 429.
195. *Confederate Veteran*, February 1902, pp. 84-85.
196. *Confederate Veteran*, August 1930, p. 313.
197. *Confederate Veteran*, January 1902, p. 33.
198. *Confederate Veteran*, June 1900, p. 280.
199. For details on Van Dorn's death, see Seabrook, TMOCP, p. 355.
200. *Confederate Veteran*, April 1929, p. 147.
201. *Confederate Veteran*, July 1909, p. 356.
202. *Confederate Veteran*, February 1910, p. 84. Note: Some of this information is from my personal family tree.
203. *Confederate Veteran*, January 1923, p. 28.
204. *Confederate Veteran*, February 1925, p. 66.
205. *Confederate Veteran*, March 1910, p. 136.
206. *Confederate Veteran*, March 1906, p. 135.
207. *Confederate Veteran*, March 1903, p. 130. Note: His initials are also given as "S.C." It is not known which is correct.
208. For a detailed discussion on this important legal right, see Seabrook, AWAITBLA.
209. *Confederate Veteran*, October 1900, pp. 452-453.
210. *Confederate Veteran*, May 1927, p. 183.
211. *Confederate Veteran*, March 1911, p. 137.
212. *Confederate Veteran*, April 1908, p. xxiii.
213. *Confederate Veteran*, August 1916, p. 366.
214. *Confederate Veteran*, May 1906, p. 219.
215. *Confederate Veteran*, July 1915, p. 326.
216. *Confederate Veteran*, April 1927, p. 157.
217. *Confederate Veteran*, March 1904, p. 129.
218. *Confederate Veteran*, February 1901, p. 132.
219. *Confederate Veteran*, November 1911, p. 536.
220. *Confederate Veteran*, September 1919, p. 346.
221. *Confederate Veteran*, August 1902, p. 352.
222. *Confederate Veteran*, November 1929, p. 427.
223. U.S.W.D., MRTTGO, p. 29; Warner, GIG, s.v. "Samuel Jameson Gholson."
224. *Confederate Veteran*, July 1914, p. 329.
225. *Confederate Veteran*, August 1911, pp. 388-389.
226. *Confederate Veteran*, June 1916, p. 287.
227. *Confederate Veteran*, August 1898, p. 380.
228. *Confederate Veteran*, September 1929, p. 349.
229. *Confederate Veteran*, November 1901, p. 502.
230. *Confederate Veteran*, June 1902, p. 270.
231. *Confederate Veteran*, July 1908, p. 356.
232. *Confederate Veteran*, December 1920, p. 469.
233. *Confederate Veteran*, March 1926, p. 108.
234. Seabrook, ARB, p. 277 (2011 paperback edition).
235. *Confederate Veteran*, January 1929, p. 28.
236. *Confederate Veteran*, September 1901, p. 418.
237. *Confederate Veteran*, October 1914, p. 477. His widow was living in Afton, Texas, in 1914.
238. *Confederate Veteran*, July 1903, p. 370.
239. *Confederate Veteran*, September 1924, p. 351.
240. *Confederate Veteran*, May 1920, pp. 186-187.
241. *Confederate Veteran*, March 1902, p. 122.
242. *Confederate Veteran*, April 1896, p. 135.
243. *Confederate Veteran*, June 1925, pp. 226-227.
244. *Confederate Veteran*, July 1907, p. 320.

245. *Confederate Veteran*, January 1904, p. 38.
246. For a discussion on this subject, see Seabrook, ALWALJDWAC.
247. *Confederate Veteran*, September 1929, p. 346.
248. *Confederate Veteran*, May 1911, p. 234.
249. *Confederate Veteran*, March 1902, p. 128.
250. *Confederate Veteran*, October 1903, pp. 469-470.
251. *Confederate Veteran*, June 1920, p. 228.
252. *Confederate Veteran*, March 1907, p. 128.
253. *Confederate Veteran*, September 1898, p. 434.
254. For details on Van Dorn's death, see Seabrook, TMOCP, p. 355.
255. *Confederate Veteran*, November 1919, pp. 430-432.
256. *Confederate Veteran*, August 1901, p. 372.
257. *Confederate Veteran*, January 1924, p. 24.
258. *Confederate Veteran*, August 1909, p. 415.
259. Some Conservative late 19th- and early 20th-Century Southerners, who had always been Democrats, were not fully aware of the dramatic change that took place between the two parties in 1896, the year that the once Conservative Democrat Party switched to a Liberal platform, while the once Liberal Republican Party switched to a Conservative platform. This resulted in the odd phenomenon of "Conservative Democrats," such as George Wallace. For more on this fascinating and important topic, see Seabrook, ALWALJDWAC.
260. *Confederate Veteran*, June 1920, p. 226.
261. *Confederate Veteran*, April 1907, p. 182.
262. *Confederate Veteran*, December 1919, p. 468.
263. *Confederate Veteran*, September 1920, p. 398.
264. *Confederate Veteran*, March 1907, p. 129.
265. *Confederate Veteran*, December 1924, p. 473.
266. *Confederate Veteran*, March 1932, pp. 104-105.
267. *Confederate Veteran*, August 1906, p. 373.
268. *Confederate Veteran*, October 1924, p. 395.
269. *Confederate Veteran*, November 1924, p. 433.
270. *Confederate Veteran*, February 1925, p. 67.
271. *Confederate Veteran*, August 1904, p. 398.
272. *Confederate Veteran*, October 1921, p. 389.
273. *Confederate Veteran*, May 1924, p. 184.
274. *Confederate Veteran*, January 1914, p. 45.
275. *Confederate Veteran*, September 1907, pp. 420-421.
276. *Confederate Veteran*, January 1917, p. 32.
277. *Confederate Veteran*, May 1904, p. 236.
278. *Confederate Veteran*, July 1923, p. 263.
279. *Confederate Veteran*, May 1902, p. 226.
280. *Confederate Veteran*, October 1906, p. 470.
281. *Confederate Veteran*, November 1919, p. 426.
282. *Confederate Veteran*, September 1926, p. 346.
283. *Confederate Veteran*, March 1923, p. 108.
284. *Confederate Veteran*, November 1913, p. 547.
285. *Confederate Veteran*, June 1922, p. 210.
286. Like many other politically Conservative Confederate veterans, Hows did not seem to be aware that the Democrats (the main Conservative party since the time of Andrew Jackson) switched platforms with the Republican Party in 1896, becoming the Liberal party from that time forward (while the Republicans became the Conservative party from that time forward). To learn more about this important shift in American politics, see Seabrook, ALWALJDWAC.
287. *Confederate Veteran*, October 1928, p. 387.
288. *Confederate Veteran*, July 1903, p. 330.
289. *Confederate Veteran*, June 1910, p. 287.

290. *Confederate Veteran*, February 1905, p. 84.
291. *Confederate Veteran*, August 1923, p. 306.
292. *Confederate Veteran*, February 1924, p. 67.
293. *Confederate Veteran*, March 1917, p. 134.
294. *Confederate Veteran*, March 1922, p. 110.
295. *Confederate Veteran*, March 1926, p. 119.
296. *Confederate Veteran*, September 1929, p. 346.
297. *Confederate Veteran*, October 1924, p. 396.
298. *Confederate Veteran*, November 1925, p. 428.
299. *Confederate Veteran*, February 1923, p. 77.
300. *Confederate Veteran*, August 1919, p. 308.
301. *Confederate Veteran*, December 1930, p. 477.
302. For the details behind Van Dorn's death, see Seabrook, TMOCP, p. 355.
303. *Confederate Veteran*, April 1908, p. xxii.
304. *Confederate Veteran*, March 1895, pp. 76-77.
305. U.S.W.D., MRTTGO, p. 25; *Confederate Veteran*, May 1903, pp. 232-233.
306. *Confederate Veteran*, July 1905, p. 323.
307. *Confederate Veteran*, January 1919, p. 28. My emphasis.
308. *Confederate Veteran*, August 1911, p. 392.
309. *Confederate Veteran*, October 1913, p. 502.
310. *Confederate Veteran*, July 1923, p. 282.
311. Warner, GIG, s.v. "Adam Rankin 'Stovepipe' Johnson."
312. U.S.W.D., MRTTGO, p. 32; *Confederate Veteran*, March 1900, pp. 117-118.
313. Indeed, hundreds of General Forrest's own former servants stayed on with him, or returned to work for him, after the War. For more on Forrest and blacks, see Seabrook, NBFAAA. For an in-depth discussion on American slavery and the South, see Seabrook, EYWTAASIW.
314. For more on the Reconstruction period, see Seabrook, AL.
315. *Confederate Veteran*, March 1919, p. 107.
316. *Confederate Veteran*, March 1932, p. 105.
317. *Confederate Veteran*, May 1910, p. 246.
318. Seabrook, EYWTAAAATCWIW, pp. 231-232. My emphasis.
319. *Confederate Veteran*, May 1923, p. 186.
320. *Confederate Veteran*, August 1907, p. 347.
321. *Confederate Veteran*, June 1908, p. 293.
322. My emphasis. For a detailed discussion on this topic, see Seabrook, NBFATKKK.
323. *Confederate Veteran*, June 1926, p. 225. Emphasis mine.
324. *Confederate Veteran*, May 1908, p. xxxvii.
325. *Confederate Veteran*, December 1904, p. 598.
326. *Confederate Veteran*, June 1925, p. 229.
327. *Confederate Veteran*, September 1896, p. 309.
328. *Confederate Veteran*, April 1919, p. 149.
329. *Confederate Veteran*, July 1898, p. 337.
330. *Confederate Veteran*, August 1909, p. 421.
331. *Confederate Veteran*, May 1897, p. 206.
332. *Confederate Veteran*, February 1923, p. 69.
333. *Confederate Veteran*, February 1912, p. 77.
334. *Confederate Veteran*, June 1909, p. 294.
335. *Confederate Veteran*, March 1932, p. 122.
336. *Confederate Veteran*, April 1916, p. 174.
337. *Confederate Veteran*, November 1911, pp. 534-535.
338. *Confederate Veteran*, September 1925, p. 347.
339. *Confederate Veteran*, May 1930, p. 197.
340. *Confederate Veteran*, February 1916, p. 83.

341. The Confederate Battle Flag was never "forever folded," and never will be. In fact, the conservative constitutional principles it stood for are more relevant now than ever before. For a full discussion on this topic, see Seabrook, CFF; Seabrook, LW.
342. *Confederate Veteran*, July 1919, p. 268.
343. *Confederate Veteran*, June 1897, p. 251.
344. *Confederate Veteran*, June 1897, p. 250.
345. *Confederate Veteran*, June 1897, pp. 250-251.
346. *Confederate Veteran*, December 1920, p. 469.
347. *Confederate Veteran*, September 1915, p. 419.
348. *Confederate Veteran*, August 1928, p. 306.
349. *Confederate Veteran*, September 1909, p. 470.
350. *Confederate Veteran*, May 1908, p. 238.
351. *Confederate Veteran*, July 1911, p. 351.
352. *Confederate Veteran*, March 1917, p. 133.
353. *Confederate Veteran*, July 1924, p. 270.
354. *Confederate Veteran*, November 1915, p. 516.
355. *Confederate Veteran*, June 1898, p. 276.
356. *Confederate Veteran*, January 1912, p. 32.
357. *Confederate Veteran*, January 1932, p. 28.
358. *Confederate Veteran*, September 1901, p. 418.
359. *Confederate Veteran*, November 1928, p. 405.
360. *Confederate Veteran*, August 1931, p. 306.
361. *Confederate Veteran*, January 1905, pp. 38-39.
362. For a detailed discussion on this topic, see Seabrook, NBFATKKK.
363. *Confederate Veteran*, July 1916, p. 321.
364. *Confederate Veteran*, March 1916, p. 132.
365. *Confederate Veteran*, March 1918, p. 124.
366. *Confederate Veteran*, April 1907, p. 186.
367. *Confederate Veteran*, May 1913, p. 244.
368. *Confederate Veteran*, February 1931, p. 69.
369. *Confederate Veteran*, August 1915, p. 369.
370. *Confederate Veteran*, March 1926, p. 104.
371. *Confederate Veteran*, February 1921, p. 67.
372. U.S.W.D., MRTTGO, p. 29; *Confederate Veteran*, December 1907, pp. 560-561.
373. OR, Ser. 1, Vol. 45, Pt. 2, p. 635.
374. *Confederate Veteran*, June 1912, pp. 281-282. My emphasis.
375. For a in-depth discussion on this topic, see Seabrook, ALWALJDWAC.
376. *Confederate Veteran*, December 1924, p. 475.
377. *Confederate Veteran*, February 1921, p. 68.
378. *Confederate Veteran*, June 1926, p. 228.
379. *Confederate Veteran*, March 1928, p. 108.
380. *Confederate Veteran*, December 1899, pp. 560-561.
381. For an in-depth examination of the socialist *weltanschauung* of the pre-1896, 19th-Century Republican Party (then the Liberal party), see Seabrook, LW; Seabrook, ALWALJDWAC.
382. *Confederate Veteran*, October 1924, p. 397.
383. *Confederate Veteran*, December 1925, p. 444.
384. *Confederate Veteran*, May 1904, p. 239.
385. *Confederate Veteran*, September 1911, p. 441.
386. *Confederate Veteran*, March 1919, p. 106.
387. *Confederate Veteran*, March 1909, p. 135.
388. *Confederate Veteran*, June 1914, p. 287.
389. *Confederate Veteran*, July 1910, p. 343.
390. *Confederate Veteran*, February 1901, p. 82.
391. *Confederate Veteran*, April 1913, p. 181.

392. *Confederate Veteran*, March 1903, p. 114.
393. *Confederate Veteran*, January 1905, p. 35.
394. *Confederate Veteran*, June 1901, p. 276.
395. *Confederate Veteran*, December 1923, p. 471.
396. As it turns out, the Starry Cross did not go "down forever," as many Confederate veterans assumed it would at the time. Over 150 years later it continues to fly proudly over homes, businesses, cemeteries, and parks all over the world, and for good reason: the principles for which it stood, conservatism and constitutionalism, are immortal and will thus be embraced and promoted by freedom-loving patriots for eternity. For a detailed examination of the Confederate Flag, including its history and meaning, see Seabrook, CFF.
397. *Confederate Veteran*, June 1903, p. 290.
398. *Confederate Veteran*, October 1905, p. 468. My emphasis.
399. For more on the history of our two American Confederacies (the U.S.A. and the C.S.A.), see Seabrook, C101.
400. *Confederate Veteran*, January 1916, p. 31.
401. Charles O. Blakeney was the son of William W. Blakeney and Eliza Ann Evans. He was born in 1871 at Monroe, NC. My personal family tree.
402. *Confederate Veteran*, December 1914, p. 569.
403. *Confederate Veteran*, February 1919, p. 62.
404. *Confederate Veteran*, December 1900, p. 547.
405. *Confederate Veteran*, April 1915, p. 185.
406. *Confederate Veteran*, April 1916, p. 178.
407. *Confederate Veteran*, January 1899, p. 33.
408. *Confederate Veteran*, January 1910, pp. 37-38.
409. *Confederate Veteran*, March 1910, p. 130.
410. *Confederate Veteran*, April 1916, p. 180.
411. For a detailed discussion on this topic, see Seabrook, NBFATKKK.
412. The post Civil War Ku Klux Klan referred to here, which I call the Reconstruction Ku Klux Klan, has no connection to today's KKK. The former was a *temporary conservative* society organized by former Confederate soldiers to aid war widows, orphans, and vets, while protecting the homes and constitutional rights of Southerners, until it was no longer needed. This occurred in 1869, when the Reconstruction KKK was shut down. For a detailed discussion on this topic, see my book: *Nathan Bedford Forrest and the Ku Klux Klan: Yankee Myth, Confederate Fact*.
413. *Confederate Veteran*, July 1906, pp. 324-325.
414. *Confederate Veteran*, July 1917, p. 323.
415. *Confederate Veteran*, May 1924, p. 187.
416. *Confederate Veteran*, February 1930, p. 42.
417. *Confederate Veteran*, September 1929, p. 349.
418. *Confederate Veteran*, July 1913, p. 350.
419. *Confederate Veteran*, May 1924, p. 185.
420. *Confederate Veteran*, November 1931, pp. 424-425.
421. *Confederate Veteran*, April 1911, p. 178.
422. *Confederate Veteran*, October 1929, p. 389.
423. *Confederate Veteran*, March 1922, p. 106.
424. *Confederate Veteran*, November 1928, p. 429.
425. *Confederate Veteran*, August 1899, p. 368.
426. *Confederate Veteran*, October 1914, p. 478. His widow was living in Austin, Texas, in 1914.
427. *Confederate Veteran*, November 1925, p. 427.
428. *Confederate Veteran*, April 1912, p. 181.
429. *Confederate Veteran*, January 1926, p. 39.
430. *Confederate Veteran*, May 1929, p. 199.
431. *Confederate Veteran*, February 1910, p. 83.
432. *Confederate Veteran*, November 1926, p. 427.
433. *Confederate Veteran*, April 1918, p. 167.
434. For more on this topic, see Seabrook, EYWTAAAATCWIW.

435. U.S.W.D., MRTTGO, p. 26; Warner, GIG, s.v. "John Tyler Morgan."
436. *Confederate Veteran*, February 1924, p. 66.
437. Seabrook, TGOW, pp. 116-118.
438. *Confederate Veteran*, September 1911, pp. 444-445.
439. *Confederate Veteran*, July 1924, p. 274.
440. For a detailed discussion of the original KKK (1865-1869), see Seabrook, NBFATKKK.
441. *Confederate Veteran*, November 1917, p. 516.
442. *Confederate Veteran*, June 1910, p. 293.
443. *Confederate Veteran*, February 1912, p. 76.
444. *Confederate Veteran*, December 1915, p. 553.
445. *Confederate Veteran*, August 1919, p. 319.
446. *Confederate Veteran*, December 1911, pp. 586-587.
447. *Confederate Veteran*, June 1927, p. 226.
448. *Confederate Veteran*, March 1927, p. 107.
449. *Confederate Veteran*, July 1918, p. 312.
450. *Confederate Veteran*, October 1913, p. 500.
451. *Confederate Veteran*, April 1916, p. 180.
452. *Confederate Veteran*, April 1905, pp. 175-176.
453. *Confederate Veteran*, August 1921, p. 319.
454. For a detailed discussion of the original KKK (1865-1869), see Seabrook, NBFATKKK.
455. *Confederate Veteran*, December 1916, p. 563.
456. *Confederate Veteran*, June 1914, p. 281.
457. *Confederate Veteran*, January 1918, p. 45.
458. *Confederate Veteran*, November 1897, pp. 571-572.
459. *Confederate Veteran*, May 1908, p. 239.
460. *Confederate Veteran*, May 1927, p. 184.
461. *Confederate Veteran*, September 1929, p. 349.
462. *Confederate Veteran*, February 1901, p. 80.
463. *Confederate Veteran*, September 1928, p. 348.
464. *Confederate Veteran*, December 1915, p. 574.
465. *Confederate Veteran*, December 1905, p. 577. My emphasis.
466. *Confederate Veteran*, February 1901, p. 127.
467. *Confederate Veteran*, September 1928, p. 328.
468. Warner, GIG, s.v. "John Pegram."
469. *Confederate Veteran*, June 1906, p. 277.
470. *Confederate Veteran*, February 1931, p. 89.
471. *Confederate Veteran*, March 1930, p. 113.
472. *Confederate Veteran*, September 1915, p. 431. His widow was living in Denton, Texas, in 1915.
473. *Confederate Veteran*, November 1917, p. 519.
474. *Confederate Veteran*, June 1902, p. 269.
475. *Confederate Veteran*, May 1909, p. 245.
476. *Confederate Veteran*, January 1923, p. 2.
477. *Confederate Veteran*, July 1932, pp. 266-267.
478. *Confederate Veteran*, September 1899, p. 408.
479. *Confederate Veteran*, October 1922, p. 388.
480. *Confederate Veteran*, October 1921, p. 390.
481. *Confederate Veteran*, October 1923, p. 386.
482. *Confederate Veteran*, April 1910, p. 184.
483. *Confederate Veteran*, May 1921, p. 188.
484. *Confederate Veteran*, March 1915, p. 141. His widow was living in Myra, Texas, in 1915.
485. *Confederate Veteran*, August 1905, p. 375.
486. *Confederate Veteran*, August 1923, p. 307.
487. *Confederate Veteran*, April 1898, p. 176.
488. For details on Van Dorn's death, see Seabrook, TMOCP, p. 355.

489. *Confederate Veteran*, July 1922, p. 271.
490. *Confederate Veteran*, June 1908, p. 292.
491. *Confederate Veteran*, January 1903, p. 36.
492. *Confederate Veteran*, June 1908, p. 288.
493. *Confederate Veteran*, December 1916, p. 560.
494. U.S.W.D., MRTTGO, p. 18; *Confederate Veteran*, February 1916, p. 95.
495. *Confederate Veteran*, March 1914, p. 135.
496. *Confederate Veteran*, June 1923, p. 224.
497. *Confederate Veteran*, April 1931, p. 147.
498. *Confederate Veteran*, August 1915, p. 371.
499. *Confederate Veteran*, June 1916, p. 269.
500. *Confederate Veteran*, February 1911, p. 72.
501. *Confederate Veteran*, August 1912, p. 387.
502. *Confederate Veteran*, September 1901, p. 419.
503. U.S.W.D., MRTTGO, p. 28; Warner, GIG, s.v. "Robert Vinkler Richardson."
504. *Confederate Veteran*, September 1912, p. 414.
505. The Conservative South's postwar campaign to overturn Liberal, scallywag, carpetbag rule was, quite misleadingly, referred to as "white supremacy" in Dixie at the time. Their violent and illegal oppression during so-called Reconstruction—basically, a second "Civil War" against the South that lasted three times as long (12 years)—provoked an understandable counter-reaction by white Southerners, who had, up to that time, rightfully considered themselves "the best friends the black man ever had." Antebellum, bellum, and postbellum Northern Liberals, in contrast, used African-Americans as nothing more than political pawns in their attempt to attain and maintain power in Washington, the same ploy still used by Liberals, socialists, communists, and collectivists today. For more on these topics, see Seabrook, EYWTAAAATCWIW; Seabrook, EYWTAASIW.
506. For a detailed examination of this topic, see Seabrook, ALWALJDWAC.
507. *Confederate Veteran*, July 1923, p. 262.
508. *Confederate Veteran*, July 1924, p. 272.
509. Seabrook, ARB, p. 277 (2011 paperback edition).
510. *Confederate Veteran*, January 1924, p. 28.
511. U.S.W.D., MRTTGO, p. 26; Warner, GIG, s.v. "Philip Dale Roddey."
512. *Confederate Veteran*, September 1902, p. 423.
513. *Confederate Veteran*, June 1923, p. 224.
514. *Confederate Veteran*, March 1908, p. 137.
515. *Confederate Veteran*, November 1918, p. 492.
516. *Confederate Veteran*, April 1912, pp. 176-177.
517. U.S.W.D., MRTTGO, p. 28; Warner, GIG, s.v. "Lawrence Sullivan Ross."
518. *Confederate Veteran*, May 1924, pp. 163-164.
519. Seabrook, ARB, p. 17 (paperback, 2011 edition).
520. *Confederate Veteran*, May 1924, pp. 163-164. (Note: I descend from the Rucker family. L.S.)
521. *Confederate Veteran*, October 1927, p. 388.
522. *Confederate Veteran*, July 1903, p. 369.
523. *Confederate Veteran*, March 1928, p. 109.
524. *Confederate Veteran*, November 1925, p. 425.
525. *Confederate Veteran*, July 1924, p. 272.
526. *Confederate Veteran*, April 1930, p. 156.
527. *Confederate Veteran*, January 1910, p. 39.
528. *Confederate Veteran*, June 1924, p. 232.
529. *Confederate Veteran*, February 1931, p. 82.
530. *Confederate Veteran*, December 1927, p. 426.
531. *Confederate Veteran*, December 1916, p. 563.
532. *Confederate Veteran*, May 1911, p. 235.
533. *Confederate Veteran*, May 1918, p. 220.
534. *Confederate Veteran*, March 1918, p. 120.

535. *Confederate Veteran*, May 1927, p. 187.
536. *Confederate Veteran*, September 1931, p. 322.
537. *Confederate Veteran*, February 1924, p. 67.
538. *Confederate Veteran*, June 1920, p. 226.
539. *Confederate Veteran*, June 1923, p. 228.
540. *Confederate Veteran*, May 1930, p. 196.
541. *Confederate Veteran*, July 1900, p. 355.
542. *Confederate Veteran*, June 1927, p. 227.
543. *Confederate Veteran*, November 1914, p. 517.
544. *Confederate Veteran*, June 1902, p. 273.
545. *Confederate Veteran*, August 1919, p. 309.
546. *Confederate Veteran*, November 1906, p. 516. My emphasis.
547. *Confederate Veteran*, August 1923, p. 306.
548. *Confederate Veteran*, May 1928, p. 162.
549. *Confederate Veteran*, February 1901, p. 130.
550. *Confederate Veteran*, October 1899, p. 447.
551. *Confederate Veteran*, March 1921, pp. 107-108.
552. *Confederate Veteran*, January 1916, p. 32.
553. *Confederate Veteran*, December 1927, p. 429.
554. *Confederate Veteran*, June 1924, p. 231.
555. *Confederate Veteran*, June 1906, p. 275.
556. U.S.W.D., MRTTGO, p. 22; Warner, GIG, s.v. "Peter Burwell Starke."
557. *Confederate Veteran*, June 1928, p. 226.
558. *Confederate Veteran*, August 1923, p. 305.
559. *Confederate Veteran*, March 1902, p. 127.
560. *Confederate Veteran*, July 1926, p. 265.
561. *Confederate Veteran*, April 1899, pp. 176-177.
562. *Confederate Veteran*, March 1912, p. 128.
563. *Confederate Veteran*, April 1905, p. 235.
564. *Confederate Veteran*, June 1923, p. 228.
565. *Confederate Veteran*, December 1914, p. 569.
566. *Confederate Veteran*, March 1909, p. 131.
567. *Confederate Veteran*, May 1932, p. 189.
568. *Confederate Veteran*, November 1899, p. 514.
569. *Confederate Veteran*, August 1908, p. 414.
570. *Confederate Veteran*, May 1911, p. vii-191.
571. *Confederate Veteran*, November 1924, p. 432.
572. *Confederate Veteran*, December 1902, pp. 562-563.
573. *Confederate Veteran*, September 1913, p. 453.
574. *Confederate Veteran*, November 1906, pp. 516-517.
575. *Confederate Veteran*, April 1928, p. 145.
576. *Confederate Veteran*, October 1900, p. 453. Note: This entry was written by Capt. Thomson's daughter, Dora Sifford.
577. *Confederate Veteran*, July 1908, p. 357.
578. *Confederate Veteran*, September 1923, p. 345.
579. *Confederate Veteran*, February 1901, pp. 81-82.
580. *Confederate Veteran*, May 1912, p. 233.
581. *Confederate Veteran*, April 1910, p. 183.
582. *Confederate Veteran*, November 1909, p. 566.
583. *Confederate Veteran*, October 1917, p. 470.
584. *Confederate Veteran*, June 1909, p. 288.
585. *Confederate Veteran*, June 1915, p. 277.
586. *Confederate Veteran*, February 1925, p. 65.
587. *Confederate Veteran*, September 1927, p. 347.

588. *Confederate Veteran*, June 1929, p. 225.
589. *Confederate Veteran*, July 1898, p. 336.
590. *Confederate Veteran*, January 1927, p. 26.
591. L. Seabrook.
592. *Confederate Veteran*, April 1908, p. xxv.
593. *Confederate Veteran*, January 1906, p. 17.
594. For a detailed discussion of the original KKK (1865-1869), see Seabrook, NBFATKKK.
595. *Confederate Veteran*, March 1928, p. 109.
596. *Confederate Veteran*, May 1920, p. 187.
597. *Confederate Veteran*, June 1909, p. 292.
598. *Confederate Veteran*, June 1909, p. 288.
599. For more on this important event, see Seabrook, ALWALJDWAC.
600. *Confederate Veteran*, July 1898, pp. 305-307. See also, U.S.W.D., MRTTGO, pp. 12, 25.
601. *Confederate Veteran*, December 1928, p. 468.
602. *Confederate Veteran*, September 1928, p. 347.
603. *Confederate Veteran*, January 1918, p. 30. My emphasis.
604. *Confederate Veteran*, March 1908, p. 131.
605. *Confederate Veteran*, April 1931, p. 149.
606. *Confederate Veteran*, April 1921, p. 148.
607. *Confederate Veteran*, January 1911, p. 39.
608. *Confederate Veteran*, March 1925, p. 102.
609. *Confederate Veteran*, April 1908, p. xxiv.
610. U.S.W.D., MRTTGO, pp. 10, 24; Warner, GIG, s.v. "John Austin Wharton."
611. *Confederate Veteran*, May 1919, p. 199.
612. *Confederate Veteran*, October 1916, p. 464.
613. *Confederate Veteran*, December 1899, pp. 561-562. My emphasis.
614. *Confederate Veteran*, December 1910, p. 578.
615. *Confederate Veteran*, December 1909, p. 609.
616. *Confederate Veteran*, February 1930, p. 68.
617. *Confederate Veteran*, November 1907, p. 511.
618. *Confederate Veteran*, February 1929, p. 66.
619. *Confederate Veteran*, February 1903, p. 81.
620. Seabrook, ARB, p. 277 (2011 paperback edition).
621. *Confederate Veteran*, March 1895, p. 76.
622. *Confederate Veteran*, May 1910, p. 253.
623. *Confederate Veteran*, November 1922, p. 432.
624. *Confederate Veteran*, May 1923, p. 185.
625. *Confederate Veteran*, October 1902, p. 438.
626. *Confederate Veteran*, December 1923, p. 470.
627. *Confederate Veteran*, June 1905, p. 283.
628. *Confederate Veteran*, May 1906, p. 224.
629. *Confederate Veteran*, December 1923, p. 471.
630. *Confederate Veteran*, February 1927, p. 67.
631. *Confederate Veteran*, June 1923, p. 228.
632. *Confederate Veteran*, January 1921, p. 28.
633. *Confederate Veteran*, July 1905, p. 323.
634. From the author's personal records, and *Confederate Veteran*, June 1901, p. 252.
635. *Confederate Veteran*, November 1918, p. 491. My emphasis.
636. *Confederate Veteran*, January 1928, p. 26.
637. *Confederate Veteran*, November 1916, p. 515.
638. *Confederate Veteran*, February 1920, p. 71.
639. *Confederate Veteran*, July 1908, p. 356.
640. *Confederate Veteran*, July 1914, p. 327.

641. *Confederate Veteran*, September 1904, p. 426. Note: This list was furnished by J. N. Taylor, Secretary of Forrest's staff and escort.
642. *Confederate Veteran*, October 1906, p. 441.
643. *Confederate Veteran*, April 1910, pp. 170-172.
644. *Confederate Veteran*, May 1913, p. 213.
645. *Confederate Veteran*, May 1916, p. 240.
646. *Confederate Veteran*, May 1920, p. 197.
647. *Confederate Veteran*, November 1923, pp. 428-429.
648. *Confederate Veteran*, August 1928, p. 284.

BIBLIOGRAPHY

And Suggested Reading

Note: My pro-South readers are to be advised that many of the books listed here are anti-South in nature (some extremely so), and were written primarily by Liberal elitist, socialist, communist, and Marxist authors who loathe the South, and typically the United States and the U.S. Constitution as well. Despite this, as a scholar I find these titles indispensable, for *an honest evaluation of Lincoln's War is not possible without studying both the Southern and the Northern versions*—an attitude, unfortunately, completely lacking among pro-North historians (who read and study only their own ahistorical version). Still, it must be said that the material contained in these often mean-spirited works is largely the result of a century and a half of Yankee myth, falsehoods, cherry-picking, slander, redaction, sophistry, editorializing, anti-South propaganda, outright lies, and junk research, as modern pro-North writers merely copy one another's errors without ever looking at the original 19th-Century sources. This type of literature, filled as it is with both misinformation and disinformation, is called "scholarly" and "objective" by pro-North advocates. In the process, the mistakes and lies in these fact-free, fault-ridden, South-shaming, historically inaccurate works have been magnified over the years, and the North's version of the "Civil War" has come to be accepted as the only legitimate one. Indeed, it is now the only one known by most people. That over 95 percent of the titles in most of my bibliographies fall into the anti-South category is simply a reflection of the enormous power and influence that the pro-North movement—our nation's cultural ruling class—has long held over America's education system, libraries, publishing houses, and media (paper and electronic). My books serve as a small rampart against the overwhelming tide of anti-South Fascists, Liberals, cultural Marxists, and political elites, all who are working hard to obliterate Southern culture and guarantee that you will never learn the Truth about Lincoln and his War on the Constitution and the American people.

Ashe, Captain Samuel A'Court. *A Southern View of the Invasion of the Southern States and War of 1861-1865.* 1935. Crawfordville, GA: Ruffin Flag Company, 1938 ed.
Benson, Al, Jr., and Walter Donald Kennedy. *Lincoln's Marxists*. Gretna, LA: Pelican, 2011.
Boatner, Mark Mayo. *The Civil War Dictionary*. 1959. New York, NY: David McKay Co., Inc., 1988 ed.
Bowman, John S. *The Civil War Day by Day: An Illustrated Almanac of America's Bloodiest War.* 1989. New York, NY: Dorset Press, 1990 ed.
——. (ed.) *Encyclopedia of the Civil War.* 1992. North Dighton, MA: JG Press, 2001 ed.
Boyd, James P. *Parties, Problems, and Leaders of 1896: An Impartial Presentation of Living National Questions.* Chicago, IL: Publishers' Union, 1896.
Bradley, Michael R. *Nathan Bedford Forrest's Escort and Staff.* Gretna, LA: Pelican Publishing Co., 2006.
Brock, Robert Alonzo (ed.). *Southern Historical Society Papers.* 52 vols. Richmond, VA: Southern Historical Society, 1876-1943.
Browder, Earl. *Lincoln and the Communists.* New York, NY: Workers Library Publishers, Inc., 1936.
Bryan, William Jennings. *The First Battle: A Story of the Campaign of 1896.* Chicago, IL: W. B. Conkey Co., 1896.
Burns, James MacGregor. *The Vineyard of Liberty.* New York, NY: Alfred A. Knopf, 1982.
Christian, George Llewellyn. *Abraham Lincoln: An Address Delivered Before R. E. Lee Camp, No. 1 Confederate Veterans at Richmond, VA, October 29, 1909.* Richmond, VA: L. H. Jenkins, 1909.

———. *A Capitol Disaster: A Chapter of Reconstruction in Virginia.* Richmond, VA: self-published, 1915.
———. *Confederate Memories and Experiences.* Richmond, VA: self-published, 1915.
Confederate Veteran (Sumner A. Cunningham, ed.). 40 vols. Nashville, TN: Confederate Veteran, 1893-1932.
Davis, Jefferson. *The Rise and Fall of the Confederate Government.* 2 vols. New York, NY: D. Appleton and Co., 1881.
Dinkins, James. *1861 to 1865, by an Old Johnnie: Personal Recollections and Experiences in the Confederate Army.* Cincinnati, OH: The Robert Clark Co., 1897.
Dodd, Bella. *School of Darkness.* New York, NY: P. J. Kennedy and Sons, 1954.
Drake, Francis S. *Dictionary of American Biography.* Boston, MA: Houghton, Osgood, and Co., 1879.
Duncan, Thomas D. *Recollections of Thomas D. Duncan: A Confederate Soldier.* Nashville, TN: self-published, 1922.
Encyclopedia Britannica: A New Survey of Universal Knowledge. 1768. Chicago, IL/London, UK: Encyclopedia Britannica, 1955 ed.
Evans, Clement Anselm (ed.). *Confederate Military History.* 12 vols. Atlanta, GA: Confederate Publishing Co., 1899.
Faust, Patricia L. (ed.). *Historical Times Illustrated Encyclopedia of the Civil War.* New York, NY: Harper and Row, 1986.
Franklin, John Hope. *Reconstruction After the Civil War.* Chicago, IL: University of Chicago Press, 1961.
Hale, Will Thomas, and Dixon Lanier Merritt. *A History of Tennessee and Tennesseans: The Leaders and Representative Men in Commerce, Industry and Modern Activities.* 8 vols. Chicago, IL: The Lewis Publishing Co., 1913.
Hancock, Richard R. *Hancock's Diary: Or, A History of the Second Tennessee Cavalry, With Sketches of First and Seventh Battalions.* 2 vols. in one. Nashville, TN: self-published, 1887.
Hasselberg, P. D. (ed.). *Parliamentary Debates: First Session, Fortieth Parliament, 1982, House of Representatives* (Vol. 445). Wellington, New Zealand: Government Printer, 1982.
Homans, James E. (ed.). *The Cyclopedia of American Biography.* New York, NY: The Press Association Compilers, 1918.
Johnson, Robert Underwood, and Clarence Clough Buel (eds.). *Battles and Leaders of the Civil War.* 4 vols. New York, NY: The Century Co., 1884-1888.
Johnstone, Huger William. *Truth of War Conspiracy, 1861.* Idylwild, GA: H. W. Johnstone, 1921.
Jones, John William. *The Davis Memorial Volume; Or Our Dead President, Jefferson Davis and the World's Tribute to His Memory.* Richmond, VA: B. F. Johnson, 1889.
Jordan, Thomas, and John P. Pryor. *The Campaigns of General Nathan Bedford Forrest and of Forrest's Cavalry.* New Orleans, LA: Blelock and Co., 1868.
La Bree, Ben (ed.). *The Confederate Soldier in the Civil War, 1861-1865.* Louisville, KY: Prentice Press, 1897.
Lenin, Vladimir. *"Left Wing" Communism: An Infantile Disorder.* Detroit, MI: The Marxian Educational Society, 1921.
LeVert, Suzanne. *The Civil War Society's Encyclopedia of the Civil War.* New York, NY: Wings Books, 1997.
Livermore, Thomas L. *Numbers and Losses in the Civil War in America, 1861-65.* 1900. Carlisle, PA: John Kallmann, 1996 ed.
Magliocca, Gerard N. *The Tragedy of William Jennings Bryan: Constitutional Law and the*

Politics of Backlash. New Haven, CT: Yale University Press, 2011.
Marx, Karl, and Frederick Engels. *Manifesto of the Communist Party*. Chicago, IL: Charles H. Kerr and Co., 1906.
McCarty, Burke (ed.). *Little Sermons in Socialism by Abraham Lincoln*. Chicago, IL: The Chicago Daily Socialist, 1910.
McMurray, William Josiah. *History of the Twentieth Tennessee Regiment Volunteer Infantry, C.S.A.* Nashville, TN: The Publication Committee, 1904.
McPherson, James M. *Abraham Lincoln and the Second American Revolution*. New York, NY: Oxford University Press, 1991.
Meriwether, Elizabeth Avery (pseudonym, "George Edmonds"). *Facts and Falsehoods Concerning the War on the South, 1861-1865*. Memphis, TN: A. R. Taylor and Co., 1904.
Miller, Francis Trevelyan, and Robert S. Lanier (eds.). *The Photographic History of the Civil War*. 10 vols. New York, NY: The Review of Reviews Co., 1911.
Minutes of the Eighth Annual Meeting and Reunion of the United Confederate Veterans, Atlanta, GA, July 20-23, 1898. New Orleans, LA: United Confederate Veterans, 1907.
Minutes of the Ninth Annual Meeting and Reunion of the United Confederate Veterans, Charleston, SC, May 10-13, 1899. New Orleans, LA: United Confederate Veterans, 1907.
Minutes of the Twelfth Annual Meeting and Reunion of the United Confederate Veterans, Dallas, TX, April 22-25, 1902. New Orleans, LA: United Confederate Veterans, 1907.
Morton, John Watson. *The Artillery of Nathan Bedford Forrest's Cavalry*. Nashville, TN: The M. E. Church, 1909.
Muzzey, David Saville. *The United States of America: Vol. 1, To the Civil War*. Boston, MA: Ginn and Co., 1922.
———. *The American Adventure: Vol. 2, From the Civil War*. 1924. New York, NY: Harper and Brothers, 1927 ed.
Neilson, William (ed.). *Webster's Biographical Dictionary*. Springfield, MA: G. & C. Merriam Co., 1943.
Nicolay, John G., and John Hay (eds.). *Abraham Lincoln: A History*. 10 vols. New York, NY: The Century Co., 1890.
———. *Complete Works of Abraham Lincoln*. 12 vols. 1894. New York, NY: Francis D. Tandy Co., 1905 ed.
———. *Abraham Lincoln: Complete Works*. 12 vols. 1894. New York, NY: The Century Co., 1907 ed.
Oglesby, Thaddeus K. *Some Truths of History: A Vindication of the South Against the Encyclopedia Britannica and Other Maligners*. Atlanta, GA: Byrd Printing, 1903.
ORA (full title: *The War of the Rebellion: A Compilation of the Official Records of the Union and Confederate Armies*). 70 vols. Washington, DC: Government Printing Office, 1880.
ORN (full title: *Official Records of the Union and Confederate Navies in the War of the Rebellion*). 30 vols. Washington, DC: Government Printing Office, 1894.
Parry, Melanie (ed.). *Chambers Biographical Dictionary*. 1897. Edinburgh, Scotland: Chambers Harrap, 1998 ed.
Phillips, Robert S. (ed.). *Funk and Wagnalls New Encyclopedia*. 1971. New York, NY: Funk and Wagnalls, 1979 ed.
Pollard, Edward Alfred. *The Lost Cause*. New York, NY: E. B. Treat and Co., 1867.
Richardson, John Anderson. *Richardson's Defense of the South*. Atlanta, GA: A. B. Caldwell, 1914.
Rogers, William P. *The Three Secession Movements in the United States: Samuel J. Tilden, the*

Democratic Candidate for Presidency; the Advisor, Aider and Abettor of the Great Secession Movement of 1860; and One of the Authors of the Infamous Resolution of 1864; His Claims as a Statesman and Reformer Considered. Boston, MA: John Wilson and Son, 1876.

Rosenbaum, Robert A. (ed). *The New American Desk Encyclopedia.* 1977. New York, NY: Signet, 1989 ed.

Rosenbaum, Robert A., and Douglas Brinkley (eds.). *The Penguin Encyclopedia of American History.* New York, NY: Viking, 2003.

Rove, Karl. *The Triumph of William McKinley: Why the Election of 1896 Still Matters.* New York, NY: Simon and Schuster, 2015.

Rutherford, Mildred Lewis. *Truths of History: A Fair, Unbiased, Impartial, Unprejudiced and Conscientious Study of History.* Athens, GA: n.p., 1920.

Seabrook, Lochlainn. *Carnton Plantation Ghost Stories: True Tales of the Unexplained from Tennessee's Most Haunted Civil War House!* 2005. Franklin, TN, 2016 ed.

——. *Nathan Bedford Forrest: Southern Hero, American Patriot.* 2007. Franklin, TN, 2010 ed.

——. *Abraham Lincoln: The Southern View.* 2007. Franklin, TN: Sea Raven Press, 2013 ed.

——. *The McGavocks of Carnton Plantation: A Southern History - Celebrating One of Dixie's Most Noble Confederate Families and Their Tennessee Home.* 2008. Franklin, TN, 2011 ed.

——. *A Rebel Born: A Defense of Nathan Bedford Forrest.* 2010. Franklin, TN: Sea Raven Press, 2011 ed.

——. *A Rebel Born: The Screenplay* (for the film). 2011. Franklin, TN: Sea Raven Press.

——. *Everything You Were Taught About the Civil War is Wrong, Ask a Southerner!* 2010. Franklin, TN: Sea Raven Press, revised 2014 ed.

——. *The Quotable Jefferson Davis: Selections From the Writings and Speeches of the Confederacy's First President.* Franklin, TN: Sea Raven Press, 2011.

——. *The Quotable Robert E. Lee: Selections From the Writings and Speeches of the South's Most Beloved Civil War General.* Franklin, TN: Sea Raven Press, 2011 Sesquicentennial Civil War Edition.

——. *Lincolnology: The Real Abraham Lincoln Revealed In His Own Words.* Franklin, TN: Sea Raven Press, 2011.

——. *The Unquotable Abraham Lincoln: The President's Quotes They Don't Want You To Know!* Franklin, TN: Sea Raven Press, 2011.

——. *Honest Jeff and Dishonest Abe: A Southern Children's Guide to the Civil War.* Franklin, TN: Sea Raven Press, 2012.

——. *Encyclopedia of the Battle of Franklin - A Comprehensive Guide to the Conflict that Changed the Civil War.* Franklin, TN: Sea Raven Press, 2012.

——. *The Quotable Nathan Bedford Forrest: Selections From the Writings and Speeches of the Confederacy's Most Brilliant Cavalryman.* Spring Hill, TN: Sea Raven Press, 2012.

——. *Forrest! 99 Reasons to Love Nathan Bedford Forrest.* Spring Hill, TN: Sea Raven Press, 2012.

——. *Give 'Em Hell Boys! The Complete Military Correspondence of Nathan Bedford Forrest.* Spring Hill, TN: Sea Raven Press, 2012.

——. *The Constitution of the Confederate States of America Explained: A Clause-by-Clause Study of the South's Magna Carta.* Spring Hill, TN: Sea Raven Press, 2012 Sesquicentennial Civil War Edition.

——. *The Great Impersonator: 99 Reasons to Dislike Abraham Lincoln.* Spring Hill, TN: Sea Raven Press, 2012.

——. *The Old Rebel: Robert E. Lee As He Was Seen By His Contemporaries.* Spring Hill, TN:

Sea Raven Press, 2012 Sesquicentennial Civil War Edition.

———. *The Quotable Stonewall Jackson: Selections From the Writings and Speeches of the South's Most Famous General.* Spring Hill, TN: Sea Raven Press, 2012 Sesquicentennial Civil War Edition.

———. *Saddle, Sword, and Gun: A Biography of Nathan Bedford Forrest for Teens.* Spring Hill, TN: Sea Raven Press, 2013.

———. *The Alexander H. Stephens Reader: Excerpts From the Works of a Confederate Founding Father.* Spring Hill, TN: Sea Raven Press, 2013.

———. *The Quotable Alexander H. Stephens: Selections From the Writings and Speeches of the Confederacy's First Vice President.* Spring Hill, TN: Sea Raven Press, 2013 Sesquicentennial Civil War Edition.

———. *Give This Book to a Yankee! A Southern Guide to the Civil War for Northerners.* Spring Hill, TN: Sea Raven Press, 2014.

———. *The Articles of Confederation Explained: A Clause-by-Clause Study of America's First Constitution.* Spring Hill, TN: Sea Raven Press, 2014.

———. *Confederate Blood and Treasure: An Interview With Lochlainn Seabrook.* Spring Hill, TN: Sea Raven Press, 2015.

———. *Nathan Bedford Forrest and the Battle of Fort Pillow: Yankee Myth, Confederate Fact.* Spring Hill, TN: Sea Raven Press, 2015.

———. *Everything You Were Taught About American Slavery War is Wrong, Ask a Southerner!* Spring Hill, TN: Sea Raven Press, 2015.

———. *Confederacy 101: Amazing Facts You Never Knew About America's Oldest Political Tradition.* Spring Hill, TN: Sea Raven Press, 2015.

———. *The Great Yankee Coverup: What the North Doesn't Want You to Know About Lincoln's War!* Spring Hill, TN: Sea Raven Press, 2015.

———. *Slavery 101: Amazing Facts You Never Knew About America's "Peculiar Institution."* Spring Hill, TN: Sea Raven Press, 2015.

———. *Confederate Flag Facts: What Every American Should Know About Dixie's Southern Cross.* Spring Hill, TN: Sea Raven Press, 2016.

———. *Nathan Bedford Forrest and the Ku Klux Klan: Yankee Myth, Confederate Fact.* Spring Hill, TN: Sea Raven Press, 2016.

———. *Seabrook's Bible Dictionary of Traditional and Mystical Christian Doctrines.* Spring Hill, TN: Sea Raven Press, 2016.

———. *Everything You Were Taught About African-Americans and the Civil War is Wrong, Ask a Southerner!* Spring Hill, TN: Sea Raven Press, 2016.

———. *Nathan Bedford Forrest and African-Americans: Yankee Myth, Confederate Fact.* Spring Hill, TN: Sea Raven Press, 2016.

———. *Women in Gray: A Tribute to the Ladies Who Supported the Southern Confederacy.* Spring Hill, TN: Sea Raven Press, 2016.

———. *Lincoln's War: The Real Cause, the Real Winner, the Real Loser.* Spring Hill, TN: Sea Raven Press, 2016.

———. *The Unholy Crusade: Lincoln's Legacy of Destruction in the American South.* Spring Hill, TN: Sea Raven Press, 2017.

———. *Abraham Lincoln Was a Liberal, Jefferson Davis Was a Conservative: The Missing Key to Understanding the American Civil War.* Spring Hill, TN: Sea Raven Press, 2017.

———. *All We Ask is to be Let Alone: The Southern Secession Fact Book.* Spring Hill, TN: Sea Raven Press, 2017.

———. *The Ultimate Civil War Quiz Book: How Much Do You Really Know About America's Most Misunderstood Conflict?* Spring Hill, TN: Sea Raven Press, 2017.

———. *Rise Up and Call Them Blessed: Victorian Tributes to the Confederate Soldier, 1861-1901.*

Spring Hill, TN: Sea Raven Press, 2017.
——. *Victorian Confederate Poetry: The Southern Cause in Verse, 1861-1901*. Spring Hill, TN: Sea Raven Press, 2018.
——. *Confederate Monuments: Why Every American Should Honor Confederate Soldiers and Their Memorials*. Spring Hill, TN: Sea Raven Press, 2018.
——. *The God of War: Nathan Bedford Forrest as He Was Seen by His Contemporaries*. Spring Hill, TN: Sea Raven Press, 2018.
——. *The Battle of Spring Hill: Recollections of Confederate and Union Soldiers*. Spring Hill, TN: Sea Raven Press, 2018.
Simmons, Henry E. *A Concise Encyclopedia of the Civil War*. New York, NY: Bonanza Books, 1965.
Steel, Samuel Augustus. *The South Was Right*. Columbia, SC: R. L. Bryan Co., 1914.
Stephens, Alexander Hamilton. *Speech of Mr. Stephens, of Georgia, on the War and Taxation*. Washington, D.C.: J & G. Gideon, 1848.
——. *A Constitutional View of the Late War Between the States; Its Causes, Character, Conduct and Results*. 2 vols. Philadelphia, PA: National Publishing, Co., 1870.
——. *Recollections of Alexander H. Stephens: His Diary Kept When a Prisoner at Fort Warren, Boston Harbour, 1865*. New York, NY: Doubleday, Page, and Co., 1910.
The Oxford English Dictionary. Compact edition, 2 vols. 1928. Oxford, UK: Oxford University Press, 1979 ed.
Thompson, Holland. *The New South: A Chronicle of Social and Industrial Evolution*. New Haven, CT: Yale University Press, 1920.
U.S.W.D. (United States War Department). *Memorandum Relative to the General Officers Appointed by the President in the Armies of the Confederate States, 1861-1865*. Washington, D.C.: Government Printing Office, 1905.
U.S.W.D. (United States War Department). *Bibliography of State Participation in the Civil War, 1861-1866*. Washington, D.C.: Government Printing Office, 1913.
U.S.W.D. (United States War Department). *List of Field Officers, Regiments, and Battalions in the Confederate States Army, 1861-1865*. Washington, D.C.: Government Printing Office, 1891.
U.S.W.D. (United States War Department). *List of Staff Officers of the Confederate States Army, 1861-1865*. Washington, D.C.: Government Printing Office, 1891.
Warner, Ezra J. *Generals in Gray: Lives of the Confederate Commanders*. 1959. Baton Rouge, LA: Louisiana State University Press, 1989 ed.
——. *Generals in Blue: Lives of the Union Commanders*. 1964. Baton Rouge, LA: Louisiana State University Press, 2006 ed.
Watts, Peter. *A Dictionary of the Old West*. 1977. New York, NY: Promontory Press, 1987 ed.
Wilson, Charles Reagan, and William Ferris. *Encyclopedia of Southern Culture* (Vol. 1). New York, NY: Anchor, 1989.
Woods, Thomas E., Jr. *The Politically Incorrect Guide to American History*. Washington, D.C.: Regnery, 2004.

INDEX

Of Encyclopedia Entries Only

Abernathy, Thomas E., 23
Adams, William W., 23
Aden, James S., 24
Alcorn, Milton S., 24
Aldrich, Ed, 25
Alexander, J. P., 25
Alexander, Samuel J., 26
Allen, J. G., 26
Allen, Samuel, 27
Allen, Wade, 27
Alley, Richard B., 27
Allison, Robert A., 28
Allison, Thomas F. P., 29
Anderson, Charles W., 30
Anderson, DeWitt, 30
Armstrong, Frank C., 31
Arnold, James, 31
Arnold, James M., 32
Ashcraft, John W., 32
Ashworth, Carlton, 33
Atkisson. G. J., 33
Babb, D. W., 35
Balch, L. C., 35
Bankhead, L. J., 36
Barger, W. G., 36
Barlow, Joseph C., 37
Barnett, John W., 37
Barron, S. B., 37
Baskerville, George B., 39
Bazzell, Robert I., 39
Bell, Isaac T., 40
Bell, Tyree H., 41
Bemiss, James H., 42
Bennett, W. H., 43
Berry, T. F., 43
Bethell, William D., 44
Bidwell, Bell G., 45
Biggs, George T., 46
Birdsong, Thomas L., 46
Bishop, David, 47
Bittick, John H., 47
Black, Robert J., 48
Black, William F., 48
Blackburn, James K. P., 49

Blanton, J. C., 49
Boggs, David C., 50
Bogy, Joseph V., 50
Boling, M. L., 51
Bomar, William S., 51
Bone, H. P., 51
Bonner, N. S., 52
Boone, Hugh L. W., 53
Boone, Nathan S., 53
Booton, Daniel F., 53
Bottom, Thomas A., 54
Bowles, John J., 55
Boyd, J. C., 55
Bradwell, Thomas M., 55
Bragg, Henry T., 56
Breathitt, John B., 57
Brian, James P., 57
Briggs, Joseph B., 58
Brown, Joseph T., 58
Brown, Joshua, 59
Brown, R. U., 60
Brown, Tully, 60
Brown, William H., 60
Bruce, James B. F., 61
Buchanan, Charles M., 61
Buchanan, William F., 61
Buford, Abraham, 61
Burke, Michael, 62
Busby, John S., 62
Bush, William G., 62
Callaway, William A., 65
Campbell, Alexander W., 66
Campbell, Thomas, 66
Campbell, William A., 66
Carmichael, George W., 67
Carney, John L., 68
Carter, Joe W., 69
Castleberry, Charles C., 69
Chadick, W. D., 70
Chalmers, James R., 70
Cheairs, Thomas G., 71
Claybrooke, Samuel P., 71
Clayton, Solomon S., 72
Clayton, Wiley M., 73

Clements, G. D., 73
Clift, Moses H., 73
Clinton, Samuel H., 76
Cobb, Thomas W., 76
Coker, George W., 76
Coleman, Preston B., 77
Coley, William H., 77
Collier, William A., 78
Conklin, Elijah, 80
Cook, Barnett M., 80
Cook, Virgil Y., 81
Corman, J. W., 81
Cornwall, Richard O., 82
Couch, E., 82
Cowan, George L., 82
Cowan, James B., 83
Cox, F. M., 85
Coyle, Ben L., 85
Crawley, A. B., 85
Critz, Frank A., 86
Croft, W. C., 86
Crossland, Edward, 87
Crump, Marcus V., 88
Culbreath, J. M., 88
Dashiel, George, 89
Davenport, Z. T., 89
Davidson, Elijah A., 90
Davis, Ben, 90
Davis, Carroll M., 90
Davis, Columbus J., 91
Davis, J. A., 92
Davis, J. K., 92
Davis, Robert N., 92
Davis, William H., 93
Dawson, W. A., 93
Dean, Marcus L., 94
Deaton, John W., 94
DeLoach, William R., 95
DeVaughn, James E., 96
Dew, Arthur T., 97
DeWoody, William L., 97
Dibrell, George G., 98
Dickenson, R. D., 98
Dilbeck, J. D., 98
Dinkins, James, 99
Dismukes, John L., 99
Dodge, D. F., 100
Doerner, George W., 100
Douglas, Edwin H., 100
Douglass, Thomas J., 101

Douthit, Thomas E., 102
Dowdy, Jesse L., 102
Dozier, Nathaniel B., 102
Dry, Michael A., 103
Dudley, Richard H., 104
Duffy, J. W., 105
Dugan, George M., 106
Duncan, Green C., 106
Duncan, Thomas D., 107
Duncan, W. D. L., 107
Dunlap, R. A. D., 107
Dunlap, W. N. L., 108
Dunning, Levi S., 109
Dye, Shelby, 109
Eaves, Joseph C., 111
Edgman, John L., 111
Edmondson, Henry C., 112
Elcan, Archibald L., 112
Enochs, M. A. L., 113
Evans, G. W., 114
Evans, Thomas, 115
Evins, Robert H., 115
Ewing, Benjamin D., 116
Fail, W. E., 117
Faris, Charles A. D., 117
Farrow, G. F., 118
Fatheree, L. L., 119
Fay, R. E., 119
Ferguson, Lon, 119
Ferrell, Lucillius S., 119
Field, H. C., 120
Fisher, William H., 120
Fletcher, John D., 120
Ford, Cornelius Y., 121
Forrest, Car, 121
Forrest, William M., 122
Foster, George W., 122
Fowlkes, John A., 123
Francis, John, 123
Francis, Joseph H., 123
Franklin, L. C., 124
Freeman, H. M., 124
Frensley, Harrison M., 125
Frizzell, Samuel W., 125
Fuqua, John F., 125
Fussell, Joseph H., 125
Galbraith, T. J., 127
Gardner, W. M., 127
Garrett, Elijah, 127
Garrett, William R., 127

Gay, A. T., 128
Gee, James L., 129
George, Henry, 129
George, J. H., 130
George, J. T., 131
Gholson, Samuel J., 132
Gibbs, George R., 132
Gillespie, James W., 133
Girtman, J. W. D., 133
Gloster, A. W., 133
Goodman, John, 134
Graber, Henry W., 134
Granbery, J. L., 136
Gray, H. T., 136
Green, Thomas W., 136
Greer, B. T., 137
Greer, Jones, 137
Griffith, Joseph D., 137
Grizzard, R. E., 138
Grizzle, Robert A., 138
Guerrant, P. M., 138
Gunn, Lundie B., 139
Gurley, Frank B., 139
Gustavus, W. V., 141
Gwyn, James, 141
Hails, George W., 143
Halbert, P. W., 144
Hale, Henry S., 144
Hall, G. H., 145
Hall, J. P., 146
Hall, John W., 146
Hall, Lafayette B., 146
Hamblett, James G., 147
Hancock, Richard R., 148
Hanner, James P., 148
Hardison, W. T., 149
Hardman, Charles T., 152
Hargis, J. H., 152
Harper, W. B., 153
Harrell, Reuben G., 153
Harris, C. C., 153
Harris, Gideon D., 153
Harris, John W., 154
Harris, W. W. S., 154
Harrison, Needham F., 155
Hatfield, John H., 156
Hawkins, A. G., 156
Hawkins, Benjamin F., 157
Hawkins, Hiram P., 157
Haynie, Houston, 158

Hendricks, James A., 159
Hibbler, James E., 159
Hight, J. P., 160
Hindman, Joseph, 161
Holland, Addison D., 161
Holleman, L. F. A., 161
Hollowell, Thomas R., 162
Holman, Jesse A., 162
Holt, Joseph D., 163
Hood, Bynum H., 163
Hooper, Charles W., 163
Hoskins, James, 164
House, Sam J., 164
Howard, Luther M., 165
Howell, F. A., 166
Hows, Stephen H., 166
Howse, Ambrose, 166
Howse, L. C., 167
Hubbard, David, 167
Hudson, C. T., 167
Hudson, Thomas, 168
Hudson, William, 168
Hughen, James H., 168
Hughes, C. B., 169
Hughes, James D., 169
Humphreys, John P., 169
Hunt, Thomas W., 170
Hunter, Thomas, 170
Ijams, J. C., 171
Ireland, Rufus M., 172
Irvine, Adam C., 172
Irwin, James W., 173
Jackson, WIlliam H., 175
James, John A., 177
Jarvis, Richard A., 177
Jennings, W. B., 178
Jetton, Charles W., 178
Jobe, William L., 179
Johnson, Adam R., 179
Johnson, Daniel S., 181
Johnson, John N., 182
Johnson, Sidney S., 182
Johnson, William, 183
Johnston, William A., 184
Jones, A. M., 185
Jones, James C., 185
Jones, James M., 186
Jones, John M., 186
Jones, Timothy P., 187
Jones, William B., 187

Jordan, M. D. L., 188
Juniel, James W., 189
Kelley, David C., 191
Kelly, J. O., 192
Kelly, William C., 193
Kemp, John R., 193
Kennedy, T. J., 194
Kimbro, John, 194
King, B. F., 194
King, James W., 195
Kinsolving, William C., 196
Kittrell, Robert H., 197
Klyce, H. C., 197
Knoedler, Lewis P., 198
Knox, J. P., 198
Knox, John L., 199
Knox, Richard M., 199
Lachlison, James, 201
Landman, J. H., 202
Lankford, Peter L., 203
Latham, John C., 204
Lauderdale, John M., 205
Lawrence, James J., 205
Lee, James C., 206
Leiper, John, 206
Lewis, Thomas W., 207
Lindsey, Livingston, 208
Linn, J. Z., 208
Linton, John W., 208
Lipscomb, Thomas C., 208
Little, T. C., 209
Littleton, Isaac F., 209
Livingston, James L., 210
Loggins, William E., 210
Lollar, D. F., 210
Long, B. R., 211
Long, Lemuel, 211
Loving, A. B., 212
Luckett, H. C., 212
Lunsford, T. A., 213
Lyerly, Charles A., 213
Lynn, L. C., 214
Lyon, Hylan B., 215
Mabry, Hinchie P., 217
Mackey, Benjamin F., 219
MacMurry, James A., 220
Mahon, James N., 220
Marshall, F. L., 221
Martin, Jacob T., 221
Martin, Jonathan M., 223

Martin, P. T., 223
Martin, Richard W., 224
Martin, William P., 225
Masengill, John D., 225
Mason, James M., 226
May, Augustus M., 227
Mays, Samuel T., 227
McClerkin, Luther C., 228
McClure, Baker W., 228
McConnell, W. M., 229
McCulloch, Robert, 229
McCutchan, A. C., 230
McDaniel, Tubal E., 230
McDowell, Lucien, 231
McDowell, William W., 232
McGann, James L., 233
McGaughy, J. B., 234
McGlathery, James M., 234
McGowan, John L., 235
McGregor, Augustus S., 236
McIntosh, W. D., 236
McKissack, A. C., 237
McKnight, Moses W., 237
McLaughlin, James W., 238
McLean, William H., 239
McMurray, W. J., 239
McNeill, Malcolm, 241
McNeilly, Felix C., 242
McRea, Jesse W., 243
McRee, F. M., 243
McRee, N. L., 243
Metcalfe, John, 243
Michie, Robert W., 244
Mills, John R., 244
Mills, N. P., 245
Milner, T. J., 246
Mobley, I. H., 246
Mobley, M. M., 246
Moffett, S. L., 246
Monroe, Frank, 247
Montgomery, Victor, 247
Mooneyham, B. H., 249
Moore, Lafayette, 249
Moore, P. W., 249
Morehead, Joseph M., 249
Morgan, D. M., 249
Morgan, John T., 250
Morris, William D., 250
Morton, John W., 251
Mumford, Francis M., 253

Murphy, J. H., 254
Myers, Henry C., 254
Nance, James W., 257
Neill, Hal H., 258
Nichol, Jonathan W., 259
Nicholson, John C., 261
Noland, Robert C., 261
Nolen, Columbus L., 261
Norfleet, John R., 262
Nowlin, John A., 262
Nunn, Ira D., 263
O'Brien, Robert, 265
O'Donnell, Jack, 265
Orand, T. A., 266
Orr, Carson T., 266
Osteen, John J., 266
Ownby, W. P., 267
Palmer, Joseph B., 269
Palsgrove, Abner S., 270
Park, George W., 271
Parker, Samuel R., 271
Paschall, N. J., 271
Pascoe, William H., 272
Patterson, Frank, 272
Peak, C. S., 272
Peak, Robert T., 273
Pearson, Archibald A., 273
Pegram, John, 274
Peters, Thomas H., 275
Pettus, W. G., 275
Pierce, Rice A., 275
Pitman, R. W., 276
Pitts, James M., 276
Pool, James M., 277
Pope, William H., 277
Porter, David C., 278
Porter, William N., 278
Powell, B. C., 279
Powell, J. G., 279
Price, George W., 280
Price, John H., 281
Price, Sidney T., 281
Priest, T. R., 281
Pryor, J. P., 282
Ptomey, John W., 282
Pullen, J. B., 282
Purdon, S. H., 282
Putch, William, 282
Pyrom, S. B., 283
Quinn, W. S., 285

Ramsey, Charles A., 287
Randle, E. H., 287
Randolph, George W., 287
Reagan, William B. L., 288
Reed, Thomas C., 288
Reese, David N., 289
Reynolds, Alfred C., 290
Rhodes, Robert J., 290
Rice, Robert H., 291
Richards, Daniel R., 291
Richardson, Robert V., 292
Richmond, B., 292
Roane, Archibald T., 292
Roark, W. H., 293
Roberts, Preston, 293
Robertson, George M., 293
Roddey, Philip D., 294
Rogers, Benjamin A., 294
Rogers, R. E., 295
Rogers, William J., 295
Rose, T. A., 296
Ross, Edward B., 296
Ross, Lawrence S., 299
Rucker, Edmund W., 299
Rucker, J. M., 301
Rutledge, Wade P., 301
Sampson, John, 303
Sanders, Harvey C., 303
Sanders, J. A., 304
Sanders, James W., 304
Sanford, J. B., 304
Sanford, William, 304
Saunders, Francis M., 305
Scales, David C., 305
Scanland, William H., 306
Scott, Burgess H., 306
Scott, Frank T., 308
Sea, Andrew M., 309
Searcy, John N., 310
Sexton, H. M., 311
Shearer, John, 311
Sheldon, Charles A., 312
Shepherd, James M., 312
Sherrill, Richard E., 313
Shreve, Robert S., 313
Sigman, T. F., 314
Simmons, John S., 314
Sims, W. E., 314
Smith, Baxter, 315
Smith, J. D., 316

Smith, John P., 316
Smith, Joseph P., 317
Smithson, George W., 317
Smoot, John N., 317
Sneed, John H., 319
Snell, John A., 319
Somerville, William B., 319
Stafford, John, 320
Stanfield, N. B., 320
Starke, Peter B., 321
Steele, William A., 321
Steger, John C. W., 321
Stewart, James T., 322
Stewart, Thomas W., 323
Stockdale, Thomas R., 324
Stone, Eli N., 326
Stone, James J., 327
Storm, J. L., 327
Strong, Julius L., 328
Stuart, A. J., 328
Stubbs, James W., 328
Sullivan, John E., 329
Swearingen, G. B., 329
Sykes, Edward T., 329
Tandy, C. W., 333
Taylor, R. Z., 334
Tedford, Sanford W., 334
Terry, Ben D., 335
Thomas, W. E., 335
Thomson, Tom D., 336
Tipton, Pleas, 336
Traylor, R. M., 337
Traylor, Thomas B., 337
Treanor, John O., 338
Trent, John, 339
Tribble, R. W., 340
Trigg, John A., 340
Tucker, John W., 340
Tyler, Henry A., 341
Tyree, Lemuel H., 342
Vance, James D., 345
Vanderslice, William, 345
Vaughan, A. J., 345
Vaughn, William C., 347
Vaulx, Joseph, 347
Wade, William B., 349
Wagner, William M., 350
Walker, J. H., 352
Walker, William B., 352
Wall, Robert B., 352

Walthall, Edward C., 353
Ward, Frank F., 356
Wardlaw, Zack, 356
Warren, Walter M., 358
Watkins, George W., 358
Watson, Mack G., 359
Watson, William F., 359
Weakley, Richard W., 359
Weatherley, W. M., 360
Weems, Robert D., 360
Wharton, John A., 360
Whisenant, Jacob W., 361
Whitaker, William B., 361
White, Benjamin F., 361
White, John B., 362
White, R. L. C., 362
White, William H., 363
Whittle, R. M., 364
Wilhoite, William M., 364
Wilkerson, Thomas O., 364
Wilkes, Nim, 364
Williams, James, 365
Willingham, William J., 365
Wilson, William H., 366
Winfree, William P., 366
Wingo, Thomas R., 367
Winn, Francis M., 368
Winston, James M., 368
Wisdom, Dew M., 369
Wiseman, W. J., 370
Withers, Emile Q., 370
Wood, N. E., 371
Woods, Clayton R., 371
Wright, Wilford F., 372
Wyeth, John A., 372
Wynn, J. A., 373
Yarbrough, Abner, 375
Young. G. W., 375
Young, Samuel, 376
Youngblood, G. W., 377
Zollinger, Augustus L., 379

LOCHLAINN SEABROOK ∼ 421

If you enjoyed this book you will be interested in Colonel Seabrook's other popular related titles:

- ABRAHAM LINCOLN WAS A LIBERAL, JEFFERSON DAVIS WAS A CONSERVATIVE
- EVERYTHING YOU WERE TAUGHT ABOUT THE CIVIL WAR IS WRONG, ASK A SOUTHERNER!
- ALL WE ASK IS TO BE LET ALONE: THE SOUTHERN SECESSION FACT BOOK
- EVERYTHING YOU WERE TAUGHT ABOUT AMERICAN SLAVERY IS WRONG, ASK A SOUTHERNER!
- CONFEDERATE FLAG FACTS: WHAT EVERY AMERICAN SHOULD KNOW ABOUT DIXIE'S SOUTHERN CROSS
- LINCOLN'S WAR: THE REAL CAUSE, THE REAL WINNER, THE REAL LOSER

Available from Sea Raven Press and wherever fine books are sold

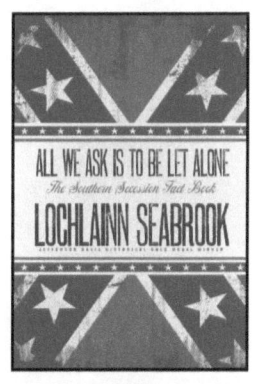

ALL OF OUR BOOK COVERS ARE AVAILABLE AS 11" X 17" POSTERS, SUITABLE FOR FRAMING

SeaRavenPress.com • NathanBedfordForrestBooks.com

MEET THE AUTHOR

"DEMANDING THAT THE PATRIOTIC SOUTH STOP HONORING HER CONFEDERATE ANCESTORS IS LIKE DEMANDING THE SUN NOT TO SHINE." — COLONEL LOCHLAINN SEABROOK

LOCHLAINN SEABROOK, a neo-Victorian and world acclaimed man of letters, is a Kentucky Colonel and the winner of the prestigious Jefferson Davis Historical Gold Medal for his "masterpiece," *A Rebel Born: A Defense of Nathan Bedford Forrest*. A classic littérateur and an unreconstructed Southern historian, he is an award-winning author, "Civil War" scholar, Confederate culture expert, Bible authority, the leading popularizer of American Civil War history, and a traditional Southern Agrarian of Scottish, English, Irish, Dutch, Welsh, German, and Italian extraction.

A child prodigy of Revolutionary, Southern, and Confederate blood, Seabrook is today a true Renaissance Man whose occupational titles also include encyclopedist, lexicographer, musician, artist, graphic designer, genealogist, photographer, and award-winning poet. Also a songwriter and a screenwriter, he has a 40 year background in historical nonfiction writing and is a member of the Sons of Confederate Veterans, the Civil War Trust, and the National Grange.

Known to his many fans as the "voice of the traditional South," due to similarities in their writing styles, ideas, and literary works, Seabrook is also often referred to as the "new Shelby Foote," the "Southern Joseph Campbell," and the "American Robert Graves" (his English cousin). Seabrook coined the terms "South-shaming" and "Lincolnian liberalism," and holds the world's record for writing the most books on Nathan Bedford Forrest. In addition, Seabrook is the first Civil War scholar to connect the early American nickname for the U.S., "The Confederate States of America," with the Southern Confederacy that arose eight decades later, and the first to note that in 1860 the party platforms of the two major political parties were the opposite of what they are today (Victorian Democrats were Conservatives, Victorian Republicans were Liberals).

Above, Colonel Lochlainn Seabrook, "the voice of the traditional South," award-winning Civil War scholar and unreconstructed Southern historian. America's most popular and prolific pro-South author, his many books have introduced hundreds of thousands to the truth about the War for Southern Independence. He coined the phrase "South-shaming" and holds the world record for writing the most books on Nathan Bedford Forrest.

The son of a Kentucky trainman and the grandson of Appalachian coal-mining and farming families, Seabrook is a seventh-generation Kentuckian whose European ancestors came from Virginia, North Carolina, and Tennessee, settling in the Bluegrass State in the early 1700s, thereafter spreading into West Virginia, the Midwest, and finally the West. He has over a dozen ancestors who fought in the American Revolutionary War, including such family surnames as Bentley, Combs, Mullins, Crase/Kress, Adkins, Kelly, Nelson, Shannon, McBrayer, Hutchinson, and Leslie.

Seabrook is co-chair of the Jent/Gent Family Committee (Kentucky), founder and director of the Blakeney Family Tree Project, and a board member of the Friends of Colonel Benjamin E. Caudill. His literary works have been endorsed by leading authorities, museum curators, award-winning historians, bestselling authors, celebrities, filmmakers, noted scientists, well regarded educators, TV show hosts and producers, renowned military artists, esteemed Southern organizations, and distinguished academicians from around the world.

Seabrook has authored over 60 popular adult books on the American Civil War, American and international slavery, the U.S. Confederacy (1781), the Southern Confederacy (1861), religion, theology, thealogy, Jesus, the Bible, the Apocrypha, the Law of Attraction, alternative health, spirituality, ghost stories, the paranormal, ufology, social issues, and cross-cultural studies of the family and marriage. His Confederate biographies, pro-South studies, Victorian Southern literature titles, genealogical monographs, family histories, biographical and military encyclopedias, self-help guides, and etymological dictionaries have received wide acclaim.

Seabrook's eight children's books include a Southern guide to the "Civil War," a biography of Nathan Bedford Forrest, a dictionary of religion and myth, a rewriting of the King Arthur legend (which reinstates the original pre-Christian motifs), two bedtime stories for preschoolers, a naturalist's guidebook to owls, a worldwide look at the family, and an examination of the Near-Death Experience.

Of blue-blooded Southern stock through his Kentucky, Tennessee, Virginia, North Carolina and West Virginia ancestors, he is a direct descendant of European royalty via his 6th great-grandfather, the Earl of Oxford, after which London's famous Harley Street is named. Among his celebrated male Celtic ancestors is Robert the Bruce, King of Scotland, Seabrook's 22nd great-grandfather. The 21st great-grandson of Edward I "Longshanks" Plantagenet), King of England, Seabrook is a 17th-generation Southerner through his descent from the colonists of Jamestown, Virginia (1607).

The 2nd, 3rd, and 4th great-grandson of dozens of Confederate soldiers, one of his closest connections to Lincoln's War is through his 3rd great-grandfather, Elias Jent Sr., who fought for the Confederacy in the Thirteenth Cavalry Kentucky under Seabrook's 2nd cousin, Colonel

(Photo © Lochlainn Seabrook)

Benjamin E. Caudill. The Thirteenth, also known as "Caudill's Army," fought in numerous conflicts, including the Battles of Saltville, Gladsville, Mill Cliff, Poor Fork, Whitesburg, and Leatherwood.

Seabrook is a direct descendant of the families of Alexander H. Stephens, John Singleton Mosby, William Giles Harding, and Edmund Winchester Rucker, and is related to the following Confederates and other 18th- and 19th-Century luminaries: Robert E. Lee, Stephen Dill Lee, Stonewall Jackson, Nathan Bedford Forrest, James Longstreet, John Hunt Morgan, Jeb Stuart, Pierre G. T. Beauregard (approved the Confederate Battle Flag design), George W. Gordon, John Bell Hood, Alexander Peter Stewart, Arthur M. Manigault, Joseph Manigault, Charles Scott Venable, Thornton A. Washington, John A. Washington, Abraham Buford, Edmund W. Pettus, Theodrick "Tod" Carter, John B. Womack, John H. Winder, Gideon J. Pillow, States Rights Gist, Henry R. Jackson, John Lawton Seabrook, John C. Breckinridge, Leonidas Polk, Zachary Taylor, Sarah Knox Taylor (first wife of Jefferson Davis), Richard Taylor, Davy Crockett, Daniel Boone, Meriwether Lewis (of the Lewis and Clark Expedition) Andrew Jackson, James K.

Polk, Abram Poindexter Maury (founder of Franklin, TN), Zebulon Baird Vance, Thomas Jefferson, Edmund Jennings Randolph, George Wythe Randolph (grandson of Jefferson), Felix K. Zollicoffer, Fitzhugh Lee, Nathaniel F. Cheairs, Jesse James, Frank James, Robert Brank Vance, Charles Sidney Winder, John W. McGavock, Caroline E. (Winder) McGavock, David Harding McGavock, Lysander McGavock, James Randal McGavock, Randal William McGavock, Francis McGavock, Emily McGavock, William Henry F. Lee, Lucius E. Polk, Minor Meriwether (husband of noted pro-South author Elizabeth Avery Meriwether), Ellen Bourne Tynes (wife of Forrest's chief of artillery, Captain John W. Morton), South Carolina Senators Preston Smith Brooks and Andrew Pickens Butler, and famed South Carolina diarist Mary Chesnut.

Seabrook's modern day cousins include: Patrick J. Buchanan (conservative author), Cindy Crawford (model), Shelby Lee Adams (Letcher Co., Kentucky, photographer), Bertram Thomas Combs (Kentucky's 50th governor), Edith Bolling (second wife of President Woodrow Wilson), and actors Andy Griffith, Riley Keough, George C. Scott, Robert Duvall, Reese Witherspoon, Lee Marvin, Rebecca Gayheart, and Tom Cruise.

Seabrook's screenplay, *A Rebel Born*, based on his book of the same name, has been signed with acclaimed filmmaker Christopher Forbes (of Forbes Film). Set for release as a full-length feature film, it is in pre-production, awaiting the necessary funding. This will be the first movie ever made of Nathan Bedford Forrest's life story, and as a historically accurate project written from the Southern perspective, is destined to be one of the most talked about Civil War films of all time.

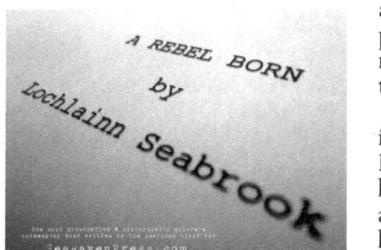

Born with music in his blood, Seabrook is an award-winning, multi-genre, BMI-Nashville songwriter and lyricist who has composed some 3,000 songs (250 albums), and whose original music has been heard in film (*A Rebel Born, Cowgirls 'n Angels, Confederate Cavalry, Billy the Kid: Showdown in Lincoln County, Vengeance Without Mercy, Last Step, County Line, The Mark*) and on TV and radio worldwide. A musician, producer, multi-instrumentalist, and renown performer—whose keyboard work has been variously compared to pianists from Hargus Robbins and Vince Guaraldi to Elton John and Leonard Bernstein—Seabrook has opened for groups such as the Earl Scruggs Review, Ted Nugent, and Bob Seger, and has performed privately for such public figures as President Ronald Reagan, Burt Reynolds, Loni Anderson, and Senator Edward W. Brooke. Seabrook's cousins in the music business include: Johnny Cash, Elvis Presley, Lisa Marie Presley, Billy Ray and Miley Cyrus, Patty Loveless, Tim McGraw, Lee Ann Womack, Dolly Parton, Pat Boone, Naomi, Wynonna, and Ashley Judd, Ricky Skaggs, the Sunshine Sisters, Martha Carson, and Chet Atkins.

Seabrook lives with his wife and family in historic Middle Tennessee, the heart of Forrest country and the Confederacy, where his conservative Southern ancestors fought valiantly against Liberal Lincoln and the progressive North in defense of Jeffersonianism, constitutional government, and personal liberty.

LochlainnSeabrook.com

Why the South fought . . .

www.ingramcontent.com/pod-product-compliance
Lightning Source LLC
Chambersburg PA
CBHW030516230426
43665CB00010B/636